Jesus

David F. Ford is Regius Professor of Divinity in the University of
Cambridge. His publications include *Jubilate: Theology in Praise* (with
Daniel W. Hardy, 1984), *Meaning and Truth in 2 Corinthians* (with F. M.
Young, 1988), *The Modern Theologians* (editor, 2nd edn., 1997), *The Shape
of Living* (1997), and *Self and Salvation: Being Transformed* (1999).

Mike Higton is Lecturer in Theology in the Departments of Lifelong
Learning and Theology in the University of Exeter. He is working on
several projects at the moment, including *Conversing with Barth* (edited
with John C. McDowell, forthcoming 2002) and *Christ and History: The
Theology of Hans W. Frei* (forthcoming, 2002).

OXFORD **READERS**

....

The Oxford Readers series represents a unique resource which brings together extracts of texts from a wide variety of sources, primary and secondary, on a wide range of interdisciplinary topics.

Available

Aesthetics
Edited by Patrick Maynard and Susan Feagin

The British Empire
Edited by Jane Samson

Class
Edited by Patrick Joyce

Classical Philosophy
Edited by Terence Irwin

Ethics
Edited by Peter Singer

Ethnicity
Edited by John Hutchinson and Anthony D. Smith

Evolution
Edited by Mark Ridley

Faith and Reason
Edited by Paul Helm

Fascism
Edited by Roger Griffin

Feminisms
Edited by Sandra Kemp and Judith Squires

Jesus
Edited by David F. Ford and Mike Higton

The Mind
Edited by Daniel Robinson

Nationalism
Edited by John Hutchinson and Anthony D. Smith

Nazism
Edited by Neil Gregor

Political Thought
Edited by Michael Rosen and Jonathan Wolff

Racism
Edited by Martin Bulmer and John Solomos

Sexuality
Edited by Robert A. Nye

Slavery
Edited by Stanley Engerman, Seymour Drescher, and Robert Paquette

War
Edited by Lawrence Freedman

Forthcoming

Anti-Semitism
Edited by Paul Lawrence Rose

Consciousness
Edited by Geoffrey Underwood

Revolution
Edited by Jack Goldstone

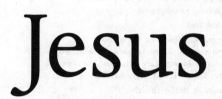

OXFORD **READERS**

Jesus

Edited by David F. Ford and Mike Higton

OXFORD
UNIVERSITY PRESS

OXFORD

UNIVERSITY PRESS

Great Clarendon Street, Oxford OX2 6DP

Oxford University Press is a department of the University of Oxford.
It furthers the University's objective of excellence in research, scholarship,
and education by publishing worldwide in

Oxford New York

Athens Auckland Bangkok Bogotá Buenos Aires Cape Town
Chennai Dar es Salaam Delhi Florence Hong Kong Istanbul Karachi
Kolkata Kuala Lumpur Madrid Melbourne Mexico City Mumbai Nairobi
Paris São Paulo Shanghai Singapore Taipei Tokyo Toronto Warsaw

with associated companies in Berlin Ibadan

Oxford is a registered trade mark of Oxford University Press
in the UK and in certain other countries

Published in the United States
by Oxford University Press Inc., New York

Editorial matter and Selection © David F. Ford and Mike Higton 2002

The moral rights of the authors have been asserted
Database right Oxford University Press (maker)

First published 2002

British Library Cataloguing in Publication Data

Data available

Library of Congress Cataloging in Publication Data

Data available

ISBN 0–19–289316–5

1 3 5 7 9 10 8 6 4 2

Typeset in Dante and Franklin Gothic
by RefineCatch Limited, Bungay, Suffolk
Printed in Great Britain by
T. J. International Ltd., Padstow, Cornwall

Preface

There are countless texts concerning Jesus of Nazareth to choose from, and any attempt to navigate the vast sea of possibilities is bound to be debatable. Even if one were to restrict attention to straightforward biographies, there are several thousand to choose from—and we have cast our net far more widely than that. Inevitably, we will have missed out many examples that others think vital, and have included much that others think strange. We hope, of course, that our selection will be a useful resource for those wishing to survey major continuities and developments in the history of responses to Jesus, but we also hope that it will spring at least one surprise on every reader, and that it will bring some neglected voices back into the ongoing conversation about Jesus of Nazareth's identity and significance.

Work on the Reader has been collaborative from the start, and we wish to offer our thanks to many people who have been involved. In the first place, David Ford would like to thank Mike Higton for undertaking the lion's share of the spadework for the book. Mike Higton would like to thank the Master and Fellows of St John's College, Cambridge, for allowing him to do much of that spadework while holding the Naden Studentship there. Both of us would like to thank all of those who advised us: Hilarion Alfeyev, Sebastian Brock, Jon Cooley, Caitríona Ó Dochartaigh, John England, Victoria Goodman, Tim Gorringe, Daniel Hardy, Douglas Hedley, Hester Higton, Steve Holmes, Timothy Jenkins, Tarif Khalidi, Alastair Logan, Winrich Löhr, John McDowell, Susan Parsons, Chad Peckhold, Brian Stanley, John Sweet, Margie Tolstoy, Lionel Wickham. We also owe thanks to the staff of two institutions: to those in Cambridge University Library who have been unfailingly helpful, particularly in the tea room, and to those at Oxford University Press who have overseen the project: George Miller, Fiona Kinnear, and Jo Stanbridge.

D.F.F.
M.A.H.

May 2001

Contents

General Introduction   I

PART I. Biblical and Patristic: To AD 451

A. The Life of Jesus

I. Canonical   13

  1 The Birth of the Messiah   13
  2 Jesus' Baptism   14
  3 Parables of the Kingdom   14
  4 The Beatitudes   15
  5 The Lord's Prayer   15
  6 The Little Apocalypse   16
  7 Casting out Demons   16
  8 Healing the Sick   17
  9 The Feeding of the Five Thousand   18
10 Calming the Storm   18
11 Peter's Confession   19
12 The Transfiguration   19
13 The Way, the Truth, and the Life   20
14 The Last Supper   21
15 The Garden of Gethsemane   21
16 The Crucifixion   22
17 The Resurrection   22
18 The Road to Emmaus   23
19 The Great Commission   24
20 The Ascension   25

II. Extra-Canonical   25

21 Other Words   26
22 Other Deeds   26
23 Jesus as a Child   27
24 Jesus as Gnostic Teacher   28
25 Jesus' Appearance   30
26 Jesus Rising   31

B. Jesus the Saviour

I. Jesus Saves   33

27 God's Light   33
28 The Enduring Rock   34
29 The Sacrificial Lamb   35
30 Our King and Helper   36
31 The Variety of Salvation   37
32 Adoring the Cross   38

II. Participating in Christ   39

33 Christ in his People   39
34 The Body of Christ   40
35 Dying with Christ   41
36 Eating Christ   42
37 Helping Christ   43
38 The Whole Christ   44

III. The Sweet Exchange   46

39 Emptying and Exaltation   46
40 The Sweet Exchange   46
41 Likeness for Likeness   48
42 Washing the Washer   48
43 Born for Rebirth   49
44 Enslaved for Slaves   49

IV. Unveiling   50

45 The Unveiling of Christ   50
46 Baptismal Renovation   51
47 Restoring the Image   52
48 Desire and Knowledge   54
49 Christ the Sun   56

V. Christ and the Cosmos   56

50 Christ and Creation   57
51 Recapitulation   57
52 Reversing Adam   59

C. Typology and Apology

I. Jesus and Judaism   60

53 The Servant of the Lord Foretold   60
54 Shadow and True Form   61
55 The True Passover   62
56 Spiritual Meaning   64

57 A Jewish Report   66
58 Yeshu's Guilt   66

II. Against the Pagans   **67**

59 The Foolishness of Wisdom   67
60 The Offence of Incarnation   68
61 Roman Persecution   68
62 Christ the Judge Foretold   70
63 The Seeds of the Logos   71
64 A Vergilian Baptism   72
65 The Fount of Light   73

D. The Development of Christology

66 In the Beginning   76

I. True Humanity   **77**

67 True Suffering   77
68 Christ Uncrucified   78
69 Jesus' Continence   79
70 True Flesh   80
71 True Embodiment?   82

II. True Divinity   **84**

72 The Paradox of Incarnation   84
73 The Ineffability of Incarnation   85
74 The Making of the Son   86
75 Against Arius   87
76 The Consubstantial Son   88
77 Arianism Resurgent   88
78 Homoian Arianism   89
79 Neo-Arianism   90
80 Nicene Renaissance   91

III. Towards Chalcedon   **91**

81 Full Humanity   91
82 Divinity and Humanity in the Gospels   93
83 The Birth of the Messiah   95
84 Assumption of Humanity   96
85 Two Natures United   98
86 Unconfused and Inseparable   100

PART 2. Byzantine and Early Medieval: 451–1208

A. Contemplating Christ

I. Transfiguration and Ascent   **105**

87 The Light of Christ's Face   105
88 The Hope of Glory   106
89 A Shining Garment   107
90 Eagerly Seeking Christ   108
91 Illumined by the Passion   110

II. Jesus Prayer   **111**

92 Ceaseless Meditation   111
93 The Heart's Occupation   112

III. Meditation and Humility   **113**

94 We Beheld his Glory   113
95 Let us Follow   114
96 Sharing Christ's Anguish   115
97 Christ Born in the Soul   116
98 Christ Little and Weak   117

B. Christ and Culture

99 The Unburning Coal   118
100 Son of the Cool Wind   119
101 Helm of Heaven   120
102 Our Chevalier   121

C. Byzantine and Early Medieval Debates

I. After Chalcedon   **123**

103 Christ is not Two   123
104 The Diversity in Christ   124
105 The Hypostatic Union   126
106 Two Wills in Christ   127
107 The Orthodox Faith   128

II. Adoring Christ's Humanity   **129**

108 On Divine Images   130
109 Mementoes of Christ   131

III. Western Christology   **132**

110 Against Ambiguity   133
111 Christ's Adoptive Humanity   134

112 Christ's Adopted Body   135
113 A Christological Vision   136
114 Christ's Death a Satisfaction   137
115 Christ's Death the Fount of Love   139
116 Against Adoption   140

IV. The Eucharist   **142**

117 Tasting Flesh and Blood   142
118 The Figure of a Mystery   143
119 Making Christ's Body   144

D. Christ beyond Christianity

I. Jewish   **146**

120 Discrediting Jesus   146
121 Disputing Christ   149

II. Zoroastrian   **150**

122 The Implausibility of Incarnation   150

III. Islamic   **151**

123 The Qur'ān   151
124 Muhammad and Christ   152
125 Christ and Sufism   153
126 The Wisdom of Jesus   153

PART 3. Later Medieval and Renaissance: 1209–1516

A. Following Christ

I. Remembrance   **157**

127 Bethlehem at Greccio   157
128 Gifts of the Magi   158
129 Christ's Appearance   161
130 Jesus the Prophet   162
131 Jesus' Escape from Folly   163
132 The Magnitude of Christ's Sorrow   165
133 Christ's Seven Afflictions   166
134 Savage Torture   169
135 The Crucifixion Deception   171
136 The Return to Heaven   172
137 Christ Triumphant   172

II. Meditation   **174**

138 Intoxicated by Christ   174
139 Suckling Christ   175
140 Continuous Contemplation   175
141 To See the Face of Christ   177
142 The Soul's Journey into God   178
143 Christ's Sweet Mercy   180
144 Drinking from Christ   182

III. Imitation   **183**

145 Imitating the Humility   183
146 Wounded with Christ   184
147 Imitation over Contemplation   184
148 Modern Devotion   185
149 Christ a Ladder   186
150 Attaining to the Likeness of Christ   187
151 Passing through Christ's Life   189

IV. The Love of Christ   **189**

152 Christ our Mother   189
153 Christ's Labour Pains   191
154 Jesus the Friend   192

B. The Benefits of Christ's Passion

155 Christ's Daily Humility   194
156 Transubstantiation   195
157 Corpus Christi   195
158 Merit and Satisfaction   197
159 Christ's Heartbeats   200
160 Christ's Maximal Humanity   201

C. Jesus and Judaism

161 No Revelation in Jesus   203
162 The Jews not Deicides   204

PART 4. Reformation and Counter-Reformation: 1517–1600

A. Christ and his Benefits

163 Against Scholasticism   209

164 Sin, Grace, and Salvation   210
165 Salvation and the Creed   211
166 Only Faith   214
167 Victim and Victor   215
168 Theology of the Cross   216
169 The Bitter Christ   217
170 Free Election   218

B. Christ in Word and Sacrament

171 Christ and the Word   220
172 Christ's Absence   221
173 Exhibiting without Containing Grace   223
174 Eating, Dwelling, and Washing   226
175 The Sacrifice of the Mass   226
176 Torture and the Eucharist   228

C. Christ in Two Natures

177 The Unity of the Natures   230
178 The Immeasurable and the Measurable   232
179 Ubiquitous Humanity?   233
180 Errors concerning the Union   235
181 Communication between the Natures   236
182 King amid the Kine   238

D. Pursuing Christ

183 Filling up Christ   240
184 Hunting Christ   241
185 Imitating Christ   243
186 Imagining Christ   245
187 Awakened by Christ   246
188 Dancing with Christ   248
189 Reading Christ   249

PART 5. Early Modernity: 1601–1789

A. The Drama of Christ

190 Christ's Stage   255
191 Dialogue with the Devil   256
192 Christ Narcissus   259

B. Crucified for Me

193 Christ's Blood   262

I. The School of Love   **262**

194 Love Defined   263
195 Love so Amazing   263
196 Love Christ's Name and Nature   264
197 Love Unknown   266

II. The Power of the Cross   **267**

198 The Punishing Cross   268
199 Crucified with Christ   269
200 Blest Cross   271

C. Union with Christ

I. Pietist   **272**

201 The Bridegroom's Arrival   272
202 All for Sinner's Gain   274
203 Hearts Submitting to Christ   276
204 Nothing but Jesus   278
205 Christ in Me   279

II. Catholic   **280**

206 Christ's Second Body   281
207 Christ the Door   282

III. Anglican   **284**

208 Keeping Close to the Union   284
209 No Union so Knitteth   285

IV. Puritan   **285**

210 Christ's Kisses   286
211 The Bridegroom's Departure   287
212 One with Christ   289

V. Radical   **290**

213 Christ Born in the Soul   290
214 The Birth of Christ in the Believer   291
215 The Spiritual Dispensation   292

D. Discussing Doctrine

216 The Father's Self-Knowledge   294
217 An Outline of Christology   296
218 Humiliation and Exaltation   298
219 The Limitations of Atonement   300

E. The Enlightenment

220 Copernican Christ   303
221 Christ Simplified   304
222 Christ and Archimedes   305
223 Against Atonement   307
224 Christ Falsified   309
225 Jesus the Jew   311
226 Christ the Charlatan   313
227 Christ's Distance   315
228 The Revolutionary Christ   317

PART 6. The Nineteenth Century: 1790–1913

A. The Historical Jesus

I. The Invention of Christ?

321

229 The Idea of the Son of God   321
230 Christ in the Unfolding of Spirit   324
231 The Last Wish of Religion   326
232 The Heart's Invention   327
233 A Translation of the Rule of Virtue   329
234 Inventing Jesus   330
235 Christ's Unavoidable Historicity   331

II. Reconstructing Jesus

333

236 Another Testament of Christ   333
237 A Mythical Transfiguration   335
238 A Rational Transfiguration   337
239 The Historical Kernel   338
240 Hero of the Passion   340
241 Christ the Communist   341
242 Jesus the Jew   342
243 One Unknown   344

B. Humility

I. Jesus the Child

347

244 The Creator in the Cradle   347
245 The Wounded Child   348
246 The Crown of Roses   350
247 Little Jesus   351

II. Divinity and the Limitations of Humanity | 352

248 Lowly Majesty | 352
249 The Self-Limitation of the Divine | 353
250 The Development of God-Humanity | 355
251 Christ Only Human | 356

III. Against Humility | 358

252 Was Jesus Gentle? | 358
253 The Anti-Christ | 360

C. Christ and the Spirit

I. The Spirit of Christ | 364

254 Christ's Fallen Nature | 364
255 Christ's Spiritual Presence | 366
256 The Power of God in Christ | 369
257 The Impact of Christ's Spirit | 370

II. The Development of Doctrine | 371

258 Preserving the Picture | 372
259 Christ Advancing | 373
260 Christ's Enduring Words | 375
261 The Gospel's Embodiment | 377
262 Freeing the Kernel | 379
263 Christ Betrayed | 381
264 Jesus' Simple Teaching | 382
265 Deeds not Doctrine | 383
266 The Teacher of True Morality | 385

D. Life in Christ

I. Conversion | 388

267 Personal Saviour | 388
268 Jesus Taking Possession | 389
269 Ongoing Conversion | 391
270 Contemporaneity with Christ | 391

II. Participation | 394

271 Christ's Second Incarnation | 394
272 Incorporation and Unification | 395
273 Breathing Christ | 397
274 Created for Christ | 397
275 Representing the King | 398
276 A Vocation of Love | 400

E. Looking Eastwards

277 Returning Christ Eastwards   402
278 Translating Christ   404
279 Incorporating Christ   405
280 Embracing Christ   407

PART 7. The Twentieth Century: 1914–2000

A. Crisis

281 Christ the Crisis   413

B. The Historical Jesus?

I. Against History?   417

282 The Message not the Man   417
283 The Earthly Jesus and the Exalted Lord   419
284 Faith-Image and History   421

II. Questing for the Historical Jesus   423

285 A Framework   423
286 A Mediterranean Jewish Peasant   425
287 A Marginal Jew   427
288 The Jesus Revolution   429
289 The Sacred Mushroom   431

C. Christ and Salvation

I. Justification and Sanctification   434

290 Christ and New Being   434
291 Substitutionary Atonement   436
292 Jesus as Lord   437
293 Becoming Lesser Christs   439
294 The Crucified and the Crusading Mind   440
295 Christ's Mercy   441

II. Liberation   443

296 Recognizing the Poor   443
297 Liberating Jesus   444
298 Hiding Jesus   446
299 The Refusal of Tyranny   447
300 Liberation Christology   449
301 Christ and the Crowd   451

302 Soulful Christianity   452
303 Liberation and Healing   454
304 Jesus, Master of Initiation   456
305 Christ the Ancestor   458
306 Black Jesus   459
307 Christ for the Enslaved   460
308 Captivity   461

III. Ethics   **462**

309 Life with Christ   463
310 Virtue and Obedience   465
311 Christ the Norm   467
312 Christ's Community   468

D. Retelling the Story

I. In Literature   **471**

313 Journey of the Magi   471
314 The Gospel according to the Son   472
315 The Man who Died   474
316 The Lion, the Witch, and the Wardrobe   476

II. In Theology   **478**

317 Emmaus and Us   478
318 Jesus in Gethsemane   481

E. God Incarnate

I. Debating Incarnation   **486**

319 Incarnation Unnecessary   486
320 Anti-Logos   488
321 Yes to the Mystery   490
322 Grace and Incarnation   492
323 Alpha and Omega   493
324 Christ beneath All   494
325 Meekness and Majesty   495

II. A Male Christ?   **496**

326 Beyond Christolatry   496
327 Christ beyond Jesus   497
328 An Inclusive Christ   499

III. Incarnation, Cross, Resurrection, Trinity   **501**

329 The Crucified God-Man   502
330 God on the Cross   503
331 The Christlikeness of God   505

332 Saved by the Cross 506
333 The Triumphant Death 508

F. Jesus beyond Christianity

I. The Uniqueness of Christ 510

334 No Un-Christlikeness at All 510
335 Jesus and Buddha 511
336 Christ and Ramakrishna 513
337 Hinduism and Christ 514

II. Jesus and Judaism 515

338 A Jewish Teacher 516
339 Who Killed Christ? 517
340 Jesus the Jew 519
341 Judaism and Incarnation 520

G. The Face of Christ

342 Christ's Beauty 523
343 The Overwhelming Face 524

Notes 526
References 531
Further Reading 548
Acknowledgements 551
Index 555

General Introduction

The things are open and obvious to all; but the right apprehension of them inaccessible.

(Thomas Traherne, 208)

Selecting the contents of this Reader on Jesus has been a remarkable experience. We were faced with sources of astonishing variety: as we explored century after century, East and West, different Church traditions, 'orthodoxy' and 'heresy', popular and high culture, responses from those of non-Christian faiths and no faith, and an array of forms of writing from sophisticated arguments to children's verse, we were overwhelmed by the wealth of material. We had to make painful exclusions, cutting out whole aspects, in order to meet the word limit; but even this reduced selection feels beyond any coherence.

We decided to choose short extracts, and are all too aware of the dangers involved in removing these texts from their contexts. Nevertheless, we have done so in order to place each extract in another vital context: that of the variety and development of responses to Jesus of Nazareth over the centuries. Only when those responses are seen together, jostling each other for attention, can we begin to grasp the breadth and depth of this man's significance.

It is the task of this Introduction (with the assistance later of the introductions to each section and each individual extract) to try to help readers make some sense of the diverse contents.

Modes of Engagement with the New Testament Jesus

COMMENTING AND CONVERSING

The most obvious way to begin to make sense of these responses to Jesus is through the relationship to the New Testament which nearly all of them exhibit, directly or indirectly. The primary sources on Jesus going back to the first century are, by comparison with later centuries, very few. There is not much for certain other than what is in the New Testament, though there is debate about this as about nearly everything else concerning him. Most of the texts we have included from later centuries owe something to the New Testament, and especially to the four Gospels of Matthew, Mark, Luke, and John (see e.g. **94, 237, 318**). So 'commentary' is perhaps the most embracing category for our collection. In some way or other they 'comment' on the

New Testament: they read it and re-read it, emphasize some aspects of it, meditate on it, argue with it, suspect it, reject it, defend it, improvise upon it, edit it, judge it, pray through it, reimagine it, apply it, or just savour it.

Commentaries in the narrow sense of discussions of the meaning of specific passages are just one obvious form this activity takes. A broader understanding is of 'conversations and deliberations around the texts'. Intensive discussion of Scripture was part of Jesus' life (cf. **18**). In addition, the way Jesus is presented in the New Testament is itself the outcome of testimonies to him that are informed by interpretations of the Jewish Scriptures which Christians came to call the Old Testament (see e.g. **53, 54**). There followed century after century of conversations and deliberations around the Old and New Testaments. These were carried on in many settings, ranging from interior meditative conversations (e.g. **143, 214**), through educational settings (e.g. **165, 217**), official deliberations about doctrine (e.g. **86, 164**), and court-room interrogation leading to execution (e.g. **176**), to the creative processes that produced hymns, poems, and novels (e.g. **64, 182, 313**).

This is one way into understanding the diversity of texts about Jesus. Here is a man already steeped in scriptural debate whose followers write of him in ways shot through with interpretations of Scripture. Then their writings in the New Testament and beyond become in turn the focus for learning of him in future generations, who produce more and more responses. Each text, action, or life risks an interpretation of texts, actions, or lives which precede it; each inspires multiple further interpretations.

But each of these interpretations is a point of intersection for many strands. It is not only a matter of what can be taken for granted in any interpretation: that each interpreter's own context, biases, and concerns will help to shape the interpretation, and so will multiply diversity. Jesus is believed by his followers to be of limitless significance, and involved with the origins and destiny of the whole of creation and of each person. So the conversations about him need to be connected with an endless range of other conversations, and to be seen as formative in one's world-view as well as in personal and social identity. And if one resists this account of his significance, there is still a challenge to give alternative interpretations. Jesus generated debate and dispute from the start, and as increasing numbers of people, cultures, periods, faiths and disciplines have responded to him, so the conversations have multiplied. Making sense of the conversations involves entering, whether in person or through study, into the communities, traditions, contexts, and texts that carry them.

Recognizing the range of commenting and conversing with reference to New Testament texts is a good antidote to any notion of an overview of Jesus or of a systematic account of him. The New Testament itself has four basic accounts of him in the Gospels, and many other angles elsewhere. It can be seen as setting up a conversation between diverse commenting voices. Christians and others have repeatedly tried to arrive at a definitive 'right apprehension' of him, only to find (or to have others find) that it is, as Traherne says, 'inaccessible'. In gathering the material for this Reader we have been more than ever struck by the resistance of Jesus to our own and others' categories, yet also by the irresistible challenge to try again and again to do justice to him.

PERFORMING AND CELEBRATING

For all their advantages, 'commenting and conversing' fail to do full justice to a great deal in this Reader. There is need for categories which give more scope to the intensity of response to Jesus in devotion, discipleship, and celebration. Testimonies to Jesus have inspired the lives of whole communities and their members. The biblical texts have often been used like scripts for performances of worship and of a life understood as 'following Jesus', 'in Christ', 'before Christ', or 'in imitation of Christ'. History has been seen in terms of a drama whose plot is given by Scripture, with Christian living as participation in the ongoing drama.

Perhaps the most influential forms of performance and celebration have been the sacraments of baptism and Eucharist (or Lord's Supper, or Holy Communion, or Mass). Baptism performs a recollection of the baptism of Jesus (cf. **46**) and an identification with his life, death, and Resurrection as an initiation into the Christian community. The Eucharist performs a recollection of Jesus' Last Supper with his disciples (cf. **14**) and a celebration of his life, death, Resurrection, and continuing presence. We have chosen several texts which indicate how the Eucharist has been an ongoing means of participation in the drama of Jesus Christ, with all the passionate controversy that has surrounded it (e.g. **118, 155, 157, 172–6, 284**).

We have also tried to represent something of the variety of ways of living lives in correspondence with Jesus: martyrdom (e.g. **35**), imitation (e.g. **145, 148, 185**), imagination (e.g. **186**), mission (e.g. **275**), love (e.g. **276**), prayer (e.g., **92, 269**), chastity (e.g. **41, 271**), and communism (e.g. **215, 241**).

Then there are the artistic ways of performing the drama or variations on it. We do not attempt to include oratorios, paintings, statues, musicals, films, mimes, buildings, and other arts not well suited to a word-based Reader. But there are hymns and songs (e.g. **30, 195, 202, 325**), drama (e.g. **128, 192, 297**), novels (e.g. **239–41, 314–15**), and poems (e.g. **64, 99, 184, 193, 244, 298**).

ENCOUNTERING

Yet even performance and celebration do not quite reach the heart of some extracts. The core testimony of many of them is to meeting with Jesus. The

Gospels are mainly about encounters with Jesus (cf. **7**, **8**, **9**, **18**). Paul's conversion (see **33**) is pivotal for the early Church. The theme of transformative encounter frequently recurs in many modes—conversion (e.g. **267–70**), vision (e.g. **134**, **152**), mystical prayer (e.g. **88**, **142**). The variety ensures that this is not about a normative Christian experience—even though some traditions have attempted to do so, it is hard to maintain plausibly that there is a standard form of 'encounter experience' without which one cannot claim to be Christian.

Dietrich Bonhoeffer (see **320**) suggests the reason why for Christians this category of personal encounter has been so central. If Jesus Christ is affirmed to have lived, died, and risen from the dead, then he is free to be present in person. In the presence of a free and living person the most appropriate core questions are not so much 'how' or 'what' questions but 'who' questions which assume that the person addressed is the decisive source of understanding. 'Who are you?' is therefore the way into understanding him; and, even more fundamentally, there is the reversal of that question when he asks: 'Who are *you*?'

In that reversal, from addressing to being addressed, there is perhaps a clue to something of pivotal centrality for Christians in the midst of all the complexity and variety. It is the characteristically Christian recognition of the prior initiative of God in this person. This is the radical passivity of being addressed, being loved, being known, being judged, and being transformed by him. Even in the activity of responding to this initiative there is never a symmetrical relationship: 'Jesus is Lord' (cf. **39**, **334**) is perhaps the most succinct summary of Christian faith. This 'active passivity' in encounter with Jesus is a mystery that has been repeatedly explored and debated in discussions of grace (e.g. **40**, **94**, **322**), the Holy Spirit (e.g. **178**, **254**, **257**), prayer (e.g. **92**, **295**), the Eucharist (e.g. **172–175**), and ethics (e.g. **309–12**). The discussions have often been concerned with complex 'how' and 'what' questions, but Bonhoeffer's 'who' question points to their unifying focus in an encounter which for him is first of all to be acknowledged in silence.

That 'who' question also leads on into the ultimate 'encounter' question relating to Jesus: God's engagement with humanity in this person. The doctrine of the Incarnation, that in Jesus God became human, runs through a great many of the extracts. We have tried to indicate some of its biblical roots (e.g. **39**, **50**, **66**), the controversies surrounding its articulation and reception (e.g. **72–80**), and the repeated recurrence of discussion of it, including attempts to understand Jesus while denying it (e.g. **251**, **319**). We were sometimes tempted to play down this theme, which accounts for some of the more abstruse extracts (e.g. **103**, **105**, **116**), but it is so fundamental and enduring, and so essential to grasping the significance of Jesus for Christians and others, that again and again its right to be heard had to be acknowledged and

the reader invited to make the intellectual and imaginative effort to appreciate a doctrine which from the first has challenged received ideas of both God
and humanity.

Key Themes

The attempt to give some coherence to the extracts in the Reader through
the identification of three forms of engagement with Jesus—commenting
and conversing, performing and celebrating, and encountering—can be taken
further by noticing some key recurrent themes in the Reader.

NARRATIVE

The most obvious and persistent theme is the identification of Jesus by his
story. This runs through all the modes of responding and it is dominant in the
New Testament too. There, the four Gospels differ in many respects, but the
most deeply embedded feature of their testimonies to Jesus is a three-part
pattern: his life (including announcing the Kingdom of God, teaching,
conflict, and embodying his message through gathering disciples, healings,
and other actions); his death by crucifixion; and his Resurrection.

Further, the New Testament stories integrate the message and ministry of
Jesus with his person. John's Gospel is especially explicit about this (cf. its 'I
am' sayings, 13); but the other ('Synoptic') Gospels also show, in their treatment of his birth (1), baptism (2), Transfiguration (12), death (16), Resurrection (17), and Ascension (20), how inextricable are his words, actions, and
person.

In addition, this core story, identifying Jesus primarily through what he
does, says, and suffers, is set within the larger story of God in relation to
Israel, and Jewish Scriptures and traditions are pervasively important in
describing him.

How are these stories treated in the extracts from outside the Bible? Tracing
that is a fascinating task. Repetitions or summaries of the stories have always
been essential to Christian worship, and the Eucharist, the principal liturgy
for the majority of the world's Christians, retells the culminating events of
the story of Jesus. It says a great deal about a liturgy, a spirituality, a theology,
a period of history, or a Christian tradition what aspects of the story are
especially emphasized by them. One of the most balanced brief statements is
that of Bonhoeffer (see 309), suggesting the simultaneous and maximal significance of Jesus' Incarnation, death, and Resurrection. Sometimes one
dimension or event is intensively focused upon and becomes the lens through
which all else is seen (cf. 169 on the death of Jesus, 264 on Jesus' teaching, 89
on the Transfiguration).

The story can also be amended or challenged. Within Christianity Marcion early on questioned the way fellow Christians affirmed the Old Testament story, and variations on his reservations have continually resurfaced. An even more radical challenge to the early Church came from the Gnostics (see 68, 69) whose dualism devalued the importance of any historical events, and who had special problems with the Crucifixion of Jesus. The latter has also been a key concern of Muslim interpretation of Jesus (e.g. 123, 135). The most common challenges to the story of Jesus in recent centuries in the West have been aimed at miracles, the virgin birth, and the Resurrection.

FRAMEWORK

It is always instructive to notice the framework of reality within which Jesus is understood. The Reader shows the main elements of the mainstream Christian framework being worked out, often through hard-fought argument. The single most important development was the articulation of the relationship of Jesus to God. This involved affirming continuity with the Old Testament identification of God but also deciding that Jesus was fully divine, the incarnation of God (cf. 74, 86, 321). It led to the doctrine of God as Trinity (Father, Son, and Holy Spirit) becoming the embracing Christian framework for acknowledging Jesus (e.g. 80). He was affirmed as the self-expression and self-gift of God in history, and this was reflected in creeds, prayers, liturgies, catechisms, doctrines, hymns, poems, and other expressions of the faith.

Often the way it was reflected was more implicit than explicit, and most believers were not very conscious of the doctrine of the Trinity. They were more aware of other frameworks, especially those to do with the overarching narrative from creation to the last Judgement and eternal life, or to do with prayer, worship, and ethics. It was always a sensitive matter how far such conceptions and practices were in line with the doctrines of Incarnation and Trinity, and the Reader shows some of the debates which resulted (e.g. 108 on icons, 326–8 on the feminist Jesus). Even when there was no question raised about the compatibility of a doctrine or practice with the Incarnation or the Trinity, as in the eucharistic controversies (e.g. 118, 156, 172–6) or the Calvinist doctrine of election (that God had predestined some to be saved through Jesus Christ and others to be damned; cf. 170), there could be deep differences which amounted to a conflict about the whole framework for belief in Jesus. Further issues are raised by attempts to think about Jesus in philosophical (e.g. 230, 290), cosmological (e.g. 323), political (e.g. 215, 300), or cultural (e.g. 305) terms. Repeatedly these reconceptions of Jesus have been questioned as to whether they distort, domesticate, or even manipulate Jesus in the interests of an alien agenda. They have often in reply not only appealed to the need to show his relevance to philosophy, cosmology, politics, or different cultures, but have also engaged in critiques of the frameworks through which he has been conceptualized in the past. Especially in recent centuries, massive shifts in world-view and in many aspects of human society have raised sharp prob-lems for any understanding rooted in premodernity. The result has been a continuing tension between such efforts to work out the relevance of Jesus and the critics who suspect that modern frameworks take over and violate the identity of Jesus.

There have also, of course, been many frameworks for understanding Jesus which reject or ignore the main strands of Christian orthodoxy. Some of these are rooted in other faith traditions, such as Judaism (e.g. **120**, **161**), Zoroastrianism (e.g. **122**), or Islam (e.g. **123–6**). Others explicitly express no faith, while dealing with Jesus aesthetically (e.g. **315**), ethically (e.g. **233**), or intellectually (much modern biblical and historical scholarship, as in **285**). And many ancient and modern non-religious world-views have produced interpretations of Jesus (e.g. **60**, **241**). Together, all these constitute an interrogative accompaniment to Christianity which has provoked a great deal of polemic (e.g. **58**, **120**) and increasing amounts of dialogue (e.g. **277**, **341**).

IMAGE

From the start Jesus has been described in images, often with startling free-dom. The chief source of imagery has always been the Old Testament, and appreciating it is therefore the main way to understand the imaginative 'logic' of a great deal in the New Testament and later literature and art. Just to take some of the key images in Sections 1.B and C—light, rock, lamb, king, sun, wisdom, judge, and word—all are common currency, but without knowing their Old Testament resonances their meaning is likely to be missed or only partly understood.

We have also given some tastes of the rich and sometimes wild variety of imaginative inventions Jesus has evoked. He is seen as an unburning coal (**99**), ladder (**149**), mother (**152**), Narcissus (**192**), communist (**241**), and fairytale lion (**316**). Sometimes the response of a culture or period is powerfully expressed in an image—Jesus as Son of the Cool Wind in China (**100**), as a chevalier taking up and transforming the idiom of courtly romance (**102**), as master of initiation in Africa (**304**), or as black in America (**306**).

There is one image to which we have paid special attention. The face of Christ is a biblical image (e.g. **12**, **45**), and can be followed through Church history (e.g. **87**, **108**, **129**, **141**, **342**, **343**). It resonates with Old Testament references to the face of God, it can be an imaginative focus for key New Testament events (from the face of the baby to the glorified face of the risen Jesus), and it allows for the intensities of agony, celebration, and face-to-face encounter.

JOURNEYS OF INTENSIFICATION

Finally, there are what might be summed up in the American theologian David Tracy's phrase as 'journeys of intensification'—ways of engaging with Jesus which are intensively immersed in a distinctive experience, activity, or symbolic mode. Much of what has already been talked about can come under this heading: an intensively debated text, concept, or doctrine; baptism and Eucharist; tropes of union with, participation in, following after, or dwelling in Christ; major events in the story of Jesus, understood as 'mysteries' to be indwelt and lived through.

But there are many others, and depth of commitment is often accompanied by such intensities. Whole traditions have their favourites, and we have given a range of instances. Martyrdom (e.g. **35**) profoundly shaped the Church in the early centuries. Contemplation of Christ (e.g. Section 2.A) was especially developed in the Byzantine and early medieval period, and in later medieval spirituality (e.g. Section 3.A) often focused especially on the suffering and death of Christ. The characteristic Reformation journey of intensification was 'justification by grace through faith' (e.g. Section 4.A), and the Counter-Reformation produced its own fresh intensities, as in the Spiritual Exercises of Ignatius Loyola (**186**). Love and marriage imagery (cf. Sections 5.B and C and **276**) has constantly recurred, as have concentrations in the modes of politics (e.g. Section 7.C.II), ethics (e.g. Section 7.C.III), and beauty (e.g. Section 7.G). Suspicion of Jesus, as in Feuerbach (**231**) or Nietzsche (**253**), can have this intensity too, as can scholarly hypotheses (e.g. **277, 243, 286, 289**).

Plan of the Book

The suggestions we have made about modes of engagement and key themes will, we hope, assist in making this Reader's diverse extracts more comprehensible and coherent. But the most straightforward approach is through the way we have arranged the extracts. We conclude this introduction with some comments on the sections of the book.

The seven main sections are chronological. Such divisions are always debatable, but we have aimed at periods appropriate to shifts in the way Jesus has been regarded, followed, or studied. Some broad themes figure in extracts in all of the seven periods: Jesus as Saviour; devotion to Jesus; Jesus as human and divine; living as a follower of Jesus; and responses of critics and non-Christians to him.

Other themes are more distinctive of particular periods, or have been highlighted by us because of their special significance then. In the biblical and patristic period the canonical material is obviously fundamental (Section 1.A.I), and the extracts from outside the canon are also of special interest

(Section 1 .A.II). That was also the time when the decisive developments in Christology happened (Section 1.D).

The Byzantine and early medieval period was perhaps most fruitful in the sphere of devotion, and this is reflected in the space given to 'contemplating Christ', 'adoring Christ's humanity', and eucharistic prayer and understanding. The later medieval and Renaissance period continued this fruitfulness in devotion and in forms of discipleship, embodied above all in Francis of Assisi and his movement of friars (cf. **127, 138, 142, 145, 155**). It was also a time of immense intellectual rigour (only hinted at in Section 3.B, since short extracts are unsuited to lengthy, interrelated discussions using technical terms).

The Reformation and Counter-Reformation are represented by four sections on salvation, word, and sacrament, the person of Christ, and discipleship. Those are fundamental, inescapable themes in relation to Jesus, and their rethinking is a sign of how the very foundations of the Christian Church in the West were being shaken.

The shaking continued in early modernity, as seen above all in Enlightenment critiques and reinterpretations (Section 5.E). The response was partly through fresh forms of Christ-centred spirituality (Sections 5.A, B, C), but also in rigorous dogmatics (Section 5.D) and some imaginative reconceptions of faith in Christ (e.g. **220, 222**).

The nineteenth century was perhaps the period of most radical shaking in the past two millennia. Section 6.A (cf. 6.C.II) gives soundings in the debate about the historical Jesus and the associated massive challenges to classical Christology, often framed within comprehensive theories that were allied to developments in the sciences and deeply suspicious of religion. Further profound questions were being raised by the growing awareness of Eastern religions (Section 6.E). There was a wide range of Christian intellectual, devotional, and artistic responses (Sections 6.A.II, B, C, D) as well as a huge missionary movement which was to make Christianity not only the most numerous but also the most widely spread of the world's religions.

The twentieth century saw the continuation of the critical and negative thrusts of the nineteenth century, but the main fresh developments were more constructive. Who would have predicted at the end of the nineteenth century that academic study by the end of the twentieth century would find so much to affirm about the historical Jesus (Section 7.B.II)? Or that there would be a multifaceted revival in classical Christology complete with the doctrine of the Trinity (Sections 7.A, B.I, C.I, III)? Or that the political and ethical Jesus would have a profound impact in most continents (Sections 7.C.II, III)? Or that in the Holocaust there would occur the most traumatic event in the history of Judaism, but that this would both help many Christians to face and repent of their terrible history of contempt for Jews and persecution of them, and would also be an incentive to Jewish scholars to study Jesus afresh (Section 7.F.II)? Or that perhaps the most far-reaching of all transformations in Christianity would be to do with feminism, the position of women, relations between men and women—and the question of the maleness of Christ (Section 7.E.II)?

A final comment on the twentieth century: it was especially effective (in line with the whole 'modern' period) both in perpetrating and discerning injustice, oppression, hidden and overt violence, and distortions of truth and of life, and also in attempting to deal with them. In a word, suffering was a core concern. This was also so in its responses to Jesus. From the Russian Orthodox tradition, which suffered more martyrdoms in that century than perhaps any other Church in history, comes Archbishop Anthony Bloom's summary of the Gospel through the Jesus Prayer and especially through the mercy, healing, and tender love of Jesus Christ (**295**). More personal, and more sharply focused through an extremity of physical suffering, is Margaret Spufford's testimony. She is an academic who has internalized the suspicion and scepticism that are second nature to many modern Westerners, but through all that she combines an utter realism about suffering with a classical insight into the relationship of Jesus to it:

It was months before I dared tell even my husband, who was not likely to feel that I had suddenly been afflicted with religious mania, and knew I did not go in for pious or saccharine imagery, that quite extraordinarily at that moment of unreachability, I had suddenly been aware, even as I screamed, of the presence of the Crucified. He did not cancel the moment, or assuage it, but was inside it (**324**).

For the sake of consistency and readability, we have made minor editorial changes to some of the extracts, changing capitalization, spelling, and punctuation to match modern practice. If any larger-scale changes have been made, this is noted in the References.

PART I

Biblical and Patristic: To AD 451

Jerusalem is a long way from Byzantium; four hundred years is a long time. A huge distance separates the execution of a controversial Jewish healer and preacher outside the former city from the gathering outside the latter of several hundred men intent on defining his nature. The distance seems still greater when we realize that the Council of Chalcedon, held near Byzantium in AD 451, was a gathering of men with power and standing in the same empire which had executed this Jewish prophet, and which had soon afterwards stamped on the buzzing annoyance of Jerusalem, his homeland's capital city. How shall we account for such a journey?

In the early years communities of followers of the executed man had flourished, at first in Jewish Palestine and then beyond its borders, springing up quickly along the trade routes and marching paths of the Roman Empire. Men and women found themselves captivated by the life or the message of this man's followers, or found themselves drawn inside these communities by the accidents of birth, friendship, or curiosity. They learned, told, shaped, and passed on stories about the man (1–26); they participated in practices designed to link them to him (e.g. 35–6, 46); they shaped their common and individual lives as they thought allegiance to him demanded, schooling their desires and moulding their hopes (e.g. 48). They read the Jewish Scriptures to understand the man better, and learned to find him hidden beneath the surface of the text (Section C.I). They collected writings from the earliest years of their movement and began to shape their own authoritative canons, setting off the snowballing roll of commentary upon commentary (e.g. 38, 55). Above all, they died for their faith (35). In the first three centuries the sporadic and inefficient but widespread and brutal persecution of believers by the Roman authorities supplied an army of saints who had been united to their executed master in the most intimate way possible. Fuelled by these fires, what had been a movement for reform among the peasants and artisans of Palestinian Judaism spread to the wide Jewish diaspora, to the Gentile Greeks and Romans, up the ranks of worldly authority, to touch the limits of the known world (section C.II).

In all this the followers of the executed man developed ways of talking about his nature and significance, common motifs or formulas which helped them to organize their understanding and description of the life they were sharing (e.g. 40, 75). They searched for explanations or clarifications which would show how their beliefs and practices made sense, how they could cohere with their other commitments and responsibilities. They developed or discovered forms of expression which, to many of them (though not all), seemed to support and cast into relief the practices and experiences of their communities, to direct and intensify attention to its Scriptures, and to satisfy their desire for a coherent and comprehensive world in which to pursue this life. Members and communities argued over the best ways to ground and emphasize these motifs and formulas, and they found themselves differing over the appropriate ways of preserving, practising, and passing on their allegiance. Many groups found the accounts and practices they had developed to supplement and support their shared faith seemed to have such retrospective inevitability that to abandon them was to undermine the faith itself.

As the institutional organization of the spreading Church developed, and was held together in significant part by networks of arguing bishops, these accounts and practices, formulas and traditions, were rubbed against one another. Eventually large numbers of them coalesced into an evolving 'orthodoxy', a main stream of worship, conversation, and argument which criss-crossed the empire.

When, in the fourth century, the fortunes of Christianity changed and the upstart religion became first acceptable and then official in the Roman world, Christians had to come to terms with the end of martyrdom, and the beginning of more ambiguous relations with the pagan heritage of a sometimes superficially Christian empire. They also had to come to terms with power. The arguments and coalitions of Christian Churches became imperial business, and one emperor after another involved himself in the debates about Jesus, taking recalcitrant bishops in hand, calling together councils and requiring the gathered men to make up their minds, for the peace of the empire. The understanding of Christ became a matter of high politics (76, 80). Yet it was still the same Christ who was being argued about, and when the Eastern emperor Marcian called several hundred bishops together at Chalcedon to police the boundaries of the orthodox peace by clarifying their Christology and rejecting deviations from it, it was in many ways simply one more episode in the heated, schismatic, centuries-long conversation about the significance of the carpenter's son from Nazareth which had spread to engulf even the highest echelons of the imperial power which controlled his homeland (86).

Section A

....

The Life of Jesus

....

That we know about Jesus of Nazareth at all is due primarily to the sayings and stories which were the currency of the early Church, handed on, shaped, collected, and in time written down by his first followers. The writings that emerged from this process have presented all subsequent generations with the main wells from which images of Jesus are drawn, and have been followed by an endless succession of commentaries. Much of the rest of the material in this book is, in one way or another, made up of commentaries upon these foundational texts.

I. Canonical

Four of the writings about Jesus produced in the first century were accepted by the early Church as having unavoidable authority, and eventually joined other texts to form the New Testament: the three closely related 'Synoptic Gospels', known as Matthew, Mark, and Luke, and the rather different 'fourth Gospel', known as John. For much of Church history 'Jesus' meant simply 'the one whose life, death, Resurrection, and Ascension are rendered here'.

1   The Birth of the Messiah

....

Stories about Jesus' birth appear only in Matthew and Luke among the canonical Gospels; Mark begins instead with the story of Jesus' baptism (**2**) and John with an astonishing cosmological prologue (**66**). Matthew presents the miracle of the virgin birth in the context of an enduring emphasis on continuity—the use of the words of the prophet Isaiah (cf. **53**), and of the title 'Messiah' witnessing to the faithfulness of Israel's God.[1] (Cf. **100, 182, 244**.)

Now the birth of Jesus the Messiah took place in this way. When his mother Mary had been engaged to Joseph, but before they lived together, she was found to be with child from the Holy Spirit. Her husband Joseph, being a righteous man and unwilling to expose her to public disgrace, planned to dismiss her quietly. But just when he had resolved to do this, an angel of the Lord appeared to him in a dream and said, 'Joseph, son of David, do not be afraid to take Mary as your wife, for the child conceived in her is from the Holy Spirit. She will bear a son, and you are to name him Jesus, for he will save his people from their sins.'[2]

All this took place to fulfil what had been spoken by the Lord through the prophet: 'Look, the virgin shall conceive and bear a son, and they shall name him Emmanuel' [Isa. 7: 14] which means, 'God is with us.'

Matthew 1: 18–23 (1st century)

2   Jesus' Baptism

In all four canonical Gospels we meet John the Baptizer, whose wilderness ministry of preaching and baptizing in the face of God's coming wrath is presented as a preparation for the ministry of Jesus himself. The story of Jesus' baptism by John, with its tantalizing glimpses of the Father and the Spirit (cf. **12**) provided a rich source for later doctrinal and devotional developments. (Cf. **46**.)

In those days Jesus came from Nazareth of Galilee and was baptised by John in the Jordan. And just as he was coming up out of the water, he saw the heavens torn apart and the Spirit descending like a dove on him. And a voice came from heaven, 'You are my Son, the beloved; with you I am well pleased.'

And the Spirit immediately drove him out into the wilderness. He was in the wilderness forty days, tempted by Satan; and he was with the wild beasts; and the angels waited on him.

Mark 1: 9–13 (1st century)

3   Parables of the Kingdom

The canonical Gospels present Jesus' teachings in a number of ways. In the Synoptics, the most characteristic form is the parable: a fresh, pithy, and often paradoxical story set in the everyday world of Jesus' time, and used above all to develop Jesus' key theme: the kingdom of God (or 'kingdom of heaven'). (Cf. **287, 288**.)

He put before them a parable: 'The kingdom of heaven is like a mustard seed that someone took and sowed in his field; it is the smallest of all the seeds, but when it has grown it is the greatest of shrubs and becomes a tree, so that the birds of the air come and make nests in its branches.'

He told them another parable: 'The kingdom of heaven is like yeast that a woman took and mixed in with three measures of flour until all of it was leavened.' Jesus told the crowds all these things in parables; without a parable he told them nothing.

Matthew 13: 31–4 (1st century)

4 The Beatitudes

Alongside parables (**3**), longer discourses appear on Jesus' lips, the most famous being Matthew's 'Sermon on the Mount', which has become, particularly in recent centuries, *the* focus for discussion of Jesus' ethical teaching. (Cf. **90, 264**.)

When Jesus saw the crowds, he went up the mountain; and after he sat down, his disciples came to him. Then he began to speak, and taught them, saying:

'Blessed are the poor in spirit, for theirs is the kingdom of heaven.
Blessed are those who mourn, for they will be comforted.
Blessed are the meek, for they will inherit the earth.
Blessed are those who hunger and thirst for righteousness, for they will be filled.
Blessed are the merciful, for they will receive mercy.
Blessed are the pure in heart, for they will see God.
Blessed are the peacemakers, for they will be called children of God.
Blessed are those who are persecuted for righteousness' sake, for theirs is the kingdom of heaven.

Blessed are you when people revile you and persecute you and utter all kinds of evil against you falsely on my account. Rejoice and be glad, for your reward is great in heaven, for in the same way they persecuted the prophets who were before you.'

Matthew 5: 1–12 (1st century)

5 The Lord's Prayer

Jesus is presented in the canonical Gospels as a man of prayer, spending time alone in prayer, and teaching about its proper practice; here in his most famous prayer (presented with slight differences also in Matt. 6: 9–13), we again see him teaching his disciples to pray for the coming of God's kingdom (cf. **3**), and to anticipate its arrival by practising forgiveness.

He was praying in a certain place, and after he had finished, one of his disciples said to him, 'Lord, teach us to pray, as John taught his disciples.'
He said to them, 'When you pray, say:

"Father, hallowed be your name.
Your kingdom come.
Give us each day our daily bread.
And forgive us our sins,
for we ourselves forgive everyone indebted to us.
And do not bring us to the time of trial."'

Luke 11: 1–4 (1st century)

Jesus' teaching and action is charged with expectation of God's coming intervention in the world's course, to bring about the establishment of his kingdom on earth (5). At times the Gospels present that kingdom as having already come in Jesus' ministry, but such affirmations jostle with strong currents of expectation pointing to a future cataclysmic fulfilment. (Cf. **62**, **243**, **262**, **288**.)

Jesus began to say to them, 'Beware that no one leads you astray. Many will come in my name and say, "I am he!" and they will lead many astray. When you hear of wars and rumours of wars, do not be alarmed; this must take place, but the end is still to come. For nation will rise against nation, and kingdom against kingdom; there will be earthquakes in various places; there will be famines. This is but the beginning of the birth pangs.

'As for yourselves, beware; for they will hand you over to councils; and you will be beaten in synagogues; and you will stand before governors and kings because of me, as a testimony to them. And the good news must first be proclaimed to all nations. When they bring you to trial and hand you over, do not worry beforehand about what you are to say; but say whatever is given you at that time, for it is not you who speak, but the Holy Spirit. [Cf. **171**.] Brother will betray brother to death, and a father his child, and children will rise against parents and have them put to death; and you will be hated by all because of my name. But the one who endures to the end will be saved.'

Mark 13: 5–13 (1st century)

Exorcisms are a striking feature of Jesus' ministry as presented in the canonical Gospels, presenting in microcosm Jesus' anticipation of God's coming rout of the forces of evil, his bringing in to communion of those whom society has placed beyond the pale. (Cf. **287**.)

A man of the city who had demons met [Jesus]. For a long time he had worn no clothes, and he did not live in a house but in the tombs. When he saw Jesus, he fell down before him and shouted at the top of his voice, 'What have you to do with me, Jesus, Son of the most high God? I beg you, do not torment me'—for Jesus had commanded the unclean spirit to come out of the man. (For many times it had seized him; he was kept under guard and bound with chains and shackles, but he would break the bonds and be driven by the demon into the wilds.)

Jesus then asked him, 'What is your name?'

He said, 'Legion'; for many demons had entered him. They begged him not to order them to go back into the abyss. Now there on the hillside a large herd of swine was feeding; and the demons begged Jesus to let them enter these. So he gave them permission. Then the demons came out of the man and entered the swine, and the herd rushed down the steep bank into the lake and was drowned.

Luke 8: 27–33 (1st century)

8 Healing the Sick

Jesus' ministry was one of healing—both in the obvious sense that he was known as a miracle-worker who could overcome physical ailments, and in the more radical sense that he offered forgiveness (5), stepping over the barriers which separated people from full fellowship with one another and with God. (Cf. 7, 287, 288.)

When [Jesus] returned to Capernaum after some days, it was reported that he was at home. So many gathered around that there was no longer room for them, not even in front of the door; and he was speaking the word to them. Then some people came, bringing to him a paralysed man, carried by four of them. And when they could not bring him to Jesus because of the crowd, they removed the roof above him; and after having dug through it, they let down the mat on which the paralytic lay.

When Jesus saw their faith, he said to the paralytic, 'Son, your sins are forgiven.'

Now some of the scribes were sitting there, questioning in their hearts, 'Why does this fellow speak in this way? It is blasphemy! Who can forgive sins but God alone?'

At once Jesus perceived in his spirit that they were discussing these questions among themselves; and he said to them, 'Why do you raise such questions in your hearts? Which is easier, to say to the paralytic, "Your sins are forgiven," or to say, "Stand up and take your mat and walk"? But so that you may know that the Son of Man has authority on earth to forgive sins'—he said to the paralytic—'I say to you, stand up, take your mat and go to your home.'

And he stood up, and immediately took the mat and went out before all of them; so that they were all amazed and glorified God, saying, 'We have never seen anything like this!'

Mark 2: 1–12 (1st century)

9 The Feeding of the Five Thousand

Jesus' miracles are presented in the canonical Gospels as signs not just of his compassion, but also of his extraordinary power and authority. This is particularly true of some of those miracles which are neither healings nor exorcisms but demonstrations of Jesus' ability to provide whatever is necessary. (Cf. **10, 82**.)

When he looked up and saw a large crowd coming toward him, Jesus said to Philip, 'Where are we to buy bread for these people to eat?' He said this to test him, for he himself knew what he was going to do.

Philip answered him, 'Six months' wages would not buy enough bread for each of them to get a little.'

One of his disciples, Andrew, Simon Peter's brother, said to him, 'There is a boy here who has five barley loaves and two fish. But what are they among so many people?'

Jesus said, 'Make the people sit down.' Now there was a great deal of grass in the place; so they sat down, about five thousand in all. Then Jesus took the loaves, and when he had given thanks, he distributed them to those who were seated; so also the fish, as much as they wanted. When they were satisfied, he told his disciples, 'Gather up the fragments left over, so that nothing may be lost.' So they gathered them up, and from the fragments of the five barley loaves, left by those who had eaten, they filled twelve baskets. When the people saw the sign that he had done, they began to say, 'This is indeed the prophet who is to come into the world.'

John 6: 5–14 (1st century)

10 Calming the Storm

As with the feeding of the five thousand (**9**), the story of Jesus' calming of the storm is presented as a demonstration of his overwhelming authority, his connection to the God who commanded the waters in creation (Gen. 1: 6–7).

One day [Jesus] got into a boat with his disciples, and he said to them, 'Let us go across to the other side of the lake.'

So they put out, and while they were sailing he fell asleep. A windstorm swept down on the lake, and the boat was filling with water, and they were in danger. They went to him and woke him up, shouting, 'Master, Master, we are perishing!'

And he woke up and rebuked the wind and the raging waves; they ceased, and there was a calm. He said to them, 'Where is your faith?'

They were afraid and amazed, and said to one another, 'Who then is this, that he commands even the winds and the water, and they obey him?'

Luke 8: 22–5 (1st century)

11 Peter's Confession

In the Synoptics, the story of Peter's confession at Caesarea Philippi is part of a transition from Jesus' ministry in the Galilee area to his long journey to Jerusalem and the looming Cross. Another seminal passage, it has long been a key resource in debates about the relationship between Jesus' authority and authority in the Church which bears his name. (Cf. **296**.)

Now when Jesus came into the district of Caesarea Philippi, he asked his disciples, 'Who do people say that the Son of Man is?'

And they said, 'Some say John the Baptist, but others Elijah, and still others Jeremiah or one of the prophets.'

He said to them, 'But who do you say that I am?'

Simon Peter answered, 'You are the Messiah,[3] the Son of the living God.'

And Jesus answered him, 'Blessed are you, Simon son of Jonah! For flesh and blood has not revealed this to you, but my Father in heaven. And I tell you, you are Peter, and on this rock I will build my church, and the gates of Hades will not prevail against it. I will give you the keys of the kingdom of heaven, and whatever you bind on earth will be bound in heaven, and whatever you loose on earth will be loosed in heaven.' Then he sternly ordered the disciples not to tell anyone that he was the Messiah.

Matthew 16: 13–20 (1st century)

12 The Transfiguration

In Orthodox Christianity in particular the story of the Transfiguration has had a pervasive influence on the way that Jesus is presented and understood, from gold-swathed icons to the dogmatic pronouncements of councils (**73**, **88**, **89**); along with the baptism (**2**) it has also been seen as a key moment at which the story of Jesus unfolds the nature of God as trinity (**295**). (Cf. **56**, **238**, **237**.)

Jesus took with him Peter and James and John, and led them up a high mountain apart, by themselves. And he was transfigured before them, and his clothes became dazzling white, such as no one on earth could bleach them. And there appeared to them Elijah with Moses, who were talking with Jesus. Then Peter said to Jesus, 'Rabbi, it is good for us to be here; let us make three dwellings, one for you, one for Moses, and one for Elijah.' He did not know what to say, for they were terrified.

Then a cloud overshadowed them, and from the cloud there came a voice, 'This is my Son, the Beloved; listen to him!' Suddenly when they looked around, they saw no one with them any more, but only Jesus.

Mark 9: 2–8 (1st century)

13   The Way, The Truth, and the Life

In John, Jesus' teaching orbits around a set of 'I am' sayings, in which Jesus proclaims his identity and significance. In this extract one such saying leads in to a series of dynamic and riddling statements in which Jesus draws his disciples into an awareness of his unparalleled relationship with his heavenly Father.

[Jesus said,] 'Do not let your hearts be troubled. Believe in God, believe also in me. In my Father's house there are many dwelling places. If it were not so, would I have told you that I go to prepare a place for you? And if I go and prepare a place for you, I will come again and will take you to myself, so that where I am, there you may be also.

'And you know the way to the place where I am going.'

Thomas said to him, 'Lord, we do not know where you are going. How can we know the way?'

Jesus said to him, 'I am the way, and the truth, and the life. No one comes to the Father except through me. If you know me, you will know my Father also. From now on you do know him and have seen him.'

Philip said to him, 'Lord, show us the Father, and we will be satisfied.'

Jesus said to him, 'Have I been with you all this time, Philip, and you still do not know me? Whoever has seen me has seen the Father. How can you say, "Show us the Father"? Do you not believe that I am in the Father and the Father is in me? The words that I say to you I do not speak on my own; but the Father who dwells in me does his works. Believe me that I am in the Father and the Father is in me; but if you do not, then believe me because of the works themselves.'

John 14: 1–11 (1st century)

14 The Last Supper

In the canonical Scriptures it is not only in the four Gospels that we find descriptions of Jesus' words and deeds. Although on the whole he has little explicit to say about the details of Jesus teaching and ministry, Paul, the dramatically converted Apostle to the Gentiles, hands on in his correspondence with the Church in Corinth a tradition about Jesus' actions at his last meal with his disciples. (Cf. 36, 117–19, 155–7, 172–6, 273.)

For I received from the Lord what I also handed on to you, that the Lord Jesus on the night when he was betrayed took a loaf of bread, and when he had given thanks, he broke it and said, 'This is my body that is for you. Do this in remembrance of me.' In the same way he took the cup also, after supper, saying, 'This cup is the new covenant in my blood. Do this, as often as you drink it, in remembrance of me.' For as often as you eat this bread and drink the cup, you proclaim the Lord's death until he comes.

1 Corinthians 11: 23–6 (1st century)

15 The Garden of Gethsemane

The last meal with his disciples over (14), Jesus is shown in the Gospels making his way to a secluded retreat outside the walls of Jerusalem, there to confront in anguished prayer the sufferings which he was soon to undergo physically. Perhaps more than any other, this passage has forced Christian theologians and their opponents to think about the humanity of Christ, his ability to suffer not just wounds to his flesh but mental torment and fear. (Cf. 132, 318.)

Jesus went with [the disciples] to a place called Gethsemane; and he said to his disciples, 'Sit here while I go over there and pray.'

He took with him Peter and the two sons of Zebedee, and began to be grieved and agitated. Then he said to them, 'I am deeply grieved, even to death; remain here, and stay awake with me.' And going a little farther, he threw himself on the ground and prayed, 'My Father, if it is possible, let this cup pass from me; yet not what I want but what you want.'

Then he came to the disciples and found them sleeping; and he said to Peter, 'So, could you not stay awake with me one hour? Stay awake and pray that you may not come into the time of trial; the spirit indeed is willing, but the flesh is weak.'

Again he went away for the second time and prayed, 'My Father, if this cannot pass unless I drink it, your will be done.' Again he came and found them sleeping, for their eyes were heavy. So leaving them again, he went

away and prayed for the third time, saying the same words. Then he came to
the disciples and said to them, 'Are you still sleeping and taking your rest?
See, the hour is at hand, and the Son of Man is betrayed into the hands of
sinners. Get up, let us be going. See, my betrayer is at hand.'

Matthew 26: 36–46 (1st century)

16   The Crucifixion

> Everything in the Gospels leads to the bare summit of Golgotha, the 'place of
> the skull', where Jesus is executed in humiliation. All the pathways of later
> response to this man ultimately meet here, in a broken body suffering and
> then dead. (Cf. **67, 68, 70, 132–5, 143–6, 187, 192–5, 198–200, 202, 291, 329–32.**)

And they crucified him, and divided his clothes among them, casting lots to
decide what each should take. It was nine o'clock in the morning when they
crucified him. The inscription of the charge against him read, 'The King of
the Jews.' And with him they crucified two bandits, one on his right and one
on his left. Those who passed by derided him, shaking their heads and saying,
'Aha! You who would destroy the temple and build it in three days, save
yourself, and come down from the cross!' In the same way the chief priests,
along with the scribes, were also mocking him among themselves and saying,
'He saved others; he cannot save himself. Let the Messiah, the King of Israel,
come down from the cross now, so that we may see and believe.' Those who
were crucified with him also taunted him.

When it was noon, darkness came over the whole land until three in the
afternoon. At three o'clock Jesus cried out with a loud voice, 'Eloi, Eloi, lema
sabachthani?' which means, 'My God, my God, why have you forsaken me?'
When some of the bystanders heard it, they said, 'Listen, he is calling for
Elijah.' And someone ran, filled a sponge with sour wine, put it on a stick,
and gave it to him to drink, saying, 'Wait, let us see whether Elijah will come
to take him down.' Then Jesus gave a loud cry and breathed his last. And the
curtain of the temple was torn in two, from top to bottom.

Now when the centurion, who stood facing him, saw that in this way he
breathed his last, he said, 'Truly this man was God's Son!'

Mark 15: 24–39 (1st century)

17   The Resurrection

> After the stark summit of the Cross, the Gospel authors move to a kaleido-
> scope of stories and incidents in which the crucified one is shown to have
> risen—a claim which has reverberated across the world since then. In Luke's

story, having hurriedly buried him in a nearby tomb before the sabbath, some of the women who were Jesus' friends and followers return later to complete their task. (Cf. **26**.)

But on the first day of the week, at early dawn, they came to the tomb, taking the spices that they had prepared. They found the stone rolled away from the tomb, but when they went in, they did not find the body. While they were perplexed about this, suddenly two men in dazzling clothes stood beside them. The women were terrified and bowed their faces to the ground, but the men said to them, 'Why do you look for the living among the dead? He is not here, but has risen. Remember how he told you, while he was still in Galilee, that the Son of Man must be handed over to sinners, and be crucified, and on the third day rise again.'

Then they remembered his words, and returning from the tomb, they told all this to the eleven and to all the rest. Now it was Mary Magdalene, Joanna, Mary the mother of James, and the other women with them who told this to the apostles. But these words seemed to them an idle tale, and they did not believe them. But Peter got up and ran to the tomb; stooping and looking in, he saw the linen cloths by themselves; then he went home, amazed at what had happened.

Luke 24: 1–12 (1st century)

18 The Road to Emmaus

One of the Resurrection stories (**17**) most pregnant with possibilities for future elaboration and reflection is this story from Luke, with its resonances of preaching and the Eucharist, Christocentric biblical interpretation and conversion. (Cf. **255**, **286**, **317**.)

Now on that same day two of them were going to a village called Emmaus, about seven miles from Jerusalem, and talking with each other about all these things that had happened. While they were talking and discussing, Jesus himself came near and went with them, but their eyes were kept from recognising him. And he said to them, 'What are you discussing with each other while you walk along?'

They stood still, looking sad. Then one of them, whose name was Cleopas, answered him, 'Are you the only stranger in Jerusalem who does not know the things that have taken place there in these days?'

He asked them, 'What things?'

They replied, 'The things about Jesus of Nazareth, who was a prophet mighty in deed and word before God and all the people, and how our chief priests and leaders handed him over to be condemned to death and crucified him. But we had hoped that he was the one to redeem Israel. Yes, and besides all this, it is now the third day since these things took place. Moreover, some women of our group astounded us. They were at the tomb early this morning, and when they did not find his body there, they came back and told us that they had indeed seen a vision of angels who said that he was alive. Some of those who were with us went to the tomb and found it just as the women had said; but they did not see him.'

Then he said to them, 'Oh, how foolish you are, and how slow of heart to believe all that the prophets have declared! Was it not necessary that the Messiah should suffer these things and then enter into his glory?' Then beginning with Moses and all the prophets, he interpreted to them the things about himself in all the scriptures.

As they came near the village to which they were going, he walked ahead as if he were going on. But they urged him strongly, saying, 'Stay with us, because it is almost evening and the day is now nearly over.' So he went in to stay with them. When he was at the table with them, he took bread, blessed and broke it, and gave it to them. Then their eyes were opened, and they recognised him; and he vanished from their sight. They said to each other, 'Were not our hearts burning within us while he was talking to us on the road, while he was opening the scriptures to us?'

Luke 24: 13–32 (1st century)

19 The Great Commission

The story told in the Gospels which has led through Crucifixion (16) to the Resurrection (17) does not close there, but runs on into the mission of disciples propelled to bear witness to their risen Lord. (Cf. 275.)

Now the eleven disciples went to Galilee, to the mountain to which Jesus had directed them. When they saw him, they worshipped him; but some doubted. And Jesus came and said to them, 'All authority in heaven and on earth has been given to me. Go therefore and make disciples of all nations, baptising them in the name of the Father and of the Son and of the Holy Spirit, and teaching them to obey everything that I have commanded you. And remember, I am with you always, to the end of the age.'

Matthew 28: 16–20 (1st century)

20 | The Ascension

Luke summarizes his account of the Resurrection appearances (17) of Jesus at the beginning of Acts, the second part of his history of the faith, and then sketches the overarching context for his history of the Church's mission by describing Jesus' final commission, his departure, and the hope of his return. (Cf. 14.)

After his suffering he presented himself alive to them by many convincing proofs, appearing to them during forty days and speaking about the kingdom of God. While staying with them, he ordered them not to leave Jerusalem, but to wait there for the promise of the Father. 'This,' he said, 'is what you have heard from me; for John baptised with water, but you will be baptised with the Holy Spirit not many days from now.'

So when they had come together, they asked him, 'Lord, is this the time when you will restore the kingdom to Israel?'

He replied, 'It is not for you to know the times or periods that the Father has set by his own authority. But you will receive power when the Holy Spirit has come upon you; and you will be my witnesses in Jerusalem, in all Judea and Samaria, and to the ends of the earth.'

When he had said this, as they were watching, he was lifted up, and a cloud took him out of their sight. While he was going and they were gazing up toward heaven, suddenly two men in white robes stood by them. They said, 'Men of Galilee, why do you stand looking up toward heaven? This Jesus, who has been taken up from you into heaven, will come in the same way as you saw him go into heaven.'

Acts 1: 3–11 (1st century)

II. Extra-Canonical

The canonical Scriptures do not exhaust all that the early Christians preserved concerning Jesus or attributed to him. There are other memories preserved in the documents of the first centuries, and other attempts to write the story of the man from Nazareth. The process by which these writings were sifted, and a canon defined of those deemed most authoritative, most capacious for the unfolding of Christian practice and reflection, is crucial in the Church's early centuries.

In various places in the documents of the early Church sayings are attributed to Jesus beyond those we find in the four Gospels. Some of them plausibly come from Jesus himself.

'To give is more blessed than to receive.'

Acts 20: 35 (1st century)

'No one can attain the kingdom of heaven who has not gone through temptation.'

Tertullian (Quintus Septimius Florens Tertullianus) (cf. 70), De Baptismo
20. 2 (c.205)

'He who is near me is near the fire; he who is far from me is far from the kingdom.'

Origen (cf. 73), Homilies on Jeremiah 20: 3 (c.240) = The Gospel of Thomas (cf. 24),
Logion 82 (2nd century)

When on the same day he saw a man doing work on the Sabbath, he said to him, 'If you know what you are doing, blessed are you! But if you do not know, you are cursed and a transgressor of the law.'

Luke 6: 5 according to Codex D (5th or 6th century)

In 1905 a page of papyrus covered with tiny writing was discovered in Egypt. It contained the following passage from an otherwise unknown Gospel. The papyrus is from the fourth or fifth century (and may have been used as an amulet), but the text is plausibly much older.

He took the disciples with him into the place of purification itself and walked about in the Temple court, and a Pharisaic chief priest, Levi by name, fell in with them and said to the Saviour, 'Who gave you leave to walk in this place of purification and to look upon these holy utensils without having bathed yourself and even without your disciples having washed their feet? On the contrary, you have walked the Temple court whilst defiled, this clean place, although no one who has not first bathed himself or changed his clothes may tread it and venture to view these holy utensils!'

Then the Saviour stood still with his disciples and answered, 'What about you? For you are also here in the Temple court. Are you clean?'

The Levite answered, 'I am clean: I have bathed myself in the pool of David and have gone down by one stair and come up by the other; I have put on white and clean clothes; and only then have I come here and viewed the holy utensils.'

Then the Saviour said to him, 'Woe to you who are blind and do not see. You have bathed yourself in water that has been poured out, in which dogs and swine lie night and day, and you have washed yourself and have chafed your outer skin, which prostitutes and flute-girls also anoint, bathe, chafe and rouge in order to arouse desire in men even though within they are full of scorpions and every kind of evil. But I and my disciples, who you say have not been immersed, have been immersed in the living water which comes down from heaven.'

Papyrus Ox 840, extract (date unknown)

23   Jesus as a Child

The stretches of Jesus' life over which the canonical Gospels pass in silence provided later imagination with an open field. Jesus' childhood was the scene for many stories, such as these rather brutal stories from the (probably) second-century *Infancy Story of Thomas*, a popular work depicting a vaguely docetic Jesus (cf. **25**, **26**).[4]

When the boy Jesus was five years old he was playing at the ford of a brook, and he gathered together into pools the water that flowed by, and made it at once clean, and commanded it by his word alone. He made soft clay and fashioned from it twelve sparrows. And it was the sabbath when he did this. And there were also many other children playing with him. Now when a certain Jew saw what Jesus was doing in his play on the sabbath, he at once went and told his father Joseph: 'See, your child is at the brook, and he has taken clay and fashioned twelve birds and has profaned the sabbath.' And when Joseph came to the place and saw it, he cried out to him, saying: 'Why do you do on the sabbath what ought not to be done?' But Jesus clapped his hands and cried to the sparrows: 'Off with you!' And the sparrows took flight and went away chirping. The Jews were amazed when they saw this, and went away and told their elders what they had seen Jesus do. [. . .]

After this again he went through the village, and a lad ran and knocked against his shoulder. Jesus was exasperated and said to him: 'You shall not go further on your way', and the child immediately fell down and died. But some, who saw what took place, said: 'From where does this child spring, since his every word is an accomplished deed?' And the parents of the dead child came to Joseph and blamed him and said: 'Since you have such a child, you cannot dwell with us in the village; or else teach him to bless and not to curse. For he is slaying our children.'

And Joseph called the child aside and admonished him saying: 'Why do you do such things that these people must suffer and hate us and persecute us?' But Jesus replied: 'I know that these words are not yours; nevertheless for your sake I will be silent. But they shall bear their punishment.' And immediately those who had accused him became blind. And those who saw it were greatly afraid and perplexed, and said concerning him: 'Every word he speaks, whether good or evil, was a deed and became a marvel.' And when Joseph saw that Jesus had so done, he arose and took him by the ear and pulled it hard. And the child was angry and said to him: 'It is sufficient for you to seek and not to find, and most unwisely have you acted. Do you not know that I am yours? Do not vex me.'

Now a certain teacher, Zacchaeus by name, who was standing there, heard in part Jesus saying these things to his father, and marvelled greatly that, being a child, he said such things. And after a few days he came near to Joseph and said to him: 'You have a clever child, and he has understanding. Come, hand him over to me that he may learn letters, and I will teach him with the letters all knowledge, and to salute all the older people and honour them as grandfathers and fathers, and to love those of his own age.' And he told him all the letters from Alpha to Omega clearly, with much questioning. But he looked at Zacchaeus the teacher and said to him: 'How do you, who do not know the Alpha according to its nature, teach others the Beta? Hypocrite, first if you know it, teach the Alpha, and then we shall believe you concerning the Beta.' Then he began to question the teacher about the first letter, and he was unable to answer him. And in the hearing of many the child said to Zacchaeus: 'Hear, teacher, the arrangement of the first letter, and pay heed to this, how it has lines and a middle mark which goes through the pair of lines which you see, how these lines converge, rise, turn in the dance, three signs of the same kind, subject to and supporting one another, of equal proportions; here you have the lines of the Alpha.'

The Infancy Story of Thomas 2–6, extracts (2nd century?)

24   Jesus as Gnostic Teacher

The full text of The Gospel of Thomas was discovered in 1945 in Egypt, and may date from the middle of the second century. It is a collection of sayings of Jesus, shorn of most narrative setting, and often Gnostic in feel (cf. 68–9), presenting Jesus as a teacher of esoteric wisdom. Its value as a historical record has been much debated, but it certainly seems to represent an early and distinctive tradition of reflection on Jesus' meaning and message.

Jesus said, 'If those who lead you say to you, "Behold, the Kingdom is in heaven," then the birds of the heaven will be before you. If they say to you, "It is in the sea," then the fish will be before you. But the Kingdom is within you, and it is outside of you. When you know yourselves, then shall you be known, and you shall know that you are the sons of the living Father. But if you do not know yourselves, then you are in poverty, and you are poverty.'

Logion 3

Jesus said, 'I have cast fire upon the world, and behold, I guard it until it is ablaze.'

Logion 10

Jesus said to his disciples, 'Make a comparison to me, and tell me whom I am like.' Simon Peter said to him, 'You are like a righteous angel.' Matthew said to him, 'You are like a wise man of understanding.' Thomas said to him, 'Master, my mouth will in no way let me say whom you are like.' Jesus said, 'I am not your master, because you have drunk, you have become drunk from the bubbling spring which I have measured out.' And he took him, went aside, and spoke to him three words. Now when Thomas came to his companions, they asked him: 'What did Jesus say to you?' Thomas said to them, 'If I tell you one of the words which he said to me, you will take up stones and throw them at me; and a fire will come out of the stones and burn you up.'

Logion 13

Jesus said, 'I stood in the midst of the world, and I appeared to them in flesh. I found them all drunk. I found none among them thirsting; and my soul was afflicted for the sons of men, for they are blind in their heart and they do not see. For they came empty into the world, seeking also to depart empty from the world. But now they are drunk. When they have thrown off their wine, then they will repent.'

Logion 28

Jesus said, 'Become passers-by.'

Logion 42

Jesus said, 'If two make peace with one another in this one house, they shall say to the mountain, "Be moved!" and it shall be moved.'

Logion 48

Jesus said, 'Blessed is the man who has suffered; he has found the life.'

Logion 58

Jesus said, 'He who knows the All but fails to know himself lacks everything.'

Logion 67

Jesus said, 'I am the light that is over them all. I am the All; the All has come forth from me, and the All has attained unto me. Cleave a piece of wood: I am there. Raise up a stone, and you shall find me there.'

Logion 77

Jesus said, 'He who shall drink from my mouth shall become like me; I myself will become he, and the hidden things shall be revealed to him.'

Logion 108

His disciples said to him: 'On what day will the kingdom come?' Jesus said, 'It does not come with observation. They will not say, "Look, here!" or "Look, there!" But the kingdom of the Father is spread out upon the earth, and men do not see it.'

Logion 113

The Gospel of Thomas (2nd century?)

25   Jesus' Appearance

Passed over in silence by the writings of the New Testament, Jesus' appearance has been a constant source of fascination for later generations (cf. **129**, **342–3**). In the docetic[5] *Acts of John* (second or early third century), supposedly an account of the life and teaching of John the Evangelist, the bodily reality of Christ's humanity is called into doubt. (Cf. **26**.)

When Jesus had chosen Peter and Andrew, who were brothers, he came to me and to my brother James, saying, 'I need you; come with me!' And my brother said this to me: 'John, what does he want, this child on the shore who called us?' And I said, 'Which child?' And he answered me, 'The one who is beckoning to us.' And I said, 'This is because of the long watch we have kept at sea. You are not seeing straight, brother James. Do you not see the man standing there who is handsome, fair and cheerful-looking?' But he said to me, 'I do not see that man, my brother. But let us go, and we will see what this means.'

And when we had brought the boat to land we saw how he also helped us to beach the boat. And as we left the place, wishing to follow him, he appeared to me again as rather bald but with a thick flowing beard, but to James as a young man whose beard was just beginning. So we wondered both of us about the meaning of the vision we had seen. Then as we followed him we became gradually more perplexed about this matter.

But then there appeared to me a yet more amazing sight; I tried to see him as he was, and I never saw his eyes closing but always open. But he sometimes appeared to me as a small man with no good looks, and then again as looking up to heaven. And he had another strange property; when I reclined at table he would take me to his own breast, and I held him fast; and sometimes his breast felt to me smooth and soft, but sometimes hard like rock; so that I was perplexed in my mind and said, 'Why do I find it so?' [. . .]

Again he took us three likewise up the mountain, saying, 'Come with me.' And again we went; and we saw him at a distance praying. Then I, since he loved me, went quietly up to him, as if he could not see, and stood looking at his hinder parts; and I saw him not dressed in clothes at all, but stripped of those that we usually saw upon him, and not like a man at all. And I saw that his feet were whiter than snow, so that the ground there was lit up by his feet; and that his head stretched up to heaven, so that I was afraid and cried out; and he, turning about, appeared as a small man and caught hold of my beard and pulled it and said to me, 'John, do not be faithless, but believing—and not inquisitive.'

The Acts of John 89–90, extracts (2nd century?)

26   Jesus Rising

The legendary (and anti-Semitic) *Gospel of Peter* (probably from the middle of the second century) exists only in fragments. Like *The Acts of John* (**25**), *The Infancy Story of Thomas* (**23**), and many other second-century texts, it has a docetic flavour.[6] (Cf. **17**.)

Now in the night in which the Lord's day dawned, when the soldiers, two by two in every watch, were keeping guard, there rang out a loud voice in heaven, and they saw the heavens opened and two men come down from there in a great brightness and draw nigh to the sepulchre. That stone which had been laid against the entrance to the sepulchre started of itself to roll and gave way to the side, and the sepulchre was opened, and both the young men entered in. When now those soldiers saw this, they awakened the centurion and the elders—for they also were there to assist at the watch. And whilst they were relating what they had seen, they saw again three men come out from the sepulchre, and two of them sustaining the other, and a cross following them, and the heads of the two reaching to heaven, but that of him who was led of them by the hand overpassing the heavens. And they heard a voice out of the heavens crying, 'Thou hast preached to them that sleep?' and from the cross there was heard the answer, 'Yea'.

Those men therefore took counsel with one another to go and report this to Pilate. And whilst they were still deliberating, the heavens were again seen to open, and a man descended and entered into the sepulchre. When those who were of the centurion's company saw this, they hastened by night to

Pilate, abandoning the sepulchre which they were guarding, and reported everything that they had seen, being full of disquietude and saying, 'In truth he was the Son of God.'

The Gospel of Peter 35–45 (2nd century)

Section B

Jesus the Saviour

The driving force behind the growth of all Christian devotion, reflection, and debate concerning Jesus of Nazareth was the conviction that, somehow, he was the site of human salvation. We will look at a selection from the huge variety of ways in which that salvation was understood and expressed, before homing in on some ideas about Jesus and salvation which were particularly generative in the development of Christology.

I. Jesus Saves

In hymns and prayers and liturgies Christians of the first few centuries reiterated their basic conviction: Jesus saves; this man is, in one way or another, the means by which God has shown his love and truth, rescued us from evil, sin, and death, and drawn us into fellowship. A bewildering succession of images, narratives, explanations, and descriptions are used to give this conviction shape.

27 | God's Light

In the midst of a deep discourse about his relation to the Father, the Gospel of John has Jesus deliver what has become one of the best-known affirmations about God's salvation of the world through him; light against darkness, salvation against condemnation, truth against evil.

Very truly, I tell you, we speak of what we know and testify to what we have seen; yet you do not receive our testimony. If I have told you about earthly things and you do not believe, how can you believe if I tell you about heavenly things? No one has ascended into heaven except the one who descended from heaven, the Son of Man. And just as Moses lifted up the serpent in the wilderness, so must the Son of Man be lifted up, that whoever believes in him may have eternal life.

For God so loved the world that he gave his only Son, so that everyone who believes in him may not perish but may have eternal life. Indeed, God did not send the Son into the world to condemn the world, but in order that the world might be saved through him. Those who believe in him are not condemned; but those who do not believe are condemned already, because they have not believed in the name of the only Son of God. And this is the judgment, that the light has come into the world, and people loved darkness rather than light because their deeds were evil. For all who do evil hate the light and do not come to the light, so that their deeds may not be exposed. But those who do what is true come to the light, so that it may be clearly seen that their deeds have been done in God.

John 3: 11–21 (1st century)

28   The Enduring Rock

 The *Odes of Solomon* are forty-two hymns, probably from second-century Syria or Palestine, which were known only in fragments until the discovery of a Syriac manuscript in 1908 (although Syriac is unlikely to have been their original language). Jesus is the one who overcomes, the unshaken rock, the foundation upon which our lives can be built, safe against the storm.

> Chasms vanished before the Lord,
> And darkness dissipated before his appearance.
>
> Error erred and perished on account of him;
> And contempt received no path,
> For it was submerged by the truth of the Lord.
>
> He opened his mouth and spoke grace and joy;
> And recited a new chant to his name.
>
> Then he lifted his voice towards the Most High,
> And offered to him those that had become sons through him.
>
> And his face was justified,
> Because thus his holy Father had given to him.
>
> (Christ speaks)
>
> Come forth, you who have been afflicted,
> And receive joy.
>
> And possess yourselves through grace,
> And take unto you immortal life.
>
> And they condemned me when I stood up,
> Me who had not been condemned.
>
> Then they divided my spoil,
> Though nothing was owed them.
>
> But I endured and held my peace and was silent,
> That I might not be disturbed by them.
>
> But I stood undisturbed like a solid rock,
> Which is continuously pounded by columns of waves and endures.

And I bore their bitterness because of humility;
That I might redeem my nation and instruct it.

And that I might not nullify the promises to the patriarchs,
To whom I was promised for the salvation of their offspring.
Hallelujah.

The Odes of Solomon, Ode 31 (2nd century)

29   The Sacrificial Lamb

The celebration of Eucharist has had an incalculable impact on the Christian experience and understanding of salvation, as it has been prayed, proclaimed, and consumed in an uncountable series from the earliest days of the faith until now. Eucharistic liturgies have lent themselves in particular to the understanding of Jesus' death as a sacrifice on our behalf. This is from an early Syriac liturgy and, unusually, is addressed directly to Christ. (Cf. **14**.)

PRIEST: We make memorial, Lord, of your passion, just as you have taught us: for on that night when you were handed over to those who crucified you, Lord, you took bread in your pure and holy hands and gazed up to heaven towards your glorious Father, you blessed and signed it, consecrated and broke it, you gave it to your disciples, the blessed apostles, saying, 'This bread is my body which is broken and given for the life of the world, and is for those who partake of it the source of pardon of wrongs and forgiveness of sins; take and eat of it, and it shall be to you for eternal life.'

Likewise over the cup you gave thanks and praise in the same way, and you said, Lord, 'This cup is my blood of the new covenant which is shed on behalf of many for the forgiveness of sins; take and drink of it, all of you, and it shall be to you for the pardoning of wrongs and the forgiveness of sins, and for everlasting life.' Amen.

Whenever you eat of this holy body and drink of this cup of life and salvation, you should be recalling the death and resurrection of your Lord, until the great day of his coming.

PEOPLE: We call to mind your death, Lord.

PRIEST: We worship you, the Only-Begotten of the Father, the firstborn of the divine Being, the spiritual Lamb who has descended from the heights to the depths to become a sacrifice of forgiveness for all humanity, to take away their wickedness by your own will, to bring forgiveness through your blood to sinners, and to make the unclean holy through your being sacrificed: give life to us, Lord, by means of your true life, purify us by means of your spiritual cleansing, grant that we may acquire life through your life-giving death, and may we stand before you in purity, ministering to you in holiness and making this offering to your divinity; may the good pleasure of your majesty be pleased at it, and may your mercies be poured out upon us all.

Yes, we beg of you, Only-Begotten of the Father, through whom peace has been uttered to us, child of the Most High through whom those on high have been reconciled with those below, the Good Shepherd who laid down his life for his sheep, rescuing them from ravening wolves, O compassionate Lord who cried out on the Cross and gathered us in from wandering after vanity, El, the God of spirits and of all flesh, may our prayers be raised up to you, and may your mercies descend in response to our supplications; may this offering which we make in memorial of your passion on your altar that gives forgiveness be accepted in your presence; may your divinity be pleased at it, may your will be fulfilled by it; through it may our wrongs be pardoned and our sins forgiven; at it may our departed be commemorated; and may we give thanks to you, worshipping and glorifying you and your Father who sent you for our salvation, and your living and holy Spirit, now and always, Amen.

'Anaphora of St. Peter,' from the archaic Maronite liturgy *Sharrar*, extract (3rd century?)

30   Our King and Helper

The 'Te Deum' is a Latin hymn traditionally ascribed to Ambrose (**42**, **48**) or Augustine (**38**), but which is more likely to be by Niceta, Bishop of Remesiana, in modern Serbia (d. *c*.414). It may have been composed as part of a liturgy; it has certainly found a home in various liturgies, notably those for Matins, from an early date.

You are a glorious King, O Christ, the Father's eternal Son; yet at your coming to take upon you the human nature that you would release, a virgin's womb had no dismay for you. Drawing death's sting, you opened the kingdom of heaven to all who would believe. You sit at God's right hand, sharing the Father's glory; and we believe that you will come and judge us. We beg you, therefore, help your servants, since you have redeemed them with your precious blood. With the saints be our lot in eternal glory.

Save your people, Lord, bless the race of your choice; guide and support them always. Day by day we bless you; we will praise your name for ever, yes, for ever.

Out of your goodness, Lord, keep us from sin today. Have mercy on us, Lord, have mercy on us. Lord, let your mercy rest on us, for we put our trust in you. In you, Lord, we place our confidence; may we never be disappointed.

'Te Deum', extract (late 4th century?)

31   The Variety of Salvation

St Macrina the Younger (c.327–79) was the sister of Basil the Great and Gregory of Nyssa (46), and eventually became head of a small ascetic community they founded in Pontus. The latter wrote a hagiographic *Life* of his sister, and recorded this prayer from her deathbed, in which she piles biblical image upon biblical image to convey her trust in Christ her Saviour.

You have released us, O Lord, from the fear of death. You have made the end of life here on earth a beginning of true life for us. You let our bodies rest in sleep in due season and you awaken them again at the sound of the last trumpet. You entrust to the earth our bodies of earth which you fashioned with your own hands and you restore again what you have given, transforming with incorruptibility and grace what is mortal and deformed in us. You redeemed us from the curse and from sin, having become both on our behalf. You have crushed the heads of the serpent who had seized man in his jaws because of the abyss of our disobedience. You have opened up for us a path to the resurrection, having broken down the gates of hell and reduced to impotence the one who had power over death. You have given to those who fear you a visible token, the sign of the holy cross, for the destruction of the Adversary and for the protection of our life.

God eternal, upon whom I have cast myself from my mother's womb, whom my soul has loved with all its strength, to whom I have consecrated flesh and soul from my infancy up to this moment, put down beside me a shining angel to lead me by the hand to the place of refreshment where is the water of repose near the lap of the holy fathers. You who have cut through the flame of the fiery sword and brought to paradise the man who was crucified with you, who entreated your pity, remember me also in your kingdom, for I too have been crucified with you, for I have nailed my flesh out of reverence for you and have feared your judgements. Let not the dreadful abyss separate me from your chosen ones. Let not the Slanderer stand against me on my journey. Let not my sin be discovered before your eyes if I have been overcome in any way because of our nature's weakness and have sinned in word or deed or thought. You who have on earth the power to forgive sins [cf. **8**], forgive me, so that I may draw breath again and may be found before you in the stripping off of my body without stain or blemish in the beauty of my soul, but may my soul be received blameless and immaculate into your hands as an incense offering before your face.

Gregory of Nyssa, *The Life of St Macrina* 397–8 (late 4th century)

Egeria (or Etheria) was a fourth-century pilgrim, a wealthy and educated Spanish nun who travelled to Egypt and Palestine, and reported back to other members of her community on the liturgical riches she found there. Here she describes the rituals which took place in Holy Week in Jerusalem, on the supposed sites of the events of Christ's Passion. (Cf. **52**.)

A chair is placed for the bishop in Golgotha behind the Cross, which is now standing; the bishop duly takes his seat in the chair, and a table covered with a linen cloth is placed before him; the deacons stand round the table, and a silver-gilt casket is brought in which is the holy wood of the Cross. The casket is opened and the wood is taken out, and both the wood of the Cross and the title [see **16**] are placed upon the table. Now, when it has been put upon the table, the bishop, as he sits, holds the extremities of the sacred wood firmly in his hands, while the deacons who stand around guard it. It is guarded thus because the custom is that the people, both faithful and catechumens, come one by one and, bowing down at the table, kiss the sacred wood and pass through. And because, I know not when, some one is said to have bitten off and stolen a portion of the sacred wood, it is thus guarded by the deacons who stand around, lest any one approaching should venture to do so again [cf. **109**].

And as all the people pass by one by one, all bowing themselves, they touch the Cross and the title, first with their foreheads and then with their eyes; then they kiss the Cross and pass through, but none lays his hand upon it to touch it. When they have kissed the Cross and have passed through, a deacon stands holding the ring of Solomon and the horn from which the kings were anointed; they kiss the horn also and gaze at the ring . . . all the people are passing through up to the sixth hour, entering by one door and going out by another; for this is done in the same place where, on the preceding day, that is, on the fifth weekday, the oblation was offered.

And when the sixth hour has come, they go before the Cross, whether it be in rain or in heat, the place being open to the air, as it were, a court of great size and of some beauty between the Cross and the Anastasis; here all the people assemble in such great numbers that there is no thoroughfare. The chair is placed for the bishop before the Cross, and from the sixth to the ninth hour nothing else is done, but the reading of lessons, which are read thus: first from the psalms wherever the Passion is spoken of, then from the Apostle, either from the epistles of the Apostles or from their Acts, wherever they have spoken of the Lord's Passion; then the passages from the Gospels, where he suffered, are read. Then the readings from the prophets where they foretold that the Lord should suffer, then from the Gospels where he mentions his Passion. Thus from the sixth to the ninth hours the lessons are so read and the hymns said, that it may be shown to all the people that what-soever the prophets foretold of the Lord's Passion is proved from the Gospels and from the writings of the Apostles to have been fulfilled [cf. Section C. I]. And so through all those three hours the people are taught that nothing was done which had not been foretold, and that nothing was foretold which was not wholly fulfilled. Prayers also suitable to the day are interspersed throughout.

The emotion shown and the mourning by all the people at every lesson and prayer is wonderful; for there is none, either great or small, who, on that day during those three hours, does not lament more than can be conceived, that the Lord had suffered those things for us.

The Pilgrimage of Egeria 37: 2–7 (4th century)

II. Participating in Christ

One of the strangest but most profound affirmations made by early theologians is that to be saved is to be *in* Christ, to participate somehow in his life. The life we live is no longer our own, but is a life caught up in, animated by, representing, or extending his life. In thinking salvation through like this, they found themselves thinking differently of humanity, and the grounds and possibilities of human community.

33   Christ in his People

The Apostle Paul (also known as Saul) traced his calling back to his encounter, when still an enemy of the Christian Church, with the risen Christ. The form in which that encounter is presented in the book of Acts has provided later generations of Christians with a vital resource for thinking about Christ's identification with them. (Cf. **38**.)

Saul, still breathing threats and murder against the disciples of the Lord, went to the high priest and asked him for letters to the synagogues at Damascus, so that if he found any who belonged to the Way, men or women, he might bring them bound to Jerusalem. Now as he was going along and approaching Damascus, suddenly light from heaven flashed around him. He fell to the ground and heard a voice saying to him, 'Saul, Saul, why do you persecute me?'

He answered, 'Who are you, Lord?'

The reply came, 'I am Jesus, whom you are persecuting. But get up and enter the city, and you will be told what you are to do.'

The men who were travelling with him stood speechless because they heard the voice but saw no one. Saul got up from the ground, and though his eyes were open, he could see nothing; so they led him by the hand and brought him into Damascus.

Acts 9: 1–8 (1st century)

34   The Body of Christ

Paul's own writings are the classic source for reflection on life 'in Christ'. Here, he presents a thoroughly corporate theology—in both 'social' and 'bodily' senses of the word. (Cf. **112, 272.**)

For just as the body is one and has many members, and all the members of the body, though many, are one body, so it is with Christ. For in the one Spirit we were all baptised into one body—Jews or Greeks, slaves or free—and we were all made to drink of one Spirit.

Indeed, the body does not consist of one member but of many. If the foot would say, 'Because I am not a hand, I do not belong to the body,' that would not make it any less a part of the body. And if the ear would say, 'Because I am not an eye, I do not belong to the body,' that would not make it any less a part of the body. If the whole body were an eye, where would the hearing be? If the whole body were hearing, where would the sense of smell be? But as it is, God arranged the members in the body, each one of them, as he chose. If all were a single member, where would the body be? As it is, there are many members, yet one body. The eye cannot say to the hand, 'I have no need of you,' nor again the head to the feet, 'I have no need of you.' On the contrary, the members of the body that seem to be weaker are indispensable, and those members of the body that we think less honourable we clothe with greater honour, and our less respectable members are treated with greater respect; whereas our more respectable members do not need this. But God has so arranged the body, giving the greater honour to the inferior member, that there may be no dissension within the body, but the members may have the same care for one another. If one member suffers, all suffer together with it; if one member is honoured, all rejoice together with it. Now you are the body of Christ and individually members of it.

1 Corinthians 12: 12–27 (1st century)

35 | Dying with Christ

⌈Christianity in the first three centuries was a religion of martyrdom. The paradigmatic form of participation in Christ in the patristic period was to die with him.⌉ In dying as a witness (the meaning of 'martyr') to Christ, a Christian participated in a sense in his Crucifixion, and shared the form which his selfless life had taken in a hostile world. This is one of the many accounts of martyrdom in the early Church. (Cf. **61**.)

When the proconsul observed the extraordinary patience [of Carpus and Papylus] he ordered them to be burnt alive, and going down they both hastened to the amphitheatre that they might all the more quickly depart from the world. First of all Papylus was nailed to a stake and lifted up, and after the fire was brought near he prayed in peace and gave up his soul. After him Carpus smiled as he was nailed down. And the bystanders were amazed and said to him: 'What are you laughing at?'

And the blessed one said 'I saw the glory of the Lord and I was happy. Besides I am now rid of you and have no share in your sins.'

A soldier piled up wood and lit it, and the saintly Carpus said to him as he was hanging 'We too were born of the same mother, Eve, and we have the same flesh. Let us endure all things looking forward to the judgement seat of truth.' After he had said this, as the fire came close he prayed aloud saying, 'Blessed are you, Lord Jesus Christ, Son of God, because you thought me, a sinner, worthy of having this share in you!' And with these words he gave up his spirit.

There was a woman named Agathonicé standing there who saw the glory of the Lord as Carpus said he had seen it, realising that this was a call from heaven she raised her voice at once: 'Here is a meal that has been prepared for me. I must partake and eat of this glorious repast!'

The mob shouted out 'Have pity on your son!'

And the blessed Agathonicé said: 'He has God who can take pity on him; for he has providence over all. Let me do what I've come for!' And taking off her cloak, she threw herself joyfully upon the stake.

Those who witnessed this lamented it, saying, 'It is a terrible sentence; these are unjust decrees!'

Then she was raised up and as soon as she was touched by the fire she shouted aloud three times: 'Lord, Lord, Lord, assist me! For you are my refuge.' And thus she gave up her spirit and died together with the saints. And the Christians secretly collected their remains and protected them for the glory of Christ and the praise of his martyrs; for to him belong glory and power, to the Father, the Son, and the Holy Spirit, now and for ever and for all the ages to come. Amen.

The Martyrdom of Saints Carpus, Papylus and Agathonicé, extract (c.170?)

A strikingly realistic view of the body of Christ in the eucharist is provided in this story from Abba Daniel, an ascetic 'desert father' and disciple of another desert father, Abba Arsenius, who died in 449. (Cf. **117**, **194**.)

This is what Abba Daniel, the Pharanite, said: Our Father Abba Arsenius told us of an inhabitant of Scetis, of notable life and of simple faith; through his naiveté he was deceived and said, 'The bread which we receive is not really the body of Christ, but a symbol.' Two old men having learnt that he had uttered this saying, knowing that he was outstanding in his way of life, knew that he had not spoken through malice, but through simplicity. So they came to find him and said, 'Father, we have heard a proposition contrary to the faith on the part of someone who says that the bread which we receive is not really the body of Christ, but a symbol.' The old man said, 'It is I who have said that.' Then the old men exhorted him saying, 'Do not hold this position Father, but hold one in conformity with that which the catholic Church has given us. We believe, for our part, that the bread itself is the body of Christ and that the cup itself is his blood and this in all truth and not a symbol. But as in the beginning, God formed man in his image, taking the dust of the earth, without anyone being able to say that it is not the image of God, even though it is not seen to be so; thus it is with the bread of which he said that it is his body; and so we believe that it is really the body of Christ.' The old man said to them, 'As long as I have not been persuaded by the thing itself I shall not be fully convinced.' So they said, 'Let us pray God about this mystery throughout the whole of this week and we believe that God will reveal it to us.' The old man received this saying with joy and he prayed in these words, 'Lord, you know that it is not through malice that I do not believe and so that I may not err through ignorance, reveal this mystery to me, Lord Jesus Christ.'

The old men returned to their cells and they also prayed God, saying, 'Lord Jesus Christ, reveal this mystery to the old man, that he may believe and not lose his reward.' God heard both the prayers. At the end of the week they came to church on Sunday and sat all three on the same mat, the old man in the middle. Then their eyes were opened and when the bread was placed on the holy table, there appeared as it were a little child to these three alone. And when the priest put out his hand to break the bread, behold an angel descended from heaven with a sword and poured the child's blood into the chalice. When the priest cut the bread into small pieces, the angel also cut the child in pieces. When they drew near to receive the sacred elements the old man alone received a morsel of bloody flesh. Seeing this he was afraid and cried out, 'Lord, I believe that this bread is your flesh and this chalice your blood.' Immediately the flesh which he held in his hand became bread, according to the mystery and he took it, giving thanks to God. Then the old men said to him, 'God knows human nature and that man cannot eat raw flesh and that is why he has changed his body into bread and his blood into wine, for those who receive it in faith.' Then they gave thanks to God for the old man, because he had allowed him not to lose the reward of his labour. So all three returned with joy to their own cells.

Sayings of the Desert Fathers, Daniel 7 (5th century)

37 Helping Christ

Martin of Tours (*c*.316–97), founder of the first monastery in Gaul, was at the time of the following story a soldier in the Roman army who had become enamoured of Christianity and entered catechetical training. Sulpicius Severus (*c*.360–*c*.420) describes the encounter with Christ which persuaded Martin to leave the army and be baptized.

It came about that one day when he had nothing on him but his weapons and his uniform, in the middle of a winter which had been fearfully hard beyond the ordinary, so that many were dying of the intense cold, he met at the city gate of Amiens a coatless beggar. This beggar had been asking the passers-by to take pity on him but all had gone past the unfortunate creature. Then the God-filled man understood, from the fact that no one else had had pity, that this beggar had been reserved for him. But what was he to do? He had nothing with him but the cape which he had on, for he had already used up what else he had, in similar good works. So he took the sword he was wearing and cut the cape in two and gave one half to the beggar, putting the rest on himself again.

This raised a laugh from some of the bystanders, for he looked grotesque in the mutilated garment; but many had more sense, and sighed to think that they had not done something of the kind; indeed, having more to give, they could have clothed the beggar without stripping themselves. And that night, in his sleep, Martin saw Christ wearing the half of his cape with which he had clothed the beggar. He was told to look carefully at our Lord and take note that it was the garment he had given away. Then he heard Jesus say aloud to the throng of angels that surrounded him: 'Martin is only a catechumen but he has clothed me with this garment.'

But our Lord himself had once said, 'In doing it to one of these least regarded ones, you were doing it to me' [Matt. 25: 40], and he was only acting on his own words when he declared that he had been clothed in the person of the beggar and reinforced his testimony to so good a deed by graciously showing himself in the very garment that the beggar had received. But this most blessed man was not puffed up with vainglory by the vision but saw

God's goodness in his own good deed. And being then twenty-two years old, he flew to be baptised.

Sulpicius Severus, *The Life of St. Martin*, III (early 5th century)

38   The Whole Christ

> Augustine (354–430), the resolute bishop–theologian of Hippo whose thought has coloured the whole of the Western tradition, comments here on 1 John 4. Not far from his mind was his battle with the schismatic Donatists, whose vision of a pure Church led them to cut themselves off from the sometimes faithless impurity of others who claimed the name 'Christian'. For Augustine, this is simply impossible. (Cf. **34**, **112**.)

No one can love the Father unless he should love the Son, and he who loves the Son loves also the sons of God. What sons of God? The members of the Son of God. And by loving he also himself becomes a member and by love comes to be situated in the structure of the body of Christ, and there will be one Christ loving himself. For when the members love one another, the body loves itself. 'And if one member suffers, all the members suffer with it; and if one member glories, all the members glory with it.' And what did he continue on and say? 'Now you are the Body of Christ and the members.' [Cf. **34**.]

A little before, John was speaking about brotherly love and he said, 'He who does not love his brother whom he has seen, how can he love God whom he does not see?' [1 John 4: 20] But if you love your brother, do you perhaps love your brother and not love Christ? How, when you love Christ's members? Therefore when you love Christ's members, you love Christ. When you love Christ, you love the Son of God. When you love the Son of God, you love the Father also. Love, therefore, cannot be split into parts. Choose for yourself what you love; the rest follow you. You might say, 'I love God alone, God the Father.' You lie; if you love, you do not love the one alone, but if you love the Father, you also love the Son. 'Look,' you say, 'I love the Father and I love the Son, but only this: God the Father and God the Son and our Lord, Jesus Christ, who ascends into the heavens and sits at the right hand of the Father, that Word by whom all things were made, and the Word was made flesh and dwelt among us, this alone I love.' [Cf. **66**.] You lie. For if you love the head, you love also the members; but if you do not love the members, you do not love the head. Are you not frightened by the voice of the head crying out from heaven on behalf of the members, 'Saul, Saul, why do you persecute me?' [Cf. **33**.] He called the persecutor of his members his persecutor. He called the lover of his members his lover. Now you know what his members are, brothers; they are the very church of God. [. . .]

Extend love through the whole world if you wish to love Christ, because Christ's members lie throughout the world. If you love apart, you have been divided. If you have been divided, you are not in the body. If you are not in the body, you are not under the head.

What good does it do that you believe and yet blaspheme? You adore him in the head, you blaspheme him in the body. He loves his body. If you have cut yourself off from his body, the head has not cut himself off from his body. 'In vain you honour me,' the head shouts to you from above, 'in vain do you honour me.' Or if someone should wish to kiss your head and trample on your feet, perhaps with nailed boots he would crush your feet wishing to take hold of your head and kiss you. Would you not amid his words, as he honoured you, shout out and say 'What are you doing, man? You are trampling me!' [. . .]

Therefore our Lord Jesus Christ, ascending into heaven on the fortieth day [20], for this reason commended to us his body, where it would have to lie, because he saw that many would honour him because he ascended into heaven; and he saw that this honour would be useless if they trampled his members on earth. And, that no one might err, and while he honoured the head in heaven, would trample the feet on earth, he said where his members were. For as he was about to ascend, he said his last words; after these very words he did not speak on earth. The head, about to ascend into heaven, commended the members on earth and departed. Now you do not find Christ speaking on earth; you find him speaking, but in heaven. For to the persecutor Saul he said from above, 'Saul, Saul, why do you persecute me?' I ascended into heaven, but I still lie on the earth. Here I sit at the Father's right hand; there I still eat, thirst, and am a pilgrim.' How, then, did he, about to ascend, commend the Body on earth? When the disciples asked him, 'Lord, will you present yourself at this time and when is the kingdom of Israel?' as he was about to go, he answered, 'It is not for you to know the time that the Father has put in his own power. But you will receive the strength of the Holy Spirit coming upon you and you will be witnesses to me.' See how he spreads out his Body, see where he does not wish himself to be trampled: 'You will be witnesses to me in Jerusalem, and in all Judaea and Samaria, and even in all the earth' [Acts 1: 6–8]. Look where I who answered lie. For I ascend because I am the head; my body still lies. Where does it lie? Through the whole earth. Beware that you do not strike, beware that you do no violence, beware that you do not trample: the last words of Christ, about to go into heaven, are these.

Augustine of Hippo, *Tractates on the First Epistle of St. John*, Tractates 10. 3. 1–2; 8. 1–2; 9. 1, extracts (*c*.415)

III. The Sweet Exchange

Christ's descent into suffering and death, and its strange fruit—his ascent with us to God—provided a motif which captivated many patristic writers: the strange reversal by which defeat of the innocent one became victory for the guilty, the death of the holy one life for the unholy. The symmetry of the motif urged patristic thought to match the complete salvation of humanity for which they hoped with acknowledgement of the complete abasement of Christ.

39 Emptying and Exaltation

In this passage from the letter to the Philippians, Paul may well be drawing on an earlier hymn, in which case it would be among the earliest evidences we have for Christian worship. The double movement is already here: emptying and exaltation. (Cf. **249**.)

Let the same mind be in you that was in Christ Jesus, who, though he was in the form of God, did not regard equality with God as something to be exploited, but emptied himself, taking the form of a slave, being born in human likeness.[7] And being found in human form, he humbled himself and became obedient to the point of death—even death on a cross.

Therefore God also highly exalted him and gave him the name that is above every name, so that at the name of Jesus every knee should bend, in heaven and on earth and under the earth, and every tongue should confess that Jesus Christ is Lord, to the glory of God the Father.

Philippians 2: 5–11 (1st century)

40 The Sweet Exchange

In the second century an anonymous author wrote to the enquirer Diognetus, explaining the nature of Christianity. He set the pattern of exchange firmly within the providential purposes of God always working, whether hidden or in the open, for our salvation.

God, the Lord and creator of all, who made all things and set them in order, was not merely a lover of mankind, but was full of compassion. Mild and good, calm and true—he always was and is and will be; he alone is good. The great and ineffable idea which he conceived he communicated to his Son alone. For a time, indeed, he kept the plan of his wisdom to himself and guarded it as a mystery; and thus he seemed to have no care and thought for us. But when, through his beloved Son, he removed the veil and revealed what he had prepared from the beginning, he gave us all at once—participation in his gifts, the graces of being able to see and understand things beyond all our expectations.

In himself and with his Son, his providence had all things arranged. If, for a time before he came, he allowed us to be carried along by our own whims and inordinate desires, to be led astray by pleasures and lusts, it was in no sense because he took any joy in our sins—he merely permitted them. He did not approve of the period of our wickedness in the past; he was merely preparing the present reign of grace. He wanted us who, in times past, by our own sins, were convicted of being unworthy, to become now, by the goodness of God, worthy of life. He wanted us who proved that, by ourselves, we could not enter into the kingdom of God, to become able, by the power of God, to enter in. Once the measure of our sin had become full and overflowing, and it was perfectly clear that nothing but punishment and death could be expected as the wages of sin, the time came which God had foreordained. Henceforth he would reveal his goodness and grace—and O! how exceeding great is God's love and friendship for men. Instead of hating us and rejecting us and remembering our sins, he was compassionate and patient and took upon himself our sins. He gave us his own Son for our redemption.

For us who were sinful, he gave up the holy one; for the wicked the innocent one; the just one for the unjust; the incorruptible one for corruptible men; and for us mortals the immortal one.

For, what else but his righteousness could have concealed our sin? In whom, if not in the only Son of God, could we lawless and sinful men have been justified? What a sweet exchange! What an inexplicable achievement! What unexpected graces! that in one who was just the sin of many should be concealed, that the righteousness of one should justify many sinners. In the former time he proved the inability of our nature to obtain life, and now he has revealed a Saviour capable of saving the incapable. For both these reasons he wanted us to believe in his goodness and to look upon him as guardian, father, teacher, adviser, and physician, as our mind, light, honour, glory, strength, and life, and to have no solicitude about what we wear and eat.

Epistle to Diognetus, 8–9, extract (2nd or 3rd century)

Methodius of Olympus (d. *c.*311), opponent of Origen (cf. **73**) and (it is thought) a martyr under Diocletian, wrote the *Symposium*, a dialogue, as an exhortation to purity. Here, in a beautiful image which combines the motifs of the sweet exchange and of unveiling (**47**), he shows how we were taught purity by one who sullied himself for our sake.

In antiquity man was not yet perfect and hence did not have the capacity to comprehend the perfect, that is, virginity.[8] For being made in the image of God, man had yet to receive that which was according to his likeness. And this was precisely what the Word was sent into the world to accomplish; he took upon himself our form, spotted and stained as it was by our many sins, in order that we might be able to receive in turn the divine form which he bore for our sake. For then is it possible for us truly to fashion ourselves in the likeness of God when like skilled painters we express his features in ourselves as on a panel, and thus possess them in innocence, learning to follow the path he showed to us. This was why, although he was God, he chose to put on human flesh, that, by looking upon God's representation of our life as in a painting, we might be able to imitate him who painted it. Thus there is no discrepancy between his thoughts and his actions, nor between what he thought to be right and what he actually taught us. He both taught and did those things which were truly both right and useful.

Methodius of Olympus, *The Symposium; or, Banquet of the Ten Virgins* (early 4th century?)

42 **Washing the Washer**

Ambrose of Milan (d. 397) (cf. **48**) draws on the story of Jesus washing the disciples' feet (John 13: 1–17) and of Jesus having his feet washed by the tears of the penitent woman (Luke 7: 37–8) to produce his own version of the sweet exchange.

Jesus, I wish you would let me wash your feet, since it was through walking about in me that you soiled them. I wish you would give me the task of wiping the stains from your feet, because it was my behaviour that put them there. But where can I get the running water I need to wash your feet? If I have no water, at least I have tears: let me wash your feet with them, and wash myself at the same time.

Ambrose of Milan, 'Prayer for Forgiveness' (4th century)

43   Born for Rebirth

Ephrem the Syrian (c.306–73) was a prolific author of commentaries, dog-matic works, and ascetic treatises in Syriac verse. Repetitive and riddling, his hypnotic writings were extremely popular in the Syriac Church.

Just as he, a spiritual being, could not become bodily until he had come to bodily birth, so too bodily beings cannot become spiritual unless they are reborn in another kind of birth. The Son whose birth from the Father is unsearchable was born in another birth which can be searched out.

By the one birth we should learn that his greatness has no limits, by the other we may recognise that his grace has no measure. His grace is poured out without any limit, seeing that his other birth is proclaimed by every mouth. This is he who was born from the Godhead in accordance with his nature, from humanity, not after his nature; from baptism, not after his custom. All this was in order that we might be born from human-ity, in accordance with our nature, from the Godhead, not after our nature, from the Spirit, not after our custom. So he who came to second birth was born of the Godhead, so that he might bring what belongs to us to rebirth.

His birth from the Father is to be believed, not searched out; his birth from a woman is to be exalted in honour, not despised; his death on the Cross testifies to his birth from a woman, for a person who has died was also born.

Ephrem the Syrian, *Homily on Our Lord*, extract (c.370)

44   Enslaved for Slaves

Paulinus of Nola (353/4–431), a correspondent who spread webs of friendship over the whole unstable Western empire embracing Ambrose (cf. **42**), Augus-tine (cf. **38**), Anastasius I (cf. **89**), and many others, was considered one of the finest Latin poets in the patristic period.

Look on thy God, Christ hidden in our flesh.
A bitter word, the cross, and bitter sight:
Hard rind without, to hold the heart of heaven.
Yet sweet it is; for God upon that tree
Did offer up his life: upon that rood
My life hung, that my life might stand in God.
Christ, what am I to give thee for my life?
Unless take from thy hands the cup they hold,
To cleanse me with the precious draught of death.
What shall I do? My body to be burned?
Make myself vile? The debt's not paid out yet.
Whate'er I do, it is but I and thou,

And still do I come short, still must thou pay
My debts, O Christ; for debts thyself hadst none.
What love may balance thine? My Lord was found
In fashion like a slave, that so his slave
Might find himself in fashion like his Lord.
Think you the bargain's hard, to have exchanged
The transient for the eternal, to have sold
Earth to buy heaven? More dearly God bought me.

Paulinus of Nola, 'The Word of the Cross' (after 395)

IV. Unveiling

In the patristic period salvation and revelation were frequently thought together. The truth about God, the world, and the self has been long hidden by sin, and we labour under multiple misapprehensions. When God reveals the truth about these things, it does not lead simply to intellectual assent, to the unlocking of a philosophical problem, but to the transformation of the recipient, a movement from darkness into the light of salvation.

45 The Unveiling of Christ

Writing to the Church in Corinth, Paul, in the middle of a defence of the transparency and truth of his teaching, draws upon the metaphor of light, and upon scriptural language about glory, to convey the transformative revelation of God in Jesus Christ, contrasting it with what he saw as the limited revelation of the same glory in Israel's law. (Cf. section C.I.)

Moses put a veil over his face to keep the people of Israel from gazing at the end of the glory that was being set aside. But their minds were hardened. Indeed, to this very day, when they hear the reading of the old covenant, that same veil is still there, since only in Christ is it set aside. Indeed, to this very day whenever Moses is read, a veil lies over their minds; but when one turns to the Lord, the veil is removed. Now the Lord is the Spirit, and where the Spirit of the Lord is, there is freedom. And all of us, with unveiled faces, seeing the glory of the Lord as though reflected in a mirror, are being transformed into the same image from one degree of glory to another; for this comes from the Lord, the Spirit.

[. . .] If our gospel is veiled, it is veiled to those who are perishing. In their case the god of this world has blinded the minds of the unbelievers, to keep them from seeing the light of the gospel of the glory of Christ, who is the image of God.

[. . .] For it is the God who said, 'Let light shine out of darkness,' who has shone in our hearts to give the light of the knowledge of the glory of God in the face of Jesus Christ.

2 Corinthians 3: 13–18; 4: 3–4, 6 (1st century)

46 Baptismal Renovation

Gregory of Nyssa (*c.*330–*c.*395) (cf. **31**), one of the Cappadocian Fathers (cf. **81–2**), was a champion of Nicene theology (**76**) at the Council of Constantinople (**80**); he was a considerable theologian, a fine orator, a skilled exegete, and a devout ascetic. The following extract is from a sermon preached on the feast of Christ's baptism, probably in AD 376.

We have come, in the course of time, to the remembrance of holy mysteries, which purify humanity—mysteries which purge out from soul and body even that sin which is hard to cleanse away, and which bring us back to that fairness of our first estate which God, the best of artificers, impressed upon us. Therefore it is that you, the initiated people,[9] are gathered together; and you bring also that people who have not made trial of them, leading, like good fathers, by careful guidance, the uninitiated to the perfect reception of the faith. I for my part rejoice over both—over you that are initiated, because you are enriched with a great gift: over you that are uninitiated, because you have a fair expectation of hope—remission of what is to be accounted for, release from bondage, close relation to God, free boldness of speech, and in place of servile subjection equality with the angels. For these things, and all that follow from them, the grace of baptism secures and conveys to us. [. . .]

Christ, then, was born as it were a few days ago[10]—he whose generation was before all things, sensible and intellectual [cf. **76**]. To-day he is baptised by John that he might cleanse him who was defiled, that he might bring the Spirit from above, and exalt man to heaven, that he who had fallen might be raised up and he who had cast him down might be put to shame. And do not marvel that God showed so great earnestness in our cause: for it was with care on the part of him who did us wrong that the plot was laid against us; it is with forethought on the part of our Maker that we are saved.

The evil charmer, framing his new device of sin against our race, drew along his serpent train, which was a disguise worthy of his own intent, entering in his impurity into what was like himself, dwelling, earthly and mundane as he was in will, in that creeping thing. But Christ, the repairer of his evil-doing, assumes manhood in its fullness, and saves man, and becomes the type and figure of us all, to sanctify the first-fruits of every action, and leave to his servants no doubt in their zeal for the tradition. Baptism, then, is a purification from sins, a remission of trespasses, a cause of renovation and regeneration.

Gregory of Nyssa, 'On the Baptism of Christ: A Sermon for the Day of Lights', extracts (376)

47   Restoring the Image

About 318 the young Athanasius of Alexandria (c.296–373) wrote a short treatise in which he presented the story of humanity's fall and salvation in terms of the loss of the image of God and its restoration through the incarnation of God's Word. It was not long before, holding fast to the assumption made here that the divinity revealed in Christ is true and full divinity, he plunged into controversy with the followers of Arius (74, 77–9) and those he branded Arians.

God, who has power over all things, when he was making the human race through his own Word, saw the weakness of human nature. He saw that it was not sufficient on its own to know its maker, nor to get any idea at all of God; because God is uncreated but creatures are created out of nothing, and God is incorporeal but human beings are fashioned in a lower, bodily way, and because in every way things made fall far short of being able to comprehend and know their maker. Taking pity, I say, on the human race, for he is good, he did not leave them destitute of knowledge of himself, for then they would find no profit in existing at all. For what profit is there for creatures if they do not know their maker? Or how can they be rational without knowing the Word and Reason of the Father, in whom they receive their very being? For there is nothing to distinguish them even from brute creatures if they have knowledge of nothing but earthly things. No—why did God make them at all, if he does not wish to be known by them?

Therefore, this being so, he gave them a share in his own image, our Lord Jesus Christ, and made them after his own image and after his own likeness; so that perceiving the image (that is, the Word of the Father) by such grace they may be able through him to get an idea of the Father, and knowing their maker, live the happy and truly blessed life.

But the human race once more having despised in their perversity, in spite of all this, the grace given them, so wholly rejected God, and so darkened their soul, as not merely to forget their idea of God, but to fashion for themselves instead one invention after another.

[Athanasius then describes the descending spiral of this apostasy and explains how humanity came to trample the reminders of the truth which

God placed in creation, in the law, and in the prophets. Yet God's goodness
and loving-kindness were too great.]

What then was God to do? What was to be done except the renewing of that
which was in God's image, so that by it human beings might once more be
able to know him? But how could this have come to pass except by the
presence of the true image of God, our Lord Jesus Christ? By human means it
was impossible, since humans are only made *after* an image; nor was it
possible by angelic means, for not even they are God's images. Therefore the
Word of God came in his own person, that, as he *was* the image of the Father,
he might be able to create afresh humanity *after* the image.

However, this could not have taken place had not death and corruption
been done away with. Therefore the Word took, in natural fitness, a mortal
body, so that in it death might be once for all done away with, and humanity
made after his image might once more be renewed. Only the image of the
Father was sufficient to meet this need.

Just as, when the likeness painted on a panel has been effaced by stains
from elsewhere, he whose likeness it is needs to come once more to enable
the portrait to be renewed on the same wood (for the sake of his picture,
even the wood on which it is painted is not thrown away, but is kept so that
the outline can be renewed upon it), in the same way the most holy Son of
the Father, being the image of the Father, came to our region to renew the
humanity once made in his likeness, to find the lost ones by the remission of
sins. [. . .]

Who, then, was needed, except the Word of God, who sees both soul and
mind, and who gives movement to all things in creation, and by them makes
known the Father? For the one who taught human beings about the Father by
his own providence and ordering of all things was the very one who could
also renew this same teaching. How, then, could this have been done? Some
might say that the same means were available as before; that he could demonstrate the truth about the Father by means of the work of creation again.
But this was no longer a sure means; in fact, quite the contrary—for human
beings missed seeing this before, and turned their eyes downward instead of
upward. So, naturally, willing to profit humanity, he sojourned here as a man,
taking to himself a body like theirs, and from things of earth (that is, by the
works of his body) he taught them, so that although they would not know
him from his providence and rule over all things, they might, from the works
done by his actual body, know the Word of God which is in the body, and
through him the Father.

Just as a kind teacher who cares for his disciples comes down to their level,
if some of them cannot profit by higher subjects, and teaches them by
simpler routes; so also did the Word of God. As Paul also says: 'For seeing
that in the wisdom of God the world through its wisdom did not know God,

it was God's good pleasure through the foolishness of the Word preached to save those who believe' [1 Cor. 1: 21]. Seeing that human beings, having rejected the contemplation of God, and with their eyes downward, as though sunk in the deep, were seeking about for God in nature and in the world of sense, feigning gods for themselves out of mortal human beings and demons; the loving and general Saviour of all, the Word of God, took to himself a body, and walked among human beings as human, and met the senses of all humanity half-way. He did this, as I said, in order that they who think that God is corporeal may from what the Lord does in the body perceive the truth, and through him recognise the Father.

So, human as they were, and human in all their thoughts, on whatever objects they fixed their senses, there they saw themselves met half-way, and taught the truth from every side. For if they looked with awe upon creation, yet they saw how she confessed Christ as Lord [cf. 9]; or if their mind was swayed toward human beings, and thought of them as gods, yet the Saviour's works, when compared with those of other people, confirmed that the Saviour alone appeared Son of God, for there were no such works done among the rest as have been done by the Word of God. Or if they were biased toward evil spirits, even? Seeing them cast out by the Word, they would know that he alone, the Word of God, was God, and that the spirits were not. Or if their mind had already sunk as far as the dead, so as to worship heroes, and the gods spoken of in the poets, nevertheless, seeing the Saviour's resurrection, they would confess the dead to be false gods, and confess that the Lord alone is true, the Word of the Father, who is Lord even of death. For this reason he was both born and appeared as a human being, and died, and rose again, dulling and casting into the shade the works of all former people by his own, so that in whatever direction the bias of human beings might be, he might recall them from it, and teach them of his own true Father, as he himself said: 'I came to save and to find that which was lost' [Luke 19: 10].

Athanasius of Alexandria, *On the Incarnation of the Word of God* 11. 1–4, 13. 7–14. 2,
14. 6–15. 7, extracts (*c*.318)

48   Desire and Knowledge

That knowledge was by no means a matter simply of 'dry intellect' is evident in this work of mystical theology (cf. 87, 88, 90) by Ambrose of Milan (*c*.339–97) (cf. 42), a formidable Roman lawyer turned bishop, who was instrumental in the conversion of Augustine (48). This extract is a commentary upon the Song of Songs 1: 2–4 (cf. 210).

What does it mean, then: 'Let him kiss me with the kisses of his mouth' (S. of S. 1: 2)? Think upon the church, in suspense over many ages at the coming of the Lord, long promised her through the prophets. And think upon the soul, lifting herself up from the body and rejecting indulgence and fleshly delights and pleasures and laying aside as well her concern for worldly vanities. For a long time now she has desired to be infused with God's presence and has desired, too, the grace of the Word of salvation, and has wasted away, because he is coming late, and has been struck down, wounded with love as it were [cf. **184**], since she cannot endure his delays. Turning to the Father, she asks that he send to her God the Word, and giving the reason why she is so impatient, she says, 'Let him kiss me with the kisses of his mouth.' She asks, not for one kiss, but for many kisses, so that she may fulfil her desire. For as a lover, she is not satisfied with the meagre offering of a single kiss, but demands many, claims many as her right, and thus has grown accustomed to recommend herself the more to her beloved. Indeed she has gained approval in the Gospel, for 'she has not ceased to kiss my feet.' And so 'her sins, many as they are, are forgiven her, because she has loved much' [Luke 7: 45–7].

Therefore such a soul also desires many kisses of the Word, so that she may be enlightened with the light of the knowledge of God. For this is the kiss of the Word, I mean the light of holy knowledge. God the Word kisses us, when he enlightens our heart and man's very governing faculty with the spirit of the knowledge of God. The soul that has received this gift exults and rejoices in the pledge of wedded love and says, 'I opened my mouth and panted' [Ps. 119: 131]. For it is with the kiss that lovers cleave to each other and gain possession of the sweetness of grace that is within, so to speak. Through such a kiss the soul cleaves to God the Word, and through the kiss the spirit of him who kisses is poured into the soul, just as those who kiss are not satisfied to touch lightly with their lips but appear to be pouring their spirit into each other. Showing that she loves not only the appearance of the Word, and his face, as it were, but all his inner parts, she adds to the favour of the kisses: 'Your breasts are better than wine and the fragrance of your ointments is above all perfumes' [S. of S. 1: 2–3]. She sought the kiss, God the Word poured himself into her wholly and laid bare his breasts to her, that is, his teachings and the laws of the wisdom that is within, and was fragrant with the sweet fragrance of his ointments. Captive to these, the soul is saying that the enjoyment of the knowledge of God is richer than the joy of any bodily pleasure. For there breathes in the Word the fragrance of grace and the forgiveness of sins. Poured out into all the world, this forgiveness has filled all things and the ointment has been emptied out, as it were, in wiping away the heavy dregs of vice among all men.

'Therefore young maidens have loved you. Draw us, let us run after the fragrance of your ointments' [S. of S. 1: 3–4]. [. . .] Do not consider shameless her statement, 'Draw us,' but hear him as he says, 'Come to me, all you who labour and are burdened, and I will give you rest' [Matt. 11: 28]. You see how gladly he draws us, so that we may not be left behind as we follow. But let him who desires to be drawn so run as to obtain, and let him run forgetting the things that are past and seeking those that are better, for thus he will be able to obtain Christ. On this account the Apostle also says, 'So run that you all obtain' [1 Cor. 9: 24]. The soul too wishes to arrive at the prize that she longs to obtain. And so she wisely asks that she be drawn, because not all are able to follow.

Ambrose of Milan, *Isaac; or, The Soul*, 3. 8–10, extracts (*c.*390)

49   Christ the Sun

Prudentius (348–*c.*405), a Spanish civil servant at the court of Emperor Theodosius, produced on his retirement a book of Latin poems for the liturgical hours which secured his fame, and earned him a place in the Roman breviary. Sunrise provides an irresistible reminder of the triumph of Christ over darkness (cf. **220**).

> O Night and Dark,
> O huddled sullen clouds,
> Light enters in: the sky
> Whitens.
> Christ comes! Depart! Depart!
>
> The mist sheers apart
> Cleft by the sun's spear.
> Colour comes back to things
> From his bright face.

Aurelius Clemens Prudentius, *Cathemerinon* 11. 1–8, 'Hymn for Morning' (*c.*400)

V. Christ and the Cosmos

The revelation which took place in Christ, and the great salvific exchange by which his descent made for our ascent, were understood not as one more episode in the dealings of God with the world, but as the keystone of the providential structure of creation, the clue which deciphers the whole cosmic plan of God from creation to consummation. Patristic writers constantly turned their readings of Christ and salvation into readings of everything—of the whole of history, the whole created order—and sought to find in him a guide to the riddling turnings of the world. (Cf. **47**, **40**.)

50   Christ and Creation

Another Pauline passage which may draw on an earlier hymn (cf. **39**), this stands alongside the prologue of John (**66**) as the broadest canonical affirmation of the place of Christ in God's cosmic plan. It is a fantasia on a theme from Genesis: 'In the beginning', Christ is the beginning, the head, the first-born; creation is in, through, and for *him*.

He is the image of the invisible God, the firstborn of all creation; for in him all things in heaven and on earth were created, things visible and invisible, whether thrones or dominions or rulers or powers—all things have been created through him and for him. He himself is before all things, and in him all things hold together. He is the head of the body, the church; he is the beginning, the firstborn from the dead, so that he might come to have first place in everything. For in him all the fullness of God was pleased to dwell, and through him God was pleased to reconcile to himself all things, whether on earth or in heaven, by making peace through the blood of his cross.

Colossians 1: 15–20 (1st century)

51   Recapitulation

Irenaeus of Lyons (*c*.130–*c*.200) was the greatest theologian of his century. He wrote pungently against Gnosticism (cf. **68**, **69**) and other heresies, and in the course of his polemic unfolded a story of salvation of breathtaking coherence and scope. In Christ the creation of humanity in Adam rings out again in a major key, catching all the seemingly disparate elements of creation and history into a fitting harmony. (Cf. **52**.)

The prophets were sent by God through the Holy Spirit, and they instructed the people and turned them to the God of their fathers, the Almighty; and they became heralds of the revelation of our Lord Jesus Christ the Son of God, declaring that from the posterity of David his flesh should blossom forth, that according to the flesh he might be the son of David, who was the son of Abraham by a long succession; but according to the spirit Son of God, pre-existing with the Father, begotten before all the creation of the world, and at the end of the times appearing to all the world as man, the Word of God gathering up in himself all things that are in heaven and that are on earth.

So then he united man with God, and established a community of union between God and man, since we could not in any other way participate in incorruption than by his coming among us. For so long as incorruption was invisible and unrevealed, it helped us not at all; therefore it became visible, that in all respects we might participate in the reception of incorruption.

And, because in the original formation of Adam all of us were tied and bound up with death through his disobedience, it was right that through the obedience of him who was made man for us we should be released from death. And because death reigned over the flesh, it was right that through the flesh it should lose its force and let man go free from its oppression. So the Word was made flesh [66], that, through that very flesh which sin had ruled and dominated, it should lose its force and be no longer in us. And therefore our Lord took that same original formation as his entry into flesh, so that he might draw near and contend on behalf of the fathers, and conquer by Adam that which by Adam had stricken us down.

Whence then is the substance of the first-formed man? From the will and the wisdom of God, and from the virgin earth. For God had not sent rain, the Scripture says, upon the earth, before man was made; and there was no man to till the earth. From this, then, whilst it was still virgin, God took dust of the earth and formed the man, the beginning of mankind. So then the Lord, summing up afresh this man, took the same dispensation of entry into flesh, being born from the Virgin by the will and the wisdom of God; that he also should show forth the likeness of Adam's entry into flesh, and there should be that which was written in the beginning, man after the image and likeness of God.

Again, just as through a disobedient virgin man was stricken down and fell into death, so through the Virgin who was obedient to the Word of God man was reanimated and received life. For the Lord came to seek again the sheep that was lost; and it was man that was lost: and for this cause it was not some other formation which was made, but that same formation which had its descent from Adam; he preserved the likeness of the first formation. For it was necessary that Adam should be summed up in Christ, that mortality might be swallowed up and overwhelmed by immortality; and Eve summed up in Mary, that a virgin should be a virgin's intercessor, and by a virgin's obedience undo and put away the disobedience of a virgin.

And the trespass which came by the tree was undone by the tree of obedience, when, hearkening unto God, the Son of man was nailed to the tree; thereby putting away the knowledge of evil and bringing in and establishing the knowledge of good (for evil is to disobey God, and good is hearkening unto God). And for this cause the word spoke by Isaiah the prophet, announcing beforehand that which was to come [. . .]: 'I refuse not, nor gainsay: I gave my back to scourging, and my cheeks to smiting; and my face I turned not away from the shame of spitting.' So then by the obedience by which he obeyed even unto death [cf. 39], hanging on the tree, he put away the old disobedience which was wrought in the tree.

Now seeing that he is the Word of God Almighty, who in an unseen way in our midst is universally extended in all the world, and encompasses its length and breadth and height and depth, for by the Word of God the whole universe is ordered and disposed—in it is crucified the Son of God, inscribed crosswise upon it all: for it is right that he, being made visible, should set upon all things visible the sharing of his cross, that he might show his operation on visible things through a visible form. For he it is who illuminates the height, that is the heavens; and encompasses the deep which is beneath the earth; and stretches and spreads out the length from east to west; and steers across the breadth of north and south; summoning all that are scattered in every quarter to the knowledge of the Father.

Moreover he fulfilled the promise made to Abraham, which God had promised him, to make his seed as the stars of heaven [. . .] And he fulfilled the promise to David; for to him God had promised that of the fruit of his body he would raise up an eternal King, whose kingdom should have no end. And this King is Christ, the Son of God, who became the Son of man; that is, who became the fruit of that Virgin who had her descent from David. [. . .]

Thus then he gloriously achieved our redemption, and fulfilled the promise of the fathers, and abolished the old disobedience. The Son of God became Son of David and Son of Abraham; perfecting and summing up this in himself, that he might make us to possess life.

Irenaeus of Lyons, *The Demonstration of the Apostolic Preaching* 30–7, extracts (late 2nd century)

52   Reversing Adam

Paula (347–404) and her virgin daughter Julia Eustochium (370–c.419) were women of senatorial class who, after the death of Paula's husband, lived an ascetic life in Rome before settling in Bethlehem under the guidance of Jerome (cf. 56). Through him they wrote a letter to Marcella extolling the virtues of their new home, right by Jerusalem. (Cf. 51.)

Tradition has it that in this city, nay, more, on this very spot, Adam lived and died. The place where our Lord was crucified is called Calvary, because the skull of the primitive man was buried there. So it came to pass that the second Adam, that is the blood of Christ, as it dropped from the cross, washed away the sins of the buried protoplast, the first Adam, and thus the words of the apostle were fulfilled: 'Awake, thou that sleepest, and arise from the dead, and Christ shall give thee light.'

Paula and Julia Eustochium, Letter, extract (386)

Section C

Typology and Apology

The development of patristic responses to Jesus of Nazareth took place in a constant struggle with Judaism on the one hand and with Graeco-Roman culture on the other. Growing from the soil provided by one in the atmosphere of the other, Christians constantly borrowed from both Jewish and pagan culture, while learning to distinguish themselves from them. In both cases, the claims Christians made about the man Jesus of Nazareth were central to the sense of their own identity which they developed.

I. Jesus and Judaism

Although it began as a movement firmly embedded within first-century Judaism, as the proportion of Gentile believers grew, and especially after Judaism itself underwent the convulsion of the destruction of the temple (AD 70), Christianity increasingly came to have a distinct identity. That identity was never without Jewish roots, however—even those who thought the God of the Old Testament foreign to Christianity had the lines of their theology set by this rejection. This debt is most obviously seen in the constant Christian attempts to understand Jesus of Nazareth against the background of the Jewish Scriptures; it is also seen in the growth of Christian anti-Semitism. (Cf. 120–1, 161–2, 225, 242, 338–41.)

53 The Servant of the Lord Foretold

One of the passages of the Hebrew Scriptures frequently taken to predict Christ, or to provide the categories within which Jesus' saving work can be understood, has been the fifth-century BC prophecy of Isaiah concerning Yahweh's servant.

See, my servant shall prosper; he shall be exalted and lifted up, and shall be very high. Just as there were many who were astonished at him—so marred was his appearance, beyond human semblance, and his form beyond that of mortals—so he shall startle many nations; kings shall shut their mouths because of him; for that which had not been told them they shall see, and that which they had not heard they shall contemplate.

Who has believed what we have heard? And to whom has the arm of the

Lord been revealed? For he grew up before him like a young plant, and like a root out of dry ground; he had no form or majesty that we should look at him, nothing in his appearance that we should desire him. He was despised and rejected by others; a man of suffering and acquainted with infirmity; and as one from whom others hide their faces he was despised, and we held him of no account. Surely he has borne our infirmities and carried our diseases; yet we accounted him stricken, struck down by God, and afflicted.

But he was wounded for our transgressions, crushed for our iniquities; upon him was the punishment that made us whole, and by his bruises we are healed. All we like sheep have gone astray; we have all turned to our own way, and the Lord has laid on him the iniquity of us all.

He was oppressed, and he was afflicted, yet he did not open his mouth; like a lamb that is led to the slaughter, and like a sheep that before its shearers is silent, so he did not open his mouth. By a perversion of justice he was taken away. Who could have imagined his future? For he was cut off from the land of the living, stricken for the transgression of my people. They made his grave with the wicked and his tomb with the rich, although he had done no violence, and there was no deceit in his mouth.

Yet it was the will of the Lord to crush him with pain. When you make his life an offering for sin, he shall see his offspring, and shall prolong his days; through him the will of the Lord shall prosper. Out of his anguish he shall see light; he shall find satisfaction through his knowledge. The righteous one, my servant, shall make many righteous, and he shall bear their iniquities. Therefore I will allot him a portion with the great, and he shall divide the spoil with the strong; because he poured out himself to death, and was numbered with the transgressors; yet he bore the sin of many, and made intercession for the transgressors.

Isaiah 52: 13–53: 12 (5th century BC)

54　Shadow and True Form

One of the ways in which the relation of Christianity to Judaism was worked out was in terms of the metaphor of shadow and reality. Israel with its law was considered as a shadow in which the shape of God's consummate work could be dimly discerned, but which was only properly understood when seen spread at the feet of the one whose shadow it was. The author of Hebrews interprets the Jewish sacrificial system in this way.

Since the law has only a shadow of the good things to come and not the true form of these realities, it can never, by the same sacrifices that are continually offered year after year, make perfect those who approach. Otherwise, would they not have ceased being offered, since the worshippers, cleansed once for all, would no longer have any consciousness of sin? But in these sacrifices there is a reminder of sin year after year. For it is impossible for the blood of bulls and goats to take away sins.

Consequently, when Christ came into the world, he said, 'Sacrifices and offerings you have not desired, but a body you have prepared for me; in burnt offerings and sin offerings you have taken no pleasure. Then I said, "See, God, I have come to do your will, O God. (In the scroll of the book it is written of me.)"' [Ps. 40: 6–8.]

When he said above, 'You have neither desired nor taken pleasure in sacrifices and offerings and burnt offerings and sin offerings' (these are offered according to the law), then he added, 'See, I have come to do your will.' He abolishes the first in order to establish the second. And it is by God's will that we have been sanctified through the offering of the body of Jesus Christ once for all.

And every priest stands day after day at his service, offering again and again the same sacrifices that can never take away sins. But when Christ had offered for all time a single sacrifice for sins, he sat down at the right hand of God, and since then has been waiting 'until his enemies would be made a footstool for his feet' [Ps. 110: 1]. For by a single offering he has perfected for all time those who are sanctified.

Hebrews 10: 1–14 (1st century)

55   The True Passover

We know little of Melito of Sardis (d. c.190) except what can be gleaned from his rhythmic liturgical treatise *On the Pasch*.[11] Melito appropriates the Jewish Scriptures, drawing in particular on Exodus 12, and makes them speak in a rich polyphony of Jesus Christ (cf. **18**, **32**). He also includes repeated polemics against the Jews who 'murdered Jesus' (see **162**, **339**).

The Lord made prior arrangements for his own sufferings in patriarchs and in prophets and in the whole people, setting his seal to them through both law and prophets. For the thing which is to be new and great in its realisation is arranged for well in advance, so that when it comes about it may be believed in, having been foreseen well in advance. Just so also the mystery of the Lord, having been prefigured well in advance and having been seen through a model, is today believed in now that it is fulfilled, though considered new by men. For the mystery of the Lord is new and old: old according to the law, but new with reference to the grace. But if you look carefully at the model, you will perceive him through the final outcome. Therefore if you wish to see the mystery of the Lord, look at Abel who is similarly murdered, at

Isaac who is similarly bound, at Joseph who is similarly sold, at Moses who is similarly exposed, at David who is similarly persecuted, at the prophets who similarly suffer for the sake of Christ. Look also at the sheep which is slain in the land of Egypt, which struck Egypt and saved Israel by its blood. [. . .]

It is Christ who, coming from heaven to the earth because of the suffering one, and clothing himself in that same one through a virgin's womb, and coming forth a man, accepted the passions of the suffering one through the body which was able to suffer, and dissolved the passions of the flesh; and by the Spirit which could not die he killed death the killer of men. For, himself led as a lamb and slain as a sheep, he ransomed us from the world's service as from the land of Egypt, and freed us from the devil's slavery as from the hand of Pharaoh; and he marked our souls with his own Spirit and the members of our body with his own blood. It is he that clothed death with shame and stood the devil in grief as Moses did Pharaoh. It is he that struck down crime and made injustice childless as Moses did Egypt. It is he that delivered us from slavery to liberty, from darkness to light, from death to life, from tyranny to eternal royalty, and made us a new priesthood and an eternal people personal to him.

He is the Pascha of our salvation. It is he who in many endured many things: it is he that was in Abel murdered, and in Isaac bound, and in Jacob exiled, and in Joseph sold, and in Moses exposed, and in the lamb slain, and in David persecuted, and in the prophets dishonoured. It is he that was enfleshed in a virgin, that was hanged on a tree, that was buried in the earth, that was raised from the dead, that was taken up to the heights of the heavens. He is the lamb being slain; he is the lamb that is speechless [cf. 53]; he is the one born from Mary the lovely ewe-lamb; he is the one taken from the flock, and dragged to slaughter, and sacrificed at evening, and buried at night; who on the tree was not broken, in the earth was not dissolved, arose from the dead, and raised up man from the grave below.

It is he that has been murdered. And where has he been murdered? In the middle of Jerusalem. By whom? By Israel. Why? Because he healed their lame and cleansed their lepers and brought light to their blind and raised their dead, that is why he died.

Melito of Sardis, Peri Pascha 57–60, 66–72 (2nd century)

Jerome (c.342–420) was an ascetic and a prolific scholar who, along with many other works, produced a new Latin translation of the Bible from the original Hebrew, Aramaic, and Greek. This formed the basis for the Vulgate, and eventually gave the Latin West its lingua franca. Here, while explaining the 'spiritual meaning' of the stories of the Transfiguration, he shows how Christians cannot stop short with the literal meaning if they wish to appropriate the Old Testament, but must bring all things in subjection to Christ.

If we read and take all this [i.e. the Transfiguration story; 12] literally, what is the value of 'shining,' of 'white,' of 'on high'? If we ponder it spiritually, Holy Writ, that is, the clothing of the word, is transformed immediately and becomes as white as snow: 'as no fuller on earth can whiten.' Take any prophetical witness, any evangelical parable, if you consider merely the letter, there is nothing shining in it, nothing white. If, however, you follow the apostle with deep spiritual perception, immediately the clothing of the word is changed and becomes white; Jesus is completely transformed on the mountain, and his garments become exceedingly white as snow: 'as no fuller on earth can whiten.' The earthly man cannot whiten his garments; but he who abandons the world and ascends the mountain with Jesus, and meditating mounts to heavenly contemplations, that man is able to make his garments white as no fuller on earth can do. [. . .]

'There appeared to them Elias with Moses, and they were talking with Jesus.' Until they had seen Jesus transfigured, until they had seen his white garments, they could not see Moses and Elias. 'They were talking with Jesus.' As long as we limit our perception as do the Jews, and follow only the letter that kills, Moses and Elias are not talking with Jesus; they do not know the Gospel. If, however, they shall have followed Jesus and have deserved to see the Lord transfigured with his white garments and to penetrate the Sacred Scripture with spiritual insight, at once, Moses and Elias come—that is, the Law and the prophets—and talk with the Word. 'There appeared to them Elias with Moses, and they were talking with Jesus.' The Gospel according to Luke adds: 'They spoke to him of his death, which he was about to fulfil in Jerusalem.' That is what Moses and Elias are discussing, and they speak with Jesus, that is, with the Word, and announce to him what he is going to suffer in Jerusalem, for the Law and the prophets proclaim the passion of Christ. Do you see how the spiritual interpretation benefits our soul? Moses and Elias, notice, also appear in white garments. As long as they are not with Jesus, they do not have white garments. If you should read the Law, which is Moses, and the prophets, which is Elias, and do not appreciate them in Christ, nor comprehend how Moses and Elias speak with Jesus; but accept Moses and Elias without him and do not perceive that they are announcing to him the

Passion, then, Moses and Elias do not ascend the mountain, nor do they have white garments, but those that are still soiled.

If you follow the letter as do the Jews, what does it profit you to read that Judah has relations with Tamar, his daughter-in-law? What profit to you that Noah became intoxicated and exposed his nakedness? What profit that Onan, the son of Judah, committed so disgraceful an act that I blush to mention it; what, I ask, does it profit you? But if you have spiritual discernment, do you see how the soiled garments of Moses are made white? Peter, James, and John, who had seen Moses and Elias before without Jesus, now that they have seen them in white garments talking with him, realise that they are themselves on the mountain. Truly, we are standing on the mountain with them when we understand the Scriptures spiritually. If I read Genesis, Exodus, Leviticus, Numbers, Deuteronomy, as long as I read carnally I seem to be down below, but if I grasp their spiritual significance, I am climbing to the top of the mountain. You see, therefore, how Peter, James, and John recognise that they are on the mountain—in the discernment of the spirit—and despise, therefore, the lowly and the human, and long for the lofty and divine. They do not want to descend to earth, but to remain wholly with the spiritual. [. . .]

'This is my beloved Son; hear him,' my Son, not Moses nor Elias. They are servants; this is the Son. This is my Son, of my nature, of my substance, abiding in me, and he is all that I am. This is my beloved Son. They, too, indeed are dear to me, but he is my beloved; hear him, therefore. They proclaim and teach him, but you, hear him; he is the Lord and Master, they are companions in servitude. Moses and Elias speak of Christ; they are your fellow servants; he is the Lord; hear him. Do not render the same honour to fellow servants as to the Lord and Master. Hear only the Son of God.

While the Father is speaking thus and saying: 'This is my beloved Son; hear him,' it has not been evident who was speaking. There was a cloud; a voice was heard; it said: 'This is my beloved Son; hear him.' Peter could have said, in error: It speaks of Moses or of Elias, but lest there be any doubt, the two vanish while the Father is speaking and Christ alone remains. 'This is my beloved Son; hear him.' Peter muses in his heart: Who is his Son? I see three; do you have any idea of whom he is speaking? While he is seeking to know whom to choose, he sees only one. Suddenly looking round expecting to see three, they find only one; nay more, losing three, they find one; I may even say by way of amplification, in one they find three. Moses, in fact, and Elias, too, are more apt to be found if they are brought together in one with Christ.

'Suddenly looking round, they no longer saw anyone with them.' When I read the Gospel and see there testimony from the Law and the prophets, I contemplate Christ alone. I have looked at Moses and Elias only that I might understand them as they speak of Christ. Finally, when I come to the splendour of Christ, and behold, as it were, the exceedingly brilliant light of the bright sun, I cannot see the light of the lamp. Can a lamp give light if you light it in the daytime? If the sun is shining, the light of the lamp is not visible, so when Christ is present, the Law and the prophets, by comparison, are not even visible. I am not detracting from the Law and the prophets, rather I am praising them, for they proclaim Christ; I so read the Law and the prophets that I do not remain in them, but through them arrive at Christ.

Jerome (Eusebius Hieronymus), *Homilies on St. Mark*, 80, extracts (late 4th century)

57   A Jewish Report

It is harder, in the patristic period, to find evidence for Jewish views of Christianity than vice versa. We find the following extract by Josephus (*c.*37–*c.*100), a Jewish historian, in his *Antiquities of the Jews*, but it has been expanded by an anonymous Christian author. The passages in italics below are likely to come from the anonymous interpolator.

Now there was about this time [i.e. about the time of the rising against Pilate who wished to extract money from the Temple for the purpose of bringing water to Jerusalem from a distant spring] Jesus, a wise man, *if it be lawful to call him a man*. For he was a doer of wonderful works, a teacher of such men as receive the truth with pleasure. He drew over to him both many of the Jews and many of the Gentiles. *He was the Christ* and when Pilate, at the suggestion of the principal men among us, had condemned him to the cross, those that loved him at the first did not forsake him, *for he appeared to them alive again on the third day, as the divine Prophets had foretold these and ten thousand other wonderful things concerning him*; and the tribe of Christians, so named from him, are not extinct even now.

Flavius Josephus, *Antiquities of the Jews* 18. iii. 3 (*c.*94)

58   Yeshu's Guilt

Jewish interpretation of Scripture in the early patristic period circulated in collections called *mishnayot*, eventually collected in the second or early third century into an authoritative collection, the Mishnah. This then formed the basis for further debate and discussion and elaboration, leading to the collections called, collectively, Gemara over the next few centuries. In the fifth century the Mishnah and Gemara were themselves collected in authoritative forms in the Babylonian and Palestinian Talmuds, although the Babylonian Talmud did not achieve its final form for some time. Buried within the Babylonian Talmud, and almost impossible to date, there are references which appear to refer to Jesus, such as the following discussion of his trial.

MISHNAH: If then they find him innocent, they discharge him; but if not, he goes forth to be stoned. And a herald precedes him crying: 'And so, the son of so and so, going forth to be stoned because he committed such and such an offence, and so and so are his witnesses. Whoever knows anything in his favour, let him come and state it.'

GEMARA: Abaye said: It must also be announced: On such and such a day, at such and such an hour, and in such and such a place the crime was committed, in case there are some who know to the contrary, so that they can come forward and prove the witnesses.

'And a herald precedes him' etc. This implies, only immediately before the execution, but not previous thereto. In contradiction to this it was taught: On the eve of the Passover Yeshu was hanged. For forty days before the execution took place, a herald went forth and cried, 'He is going forth to be stoned because he has practised sorcery and enticed Israel to apostasy. Any one who can say anything in his favour, let him come forward and plead on his behalf.' But since nothing was brought forward in his favour he was hanged on the eve of the Passover!—Ulla retorted: Do you suppose that he was one for whom a defence could be made? Was he not an enticer concerning whom Scripture says, 'Neither shalt thou spare, neither shalt thou conceal him?' [Deut. 13: 9.] With Yeshu however it was different, for he was connected with the government.

Babylonian Talmud, *Sanhedrin* 43a (date unknown)

II. Against the Pagans

If the primary soil in which Christianity grew was Jewish, the air around it was soon pagan. Christians, whether at times of explicit persecution or simply when living peacefully among pagans, explained themselves to, distinguished themselves from, made their faith attractive for, and unconsciously or consciously assimilated the language and ideas of, the pagan world.

59   The Foolishness of Wisdom

Paul (cf. 14, 39, 45, 50), himself a Roman citizen as well as originally a devout Jew, contrasted the offensive weakness of the Christian faith with the dominant and dominating wisdom of the Graeco-Roman world.

For the message about the cross is foolishness to those who are perishing, but to us who are being saved it is the power of God. For it is written, 'I will destroy the wisdom of the wise, and the discernment of the discerning I will thwart' [Isa. 29: 14]. Where is the one who is wise? Where is the scribe? Where is the debater of this age? Has not God made foolish the wisdom of the world? For since, in the wisdom of God, the world did not know God through wisdom, God decided, through the foolishness of our proclamation, to save those who believe. For Jews demand signs and Greeks desire wisdom, but we proclaim Christ crucified, a stumbling block to Jews and foolishness to Gentiles, but to those who are the called, both Jews and Greeks, Christ the power of God and the wisdom of God. For God's foolishness is wiser than human wisdom, and God's weakness is stronger than human strength.

1 Corinthians 1: 18–25 (1st century)

60   The Offence of Incarnation

Porphyry (c.232–c.303) was a Neoplatonist philosopher and writer against popular superstitions. He wrote a stinging attack entitled *Against the Christians* in fifteen books which survives only in the fragments quoted by the many theologians who wrote the case for the defence; the rest was condemned to the flames in AD 448. Here he attacks one of the aspects of Christian belief most ridiculous to a Greek philosopher. (Cf. **1, 70, 161.**)

Even supposing some Greeks are so foolish as to think that the gods dwell in the statues, even that would be a much purer concept of religion than to admit that the divine power should descend into the womb of the Virgin Mary, that it became an embryo and after birth was wrapped in rags, soiled with blood and bile, and even worse.

Porphyry, *Against the Christians*, fr. 77 (c.290)

61   Roman Persecution

Pliny the Younger (c.61–c.112), an urbane and refined governor of Bithynia, wrote to the emperor Trajan in c.112, asking for his advice in dealing with these Christians. Despite the hints of tolerance which emerge, the correspondence makes chilling reading. (Cf. **35.**)

It is my custom to refer all my difficulties to you, Sir, for no one is better able to resolve my doubts and to inform my ignorance.

I have never been present at an examination of Christians. Consequently, I do not know the nature or the extent of the punishments usually meted out to them, nor the grounds for starting an investigation and how far it should be pressed. Nor am I at all sure whether any distinction should be made between them on the grounds of age, or if young people and adults should be treated alike; whether a pardon ought to be granted to anyone retracting his beliefs, or if he has once professed Christianity, he shall gain nothing by renouncing it; and whether it is the mere name of Christian which is punishable, even if innocent of crime, or rather the crimes associated with the name.

For the moment this is the line I have taken with all persons brought before me on the charge of being Christians. I have asked them in person if they are Christians, and if they admit it, I repeat the question a second and third time, with a warning of the punishment awaiting them. If they persist, I order them to be led away for execution; for, whatever the nature of their admission, I am convinced that their stubbornness and unshakeable obstinacy ought not to go unpunished. There have been others similarly fanatical who are Roman citizens. I have entered them on the list of persons to be sent to Rome for trial.

Now that I have begun to deal with this problem, as so often happens, the charges are becoming more widespread and increasing in variety. An anonymous pamphlet has been circulated which contains the names of a number of accused persons. Among these I considered that I should dismiss any who denied that they were or ever had been Christians when they had repeated after me a formula of invocation to the gods and had made offerings of wine and incense to your statue (which I had ordered to be brought into court for this purpose along with the images of the gods), and furthermore had reviled the name of Christ: none of which things, I understand, any genuine Christian can be induced to do.

Others, whose names were given to me by an informer, first admitted the charge and then denied it; they said that they had ceased to be Christians two or more years previously, and some of them even twenty years ago. They all did reverence to your statue and the images of the gods in the same way as the others, and reviled the name of Christ. They also declared that the sum total of their guilt or error amounted to no more than this: they had met regularly before dawn on a fixed day to chant verses alternately among themselves in honour of Christ as if to a god, and also to bind themselves by oath, not for any criminal purpose, but to abstain from theft, robbery and adultery, to commit no breach of trust and not to deny a deposit when called upon to restore it. After this ceremony it had been their custom to disperse and reassemble later to take food of an ordinary, harmless kind; but they had in fact given up this practice since my edict, issued on your instructions, which banned all political societies. This made me decide it was all the more necessary to extract the truth by torture from two slave-women, whom they call deaconesses. I found nothing but a degenerate sort of cult carried to extravagant lengths.

I have therefore postponed any further examination and hastened to consult you. The question seems to me to be worthy of your consideration, especially in view of the number of persons endangered; for a great many individuals of every age and class, both men and women, are being brought to trial, and this is likely to continue. It is not only the towns, but villages and rural districts too which are infected through contact with this wretched cult. I think though that it is still possible for it to be checked and directed to better ends, for there is no doubt that people have begun to throng the temples which had been almost entirely deserted for a long time; the sacred rites which had been allowed to lapse are being performed again, and flesh of sacrificial victims is on sale everywhere, though up till recently scarcely anyone could be found to buy it. It is easy to infer from this that a great many people could be reformed if they were given an opportunity to repent.

[Trajan replied:]

You have followed the right course of procedure, my dear Pliny, in your examination of the cases of persons charged with being Christians, for it is impossible to lay down a general rule to a fixed formula. These people must not be hunted out; if they are brought before you and the charge against them is proved, they must be punished, but in the case of anyone who denies that he is a Christian, and makes it clear that he is not by offering prayers to our gods, he is to be pardoned as a result of his repentance however suspect his past conduct may be. But pamphlets circulated anonymously must play no part in any accusation. They create the worst sort of precedent and are quite out of keeping with the spirit of our age.

Pliny, *Letters*, extracts (*c.*112)

62   Christ the Judge Foretold

If Christian relations with Judaism revolved around the appropriation of the Jewish Scriptures, its attempts to come to terms with paganism often involved an appropriation of pagan culture. Sometimes that took the form of showing that the Jewish Scriptures had chronological and philosophical priority over Greek writings; here instead we find a collection of works purporting to be Greek oracles from earlier centuries containing prophecies of Christ and testimonies to the truth of Judaism and Christianity. This acrostic was probably written by a second- or third-century Christian. (Cf. **6**.)

Judgement's sign appearing,   all earth in horror sweating;
Eternity's King shall enter.   From heaven, the great King coming—he
Shall judge all human people,   shall judge the whole world's nations.
Unfaithful folk and faithful,   shall see the Most High God then,
Saints in glory spread around him,   at the end of time soon coming.
Clothed with flesh beside his throne,   the souls of all the people
He shall sit over in judgement,   their earth dried up and arid.
Riches all and idols   the world's people shall abandon
Into the fire then roaring,   which, heaven, earth, sea consuming,
Spreads destroying ever wider,   to break the door of Hades,
To bring all its captured people   from the dead to light of freedom.
Gone to fire for countless ages   in torment, all the lawless;
Opened then and spoken   all dark things wrought in secret;
Dark breasts will be uncovered   by God's lights, the darkness searching.
Shrieking out and wailing,   all the lawless teeth are gnashing.
Sin's waning light occluded,   all the stars of heaven dancing;
Overcome, the light of man,   rolled away are all his heavens;
No more mountains or high hills,   all the rugged land is levelled;
Out from in among them,   all the baneful heights shall go;
Up will come all yawning chasms,   all the sea will flee away;
Removed with all its voyages,   the earth left parched behind:
Springs will all have vanished,   all the rivers will cease foaming.
A trumpet call from heaven   shall sound great lamentation,
Voicing mourning for defilement,   for the wide world's great disaster.
Infernal and abyssal,   all the earth is left with nothing.
Over all the earthly kings, then,   our God shall show his judgement,
Using burning fire for pouring,   on the sinful land with sulphur.
Revelation will arrive then,   a sign for all earth's mortals,
Showing wood among the faithful,   a horn they long expected,
Condemning all to stumbling,   while enlivening the pious,
Replenishing the faithful,   with the twelve-springed waters,
Overruling them with iron,   with the staff a shepherd works with.
Search now this acrostic,   for the one we own Divine; our
Saviour, King immortal,   who for our healing suffered.

Sibylline Oracles VII, 217–50 (2nd or 3rd century)

63 The Seeds of the Logos

Justin Martyr (*c*.100–*c*.165) converted to Christianity from paganism after a dalliance with several philosophies including Platonism. He addressed defences of Christianity to the emperor Antoninus Pius and to the Senate, seeking to make Christianity intelligible and, to an extent, acceptable to its cultured despisers. He was eventually beheaded for his faith (cf. **35**). He argued, in his Second Apology, that the Logos had sown seeds widely among human beings before he became man, and that hints and portions of truth can be found wherever that sowing Logos is present. (Cf. **66**.)

I confess that I both pray and with all my strength strive to be found a Christian; not because the teachings of Plato are different from those of Christ, but because they are not in every respect equal, as neither are those of the others, Stoics, and poets, and historians. For each person spoke well, according to the part present in him of the divine logos, the Sower, whenever he saw what was related to him as a person. But they who contradict themselves on the more important points appear not to have possessed the hidden understanding and the irrefutable knowledge. Therefore, whatever things were rightly said among all people are the property of us Christians. For next to God, we worship and love the logos who is from the unbegotten and ineffable God, since also he became man for our sakes, that, becoming a partaker of our sufferings, he might also bring us healing. For all the writers were able to see realities darkly, through the presence in them of an implanted seed of logos. For the seed and imitation of something, imparted according to capacity, is one thing, and another is the thing itself, the part possession and imitation of which is effected according to the grace coming from him.

Justin Martyr, Second Apology 13 (extract) (before 161)

64   A Vergilian Baptism

Faltonia Proba was from a noble Roman family, and was probably the wife of the proconsul Clodius Celsinus Adelphius, who was prefect in AD 351. About that time she wrote a cento poem, adopting a thoroughly classical form based on the work of Vergil and filling it with Christian content. (Cf. 2.)

A prophet, a most reliable witness,
when he espied a secluded spot far off by a cool stream, cried,
'It is the Lord's time. Behold the Lord, to him belongs the greatest faith
in world or word. Thou now shalt be the vicar,
O blessed Son, of him whom the stars obey.
Thus indeed I wondered in my mind and contemplated the future;
Thou are come, O long awaited one, our hope and our comfort.'
When he had uttered these words, the prophet
received him into the waters of salvation and baptised him with gentle waters:
The rivers rejoiced and suddenly a dove, inspired,
flew down and hesitated over his hair; then she skims
the liquid air, moving not her swift wings.
Hither ran the whole crowd, rushing to the banks
vying with one another to pour the abundant waters over their shoulders.
Then the Father addressed his Son with loving words:
'My Son, you alone are my strength, my mighty power;
you are about to bring sweet glory to your Sire,
All things begin and end with you. Accept, I implore,

O my son, both oceans which the sun surveys
in its rounds. Once your task is completed,
in joy you shall behold all things revolving beneath your feet.
Rule your people with authority, both men and women.
Already you calm their pride and their hearts grown cold,
And with me you have compassion for slothful humans, those ignorant of the way.
Go forth and become used to being invoked with prayers.'
God had spoken. He prepared to obey the commands
of his Almighty Father, eager for his task and the kingdom to come.
Alas for holiness, alas for old-time faith! What thanks
shall I commence to offer, if it is permissible to return a pittance for such great
    things?
For me there was no longer hope of seeing the ancient fatherland,
no hope for freedom, no concern for salvation.
He was the first to give answer to my petition;
he removed the inborn stain and left a pure,
spiritual sensation, and he sent me back to my realms.
I would follow him through flames were I an exile in Africa,
through misfortunes of all sorts, though a thousand missiles come at me,
withersoever situations tended, him alone, because of his great name,
I would follow, and I would strew his altars with gifts.
At his coming, in honour of such great praises,
the mountains and their woods raise their voices
to the stars in joy. The valleys echo it all.

Falconia Proba, 'Cento', 388–428 (c.351)

65 The Fount of Light

Synesius of Cyrene (c.370–c.414), Libyan ambassador to Constantinople, married a Christian wife and was chosen Bishop of Ptolemais before he had been baptized as a Christian. He composed poetry which combined his adopted Christianity with classical forms and motifs (cf. 64, 137, 182), demonstrating the porous boundaries between pagan and Christian culture. Note particularly the Neoplatonic[12] images in the fourth stanza of this poem.

Sing we her Son whom wedlock
bound to no human bed.
The Father's hidden counsels
decreed the birth of Christ,
the virgin lent her labour
and gave him human shape:
he came and brought us mortals
light, the fount of light.

Before the seed of time took root,
you were born mysteriously.

O well of light, O splendour
shining with the Father,
the murk of matter breaks before you,
you shine in souls that are pure.

Creator of the universe—
the wheels of noble stars,
the centre of the rooted earth—
you the Saviour of men:
for you the great sun goes riding,
unscorched by his fiery horses,
the heifer-headed moon for you
whitens the gloom of night,
the crops increase and grow for you,
for you the cattle graze.
From the secret fountain of you,
vitalising brightness
flows to fecundate the world;
from your bosom light is born,
soul and understanding.
Have compassion on your daughter
in her fleshly prison,
the measure of her mortal lot.
Keep from the touch of disease
the vigour of our limbs unscathed.
Grant us words to persuade
and deeds to win men's reverence,
that they make speak of us
as once of Sparta and Cyrene.

May sorrow never walk the ways
of my soul, but leave my life
in peace, my vision undisturbed,
set on your splendour.
May matter not impede me. Speed me
along unswerving paths,
far from this bitter earth, and plunge me
into the source of my being.
So may he spotless be who makes
music for your praising.

Now as I sing my hymns to you,
to your great Father's glory
and to the Spirit throned together
with Father and with Son,
now as I sing the Father's power
and bring my hymns to you,
my soul conceives a son of its own
and breathes its own spirit.

Hail Father, source of the Son,
Son, the Father's image,
Father, the ground where the Son stands,
Son, the Father's seal,
Father, the power of the Son,
Son, the Father's beauty,
spotless Spirit, bond between
the Father and the Son.
Send, O Christ, the Spirit, send
the Father to my soul;
steep my dry heart in this dew
the best of all your gifts.

Synesius of Cyrene, 'Hymn to Christ' (early 5th century)

Section D

The Development of Christology

Much if not all that has appeared in the preceding extracts could appropriately be considered part of the development of 'Christology'. In this section, however, we shall focus more narrowly on the question of Christ's divinity and humanity, as it emerged, was slowly clarified and debated, and eventually received classic (if controversial) official expression. From the very beginning, Christians were not and could not be engaged simply in the retelling of the stories which they had received and the repetition of the practices they had learned. Speculation and polemic, improvisations in the face of ever new circumstances pregnant with possibilities and threats, were inevitable. Speculation occurred wherever Christians tried to gain a clearer glimpse of the deep truths about God and the world which undergirded the practice and beliefs of their faith. Polemic occurred wherever they defended their speculations, and the practices and beliefs which those speculations supported, against those who differed.

66 In the Beginning

> The startling prologue to John's Gospel, introducing Jesus as the enfleshed Word of God, drew on Old Testament imagery (e.g. Gen. 1, Prov. 8) in a way which threw doors open to later elaboration in terms drawn from Greek philosophy. It is, alongside the hymns in Paul's letters to the Philippians (**39**) and Colossians (**50**), one of the seminal texts in the development of Christology. (Cf. **63**, **94**.)

In the beginning was the Word, and the Word was with God, and the Word was God. He was in the beginning with God. All things came into being through him, and without him not one thing came into being. What has come into being in him was life, and the life was the light of all people. The light shines in the darkness, and the darkness has not overcome it.

There was a man sent from God, whose name was John. He came as a witness to testify to the light, so that all might believe through him. He himself was not the light, but he came to testify to the light.

The true light, which enlightens everyone, was coming into the world. He was in the world, and the world came into being through him; yet the world did not know him. He came to what was his own, and his own people did not accept him. But to all who received him, who believed in his name, he gave power to become children of God, who were born, not of blood or of the will of the flesh or of the will of man, but of God.

And the Word became flesh and lived among us, and we have seen his glory, the glory as of a father's only son, full of grace and truth.

John 1: 1–14 (1st century)

I. True Humanity

There was a tendency in the first-century world for heroes to be elevated above the constraints of humanity; for their powers and virtues to be emphasized in ways which called into question their likeness to us mere mortals. The same tendency affected many portrayals of Jesus (cf. **25, 26**), and the attempt to overcome it is one of the distinctive features of the development of Christology.

67   True Suffering

Ignatius of Antioch (c.35–107) wrote a remarkable series of letters while on his way to martyrdom. Far from dreading his coming death, he was eager to be counted worthy to share Christ's Crucifixion. In such a martyr's faith, there is no room to disparage Christ's suffering. (Cf. **35, 61**.)

I give glory to Jesus Christ, the God who has imbued you with such wisdom. I am well aware that you have been made perfect in unwavering faith, like men nailed, in body and spirit, to the Cross of our Lord, Jesus Christ, and confirmed in love by the blood of Christ. In regard to our Lord, you are thoroughly convinced that he was of the race of David according to the flesh, and the Son of God by his will and power; that he was truly born of the Virgin and baptised by John in order that all due observance might be fulfilled by him; that in his body he was truly nailed to the Cross for our sake under Pontius Pilate and Herod, the tetrarch—of his most blessed passion we are the fruit—so that, through his resurrection, he might raise, for all ages, in the one body of his Church, a standard for the saints and the faithful, whether among Jews or Gentiles.

For he suffered all these things for us, that we might be saved. And he suffered truly, and just as truly raised himself from the dead. He did not suffer merely in appearance, as some of the unbelievers say—they themselves being merely in appearance; for it will be their fate, in accordance with their faith, to be bodiless and ghostlike.

As for me, I know that even after his resurrection he was in the flesh, and I believe this to be true. For, when he came to those who were with Peter, he said to them: 'Take hold on me and handle me and see that I am not a spirit without a body' [Luke 24: 39]. And, as soon as they touched him and felt his flesh and pulse, they believed. It is for this reason that they despised death and even showed themselves superior to death. After his resurrection he ate and drank with them like anyone else with a body, although in his spirit he was one with the Father.

Ignatius of Antioch, *Epistle to the Smyrnaeans*, 6. 1–3 (*c*.107)

68   Christ Uncrucified

Basilides (*fl. c*.132–5) was a Gnostic from Alexandria whose teachings we know primarily from the summary provided by his opponent Irenaeus (cf. **51**). Gnosticism was a varied set of interrelated movements rather than a unified creed, but tended to involve the belief that the messy biological existence of humanity was the product not of an act of creation but a complex, layered fall ever further from the purity of the divine unity; that some or all human beings contained within their brutish physicality a spark of that original divinity; and that salvation consisted in release of that spark from the constraints of its fleshly prison. For Basilides, Jesus' role in this salvation is only secured at the cost of denying his full involvement in bodily life, particularly in suffering. (Cf. **67, 123, 135**.)

First, by the unengendered parent there was engendered intellect. And from it was engendered verbal expression (*word*). From the verbal expression, prudence. From prudence, wisdom (*sophia*) and power. And out of power together with wisdom there were engendered authorities, rulers, angels. These authorities, rulers, and angels he calls 'first' ones. And by them the first heaven was crafted.

By an act of emission on their part, other angels came into being, and they made another heaven closely resembling the first one. Then, in turn, by an act of emission on the part of these, there were produced other angels, corresponding to those that were above them, and they stamped a corresponding third heaven. And from the third level of descendants was produced a fourth, and thereafter in like manner were made still other rulers and angels, up to a total of 365 heavens. And it is because of them that the year has that quantity of days, corresponding to the number of heavens.

Moreover, the angels who occupy the last heaven, the one that is visible to us, crafted all the things that are within the world; and among themselves they divided up the earth and the nations that are upon it.

Now, their chief is the one who is known as the god of the Jews. And since the latter wanted to subject all nations to its own, the Jews, all the rest of the rulers resisted and opposed it; and so all the other nations, too, resisted the Jewish god's nation.

Then the unengendered, unnameable parent saw their ruin, and sent its first-born, the intellect, called Christ, to save people who believed in it, from the authority of the beings that had crafted the world. And unto the nations belonging to them it appeared on earth as a man, and he performed deeds of power. Hence he did not suffer. Rather, a certain Simon of Cyrene was forced to bear his cross for him, and it was he who was ignorantly and erroneously crucified, being transformed by the other, so that he was taken for Jesus; while Jesus, for his part, assumed the form of Simon and stood by, laughing at them. For because he was an incorporeal power and was the intellect of the unengendered parent, he was transformed however he willed. And thus he ascended to the one who had sent him, mocking them. For he could not be held back and was invisible to all.

Therefore people who know these things have been set free from the rulers that crafted the world. One should not acknowledge the man who was crucified, but rather the one who came in the form of a man, was thought to have been crucified, was named Jesus, and was sent by the parent so that by this providential arrangement of events he might destroy the works of the craftsmen of the world. Thus, he says, anyone who confesses the man who was crucified is still a slave and is still under the authority of the beings that created bodies; while anyone who denies him is both freed from them and has acquaintance with the unengendered parent's providential arrangement of events.

From Irenaeus, Against Heresies 1. 24. 3–4 (late 2nd century)

69 Jesus' Continence

Offence at the constraints of bodiliness most often fastens on suffering, ignorance, or weakness, but from time to time bodily functions like excretion have provoked theologians, as in this fragment from the Gnostic (cf. **68**) Valentinus (*c.*100–*c.*175). For an antidote, see **109**.

He was continent, enduring all things. Jesus digested divinity: he ate and drank in a special way without excreting his solids. He had such a great capacity for continence that the nourishment within him was not corrupted, for he did not experience corruption.

Valentinus, 'Epistle to Agathapous' (fragment), preserved in Clement of Alexandria,
Miscellanies 3. 59. 3 (2nd century)

If a rejoinder is wanted to Gnostic denials of Christ's true bodiliness (**69**), it is hard to find one more strident and thoroughgoing than that of the African Tertullian (*c*.160–*c*.225). Tertullian was eventually to become a member of the Montanists, a sect who emphasized the ecstatic workings of the Spirit, but there is nothing 'spiritualizing' here, in his attack upon Marcion (d. *c*.160), a thinker whose views, on this point at least, paralleled Gnosticism.

Beginning then with that nativity you so strongly object to, orate, attack now, the nastinesses of genital elements in the womb, the filthy curdling of moisture and blood, and of the flesh to be for nine months nourished on that same mire. Draw a picture of the womb getting daily more unmanageable, heavy, self-concerned, safe not even in sleep, uncertain in the whims of dislikes and appetites. Next go all out against the modesty of the travailing woman, a modesty which at least because of danger ought to be respected and because of its nature is sacred. You shudder, of course, at the child passed out along with his afterbirth, and of course bedaubed with it. You think it shameful that he is straightened out with bandages, that he is licked into shape with applications of oil, that he is beguiled by coddling. This natural object of reverence you, Marcion, be-spittle: yet how were you born? You hate man during his birth: how can you love any man? Yourself at least you evidently did not love when you withdrew from the Church and the faith of Christ. But it is your own concern if you are an object of displeasure to yourself, or if you were born some other way. Christ, there is no doubt of it, did care for the sort of man who was curdled in uncleannesses in the womb, who was brought forth through organs immodest, who took nourishment through organs of ridicule. For his sake he came down, for his sake he preached the gospel, for his sake he cast himself down in all humility even unto death, yea, the death of the cross [cf. **39**]. Evidently he loved him: for he redeemed him at a great price. If Christ belongs to the Creator, with good reason he loved his own: if he is from another god his love was even greater, in that he loved one who was not his own. In any case, along with man he loved also his nativity, and his flesh besides: nothing can be loved apart from that by which it is what it is. Else you must remove nativity and show me man, you must take away flesh and present to me him whom God has redeemed. If these are the constituents of man whom God has redeemed, who are you to make them a cause of shame to him who redeemed them, or to make them beneath his dignity, when he would not have redeemed them unless he had loved them? Nativity he reshapes from death by a heavenly regeneration, flesh he restores from every distress: leprous he cleanses it, blind he restores its sight, palsied he makes it whole again, devil-possessed he atones for it, dead he brings it again to life: is he ashamed to be born into it? [. . .]

But your answer is now required, murderer of the truth: Was not God truly crucified? Did he not, as truly crucified, truly die? Was he not truly raised again, seeing of course he truly died? Was it by fraud that Paul determined to know nothing among us save Jesus crucified, was it by fraud that he represented him as buried, by fraud that he insisted that he was raised up again? Fraudulent in that case is also our faith, and the whole of what we hope for from Christ will be a phantasm, you utter scoundrel, who pronounce innocent the assassins of God. For of them Christ suffered nothing, if he in reality suffered nothing. Spare the one and only hope of the whole world: why tear down the indispensable dishonour of the faith? Whatever is beneath God's dignity is for my advantage. I am saved if I am not ashamed of my Lord. Whosoever is ashamed of me, he says, of him will also be ashamed. I find no other grounds for shame, such as may prove that in contempt of dishonour I am nobly shameless and advantageously a fool. The Son of God was crucified: I am not ashamed—because it is shameful. The Son of God died: it is immediately credible—because it is silly. He was buried, and rose again: it is certain—because it is impossible. But how can these acts be true in him, if he himself was not true, if he had not truly in himself that which could be crucified, which could die, which could be buried and raised up again—this flesh, in fact, suffused with blood, scaffolded of bones, threaded through with sinews, intertwined with veins, competent to be born and to die, human unquestionably, as born of a human mother? And in Christ this flesh will be mortal precisely because Christ is man, and Son of Man. Else why is Christ called Man, and Son of Man, if he has nothing that is man's, and nothing derived from man?—unless perchance either man is something other than flesh, or man's flesh is derived from somewhere else than from man, or Mary is something other than human, or Marcion's god is a man. Unless one of these suppositions were true, Christ could not be described in the Scripture as man except with reference to his flesh, nor as Son of Man except with reference to some human parent: as neither could he be described as God without the Spirit of God, nor as the Son of God without God for his Father. Thus the official record of both substances represents him as both man and God: on the one hand born, on the other not born: on the one hand fleshly, on the other spiritual: on the one hand weak, on the other exceeding strong: on the one hand dying, on the other living. That these two sets of attributes, the divine and the human, are each kept distinct from the other, is of course accounted for by the equal verity of each nature, both flesh and spirit being in full degree what they claim to be: the powers of the Spirit of God proved him God, the sufferings proved there was the flesh of man. If the powers postulate the Spirit, no less do the sufferings postulate the flesh. If the flesh along with the sufferings was fictitious, it follows that the Spirit also along with the powers was a fraud. Why make out that Christ was half a lie? He was wholly the truth. He thought it better, I am sure, to be born than to be partially a liar, a liar too against himself, by wearing flesh without bones yet hard, without muscles yet firm, without blood yet gory, without a cloak yet clothed, flesh that hungered without appetite, ate without teeth, and spoke without a tongue, so that his discourse should be a phantasm conveyed to the ears by the ghost of a voice.

Tertullian (Quintus Septimius Florens Tertullianus), *On the Flesh of Christ* 4–5 (early 3rd century)

71   True Embodiment?

Most of the early Church's toiling over Christ's humanity took place in terms less extreme than those of the Gnostics or of Tertullian. Eusebius of Caesarea (*c*.260–*c*.340), the first great Church historian, was branded an Arian (see 74) by his opponents because they distrusted his ways of affirming Christ's true divinity. He here uses expressions which raise nagging questions about Christ's true embodiment. (Cf. 75.)

There is no need to be disturbed in mind on hearing of the birth, human body, sufferings and death of the immaterial and unembodied Word of God. For just as the rays of the sun's light undergo no suffering, though they fill all things, and touch dead and unclean bodies, much less could the unembodied power of God suffer in its essence, or be harmed, or ever become worse than itself, when it touches a body without being really embodied.

For what of this? Did he not ever and everywhere reach through the matter of the elements and of bodies themselves, as being the creative Word of God, and imprint the words of his own wisdom upon them, impressing life on the lifeless, form on that which is formless and shapeless by nature, stamping his own beauty and unembodied ideas on the qualities of matter, moving things by their own nature lifeless and immovable, earth, air, fire, in a wise and harmonious motion, ordering all things out of disorder, increasing and perfecting them, pervading all things with the divine power of reason, extending through all places and touching all, but yet receiving hurt from naught, nor defiled in his own nature.

And the same is true of his relation to men as well as nature. Of old he appeared to a few easily numbered, only the prophets who are recorded and the just men, now to one, now to another, but finally to us all, to the evil and unholy, to the Greeks as well as the Hebrews, he has offered himself as benefactor and saviour through the surpassing goodness and love of the Father, who is all-good, distinctly announcing it thus: 'They that are whole have no need of a physician, but they that are sick: I have not come to call the righteous, but sinners to repentance' [Matt. 9: 12]. Yes, the Saviour of all cried unto all, saying 'Come unto me, all ye that labour and are heavy laden, and I will refresh you' [Matt. 11: 28]. He called and healed ungrudgingly through the human organism which he had assumed, like a musician showing his skill by means of a lyre, and exhibited himself as an example of a life wholly wise, virtuous, and good, unto the souls diseased in human bodies, just as the most clever physicians heal men with remedies akin to and resembling them. [. . .]

He fulfilled all things by the humanity that he had taken, for those who only in that way were able to appreciate his divinity. In all this, then, for the advantage and profit of us all the all-loving Word of God ministered to his Father's counsels, remaining himself immaterial and unembodied, as he was before with the Father, not changing his essence, not dissolved from his own nature, not bound with the bonds of the flesh, not falling from divinity, and neither losing the characteristic power of the Word, nor hindered from being in the other parts of the universe, while he passed his life where his earthly vessel was. For it is the fact that during the time in which he lived as a man, he continued to fill all things, and was with the Father, and was in him too, and had care of all things collectively even then, of things in heaven and on earth, not being like ourselves debarred from ubiquity [cf. **179**], nor hindered from divine action by his human nature.

But he shared his own gifts with man, and received nothing from mortality in return. He supplied something of his divine power to mortals, not taking anything in return for his association with mortals. He was, therefore, not defiled by being born of a human body, being apart from body, neither did he suffer in his essence from the mortal, being untouched by suffering.

As when a lyre is struck, or its strings torn asunder, if so it chance, it is unlikely that he who played it suffers, so we could not say truly that, when some wise man is punished in his body, the wisdom in him, or the soul in his body, is struck or burned. Much less is it reasonable to say that the nature or power of the Word received any hurt from the sufferings of the body. For it was granted in our illustration of light that the rays of the sun sent down to earth from heaven are not defiled by touching all the mud and filth and garbage. We are not even debarred from saying that these things are illuminated by the rays of light. Whereas it is impossible to say that the sun is defiled or rendered muddy by contact with these materials. And these things could not be said to be foreign to one another. Whereas the immaterial and unembodied Word of God, having his life and reason and everything we have said in himself, if he touch aught with divine and unembodied power, the thing touched must necessarily live and exist with the light of reason. Thus therefore, also, whatever body he touches, that body is made holy and illuminated at once, and all disease and weakness and all such things depart. Its emptiness is exchanged for the fullness of the Word. And this was why a dead body, though but a small part of it came in contact with the power of the Word, was raised up to life, and death fled from life, and darkness was dissolved by light, the corruptible put on incorruption, and the mortal immortality.

Eusebius of Caesarea, The Demonstration of the Gospel 13, extracts (c.316)

II. True Divinity

If part of the difficulty for the early Church in finding an adequate expression for all that it wished to say about Christ was the struggle many had in allowing that Christ suffered and sweated, the other part was the struggle to know what was meant when it was said that Christ was divine. What kind of divinity could be attributed to this man who grew, wept, suffered, and died?

72   The Paradox of Incarnation

> The popular second-century Acts of Peter contain a strong if unsophisti-cated attempt to express the divinity and humanity of Jesus of Nazareth. At times the affirmations of divinity drown out the affirmations of humanity, but towards the end of the passage given here, an impressive balance is attained.

When error was in full flood and many thousands of men were plunging to destruction, the Lord in his mercy was moved to show himself in another shape and to be seen in the form of a man, on whom neither the Jews nor we were worthy to be enlightened. For each one of us saw him as he was able, as he had power to see [cf. 25].

And now I will explain to you what has just been read to you. Our Lord wished me to see his majesty on the holy mountain [cf. 12]; but when I with the sons of Zebedee saw the brilliance of his light, I fell as one dead, and closed my eyes and heard his voice, such as I cannot describe, and thought that I had been blinded by his radiance. And recovering my breath a little I said to myself, 'Perhaps my Lord willed to bring me here to deprive me of my sight.' And I said, 'If this be thy will, Lord, I do not gainsay it.' And he gave me his hand and lifted me up. And when I stood up I saw him in such a form as I was able to take in.

So my dearest brethren, as God is merciful, he has borne our weaknesses and carried our sins, as the prophet says, 'He beareth our sins and is afflicted for us; yet we thought him to be afflicted and stricken with wounds' [53]. For he is in the Father and the Father in him; he also is himself the fullness of all majesty, who has shown us all his goodness.

He ate and drank for our sakes, though himself without hunger or thirst, he bore and suffered reproaches for our sakes, he died and rose again because of us. He who defended me also when I sinned and strengthened me with his greatness, will also comfort you that you may love him, this God who is both great and little, beautiful and ugly, young and old, appearing in time and yet in eternity wholly invisible; whom no human hand has grasped, yet is held by his servants, whom no flesh has seen, yet now he is seen; whom no hearing has found yet now he is known as the word that is heard; whom no suffering can reach, yet now is chastened as we are; who was never chastened, yet now is chastened; who is before the world, yet now is comprehended in time; the beginning greater than all princedom, yet now delivered to the princes; beauteous, yet appearing among us as poor and ugly [. . .]; this Jesus you have, brethren, the door, the light, the way, the bread, the water, the life, the resurrection, the refreshment, the pearl, the treasure, the seed, the abundance, the mustard-seed, the vine, the plough, the grace, the faith, the word: He is all things, and there is no other greater than he. To him be praise for ever and ever. Amen.

Acts of Peter 20, extract (2nd century)

73 The Ineffability of the Incarnation

Origen (c.185–c.254) was head of the famous Catechetical School in Alexandria, a centre for the study of the Christian faith which had a distinctive flavour, redolent of Greek philosophy. His prolific and original work has been hugely influential on many strands of Christian theology, even though it was condemned after long controversy in the fifth and sixth centuries. Here he faces squarely the difficulty of understanding the Incarnation. (Cf. 40.)

Of all the marvellous and splendid things about him there is one that utterly transcends the limits of human wonder and is beyond the capacity of our weak mortal intelligence to think of or understand, namely, how this mighty power of the divine majesty, the very Word of the Father, and the very wisdom of God, in which were created all things visible and invisible [50], can be believed to have existed within the compass of that man who appeared in Judaea; yes, and how the wisdom of God can have entered into a woman's womb and been born as a little child and uttered noises like those of crying children; and further, how it was that he was troubled, as we are told, in the hour of death, as he himself confesses when he says, 'My soul is very sorrowful, even to death' [15]; and how at the last he was led to that death which is considered by men to be the most shameful of all, even though on the third day he rose again. When, therefore, we see in him some things so human that they appear in no way to differ from the common frailty of mortals, and some things so divine that they are appropriate to nothing else but the primal and ineffable nature of deity, the human understanding with its narrow limits is baffled, and struck with amazement at so mighty a wonder knows not which way to turn, what to hold to, or whither to betake itself. If it thinks of God it sees a man; if it thinks of a man, it beholds one returning from the dead with spurs after vanquishing the kingdom of death. For this reason we must pursue our contemplation with all fear and reverence, as we seek to prove how the reality of each nature exists in one and the same person, in such a way that nothing unworthy or unfitting may be thought to reside in that divine and ineffable existence, nor on the other hand may the events of his life be supposed to be the illusions caused by deceptive fantasies. But to utter these things in human ears and to explain them by words far exceeds the powers we possess either in our moral worth or in mind and speech. I think indeed that it transcends the capacity even of the holy apostles; nay more, perhaps the explanation of this mystery lies beyond the reach of the whole creation of heavenly beings.

Origen, *On First Principles* 2. 6, extract (c.229)

74   The Making of the Son

> Arius (c.256–c.336) was a golden-tongued preacher in one of the great churches of Alexandria who became known as a champion of the idea that Christ's divinity was not in every respect the full and ineffable divinity of the unalterable Father, but was a lesser 'divinity', the absolute maximum that could be affirmed of a creaturely reality. After his condemnation, all those who drew back from the most robust affirmations of Christ's full divinity tended to be branded Arians by their opponents. (Cf. 71, 77, 78.)

God himself in himself remains mysterious. He alone has no equal, none like him, none of equal glory. We call him unoriginated in contrast to him who is originated by nature . . . we praise him as without beginning in contrast to him who has a beginning, we worship him as eternal in contrast to him who came into existence in times. He who was without beginning made the Son a beginning of all things which are produced, and he made him into a Son for himself, begetting him. He (the Son) has nothing peculiar to God according to the reality of that which is peculiarly his, and he is not equal . . . far less is he consubstantial to God. [. . .]

Certainly there is a Trinity . . . [but] their individual realities do not mix with each other, and they possess glories of different levels. The sole glory is of the Sole, infinitely more splendid in his glories. The Father is in his substance alien from the Son because he remains without beginning. Understand therefore that the Monad existed, but the Dyad did not exist before it attained existence. So the Son having not existed attained existence by the Father's will. He is only-begotten God and he is different from any others. Wisdom became Wisdom by the will of the wise God, and so he is apprehended in an uncountable number of aspects. He is God's glory and truth, and image and word. Understand too that he is apprehended as reflection also and light. The greater one is able to beget someone equal to the Son, but not someone more important or more powerful or greater. It is by the will of God that the Son has his stature and character when and whence and from what time he is from God. For he is the Mighty God (i.e. the Son) and in some degree worships the greater.

Arius, *Thalia* (*c*.320s), quoted by Athanasius, *De Synodis* 15

75 Against Arius

Although the influence of Arius himself was limited, the condemnation of his views at the Council of Nicaea in AD 325 (**76**) was the catalyst for a long and ingloriously bitter battle over the nature of God and Christ's relationship to that nature. During the fourth century there were councils and counter-councils, anathemas and condemnations, polemics and counterblasts, until a resolution was reached in Constantinople in 381 (**80**) with the triumph of Nicaea's claim that Jesus was of 'one substance' with the Father: *homoousios*. The text below is from an anti-Arian 'pre-meeting' for the Council of Nicaea, which provisionally excommunicated Eusebius of Caesarea (**71**), leaving him to defend himself at Nicaea—successfully, as it turned out.

And [we believe] in one Lord Jesus Christ, the only-begotten Son, begotten not from non-existence, but from the Father, not as made but as genuine product, and begotten unspeakably and ineffably, because only the Father who begot and the Son who was begotten knew . . . . He (i.e. Christ) always exists and did not formerly not exist [cf. **74**], for we have been taught from the holy Scriptures that he alone is an image, not unbegotten—clearly from the Father—not by appointment . . . so that we believe him to be immutable and unalterable, and that he has not been begotten or come into existence by will nor by appointment so that he should appear to be from non-existence but in the way that was proper for him to be begotten, not (an idea unholy to conceive) by resemblance or nature or association in connection with any of the things that came into existence through him. But, because he transcends all thought and conception and argument, we confess that he has been begotten from the unbegotten Father, God the Word, true Light, righteousness,

Jesus Christ, Lord of all and Saviour. For he is the image not of the will nor of anything else except the actual *hypostasis*[13] of the Father.

Council of Antioch, *Statement of Belief* (325)

76 The Consubstantial Son

A general council was called by the emperor Constantine at Nicaea, in part to deal with the argument sparked by Arius' teaching. A large number of bishops (traditionally 318) agreed the following creed. (Cf. **80**.)

We believe in one God Father Almighty Maker of all things, seen and unseen:
And in one Lord Jesus Christ the Son of God, begotten as only-begotten of the Father, that is of the substance of the Father, God of God, Light of Light, true God of true God, begotten not made, consubstantial with the Father through whom all things came into existence, both things in heaven and things on earth; who for us men and for our salvation came down and was incarnate and became man, suffered and rose again the third day, ascended into the heavens, is coming to judge the living and the dead.
And in the Holy Spirit.
But those who say 'there was a time when he did not exist', and 'Before being begotten he did not exist', and that he came into being from non-existence, or who allege that the Son of God is of another hypostasis or ousia,[14] or is alterable or changeable, these the Catholic and Apostolic Church condemns [cf. **74**].

Council of Nicaea, *Creed* (325)

77 Arianism Resurgent

The small council at Sirmium in 357 took place when the 'Arians' (cf. **74**) (as their opponents called them) were in the ascendancy, yet its Latin creed avoided making a positive statement of distinctively Arian doctrines.

It is agreed that there is one almighty God and Father, as is believed throughout the whole world, and his only Son Jesus Christ the Lord, our Saviour, born from him before the ages; but there cannot be two gods nor should they be preached, as the text runs. Therefore there is one God of all, as the apostle taught, and the rest agrees and can contain no ambiguity. But as for the fact that some, or many, are concerned about substance (which is called *ousia* in Greek), that is, to speak more explicitly, *homousion*, or *homoeusion* as it is called—there should be no mention of it whatever, nor should anyone preach it. And this is the cause and reason, that it is not included in the divine

Scriptures, and it is beyond man's knowledge nor can anyone declare the birth of the Son, and it is written on this subject. For it is clear that only the Father knows how he begot his Son, and the Son how he was begotten by the Father. There is no uncertainty about the Father being greater: it cannot be doubted by anyone that the Father is greater in honour, in dignity, in glory, in majesty in the very name of 'Father', for he himself witnesses. And nobody is unaware that this is catholic doctrine, that there are two persons of the Father and the Son, and that the Father is greater, and the Son is subjected in common with all the things which the Father subjected to him; that the Father has no beginning, is invisible, immortal and impassible; but that the Son is born from the Father, God from God, Light from Light, whose generation as Son, as has been said already, no one knows except the Father; and that the Son of God himself our Lord and God, as it is said, assumed flesh or body, that is man from the womb of the Virgin Mary, as the angel foretold. As all the Scriptures teach, and especially the teacher of the Gentiles himself, the apostle, he took human nature from the Virgin Mary, and it was through this that he suffered. But that is the summary of the whole faith and the confirmation of it that the Trinity should always be preserved, as we read in the gospel.

The Second Sirmian Creed (357)

78 Homoian Arianism

Various attempts were made to find a middle path between Arianism (cf. **74**) and Nicaea (**76**). This creed from Germinius of Sirmium (d. 367/7) represents 'Homoian Arianism', which instead of saying that the Son was 'of one being' with the Father (*homoousious*), said that the Son was 'like' the Father (*homoios*) in all things. The Homoian position was, however, unstable: Homoians soon fell out over how far this 'like' went. Eventually Germinius moved in a Nicene direction by pushing the 'like' until he could say, in a later letter, 'like in all respects to the Father, ingenerateness excepted'.

I bishop Germinius believe and confess that there is one true God the Father, eternal, almighty; and Christ his only Son and our Lord God, the true Son of God from the true God the Father, born before all things, in deity, love, majesty, power, glory, love, wisdom, knowledge, *like* in all things to the Father, since he is born perfect from the Perfect. His taking of manhood from the Virgin Mary, as the prophets predicted would happen, and as the texts of the gospels and apostles inform us to have been accomplished; his sufferings too and death and resurrection and ascension into heaven we accept, believe and profess; and that at the end of the world he will descend from heaven to judge the living and the dead and to reward each according to his works. And in the Holy Spirit, that is the Paraclete who was given to us from God the Father through the Son. That is all.

Germinius of Sirmium, Symbol (360s)

79   Neo-Arianism

'Neo-Arianism' is a name sometimes given to the followers of two theologians, Aetius and Eunomius, who attempted to provide a rigorous and philosophically robust alternative to the Nicene faith. Eunomius (d. 394) based his system on the ingenerateness and incomparability of God, making these the keystone of his theology; he would thus have found Germinius' formula 'like in all respects to the Father, *ingenerateness excepted*' all but incomprehensible (cf. **78**).

We believe in the one and only true God [. . .] [I]n every way and wholly he is one, remaining sole in the same conditions and as always. He has no sharer of his Godhead, nor participator of his glory nor joint possessor of his authority nor consort of the throne of his kingdom, for he is one and sole God almighty [. . .] In generating he has not divided his own *ousia* nor is the generator the same as the generated nor has he become both Father and Son; for he is beyond process, and he does not need in creation matter or parts or physical organs, for he is altogether independent. And we believe in the Son of God, the only-begotten God, the first-born of all creation, true Son, not ingenerate, truly generated before the ages, named Son not without coming into existence, coming into existence before the creation, not uncreated, existing in the beginning, not unbeginning [. . .] not to be measured in rank along with him who generated him nor in any point with respect to his Father's *ousia* but coming into existence by generation; glorious and the Lord of glory, and receiving his glory from the Father, not sharing his glory [. . .] Son, only-begotten and like to him who generated him uniquely alone according to his peculiar aspect. He is not Father to the Father, for there are not two Fathers, nor is he an Ingenerate to the Ingenerate, nor as a Son to the Son, for as Son he is image and seal of all the activity and power of the Almighty, seal of his counsels.

Eunomius, Confession of Faith, extracts (383)

80   Nicene Renaissance

In 381 the emperor Theodosius called another general council; some 150 bishops attended. The Creed of Nicaea (76) was, with some modifications, ratified, and was made, by imperial edict, the official faith of the Roman Empire.

We believe in one God the Father Almighty, maker of heaven and earth and of all things visible and invisible;

And in one Lord Jesus Christ the Son of God, the Only-begotten, begotten by his Father before all ages, Light from Light, true God from true God, begotten not made, consubstantial with the Father, through whom all things came into existence, who for us men and for our salvation came down from the heavens and became incarnate by the Holy Spirit and the Virgin Mary and became a man, and was crucified for us under Pontius Pilate and suffered and was buried and rose again on the third day in accordance with the Scriptures and ascended into the heavens and is seated at the right hand of the Father and will come again with glory to judge the living and the dead, and there will be no end to his kingdom;

And in the Holy Spirit, the Lord and Life-giver, who proceeds from the Father, who is worshipped and glorified together with the Father and the Son, who spoke by the prophets;

And in one holy, catholic and apostolic Church;

We confess one baptism for the forgiveness of sins;

We wait for the resurrection of the dead and the life of the coming age. Amen.

Council of Constantinople, Creed (381)

III. Towards Chalcedon

The resolution of the Nicene conflict (cf. 74–80) was not the end of Christological debate; rather it provided a framework and a terminology within which a more pointed debate about the extent of Christ's humanity, and the relation of humanity and divinity in him, could take place.

81   Full Humanity

In the late fourth century Apollinarius (*c*.310–*c*.390), a champion of Nicene Christology (76) against the Arians (74, 77, 78), secured his account of the unity of divinity and humanity in Christ by claiming that the Logos, the divine Word of God, took the place of the human spirit in Christ's humanity.

Gregory of Nazianzus (329–89) (cf. **82**), the retiring, ascetic Bishop of Nazianzus and one of the three Cappadocian Fathers (cf. **46**), penned a famous response which, although possibly unfair to Apollinarius, stated (in the second sentence below) one of the most important ground rules of orthodox Christology.

If anyone has put his trust in him as a man without a human mind, he is really bereft of mind, and quite unworthy of salvation. For that which he has not assumed he has not healed; but that which is united to his Godhead is also saved. If only half Adam fell, then that which Christ assumes and saves may be half also; but if the whole of his nature fell, it must be united to the whole nature of him that was begotten, and so be saved as a whole. Let them not, then, begrudge us our complete salvation, or clothe the Saviour only with bones and nerves and the portraiture of humanity. For if his manhood is without soul, even the Arians admit this, that they may attribute his passion to the Godhead, as that which gives motion to the body is also that which suffers. But if he has a soul, and yet is without a mind, how is he man, for man is not a mindless animal? And this would necessarily involve that while his form and tabernacle was human, his soul should be that of a horse or an ox, or some other of the brute creation. This, then, would be what he saves; and I have been deceived by the truth, and led to boast of an honour which had been bestowed upon another. But if his Manhood is intellectual and not without mind, let them cease to be thus really mindless.

But, says such a one, the Godhead took the place of the human intellect. How does this touch me? For Godhead joined to flesh alone is not man, nor to soul alone, nor to both apart from intellect, which is the most essential part of man. Keep then the whole man, and mingle Godhead therewith, that you may benefit me in my completeness. But, he asserts, he could not contain two perfect natures. Not if you only look at him in a bodily fashion. For a bushel measure will not hold two bushels, nor will the space of one body hold two or more bodies. But if you will look at what is mental and incorporeal, remember that I in my one personality can contain soul and reason and mind and the Holy Spirit; and before me this world, by which I mean the system of things visible and invisible, contained Father, Son, and Holy Ghost. For such is the nature of intellectual existences, that they can mingle with one another and with bodies, incorporeally and invisibly. For many sounds are comprehended by one ear and the eyes of many are occupied by the same visible objects, and the smell by odours; nor are the senses narrowed by each other, or crowded out, nor the objects of sense diminished by the multitude of the perceptions. [. . .]

Further let us see what is their account of the assumption of manhood or the assumption of flesh as they call it. If it was in order that God otherwise incomprehensible might be comprehended and might converse with men through his flesh as through a veil, their mask and the drama which they represent is a pretty one, not to say that it was open to him to converse with us in other ways as of old in the burning bush and in the appearance of a man. But if it was that he might destroy the condemnation by sanctifying like by like then as he needed flesh for the sake of the flesh which had incurred condemnation and soul for the sake of our soul so too he needed mind for the sake of mind which not only fell in Adam but was the first to be affected, as the doctors say of illnesses. For that which received the command was that which failed to keep the command and that which failed to keep it was that also which dared to transgress and that which transgressed was that which stood most in need of salvation and that which needed salvation was that which also he took upon him. Therefore mind was taken upon him. This has now been demonstrated, whether they like it or not, by, to use their own expression, geometrical and necessary proofs.

> Gregory of Nazianzus, Epistle to Cledonius 'against Apollinarius', extracts (late 4th century)

82 Divinity and Humanity in the Gospels

> Gregory (cf. **81**) had been summoned to Constantinople in 379 and was instrumental in the reaffirmation of Nicene Christology (**80**). This is from one of the great 'Theological Orations' which he preached while there, speeches which have become known as bastions of Trinitarian and Christological orthodoxy.

He whom you now treat with contempt was once above you. He who is now man was once the uncompounded. What he was he continued to be; what he was not he took to himself. In the beginning he was, uncaused; for what is the cause of God? But afterwards for a cause he was born. And that cause was that you might be saved, who insult him and despise his Godhead, because of this, that he took upon him your denser nature, having converse with flesh by means of mind. His inferior nature, the humanity, became God, because it was united to God, and became one person because the higher nature prevailed . . . in order that I too might be made God so far as he is made man.

He was born—but he had been begotten; he was born of a woman—but she was a virgin. The first is human, the second divine. In his human nature he had no Father, but also in his divine nature no Mother. Both these belong to Godhead. He dwelt in the womb but he was recognised by the prophet, himself still in the womb, leaping before the Word for whose sake he came into being. He was wrapped in swaddling clothes—but he took off the swathing bands of the grave by his rising again [cf. **17**]. He was laid in a manger [cf. 1]—but he was glorified by angels, and proclaimed by a star, and worshipped by the Magi. Why are you offended by that which is presented to your sight, because you will not look at that which is presented to your mind? He was driven into exile into Egypt—but he drove away the Egyptian idols.[15] He had no form nor comeliness in the eyes of the Jews [53]—but to David he is fairer than the children of men. And on the mountain he was bright as the lightning [12], and became more luminous than the sun, initiating us into the mystery of the future.

He was baptised as man [cf. 2]—but he remitted sins as God [cf. 8], not because he needed purificatory rites himself, but that he might sanctify the element of water. He was tempted as man [cf. 2], but he conquered as God; yes, he bids us be of good cheer, for he has overcome the world. He hungered—but he fed thousands; yes, he is the bread that gives life, and that is of heaven. He thirsted—but he cried, 'If any man thirst, let him come unto me and drink.' Yes, he promised that fountains should flow from them that believe. He was wearied, but he is the rest of them that are weary and heavy laden. He was heavy with sleep, but he walked lightly over the sea. He rebuked the winds, he made Peter light as he began to sink. He pays tribute but it is out of a fish; yes, he is the King of those who demanded it.

He is called a Samaritan and a demoniac—but he saves him that came down from Jerusalem and fell among thieves; the demons acknowledge him, and he drives out demons, and sinks in the sea legions of foul spirits, and sees the prince of the demons failing like lightning. He is stoned but is not taken. He prays, but he hears prayer. He weeps, but he causes tears to cease. He asks where Lazarus was laid, for he was man; but he raises Lazarus, for he was God. He is sold, and very cheap, for it is only for thirty pieces of silver; but he redeems the world, and that at a great price, for the price was his own blood. As a sheep he is led to the slaughter [cf. 53], but he is the Shepherd of Israel, and now of the whole world also. As a lamb he is silent, yet he is the Word, and is proclaimed by the voice of one crying in the wilderness. He is bruised and wounded, but he heals every disease and every infirmity [cf. 53]. He is lifted up and nailed to the tree, but by the tree of life he restores us; yes, he saves even the robber crucified with him; yes, he wrapped the visible world in darkness [cf. 16]. He is given vinegar to drink mingled with gall [cf. 16]. Who? He who turned the water into wine, who is the destroyer of the bitter taste, who is sweetness and altogether desire. He lays down his life, but he has power to take it again; and the veil is rent, for the mysterious doors of heaven are opened; the rocks are cleft, the dead arise. He dies, but he gives life, and by his death destroys death. He is buried, but he rises again [cf. 17]; he goes down into hell, but he brings up the souls; he ascends to Heaven [cf. 20], and shall come again to judge the quick and the dead, and to put to the test such words as yours. If the one give you a starting point for error, let the others put an end to it.

Gregory of Nazianzus, 'Third Theological Oration', 19–20 (380)

83 The Birth of the Messiah

If the views of Apollinarius were one of the key goads to further Christological discussion after Constantinople (**80**), the views of Nestorius (d. 451) were another. Nestorius was a monk of Antioch, and later Bishop of Constantinople. He taught that we must carefully distinguish what we attribute to Christ's humanity, what to his divinity (cf. **82**), yet appeared to allow little room for the balancing affirmation that those things which Christ suffered in his humanity were suffered by the one person who was human and divine, and thus are not *distant* from Christ's divinity (cf. **86**). Thus, for instance, Nestorius could not say that Christ's divinity was in any sense in the womb of Mary with his humanity: she was not, in a phrase then already ancient, 'Theotokos': God-bearer (cf. **99**).

Everywhere in sacred Scripture whenever it makes mention of the 'economy' of the Lord, the birth for our sake and the passion are ascribed, not to the divinity, but to the humanity of Christ. So according to the most precise appellation, the Holy Virgin is called the Mother of Christ, not the Mother of God. Listen to these words of the Gospels that say, 'The book of the generation of Jesus Christ, the son of David, the son of Abraham' [Matt. 1: 1]. It is plain that God the Word was not the son of David. Accept another testimony, if you please, 'Jacob begot Joseph the husband of Mary, and of her was born Jesus who is called Christ' [Matt. 1: 16]. Notice yet another voice testifying for us, 'Now the origin of Christ was in this wise. When Mary his mother had been betrothed to Joseph, she was found to be with child by the Holy Spirit' [Matt. 1: 18]. Whoever would assume that the divinity of the only begotten was a creation of the Holy Spirit? What need to say, 'The mother of Jesus was there' [John 2: 1], and again, 'with Mary the Mother of Jesus' and, 'that which is begotten in her is of the Holy Spirit' [cf. Matt. 1: 20] and, 'take the child and his mother and flee into Egypt' [Matt. 2: 13] and, 'concerning his Son who was born according to the flesh of the offspring of David' [Rom. 1: 3]? And again concerning his passion, 'Since God sent his Son in the likeness of sinful flesh, and concerning sin he has condemned sin in the flesh' [Rom. 8: 3] and again, 'Christ died for our sins' [1 Cor. 15: 3] and, 'since Christ suffered in the flesh' [1 Pet. 4: 1] and, 'This is (not my divinity, but) my body, which is broken for you' [**14**], And heed the countless other voices testifying to the human race that they should not think that the divinity of the Son was recent, or capable of receiving bodily suffering, but that the flesh was, which was joined to the nature of the divinity. Wherefore, also, Christ calls himself both David's Lord and Son, for he says, 'What do you think of the Christ? Whose son is he?' They say to him, 'David's'. Jesus answered and said to them, 'How then does David in the Spirit call him Lord saying, "The Lord said to my Lord, sit at my right hand"' [Matt. 22: 42–4] as he is the Son of David by all means according to the flesh, but his Lord according to his divinity.

Therefore, it is right and worthy of the Gospel traditions to confess that the body is the temple of the Son's divinity and a temple joined to the divinity according to a certain sublime and divine union, and that his divine nature makes his own the things of his body. But in the name of this relationship to attribute also to his divinity the properties of the united flesh, I mean birth, suffering, and death, is, my brother, the act of a mind truly led astray like the pagans or diseased like the minds of that mad Apollinaris, Arius, and the other heresies, but rather more grievously than they. For it is necessary that such as are dragged into error by the word relationship make the Word God partake of the nourishment of milk through the relationship, and have a share in growing, little by little, and of fear at the time of his passion [cf. 15], and be in need of angelic assistance. And I pass over in silence that circumcision, sacrificing, sweat, hunger, and thirst, which happened to his body on account of us, are worshipfully united to the divinity. If these are taken with reference to the divinity, and falsely, there is a cause for just condemnation against us as slanderers.

Nestorius, Letter 5. 7–8 (Nestorius to Cyril) (early 5th century)

84   Assumption of Humanity

Cyril of Alexandria (d. 444) was the chief opponent of Nestorius, and a theologian whose work proved to be a source of both illumination and disagreement in subsequent Christology (cf. 83). The terminology which he used in attacking Nestorius' apparent separation of humanity and divinity in Christ meant that Cyril's work was used extensively by the monophysite (cf. 103–4) opponents of the Council of Chalcedon, yet his work was also one of the most important ingredients in that very Chalcedonian settlement (86). (Cf. 105.)

There is one Lord Jesus Christ, personally the only-begotten Word of God, become man without departure from being what he was; for even in manhood he has remained God, even in slave's form master, even in human self-emptying possessor of full deity, even in fleshly weakness lord of spiritual powers and even within the compass of manhood owner of transcendence over the whole creation. What he was before incarnation (he was God, true only-begotten Son, light, life and power) he maintains without loss; what he was not, he is seen to have assumed for the sake of the divine plan. He made the properties of the flesh his own, for the flesh united in expressibly mysterious fashion with him was his and no other's. This is what wise John means when he says 'the Word was made flesh': he has become flesh not by changing into the nature of flesh by way of transference, variation or alteration, nor by undergoing mingling, mixture or the 'consubstantiation' some people prate about (an impossibility, seeing that he exists unvarying and unalterable!) but, as I said, by taking flesh endowed with mental life from a spotless virginal body and making it his own. [. . .]

So the Word has become man without ceasing to be what he was; he has remained God when manifest in our shape. Moreover, Christ is not to be thought of as a man who later proceeded to become God; the Word who is God has become man, so that we recognise him as being at once God and man. Yet those who divide him into two sons, who venture to assert that God the Word joined the man of David's stock to himself, gave him a share of his dignity, honour and rank of sonship, made him undergo the cross, die, come to life again, ascend to heaven and sit at the Father's right hand so that he is worshipped by all creation as the recipient of metaphorical divine honours—these start by propounding two sons and proceed to an ignorant distortion of the meaning of the mystery. Christ, as I said, has not been made God after being man, but the Word who is God has been made flesh, that is to say man; it is affirmed that he has been 'emptied' because before the 'emptying' he had in his own nature the fullness whereby he is recognised as God. He is not someone who attained fullness after being empty; instead he abased himself from his divine heights and unspeakable glory. He is not a lowly man who was exalted in glory, but free, he took slave's form. He is not a slave who made a leap up to the glory of freedom; he who is in the Father's form, in equality with him, has been made in the likeness of men—he is not a man who has come to share the riches of God's likeness. [. . .]

Consequently we follow the fathers' confession without deviation and affirm that the Father's only-begotten Son, begotten of God the Father, was personally incarnate and made man, that he suffered, died and rose again from the dead on the third day. God's Word is, of course, undoubtedly impassible in his own nature and nobody is so mad as to imagine the all-transcending nature capable of suffering; but by very reason of the fact that he has become man making flesh from the holy Virgin his own, we adhere to the principles of the divine plan and maintain that he, who as God transcends suffering, suffered humanly in his own flesh. If whilst being God he has become man yet has not departed from any aspect of his being God; if he has been made part of creation and yet abides above creation; if whilst being as God the giver of law he has been made under law and yet was still giver of law, and whilst being, divinely, master he put on slave's form, and yet retains unimpaired the dignity of mastership; if whilst being only-begotten he has been made the first-born among many brethren and yet is still only-begotten, does it tax credibility if by the same token he suffered humanly and yet is seen as divinely impassible? [. . .]

Why, then, our opponents, who in their extreme folly do not forbear to hold or express the views of Nestorius and Theodore, must answer our question: 'Do you refuse to allow him who is of the Holy Virgin his being God and true Son of God the Father? Do you allot the suffering to him alone, fending it off from God the Word to avoid God's being declared passible?' This is the point of their pedantic, muddle-headed fictions. In that case, the Word of God the Father on his own and by himself should not be called 'Christ'; for just as suffering is out of character with him when he is considered in isolation from the flesh, so is anointing an inconsistent feature alien to him. For God anointed Jesus of Nazareth with the Holy Ghost, but the Word of God is utterly complete in himself and required no anointing through the Holy Ghost. In which case, deny God's plan, banish the Only-begotten from any love towards the world! 'Christ' you must not call him. Was not his created existence within human limitations a lowly thing? In which case, seeing that *that* is out of character with him, nobody must acknowledge that he has become man, with the result that Christ can tell them, 'You err, knowing neither the scriptures nor God's power'. Let us, then, deem the holders of opinions like this Truth's enemies and shun their baleful vanities; let us instead follow the views of the holy fathers and the tradition of the holy apostles and evangelists. The Word made man was, indeed, he who spoke in them, and through him and with him be honour, glory and power to God the Father with the Holy Ghost for ever and ever. Amen.

Cyril of Alexandria, *On the Holy Creed*, extracts (440s)

85   Two Natures United

Leo the Great (d. 461), an energetic Pope, was not himself a brilliant theologian but he was a forceful and persuasive presenter of existing views. When the Eastern Church sought to resolve its Christological wrangles at Chalcedon (**86**), Leo weighed in with his *Tome*, written in 449.

While the distinctness of both natures and substances was preserved, and both met in one person, lowliness was assumed by majesty, weakness by power, mortality by eternity; and in order to pay the debt of our condition, the inviolable nature was united to the passible, so that as the appropriate remedy for our ills one and the same 'Mediator between God and man the man Christ Jesus' [1 Tim. 2: 5] might from one element be capable of dying and also from the other be incapable. Therefore in the entire and perfect nature of very man was born very God, whole in what was his, whole in what was ours. By 'ours' we mean what the Creator formed in us at the beginning and what he assumed in order to restore; for of that which the deceiver brought in, and man, thus deceived, admitted, there was not a trace in the Saviour and the fact that he took on himself a share in our infirmities did not make him a partaker in our transgressions. He assumed 'the form of a servant' [39] without the defilement of sin, enriching what was human not impairing what is divine: because that 'emptying of him-self' whereby the Invisible made himself visible and the Creator and Lord of all things willed to be one among mortals, was a stooping down in compassion, not a failure of power. Accordingly, the same who, remaining in the form of God, made man, was made man in the form of a servant. For each of the natures retains its proper character without defect; and as the form of God does not take away the form of a servant, so the form of a servant does not impair the form of God. For since the devil was glorying in the fact that man, deceived by his craft, was bereft of divine gifts and, being stripped of his endowment of immortality, had come under the grievous sentence of death, and that he himself, amid his miseries, had found a sort of consolation in having a transgressor as his companion, and that God, according to the requirements of the principle of justice had changed his own resolution in regard to man, whom he had created in so high a position of honour; there was need of a dispensation of secret counsel, in order that the unchangeable God, whose will could not be deprived of its own benignity, should fulfil by a more secret mystery his original plan of loving-kindness toward us [cf. 47], and that man, who had been led into fault by the wicked subtlety of the devil should not perish contrary to God's purpose. Accordingly, the Son of God descending from his seat in heaven, and not departing from the glory of the Father, enters this lower world, born after a new order by a new mode of birth [cf. 43]. After a new order, because he who in his own sphere is invisible, became visible in ours; he who could not be enclosed in space, willed to be enclosed; continuing to be before times, he began to exist in time; the Lord of the universe allowed his infinite majesty to be overshadowed, and took upon him the form of a servant; the impassible God did not disdain to be passible man and the immortal One to be subjected to the laws of death. And born by a new mode of birth; because inviolate virginity, while ignor-ant of concupiscence, supplied the matter of his flesh. What was assumed from the Lord's mother was nature not fault; nor does the wondrousness of the nativity of our Lord Jesus Christ, as born of a Virgin's womb, imply that his nature is unlike ours. For the selfsame who is very God, is also very man; and there is no illusion in this union, while the lowliness of man and the loftiness of Godhead meet together. For as 'God' is not changed by the compassion exhibited, so 'Man' is not consumed by the dignity bestowed. For each 'form' does the acts which belong to it, in communion with the other; the Word, that is, performing what belongs to the Word, and the flesh carrying out what belongs to the flesh; the one of these shines out in miracles, the other succumbs to injuries. And as the Word does not withdraw from equality with the Father in glory, so the flesh does not abandon the nature of our kind. For, as we must often be saying, he is one and the same, truly Son of God, and truly Son of Man. God, inasmuch as 'in the beginning was the Word, and the Word was with God, and the Word was God.' Man, inasmuch as 'the Word was made flesh, and dwelt among us' [66]. God, inasmuch as 'all things were made by him, and without him nothing was made' [66]. Man, inasmuch as he was 'made of a woman, made under the law' [Gal. 4: 4]

Leo the Great, *Tome*, extract (449)

86   Unconfused and Inseparable

The Council of Chalcedon (451) marks the culmination of patristic Christology, not because it answered all Christological questions and tied up all the loose ends, but because it provided later generations with a formula which they had either to accept or to reject, but which they could not ignore. After Chalcedon, the Eastern Church was riven by divisions pro and contra for centuries; after Chalcedon the Western Church had little to do with Eastern Christological debates. Chalcedon, with its remarkable balancing act of near-contradictory affirmations and denials, was a turning point. (Cf. 103–7, 112, 319–25.)

Following the holy Fathers we teach with one voice that the Son and our Lord Jesus Christ is to be confessed as one and the same, that he is perfect in Godhead and perfect in manhood, very God and very man, of a reasonable soul and body consisting, consubstantial with the Father as touching his Godhead and consubstantial with us as touching his manhood; made in all things like unto us sin only excepted; begotten of his Father before the worlds according to his Godhead but in these last days for us men and for our salvation born of the Virgin Mary the Mother of God according to his manhood. This one and the same Jesus Christ, the only-begotten Son, must be confessed to be in two natures, unconfusedly, immutably, indivisibly, distinctly, inseparably, and that without the distinction of natures being taken away by such union, but rather the peculiar property of each nature being preserved and being united in one person and subsistence, not separated or divided into two persons, but one and the same Son and only-begotten, God the Word, our Lord Jesus Christ, as the prophets of old time have spoken concerning him, and as the Lord Jesus Christ hath taught us, and as the Creed of the Fathers hath delivered to us.

Council of Chalcedon, Definition of Faith, extract (451)

PART 2

Byzantine and Early Medieval: 451–1208

After 451 it becomes clear that our story has split into two. 1054 is the usual date at which the split between the Eastern and the Western halves of the Roman Empire and the Roman Church is said to have become official, but the de facto split was, by then, already old. The two had begun to grow apart in the fourth century, and the story of the Byzantine Empire between 451 and 1208 differs radically from the story of its Western neighbours. The East at the time of Chalcedon and for long afterwards was confident and coherent, a worthy continuation of the glories of the Roman Empire; the Western half of the Empire saw the sway of Roman rule totter and fall, if not into the 'dark ages' passed over by earlier historians, then at least into a patchwork of disparate communities which, however energetic they were, could not match the scope of the Roman world. Three-quarters of a millennium later the balance of power had completely reversed: the most devastating blow to relations between East and West was struck by the Western armies of the Fourth Crusade, who in 1204 subdued Constantinople and imposed a pyrrhic East–West unity which scarcely concealed the irrevocable breakdown of relations between the two—and the fatal weakening of Eastern Christendom in the face of Islamic expansion.

In the East the story we left at Chalcedon carried on in much the same key: a volatile mix of complex theological definition and high politics is seen in one heated controversy after another (e.g. **105**, **108**), one definitive council after another (e.g. **106**). For a long time it was the Council of Chalcedon itself which was at stake: the acceptance, clarification, or amelioration of that council's definition occupied generations of Eastern theologians; the attempt to find appropriate ways of speaking of what was two in Christ, what was one.

Accompanying and sustaining the arguments of the theologians, the East echoed to the ongoing cycles of ascending meditation (e.g. **87**, **88**) and the rhythms of the Jesus Prayer (e.g. **92**, **93**). In the monasteries (which, in the East, were first and foremost schools of mystical prayer) and among the holy men, heroes of prayer, eyes were turned upwards, straining to catch glimpses of the same light with which Christ was transfigured on Tabor (cf. **87**, **90**). The Christological debates and this fierce devotion walked hand in hand.

By the time the next great controversy emerged, over the use and abuse of icons (**108**) in the Church's worship, another force was concentrating Eastern minds: Islam. With extraordinary swiftness, the energy released by the prophet Muhammad in the dying years of the sixth century spilled through Arabia, Syria (overwhelming struggling Byzantine defences there), Egypt, and Iraq (subjugating the Persian Sassanid

Empire)—then, in the early eighth century, along the shores of northern Africa and over the straits to Spain, and, at the same time, right up to the gates of Constantinople. This Islam, which had drawn at its inception on popular Arabian Christianity, fostered a rich variety of stories about and attitudes to Jesus, very different views of Jesus from those debated in the council chambers and churches of Constantinople; for a time in the eighth century it must have looked as if Christian images of Jesus would be supplanted by these Islamic alternatives in both West and East (e.g. **123–6**).

In the West the overarching structures of Roman rule, which had done much to hold the different peoples and Churches of the empire together in one ongoing conversation, disintegrated. The Church found itself the repository of much that had previously been the province of secular authority, and, to some extent, the preserver of what remained of pan-European communication. But the Christian faith also adapted to the situation of fragmentation, and developed in new local forms which meshed with the cultures of the peoples who arrived or emerged with the removal of Roman rule. North Africa and much of Spain were lost to Islam, but Germanic and Scandinavian peoples arrived, and were converted, and Christian missionaries spread the faith northwards and eastwards, or re-established it in places where the barbarians had trampled it. The face of Jesus appears in new guises in these new cultures, looking at us through eyes now Frankish, now German, now Northumbrian, now Irish, now Norman (e.g. **101, 102**).

A large part of the story of Christianity in the West in these years, and the most prominent source for the period's representations of Jesus, is monastic. Monastic communities sprang up across the West, providing a resilient mesh into which the fabric of the medieval church was woven. When waves of reform came, they were often transmitted across Europe from monastery to monastery: the late seventh-century 'Northumbrian revival' was felt first and foremost in the monasteries; Charlemagne's attempts to reunify Western Europe and the resulting 'Carolingian revival' included the imposition of a uniform Benedictine rule for monastic life, and the dispersion of new learning to monasteries now become houses of education (cf. **111**). In the eleventh and twelfth centuries a new religious vigour, a new devotion centred on Christ's humble humanity, was spread by the Cistercian order, hundreds of houses being founded in its first hundred years (e.g. **94–8**).

The monasteries were also the birthplace of scholasticism. Although there are hints and portents of scholastic method much earlier (**110**), it is not until the end of the eleventh century, and the work of Anselm of Canterbury (**114**) and Peter Lombard (**116**), that we begin to see scholasticism proper emerge. Many monasteries became places where, enveloped in the context provided by the liturgy, spaces for debate were opened up, where the arrangement, coherence, implications, and proper understanding of the faith celebrated in the liturgy could be explored, monastic faith seeking rational understanding.

When we meet Jesus in the medieval West, it is, in these and other ways, most often as the Christ of the cloisters.

Section A

Contemplating Christ

I n all periods of Christian history there have been writings which call us to let attentiveness to Christ percolate through our lives, but in each place and time this common call has taken a particular shape. The Byzantine Church (despite those fringes of the Eastern mystical tradition which stood in danger of downplaying reference to the incarnate Christ) was captivated by the image of a purifying ascent into the light of God's glory led, supported, and accompanied by Christ. The story of Christ's Transfiguration on the mountain (12) provided a concentrated symbol of the glorious beholding of Christ to which Christians are called, and the Jesus Prayer provided an accompanying practice, imparting an unceasing Christocentric rhythm to the devout life. In the Western tradition the contemplation of Christ appears more often in the cultivation of humility, practised in the monastic arks in which much Latin Christian culture weathered the storms of the empire's collapse, and which later provided the platform for a resurgence of Western Christianity.

I. Transfiguration and Ascent

Ascent and light are linked motifs which run like the helices of DNA through the genes of Byzantine Christianity. The Christian ascends towards a true relationship with and understanding of God in Christ, drawn upwards by the beauty of God, the dross of disobedience and error being burned away in the fierceness of the divine light.

87 The Light of Christ's Face

Eastern spirituality in the Byzantine period was strongly swayed by two bodies of writing: the writings of Evagrius of Pontus (346–99) and a set of writings attributed none too securely to Macarius of Egypt (*c.*300–*c.*390), one of the pioneers of Egyptian monasticism. The latter are almost certainly of a rather later date than this attribution implies, and unlike the writings of Evagrius, they have a strong emphasis on the contemplation of Christ incarnate. The following extract is part of a commentary on Ezekiel's vision (Ezek. 1). (Cf. **27, 45, 237**.)

The soul that has been deemed worthy by the Spirit to participate in his light and that has been illumined by the splendour of his ineffable glory, when he has prepared it to become the throne of his glory, becomes wholly light, wholly face, wholly eyes, and there remains no further part of itself that is not filled with the spiritual eyes of light. That is to say, it has nothing of darkness, but it is wholly light and spirit, wholly full of eyes, having now no back, but presenting its face on all sides, the ineffable beauty of the glory of the light of Christ having come into it and dwelling in it. Just as the sun is wholly like itself, having no other side, no inferiority, but is wholly resplendent with light, is wholly light and equally so in all its parts, or as, in the fire, the light of the fire is wholly like itself, having nothing primary or secondary, greater or smaller, so the soul, that has been fully illuminated by the ineffable beauty of the glory of the light of the face of Christ and filled with the Holy Spirit, worthy to become the dwelling and the temple of God, is wholly eye, wholly light, wholly face, wholly glory and wholly spirit, Christ in this way adorning it, carrying it, directing it, sustaining it and leading it and so illuminating it and decorating it with spiritual beauty.

Pseudo-Macarius, First Homily, 11 (5th century?)

88. The Hope of Glory

At some time towards the beginning of the sixth century an author in Syria wrote an extraordinary series of works of mystical theology. The works were attributed to Dionysius (or Denys) the Areopagite, whose conversion is described in Acts 17: 34, and now go under the heading 'Pseudo-Dionysius' or 'Pseudo-Denys'. The writings, which mix Christian doctrine and Neoplatonic ideas (cf. **65**), became another major influence on the development of mystical theology, this time particularly in the West; Dionysius was a leading theological authority for about a thousand years. One of the author's chief emphases was the ways in which we are drawn to know God, who is beyond every thought, name, and image, through the many names and images with which God provides us. (Cf. **142**, **149**.)

We have also been initiates in all the other divine enlightenments, which the secret tradition of our inspired teachers has granted to us by mystic interpretation in accordance with the scriptures. We have apprehended these things in this present life, according to our powers, through the sacred veils of that loving kindness which in the scriptures and hierarchical traditions wraps up spiritual truths in terms drawn from the world of sense, and hyper-essential truths in terms that are drawn from essence; clothing shapeless things that are formless in shapes and forms and fashioning manifold attributes for the supernatural imageless simplicity by a variety of separable symbols. But hereafter when we are incorruptible and immortal and attain that blessed lot of being like Christ, then, as scripture tells us, we shall all be for ever with the Lord. We shall be fulfilled with his visible theophany in holy contemplations, and it shall shine round about us with radiant beams of glory just as of old it once shone round the disciples at the divine Transfiguration [12]. And then, with our mind made impassible and spiritual, we shall participate in a spiritual illumination from him, and in a union that transcends our mental faculties. There, amidst the blinding blissful impulses of his dazzling rays we shall be made like to the heavenly intelligences in a more divine manner than at present. As the infallible scripture says, we shall be equal to the angels and shall be sons of God, being sons of the Resurrection. But as for the present we employ, so far as in us lies, appropriate symbols for divine realities.

Pseudo-Dionysius the Areopagite, The Divine Names 1. 4 (6th century?)

89   A Shining Garment

> Anastasius I of Antioch (d. 599) was a man known for his learning and his asceticism—and for his opposition to the dabblings in theology of the emperor Justinian. Anastasius uses transfiguration and radiance as organizing motifs for a complete concise Christology. (Cf. **12**.)

Of old Jesus the Saviour was transfigured, not in the presence of men, but in the presence of his own father when he did not think it a thing to be grasped to be equal to God, but emptied himself out, taking the form of a slave, he who was in the form of God [**39**]. And so, he formerly covered up the divine form when he was transfigured into the form of a slave but now he restores that form of the slave to its natural state, not laying aside the servile nature but rather brightening it with divine properties. Thus he was transfigured before them to show them that in this way he will refashion the body of our lowliness then and make it conform to the body of his own glory. And it says that 'his face shone like the sun and his garments became as white as snow' [Matt. 17: 2; cf.**12**]. These things are written not because he can be compared to the sun or the snow (for to what can you compare the incomparable?) but because there is nothing among material things that is brighter than the sun or whiter than snow, and he wished to give a suitable description of the immensity and splendour of the light by reference to something we know about. The radiance of his garments signifies the change of our bodies; for we shall become a garment for him, since he put on the vesture of our flesh. Or perhaps 'his face shone like the sun' symbolically designates his own body and 'his garments became as white as snow' signifies those who are cleansed by him through his refashioning and transforming power, because this spiritual garment can also be likened to snow since it too is refashioned and evaporates from water to become snow. And because our own nature became his garment, and shall be so again, so we hear Isaiah speaking to him in the person of God: 'For you shall put on all of these as vesture, and gird yourself in them as a bridal ornament' [Isa. 49: 18].

Anastasius I of Antioch, *Homily on the Transfiguration* 4, extract (6th century)

90   Eagerly Seeking Christ

Simeon the New Theologian (949–1022) was an abbot in Constantinople and then, after his works provoked controversy, a recluse in Asia Minor. He stood squarely in the tradition represented by our extract from 'Macarius' (**87**), focused on the divine light and its radiance of Jesus of Nazareth. Here he seeks to move the monks to greater desire for Christ. (Cf. **48**, **210**.)

My brother, if you wish to attain that which you strive for and long after, that is, the good things of God, and from among men become an angel on earth, you must love bodily affliction and embrace suffering. As for trials, love them as the means of obtaining every blessing. Tell me, what is more beautiful than a soul undergoing tribulation, which knows that by enduring it will inherit joy in all things? What is more courageous than 'a humble and contrite heart' [Ps. 51: 19]? Without difficulty it routs the massed troops of devils and pursues them to their end. What is more glorious than spiritual poverty, which is the means of obtaining the kingdom of heaven [Cf. **4**]? Can anything equal it either now or in the world to come? To have no care for any earthly thing for oneself but to have one's mind wholly set on Christ, how great are the eternal benefits that you think this will procure, how great an angelic state? To despise all temporal things alike, including even the urgent needs of the body, yet without any rivalry with anyone on this account, so that peace and love may be preserved undiminished in a tranquil state of mind, what rewards will this not deserve, what crowns and prizes? In truth the commandment is beyond nature and its rewards beyond words. For such, Christ will become all and take the place of all things.

'Christ'—as you hear this do not heed the simplicity of the word or the brevity of the expression. Rather, join with me in thinking of the glory of the Godhead, which is beyond thought and understanding. Think of God's unutterable power, his immeasurable mercy, his inconceivable riches, which he generously and bountifully gives to men. These will suffice them in place of all other things, as they receive into themselves him who is the cause and the bestower of all blessing. He who has been found worthy to see him and contemplate him has no desire for anything else, nor can he who has been filled with the love of God have more love for anyone on earth.

Let us therefore, my beloved brethren, be eager to find Christ and see him as he is, in his beauty and attractiveness. We see many men who are moved by the desire of transitory things to endure many toils and labours. They will travel great distance and even disregard wife and children and every other glory and enjoyment, and prefer nothing to their purpose in order that they may secure the attainment of their goal. If, then, there are some who make every effort to attain transitory and temporal ends even to the point of laying down their very lives, shall we not deliver our souls and bodies to death for the sake of the King of kings and Lord of lords, the creator and sovereign of all things? Whither shall we go, brethren, 'whither shall we flee from his face? If we go up to heaven, there we shall find him; if we go down to hell, there he is present. If we go to the uttermost part of the sea, we shall not escape his hand, but his right hand will encompass' [Ps. 139: 7–10] our souls and bodies. Since then, brethren, we cannot withstand the Lord or flee from his face, come, let us give ourselves as slaves to him, our Lord and God, who for our sakes 'took on himself the form of a slave' and died for us [**39**]. Come, let us be humbled under his mighty hand, which makes eternal life to spring forth for all, and imparts it abundantly through the Spirit to those who seek it.

O my dear brethren, with what pain and sorrow my heart is filled when I want to proclaim the wondrous deeds of God's hand and its ineffable beauty, so that you may know and learn its greatness and seek to receive him within yourselves! Yet I see that some of you lack the desire of fervour to heed what I say and strive for the enjoyment of such glory! This is the reason why I remain altogether tongue-tied; I am quite unable to tell or explain to anyone the glory of Christ our God, which he bestows on those who seek him with all their soul. How it fills me with amazement! How great are God's gifts! He has left behind the wisdom, the power, and the wealth of the world, and has chosen its weakness, foolishness, and poverty [1 Cor. 1: 27], out of his great and ineffable goodness. For this alone who is capable of giving him worthy thanks? Nearly all men reject the weak and the poor as objects of disgust; an earthly king cannot bear the sight of them, rulers turn away from them, while the rich ignore them and pass them by when they meet them as though they did not exist; nobody thinks it desirable to associate with them. But God, who is served by myriads of powers without number, who 'sustains all things by the word of his power' [Heb. 1: 3], whose majesty is beyond anyone's endurance, has not disdained to become the father, the friend, the brother of those rejected ones. He willed to become incarnate so that he might become 'like unto us in all things except for sin' [Heb. 4: 15] and make us to share in his glory and his kingdom. What stupendous riches of his great goodness! What an ineffable condescension on the part of our Master and our God!

Symeon the New Theologian, *Discourses* II. 2–4 (10th century)

Contemplation of Christ's radiant glory could be taken in such a way as to point away from the suffering Christ, but this need not be so. We know little of Peter of Damaskos (12th century), except that he wrote many works for and about monastic life. He balances imaginative contemplation of Christ's Passion with calls to ascetic efforts, regarding each as balancing and correcting the dangers of the other.

So that we will not think that we are doing something great through our ascetic efforts and our many sighs and tears, we are given knowledge of the sufferings of Christ and his saints. Meditating on these we are astonished, and in our amazement we exhaust ourselves through our ascetic labours. For by contemplating the numberless trials that the saints joyfully accepted and the many sufferings that the Lord endured on our behalf, we become aware of our own feebleness. At the same time we are illumined by the knowledge of what the Lord did and said. And by understanding what is stated in the Gospel, we begin sometimes to mourn bitterly in sorrow, sometimes to rejoice spiritually in thanksgiving. Not because we think that we have done anything good, for that would be self-conceit; but because, in spite of being such sinners, we have been granted the contemplation of these things.

In this way we become all the more humble in action and thought, practising the seven forms of bodily discipline of which we have spoken, as well as the moral virtues, that is to say, the virtues of the soul; and we guard the five senses and keep the Lord's commandments. We do not regard these as good works deserving reward; rather we view them as a debt to be paid. Nor do we hope in any way to be released from the debt, for we recognise how enormous are the gifts of knowledge that we have received. We become, as it were, captive to the meaning of what we read and the message of what we chant; and in our delight we often unconsciously forget our sins, and in our joy we begin to shed tears that are sweet as honey. But then, fearful of being deluded in case this is all premature, we restrain ourselves; and recalling our former way of life, we again weep bitterly. In this manner we oscillate between these two kinds of tears, the sweet and the bitter.

So we go forward, provided we are attentive and always consult someone of experience, and provided we come before God with the pure prayer that is appropriate for one practising the virtues, while at the same time we withdraw our intellect from all that it has known or heard, and concentrate it on the remembrance of God, asking only that God's will may be done in all our thoughts and undertakings. But if we fail to do this, then we are liable to be deluded, thinking that we will see an apparition of one of the holy angels, or of Christ. We fail to realise that he who seeks to see Christ should look not outside himself, but within himself, emulating Christ's life in this world, and becoming sinless in body and soul, as Christ was. His intellect should apprehend everything through Christ.

Peter of Damaskos, A Treasury of Divine Knowledge II. 24: 'The Remembrance of Christ's
Sufferings', extract (12th century)

II. Jesus Prayer

The Jesus Prayer, the constant repetition of a short plea addressed to Christ (in its most common, later form: 'Lord Jesus Christ, Son of God, have mercy on me, a sinner'), is a distinctive and pervasive feature of Eastern spirituality from the middle ages onwards. (Cf. **269**, **295**.)

92   Ceaseless Meditation

Diadochus of Photike (*c*.400 – before 486) is one of the figures who stands at the head of the Jesus Prayer tradition. An heir of the desert fathers (cf. **36**), he was deeply concerned with the 'practice of the presence of Jesus'' through ceaseless prayer.

If we close down all the intellect's outlets in order to remember God, we find that it nags at us for something which will satisfy its need to be doing something. It must therefore be given the prayer 'Lord Jesus', the only occupation which will meet its requirements completely. [. . .] The intellect should contemplate this phrase, with its own riches single-mindedly, not turning away from it in the direction of any other imaginative acts at all. All those who meditate ceaselessly upon this holy and glorious name in the depths of their hearts can in the end come to see by the light of their own intellect because, sustained by thought's strict attentions, the name consumes, with an intense feeling, all the dross that covers the surface of the soul; as it is said, 'Our God is a devouring fire' [Deut. 4: 24]. After that, the Lord will draw the soul to great love by his own glory; while it remains by intellectual memory in the fervour of the heart, this glorious, so desirable name implants within us the habit of loving its goodness, which nothing henceforth can resist. This is, indeed, the precious pearl that a man can buy by selling all his goods, so as to enjoy an ineffable joy at its unearthing. [. . .]

[Such a] soul bears the true grace of meditation which cries out with her 'Lord Jesus', just as a mother would teach her child the word 'Father' by repeating it with him until, in the place of any other infantile babble, she has brought him to the habit of distinctly calling for his father, even in his sleep. This is what the Apostle says, 'Similarly, the Spirit comes to aid our weakness, for we do not know how to pray as we should, but the Spirit himself intercedes for us with unimaginable groanings' [Rom. 8: 26]. Indeed, we are children in relation to perfection in the practice of prayer, and we have utter need of the Spirit's help, so that all our mental activity may be shot through and softened by his ineffable gentleness, and so that, in all the movements of our affections, we are borne to the memory and love of our God and Father. It is thus that we cry out in him, as the divine Paul himself once again said, marking the cadence for our unceasing call on God as Father: 'Abba Father' [Rom. 8: 15].

Diadochus of Photike, One Hundred Gnostic Chapters 59, 61 (5th century)

93   The Heart's Occupation

> Abba Philimon lived in Egypt, perhaps in the sixth or seventh century; if this dating is right, he is the first to cite the Jesus Prayer in something like its standard form.

A brother named John came from the coast to Father Philimon and, clasping his feet, said to him: 'What shall I do to be saved? For my intellect vacillates to and fro and strays after all the wrong things.'

After a pause, the father replied: 'This is one of the outer passions and it stays with you because you still have not acquired a perfect longing for God. The warmth of this longing and of the knowledge of God has not yet come to you.'

The brother said to him: 'What shall I do, father?'

Abba Philimon replied: 'Meditate inwardly for a while, deep in your heart; for this can cleanse your intellect of these things.'

The brother, not understanding what was said, asked the Elder: 'What is inward meditation, father?'

The Elder replied: 'Keep watch in your heart; and with watchfulness say in your mind with awe and trembling: "Lord Jesus Christ, have mercy upon me." For this is the advice which the blessed Diadochos [92] gave to beginners.'

The brother departed; and with the help of God and the Elder's prayers he found stillness and for a while was filled with sweetness by this meditation. But then it suddenly left him and he could not practise it or pray watchfully. So he went again to the Elder and told him what had happened. And the Elder said to him: 'You have had a brief taste of stillness and inner work, and have experienced the sweetness that comes from them. This is what you should always be doing in your heart: whether eating or drinking, in company or outside your cell, or on a journey, repeat that prayer with a watchful mind and an undeflected intellect; also chant, and meditate on prayers and psalms. Even when carrying out needful tasks, do not let your intellect be idle but keep it meditating inwardly and praying. For in this way you can grasp the depths of divine Scripture and the power hidden in it, and give unceasing work to the intellect, thus fulfilling the apostolic command: "Pray without ceasing" [I Thess. 5: 17]. Pay strict attention to your heart and watch over it, so that it does not give admittance to thoughts that are evil or in any way vain and useless. Without interruption, whether asleep or awake, eating, drinking, or in company, let your heart inwardly and mentally at times be meditating on the psalms, at other times be repeating the prayer, "Lord Jesus Christ, Son of God, have mercy upon me." And when you chant, make sure that your mouth is not saying one thing while your mind is thinking about another.'

Abba Philimon, Discourse, extract (6th or 7th century?)

III. Meditation and Humility

The practice of meditation on Christ, particularly in so far as it led to humility—as is assumed in Paul's appeal to the great Christological hymn in Philippians (39)—did not in the early medieval West produce texts as powerful and graphic as we find in later medieval sources (cf. 133, 134), but it was nevertheless a constant heart-beat within early medieval devotion—particularly within the Cistercian movement (cf. 97).

94   We Beheld his Glory

Rupert of Deutz (c.1075–1129) was a prolific monastic theologian, a protégé of William of St-Thierry. About 1114 he wrote a series of extended homilies on the book of John. This comes from the commentary on John 1: 14 (66). Rupert gives a brief overview of the life of Christ in terms of 'glory', with a very different feel from the Eastern writers included above (87–9).

God or his Word, since he is reason itself, is not influenced by any of our feelings and does not avoid or hate any creature or any nature which certainly he and not another made; he avoids and hates only the corruption of nature. It is therefore even more appropriate faithfully and devoutly to believe that he did not abhor the inviolate womb of the Virgin [cf. 70]. Thus God the Word dwelt among us and sojourned for nine months without taint of sin in the privacy of female nature from which no one of us has emerged without sin. From that place 'like a bridegroom leaving his chamber and setting his tent in the sun' [Ps. 19: 4], he dwelt among us [66], enveloped in tender flesh as a child and uttering the cries of infancy, made under the law, subordinate to Joseph and Mary, circumcised and purified with sacrifice according to the law like any sinner [cf. **161**], enduring hunger and undergoing the artifices of the tempter [cf. **2**], suffering also persecution at the hands of men, saddened unto death, fleeing from place to place, and at the very last made obedient even to death [**39**].

To what end did this humiliation and weakness at length arrive? John answers, 'And we beheld his glory, glory as of the only-begotten from the Father.' He says: 'We beheld his glory, and since we have seen it we can bear positive witness to it. We really began to see it by virtue of that sign whereby he changed water into wine when he was invited to a wedding. That was the beginning of signs in the presence of his disciples when he manifested his glory. Thereafter we saw him opening blind eyes, putting leprosy to flight by his touch, expelling fevers, raising the decomposing dead, loosing the dumb tongue and deaf ear [cf. **8**], walking on the waters, calming the winds [cf. **10**], stanching the flow of blood, and filling many thousands with a few loaves. We saw also the glory of his transfigured face which should be revealed only to the choirs of angels [cf. **12**]. At his last but greatest and most glorious moment we saw him rising from the dead. We saw in his hands and feet the scars of the nails; we saw, I say, we stared at, we felt, our very hands touched his side where it was pierced by the lance [cf. **16**]. We ate and drank with him, and we saw him as he ascended in glory to heaven. We received the Holy Spirit, the Paraclete promised by him. This glory we have seen, glory as of the only-begotten from the Father, that is, so great a glory as no other of all the sons of God is deemed worthy to receive. For all of God's other sons are adoptive children. This one, however, was begotten or rather only-begotten. All the others are sons by grace. This one alone is Son by nature. Rightfully therefore this one, "fairest in form of the sons of men" [Ps. 45: 2], has the glory which we have seen, a glory differing from that of all the other sons.'

Finally, let us hear the ultimate conclusion of this Gospel prologue. How glorious was the Word which you saw, O John? 'Full of grace and truth,' he replies. O noble proclamation, O noble and faithful witness! Are you seeking what kind of glory belonged to the only-begotten? It was gold, pure gold, a price worthy of our captivity. That man, rich and noble, came forth from the treasury of the Most High; his body, insignificant though it was, was a chest of precious gold. Lay hold of him, therefore, as he is cut off by the blow of death and seize the talent of grace and truth which is therein.

Rupert of Deutz, *Commentary on Saint John*, on John 1: 14, extract (c.1114)

95   Let us Follow

Peter of Celle (1115–83) was Bishop of Chartres after the more famous John of Salisbury. He was a man who delighted in escaping from the business of life into his *scriptoriolum*—a small library attached to his monastic cell. There he found that the whole life of Christ became a pattern-book for the practice of ascetic Christian virtue. (Cf. **151**).

Let us follow Jesus who was conceived of the Holy Spirit, by accepting the same Spirit's grace of inspiration. Let us follow him who was born of the Virgin Mary, when by the help of that grace we join our free wills to grace. Let us follow him who was placed in the manger, by having a humble opinion of ourselves. Let us follow him who was circumcised, by cutting off the superfluities of our first birth. Let us follow him who was offered in the temple, by making our bodies into temples of the Holy Spirit. Let us follow him who was baptised by John, by cleansing ourselves in confession. By our abstinence let us follow him who fasted in the desert. Let us follow him who was tempted, by resisting temptation. Let us follow him who preached and worked miracles, by taking our stand on the word of God and of doctrine. Let us follow him in his transfiguration, by conforming ourselves to the body of Jesus. Let us follow him in his suffering, by bearing every injury patiently. Let us follow him who was sold, by renouncing our pleasures and binding ourselves to the divine commands. Let us follow him who was crucified, by mortifying our vices. By dying to the world let us follow him who died. Let us follow him who was buried, by waiting for the future judgment in peace.

Peter of Celle, 'A Sermon for Passion Sunday' (12th century)

96 Sharing Christ's Anguish

Peter Abelard (1079–1142) (cf. **115**), whose ill-fated love affair with Héloïse has made him more famous than most Parisian nominalist philosophers, combined writings on the most abstract of theological problems with warm and affective poems and hymns. In this hymn, written for the liturgy of Good Friday, the worshippers are present at the Passion: 'This is that night', 'So may our hearts share.'

> Alone to sacrifice thou goest, Lord,
> Giving thyself to death whom thou wilt slay.
> For us thy wretched folk is any word,
> Whose sins have brought thee to this agony?
>
> For they are ours, O Lord, our deeds, our deeds.
> Why must thou suffer torture for our sin?
> Let our hearts suffer for thy passion, Lord,
> That very suffering may thy mercy win.
>
> This is that night of tears, the three days' space,
> Sorrow abiding of the eventide,
> Until the day break with the risen Christ,
> And hearts that sorrowed shall be satisfied.

So may our hearts share in thine anguish, Lord,
That they may sharers of thy glory be:
Heavy with weeping may the three days pass,
To win the laughter of thine Easter Day.

Peter Abelard, 'Good Friday: The Third Nocturn' (12th century)

97   Christ Born in the Soul

Bernard of Clairvaux (1090–1153) was the brightest star in the developing
Cistercian firmament, an order which followed a strict rule dedicated to
communal intercession, worship, and manual labour. He was a caustic
polemicist, an eloquent preacher (including support for the Second Crusade),
and a theologian whose main theme was a mysticism of love. The following
extracts are from a sermon for Christmas Eve. (Cf. 1, 204, 271.)

We have heard, my brethren, the announcement, full of sweetness and
worthy of all acceptation, that Jesus Christ, the Son of God, is born in
Bethlehem of Judah.[2] My very soul has melted at the sound of these words,
and my spirit is burning in my bosom, eager with its usual ardour of desire to
communicate to you its own joy and exultation. 'Jesus' means Saviour. What
is so necessary to the lost as a saviour? What so welcome to the miserable? To
the despairing what so useful? [. . .]

   With good reason, therefore, did your hearts leap for joy, when the voice
of this announcement sounded in your ears; with good reason did you
return thanks to God and prostrate yourselves on the floor in humble
adoration, lying together under the shadow of his shoulders and hoping
under his wings. Did not every one of you, on hearing the good tidings
of the Saviour's nativity, repeat in his heart the words of the psalm, 'It is
good for me to adhere to my God, to put my hope in the Lord God'
[Ps. 73: 28]? [. . .]

   That, my brethren, is always new which always renovates the mind. That is
never old which never ceases to fructify, which no length of time can rob of
its freshness. Such is this Holy One whom God will not 'give to see corruption' [Ps. 16: 10; Acts 2: 27, 13: 35]. He is the new Man who is incapable of ever
becoming old, and who confers true newness of life even upon those whose
'bones have all grown old,' as the Psalmist says [Ps. 31: 10]. Hence it is that in
today's most sweet announcement, we are not told, as you may have noticed,
that he *was* born, but that he *is* born, that 'Jesus Christ, the Son of God, is
born in Bethlehem of Judah.' For just as he is still daily immolated in a
mystical manner whilst we 'show forth his death' upon the altar, so also does
he seem to be newly born whilst we annually commemorate his nativity.
Tomorrow, therefore, we shall see the majesty of God, not indeed in himself

but in us. We shall see majesty in humility, power in weakness, God in man. [. . .]

Thus, therefore, is he born. But born where? 'In Bethlehem of Judah.' We must not, my brethren, pass over Bethlehem, for the shepherds did not say, 'Let us pass over Bethlehem,' but, 'Let us pass over *to* Bethlehem.' [Luke 2: 15]. What though it be but a poor insignificant village? What though it seems to be but 'a little one among the thousands of Judah' [Mic. 5: 2]. For such a birth-place is not unbefitting for him who, whereas he was rich, became poor for our sakes; Who, although he was 'the great Lord and greatly to be praised', was born for us as a little one; who said, 'Blessed are the poor in spirit, for theirs is the kingdom of heaven' [4], and, 'Unless you be converted and become as little children, you shall not enter into the kingdom of heaven' [Mt 18: 3]. Therefore did he choose the stable and the manger, a house of clay and the shelter of beasts, in order to teach us that it is he who 'lifts up the poor out of the dunghill' [Ps 113: 7], and 'preserves men and beasts' [Ps 36: 6].

Would to God that we also were each of us found to be a Bethlehem of Judah, so that Christ might condescend to be born in us, and that we might deserve to hear addressed to us the words, 'Unto you that fear my name the Sun of justice shall arise' [Mal. 4: 2]. And perhaps it is the same thing to say that a man must make himself a Bethlehem of Judah if he would have Jesus to be born in his heart, as what I remember to have remarked awhile ago, namely, that there is need of sanctification and preparation before we can see in us the majesty of God.

Bernard of Clairvaux, 'Sixth Sermon for Christmas Eve', extracts (12th century)

98   Christh Little and Weak

> Aelred, Abbot of the Cistercian monastery (cf. **97**) of Rievaulx in Yorkshire (1109–67), was pre-eminently a theologian of friendship (writing a Christian version of Cicero's *De Amicitia*), and of the suffering humanity of Christ.

Lord Jesus, in my littleness I embrace you made little, in my weakness I embrace you made weak, as a human being I embrace you become man and, I say more, a poor man. For you, O Lord, were poor, sitting on an ass and the foal of an ass. Thus, therefore, I embrace you, Lord. For my whole greatness is your littleness, my whole strength is your weakness, and all my wisdom is your foolishness.

Aelred of Rievaulx, *Mirror of Charity* I. 7, extract (12th century)

Section B

Christ and Culture

As Christianity found a home in different cultures, both because of its continued spread and because of the incursions of barbarians and invaders, the story of Jesus was told again and again in new forms, forms which absorbed the patterns of thought and expression of unfamiliar surroundings and, with varying success, drew them into Christ's service.

99 The Unburning Coal

Kassia (*c*.805–*c*.865), a noblewoman of Constantinople, became a nun about 830 (supposedly after being rejected as a possible bride by the emperor Theophilus, 829–42), founding her own monastery in 843. She was a supporter of icons during the iconoclastic controversies (cf. **108**), living to see their final reinstatement in 843. Most of all, however, she was a poet and hymn-writer, the only woman writer to have her works included in the Orthodox liturgy. In the third stanza of this hymn she explores the orthodox, anti-Nestorian idea of Mary as God-bearer, Theotokos. (Cf. **83, 244, 326**.)

> When you appeared, Christ,
> in the arms of her who bore you
> as in a pair of tongs
> you were given to Simeon the Elder a perfect child,
> a coal perceived not burning;
> when he held you in his arms
> he rejoiced full of youthful spirit
> and asked for release, 'Saviour', he cried out to you,
> 'now release me, your servant, from this world to eternal life,
> according to your word,
> for I have seen you in human form.'
>
> The undefiled Virgin
> carrying in her arms
> him whom she embodied
> delivers him to the holy elder, saying,
> 'Receive him whom the teachings
> of the prophets proclaimed,
> the child who because of compassion is now summoned
> and as the holy lawgiver fulfils the law';
> and he cried out to him,
> 'You have come who will release me

from this world to eternal life;
glory to you, Lord.'

'How can I hold you as a child,
you who holds everything together?
How do I bring you to the temple, who is beyond goodness?
How do I deliver you to the arms of the elder
who sits in the bosom of the Father?
How do you endure purification,
you who purifies the whole corrupt nature?'
So said the Virgin
the temple who contained God
marvelling at your great condescension,
Christ.

Kassia, 'February 2: The Meeting of the Lord (at Vespers)' (9th century)

100   Son of the Cool Wind

Written in the seventh century in the Nestorian (cf. **83**) Church in China, perhaps in 635, this document may have been part of an apology for the then newly arrived Christianity, addressed perhaps to the emperor T'ai-tsung. For the most part it is an attempt at the transposition of the Christian story into Chinese terms, but it contains a strong sting in the tail.

All the living beings [. . .] have turned their face away from God and committed sins and finally rebelled against the Lord of Heaven. Seeing such was their manner of living, the Lord of Heaven took great pity on them and admonished them to do good deeds, and not to trust to the old teaching. The Lord of Heaven, therefore, made the Cool Wind to enter a virgin named Mo-yen. Hereupon, the Cool Wind entered the body of Mo-yen in accordance with the instruction of the Lord of Heaven. [. . .] After her conception, Mo-yen gave birth to a son named I-shu, whose father was the Cool Wind. [. . .]

When he was born as the Mi-shih-ho, after the elapse of five times of one year, he began to talk. And afterward he preached to the people admonishing them to do good deeds. When he was over twelve years old, he came to a purifying place named Shu-nan and sought to be named. And consequently, he went to Yao-ku-hun and was immersed for washing. At first, the Mi-shih-ho submitted to Yao-ku-hun as a disciple. This sacred man dwelt in a wild ravine. He neither ate meat nor drank wine from his birth. He only lived on raw vegetables and honey—honey on the ground. At that time, there were many people who came to Yao-ku-hun. They all worshipped him, and from him they also received the precepts. And now, Yao-ku-hun thought it proper to make the Mi-shih-ho enter the To-nan. The Mi-shih-ho, after finishing the washing, came out of the water, when the Cool Wind descended from the

Heaven in appearance of a dove and sat upon the Mi-shih-ho, whilst a voice sounded in empty-space, saying: The Mi-shih-ho is my son; all the people in the world must do what is told by the Mi-shih-ho, obeying his command to do good. The Mi-shih-ho, then, showed to all the living beings that the way of heaven is no other than the decided will of the Lord of Heaven. His decided will is to make all the living beings give up serving false gods. Therefore, if any living being should hear these words, let him give up serving these false gods. Let him stop evil deeds, and forthwith do the good work in faith.

Hsü-T'ing Mi-shih-ho-ching ('Jesus-Messiah Sūtra') 148–50, 164–76 (*c*.635?)

101 Helm of Heaven

Cynewulf was an Anglo-Saxon poet of the early ninth century, who in his epic poem *Christ* poured the story of Jesus into an heroic, militaristic mould familiar to us from such other Saxon epics as *Beowulf*. Here he takes up the popular medieval theme of the harrowing of hell (1 Pet. 3: 19).

Now hath the holy one harrowed hell of tribute, of all that in the days of yore it swallowed up unrighteously into that house of torment. Now are these devil-champions all undone, cast into everlasting torture, bound in the pit of hell, despoiled of might. Nor in that battle might these foes of hell, in that clash of weapons, know success, when by his might alone the King of glory, the helm of heaven, waged battle on his olden enemies; when he led forth from thraldom, from the city of his foes, exceeding spoil, a countless train of folk, this very multitude whereon ye gaze. Now will the Saviour of souls, the very Son of God, depart unto the mercy-seat of spirits after the battle-play. Now do ye know aright who is that Lord who leadeth this array. Unto your friends go boldly glad in heart—Open, ye gates, for with no little train the all-ruling King, the author of creation, leadeth unto you, into the joy of joys, within the city, that folk which he in triumph wrested from the foes of hell. From this time forth forever shall be peace to men and angels, covenant of God and man, spiritual faith, and love, and hope of life and gladness in all light.

Lo! we have heard how by his hither-coming the Son of healing, mighty child of God, vouchsafed salvation, freed and upheld the folk beneath the clouds, that now each man of men while he dwelleth here alive may choose the shame of hell or the splendour of heaven, the gleaming light or the loathsome night, the spell of glory or the vengeance of darkness, joy with the Lord or tumult with devils, torment with fiends or bliss with the angels, or life or death, as may be dearer to him to accomplish so long as flesh and spirit dwell together in the world. And to the majesty of the Trinity be glory and eternal thanks.

Cynewulf, *Christ: Ascension*, extract (9th century)

102   Our Chevalier

Nicholas Bozon (*fl.* 1300–20) was a native of Norfolk who became a Franciscan, moved to Nottingham, and distinguished himself as a moralist and
preacher. This is a remarkable poem, in which the Gospel is retold in the
idiom of chivalric romance.

Listen, my lords, to a tale of high chivalry,
of a noble knight, who for love of his lady
strove so hard that he gave up his life
to win back his exiled bride,

(that is, the human soul that had been betrayed),
but her gentle lover did not hasten
to her rescue till she realised her folly
and the way in which she had completely debased her life.

Long did he permit her torment
so she might see how much she had declined;
yet as soon as she cried for mercy, he took pity on her,
and the more so because she had been led astray.

Alone he took to the field to rescue his love;
though victorious in battle and triumphant over all
(partly by force and partly by strategy),
He was wounded sorely on account of his jealous love.

How handsome was the knight in this test—
who for love of his mistress suffered such wounds!
And well ought she in her curtained chamber
To have hung the shield emblazoned thus:

He bore a shield of silver, stencilled with gules;
in chief, a crown of sharp thorns,
a fair white border on which were four costly signs,
and in the midst of the field, a rich fountain of blood.

Tall and strong was the steed he mounted that day.
Its coat all over was of four kinds of fur:
cypress for the body, cedar for the hooves,
olive for the back, and the great mane of palm.

On his head the knight wore a helmet of bloody locks;
his over-jerkin was bare skin, pierced through and through;
and his mail-coat of suffering was all split and riven,
but the lance he held in his hand was his deity.

And thus it was he conquered him who had conquered us all.
But to do this he had disguised his identity,
for had his enemy recognised him,
on no account would he have ridden out to battle.

But our chevalier acted wisely:
He borrowed arms of one of his knights-bachelor,

Adam by name, had them refurbished
and had a damsel arm him with them.

He entered this damsel's chamber
(she was the fairest of all);
He entered so secretly, without word or sound
that no one knew he was there save her alone.

The damsel then armed him with borrowed armour:
pure white flesh was the jerkin she gave him,
padded not with silk or cotton but with blood;
for cuisses and greaves she gave him groin and thighs.

For chauces of mail she wrapped his legs with sinews,
his leg-plates were well-fitting bones;
covering all, skin was his silken gamboison,
trimmed all about with veins.

Once armed the knight left the chamber,
nobly offering to do battle for us.
His deceitful enemy sortied from the ranks,
not knowing his true identity.

Taking one look at the armour, he sneered in disdain,
but Jesus let him carry on his vain assault,
awaiting the right moment to raise his hand;
when he was himself doomed to death, then it was he made us whole.

Then he left his armour hanging on a tree,
and took the field as a proven champion.
He found his lady in her vile prison,
and took her away with him to salvation.

Nicholas Bozon, 'Christ's Chivalry' (between 1300 and 1320)

Section C

....

Byzantine and Early Medieval Debates

....

I. After Chalcedon

Chalcedon, far from resolving the Christological debates of the East, became a bone of contention. Various kinds of Monophysite,[3] who opposed its affirmation of two 'natures', attacked it bitterly for dividing the one Christ; defenders of Chalcedon accused them of doing justice neither to Christ's humanity nor to his divinity. Various attempts were made to find a middle way, or to clarify the terminology in a way acceptable to both sides, but none were successful for long.

103   Christis not Two

....

> Sergius the Grammarian and Severus of Antioch (104) were both Mono-physites, but Sergius was the more radical. In this letter he takes Severus to task for effectively giving way to Chalcedon. They were using the terminology of *ousia* (substance) and 'propriety', instead of 'person' and 'nature', largely because it was less loaded. Sergius wished them to say that they 'did not speak of two proprieties' after the Incarnation (i.e. that there was one propriety, just as in the other terminology there was one nature); Severus had made the weaker claim that he 'did not speak of *divided* proprieties', yet this negative way of putting it would have been acceptable to any Chaledonian.

Shall we speak of two 'proprieties' [in Christ], so that we may remove the foolishness of the metousiasts,[4] flesh being understood as flesh, and divinity not descending to confusion? But this is to keep two *ousiai*, and by no means just two 'proprieties'.

For God and flesh are *ousiai*, but it is the propriety of God to be eternally, but of flesh to become and to be corrupted. [. . .] If we should say that these proprieties persist [in Christ] how will we find them, when we enquire about the facts in question? For the propriety of God, to be sure, is that he is not seen or touched—yet God came visibly, and 'was seen on earth, and had dealings with men' [Baruch 3: 38], and 'we saw him, and his appearance was not honourable, and was despised by men' [53] . . . 'that which was from the beginning, which we have heard and seen, and our hands have touched, concerning the Word of Life . . .' [1 John 1: 1].

But it is the propriety of flesh that it is brought forth from two parents, and when once it is brought forth, that it should also be corrupted. But where are these things in the case of the flesh of Life? For no man was father of Christ, for without the bush being burned, and the door being still sealed, the Lord went forth endowed with a body. Hence because he was not born in accordance with the propriety of the flesh, neither did his flesh see corruption.

[. . .] Every propriety belongs to an underlying nature, and if we speak of two proprieties, we are obliged also to speak of two natures. And if we suppose [only] that the proprieties are 'undivided'—neither do those Dyophysites divide the natures, but everywhere proclaim to us natures which are undivided. And this is the summing up of the sickness of Chalcedon [86] and the madness of Leo [85], which, while it divides the activities with the natures [cf. 82], says each form does what is proper undividedly 'in partner-ship with the other'. Therefore how shall we escape from such frenzy, we who teach one nature of the Word incarnate after the union, unless, just as we believe Christ is one from two natures,[5] so also we accept one propriety from two of God incarnate, of him who out of kindness undertakes to be seen, but transcended the human propriety by means of the supreme union: thus he walked on the waters without being dragged by the burden of the flesh into the depth of the sea. And when they sealed the sepulchre, he was not held in, and closed doors were unable to prevent his entrance.

And so henceforward, neither is any propriety of God to be recognised in his Logos, nor is any propriety of flesh to be seen in him either, but the entire manner of the economy points towards one propriety, that which is with God incarnate. For just as laughter is the propriety to 'man', and none of the other animals is like him in this, so also there is one propriety of Christ, in which no-one from those who are invisible or visible shares. For only God who was incarnate is born from the Virgin, and performed everything and suffered on our behalf, and from where he descended, there again he ascended, endowed with the flesh.

Sergius the Grammarian, Letter 1, extract (c.515)

104   The Diversity in Christ

> Severus, Patriarch of Antioch (c.465–538), replied to the more radically monophysite Sergius (cf. 103) using the analogy of a soul and a body to explain how he meant to use the language of 'propriety' and *ousia* to refer to a diversity in unity in Christ, without in any way jeopardizing the unity.

Some of the things which are done by a man like us are intellectual, and some are sensible and bodily. For example, to reckon up and think about something that should be done, and to fulfil and plan in thought, and to fix and determine intention, is a thing which is done intellectually, such as arranging how it is fitting to prepare a city or a house or a ship. But to build a house or to construct a ship, is sensible and bodily. And the man who acts in both cases is one, consisting of soul and body, and the activity is one, for the active movement is one, which is the impetus of volition, but the things which are done are diverse, for one is intellectual but the other is sensible and bodily. One can see the same in the case of Emmanuel. For there is one who acts, that is the Word of God incarnate; and there is one active movement which is activity, but the things which are done are diverse, that is the things accomplished by activity. For example, bodily to walk on the earth and to make a journey is something human, but to raise up and order to run those who are lame in the feet, and unable to use their soles, but who are prostrate and crawl like reptiles, is most proper to God. But there is one Word which was incarnate, and one activity of his, which is an active movement, which performed the one and the other. And it is not the case that, because these things which were done were of different kinds, we say that consequently there were two natures which were effecting those things, for as we have said, a single God the Word incarnate performed both of them.

And just as no-one divides the Word from the flesh, so also it is impossible to divide or separate these activities. For we also recognise a variety of utterances: for some are proper to God, while others are human, but one Word incarnate spoke both the former and the latter. For there are utterances which make known at the same time the divine character of Emmanuel and the humanity as well, as 'One Lord Jesus Christ, through whom are all things' [1 Cor. 8: 6], and 'From whom is Christ, in the flesh, who is God blessed for ever, above all things' [Rom. 9: 5]. And no-one, unless he is mad, dares to divide or distinguish into two these statements, which establish the same Christ as indivisible, being both from Israel in the flesh, and God blessed for ever. And again the same one is anointed because he was incarnate, for the act of being anointed belongs to the incarnation, and through the same one everything came into existence.

But what our Saviour said about the death of Lazarus is like those utterances as well, in that it shows at the same time the divine character and humanity: 'Lazarus our friend is asleep, but I go that I may arouse him' [John 11: 11]. For it belongs to God that he should say that he would rouse him as if he were asleep, him who for four days had been reckoned among the dead, and had wasted away, and had putrefied in the body, and in truth to change death into sleep, because of the hope of the resurrection; but it was human to say 'I go and shall awake him'. For he was able as God, even while he was far off, to do that. But he mingled the two, establishing that he is indivisibly one and the same Son and Word, who on our behalf unchangeably became man, speaking as befits God and humanly. Thus too it is often possible to see in his actions what belongs to the character of God and what is human mingled together. For how will anyone divide walking upon the water? For to run upon the sea is foreign to the human nature, but it is not proper to the divine nature to use bodily feet. Therefore that action is of the incarnate Word, to whom belongs at the same time divine character and humanity indivisibly.

Severus of Antioch, Letter 1, extract (c. 515)

105   The Hypostatic Union

Leontius of Jerusalem (*fl.* 538–44) was a theologian at the court of the emperor Justinian. He attempted to give the theology agreed at Chalcedon (**86**), which he read in the light of the work of Cyril (cf. **84**), a more detailed conceptual exposition. He established the idea that the human nature of Christ, in itself 'without hypostasis' ('anhypostatic'), was assumed by the person of the Logos, and so made hypostatic ('enhypostasic')—that is, that Christ's humanity had no individual existence proper to it independent of its assumption by the Son. (Cf. **112**.)

Just as the iron which is made red-hot in the furnace does not lose any part of its hypostasis from the species of the fire, but admits only the nature [of the fire] into its own hypostasis—for likewise the hypostasis of the fire in the furnace remains, lacking nothing, even after the fire becomes red-hot—so we say that the Logos assumed from our nature a somewhat particular nature into his own hypostasis.[6] [. . .]

Iron burned in the embers does not display a new nature or a new hypostasis. For both the hypostasis of the iron and the hypostasis of the hot charcoals remain the same; but in the hypostasis of the iron the nature of the fire, which is itself without hypostasis, is united to the nature of the iron, becoming with it one hypostasis. What then constitutes the union in Christ? Nothing other than the things which before were not united with one another, and which are now united in the one hypostasis of one of the natures that has been united. [. . .]

He is born by a certain type of generation, not by being transformed, but at the same time, he does not remain absolutely simple as he was before, nor does he remain in his simple existence, nor does he remain in the manner of existence which describes him before, but he is now with the flesh; and henceforth I dare to say his hypostasis is altered in its manner of being in this way, not because there is a change of the Logos' properties, or because there is a change in the properties of God; but because he receives and acquires the other properties of Jesus, and he acquires the properties of the human nature in the same one hypostasis of the Logos himself which increases and receives more properties. [. . .]

For the man in Christ is not particular, but it shares with the divine nature the one hypostasis of the Logos; and instead of a human hypostasis it has acquired a divine hypostasis; instead of being a term that refers to a whole hypostasis, in the hypostasis of the Logos the man is seen as a part, for this is to be sure the ultimate blessedness for the man in Christ.

Leontius of Jerusalem, Against the Nestorians I. 20, I. 49, IV. 42, V. 30, extracts (between 538 and 544)

106 Two Wills in Christ

One of the attempts made on the Chalcedonian (cf. **86**) side to produce a formula acceptable to the Monophysites was Monothelitism: the teaching that although there are two natures in Christ, there is only one 'proper activity'. There was much toing and froing about the terminology, and there was some confusion between 'activity' and 'will', and the idea that there was one *will* in Christ soon followed. After attempts simply to quash all use of this terminology, which was found to confuse rather than clarify the issues at stake, Monothelitism was condemned at the Council of Constantinople in 680. The following is an extract from the proceedings of the Council.

Following the five holy and universal synods and the holy and accepted fathers, and defining in unison, it professes our Lord Jesus Christ our true God, one of the holy Trinity, which is of one same being and is the source of life, to be perfect in divinity and perfect in humanity. [. . .] [A]t no point was the difference between the natures taken away through the union, but rather the property of both natures is preserved and comes together into a single subsistent being [. . .].

And we proclaim equally two natural volitions or wills in him and two natural principles of action which undergo no division, no change, no partition, no confusion, in accordance with the teaching of the holy fathers. And the two natural wills not in opposition, as the impious heretics said, far from it, but his human will following, and not resisting or struggling, rather in fact subject to his divine and all powerful will. For the will of the flesh had to be moved, and yet to be subjected to the divine will, according to the most wise Athanasius.[7] For just as his flesh is said to be and is flesh of the Word of God, so too the natural will of his flesh is said to and does belong to the Word of God, just as he says himself: 'I have come down from heaven, not to do my own will, but the will of the Father who sent me' [John 6: 38], calling his own will that of his flesh, since his flesh too became his own. For in the same way that his all holy and blameless animate flesh was not destroyed in being made divine but remained in its own limit and category, so his human will as well was not destroyed by being made divine, but rather was preserved, according to the theologian Gregory, who says: 'For his willing, when he is considered as saviour, is not in opposition to God, being made divine in its entirety' [Gregory of Nazianzus [cf. **82**], Oration 30]. [. . .] For of course we will not grant the existence of only a single natural principle of action of both God and creature, lest we raise what is made to the level of divine being, or indeed reduce what is most specifically proper to the divine nature to a level befitting creatures; for we acknowledge that the miracles and the sufferings are of one and the same, according to one or the other of the two natures out of which he is and in which he has his being, as the admirable Cyril said.

Constitutions of the Third Council of Constantinople, extract (680)

107 The Orthodox Faith

John of Damascus (*c.675–c.749*) was one of the great consolidators of Eastern theology. He drew upon the work of, especially, the Cappadocian Fathers (cf. **46**, **81**), Maximus the Confessor (who had been prominent in the rejection of Monothelitism, **106**), and Leontius of Jerusalem (cf. **105**), to produce a systematic and coherent statement of the Chalcedonian faith. It was hugely influential in the East, and, after being translated into Latin in 1150, influenced Peter Lombard (cf. **116**), Thomas Aquinas (cf. **158**), and many other Westerners.

After the holy Virgin had given her assent, the Holy Ghost came upon her according to the Lord's word, which the angel had spoken, and purified her and gave her the power both to receive the divinity of the Word and to beget. Then the subsistent Wisdom and Power of the Most High, the Son of God, the Consubstantial with the Father, overshadowed her like a divine seed and from her most chaste and pure blood compacted for himself a body animated by a rational and intellectual soul as first-fruits of our clay. This was not by seed, but by creation through the Holy Ghost, with the form not being put together bit by bit, but being completed all at once with the Word of God himself serving as the person to the flesh [cf. **105**]. For the divine Word was not united to an already self-subsistent flesh, but, without being circumscribed, came in his own person to dwell in the womb of the holy Virgin and from the chaste blood of the ever-virgin made flesh subsist animated by a rational and intellectual soul. Taking to himself the first-fruits of the human clay, the very Word became person to the body. Thus, there was a body which was at once the body of God the Word and an animate, rational, intellectual body. Therefore, we do not say that man became God, but that God became man. For, while he was by nature perfect God, the same became by nature perfect man. He did not change his nature and neither did he just appear to become man. On the contrary, without confusion or alteration or division he became hypostatically united to the rationally and intellectually animated flesh which he had from the holy Virgin and which had its existence in him. He did not transform the nature of his divinity into the substance of his flesh, nor the substance of his flesh into the nature of his divinity, and neither did he effect one compound nature out of his divine nature and the human nature which he had assumed. [. . .]

We say, then, that the divine Person of God the Word exists before all things timelessly and eternally, simple and uncompounded, uncreated, incorporeal, invisible, intangible, and uncircumscribed. And we say that it has all things that the Father has since it is consubstantial with him, and that it differs from the person of the Father by the manner of its begetting and by relation, that it is perfect and never leaves the person of the Father. But, at the same time, we say that in latter times, without leaving the bosom of the Father, the Word came to dwell uncircumscribed in the womb of the holy Virgin, without seed and without being contained, but after a manner known to him, and in the very same person as exists before the ages he made flesh subsist for himself from the holy Virgin. [. . .]

The whole 'he', then, is perfect God, but not wholly God, because he is not only God but also man. Likewise, the whole he is perfect man, but not wholly man, because he is not only man but also God. For the 'wholly' is indicative of nature, while the 'whole' is indicative of person, just as 'one thing' is of nature, while 'another one' is of person.

One must know, moreover, that, although we say that the natures of the Lord are mutually immanent, we know that this immanence comes from the divine nature. For this last pervades all things and indwells as it wishes, but nothing pervades it. And it communicates its own splendours to the body [cf. **181**] while remaining impassible and having no part in the affections of the body. For, if the sun communicates its own operations to us, yet has no part in our own [cf. **71**], then how much more so the Creator of the sun who is the Lord?

John of Damascus, *The Orthodox Faith* III. 1–2, 7, extracts (8th century)

II. Adoring Christ's Humanity

A controversy over the use of icons raged in the Eastern Church from the seventh century to the ninth, reaching a head in 726 when Emperor Leo III issued an edict ordering the destruction of all idols. The subsequent unrest did not finally die down until the reign of Empress Theodora in 843. This controversy is in some ways the last great Christological controversy of the East, the issues it raised about the nature of Christ's humanity going to the heart of Chalcedonian faith. The restoration of icons in 843 on the first Sunday in Lent is still celebrated as the Feast of Orthodoxy. The controversy largely passed the West by, but there were some parallels in the devotion given to relics of Christ's life.

108   On Divine Images

When icons were first banned, John of Damascus (cf. 107) wrote a series of apologies for their use, making clear the Christological issues at stake.

In former times God, who is without form or body, could never be depicted. But now when God is seen in the flesh conversing with men, I make an image of the God whom I see. I do not worship matter; I worship the Creator of matter who became matter for my sake, who willed to take his abode in matter; who worked out my salvation through matter. Never will I cease honouring the matter which wrought my salvation! I honour it, but not as God. How could God be born out of things which have no existence in themselves? God's body is God because it is joined to his person by a union which shall never pass away. The divine nature remains the same; the flesh created in time is quickened by a reason-endowed soul. Because of this I salute all remaining matter with reverence, because God has filled it with his grace and power. Through it my salvation has come to me. Was not the thrice-happy and thrice-blessed wood of the cross matter [cf. 32]? Was not the holy and exalted mountain of Calvary matter? What of the life-bearing rock, the holy and life-giving tomb, the fountain of our resurrection, was it not matter? Is not the ink in the most holy Gospel-book matter? Is not the life-giving altar made of matter? From it we receive the bread of life! Are not gold and silver matter? From them we make crosses, patens, chalices! And over and above all these things, is not the Body and Blood of our Lord matter? Either do away with the honour and veneration these things deserve, or accept the tradition of the Church and the veneration of images. Reverence God and his friends; follow the inspiration of the holy Spirit. Do not despise matter, for it is not despicable. God has made nothing despicable. To think such things is Manichaeism.[8] Only that which does not have its source in God is despicable—that which is our own invention, our wilful choice to disregard the law of God—namely, sin. [. . .]

Some would say: Make an image of Christ and of his mother, the Theotokos, and let that be enough. What foolishness! Your own impious words prove that you utterly despise the saints. If you make an image of Christ, and not of the saints, it is evident that you do not forbid images, but refuse to honour the saints. You make images of Christ as one who is glorified, yet you deprive the saints of their rightful glory, and call truth falsehood. The Lord says, 'I will glorify those who glorify me' [1 Sam. 2: 30]. The divinely inspired apostle writes, 'So through God you are no longer a slave but a son, and if a son, then an heir.' And 'if children, then heirs, heirs of God and fellow heirs with Christ, provided we suffer with him in order that we may also be glorified with him' [Rom. 8: 17]. You are not waging war against images, but against the saints themselves. St. John the Theologian, who leaned on the breast of Christ, says 'We shall become like him' [1 John 3: 2]. Just as something in contact with fire becomes fire not by its own nature, but by being united, burned, and mingled with fire, so it is also, I say, with the assumed flesh of the Son of God. By union with his person, that flesh participates in the divine nature and by this communion becomes unchangeably God; not only by the operation of divine grace, as was the case with the prophets, but by the coming of grace himself. The Scripture calls the saints gods, when it says, 'God has taken his place in the divine council; in the midst of the gods he holds judgment' [Ps. 82: 1]. Saint Gregory [cf. **81**] interprets these words to mean that God takes his place in the assembly of the saints, determining the glory due each [*Theological Orations* 40]. The saints during their earthly lives were filled with the Holy Spirit, and when they fulfil their course, the grace of the Holy Spirit does not depart from their souls or their bodies in the tombs, or from their likenesses and holy images, not by the nature of these things, but by grace and power. [. . .]

We depict Christ as our King and Lord, then, and do not strip him of his army. For the saints are the Lord's army. If the earthly emperor wishes to deprive the Lord of his army, let him also dismiss his own troops. If he wishes in his tyranny to refuse due honour to these valiant conquerors of evil, let him also cast aside his own purple. For if the saints are heirs of God and co-heirs with Christ, they will also share in the divine glory and dominion. If they have partaken of Christ's sufferings, and are his friends, shall they not receive a share of glory from the Church on earth? 'No longer do I call you servants,' God says, 'but I have called you friends' [John 15: 15]. Shall we strip them of the glory given them by the Church? What audacity! What effrontery of mind, to fight with God, refusing to follow his commands! You who refuse to bow before images also refuse to bow before the Son of God who is the living image of the invisible God [**50**], and his unchanging likeness. I bow before the images of Christ, the incarnate God; of our Lady, the Theotokos [cf. **99**] and Mother of the Son of God; and of the saints, who are God's friends.

John of Damascus, On Divine Images 1. 16, 19, 21, extracts (c.730)

109   Mementoes of Christ

A somewhat similar note is struck in a wholly different context by the following extract from the *Life* of Hugh of Lincoln (1140–1200) written by a monk of Eynsham called Adam. Hugh was influenced by Bernard [cf. **97**], and, rather than seeing it as a problem to be explained or as a barrier to faith, or even simply as a lesson in humility, he saw that the true humanity of Christ made possible forms of devotion which, in any other circumstance, would have been idolatrous. [Cf. **69**.]

Speaking when alone with his friends of the marvellous mercy of our Saviour who had so often in the gospels testified with his own divine mouth to the blessedness of those who had been most wretched on earth, as, for example when he declared that Lazarus with his sores was borne by angels to Abraham's bosom, and that he himself shared the afflictions of the afflicted, Hugh used to extol in glowing terms the author of all goodness. 'O,' he exclaimed, 'how fortunate were the companions of this gracious man! How sweet I should have found it to have beheld and kissed his footprints, or, if it had been possible, to have held close to my heart anything which his hands or any part of his body had touched! What shall I say of his excretions, if it is not impious to call an excretion what flowed from the Tree of Life? What, I say, should I feel about the sweat which perchance flowed from the Vessel of such great blessedness, owing to his assumption of our infirmity? Certainly, if I were given the chance, I would not only carefully collect it, but would devour it with my lips and imbibe it as something sweeter than honey, and would treasure it in the depths of my heart. How wretched are they who dread anything except to offend so sweet a friend! How much to be pitied are they who esteem anything else sweet, or desire anything except to cleave lovingly to such a lover, and lovingly obey him! To my mind nothing can seem hard to a man who has through meditation experienced his sweetness, and sweetly digested it in the depths of his heart.'

Adam of Eynsham, *The Life of St. Hugh of Lincoln* III, extract (13th century)

III. Western Christology

The Christological controversies of the East passed the West by, and it was not until a much later period that we find really significant Western developments in the technical expression of Christology. Nevertheless, despite this relative paucity of Christological material, narrowly defined, we do see the emergence of some features which will be characteristic of later Western Christology, particularly in the grammatical method of Boethius (**110**) and in the early scholasticism of Anselm (**114**) and Peter Lombard (**116**).

110   Against Ambiguity

Boethius (c.480–c.524) is best known for his writing *On the Consolation of Philosophy*, but he also produced several short theological works, among them a defence of Chalcedonian orthodoxy (cf. **86**), 'Against Eutyches and Nestorius' (cf. **83**). He stands at the transition between the patristic and medieval periods in the West; a statesman son of a Roman consul, he was executed for political reasons by the Ostrogothic King of Italy, Theodoric. Clarifying opposing Christological views by means of grammatical and verbal precision, he prefigured the method of later generations of Western theologians; a commentary on this work by Gilbert de la Porrée (c.1080–1154) made Boethius' influence on Western Christology felt strongly some six centuries later.

The statement that a thing consists of two natures bears two meanings; one, when we say that anything is a union of two natures, as e.g. honey and water, where the union is such that in the combination, however the elements be confounded, whether by one nature changing into the other, or by both mingling with each other, the two entirely disappear. This is the way in which according to Eutyches Christ consists of two natures.

The other way in which a thing can consist of two natures is when it is so combined of two that the elements of which it is said to be combined continue without changing into each other, as when we say that a crown is composed of gold and gems. Here neither is the gold converted into gems nor is the gem turned into gold, but both continue without surrendering their proper form.

Things then like this, composed of various elements, we say consist also *in* the elements *of* which they are said to consist. For in this case we can say that a crown consists *of* gems and gold, for gems and gold are that *in* which the crown consists. For in the former mode of composition honey and water is not that *in* which the resulting union of both consists.

Since then the catholic faith confesses that both natures continue in Christ and that they both remain perfect, neither being transformed into the other, it says with right that Christ consists both *in* and *of* the two natures; *in* the two because both continue, *of* the two because the one person of Christ is formed by the union of the two continuing natures.

But the catholic faith does not hold the union of Christ out of two natures according to that meaning which Eutyches puts upon it. For the meaning of the conjunction out of two natures which he adopts forbids him to confess that it consists *in* the two or that the two continue; but the catholic adopts such a meaning of its consisting *of* two—as comes near to that of Eutyches—yet also keeps the meaning which confesses that it consists *in* two.

To 'consist *of* two natures' is therefore an equivocal or rather an ambiguous term of double meaning denoting different things; according to one meaning the substances out of which the union is said to have been composed do not continue, according to another the union effected of the two is such that both natures continue.

When once this knot of equivocity and ambiguity has been untied, nothing further can be advanced to shake the true and solid content of the catholic faith, which is that the same Christ is perfect man, the same is God, and the same who is perfect man and God is one as God and Son of God; that, however, quaternity is not added to the Trinity by the addition of man to perfect God, but that one and the same person completes the number of the Trinity, so that, although it was the humanity which suffered, yet God may be said to have suffered, not because manhood became Godhead itself but because it was assumed by Godhead.

Anicius Manlius Severinus Boethius, *Against Eutyches and Nestorius* VII, extract (6th century)

111 Christ's Adoptive Humanity

At the end of the eighth century Elipandus, Archbishop of Toledo from 783 to 808, developed (with help from Felix, Bishop of Urgel) an account of Christology based on a peculiarity of the Spanish liturgy, which spoke of the 'adoptive man' in Christ. His views were argued against by Beatus of Liebana (cf. **112**) and by the more famous Alcuin of York, and condemned at synods in 792 and 794, convened by the emperor Charlemagne.

We confess and we believe in God the Son of God, born without beginning of the Father before all ages, co-eternal and consimilar and consubstantial not by adoption but by generation, and not by grace but by nature. To this the same Son testifies when he says, 'I and the Father are one' [John 10: 30], along with the rest of the passages which the same one, truly God and truly human, spoke for us concerning his divinity. But, toward the end of time, for the salvation of the human race, appearing to the public view out of the hidden and ineffable bosom of the Father—the invisible assuming a visible body from the Virgin—he came forth, ineffably, through the inviolably virgin members of his mother. We confess according to the tradition of the Fathers, and believe, that he was made of a woman, under the law, Son of God not by generation but by adoption, and not by nature, but by grace, as the same Lord testifies, saying, 'The Father is greater than I' [John 14: 28]. [. . .]

Why is there any hesitation to say that the Son of God, according to the form of a slave, emptied of his Godhead, corporeal and visible and palpable, is adoptive? Beatus the Unspeakable is unhappy if anyone says that Christ, according to the form of a slave, is adoptive, even though John the Apostle and Evangelist is not afraid to call the Son of God, emptied of his Godhead, an 'advocate' (that is, adopted), and in the form of a slave, 'full of grace' [66].

Elipandus of Toledo, Letter to the Bishops of Frankland, extracts (780s)

112   Christ's Adopted Body

> The Spanish monk Beatus of Liebana (d. 798) was one of the most promin-
> ent critics of the adoptionism of Elipandus (111). Elipandus denounced
> Beatus' opposition to adoptionism as heretical to his abbot; Beatus replied
> with a long discussion and condemnation of Elipandus' doctrine. He argues
> that, in order to give a proper account of Christ's mediatorial role, and of
> the Church as the body of Christ, we need to reserve the term 'adopted' for
> the Church. (Cf. 34, 38.)

The unhappy heretic is not aware that Christ is one, God and human being, and is head of his Church, in which, as a human being, he is. And God is the head of Christ, that is, the whole of the divine nature is the head of the human being whom the Son alone took up. The Son, as a human being, is the head of the Church which is joined to this Head. Thus there comes into being the whole Christ, head and body, one person. [. . .]

Only the Son was made a human being, that is, rational soul and flesh. Because of this there are indeed three substances—the Word, the soul, and the flesh—but there is one Christ who is the unique Son, our one Lord Jesus Christ, Only-begotten of God the Father, who was born of the Holy Spirit and the Virgin Mary and who was crucified under Pontius Pilate. He truly and without any falsehood has God as his Father naturally, from whom he has his deity, so that he is, thus, true God, and there is no other God beside him. Equally truly and without falsehood he has for his mother Mary, natur-ally. And there is no other human being beside him.[9] Together with the whole Church which he redeemed with his own blood, he is the one Christ, one *persona* of three substances [cf. 86]. This *persona* is not the Father's nor the Holy Spirit's, but as we have said, the Son's.

Behold the Mediator! The heretics fail to confess that there is no other God beside him, and that together with the whole Church he is one human being, and that it is not the case that the Church is one *persona*, and Christ the human being another *persona*, and the Word another *persona* (so that there would be three *personae*, the Word, the human being, and the Church, just as the Father, the Son, and the Holy Spirit are three *persona*). [Cf. 83.] [. . .]

It is from *him* that believers are called 'lords'—from *him* that they are called 'christs'. He was made servant [39] of the Father so that he might liberate us from a multitude of 'lords', that is, from the multitude of idols, and that we might have as Lord only him who was made for us a servant, that we might be free through him who alone is 'free among the dead' and who leads us to this nobility as well. There is no doubt that the highest nobility is present where there is the servitude of Christ to prove its presence. He became impoverished for us, so that we by his poverty might be made rich [. . .] And what is his poverty, but his humanity? And what are our riches, but his humanity? [. . .]

Christ is the Sun [cf. 220] [. . .] Just as the sun makes the twelve hours in a day—not the other way around—so also Christ makes and chooses his twelve Apostles. They neither made nor chose him [. . .] And thus *those who are chosen* are adoptive sons—not the one who chooses! Still, the one who chose and the ones who were chosen are one day and one light [. . .] This is the one day, that is, Christ and the Church, one *persona*.

Beatus of Liebana, *Against Elipandus*, extracts (c.786)

113   A Christological Vision

Adoptionism (cf. 111) has been called 'the last Christology of the West', but the relative paucity of Christological debate in the remainder of the early medieval period should not be overstated, nor should it be assumed to imply a universal lack of interest in Christological issues. Christological questions continue to crop up in all sorts of unexpected ways. This extract from Hildegard of Bingen (1098–1179), an abbess, is from a book of ecstatic visions, the last place where modern readers would expect to find dogmatic Christology. Hildegard also wrote an exposition of the Athanasian Creed, but the present work, a passionate call to repentance, had a far wider influence. (Cf. 136.)

And then I saw, on the south side of the wall of the building beyond the pillar of the true Trinity, a great and shadowed pillar, which protruded both inside and outside the building; and it was so obscure to my sight that I could not tell its size or height. And between this pillar and the pillar of the true Trinity there was a gap three cubits wide in the wall as mentioned above, only the foundation had been laid. [. . .]

[God explains the vision:]

In a mystical mystery, the pillar you see on the south side of the wall of the building beyond the pillar of the true Trinity signifies the humanity of the Saviour, who was conceived by the Holy Spirit and born of the sweet Virgin, the Son of the Most High; for he is the strong pillar of sanctity and holds up the whole edifice of the Church. His humanity is manifested in the ardent faith of its stones, which are the faithful people who work hard by the goodness of the Supernal Father when the Trinity has been revealed to them.

For when the Trinity in One God was made known to the believing people, the belief also appeared that the incarnate Word of God must be worshipped as true God with the Father and the Holy Spirit in the unity of the divinity of the One True God.

It is a great and shadowed pillar, which protrudes both inside and outside the building. For the great and incomprehensible holiness of the true Incarnation is so obscure to human minds that it cannot be contemplated, except insofar as it can be done by faith. It can be understood in faith and works by those who labour in the divine cult, that is, inside the building; and those who stand idle outside can know it by words and sounds.

And it is so obscure to your sight that you cannot tell its size or height. For my Son came among humans in the mortality of the flesh to undergo death for the people, and thus was in shadow because he was mortal; but he came without any spot of sin, so that his true incarnation exceeds all the power of the human intellect, incomprehensible in the mystical greatness of God's mysteries and incalculable in the might of his divine power.

And between this pillar and the pillar of the true Trinity there is a gap three cubits wide in the wall as mentioned above. This is to say that the incarnate Son of God, who is true God with the Father and the Holy Spirit is now inherent in his members; that is, the faithful people who will be born up till the end of the world and made members of their head through living works as miraculously and symbolically you were shown above. But who, how many and what kind of people they will be in the long ages to come, who will adore the Trinity in the Unity of Divinity with faithful and devout worship resides in the mystery of the ineffable Trinity; for the place of those yet to be born is empty, and the wall of their good works has not yet been built.

But the foundation has been laid, which is to say that they are in God's foreknowledge, and the faith that will save them is already strongly established; and so man must not hope and trust in anyone except God, and never despair of his mercy, since he is the strong foundation of the faithful soul.

Hildegard of Bingen, Scivias III, Vision 8: 'The Pillar of the Humanity of
the Saviour' 1, 9–11, extracts (c.1141–50)

114   Christ's Death a Satisfaction

Anselm of Canterbury (c.1033–1109) was a pivotal figure in medieval theology. In his most influential work, *Cur Deus Homo* (c.1098), he provided emerging feudal society with a theology in its own image. The whole creation is a well-ordered hierarchy, all sin a disturbance of that order, a refusal to give to others what is due to them according to their position in the whole. Redemption is the restoration of balance by the exaction of punishment or a payment in punishment's place (a 'satisfaction'), a punishment proportionate to the position in the hierarchy of the one offended. To this feudal theology Anselm adds one more element which proved seminal in the development of medieval and Reformation theology: merit. Christ graciously pays the satisfaction we owe using the coinage which accrues to him from his innocent actions. (Cf. **158, 223**.)

B Why did God become man, to save man by his death, when it seems that he could have done this in some other way? You have answered this by showing, by many necessary reasons, how it would not have been right for the restoration of human nature to be left undone, and how it could not have been done unless man paid what was owing to God for sin. But the debt was so great that, while man alone owed it, only God could pay it, so that the same person must be both man and God. Thus it was necessary for God to take manhood into the unity of his person, so that he who in his own nature ought to pay and could not should be in a person who could. Then you showed that the man who also was God was to be taken from a virgin, and by the person of the Son of God, and how he could be taken from the sinful mass without sin. Moreover, you have proved most straightforwardly that the life of this man was so sublime, so precious, that it can suffice to pay what is owing for the sins of the whole world, and infinitely more. It now remains, therefore, to be shown how it is paid to God for the sins of men. [. . .]

A Now let us consider, as fully as we can, the great reason why man's salvation follows from his death.

B My heart is struggling toward this. For although I seem to myself to understand it, I want to have the whole structure of the argument outlined by you.

A There is no need to explain what a great gift the Son gave freely.

B That is clear enough.

A You will not suppose that he who freely gives God so great a gift ought to be left unrewarded.

B On the contrary, I see how necessary it is for the Father to reward the Son. Otherwise, he would seem unjust if he were unwilling and powerless if he were unable to reward him; but both these things are foreign to God.

A He who rewards someone either gives what the latter does not have or foregoes what can be required from him. But before the Son did this great work, all that belonged to the Father belonged to him, and he never owed anything that could be remitted to him. What, then, will be given him as a reward, when he is in need of nothing and there is nothing that can be given or forgiven him?

B I see on the one hand that a reward is necessary, and on the other that it is impossible. For it is necessary for God to repay what he owes, and there is no way of making repayment.

A If such a great and merited reward is paid neither to him nor to anyone else, it will seem that the Son performed such a great work in vain.

B It is impious to think this.

A Then it must be paid to someone else, since it cannot be paid to him.

B That inevitably follows.

A If the Son willed to give to another what is owing to himself, could the Father rightly forbid him, or deny it to the other?

B On the contrary, I think that it is both just and necessary for the Father to pay it to anyone to whom the Son wills to give it, because the Son has a right to give what belongs to him, and the Father can only give what he owes him to someone else.

A To whom would it be more fitting for him to assign the fruit and recompense of his death than to those for whose salvation (as truthful reasoning has taught us) he made himself man, and to whom (as we have said) by dying he gave an example of dying for the sake of justice? For they will be his imitators in vain if they do not share in his merit. Or whom will he more justly make heirs of the debt which he does not need, and of the abundance of his own fullness, than his kinsmen and brethren, whom he sees bound by so many great debts, languishing in poverty and deepest misery—so that what they owe for their sins may be forgiven them, and what they need, on account of their sins, may be given them?

B The world can hear nothing more reasonable, nothing more delightful, nothing more desirable. Indeed, I gain such great confidence from this, that already I cannot say how great the joy is that makes my heart leap. For it seems to me that God can repel no man who draws near to him in this name.

Anselm of Canterbury, *Why God Became Man* XVIII–XIX, extracts (1090)

115 Christ's Death the Fount of Love

Peter Abelard's turbulent life (1079–1142) (cf. **96**) did not overwhelm an unwavering commitment to various key philosophical ideas, among which was a strong focus on intention and desire in ethics; it was on the back of this commitment that he developed a doctrine of the Atonement very different from Anselm's (**114**) in a commentary on Paul's Epistle to the Romans. Central to his account is an emphasis upon Christ's example winning human hearts to the love of God.

Now it seems to us that we have been justified by the blood of Christ and reconciled to God in this way: through this unique act of grace manifested to us—in that his Son has taken upon himself our nature and persevered therein in teaching us by word and example even unto death—he has more fully bound us to himself by love; with the result that our hearts should be enkindled by such a gift of divine grace, and true charity should not now shrink from enduring anything for him.

And we do not doubt that the ancient fathers, waiting in faith for this same gift, were aroused to very great love of God in the same way as men of this dispensation of grace, since it is written: 'And they that went before and they that followed cried, saying: "Hosanna to the Son of David" ' [Mark 11: 9], etc. Yet everyone becomes more righteous—by which we mean a greater lover of the Lord—after the Passion of Christ than before, since a realised gift inspires greater love than one which is only hoped for. Wherefore, our redemption through Christ's suffering is that deeper affection in us which not only frees us from slavery to sin, but also wins for us the true liberty of sons of God, so that we do all things out of love rather than fear—love to him who has shown us such grace that no greater can be found, as he himself asserts, saying, 'Greater love than this no man hath, that a man lay down his life for his friends' [John 15: 13]. Of this love the Lord says elsewhere, 'I am come to cast fire on the earth, and what will I, but that it blaze forth?' [Luke 12: 49.] So does he bear witness that he came for the express purpose of spreading this true liberty of love amongst men.

Peter Abelard, *Exposition of the Epistle to the Romans* II, on Rom. 3: 19–26, extract (12th century)

116 Against Adoption

Peter Lombard (*c.*1100–60) was a teacher at the Cathedral School in Paris, and, at the very end of his life, bishop of that city. He wrote four books of 'Sentences' (on the Trinity, on Creation and sin, on the Incarnation and virtues, and on the sacraments and last things), textbooks of theology with thousands of quotations from the Latin Fathers and from John of Damascus (cf. **107**). After the Fourth Lateran Council (cf. **156**), the *Sentences* became the standard primer of Catholic theology for much of the medieval period.

Whether Christ, as Man, is an Adopted Son [cf. **111–12**]

If it is asked whether Christ is an adopted son, as man, or in some other way, we reply that Christ is not an adopted son in any way, but only a natural Son. For he is a Son by nature, not by the grace of adoption. [. . .]

Moreover he is not an adopted son, because he did not first exist and then become adopted as son, as we are spoken of as adopted sons in that when we were born we were 'sons of wrath' but have been made 'sons of God' through grace. There never was a time when Christ was not a son and therefore he is not an adopted son.

But against this one can argue thus: If Christ is the son of man, that is of a virgin, it is either by grace or by nature, or by both. If this is so by nature, then it is either by divine nature or by human nature; but not by divine nature, therefore either by human nature or else he is not by nature the son of man. If it is not by nature, then by grace alone; and indeed, if by human nature, not thereby less through grace. If, therefore, he is the son of the virgin by grace, he seems to be an adopted son, so that the same man is a natural Son of the Father and an adopted son of the virgin.

To this it can be said that Christ is the son of the virgin by nature, or naturally, or naturally and by grace. He is not, however, the adopted son of the virgin, since it is not through adoption, but through union, that he is called the son of the virgin. For he is called son of the virgin in that in the virgin he received a man into the unity of a person; and this was by grace, not by nature.[10]

Thus Augustine [cf. 38] in *On John* says: 'That the Only-begotten is equal to the Father is not from grace but from nature. However that a man was assumed into the unity of person of the only-begotten, is from grace, not from nature' [74.3]. Christ, therefore, is the adopted son neither of God nor of man, but the Son of God naturally and the son of man naturally and by grace.

Augustine shows that he is the son of man naturally in the book *To Peter on the Faith*: 'He, namely God, who is naturally the only-begotten Son of God the Father, was made the son of man naturally' [actually Fulgentius of Ruspe, *Ad Petrum* 2. 14].

Moreover, that he is not an adopted son, and yet is son by grace, is proved by the following testimonies.

Jerome [cf. 56], in *On the Epistle to the Ephesians*, says: 'It is written about Christ Jesus, that he was always with the Father, and that the paternal will never, as it were, preceded him' [1.5]; 'and he was son by nature, we by adoption. He never was not a son; we, before we were, were predestined, and then we received the Spirit of adoption, because we believed in the Son of God' [1. 5].

Hilary too, in Book III of *On the Trinity*, says: 'The Lord saying, "Glorify thy Son," is witness that he is Son not only by name, but also by property. We are sons of God, but not like this Son. For he is true Son, in the strict sense, by Origin, not by adoption; by truth, not by name; by nativity, not by creation' [III. 11].

Augustine, in *On John*, also says: 'We are sons by grace, not by nature; the Only-begotten is by nature, not by grace. Does this also refer to the man in the Son himself? Yes, certainly' [82.4].

Ambrose [cf. 48] too, in Book I of *On the Trinity*, says: 'Christ is Son, not through adoption but through nature. We are called sons through adoption, but he is Son through the truth of nature' [cf. Ambrose, *De Fide* 1. 19. 126].

These statements make it evident that Christ is not a Son by the grace of adoption. That is the grace understood when Augustine asserts that he is not Son by grace; for by the grace, not of adoption, but rather of union, the Son of God is the son of man, and conversely.

Peter Lombard, *Sentences*, book III, Distinction x, Ch. 2 (1155–8)

IV. The Eucharist

There was more debate in the West about the Eucharist than about Christology proper. In the ninth century a Benedictine monk called Paschasius Radbertus (*c*.790–865) wrote one of the first theological discussions of the nature of the eucharistic elements, and inevitably provoked a strong reaction with his radically realistic views. In this controversy and elsewhere, the precise role of the Eucharist in mediating the presence of Jesus was probed and analysed.

117 Tasting Flesh and Blood

> Joseph the Visionary (b. *c*. 710), was born into a Zoroastrian (cf. **122**) family, captured, and sold into slavery in Iraq. There he became a Christian and, on gaining his freedom, became a monk. A world away from the Latin controversies of the ninth century, Joseph's understanding of the presence of Christ in the Eucharist is no less robustly expressed in this prayer for use before the Eucharist. (Cf. **36, 156, 194**.)

To you be praise, first-born of Being, exalted and full of awe, for, by the sacrifice of your body, you have effected salvation for the world.

O Christ, Son from the Holy Father, to you do I pray in awe at this time; of you, Lord, do I ask your will and beseech your compassion, that my whole person may be made holy through your grace, and that the enemy's constraint upon me may be rendered ineffective.

Purify my understanding in your compassion, so that my hands may stretch out in purity to receive your holy and fearful body and blood. Cleanse my hidden mind with the hyssop of your grace, for I draw near to the Holy of Holies of your mysteries. Wash from me all understanding that belongs to the flesh, and may an understanding which belongs to your Spirit be mingled within my soul. Cause to reside in me a faith that beholds your mysteries, so that I may behold your sacrifice as you are, and not as I am. Create eyes in me, and so may I see with your eyes, for I cannot see with my own eyes. May my mind travel inwards towards the hiddenness of your sacrifice, just as you have travelled out into the open and been conjoined to your mysteries.

At this moment may I be totally forgetful of myself, and remain utterly unmindful of my own person. May every bodily image be wiped away from my mind's eye, and may you alone be depicted before the eye of my mind. And now, when your Spirit descends from heaven upon your mysteries, may I ascend in spirit from earth to heaven. At this time when your power is mingled in with the bread, may my life be commingled with your spiritual life. At this moment when the wine is changed and becomes your blood, may my thoughts be inebriated with the commixture of your love. At this time when your Lamb is lying slain upon the altar, may sin cease and be utterly removed from all my limbs. At this moment when your body is being offered as a sacrifice to your Father, may I too be a holy sacrifice to you and to him who sent you, and may my prayer ascend before you together with the prayer of your priest.

Provide me with hidden hands so that with them I may carry the fiery coal. Create in me a pure heart so that your holy power may reside within me, so that, through the power of your Spirit I may in a spiritual fashion inhale your salvation. Fashion in me, Lord, eyes within my eyes, so that with new eyes I may contemplate your divine sacrifice. Lord, may I not see the outward aspect of what I am now to receive, but hold me worthy to see and recognise, as did Simon the fisherman who was called blessed for his faith [cf. 11]. Lord, may I taste not just the bread in your body, or just the cup in your blood: give me faith so that I may see your body and not the bread, and drink your living blood from the cup. Grant me that spiritual palate which is able to taste your blood and not the wine [cf. 194].

Joseph the Visionary, Prayer for Use before Communion, extract (8th century)

118   The Figure of a Mystery

> Ratramnus of Corbie (d. 868) was one of those who wrote against the realist views of the Eucharist expressed by Paschasius Radbertus. His own views have had a chequered history since then, being successively condemned at the Synod of Vercelli (1050), appealed to by Reformers and Catholics alike in the sixteenth century, banned, and reinstated. (Cf. 156, 172–6.)

While certain of the faithful say that in the mystery of the body and the blood of Christ, daily celebrated in the church, nothing takes place under a figure, under a hidden symbol, but it is performed with a naked manifestation of truth itself, others bear witness, however, that these elements are contained in the figure of a mystery, and that it is one thing which appears to the bodily sense and another which faith beholds. No small divergence is to be distinguished between them. And though the apostle writes to the faithful that they should all hold the same views and say the same things, and that no schism should appear among them, yet they are divided by great schism when they utter different views concerning the mystery of Christ's body and blood. [. . .]

If that mystery is not performed in any figurative sense, then it is not rightly given the name of mystery, since that cannot be called a mystery in which there is nothing hidden, nothing removed from the physical senses, nothing covered over with any veil. But that bread which through the ministry of the priest comes to be Christ's body exhibits one thing outwardly to human sense, and it proclaims another thing inwardly to the minds of the faithful. Outwardly it has the shape of bread which it had before, the colour is exhibited, the flavour is received, but inwardly something far different, much more precious, much more excellent, becomes known, because something heavenly, something divine, that is, Christ's body, is revealed, which is not beheld, or received, or consumed by the fleshly senses but in the gaze of the believing soul.

The wine also, which through priestly consecration becomes the sacrament of Christ's blood, shows, so far as the surface goes, one thing; inwardly it contains something else. What else is to be seen on the surface than the substance of wine? Taste it, and it has the flavour of wine; smell it, and it has the aroma of wine; look at it, and the wine colour is visible. But if you think of it inwardly, it is now to the minds of believers the liquid of Christ's blood, and when tasted, it has flavour; when looked at, it has appearance; and when smelled, it is proved to be such. Since no one can deny that this is so, it is clear that that bread and wine are Christ's body and blood in a figurative sense. For as to outward appearance, the aspect of flesh is not recognised in that bread, nor in that wine is the liquid blood shown, when however, they are, after the mystical consecration, no longer called bread or wine, but Christ's body and blood.

Ratramnus of Corbie, *Christ's Body and Blood* 2, 9–10 (9th century)

119 Making Christ's Body

Feodosiy (Theodosius) of Pechersk (d. 1074) was a monk who co-founded a monastery in a system of caves near Kiev. His biography was written by another Kievan monk, Nestor the Chronicler. This passage illustrates a more popular approach to the Eucharist.

When [blessed Theodosius] saw that often Mass could not be celebrated because there was no altar bread, he was greatly distressed and resolved humbly that he would devote himself to this work. And he kept his resolution. He began to bake altar bread and sell it; some of the money thus earned he gave to the poor, and some he kept in order to buy more wheat, which he would grind with his own hands. And in this manner his work of baking the loaves continued. Now this was according to God's will, so that the church might be provided with pure altar bread made by the hands of a chaste and innocent youth. He carried on the work for two years or more.

Boys of his own age, inspired by the enemy, ridiculed him for performing such a task. But the saint suffered all this joyfully and without complaint.

Now the enemy, who hates all that is good, seeing the humility of the God-enlightened youth triumphing over him, knew no peace; in the attempt to divert the boy from his task, he persuaded the mother that she must prevent Theodosius from pursuing his activities. The mother, who could not bear to have her son the object of ridicule, said to him gently, 'I beg of you, my son, give up this work. You are bringing disgrace upon your family; indeed it is not right for a young man to be engaged in such work.' Good Theodosius replied humbly: 'Listen to me. Our Lord Jesus Christ became poor and humbled himself, offering himself as an example, so that we should humble ourselves in his name. He suffered insults, was spat upon and beaten, for our salvation; how just it is, then, that we should suffer in order to gain Christ. As to my work, listen to me. When Jesus Christ sat with his disciples at the Last Supper, he took bread, and having blessed it, broke it, and gave it to his disciples, saying, "Take ye, and eat. This is my body." If Our Lord called bread his body, should I not rejoice that God lets me share in the making of his body?'

Nestor the Chronicler, *Life of Theodosius*, extract (12th century)

Christ Beyond Christianity

In the Byzantine and early medieval period Jewish theology and philosophy blossomed, but (understandably, given the treatment of Jews at Christian hands), there are no strong signs of a reassessment of the place of Jesus of Nazareth. Further East, encounter with the Zoroastrians of the Persian Sassanian Empire (3rd to 7th centuries) led to some debate about the significance of Jesus. The major non-Christian power from the seventh century onwards, however, was Islam, and the attention paid to Jesus by Islamic writers was rich and varied.

I. Jewish

This period was one in which Jewish theology flourished. At one end of the period stands the continuing work on the Babylonian Talmud; at the other end stands the great Moses Maimonides (1135–1204), one of the greatest Jewish thinkers. However, despite an Edict of Tolerance (*c.*600) under Gregory the Great, the treatment Jews received at Christian hands worsened. (Cf. **53–8, 161–2, 225, 242, 338–49**.)

120   Discrediting Jesus

> The *Tol'doth Yeshu* was extremely popular among medieval Jews, circulating in multiple versions. We do not know quite when or where it was written, but its purpose is reasonably clear.

A man of the house of David, resident at Bethlehem, after the fashion of his time espoused to himself the daughter of a neighbour of his. He was a man honoured by all who knew him intimately as one of the pious. He was characterised by fine respect for the commandments of his ancestral religion. He habitually revealed that reverence for God which in Jewish devotion is the natural climax of true piety. She, too, was looked on as a most fitting partner for so devout a man. She was held in high esteem as a very respectable and most humble-minded young woman. At the close of one Sabbath day, a very handsome young man accosted her. She took him for the man to whom she was espoused. Very much against her own inclination she submitted herself to him. She wondered, however, at such conduct on the part of one who had had a great reputation for piety. When later she was actually face to face with him, she expressed her astonishment at what had taken place that Sabbath. She was very soon disillusioned, and the suspicions of her husband-to-be fell on the very man who had been so attracted toward her as to do her so great a wrong. He revealed his suspicions to his rabbi, but the good man in his sorry plight was quite unable to prove his case against this assailant. In desperation and shame he took to flight. In due course a son was born—Jesus.

In many respects this child was fortunate. He was given quite exceptional opportunities of becoming acquainted with the Law of his people. He had as his teacher a scholar of more than usual ability and distinction. But he turned out in many respects very strange—as the children of illicit union so often do. In some respects he was a real problem to those who were most intimate with him. In his personal habits he made himself offensive to the official exponents of the Law of his folk. In particular, he indulged in such expositions of ancient Scripture as were peculiarly distasteful to them. At length these, in their very disgust, dubbed him *bastard* and *son of uncleanness*. This led on painfully to the confession of his mother, that he was in fact both of these at once, since his birth was due to the assault of one other than the man to whom she was betrothed, at the very time of her uncleanness. The rabbi who had been entrusted with the suspicions of the poor wronged man who had fled, thereupon recalled what his devout disciple had so long ago confided to him.

This Jesus afterward made his way to Jerusalem. In the Temple there, by trickery he gained knowledge of the Ineffable Name. This knowledge he used for the evil purpose of working wonders as a sorcerer or magician. Very soon this baneful activity on his part attracted the attention of the authorities. They held him guilty of acts of sorcery; they thought him a wicked beguiler of the common people. Still he persisted, and even began to impress favourably some of those who at first were condemning him. He moved his quarters from the South to Upper Galilee. Here his miracles drew great crowds, who followed him from place to place. There was nothing left for it but for someone to meet him on his own ground and to exceed him in his power of using the Ineffable Name. Very heroically one of the Sages became his serious competitor in the matter of doing signs and wonders before the people. At last he so far excelled Jesus in this art that Jesus became discredited, and ere long was imprisoned under sentence of death.

Before this in Bethlehem, his native place, he had succeeded in gathering round him a group of young Jews. To these young men he had presented his claim to be the Anointed, the Son of God. These and others who afterwards joined their company, as his disciples, came to believe that whatever might happen to him was just what God had willed should come upon his appointed Messiah. To their way of thinking the ancient prophets of their people had made clear beforehand everything that was to befall him. Such, too, was the enthusiasm of these disciples of his that they took the field on his behalf. They fought and rescued him out of the hands of those who had decided on his execution.

Once liberated, Jesus took flight first to Antioch. From thence he made his way to Egypt—there, if possible, to learn the art of working wonders by magic spells. But his old opponent in the use of the Ineffable Name in magic, to whose success against him he had owed his arrest and condemnation, wrought on among his disciples, and at last succeeded in robbing him of the spell of the Name. Jesus thereupon made up his mind to visit Jerusalem again, and there learn it afresh. His powerful rival gave due warning to the authorities of the Holy City, and magic suggestions for his arrest. When the opportunity came, these were carried out successfully. Jesus and his followers were in the habit of dressing in garments of the same colour. Consequently Jesus could not very easily be picked out from among them. His followers, too, had sworn that they would not say anything to any outside their number, such as would assist enemies in distinguishing their leader from themselves. His rival, however, was quite equal to surmounting this difficulty. He knew quite well which was Jesus. According to the arrangement previously come to, one day when Jesus and some of his disciples were in the courts of the Temple, this man went right up to Jesus and made his bow before him. To those near by and watching Jesus was in that fashion pointed out clearly. So his arrest.

Condemnation to death followed. Since also Jesus had by the Ineffable Name put under a curse any tree that would receive his body, when he was to be hanged, none was to be found that would bear him. As, however, the cabbage stem was not included among trees, and so was left uncursed, it was available for the purpose. On the eve of the Passover they took Jesus and hanged him on a cabbage stem. On the Sabbath's eve the body was taken down, as the Law required, and was buried. Afterward the body was taken out of the tomb by the gardener, who threw it into the garden's water-channel, where the water flowed over it. His disciples, on being unable later to find the body in the tomb, made it public that Jesus had been raised from the dead. This report, being believed in high quarters, looked like bringing swift punishment on those who had instigated what now was coming to look like the murder of the Lord's Anointed. The Jews were in great distress at this prospect and a fast was declared. Finally, by the good providence of God, the dead body of Jesus was actually found in the garden, in the very spot where it had been thrown by the gardener. The Jewish authorities ordered its removal, and to expose the deception publicly they had it dragged through the streets tied to the tail of a horse. The disciples of Jesus fled, and ultimately formed themselves into a community with religious rites and ceremonies distinct from those of the rest of the Jews.

Anonymous, *Tol'doth Yeshu* (date unknown)

121 Disputing Christ

Wecelin was a Christian cleric in Rhenish Franconia, possibly in Mainz, who converted to Judaism in 1006. He wrote a letter, using the typically acerbic polemic of his day, defending his repudiation of Christianity. The text given below is quite possibly a summary of the letter's main points, rather than the letter itself. A reply was written by a certain Henry.

Wecelin's Letter

Why do you contradict the truth, fool? Read Habakkuk the prophet, in whose book God has said: 'I am God and do not change' [cf. Mal. 3: 6]. If according to your accursed faith he did change and was produced by mingling of a woman, then the beginning of his words would not be the truth. The Lord has said to Moses: 'No man shall see me and be able to live' [Exod 33: 20]. Which son of man has he passed over? For the prophet David says: 'Put not your trust in princes, in children of men, in whom there is no salvation' [Ps. 146: 3]. And Ezekiel: 'Cursed is the man who trusts in man and makes flesh his arm; for he shall be like a tamarisk in the desert and not see the fruit when good shall come' [cf. Jer. 17: 5–6] What is it you are barking back at me, animal? Which son of man has he passed over? Surely not Peter, John or Martin or the other evil spirits whom you call saints?

In all places it says 'God of Israel' and not 'God of the nations'. What is your explanation of that? David says, 'The Lord will remember his covenant forever, the word he commanded to a thousand generations, the covenant he made with Abraham, his oath to Isaac' [Ps. 105: 8–9] That is to say his Holy Law, including circumcision, that he gave to Moses, his servant.

Henry's Letter

To reply to the calumny, unbelieving Jew, that you just now have vomited forth from your blasphemous mouth against Christ and his saints, would be easy for anyone instructed in Christian combat, were it not simpler to be able to soften stones than cleave your hearts asunder to receive the truth. For in spite of the fact that you recognised him, with cleft hearts, as your creator, when he died, you still persist with insensible hearts, although shattered and destroyed, in the obstinacy of your deep-rooted iniquity. Though the mouth of them that speak wicked things has been stopped by God's coeternal wisdom through which the world was miraculously established and even more miraculously transformed, and though your iniquity has lied to itself and it is manifest through the whole world and through the words of the prophets and examples of the saints how cursed the blind irreverence of your disbelief is and how glorified the weakness of mortality assumed by Christ, yet you Jews until now do not desist, in the stubborn wickedness of your malice, from your machinations, that is murmuring with infamous arrogance in an attempt to refute the Christian religion and taking issue once again with the erect and flourishing Church, using examples of the fathers and the words of the prophets, although you are already entirely beaten and wholly over-thrown. Therefore we must attack you with the help-giving wisdom of God, God's Word, the Son of God, but first we must make our hearts stony with him as the stone that the prophet Daniel, whom you regard as your prophet, but who is actually ours, saw rolling down the mountain without human hands and fill the whole earth. Of whom David also says: 'My heart has uttered a good word' [Ps. 45: 1] and also: 'The Lord has spoken to me: you are my son, today have I begotten you' [Ps. 2: 7], and even: 'You have made everything in wisdom.' And Solomon: 'The Lord has possessed me in the beginning of his ways' [Pr 8: 22].

Wecelin and Henry, Correspondence, extract (c.1006)

II. Zoroastrian

Zoroastrianism, which originated in the sixth century BC, has sometimes been held to be a strong influence on early Christianity, although this now seems improbable. Christianity was first forced into sustained contact with it after the third century AD, when the growth of the Persian Empire under the Zoroastrian Sassanids made the religion Christianity's strongest Eastern neighbour.

122 The Implausibility of Incarnation

Mardān Farukh was a ninth-century Zoroastrian apologist who wrote against Judaism, Christianity, and Manichaeism, in order to dispel the doubts of the 'new learner'.

There are some [. . .] who say that the Messiah is the Sacred Being himself. Yet it would be very strange if the mighty Sacred Being, the maintainer and cherisher of all existence, became of human nature, and went into the womb of a woman who was a Jew [cf. 60, 70]. To leave the lordly throne, the sky and earth, the celestial sphere and other similar objects of his providence and protection, and fall hidden into a polluted and straitened place, and, finally, deliver his own body to scourging, execution on the tree, and the hands of enemies, with much brutality and lawlessness beside the death arranged by them as well!

[However,] if they speak of his having been inside the womb of a woman in the sense that the sacred being exists in every place, then being inside the womb of a woman, as part of existence in every place, is not more problem-atic than being in any very polluted and very fetid place. Further, the faultiness of speaking of the supreme being as having the property of being in any place whatsoever is manifold, because it would be strange to speak of anything whatsoever existing beyond the presence of the sacred being.

As to their saying that the death and execution on the tree were accepted by him, as a yoke, for the sake of demonstrating the resurrection to mankind, that implies—if it were not possible for him to demonstrate the resurrection to mankind, except through that disgrace, death and brutal treatment of himself—that his omnipotence failed. Or, when no opponent and adversary whatever arose against him, why can people not be convinced with the sort of clear knowledge which is imparted by seeing the resurrection, without any necessity for this mode of demonstrating it—brutally, disgracefully, distressingly, and through the will of his enemies? Furthermore, if that death were willingly accepted by him, as a yoke [. . .], then it is unreasonable to make a woeful outcry and pour curses on his executioners, and to think wrathfully of those Jews. Rather, instead of instigating curses and imprecations of woe against them, it is fitting for them to be considered worthy of reward for that deed!

Mardān Farukh, *Sikand-Gūmānīk Vigār* ('Doubt-Dispelling Explanation') xv. 31–45 (9th century)

III. Islamic

Islam has a strong but complex relationship to Christianity. Emerging from an area and an era imbued with various popular forms of Christianity, Muhammad believed that he had been given the final revelation of God's will, in a form which called into question the debased coinage of Christianity, while nevertheless drawing on some of those popular stories and themes. Jesus played a significant positive role in Islamic belief, and there is a sizeable body of early Islamic literature concerning him.

123 The Qur'ān

Muhammad (c.570–632) claimed that the Qur'ān was the pure word of God, delivered to him by the Angel Gabriel. The material in it on Jesus accords with various sources in the Christian popular apocryphal literature, but propounds a distinctive line about Jesus' significance.

[The People of the Book have incurred divine displeasure] in that they said (in boast) 'We killed Christ Jesus the son of Mary, the messenger of Allah'—but they killed him not, nor crucified him, but so it was made to appear to them; and those who differ therein are full of doubts, with no certain knowledge, but only conjecture to follow. For, of a surety, they killed him not—nay, Allah raised him up unto himself, and Allah is exalted in power and wise. [Cf. **16, 68, 135.**] [. . .]

Allah will say: O Jesus, son of Mary! Recount my favour to thee and to thy mother. Behold, I strengthened thee with the Holy Spirit, so that thou didst speak to the people in childhood and in maturity. Behold, I taught there wisdom, the Law and the Gospel, and behold! thou makest out of clay, as it were, the figure of a bird, by my leave; and thou breathest into it, and it becometh a bird by my leave [Cf. **23**]; and thou healest those born blind, and the lepers, by my leave [Cf. **8**]. And behold, thou bringest forth the dead by my leave. And behold, I did restrain the children of Israel from violence to thee when thou didst show them the clear signs, and the unbelievers among them said, 'This is nothing but evident magic.' [. . .]

And behold, Allah will say, 'O Jesus the son of Mary! Didst thou say unto men, "Worship me and my mother as gods in derogation of Allah"?' He will say, 'Glory to thee. Never could I say what I had no right to say. Had I said such a thing, thou wouldst indeed have known it. Thou knowest what is in my heart, though I know not what is in thine. For thou knowest in full all that is hidden. Never said I to them aught except what thou didst command me. To say, to wit, "Worship Allah, my Lord and your Lord"; and I was a witness over them whilst I dwelt amongst them; when thou didst take me up thou wast the watcher over them, and thou art a witness to all things.' [. . .]

And they say, 'Allah most gracious has begotten offspring.' Glory to him! They are but servants raised to honour. They speak not before he speaks, and they act in all things by his command. He knows what is before them, and what is behind them, and they offer no intercession except for those who are acceptable, and they stand in awe and reverence of his glory. If any of them should say, 'I am a god beside him,' such a one we should reward with hell: thus do we reward those who do wrong.

Qur'ān 4: 157–8; 5: 110; 5: 116–7; 21: 26–9

124   Muhammad and Christ

Al-Bukhari (816–78) and his student Muslim (824–83) between them collected many thousands of *hadith*, traditional stories about the life of the prophet Muhammad.

Abu Huraira reported Allah's Messenger, peace and blessings of Allah be upon him, as saying, 'I am the nearest of kin to Jesus, son of Mary, in this world and the next. The prophets are brothers, sons of one father by co-wives. Their mothers are different, but their religion is one. There has been no prophet between us.'

Imam al-Bukhari and Sahih Muslim, Hadith (9th century)

125   Christ and Sufism

Sufism, which developed in the eighth century, emphasizes the mystical side of Islam, the paths to spiritual insight which it fosters. Al-Hujwiri (d. 1071) wrote one of the first great systematic expositions of Sufism in Persian. [Cf. 126.]

Sufism is founded on eight qualities exemplified in eight apostles: the generosity of Abraham, who sacrificed his son; the acquiescence of Ishmael, who submitted to the command of God and gave up his dear life; the patience of Job, who patiently endured the affliction of worms and the jealousy of the Merciful; the symbolism of Zacharias, to whom God said, 'Thou shalt not speak unto men for three days save by signs' and again to the same effect, 'When he called upon his Lord with a secret invocation'; the strangerhood of John, who was a stranger in his own country and an alien to his own kin amongst whom he lived; the pilgrimhood of Jesus, who was so detached therein from worldly things that he kept only a cup and a comb—the cup he threw away when he saw a man drinking water in the palms of his hands, and the comb likewise when he saw another man using his fingers instead of a toothpick; the wearing of wool by Moses, whose garment was woollen; and the poverty of Mohammed, to whom God Almighty sent the key of all the treasures that are upon the face of the earth, saying: 'Lay no trouble on thyself, but procure every luxury by means of these treasures'; and he answered: 'O Lord, I desire them not; keep me one day full-fed and one day hungry.' These are very excellent principles of conduct.

'Al' B. 'Uthmān Al-Jullāb' Al-Hujw'r', *The Kashf al-Mahjūb* III, extract (11th century)

126   The Wisdom of Jesus

Another great Sufi author, al-Ghazali (1058–1128), was a prolific scholar. These extracts are from his greatest work, in which he expounded the whole of Islam from a Sufi perspective. [Cf. 125.]

When Jesus was born, the demons came to Satan, and said: 'The idols have been overturned.'" He said, 'This is a mere accident that has occurred; keep still.' Then he flew till he had gone over both hemispheres, and found nothing. After that he found Jesus the son of Mary already born, with the angels surrounding him. He returned to the demons and said, 'A prophet was born yesterday; no woman ever conceived or bare a child without my presence save this one. Hope not, therefore, that the idols will be worshipped after this night, so attack mankind through haste and thoughtlessness.' [. . .]

Jesus was asked, 'Who taught you?' He answered, 'No one taught me. I saw that the ignorance of the fool was a shame, and I avoided it.' [. . .]

Jesus said, 'Devotion is of ten parts. Nine of them consist in silence, and one in solitude.' [. . .]

Malik, son of Dinar, said, 'Jesus one day walked with his apostles, and they passed by the carcass of a dog. The apostles said, "How foul is the smell of this dog!" But Jesus said, "How white are its teeth!"' [. . .]

It is recorded that one day Jesus was sore troubled by the rain and thunder and lightning, and began to seek a shelter. His eye fell upon a tent hard by, but when he came there, finding a woman inside, he turned away from it. Then he noticed a cave in a mountain, but when he came there, there was a lion there. Laying his hand upon the lion, he said, 'My God; you have given each thing a resting place, but to me you have given none!' Then God revealed to him, 'Your resting place is in the abode of my mercy, that I may wed you on the day of judgment . . . and make your bridal feast four thousand years, of which each day is like a lifetime in this present world; and that I may command a herald to proclaim, "Where are they that fast in this world? Come to the bridal feast of Jesus, who fasted in this world!"'

Al-Ghazali, *Revival of the Religious Sciences* III. 28, 52, 87, 108, 153; iv. 120, extracts (12th century)

PART 3

Later Medieval and Renaissance: 1209–1516

The Eastern empire had been fatally weakened in 1204 by the soldiers of the Fourth Crusade; from that time on it dwindled in size and power, clinging on to a precarious existence until its final collapse in 1453. The Eastern voice in this section is correspondingly weaker, and more sporadic, emerging only in a few men like Gregory of Sinai (**151**) and Theoleptos of Philadelphia (**150**).

In the Western Church the beginning of the thirteenth century was a turbulent time. Society was moving towards a new coherence with the emergence of a feudal order; the institutional strength of the Church was at its peak, with the immensely powerful Innocent III on the papal throne, spreading his authoritative fingers ever further into the business of European rulers; yet the twelfth century and the beginning of the thirteenth saw the emergence or growth of many disruptive radical movements on the fringes of the mainstream Church, groups such as the Cathars and Waldensians. Three of the most important achievements of Innocent III's career were, in one way or another, responses to the threat of these groups: the Lateran Council was convoked in 1215 (**156**) to condemn heresy and clarify the definition of true doctrine; the Dominican order of preachers dedicated to converting the heretics was founded; and, most importantly of all, the order of the 'little brothers' was recognized, perhaps largely in the hope that it would provide a respectable and controllable alternative to the heretical groups. That order, dedicated to poverty and simplicity, was founded in 1209 by Francis of Assisi (**127, 138, 145, 155**), and the friars minor, or Franciscans, changed the face of the Christian world. The face of Christ that we meet in the later medieval period is very often a Franciscan face.

The monastic orders also found room for another set of potentially disruptive, often excluded, voices: women. In the late medieval period women visionaries and mystics begin to make themselves heard, making their own fresh and powerful contributions to the medieval imagination. Whether it be in visions of the Passion of Christ (**134**), in devotion to Christ as mother (**152**), or in intense devotion to the body of Christ (**157**), the blood of Christ (**149**), or the sacred heart of Christ (**159**), the image of Christ which emerges from the later medieval West is often the embodied and abused Christ imagined by these women.

The monastic world also continued to be the primary home of scholasticism. Often portrayed as dry and hair-splitting, scholasticism at its best was the product of lively debate between opinion and counter-opinion, its dynamism captured in forms which pitted voice against voice, idea against idea, using logical distinctions and clarifications as the means by which these diverse authorities could be woven into a capacious and coherent whole (158). Of course, the question arises whether the Christ of scholasticism, the Christ of a thousand minute questions and qualifications, has any positive connection to the Jesus of Francis of Assisi, or the Jesus of the medieval women mystics—but the picture of an unbridgeable gulf between the two, or between the intellectual Dominicans and the passionate Franciscans, is one we should not accept too hastily (compare, for instance, 132 and 133); too quick a negative answer denies the possibility that, however rigorous and complex the intellectual machinery became, scholasticism was still the understanding sought by a rich and living faith.

Waves of reform and radicalism continued to break against the medieval Church, some erupting at or beyond the fringes of the Church, and some finding a place among the proliferating religious orders, and becoming part of the mainstream (148, 154). However, the main change which began to roll across the West at the end of the medieval period was not identifiable as a single movement, certainly not containable within a single order. The Renaissance was rather the slow percolation of new philosophical, scientific, political, artistic, and theological ideas and practices from cradles in rich merchant cities like Florence, spreading northward across the continent. We shall meet, briefly, an explicitly Renaissance Christ—a Christ whose story has been retold with the help of the rediscovered classical forms which fuelled so much of the Renaissance (137). The effect of Renaissance thinking was wider and more subtle than this, however—and we shall see its effects emerging only gradually over the following centuries.

Section A

Following Christ

Most divisions of history into distinct periods are in large part arbitrary, but it is possible to detect a distinctive flavour in the devotion of the later centuries of the medieval period in the West. We find a renewed concentration on the lowly birth and harsh death of Jesus of Nazareth; we find a richer flourishing of meditation designed to guide and shape the believer into conformity to and love for Christ; and we find a sterner concentration on the imitation of Christ as the shape of austere Christian living.

I. Remembrance

There is often, in the telling of the story of Jesus in the later medieval period, a particularly zealous attention to the humility and humiliation of Christ in his Passion and his birth, a zeal inflamed pre-eminently by Francis of Assisi. However, the story of Jesus took other forms as well, moulded to the rhythms of other cultures and circumstances—whether the poetry of popular drama, the sharpness of Islamic folk tales, or the erudition of Renaissance literary exercises.

127 Bethlehem at Greccio

The thirteenth century was brightly illuminated by Francis of Assisi (1181/2–1226) and his friars minor, members of monastic communities dedicated to poverty and simplicity (cf. **138, 145, 155**). A wealthy merchant's son who gave up everything for a life of prayer and preaching, Francis's impact is hard to overstate. The intensity and popular appeal of his devotion to Christ is illustrated by this incident from 1223, described in an extract from the earliest biography of Francis (1228), by Thomas of Celano (c.1190–1260). (Cf. **1, 99, 244–7**.)

There dwelt at Greccio a man named John whom Francis loved with special affection, because, having been a man of noble and honourable position in his town, he had trampled on nobility of the flesh, and followed after nobility of the mind. This man did blessed Francis send for about fifteen days before the Nativity of the Lord, and said to him: 'If thou wilt that we celebrate the present festival of the Lord at Greccio, make haste and diligently prepare what I tell thee. For I would make memorial of that child who was born in Bethlehem, and in some sort behold with bodily eyes his infant hardships: how he lay in a manger on the hay, with the ox and the ass standing by.'

When the good and faithful man heard it, he made haste and prepared in the aforesaid place all the things that Francis had told him of . . . . The holy man came, found all things ready, and rejoiced. The manger was prepared, with the hay; the ox and the ass had been brought in. The people came together, the brethren sang praises to God. The saint of God stood before the manger, full of sighs, overcome with pity, and filled with wondrous joy. The solemnities of mass were celebrated over the manger . . . and the holy man of God with sonorous voice chanted the Gospel, and then preached to the people who stood around, uttering words sweet as honey concerning the birth of the poor king and the little town of Bethlehem.

Thomas of Celano, *First Life of St. Francis* 84–5, extracts (1228)

128   Gifts of the Magi

In the later medieval period mystery plays were one popular form in which Gospel stories (particularly, but not exclusively, Passion stories) were told. They were quasi-liturgical pageants in which local guilds or other groups would stage elaborate open-air performances drawn from a stock of biblical or hagiographic themes. In this play from the Chester Mystery Cycle the three magi explain the gifts which they have brought for the infant Jesus. For an explanation of archaic words, see the phrases in italics to the right. (Cf. **313**.)

1ST KING	'King of Jews' we shall him call;	
	therefore of me have he shall—	*from*
	that am his subject and his thrall—	*servant*
	gold, or I pass.	*before; depart*
	For in our land is the manner	*custom*
	to approach no king near	
	bout dainty gifts rich and dear	*without; fine*
	after his dignity.	*according to his noble rank*
	And for a king, gold clean and clear	*pure*
	is most commendable. Therefore now here	
	to relieve him in this manner	*help; way*
	he shall have that of me.	
	Also it seems by this place	
	that little treasure his mother has.	
	Therefore to help her in this case	*situation*
	gold shall be my present.	

2ND KING   And I will offer through God's grace
           incense that noble savour has.   *perfume*
           Stink of the stable it shall waste,   *disperse*
           thereas they be lent.   *where; placed*

3RD KING   And myrrh is best my offering to be:
           to anoint him, as thinks me—   *it seems to me*
           the child's members, head and knee   *limbs*
           and other limbs all.
           Thus shall we honour him all three
           with things that falls to his degree,   *befit his rank*
           touching manhood and deity.   *pertaining to humanity*
           These gifts will well befall.   *suit*

1ST KING   You say well, lords, witterly.   *indeed*
           As touching gold, prove may I,
           it should be given him duly
           because of temporality.   *temporal power*
           Sith he shall be king most mighty,   *since*
           tribute he must have truly;
           and gold therefore witterly   *certainly*
           is best, as thinks me.   *it seems to me*

2ND KING   And sith he hath in him godhead,   *since*
           methinks best—as eat I bread—   *it seems to me*
           incense to give him through my read   *advice*
           in name of sacrifice,
           for that may no way be led.   *set aside*
           Sith he of Holy Church is head,   *since*
           more due gifts, if I should be dead,   *fitting*
           I cannot devise.

3RD KING   You say full well, sirs, both two.
           And myrrh is good, methinks also.   *it seems to me*
           sith he for Man will suffer woe   *since*
           and die on rood-tree—   *the cross*
           myrrh that puts sin him fro   *from*
           and saves Man from rotting woe;   *sad decay*
           for it is best to balm him tho,   *embalm; then*
           that shall he have of me.   *from*

1ST KING   By these gifts three of good array   *appearance*
           three things understand I may:
           a king's power, sooth to say,   *truth*
           by gold here in my hand;
           and for his godhead lasteth ay,   *for ever*
           incense we must give him today;

and bodily death also in good fay   *truly*
by myrrh I understand.

2ND KING   Gold love also may signify,
for it men given not commonly   *generally*
but those they loven heartfully—   *to those; sincerely*
this child as we done all;   *do*
and incense tokeneth, lieve I,   *signifies; believe*
orisons and prayers done devoutly;
myrrh, death that Man hath bodily.
And all these shall him fall.   *to him*

3RD KING   By gold that we to bring are boun,   *ready*
that richest metal of renown,
skilfully understand we mon   *reasonably; may*
most precious godhead;
and incense may well be said   *called*
a root of great devotion;   *source*
by myrrh, that waives corruption,   *removes*
clean flesh, both quick and dead.   *living*

And sickerly this knowen we: *certainly; know*
he wants none of these three;   *lacks*
for full godhead in him has he   *complete*
as gold may signify.
And soul devout in him must be
to come out of the Trinity;
and clean flesh we hopen to see   *sinless; expect*
in him full hastily.   *very quickly*

    [. . .]

1ST KING   Hail be thou, Lord, Christ and Messy,   *Messiah*
that from God art comen kindly,   *come; by nature*
Mankind of bale for to forbuy   *from; torment; redeem*
and into bliss bring.
We know well by prophecy
of Moses, David and Isay,   *Isaiah*
and Balaam of our ancestry,   *forefathers*
of Jews thou shalt be king.

Therefore, as falleth for thy crown,   *befits*
gold I have here ready boun   *prepared*
to honour thee with great renown
after thy royalty.
Take here, Lord, my intention   *purpose*
that I do with devotion,
and give me here thy benison   *blessing*
ere that I go from thee.   *before*

2ND KING	Hail be Christ Emmanuel!	
	Thou comen art for Man's heal	*come; well-being*
	and for to win again that weal	*happiness*
	that Adam put away.	*cast aside*
	Prophets of thee every one tell,	
	both Isay and Ezechiel;	*Isaiah*
	and Abraham might not conceal	
	the truth of thee to say.	

Bishop I wot thou must be;   *priest; know*
therefore now, as thinks me,   *it seems to me*
incense will fall best for thee;   *be most fitting*
and that now here I bring
in tokening of thy dignity   *sign; high position*
and that office of spirituality.

3RD KING   Receive here, Lord, at me   *from*
devoutly my offering.
Hail, Conqueror of all Mankind!   *champion*
To do mercy thou has mind,   *intend*
the Devil's bond to unbind
and relieve all thine.   *release*
A full fair way thou can find   *have found*
to hance us and put him behind,   *exalt*
through thy Passion to unbind
thy people that be in pine;   *torment*
for thou shalt mend us through thy might,   *restore*
die and rise the third night,
to recover again our right,   *what is rightfully ours*
and break the Devil's band.   *bond*
Myrrh to thee here have I dight   *prepared*
to balm thy body fair and bright.   *embalm; beautiful*
Receive my present, sweet wight,   *child*
and bless me with thy hand.

Anonymous, *The Chester Mystery Cycle*, The Offerings of the Three Kings
37–120, 137–80 (15th or 16th century)

129   Christ's Appearance

The canonical Gospels contain no description of Jesus' appearance, but Christians down the ages have not been slow to supply the missing details. One of the most popular written descriptions is an anonymous letter, probably thirteenth-century in origin, which was supposedly written by a Roman official in Palestine at the time of Christ's ministry. (Cf. **25, 342–3**.)

In these days there appeared, and there still is, a man of great power named Jesus Christ, who is called by the Gentiles the prophet of truth, whom his disciples call the Son of God, raising the dead and healing diseases—a man in stature middling tall, and comely, having a reverend countenance, which those who look upon may love and fear; having hair of the hue of an unripe hazelnut and smooth almost down to his ears, but from the ears in curling locks somewhat darker and more shining, flowing over his shoulders; having a parting at the middle of the head according to the fashion of the Nazareans; a brow smooth and very calm, with a face without wrinkle or any blemish, which a moderate red colour makes beautiful; with the nose and mouth no fault at all can be found; having a full beard of the colour of his hair, not long, but a little forked at the chin; having an expression simple and mature, the eyes grey, flashing, and clear; in rebuke terrible, in admonition kind and loveable, cheerful yet keeping gravity; sometimes he has wept, but never laughed; in stature of body tall and straight, with hands and arms fair to look upon; in talk grave, reserved and modest, fairer than the children of men.

Anonymous, *The Letter of Lentulus* (13th century)

130   Jesus the Prophet

Many traditions about Jesus, some recognizably related to the canonical Gospels (see in this case, Luke 18: 10–14), others drawn from the apocryphal literature of the early Church, made their way into Islamic literature, where they received a vivid colouring from Islamic ideas and devotion, and emerged in distinctive literary forms, like this folk tale from Sa'adi (c.1219–93), a Persian poet. Jesus is a prophet, one who by divine inspiration can judge the path to true wisdom.

I have heard that Jesus came out of the desert, and passed by a hermit's hut. The hermit came out of his hut, and fell at Jesus' feet with his head bowed. An unhappy sinner was also bewildered by him, like a moth dazzled in the light, waiting penitent and downcast like a dervish before a rich man. Ashamed of himself, he was apologising with burning heart, for nights passed to days in neglect. He was weeping like the rain out of sorrow and saying: 'Woe, my life has been spent in negligence. I have spent the cash of my life and have not gained any good deeds. May none like me live forever, for my death is much better than my living. Happy is the person who died in childhood, for he did not feel ashamed in old age. Forgive my sins, O Creator of the World, for if they accompany me, I shall be disappointed.' His head was cast down in disappointment, the tears of regret pouring down his face.

At this corner was crying the old sinner, saying 'O Helper, help me.' The hermit, with a proud head, frowned at the sinner from afar saying: 'Why is this wretched man after us? How is this wretched ignorant person worthy of us? You are falling in the Fire downright. You have given your life for naught.

What good comes to your selfish self, to accompany Christ and me? What were you, who took trouble ahead of you and went to hell following your deeds? I do not become concerned at your unhappy star, lest your fire also fall on me. On the Judgment Day, when all gather, O God do not put me in company with him.'

At this time a revelation came to Jesus from the Highest Virtue, saying 'The one is a learned man and the other ignorant; accept both. The man who has spent his days in sin and wretchedness, has wept to me in despair. I shall not count out any one who comes to me hopeless; out of my generosity I forgive all their evil deeds. I will take him to Paradise by my favour. And if the lover of worship is ashamed of sitting with the sinner in Paradise, tell him not to be ashamed of him in the resurrection day, or the sinner will be taken to Paradise, and he to the Fire. For [the sinner] was desperate in agony and trouble, while the other depended on his worship. The helpless man does not know that at the court of the All-Wealthy, helplessness is far better than pride and insolence. He who has a clean robe but unclean character should not have a key out for the door of hell. At this threshold, inability and poverty are far better than worship and thinking of self. You are bad if you count yourself as one of the good, for self is not involved in God. If you are a man, do not speak of your manliness, every polo-player does not win the ball! The clumsy onion became all peel for it thought it had a kernel like the pistachio. This type of worship is not good. Go bring an apology for short-comings in worship. Both the unhappy and distressed knave and the hermit making things difficult for himself do not benefit from worship, they are good to God and bad to men of God.'

Words remain as a memorial of a wise man, hear but this word from Sa'adi: The sinner who fears God is better than a godly man who parades his worship.

Sa'adi, *Persian Poetry*, extract (13th century)

131 Jesus' Escape from Folly

Jelaluddin Rumi (1207–1273) was a Persian Sufi sage, and a prolific poet. His *Mathnawi* has been called the 'Qur'ān of the Persian language'. Note how, at the very end of the following story, Rumi is concerned that his moral tale should not be read in such a way as to cast a shadow on Jesus' character.

Jesus, son of Mary, was fleeing to a mountain: you would say that a lion wished to shed his blood. A certain man ran after him and said, 'Is it well with you? There is no one in pursuit of thee: why do you flee, like a bird?' But Jesus still kept running with haste, so quickly that on account of his haste he did not answer him.

He pushed on in pursuit of Jesus for the distance of one or two fields, and then invoked Jesus with the utmost earnestness, saying, 'For the sake of pleasing God, stop one moment, for I have a difficulty concerning thy flight. From whom are you fleeing in this direction, O noble one? There is no lion pursuing thee, no enemy, and there is no fear or danger.'

Jesus said, 'I am fleeing from the fool. Begone! I am saving myself. Do not debar me!'

'Why,' said he, 'are you not the Messiah by whom the blind and the deaf are restored to sight and hearing?'

Jesus said, 'Yes.'

Said the other, 'Are you not the King in whom the spells of the Unseen World have their abode? So that when you chant those spells over a dead man, he springs up rejoicing like a lion that has caught his prey?'

Jesus said, 'Yes, I am he.'

Said the other, 'Do you not make living birds out of clay, O beauteous one?'

Jesus said, 'Yes.'

Said the other, 'Then, O pure Spirit, you do whatsoever thou wilt: of whom have you fear? With such miraculous evidence, who is there in the world that would not be one of the slaves devoted to you?'

Jesus said, 'By the holy Essence of God, the Maker of the body and the Creator of the soul in eternity; by the sanctity of the pure essence and attributes of him, for whose sake the collar of Heaven is rent, I swear that the spells and the Most Great Name which I pronounced over the deaf and the blind were good in their effects. I pronounced them over the stony mountain: it was cloven and tore upon itself its mantle down to the navel. I pronounced them over the corpse: it came to life. I pronounced them over nonentity: it became entity.

'I pronounced them lovingly over the heart of the fool hundreds of thousands of times, and it was no cure for his folly. He became hard rock and changed not from that disposition; he became sand from which no produce grows.'

Said the other, 'What is the reason that the Name of God availed there, while it had no advantage here? Physical infirmity is disease too, and this folly is a disease: why did the Name of God not become a cure for this, since it cured that?'

Jesus said, 'The disease of folly is the result of the wrath of God; physical disease and blindness are not the result of Divine wrath: they are a means of probation.'

Probation is a disease that brings Divine mercy in its train; folly is a disease that brings Divine rejection. That which is branded on the fool, God has sealed: no hand can apply a remedy to it.

Flee from the foolish, seeing that even Jesus fled from them: how much blood has been shed by companionship with fools! The air steals away water little by little: so too does the fool steal away religion from you. He steals away your heat and gives you cold, like one who puts a stone under your rump.

The flight of Jesus was not caused by fear, for he is safe from the mischief done by fools: it was for the purpose of teaching others.

Jelaluddin Rumi, Mathnawi III. 2570–99 (13th century)

132   The Magnitude of Christ's Sorrow

The following extract is from a book of meditations on Jesus' life and Passion which may be by Johann Tauler (*c.*1300–61), a popular Dominican preacher influenced by Henry Suso (cf. **147**), and a famous helper of the sick during the Black Death. There is certainly a Dominican flavour to this extract's combination of emotive concentration on the Passion with careful analysis of causes and parts. (Cf. **133**.)

When Christ had come into the garden, he began to be sorrowful and afraid and very heavy; and by reason of the vehemence of his inward pain, he trembled outwardly in all his members, nor was he ashamed to confess to his disciples this sorrow and weakness and trouble of his body, for he said, 'My soul is sorrowful even unto death' [**15**].

Let us also go and see what is the cause of so great a sorrow. And indeed, for many reasons was Christ so sad; but we will here only touch on two reasons, which may the more forcibly stir us up to compassion and love.

The first reason was, because of our many and grievous sins and obstinate malice and great ingratitude, and because we were so utterly devoid of all holy fear. For on account of these things was Jesus sorrowful. For we both read and know by experience that if God were to permit a man to see his own sins as he himself seeth them, straightway his heart would break for exceeding great sorrow; or he would lose his senses when he beheld how he had wronged and despised and thought lightly of his Maker and Redeemer, his God and Lord, and how basely and unworthily he had deformed his own beautiful and noble soul. Now of a truth, Christ took all the sins of the world upon himself, and of his own will he allowed sorrow of heart for these sins to come upon him, even as if he himself had committed them. And because of his divine wisdom which saw all things, he beheld all sins, especially those that were most hateful, that ever have been or ever will be; and at the same time he beheld the contempt and wrong which they inflicted on his Father. Who then can in any way understand how great must have been his grief and sorrow? For he was ever urged on to promote his Father's honour with his whole strength; nor did he thirst after anything, save his Father's glory and the salvation of souls. [. . .]

Of Phinees, the son of Eleazar, we read in the Bible that he avenged a wrong done to God. For when he saw a certain Israelite sinning with a Moabitish woman, he burned with anger, and thrust both of them through, and for this was beloved by God. In like manner Moses avenged a wrong done to God, thousands being put to death for adoring the golden calf, after which the Lord was appeased. What, then, was the vengeance taken by the Son of God, Jesus Christ, who was ever consumed by a burning thirst after justice, and who placed all his zeal in this one thing, namely, that he might increase his Father's glory, and turn aside and prevent whatever was contrary to his will—when he beheld not merely a single sin, but the crimes of the whole world? Who can understand how all his inward parts were shaken with grief, how all his limbs trembled by reason of his burning thirst for justice, how his whole man was moved to avenge the wrong done to his Father? Yet in this his anger he remembered mercy, for he was full not of truth only, but of grace and loving kindness. Therefore said he unto his Father, 'O my Father, you know that I have ever loved you, and done your most gracious will; you see also that my heart is just, and how exceedingly I thirst to do your will, and to avenge the wrong done to you by Adam and his posterity. Yet, as mercy is mine, and my nature is goodness, and I have come not to take vengeance, but to reconcile; not to strike, but to heal; not to kill, but to redeem; and as Adam's sin cannot pass unavenged, I beseech thee, Father in heaven, to take vengeance upon me. I take all the sins of man upon myself. If this tempest of anger hath risen up because of me, cast me into the red and bitter sea of my Passion, let me be swallowed up and overwhelmed in the abyss of a shameful death, if only thy wrath may pass away, and man's debt may be justly cancelled.'

John Tauler?, *Meditations on the Life and Passion of Our Lord Jesus Christ* VII, extract (14th century)

133 Christs Seven Afflictions

Angela of Foligno (c.1248–1309) experienced many visions (cf. **113**) while a Franciscan tertiary (one who followed a simplified Franciscan rule (cf. **127**) in the midst of an ordinary life). This particular vision is thoroughly analytical, distinguishing the multiple sources and shapes of the horror of Jesus' Passion, yet its careful distinctions are deployed in order to awake the reader to heartfelt compassion and grief. (Cf. **133**.)

God, whose plan is ineffable, foreordained that the heart of Jesus would be stricken with seven afflictions.

Christ's sufferings were unspeakable, manifold, and hidden. And his unspeakably acute sufferings originated in the ineffable wisdom of the plan of God, who foreordained it and bestowed it on him. From all eternity, in an ineffable manner, Christ was united to this divine plan, and it culminated in his experiencing the supreme degree of suffering. The more wondrous the divine plan, the more acute and intense Christ's suffering. The painful effects of the divine plan were so acute and the sufferings so unspeakable and extreme that there is no intelligence comprehensive or large enough to ever be able to understand them. The divine plan, then, was the source and origin of all the sufferings of Christ. In it they begin and end.

Some of Christ's sufferings were a consequence of the ineffable divine light granted to him. God, who is ineffable light, enlightened Christ ineffably. It was part of the divine plan for Christ to be so ineffably united to God and transformed into his divine light that the suffering he was given to endure was altogether ineffable. Christ saw in the divine light the measure of suffering allotted to him. Because of its very excessiveness and ineffability, this suffering was concealed from all creatures. This suffering, a consequence of the light given to him, had its source and origin in the divine plan.

Christ also suffered most intensely and acutely from his most wonderful compassion toward the human race he loved so much. His compassion and suffering for each person was directly in proportion to each one's offences and the punishments which he knew with utmost certitude each was incurring or had incurred. Because Christ's love for each of his elect was so ineffable and visceral, he continually felt, as if present to him, the offences they were going to commit or had committed, as well as the corresponding pain and punishment they would have to suffer for each of their great offences. Out of his compassion he took upon himself the punishments due to them, and this was for him a source of extreme suffering. The more visceral Christ's love for his elect, the more did his compassion and suffering increase as he took on their punishments and sufferings. The cause of these sufferings of Christ is to be found in the divine plan.

Some of Christ's suffering also came from his compassion toward himself. This was because he foresaw the indescribable suffering that would inevitably befall him. Because he perceived himself as the one sent by the Father to bear in his own person the sufferings and pains of all the elect, and because he knew that he could not be wrong about these indescribable and acute sufferings that would fall upon him—for he was sent to give himself totally for this purpose—Christ's compassion for himself was the source of extreme suffering. For if someone knew with absolute certainty that he would inevitably have to endure the greatest and most indescribable pain and suffering, and had the sight of this suffering constantly before him, would he not have compassion for himself in proportion to this coming suffering? [. . .] Christ, foreseeing, then, the undescribable suffering that he would inevitably have to endure, had compassion for himself at the thought of being transformed into such a state of suffering.

Some of Christ's suffering also reflects his compassion for his most dear mother. Christ loved her more than any other creature—from her alone he had received his very flesh. Christ suffered extremely because he saw the extreme suffering that was hers. For endowed with the noblest and deepest qualities, superior to any other creature, she grieved over her own true son, in her own special way, more than any other creature grieved for him. Seeing her in such great pain, Christ suffered all the more out of compassion for her. The mother of God suffered in the extreme, and Christ continually bore this suffering in himself. The foundation for this suffering is the divine plan.

Christ also suffered as a result of his compassion for his apostles and disciples, because of the intense suffering that they would have to undergo when the sweetness of his physical presence, the source of such joy, was withdrawn from them. His physical presence was truly so loving and delightful that his mother and his disciples were afflicted with indescribable suffering when he was taken away from them at the time of the passion. All these sufferings Jesus, the God-man, bore continually within himself.

Finally, Christ suffered extremely and acutely because of the gentle, most noble, and sensitive nature of his soul. The intense and acute suffering he endured was torment in direct proportion to his soul's nobility and innate sensitivity. This noblest of souls afflicted on itself the greatest suffering. And all these sufferings of Christ originate at the highest and totally ineffable levels of the divine plan. (At this point, mother, you also said: 'Because of the ineffable union between soul and body, all these sufferings dispensed by the divine plan tormented Christ's soul so terribly and intensely that each of its pains reverberated in his body, and the body, too, was most keenly afflicted.')

Five kinds of knives with which Christ's enemies tried to destroy him: There were five kinds of knives that pierced Jesus, the God and man.

The first kind of knife was the perverse cruelty of those whose hearts were set against him. Their hearts were so continually and obstinately set against him that their constant concern was to eliminate him from the face of the earth by the most shameful and ignominious means imaginable.

The second kind of knife was the knives of those who clamoured against him with most vicious tongues. Because of the constant anguish of their hate-filled and obstinate hearts, they continually spoke against him with the venom and poison of their vicious and deceitful tongues.

The third kind of knife was the immense and boundless rage directed against him. From obstinate and murderous hearts, and deadly and biting tongues intent on tearing Christ apart, came forth the most cruel rage, continually directed at him. The many thoughts directed against him were like so many knives driven into his soul. The words spoken against him and the most cruel rage and anger were like so many knives which continuously pierced his soul.

The fourth kind of knife was the perfect fulfilment of all the evil intentions of Christ's enemies, for they did with him whatever they wanted.

The fifth kind of knife with which Christ was stabbed was the terrible nails with which they nailed him to the cross. They used the largest of nails, blunted, rusty, and square, because this shape causes the most extreme pain. They did this so as to better satisfy their malice.

Angela of Foligno, *The Book of Blessed Angela* III. 1, extract (late 13th century)

134 Savage Torture

Birgitta of Sweden (*c.*1303–73) was founder of the Brigittine order, committed to prayer and to the study of holy books. She obtained acceptance of her rule in Rome in 1349, and stayed there for the remainder of her life. She was, like Angela of Foligno (cf. **133**), Mechthild of Magdeburg (cf. **136**), Margaret Ebner (cf. **138**), and others, a visionary, and her revelations, like this extraordinarily graphic portrayal of the Crucifixion, achieved high popularity after her death.

I saw how the Jews were there fixing and fastening his cross firmly in the hole in the rock of the mount with bits of wood strongly hammered in on every side in order that the cross might stand more solidly and not fall. Then, when the cross had been so solidly fastened there, at once wooden planks were fitted around the trunk of the cross to form steps up to the place where his feet were to be crucified, in order that both he and his crucifiers might be able to ascend by those plank steps and stand atop the planks in a way more convenient for crucifying him. After this, they then ascended by those steps, leading him with the greatest of mockery and scolding. He ascended gladly, like a meek lamb led to the slaughter. When he was finally on top of those planks, he at once, willingly and without coercion, extended his arm and opened his right hand and placed it on the cross. Those savage torturers monstrously crucified it, piercing it with a nail through that part where the bone was more solid. And then, with a rope, they pulled violently on his left hand and fastened it to the cross in the same manner. Finally, they extended his body on the cross beyond all measure; and placing one of his shins on top of the other, they fastened to the cross his feet, thus joined, with two nails. And they violently extended those glorious limbs so far on the cross that nearly all of his veins and sinews were bursting. Then the crown of thorns, which they had removed from his head when he was being crucified, they now put back, fitting it onto his most holy head. It pricked his awesome head with such force that then and there his eyes were filled with flowing blood and his ears were obstructed. And his face and beard were covered as if they had been dipped in that rose-red blood. And at once those crucifiers and soldiers quickly removed all the planks that abutted the cross, and then the cross remained alone and lofty, and my Lord was crucified upon it.

And as I, filled with sorrow, gazed at their cruelty, I then saw his most mournful Mother lying on the earth as if trembling and half dead. She was being consoled by John and by those others, her sisters, who were then standing not far from the cross on its right side. Then the new sorrow of the compassion of that most holy Mother so transfixed me that I felt as it were, that a sharp sword of unbearable bitterness was piercing my heart. Then at last his sorrowful Mother arose; and, as it were, in a state of physical exhaustion, she looked at her Son. Thus, supported by her sisters, she stood there all dazed and in suspense, as though dead yet living, transfixed by the sword of sorrow. When her Son saw her and his other friends weeping with a tearful voice he commended her to John. It was quite discernible in his bearing and voice that out of compassion for his Mother his own heart was being penetrated by a most sharp arrow of sorrow beyond all measure.

Then too his fine and lovely eyes appeared half dead; his mouth was open and bloody; his face was pale and sunken, all livid and stained with blood; and his whole body was as if black and blue and pale and very weak from the constant downward flow of blood. Indeed, his skin and the virginal flesh of his most holy body were so delicate and tender that after the infliction of a slight blow a black and blue mark appeared on the surface. At times however he tried to make stretching motions on the cross because of the exceeding bitterness of the intense and most acute pain that he felt. For at times the pain from his pierced limbs and veins ascended to his heart and battered him cruelly with an intense martyrdom, and thus his death was prolonged and delayed amidst grave torment and great bitterness.

Then therefore in distress from the exceeding anguish of his pain and already near to death, he cried to the Father in a loud and tearful voice saying: 'O Father, why have you forsaken me?' He then had pale lips, a bloody tongue, and a sunken abdomen that adhered to his back as if he had no viscera within. A second time also, he cried out again in the greatest of pain and anxiety: 'O Father, into your hands I commend my spirit.' Then his head, raising itself a little, immediately bowed; and thus he sent forth his spirit. When his Mother then saw these things, she trembled at that immense bitterness and would have fallen onto the earth if she had not been supported by the other women. Then, in that hour, his hands retracted slightly from the place of the nail holes because of the exceeding weight of his body; and thus his body was as if supported by the nails with which his feet had been crucified. Moreover, his fingers and hands and arms were now more extended than before; his shoulder blades, in fact, and his back were as if pressed tightly to the cross.

Then at last the Jews standing around cried out in mockery against his Mother, saying many things. For some said: 'Mary, now your Son is dead'; but others said other mocking words. And while the crowds were thus standing about, one man came running with the greatest of fury and fixed a lance in his right side with such violence and force that the lance would have passed almost through the other side of the body. Thus, when the lance was extracted from the body, at once a stream, as it were, of blood spurted out of that wound in abundance; in fact, the iron blade of the lance and a part of the shaft came out of the body red and stained with the blood. Seeing these things, his Mother so violently trembled with bitter sighing that it was quite discernible in her face and bearing that her soul was then being penetrated by the sharp sword of sorrow.

When all these things had been accomplished and when the large crowds were receding, certain of the Lord's friends took him down. Then, with pity, his Mother received him into her most holy arms; and sitting, she laid him on her knee, all torn as he was and wounded and black and blue. With tears, she and John and those others, the weeping women, washed him. And then, with her linen cloth, his most mournful Mother wiped his whole body and its wounds. And she closed his eyes and kissed them; and she wrapped him in a clean cloth of fine linen. And thus they escorted him with lamentation and very great sorrow and placed him in the sepulchre.

Birgitta of Sweden, *The Seventh Book of Revelations*, book 7, ch. 15, 4–35 (14th century)

135 The Crucifixion Deception

Al-Baydawi (d. 1276), a commentator on the Qur'ān, illustrates the opposite attitude to that of Birgitta, typical of Islam at this time: an abhorrence of the idea of a suffering Jesus. This is an expansion of the story in Qur'ān 4: 157–8. (Cf. 123.)

There is a story that a group of Jews insulted Jesus and his mother, whereupon he appealed to God against them. When God transformed those who had insulted them into monkeys and swine, the Jews took counsel to kill Jesus. Then God told Jesus that he would raise him up to heaven, and so Jesus said to his disciples: 'Who among you will agree to take a form similar to mine and die in my place and be crucified and then go straight to Paradise?' A man among them offered himself, so God changed him into a form resembling Jesus, and he was killed and crucified. Others say that a man pretended to be a believer in Jesus' presence but then went off and denounced him, whereupon God changed the man into a form similar to that of Jesus, and then he was seized and crucified.

Al-Baydawi, *Commentary on the Qur'ān* on 4: 157–8 (13th century)

136   The Return to Heaven

Mechthild of Magdeburg (*c.*1210—*c.*1280) was a member of a Beguine community (a group of lay people dedicated to an austere lifestyle and good works, but not bound by monastic vows). She, like Angela of Foligno (cf. **133**) and Hildegard of Bingen (cf. **113**), received many visions, and her powerful written descriptions of them, dominated by images of light, had a strong influence on German mysticism. (Cf. **20**.)

After Jesus Christ had come from earthly strife to the peace of Heaven, his Father received him with these words: 'Welcome, honoured Son! My hand is in your works, my honour in your power, my strength in your warfare, my praise in your victory, my will in your return, my miracle in your ascension, my anger at your judgment. The pure Bride you bring me shall be yours and shall never be separated from you. My Godhead is your crown, your humanity my sun. Our one Spirit is one will, one counsel, one power in all things, without beginning and without end. Your soul is the dearest bride of our three persons.'

Ah! how blissfully the soul of Christ plays about the One Holy Trinity, in the same way as beams play from the glorious sun, beams which none can see save those with far-seeing eyes!

Mechthild of Magdeburg, *The Revelations; or, The Flowing Light of the Godhead* 5.27 (1265)

137   Christ Triumphant

In contrast both to the passionate medieval Franciscan or Dominican portrayals and to the folk-tale Islamic portrayals given above, Juan Luis Vives (1492–1540), a Spanish thinker and writer, provides a Renaissance portrait, one which draws primarily on classical motifs and delights in the demonstration of erudition. (Cf. **64**.)

Christ, our life, rose from the dead with a penetrating, agile and immortal, body, with the sensual part of the soul freed from all passion and turmoil, free from hunger, thirst, heat, cold, pain and fatigue, to ascend into that heavenly temple as though he were climbing the road which slopes up to the Capitoline hill and the Tarpeian rock,[2] a temple indeed, which our ancestors rightly named the church triumphant. This one here on earth they called the church militant,[3] because Christ was the first to serve as a soldier in it but triumphed in the one in heaven, as we will do also. In accordance with the time-honoured custom of generals, he was carried in on a four-horse chariot and clothed in purple, a far more brilliant hue than any other. For this reason, several of those running to meet him asked in wonder, 'Who is he who has come down from Edom, from Bozrah in coloured garments?' [Isa. 63: 1.]

Four gleaming white horses pulled the triumphing general's chariot, and four youths rode upon them: on Wisdom sat the rule and order of the church militant; on Justice, peace and inward tranquillity; on Courage, martyrdom, constancy amid temptations, and a soul uplifted in times of adversity and most humble in prosperity; on Temperance, observance of divine law, continence and a certain adornment of life, as it were, restraint, and complete quelling of the perturbations of the spirit; in short, in all things the best measure. Some maidens walked ahead and others followed, all proclaiming loudly the triumphant words, 'Holy, holy, holy' [Isa. 6: 3]. Soldiers before and after cried out, 'Blessed is he who comes in the name of the Lord' [Mark 11: 9], since through him both groups had escaped the hand of the enemy. But the Crossbearer, he who was called Standard-bearer, preceded them all. Those who carried lesser symbols such as the nails, the spear, the whips, the pillar, the rod with the sponge, and other objects of that sort followed after him. So much embossed silver and gold did he bring into the treasury that our republic would never have to borrow funds or ever need money again, even were it to last for eternity. Representations of the towns he had conquered preceded him likewise. These were no doubt portraitures of both heaven and earth, over which he, as their conqueror, was given all power. Those whom he had saved followed the chariot of the illustrious leader. This custom was observed even in other triumphal processions at Rome, as was reported of the senator Terentius Culleo in the triumph of Scipio Africanus over Hannibal and the Carthaginians.[4]

There went out to meet him two most distinguished consuls, the Father and the Paraclete, and then the senators—the Cherubim, Seraphim, and Thrones. After that the knights were spread out over the countryside—the Dominations, Virtues, and Powers; and finally came the plebs, the largest crowd of all—the Principalities, Archangels, and Angels, all longing to behold the face of their sublime deliverer. Then after he had been greeted and received by the Senators and plebs, the consuls granted him the title Father of his Country. He dedicated to God, greatest and best, the ancestors in hell because they were the richest spoils, as Romulus and Aurelius Cossus had dedicated their spoils to Jupiter Feretrius.[5] The next day he presented the Senate and plebs with a banquet, his pure, stainless, and holy body, the 'bread of angels, of which man has partaken' [Ps. 78: 25], and he set chalices filled with wine before them. Senators on earth once drank from a general's cup;

those were actually the holy disciples, whose successors reflect the image of that ancient Roman senate, said to have been composed of kings, and the general's successor recalls the Roman dictator, or emperor.

In addition to all this, just as many arches and obelisks had been erected to honour Furius Camillus after Rome was restored,[6] and on all of them TO THE DEFENDER OF THE NATION was inscribed, reminding men of such a great war, so to the imperishable memory of such a great event many temples, arches, statues, columns, and obelisks were now too erected, so that the ravages of time would not bury in oblivion a war so strenuously and successfully fought, and letters were inscribed upon them as eternal witnesses to divine power. On some monuments was written TO THE DEFENDER OF THE NATION, on others TO THE FATHER OF OUR COUNTRY, or on others yet TO THE SAVIOUR AND LIBERATOR OF OUR COUNTRY, which is most pleasing of all.

Juan Luis Vives, *The Triumph of Jesus Christ* 11–14 (1514)

II. Meditation

The life of Jesus was not remembered and retold out of curiosity, but in order to guide, deepen, and challenge religious life. It seems likely that even *The Letter of Lentulus* (**129**) was produced and circulated for devotional reasons. The next set of extracts focus more squarely on the effects of considering Christ, the deep impact which it was intended to have upon the Christian heart.

138   Intoxicated by Christ

Francis of Assisi (cf. **127, 145, 155**) was a man of tempestuous and infectious devotion, whose constant concern was to let the story of Christ move him to love, to compassion, to joy, to grief. He explored, and invited others into, a new affective landscape shaped by Christ's humility and humiliation.

A short while after his conversion, as he was walking alone along the road not far from the church of St Mary of the Porziuncula, he was uttering loud cries and lamentations as he went. And a spiritually minded man who met him, fearing that he was suffering from some painful ailment, said to him, 'What is your trouble, brother?' But he replied, 'I am not ashamed to travel through the whole world in this way, bewailing the Passion of my Lord.' At this, the man joined him in his grief, and began to weep aloud. [. . .]

Intoxicated by love and compassion for Christ, blessed Francis sometimes used to act in ways like these. For the sweetest of spiritual melodies would often well up within him and found expression in French melodies, and the murmurs of God's voice, heard by him alone, would joyfully pour forth in the French tongue.

Sometimes he would pick up a stick from the ground, and laying it on his left arm, he would draw another stick across it with his right hand like a bow, as though he were playing a viol or some other instrument; and he would imitate the movements of a musician and sing in French of our Lord Jesus Christ.

But all this jollity would end in tears, and his joy would melt away in compassion for the sufferings of Christ. And at such times he would break into constant sighs, and in his grief would forget what he was holding in his hands, and be caught up in spirit into heaven.

Anonymous, *The Mirror of Perfection* VI. 92–3, extracts (13th century)

139 Suckling Christ

Margaret Ebner (1291–1351) entered a Dominican monastery in Bavaria at the age of 15. Inspired by Mechthild of Magdeburg's writings (cf. **136**), she began to write accounts of her own visionary experiences, including this striking example.

While I was writing this little book, the greatest delight and sweetest grace came upon me concerning the childhood of our Lord [. . .] I have a statue of our Lord as a child in the manger. I was powerfully attracted to it by my Lord with delight and desire and by his gracious request. This was spoken to me by my Lord: 'If you do not suckle me, then I will draw away from you and you will take no delight in me.' So I took the image out of the crib and placed it against my naked heart with great delight and sweetness, and perceived then the most powerful grace in the presence of God. [. . .]

I am set afire by the ardent love coming from him and am filled up by his presence and by his sweet grace so that I am drawn into the true enjoyment of his divine essence with all loving souls who have lived in the truth.

Margaret Ebner, *Revelations*, extract (*c*.1344)

140 Continuous Contemplation

This anonymous fourteenth-century manual for meditation on the life of Christ teaches its readers how to cultivate the story of Christ 'in the secret of the heart'. In this extract the author describes some of the main benefits to be had from such contemplation.

You will never find better instruction against vain and fleeting blandishments, against tribulation and adversity, against the temptations of enemies and vices, than in the life of Christ, which was without blemish and most perfect. Through frequent and continued meditation on his life the soul attains so much familiarity, confidence, and love that it will disdain and disregard other things and be exercised and trained as to what to do and what to avoid.

I say first that the continuous contemplation of the life of Jesus Christ fortifies and steadies the intellect against trivial and transient things, as is disclosed in the example of the Blessed Cecilia, whose heart was so permeated with the life of Christ that trivial things could not enter. Thus during the pomp of the wedding, when there was so much vanity, with the organs singing, and dishonest hearts, she attended only to God, saying, 'O Lord, may my heart and my body become pure, that I may be untroubled.'

In the second place it fortifies against trials and adversity, as is shown by the holy martyrs about whom Bernard [cf. 97] in his 61st sermon on the Canticles said, 'In this way martyrdom is endured, that you consider the wounds of Christ in all devotion and dwell in continued contemplation. In this will the martyr remain happy though his whole body be lacerated and iron torture his sides. Thus where is the soul of the martyr? Surely in the wounds of Christ, since the wounds are clearly an entrance. If it were inside himself, he would feel the iron searching him; he could not bear the pain but would feel it and recant.' [. . .] However, not only the martyrs but also the confessors bore their tribulations and infirmities with great patience, and have to this day. If you read about the Blessed Francis [cf. 127] and the Blessed virgin Clara, your mother and leader, you will discover how they remained not only patient but even cheerful throughout many tribulations, poverty, and illness. And also you will continue to see this quality in those who lead a saintly life, because their souls were not and are not in their bodies but in Christ, owing to their devoted contemplation of his life.

In the third place I declare that one should be instructed on how to avoid enemies and vices leading to fall and deception, because in this is found the perfection of virtue. Where can you find examples and teachings of charity, of great poverty, of faultless humility, of profound wisdom, of prayer, meekness, obedience, and patience, and of all the virtues to equal those in the holy life of the Lord, full of all virtues? [. . .] Therefore the heart of one who wishes to follow and win him must take fire and become animated by frequent contemplation: illuminated by divine virtue, it is clothed by virtue and is able to distinguish false things from true. Thus it is more the illiterate and simple people who have recognised in this way the greatness and intensity of divine things. Do you believe that the Blessed Francis would have attained such abundance of virtue and such illuminated knowledge of the Scriptures and such subtle experience of the deception of the enemy and of vices if not by familiar conversation with and contemplation of his Lord Jesus? With such ardour did he change himself that he had become almost one with him and tried to follow him as completely as possible in all virtues, and when he was finally complete and perfect in Jesus, by the impression of the sacred stigmata[7] he was transformed into him. Thus you see to what a high level the contemplation of the life of the merciful Jesus Christ may lead, and that a strong foundation lifts you to a higher degree of contemplation; and therefore is discovered an unction that purifies step by step and raises the soul.

Anonymous, *Meditations on the Life of Christ*, Prologue, extract (14th century)

141 · To See the Face of Christ

Antony of Padua (1195–1231) was a Franciscan friar and an eloquent preacher, the first official 'lector in theology' of the Franciscan order. Here he expounds the description of Job's sufferings in Job 16: 16–19, and applies it to Christ, then returns to the main text for his sermon: 'Blessed are the eyes that see what you see. I tell you, many prophets and kings wished to see what you see but did not see it, and to hear what you hear but did not hear it' (Luke 10: 23–24). Contemplation of Christ's humiliation distinguishes, for Anthony, those truly on the path of salvation from a corrupt and complacent Church. (Cf. **53, 168–9**.)

Christ is the dazzling bright sun who covered himself with a cloud in order to be seen: 'I have sewn sackcloth over my skin, and rubbed my brow in the dust. My face is red with tears and a veil of shadow hangs over my eyelids; although my hands are free from violence, and my prayer is sincere. Cover not my blood, O earth, afford my cry no place to rest.'

Sackcloth and *dust* express the bitterness and shoddiness of the human condition. Jesus Christ made for himself a tunic of the sackcloth of our human nature, sewing it with the needle of the subtle workings of the Holy Spirit and the thread of the faith of the Blessed Virgin. He sewed it, donned it, and embellished it with the dust of lowliness and poverty. Eyes afflicted with blindness cannot perceive this.

Look at the *face* of Jesus, swollen and bruised, and covered with his tears. He suffered 'though he had done no wrong, nor spoken any falsehood' [Isa. 53: 9]. He 'prayed at all times for sinners' [**53**], even on the cross when he asked his father to forgive those who persecuted him.

O earth (meaning you who have sinned), *cover not my blood* the price of your redemption, with the love of earthly things. I beg you to let it produce results within you. Emblazon the sign 'TAU' on your forehead with my blood so that the destroying angel cannot harm you. Do not allow the cares of this earth to cover my blood, but rather imitate Pilate who refused to change the inscription on the cross over my head, saying: 'What I have written, I have written' [John 19: 22]. [. . .]

'I say that many prophets and kings wished to see.' The prophets are the corrupt leaders of the Church, and the kings are powerful men of this earth. Both wish to see Christ in heaven, yet refuse to see him nailed to the shameful cross. They wish to reign with Christ, but at the same time they want to enjoy themselves on this earth, hoping with Balaam: 'May I die the death of the just' [Num. 23: 10]. They desire to see the glory of Christ's divinity which the apostles witnessed, without suffering the shame of the passion or the poverty of Christ which the apostles experienced [cf. **168–9**]. This is the reason they will not see him as the apostles did; with the wicked they will look 'on him whom they have pierced'. They will not hear the consoling words 'Come, you have my Father's blessing;' instead they will hear the voice thunder: 'Out of my sight, you condemned' [Matt. 25: 34, 41]. [. . .]

Blessed are the eyes that see in the face of Jesus the bitterness of his passion, swollen with bruises and tears, smeared with spittle, because one day they will see that same face 'at which the angels love to look' [1 Pet. 1: 12] in the glory of the heavenly Jerusalem. In Job we read: 'He shall see God's face with rejoicing' [Job 33: 26], that is to say, if a man can first look at the face of Christ in his suffering with bitterness in his heart, he will one day perceive the face of Christ in heaven with indescribable joy. 'The one day in your courts' which is better 'than a thousand elsewhere' [Ps. 84: 10] is the sight of Christ's face, excelling all others in brightness in heaven. 'O Lord, our protector, look upon us' should be our prayer to the heavenly Father. The protection of the Lord is many times taken for granted since we experience it ceaselessly; if it were taken away, it would show us that man amounts to nothing without it.

'O Lord, look upon the face of your anointed' [Ps. 84: 9]. Do not, O Lord, look upon our sins, but look at the face of Christ, your anointed, covered with spittle, swollen with bruises and covered with tears on our behalf. Have mercy on us, O Lord, because of the face of Christ, and be merciful to us who have been the cause of his suffering.

Anthony of Padua, To See the Face of Christ, extract (early 13th century)

142   The Soul's Journey Into God

> Bonaventure (c.1217–1274) was the greatest Franciscan theologian of the period, just as Thomas Aquinas (cf. **158**) was the greatest Dominican. Bonaventure paid more attention than Aquinas to mystical contemplation, to the process by which a believer's mind is purified and directed to the glory of God which exceeds all its capacities—and as it does so returns to its true home and identity. This ascent to God's glory and return to oneself take place, for Bonaventure, only through contemplation of Christ. (Cf. **88**, **90**.)

After our mind has beheld God outside itself through his vestiges and in his vestiges, within itself through his image and in his image, and above itself through the similitude of the divine Light shining above us and in the Light itself, insofar as this is possible in our state as wayfarers and through the exercise of our mind, when finally in the sixth stage our mind reaches that point where it contemplates in the First and Supreme Principle and in the mediator of God and men, Jesus Christ, those things whose likenesses can in no way be found in creatures and which surpass all penetration by the human intellect, it now remains for our mind, by contemplating these things, to transcend and pass over not only this sense world but even itself. In this passing over, Christ is the way and the door; Christ is the ladder and the vehicle, like the Mercy Seat placed above the ark of God and the mystery hidden from eternity.

Whoever turns his face fully to the Mercy Seat and with faith, hope and love, devotion, admiration, exultation, appreciation, praise and joy beholds him hanging upon the cross, such a one makes the Pasch, that is, the pass-over, with Christ. By the staff of the cross he passes over the Red Sea, going from Egypt into the desert, where he will taste the hidden manna; and with Christ he rests in the tomb, as if dead to the outer world, but experiencing, as far as is possible in this wayfarer's state, what was said on the cross to the thief who adhered to Christ; 'Today you shall be with me in paradise.'

This was shown also to blessed Francis, when in ecstatic contemplation on the height of the mountain—where I thought out these things I have written—there appeared to him a six-winged Seraph fastened to a cross, as I and several others heard in that very place from his companion who was with him then. There he passed over into God in ecstatic contemplation and became an example of perfect contemplation as he had previously been of action, like another Jacob and Israel, so that through him, more by example than by word, God might invite all truly spiritual men to this kind of passing over and spiritual ecstasy.

In this passing over, if it is to be perfect, all intellectual activities must be left behind and the height of our affection must be totally transferred and transformed into God. This, however, is mystical and most secret, which no one knows except him who receives it, no one receives except him who desires it, and no one desires except him who is inflamed in his very marrow by the fire of the Holy Spirit whom Christ sent into the world. And therefore the Apostle says that this mystical wisdom is revealed by the Holy Spirit. [. . .]

But if you wish to know how these things come about, ask grace not instruction, desire not understanding, the groaning of prayer not diligent reading, the Spouse not the teacher, God not man, darkness not clarity, not light but the fire that totally inflames and carries us into God by ecstatic unctions and burning affections. This fire is God, and his furnace is in

Jerusalem; and Christ enkindles it in the heat of his burning passion, which only he truly perceives who says: 'My soul chooses hanging and my bones death' [Job 7: 15]. Whoever loves this death can see God because it is true beyond doubt that man will not see me and live. Let us, then, die and enter into the darkness; let us impose silence upon our cares, our desires and our imaginings. With Christ crucified let us pass out of this world to the Father so that when the Father is shown to us, we may say with Philip: 'It is enough for us' [John 14: 8]. Let us hear with Paul: 'My grace is sufficient for you' [2 Cor. 12: 9]. Let us rejoice with David saying: 'My flesh and my heart have grown faint; You are the God of my heart, and the God that is my portion forever. Blessed be the Lord forever and all the people will say: Let it be; let it be. Amen' [Ps. 72: 26; 105: 48].

Bonaventure, The Soul's Journey Into God VII. 1–4, 6, extracts (1259)

143   Christs Sweet Mercy

> The following meditative exercise was probably written by Richard Rolle (c.1300–49), an English hermit and author of many ascetic and mystical works. The author meditates on the sweetness in the midst of bitterness of Christ's life, and asks that Christ would with his sweet mercy protect the penitent from the acids of sickness, sin, and temptation. (Cf. **132–4**.)

Sweet Lord Jesus Christ, I thank you and am grateful to you for that sweet prayer and that holy petition which you made for us on Mount Olivet before the holy passion. I beg you, sweet Lord, to listen to my prayer.

> We adore you, O Christ, and we bless you because by your holy cross you have redeemed the world.
> Our Father . . .
> Hail Mary . . .

Sweet Lord Jesus Christ, I thank you and am grateful to you for that great anxiety you had for us when you became so full of distress that an angel came from heaven to comfort you, when you sweated blood in agony [15]. I ask you Lord, and implore you, for your sweet mercy, that you may be my help in all my distress and my temptations; and send me, Lord, the angel of good counsel and comfort in all my needs, so that through that sweat I might pass out of all my sickness of soul and body into a life of health.

> We adore you . . .
> Our Father . . .
> Hail Mary . . .

[. . .] I thank you, sweet Lord Jesus Christ, for the tortures and the humiliating experiences which you endured in the presence of the bishops and lawyers, and from your enemies, and for the buffets and the blows on the neck and for many other disgraces which you suffered; and among other things, I thank you, Lord, for that look which you directed toward your disciple, Saint Peter, who had disowned you. You looked at him with a glance of compassion, when you were in your greatest distress, and in your greatest torment. Openly you revealed there the love and the holy affection which you had for us, in that neither humiliation nor torture nor anything can drag your heart away from us as far as it depends on you. Sweet Lord, full of compassion and sympathy, there we can turn to your grace by means of your blessed gaze and repent of our sins and of our misdeeds so that we are able to reach your compassion together with Saint Peter.

    We adore you . . .
    Our Father . . .
    Hail Mary . . .

[. . .] Sweet Lord Jesus Christ, I thank you for the agonies which you endured for us, and for the sweet blood which you shed for us, when you were so painfully beaten and roped to the pillar so that the blood on the pillar can still be seen. I ask and beg you as my dear Lord for that sweet blood, which you bled so generously for me, to be full deliverance for my soul.

    We adore you . . .
    Our Father . . .
    Hail Mary . . .

Sweet Lord Jesus Christ, I thank you for the injuries and disgraces which by your own dear wish you suffered for us when you were dressed up in purple to deride you, and in the crown with its thorns to torture your sweet head, and when they, kneeling in mockery, called you 'lord, king and leader,' and after saying all that spat so filthily on your sweet face, and so filthily made your lovely face slimy with the filthy stinging spitting from the filthy accursed Jews, and cuffed and struck and hammered on your sweet head with iron. Also for your tormenting wounds I thank you, for your pains and for your sweet blood which ran down and streamed from your blessed face. I ask and beg you, dear lord, to protect us from sin, and from the disgrace which we have deserved because of sin.

    We adore you . . .
    Our Father . . .
    Hail Mary . . .

[. . .] Sweet Lord Jesus Christ, I thank you for the injuries and disgraces which you endured so graciously and so gladly, now by being tugged at, now by being butted so disgracefully, now by being struck, now by being flogged so painfully and so brutally; and by carrying your own cross on your sweet, naked back, like a thief carrying his own gallows to be hanged on it himself at Mount Calvary, where people gazed at wicked men and thieves, deciding whether this one was a thief or a murderer: and there you allowed them to put you on the cross.

Richard Rolle, *Meditations on the Passion (Shorter Version)* (14th century)

144 Drinking from Christ

Lutgard of Aywières (1182–1246) was sent to a Benedictine convent as a child because her father had lost the money with which to provide a dowry for her. After visions like that described below, she became a nun, moving eventually to the stricter Cistercians. In the last years of her life she went blind, but she treated this as a gift enabling her to concentrate more fully on Christ. (Cf. **133–4, 136, 146, 149, 152, 157, 159**.)

While Lutgard was still most tender in body and age, it happened one night around the time of Matins that an intense and natural sweat overcame her. She therefore planned in her heart to rest during Matins so that afterwards she might be stronger in the service of God, for, indeed, she presumed that the sweat was helpful for her body. Suddenly a voice cried out to her in this manner: 'Get up quickly! Why are you lying down? You must now do penance for sinners who are lying in their own filth and not indulge yourself in this sweating!' She was alarmed by this voice and quickly arose and hurried to the Church although Matins had already begun. There was no delay. Christ encountered her at the very entrance of the church, all bloody and nailed to the Cross. Lowering his arm which was nailed to the Cross, he embraced her who was standing opposite and pressed her mouth against the wound in his right side. She drank in so much sweetness from that place that always afterwards she was stronger and quicker in the service of God.

Those to whom she revealed this event have reported and certified that at that time and for a long time afterwards the saliva in her mouth tasted mellower than any sweet honey. What is there to wonder in this? 'Your lips, my spouse, are a dropping honeycomb' [S. of S. 4: 11]. Thus did her heart inwardly ruminate on the honey of divinity and the milk of the humanity of Christ while her tongue was silent.

Thomas de Cantimpré (cf. **146**), *The Life of Lutgard of Aywières* 13 (13th century)

III. Imitation

Meditation on the life of Christ could fit into a variety of forms of devotion. It was practised in order to move the believer to new levels and kinds of feeling, to love and to grief; it was practised to deepen penitential fervour and plead for forgiveness; and it was practised to move the believer further along the path by which the Christ-like image of true humanity could once more be stamped upon the heart. One of the strongest accents of Christocentric devotion at this time, however, was the desire to copy the pattern of Christ's life in one's own, to play his melody again in one's own actions. This found its clearest expression in the Devotio Moderna in the fourteenth century, but was evident well before and beyond that movement.

145   Imitating the Humility

Once again, we turn to Francis (cf. **127**, **138**, **155**). His desire to be conformed by suffering and ascetic rigours to the humiliation of Christ may ring oddly in modern ears, but his delight in self-denial was aimed not at conformity to the emaciated images of a culture obsessed with unhealthy beauty, but at a life wholly given over in sacrifice to others—and in the following extract we see that this very aim could temper the excesses of the devotion.

So fervent were the love and compassion of blessed Francis for the sorrows and sufferings of Christ, and so deep was his inward and outward grief over the Passion day by day that he had never considered his own infirmities. Consequently, although he suffered from ailments of the stomach, spleen, and liver over a long period until the day of his death, and had endured constant pain in his eyes ever since his return from overseas, he was never willing to undergo any treatment for its cure.

So the Lord Cardinal of Ostia, seeing how harsh he had always been on his own body, and how he was already beginning to lose his sight because he refused to undergo a cure, urged him with great kindness and compassion, saying, 'Brother, you are not doing right in refusing treatment, for your life and health are of great value not only to the friars, but to the layfolk and the whole Church. You have always had a great sympathy for your brethren when they are sick, and have always been kindly and merciful; you must not be cruel to yourself in so great a need. I therefore order you to have yourself cured and helped.' For because the most holy Father took boundless delight in imitating the humility and example of the Son of God, he always regarded anything unpleasant to the body as welcome.

Anonymous, *The Mirror of Perfection* VI. 91 (13th century)

Margaret of Ypres (1216–37) was not a nun, but was persuaded in 1234 to adopt a form of strictly ascetic religious life by a Dominican preacher. She continued to live with her mother, and became the centre of a group of *amici spirituales* (spiritual friends). After only three years her natural frailty and the rigours of her ascetic devotions killed her. Her life was written by Thomas de Cantimpré, the coadjutor of the Bishop of Cambrai. (Cf. **146**, **149**.)

At the age of ten, she noticed the crucifix in the church and said, 'O Jesus, our true salvation, up to this time I have done nothing to repay you.' Saying this, she wept most bitterly and at once went alone into the forest and, stripping naked, wounded herself with thorns even to the shedding of blood. She did this not just once or twice but very often whenever she tearfully recalled the wounds of Christ. Once, when her guardians noticed this and said, 'Why do you afflict yourself when you are only a tender child?' she replied, 'I'm now prepared to suffer any kind of torment for Christ if the time or the place presents itself.'

Thomas de Cantimpré, *The Life of Margaret of Ypres* (1240)

147 Imitation over Contemplation

Henry Suso (c. 1295–1366) was a German Dominican mystic. Taught by the famous mystical theologian Meister Eckhart, he in turn influenced Johannes Tauler (cf. **132**) (both Dominicans), and their common emphases ring through German spirituality up to and beyond the Reformation, as well as influencing earlier movements like the Devotio Moderna (cf. **148**, **154**). Suso's concentration on imitation is intended to temper the excesses of affective contemplation.

ETERNAL WISDOM: When I was suspended on the high branch of the Cross with boundless love, for the sake of you and of all men, my whole form was most wretchedly disfigured, my clear eyes were dimmed and lost their lustre; my divine ears were filled with mockery and insult, my noble sense of smell was assailed by an evil stench, my sweet mouth with a bitter draught, my gentle sense of touch with hard blows. Then I could not find a place of rest in the whole world, for my divine head was bowed down by pain and torment; my joyful throat was rudely bruised; my pure countenance was defiled with spittle; the clear colour of my cheeks turned wan and pallid. Look, my fair form was then disfigured, as though I were a leper, and had never been fair Wisdom [cf. **53**, **141**].

THE SERVANT: O you most charming mirror of all grace, on whom the heavenly spirits feast their eyes, as on the beauty of the spring, would that I might have seen your beloved countenance in your dying hour, until I had covered it with my heartfelt tears, and gazed my fill on your fair eyes and your bright cheeks, so that I might relieve my heart's grief with profound lamentation.

Ah, beloved Lord, your sufferings affect some persons deeply, they can lament feelingly, and weep for you sincerely. Ah, Lord, would that I could lament as the spokesman of all loving hearts, that I could shed the bright tears of all eyes, and utter the lamentations of all tongues: then I would show you today how deeply the anguish of your Passion affects me!

ETERNAL WISDOM: None can better show how much my Passion affects them than those who share it with me by the testimony of their works. I would rather have a free heart, untroubled by ephemeral love, which with steadfast diligence follows that which is highest, imitating the example of my life, than that thou shouldst for ever lament for me, and shed as many tears weeping over my martyrdom as ever drops of rain fell from the sky. For I suffered the pangs of death in order that I might be imitated, however lovable are the tears, and however acceptable to me.

THE SERVANT: Alas, gentle Lord, inasmuch as a beautiful imitation of your gentle life and of your loving Passion is so very dear to you, I will in future strive rather after a loving imitation than a tearful lamentation, although according to your words, I should do both. And therefore teach me how to resemble you in this suffering.

ETERNAL WISDOM: Break your pleasure in frivolous seeing and idle hearing; let love taste good to you, and take pleasure in what has been distasteful to you; give up for my sake all bodily luxury. You shall seek all your rest in me; love bodily discomfort, suffer evil willingly, desire contempt, renounce your desires, and die to all your lusts. That is the beginning of the school of Wisdom, which is to be read in the open and wounded book of my crucified body. And look, even if man does all that is in his power, can anyone in the whole world do for me what I have done for him?

Henry Suso, *Little Book of Eternal Wisdom* III (1328 AD)

148 Modern Devotion

In fourteenth-century Holland a spiritual revival which became known as the Devotio Moderna sprang up around the earthily reforming preaching of Geert de Groote (1340–84). An extract from one of de Groote's letters follows, showing his emphasis on the imitation of Christ. The movement spread across Europe by means of lay associations devoted to education and to prayer, known as Brethren of the Common Life, and a religious order known as the Windesheim canons. Thomas à Kempis (cf. 154) was one of the most famous members of the latter. (Cf. 150, 167, 185.)

Remembrance of the passion alone avails little, if it is not accompanied by an overpowering desire to imitate Christ.

Wherefore whenever we meditate upon some aspect of Christ's passion, we ought always to hear, as from above, the voice of Christ: 'Do this and you will live' [Luke 10: 28] and, 'for this reason I suffered for you and on your account, that you might follow my steps' [1 Pet 2: 21]. When a holy mind begins to love the humanity of Christ powerfully, even beyond every delight in this world, and to suck upon the wounds of Christ [cf. **144**], as oil from a rock and honey from the hardest crag, and to draw near the inner acts of Christ—O, how much then he will yearn to be vexed, tried, and reproached so as to be made both like and pleasing to his lover. Although perhaps one still tender, a fresh novice, is not yet up to so much pressure and especially not yet able to reach what he desires, he should propose nonetheless to suffer with Christ; he should arrange, order, plead, and seek it from the Lord. Sometimes he fails and is humiliated; sometimes he sees it through, gives thanks, and presses on vigorously to what lies ahead. In this way a man denies himself, takes up his cross and follows Christ. For the cross of Christ is every voluntary assumption of the labours, pains, and reproaches by which the world is crucified to man, that is, the things of the world held in contempt by a man, and he to the world, that is, he despised and afflicted by worldly men. This is the cross of the Lord Jesus Christ, this is conformity to the cross, and from it, as a stream from a fount, as rays from the sun, it flows into us.

Geert de Groote, Letter 62: 'On Patience and the Imitation of Christ', extract (between 1374 and 1384)

149 **Christ a Ladder**

> Catherine of Siena (c. 1347–80) was an ascetic and a visionary. She became a Dominican tertiary at the age of 16, and devoted herself to good works and to prayer. She was particularly fervent in her devotion to the Precious Blood of Christ. The powerfully physical imagery of her devotion is evident in the following extract from one of her letters. (Cf. **142**, **146**, **157**.)

If you ask me the way, I will tell you to go his way, the way of abuse, suffering, torture and scourging. And how are you to go? By way of true humility, and of burning charity and ineffable love, the love with which we turn away from worldly wealth and status and so come, as I said, from humility to obedience, and thence to peace, for, by eliminating the root cause, our own will, obedience soothes away all pain and gives all delight.

Moreover, to enable the soul to attain this perfection, Christ has made his body into a staircase, with great steps. See, his feet are nailed fast to the cross; they constitute the first step because, to begin with, the soul's desire has to be stripped of self-will, for as the feet carry the body, so desire carries the soul. Reflect that no soul will ever acquire virtue without climbing this first step. Once you have done that, you come to real, deep humility. Climb the next step without delay and you reach the open side of God's Son. Within, you will find the fathomless furnace of divine charity. Yes, on this second step of the open side, there is a little shop, full of fragrant spices. Therein you will find the God-Man; therein, too, the soul becomes so satiated and inebriated as to become oblivious of self for, like a man intoxicated with wine, it will have eyes only for the blood spilt with such burning love. With eager longing it presses on upwards and reaches the last step, the mouth, where it reposes in peace and quiet, savouring the peace of obedience. Like a man who falls asleep after drinking heavily and so is oblivious of both pain and pleasure, the bride of Christ, brimming over with love, sleeps in the peace of her Bride-groom. Her own feelings are so deeply asleep that she remains unruffled when assailed by tribulation and rises above undue delight in worldly prosper-ity; for she stripped herself of all desire of that kind back on the first step. Here on the third she is conformed to Christ crucified and made one with him.

Run, then, with brave hearts, for you know where, and how, to go to reach the place where you will find a bed to rest on, a table to fill you with delight, and food to sate your desire—for he is our table, our food and our servant. You would indeed be deserving of rebuke if, through your own fault, you failed to seek this repose and foolishly kept away from this food. I want you, indeed I beg you, on behalf of Christ crucified, to warm yourselves by bathing in Christ's blood. Also, so that you are indeed made one with him, let there be no shying away from toil, for the toil is slight and the fruit is great.

Catherine of Siena, Letter 18 (1376)

150 Attaining to the Likeness of Christ

It was not only in Western Europe that the imitation of Christ was expounded as the aim of Christian life. Theoleptos of Philadelphia (1250–1326), a Byzantine abbot, wrote the following instructions in 1307 to a nun named Eirene, who had just entered monastic life at 16.

From the depths of your heart you ought to praise God because, having received from him rays of wisdom, you decided to wither the bloom of your youth with ascetic labours. In the prime of your youth, you despised its flatteries and chose the monastic life, preferring to become the bride of Christ. Therefore, since you have abandoned this mist-encumbered world to run off to the most radiant world of virtue and have made the change to a life of renewal, it is absolutely necessary that you embrace the ways both of thinking and of acting which are proper to the monastic profession. But you must also show that your change of vocation is not half-hearted, lest by bringing with you a mixture of worldly confusion you disturb the pure vision of virtue with the result that your withdrawal from the world bears no fruit.

Monastic profession is a towering and very fruitful tree whose roots consist of dissociation from all corporeal things and whose branches consist of the detachment of the soul and its refusal to have any relationship with those things from which it has fled. Its fruit is the acquisition of the virtues, divinising love and the joy which cannot be severed from these. For scripture says, 'The fruit of the Spirit is love, joy and peace' [Gal. 5: 22].

Flight from the world provides a refuge in Christ. By the world I mean attachment to sensible things and to the flesh. He who dissociates himself from these things in recognition of the truth attains to the likeness of Christ. In acquiring the love of Christ, for the sake of which he renounced all the things of this world, he purchased the pearl of great price, namely, Christ [cf. 92]. Through saving baptism you have clothed yourself in Christ, you divested yourself of defilement through the divine bath, procured for yourself the radiance of spiritual grace and through this re-creation received the noble birth of our first creation. For what has happened? Or rather, what has man suffered as a result of his self-will? By his attachment to the world he altered the divine impress. By his association with the flesh he corrupted the Image; the mist of impassioned thoughts darkened the mirror of the soul in which Christ, the spiritual sun, is visible.

By fixing your soul upon the fear of God, you recognised the darkness inherent in the vicissitudes of this world; you realised the distracting effect of turmoil upon the discursive intellect; you have noted the empty distractions that befall people who lead an overly busied life; you have been wounded by the arrow of love attained in tranquillity [cf. 184]; you have sought peace from your thoughts, for you learned, 'Seek peace and follow after it' [Ps. 34: 14]. You desired rest from all this because you heard, 'Return, my soul, to your rest' [Ps. 116: 7]. For the sake of these things, then, you took thought for the noble birth which you received by grace in baptism and in your resolution you refused to allow yourself to be called back to the world by the passions.

And, of course, you have put your good purpose into action by entering the holy convent, by clothing yourself with the precious robes of repentance and by courageously promising to remain in the monastery until death. You have now made your second commitment to God. The first you made when you came into this present life and the second as you press on towards the end of this present life. At the former time you were bound to Christ in piety; now you have conformed yourself to Christ in repentance.

Theoleptos of Philadelphia, *The Monastic Discourses* 1.2–6, extract (1307)

151   Passing through Christ's Life

Gregory of Sinai (*c.*1265–1346) was an austere hermit and monk who was a strict adherent of the Eastern tradition of inward prayer (the Jesus Prayer; cf. **92–3**), and developed a theology of joy, warmth, and rapture. Here he develops an account of the imitation of Christ which differs noticeably from that of the Devotio Moderna. (Cf. **95**.)

Everyone baptised into Christ should pass progressively through all the stages of Christ's own life, for in baptism he receives the power so to progress, and through the commandments he can discover and learn how to accomplish such progression. To Christ's conception corresponds the foretaste of the gift of the Holy Spirit, to his nativity the actual experience of joyousness, to his baptism the cleansing force of the fire of the Spirit, to his transfiguration the contemplation of divine light, to his crucifixion the dying to all things, to his burial the indwelling of divine love in the heart, to his resurrection the soul's life-quickening resurrection, and to his ascension divine ecstasy and the transport of the intellect into God. He who fails to pass consciously through these stages is still callow in body and spirit, even though he may be regarded by all as mature and accomplished in the practice of virtue.

Gregory of Sinai, Further Texts 1 (14th century)

IV. The Love of Christ

We finish this section with three texts in which the believer's relationship with Christ is portrayed in intimately personal terms. This focus gives them a modern ring to our ears, and the kind of devotion expressed here seems a harbinger of developments more familiar to us from the post-Reformation pietists, or from various forms of nineteenth- and twentieth-century devotion which focus on personal relation to Christ. Yet the texts are firmly part of the later medieval world: the first two come from the writings of visionary women mystics and the last from a rigorously ascetic monastic theologian.

152   Christ our Mother

Julian of Norwich (*c.*1342–after 1413) received a series of visions on 8 and 9 May 1373 while living the life of a hermit outside Norwich. The chief theme of the revelations, and of Julian's reflection on them in subsequent years, was divine love. The visions had clearly lost little of their power in the twenty years or so she had spent digesting them; the central, paradoxical metaphor of this extract has lost little of its power in the six centuries since she set down the fruit of those reflections. (Cf. **153**.)

Our Mother in nature, our Mother in grace, because he wanted altogether to become our Mother in all things, made the foundation of his work most humbly and most mildly in the maiden's womb. And he revealed that in the first revelation, when he brought that meek maiden before the eye of my understanding in the simple stature which she had when she conceived; that is to say that our great God, the supreme wisdom of all things, arrayed and prepared himself in this humble place, all ready in our poor flesh, himself to do the service and the office of motherhood in everything. The mother's service is nearest, readiest and surest: nearest because it is most natural, readiest because it is most loving, and surest because it is truest. No one ever might or could perform this office fully, except only him.

We know that all our mothers bear us for pain and for death. What is that? But our true Mother Jesus, he alone bears us for joy and for endless life, blessed may he be. So he carries us within him in love and travail, until the full time when he wanted to suffer the sharpest thorns and cruel pains that ever were or will be, and at the last he died. And when he had finished, and had borne us so for bliss, still all this could not satisfy his wonderful love. And he revealed this in these great surpassing words of love, 'If I could suffer more, I would suffer more.' He could not die any more, but he did not want to cease working; therefore he must needs nourish us, for the precious love of motherhood has made him our debtor.

The mother can give her child to suck of her milk, but our precious Mother Jesus can feed us with himself, and does, most courteously and most tenderly, with the blessed sacrament, which is the precious food of true life; and with all the sweet sacraments he sustains us most mercifully and graciously, and so he meant in these blessed words, where he said, 'I am he whom Holy Church preaches and teaches to you.' That is to say, 'All the health and the life of the sacraments, all the power and the grace of my word, all the goodness which is ordained in Holy Church for you, I am he.'

The mother can lay her child tenderly to her breast, but our tender Mother Jesus can lead us easily into his blessed breast through his sweet open side, and show us there a part of the godhead and of the joys of heaven, with inner certainty of endless bliss [cf. **149**]. And that he revealed in the tenth revelation, giving us the same understanding in these sweet words which he says, 'See, how I love you, looking into his blessed side, rejoicing.'

This fair lovely word 'mother' is so sweet and so kind in itself that it cannot truly be said of anyone or to anyone except of him and to him who is the true Mother of life and of all things. To the property of motherhood belong nature, love, wisdom and knowledge, and this is God. For though it may be so that our bodily bringing to birth is only little, humble and simple in comparison with our spiritual bringing to birth, still it is he who does it in the creatures by whom it is done. The kind, loving mother who knows and sees the need of her child guards it very tenderly, as the nature and condition of motherhood will have. And always as the child grows in age and in stature, she acts differently, but she does not change her love. And when it is even older, she allows it to be chastised to destroy its faults, so as to make the child receive virtues and grace. This work, with everything which is lovely and good, our Lord performs in those by whom it is done. So he is our Mother in nature by the operation of grace in the lower part, for love of the higher part. And he wants us to know it, for he wants to have all our love attached to him; and in this I saw that every debt which we owe by God's command to fatherhood and motherhood is fulfilled in truly loving God, which blessed love Christ works in us. And this was revealed in everything, and especially in the great bounteous words when he says, 'I am he whom you love.'

Julian of Norwich, *Showings* 60, extract (c.1393)

153   Christs Labour Pains

> Margaret of Oingt (1240–1310) was a nobly born French Carthusian nun who, once she had gained approval from her superiors, wrote a variety of works of remarkable vigour in Latin and Provençal. This extract is from a set of Latin meditations. (Cf. **152**.)

Are you not my mother and more than mother? The mother who bore me laboured at my birth for one day or one night, but you, my sweet and lovely Lord, were in pain for me not just one day, but you were in labour for more than thirty years. Oh, sweet and lovely Lord, how bitterly were you in labour for me all through your life! But when the time approached where you had to give birth, the labour was such that your holy sweat was like drops of blood which poured out of your body onto the ground [15].

And when the worst traitors made you a prisoner, one of them gave you such a blow that your face was left all black; and afterwards they began to mock you and bent their knees in front of you in pure mockery and greeted you by saying: hail, king of the Jews.

Oh, lovely Lord God, those could not get enough of your torments, and surely they showed this well when afterwards they tied you to the column where they whipped you so stretched out that it seemed that you were stripped of your skin, so covered with blood were you; and after they had whipped you, they put on your tender head the crown of thorns that pierced your vital parts and your eyes.

Oh, sweet Lord Jesus Christ, who ever saw any mother suffer such a birth! But when the hour of the birth came you were placed on the hard bed of the cross where you could not move or turn around or stretch your limbs as someone who suffers such great pain should be able to do; and seeing this, they stretched you out and fixed you with nails and you were so stretched that there was no bone left that could still have been disjointed, and your nerves and all your veins were broken. And surely it was no wonder that your veins were broken when you gave birth to the world all in one day.

Oh, lovely Lord God, still you were not satisfied with all the pains that you had suffered; indeed, you suffered it that they pierced your side with the spear so cruelly that your whole kind body was split and pierced; and your precious blood gushed forth with such strength that the courtyard flowed with it like a large stream, and it gushed forth with such great abundance that it must have come from a truly great stretching. [. . .]

Oh, lovely Lord God, who ever saw at any other time that a mother wanted to die such a vile death for the love of her child? Surely, no one ever saw this, since your love was beyond all other loves.

Margaret of Oingt, *Page of Meditations* 33–7, 9 (1286)

154 Jesus the Friend

Thomas à Kempis (*c.*1380–1471), the most famous proponent of the Devotio Moderna (cf. **148**), is the most probable author of *The Imitation of Christ*, one of the most popular devotional books ever written. Not until Bunyan's *Pilgrim's Progress* (**200**) did another single work of Christian instruction have such a vast impact.

That person is truly blessed who understands what it is to love Jesus and to serve him with deep humility. Jesus wishes to be loved above all things; everything else must come second. The love of anything other than Jesus is deceptive and fickle; the love of Jesus is faithful and enduring. The person who clings to anything other than Jesus falls with its falling; the person who embraces Jesus stands firm forever. Love Jesus and keep him as your friend. When all things fade he will not abandon you, nor will he allow you to perish in the end.

If necessary, you must be willing to let go of everything if Jesus asks it of you. Cling to him in life and in death, and trust yourself to his faithfulness. He alone can help you when all else fails. Your Beloved will not share you with others—that is his nature; he wants to be first in your heart, as you are in his. If you knew how to disentangle yourself from your own confused feelings, Jesus would gladly stay with you.

You will find that whatever hope you have placed in anything other than Jesus is nearly a total loss. Do not trust or lean upon a wind-blown reed, for all flesh is grass, and its glory, like the wild-flower's, will fade away. If you trust in appearances, you will quickly be deceived; if you look for comfort and gain in others, you will often be disappointed. If you seek Jesus in everything, you will surely find him, but if you seek yourself, self you will surely find, but to your own ruin. By not seeking Jesus, we hurt ourselves more than the whole world and all our enemies could hurt us.

When Jesus is with us, all is right with the world and nothing seems difficult; when he is missing, everything is hard. When Jesus does not speak to the heart, comfort is worthless; but if he speaks only one word, we feel great joy. Did not Mary Magdalen arise at once from where she was weeping when Martha said to her, 'the Master is here and is calling for you?' [John 11: 28] Oh, happy hour when Jesus calls us from tears to spiritual joy!

How dry and hard you are without Jesus! How foolish and empty if you want anything other than Jesus! Is this not a greater loss than if you were to lose the whole world? What can the world offer you without Jesus? To be without Jesus is an unbearable hell, and to be with Jesus is a sweet paradise. If Jesus is with you no foe can harm you. The person who finds Jesus finds a good treasure—indeed, a good beyond all good; the person who loses Jesus loses a very great thing, more than the whole world. It is poverty to live without Jesus; it is wealth to live with him.

To know how to talk with Jesus is a great art, and to know how to cling to him is great wisdom. Be humble and peaceful and Jesus will be with you; be devout and quiet and he will remain with you. You will quickly drive him away and lose his grace, though, if you divert your attention to your own affairs at his expense. And if you drive him away and lose him, to whom will you fly, and who will you then seek as a friend? You cannot live well without a friend, and if Jesus is not your best friend, you will end up being heartbroken and desolate. You act foolishly, then, if you centre your life on anything else. It is better to have the whole world against us than to hurt Jesus.

Thomas à Kempis, *The Imitation of Christ* 7–8 (1418)

Section B

The Benefits of Christ's Passion

If one theme can be said to dominate the Christological thinking of the late medieval West, it is the means by which Christ's Passion is effective for his followers: How is it that Christians are included in what took place in Christ on the Cross? At its crudest this becomes a quest for some mechanism by which Christ's riches are transferred to others; at its broadest it implies an exploration of the manifold ways in which God's triune life is opened up in Christ by the Spirit for the participation of creatures. In discussions of merit, the mass, the nature of Christ's intercession, or the metaphysics of his humanity, medieval minds probed the limits and logic of this participation.

155   Christ's Daily Humility

Once more, we begin with Francis (cf. **127, 138, 145**)—and this time with an extract from one of the few writings we have from the saint himself. In this, one of his admonitions to his disciples, he expresses a simple eucharistic theology in which once again Christ's humility for our sake is central, and the sense of partaking of Christ strong and realistic.

Therefore, O sons of men, how long will you be hard of heart? Why do you not recognise the truth and believe in the Son of God? See, daily he humbles himself [cf. **39**], as when he came from the royal throne into the womb of the Virgin; daily he comes to us in a humble form; daily he comes down from the bosom of the Father upon the altar in the hands of the priest.

And as he appeared to the holy apostles in true flesh, so now he reveals himself to us in the sacred bread. And as they saw only his flesh by means of their bodily sight, yet believed him to be God as they contemplated him with the eyes of faith, so, as we see bread and wine with our bodily eyes, we too are to see and firmly believe them to be his most holy body and blood living and true.

And in this way the Lord is always with his faithful, as he himself says: 'Behold I am with you even to the end of the world' [**19**].

Francis of Assisi, *Admonitions* 1. 14–22 (early 14th century)

156   Transubstantiation

At the Fourth Lateran Council in 1215, one of the greatest councils of the Western Church, the hierarchy of the Latin Church agreed a careful formulation describing the nature of Christ's eucharistic presence. The definition is bound up with an understanding of the place of the Church and the role of the priesthood. (Cf. 36, 117–19, 172–6, 194.)

There is indeed one universal church of the faithful, outside of which nobody at all is saved, in which Jesus Christ is both priest and sacrifice. His body and blood are truly contained in the sacrament of the altar under the forms of bread and wine, the bread and wine having been changed in substance, by God's power, into his body and blood, so that in order to achieve this mystery of unity we receive from God what he received from us. Nobody can effect this sacrament except a priest who has been properly ordained according to the church's keys, which Jesus Christ himself gave to the apostles and their successor.

Constitutions of the Fourth Lateran Council, extract (1215)

157   Corpus Christi

Juliana of Mont-Cornillon (1193–1258) was an orphan who entered the monastery of Mont-Cornillon in 1207; she became prioress in 1222 and tried to impose some discipline on the wayward house—eventually having to flee when this was resisted. Her most lasting contribution, however, was her development of the Feast of the Sacrament, better known as Corpus Christi, which, after initial difficulties, went on to become one of the most popular of medieval feasts.

From her youth, whenever Christ's virgin gave herself to prayer, she saw a great and marvellous sign. There appeared to her the full moon in its splendour, yet with a little breach in its spherical body. When she had seen this sign for a long time she was astonished, not knowing what it might mean. But she could not marvel enough over the fact that, whenever she was intent on prayer, the sign constantly impressed itself on her vision. After she had tried with all her might to make it go away, as she wished, and could not succeed, she began to trouble herself unduly in fear and trembling, thinking that she was being tempted. So she prayed and asked people she trusted to pray that the Lord would rescue her from a temptation she was suffering, as she said. But when she could not drive the importunate sign away by any effort, nor by any prayer of her own or other Christians, she finally began to wonder if perhaps, instead of trying so hard to drive it away, she should seek to discover some mystery in it.

Then Christ revealed to her that the moon was the present Church, while the breach in the moon symbolised the absence of a feast which he still desired his faithful upon earth to celebrate. This was his will for the increase of faith at the end of a senescent age, and also for the growth and grace of the elect: that once every year, the institution of the Sacrament of his Body and Blood should be recollected more solemnly and specifically than it was at the Lord's Supper, when the Church was generally preoccupied with the washing of feet and the remembrance of his Passion. On this feast of the memorial of the Sacrament, what was passed over lightly or negligently on ordinary days should be celebrated with greater attention.

Christ revealed these things to his virgin, therefore, and commanded her that she herself should inaugurate this feast and be the first to tell the world it should be instituted. But Juliana, considering the sublimity of the matter and observing her own lowliness and frailty, was more astonished than words can tell. She replied that she could not do what she had been commanded. Yet every time she prayed, Christ admonished her to accept the task for which he had chosen her above all mortals. And she always answered, 'Lord, release me, and give the task you have assigned me to great scholars shining with the light of knowledge, who would know how to promote such a great affair. For how could I do it? I am not worthy, Lord, to tell the world about something so noble and exalted. I could not understand it, nor could I fulfil it.' But he responded that by all means, she should be the one to initiate this feast, and from then on it should be promoted by humble people.

[Juliana then spends many years, until 1246, taking advice from her friends and colleagues.]

Juliana, strengthened by divine and human counsel, began to wonder whom she could get to compose the Office for so great a feast. When she realised that she could not have on hand the literary men, the distinguished scholars, who seemed appropriate for the task, she trusted in the aid of divine wisdom alone and decided to choose a certain John, a brother of her house, a young man but deeply innocent. He was the one, in fact, of whom Christ's virgin had long ago predicted to the recluse of St. Martin that he would help her bear the weight of trials to come. Although she was aware that he lacked literary knowledge, she knew that the power and wisdom of God, whose work she wanted to accomplish, could speak worthily through an uneducated person. So she zealously encouraged him to assemble and compose an Office for the new feast. At first he was diffident and began to excuse himself on the ground of his ignorance, but Juliana heartened the nervous and timid young man and promised divine assistance. What more should I say? Though he had no doubt that such a task exceeded the measure of his talent and knowledge—for he was indeed of very modest learning—he was overcome by the prayers and authority of the virgin, whose sanctity he well knew. So he set out to compose and arrange an Office.

He set out, I say, trusting in the help of him who says through the prophet, 'Open your mouth and I will fill it' [Ps. 81: 10]. The young brother and Christ's virgin agreed that when he began to write, she would begin to pray; in this way each would be helped by the other for their mutual comfort. Thus the brother, perusing the books of many saints like a clever bee, culled the flowers of divine quotations that were fragrant with the sweetness of the Sacrament of Christ's Body and Blood. From these he inwardly confected a honey of antiphons, responsories, hymns, and other items pertaining to the Office and stored it in the hive of his wax tablets. In these honeycombs he made the confection sweeter than before. So, more easily and skilfully than he could have hoped at the outset, he accomplished what he pleased. But he ascribed his success to the prayer of Christ's virgin rather than his own industry or labour, and when he had composed any part of the Office he would bring it to her and say, 'This is sent to you from on high, my lady. Look and see whether anything needs to be corrected in the chant or in the text.' With the wondrous knowledge infused in her, she did this with such shrewdness and subtlety when the need arose that, after her examination and correction, even the greatest masters did not need to polish it any further. And what Christ's virgin had approved, he retained or submitted to her correction.

So it happened that the whole Office for the new feast—the Night Office and the daytime Hours, with the hymns, antiphons, responsorial readings, chapters, collects, and all the other propers—was completed, while Christ's virgin prayed, the young brother composed, and God wondrously assisted. All these texts and melodies are of such beauty and sweetness that they should be able to wring devotion even from hearts of stone.

The Life of Juliana of Mont-Cornillon, ch. 2, §§6, 9, extracts (1261–4)

---

158   **Merit and Satisfaction**
....

> Thomas Aquinas (*c*.1225–74) was a Dominican friar, and a theological giant. In his *Summa Theologiae* and other works he brought a capacious and acute intellect to bear on the questions of the Christian tradition, setting in train debates which would run for centuries. The following extract is in *quaestio* form, simulating the lively debate, frequent appeal to tradition, and resolutely logical and grammatical analysis which characterized the scholastic theology of the later medieval period. Thomas discusses the place of concepts like merit and satisfaction in accounts of Christ's work. (Cf. **114, 219, 223, 291**.)

Question 48. On the efficacy of Christ's passion
Article 1: Whether Christ's passion caused our salvation by way of merit[8]

1. It would seem that Christ's passion did not cause our salvation by way of merit. The origin of suffering is not in us, and no one merits or is praised for anything except its source is within him. Thus the passion of Christ effected nothing by way of merit.
2. Moreover, Christ from the first moment of his conception merited both for himself and for us as we have said above [3a.34.3]. But to merit again what has already been merited is superfluous. So Christ did not merit our salvation.
3. Furthermore charity is the root of merit. But the love of Christ was not made greater in his passion than it was before. Hence he did not merit our salvation more by suffering than he had before.

On the other hand:

Commenting on the text, 'Therefore God exalted Christ Jesus' [39], Augustine [cf. 38] remarks that 'the lowliness of the passion calls for glory; splendour is the reward for his abasement' [Tractates in John 104]. But Christ was glorified both in himself and in his followers, as John notes [John 17: 10]. It seems then that he did merit salvation for those who believed in him.

Reply:

We have pointed out that Christ was given grace not only as an individual but in so far as he is head of the Church [3a.7.1.9,8.1.5], so that grace might pour out from him upon his members. Thus there is the same relation between Christ's deeds for himself and his members, as there is between what another man does in the state of grace and himself. Now it is clear that if anyone in the state of grace suffers for justice's sake, he by that very fact merits salvation for himself, for it is written, 'Blessed are they who suffer persecution for justice's sake' [4]. Therefore Christ by his passion merited salvation not only for himself, but for all who are his members, as well.

Hence:

1. Suffering as such comes from an extrinsic cause and from that aspect is not meritorious. But in so far as a man suffers willingly, it has an inner source and so is meritorious.
2. From the moment of his conception Christ merited eternal salvation for us. On our part, however, there were certain obstacles which prevented us from enjoying the result of his previously acquired merits. In order to remove these obstacles, then, it was necessary that Christ suffer, as we said above [3a.46.3].
3. Christ's passion had one effect which his previous merits had not. Not that the passion indicated a greater love but it was the kind of a deed suited to produce such an effect, as is clear from what we said above in regard to the fittingness of Christ's passion [3a.46.3].

Article 2. Whether Christ's passion caused our salvation by way of satisfaction.

1. It would seem that Christ's passion did not cause our salvation by way of satisfaction. It is up to one who sins to make satisfaction, as is clear from the other parts of penance; the man who sins must do the repenting and confess. But Christ did not sin; as St Peter says, 'He did no sin.' [1 Pet. 2: 22]. He therefore did not make satisfaction by his own passion.

2. No one accepts as reparation an even greater offence. But the greatest of offences was perpetrated in Christ's passion, for they sinned most gravely who put him to death, as was pointed out above [3a.47.6]. It seems therefore that reparation could not be made to God through Christ's passion.

3. Moreover, since satisfaction is an act of justice, it implies a certain equality with the fault. But Christ's passion is not, apparently, equal to all the sins of the human race, because Christ did not suffer according to his divinity but in his flesh; St Peter says, 'Christ has suffered in the flesh' [1 Pet. 4: 1]; moreover, the soul, the seat of sin, is of greater account than the flesh. Christ therefore did not by his passion satisfy for our sins.

On the other hand:
It is said of Christ, 'Then did I pay that which I took not away' [Ps. 69: 4] He does not pay, however, who does not perfectly satisfy. It therefore seems that Christ by his suffering made perfect satisfaction for our sins.

Reply:
A man effectively atones for an offence when he offers to the one who has been offended something which he accepts as matching or outweighing the former offence. Christ, suffering in a loving and obedient spirit, offered more to God than was demanded in recompense for all the sins of mankind, because first, the love which led him to suffer was a great love; secondly, the life he laid down in atonement was of great dignity, since it was the life of God and of man; and thirdly, his suffering was all-embracing and his pain so great, as has been said above [3a.46.5; cf. 132, 133]. Christ's passion, then, was not only sufficient but superabundant atonement for the sins of mankind; as John says, 'He is a propitiation for our sins, not for ours only but also for those of the whole world' [1 John 2: 2; cf. 219].

Hence:

1. The head and members form as it were a single mystical person. Christ's satisfaction therefore extends to all the faithful as to his members. When two men are united in charity, one can satisfy for the other [cf. 114, 223] [. . .]. It is not the same where confession and contrition are concerned; but

satisfaction has to do with the exterior act, and here one can make use of instruments, a category under which friends are included.[9]

2. The love of the suffering Christ more than balanced the wickedness of those who crucified him; the satisfaction he offered by his passion, there-fore, more than offset the offence committed by his executioners in killing him. Thus Christ's passion was sufficient, and more than sufficient, to satisfy for the sins even of those who crucified him.

3. The dignity of Christ's flesh should not be reckoned merely from the nature of flesh, but according to the person who assumed it; it was, in fact, the flesh of God, and on this account, of infinite value.

Thomas Aquinas, Summa Theologiae 3a.48.1–2 (1267–73)

159   Christ's Heartbeats

> Gertrude of Helfta (1256—c.1302) was a nun at the convent of Helfta, a centre of Benedictine learning and piety, from the age of 26 until her death. She was the recipient of visions, and turned her considerable intellectual energies to contemplation. She was an early proponent of devotion to the Sacred Heart of Jesus. (Cf. **144**.)

When she saw the others assembling for the sermon, [Gertrude] complained within herself and said to the Lord: 'You know, my dearest, how gladly I would now hear the sermon with all my heart, were I not held back by sickness.' To which the Lord answered, 'Would you like me to preach to you my dearest?' She answered, 'I would, very much.' Then the Lord made her lean against his heart with the heart of her soul close to his divine heart. When her soul had sweetly rested there a while, she heard in the Lord's heart two wondrous and very sweet pulsations.

The Lord said to her: 'Each of these two pulsations brings about man's salvation in three ways. The first pulsation effects the salvation of sinners; the second, that of the just. With the first pulsation, first, I address God the Father ceaselessly appeasing him and leading him to have mercy upon sinners. Second, I invoke all my saints excusing the sinner with fraternal fidelity and urging them to pray for him. Third, I address the sinner himself calling upon him to repent, and awaiting his conversion with ineffable longing.

With the second pulsation first I address God the Father, inviting him to rejoice with me for having shed my precious blood to such good purpose for the redemption of the just in whose hearts I now find so many delights. Second, I address all the heavenly hosts inviting them to praise the lives of the just and to thank me for the benefits I have already bestowed upon them and for those I will bestow in the future. Third, I address the just themselves lavishing various favours on them for their salvation and admonishing them to progress from day to day and from hour to hour. And just as the pulsations of the human heart are not impeded by seeing or hearing or by any manual work, but always maintain their regular motion, so the government and disposition of heaven and earth and the whole universe can never affect in the very least these twofold pulsations of my divine heart, still them, modify them, or in any way hinder them, till the end of time.'

Gertrude of Helfta, The Herald of Divine Love 51 (this section written by an anonymous biographer) (late 13th, early 14th century)

160 Christ's Maximal Humanity

> Nicholas of Cusa (1401–54) was a theologian and a formidable ecclesiastical politician. In *De Docta Ignorantia* (1440), as well as defending various complex theses about the nature of the knowledge of God, he tried to show how it was that what took place in Christ's human nature was not restricted to Christ himself, but happened in and for all human nature. Although the extract below is difficult to follow, Nicholas's intention is clear: to show that Christ's humanity somehow includes our own, so that although we remain individuals, we are somehow participants in Christ's humanity. Cf. Aquinas, **158**, particularly the first point under 'Hence' in each article.

Except for Christ Jesus who descended from Heaven, there was never anyone who had enough power over himself and over his own nature (which in its origin is so subject to the sins of carnal desire) to be able, of himself, to ascend beyond his own origin to eternal and heavenly things. Jesus is the one who ascended by his own power and in whom human nature (begotten not from the will of the flesh but from God [cf. **66**]) was not hindered from returning, of its own power, to God the Father. Therefore, through its union with the divine nature, the human nature in Christ was exalted to the Supreme Power and was delivered from the weight of temporal and burdensome desires.

But Christ the Lord willed to mortify completely—and in mortifying to purge—by means of his own human body all the sins of human nature which draw us toward earthly things. He did this not for his own sake (since he had committed no sin) but for our sakes, so that *all* men, of the same humanity with him, would find in him the complete purgation of their sins.

The man Christ's voluntary and most innocent, most shameful, and most cruel death on the Cross was the deletion and purgation of, and the satisfaction for, all the carnal desires of human nature. Whatever humanly can be done against neighbourly love is abundantly made up for in the fullness of Christ's love, by which he delivered himself unto death even on behalf of his enemies. Therefore, the humanity in Christ Jesus made up for all the defects of all men.

For since it is 'maximum' humanity, it encompasses the complete possibility of the species, so that it is . . . united to each man much more closely than is a brother or a very special friend. For the maximality of [Christ's] human nature brings it about that, in the case of each man who cleaves to Christ through formed faith, Christ is this very man by means of a most perfect union—[although] each's numerical distinctness is preserved.

Because of this union the following statement of Christ is true: 'Whatever you have done to one of the least of my brethren, you have done to me' [Matt. 25: 45]. And conversely whatever Christ Jesus merited by his suffering, those who are one with him also merited—different degrees of merit being preserved in accordance with the different degree of each man's union with Christ through faith formed by love. Hence, in Christ the faithful are circumcised; in him they are baptised; in him they die; in him they are made alive again through resurrection; in him they are united to God and are glorified.

Nicholas of Cusa, *On Learned Ignorance* III. 6, extract (1440)

Section C

Jesus and Judaism

161   No Revelation in Jesus

> The *Nizzahon Vetus* is a medieval Jewish handbook of arguments against Christianity. Although it incorporates earlier material, it probably dates from the early fourteenth century. Its name, 'Old Polemic', contrasts it with a later such manual produced in the 15th century. (Cf. **58, 60, 121**.)

If [Jesus] is God, why did he cover himself with flesh and why did he not appear publicly to renew his Torah and give it openly so that the people of that generation would not err and the people of the world not be misled? He should on the contrary have done his deeds openly and in a clearly recognisable fashion so that all would believe in him. Indeed the loss that resulted from this disguise outweighed the salvation; people refrained from believing in him, since the disguise involved separation from holiness and purity and association with what the Torah regards as stringent impurities. See what is written of the time when the Torah was given: 'Be ready for the third day, do not approach a woman, for on the third day the Lord will come down in the sight of all the people' [Exod 20: 15, 11]. Because of the imminent revelation of the Lord the people were sanctified in this manner. Consequently, how could this man be God, for he entered a woman with a stomach full of faeces who frequently sat him down in the privy during the nine months, and when he was born he came out dirty and filthy, wrapped in a placenta and defiled by the blood of childbirth and impure issue [cf. **70**]. The Torah, on the other hand, warns against approaching a menstruant woman, a woman who has had an impure issue, and one who has just given birth, as it is written, 'And she shall continue in the blood of purification three and thirty days; she shall touch no hallowed thing until the days of her purification be fulfilled' [Lev 12: 4]. Hence he was not worthy of association with anything sacred.

You may argue that he was not defiled in her womb since Mary had ceased to menstruate and it was the spirit that entered her; subsequently, he came out unaccompanied by pain or the defilement of blood. The answer is that you yourselves admit that she brought the sacrifice of a childbearing woman. Now, it is clear that this sacrifice is brought as a consequence of impurity from the fact that the same sacrifice of two turtle-doves or two pigeons is brought by a leper, a woman who has had an impure issue, and one who has just given birth. Indeed, to this day they call the day that she came to the Temple and brought her sacrifice, 'Light', and they fast for forty days in commemoration of the forty days that she remained impure from Christmas till 'Light', as it is written, 'If a woman be delivered and bear a manchild, then she shall be unclean seven days' [Lev 12: 2]. The additional 'three and thirty days' make forty.

Anonymous, Nizzahon Vetus, Pentateuch 6 (early 14th century?)

162   The Jews not Deicides[10]

> Joseph ibn Shem Tob was a prominent fifteenth-century Spanish Jew. He was a politician, philosopher, apologist for Judaism, theologian, and (as the extract given here illustrates) preacher. The sermon from which this is an extract was preached in 1452 in Segovia, where there had just been an anti-Jewish riot. (Cf. **55, 275, 339**.)

And now, my brothers and friends, look, and you will see how this tragedy has come upon us. You know, of course, that our hands did not shed the blood of that man in whose name our enemies in every generation have risen against us to destroy us. Rather our righteous ancestors, basing themselves upon the Torah and justice, hanged him on a tree. A court of seventy-one came to an understanding of his case. This is the legal rule: 'The false prophet is not put to death except at the order of the Great Court' [*Sanhedrin* 1: 5]. Even though it is a principle of our law that capital cases are tried in a court of twenty-three—the Small Sanhedrin—the case of the false prophet is different and more serious.

In this case of a false prophet it is necessary to judge the truth of a prophecy and to know the criteria of prophetic status. The chief of these is that the person must possess intellectual perfection in the various branches of knowledge, ethical perfection in his conduct, and perfection in the creative power of his imagination. This determination is extremely difficult. The intellectual powers of the self-proclaimed prophet may well be inadequate. Such was the case with this man and his disciples. They made errors in biblical verses that even schoolchildren understand. Their words reveal many serious and momentous mistakes. They were masters of the imagination and because of this they had dreams and delusions that made them think they had acquired true knowledge without study. [. . .]

They also did amazing things through magical tricks, just as the Egyptian magicians did before Moses. Nature can be changed either through natural causes or through divine intervention. Therefore, a miraculous act proves nothing, for it can be done through enchantment and sorcery. Even in our own time we can see masters of illusion performing amazing tricks. That is why our Torah and tradition insist that the claim to prophecy not be based on miraculous evidence. The Master of the Prophets commanded, 'If there appears among you a prophet or a dream-diviner and he gives you a sign or a portent . . . and the sign or portent comes true, on the basis of which he said to you "Let us follow and worship another god,"' the conclusion is that you should not heed him or revere him, for that prophet has spoken maliciously. It is commanded that he be put to death [Deut 13: 2–6]. [. . .]

There is no guilt either upon us or upon [those who sat in the Great Court]. This is not why evil befalls us, just as the misfortune that befell Joseph's brothers was not because they were spies. Rather we are guilty of other things, and 'The collectors make their rounds each day and exact payment' from us, whether or not we are aware of the reason. All is in accordance with a true verdict.

He is a fool who says that had it not been for that incident [the crucifixion], those murders and conflagrations and forced apostasies would never have befallen our sacred communities. Nothing prevents God from fabricating new causes and different libels to be directed against us as justification for the collection of his debt. 'He has a basis of support.' Look at the Jewish communities in Islamic lands. Murders and forced apostasies have befallen them without any libels relating to the death of that man.

Instead, we should look into our behaviour, as individuals and as a community. This is why these tragedies occur. They are brought by the collectors who make their rounds each day to collect the debts. The situation can be remedied only by removing the cause. It is a foolish physician who concentrates exclusively on treating the illness and its symptoms without removing the underlying cause. Treating the immediate cause does not necessarily cure the disease. Only removing the underlying cause will accomplish this.

Joseph ibn Shem Tob, Sermon on Abot 3: 15–16 (1452)

PART 4

Reformation and Counter-Reformation: 1517–1600

The Christian world changed in the sixteenth century. For a start, it grew: Spanish explorers had just encountered the Americas; the Portuguese travelled around the Cape and established trade routes with India (where they found the ancient Nestorian Church of St Thomas waiting for them), and on to South Asia; Russia expanded eastwards into northern Asia. In one direction it retreated—in the face of the advance of the Islamic Ottomans, who laid siege to Vienna in 1529.

In 1517 an Augustinian monk called Martin Luther posted ninety-five theses to the door of a church in Wittenberg, calling for a reform of the penitential practices of the Catholic Church. A less flexible hierarchy than that headed three centuries before by Innocent III tried to use monastic discipline to quieten him. The attempt failed, and Luther's case became a flashpoint for revolution. A dam burst which had been holding back pent-up criticisms of the current state of the Church from all sorts of people, from refined humanists steeped in the new ideas of the Renaissance to firebrand popular preachers appalled at the worldliness of the clergy; from monks and nuns eager to leave corrupt cloisters to wily politicians eager to slip from Rome's grasp. Whereas in previous centuries movements for reform had been contained within the resilient structures of the monastic system, no new order could encompass this explosion—particularly since it was in part a rejection of the monastic system itself. Politically, Europe was seeing the emergence of something like the modern nation-state, and many political leaders were eager to flex their muscles against papal control or interference. Technologically, the new printing press meant that the views of the reformers could be broadcast with staggering speed; Luther's ninety-five theses, for instance, spread throughout Germany in a fortnight.

The Christ who emerges in the Reformation is a Christ who does not fit within the structures of medieval Catholicism, a difficult Christ who does not lend himself easily to humble imitation, a bitter, unpalatable Christ who calls into question all human confidence, all attempts at self-justification, but who holds out his hands to the weak.

He is also a Christ who, at first, shrugs off the accumulation of scholastic distinctions—but who soon becomes embroiled in the most heated and detailed Christological debates since the early Byzantine centuries. The Reformation did not lead to one coherent alternative to the existing Church hierarchy, but to a variety of differing Churches who found it hard to agree, particularly over the Eucharist. The eucharistic debates swiftly became debates about the relationship between Christ's two natures, and within a few years of Philip Melanchthon's dismissal of dry debates about the 'manner of the Incarnation' (cf. 163), Protestant groups were debating just that, more fiercely than any scholastics.

The Counter-Reformation should not be understood simply as a reaction to the Protestant Reformation; it is, rather, in large part a product of the same reforming energies which fed into the latter, but harnessed within the existing structures of the Catholic Church. Reforms were undertaken at the Council of Trent (cf. 175), which overcame many late medieval abuses; new orders such as the Jesuits were founded (cf. 186); new waves of devotion sprang up (cf. 183–7). Catholic missionaries travelled with the Spanish to the Americas, with the Portuguese to India, Ceylon, Japan, and China. All this energy was, in part, sustained or shaped by new devotion to Christ; whether in the Theatine spirituality which sprang up in Rome (187), in the flourishing of Spanish mysticism (184), or in the Ignatian Spiritual Exercises of the Jesuits (186).

However, the conflict between Protestants and Catholics was all too often bloody. In the German lands in the middle of the century there was civil war, the Catholic forces of the Holy Roman Empire eventually defeating the Protestants; in France the conflict lasted for the whole of the century until the Edict of Nantes in 1598, which allowed some religious freedom to Protestants—but by that time some 2 million, Protestant and Catholic, had died.

Section A

Christ and his Benefits

The Reformation was marked by an urgent concentration on salvation. Far less concerned with, for instance, the death of Christ as an example of humility, or as a means of moving believers to grief, love, and penitence, Reformation writers focused on the death as the means by which the judgement due to sinful human beings was both made blindingly clear and diverted. It is this salvific transaction by which helpless humanity is both judged and set on a new footing, and the discussions of sin, law, grace, and justification which make sense of it, which dominate Reformation thinking about Jesus.

163 Against Scholasticism

Philip Melanchthon (1497–1560) was something of a renaissance man: a professor of Greek and a lover of classical learning. He was the first systematic theologian of the Lutheran Reformation, his *Loci Communes* its first systematic theology. The following extract is his manifesto for a theology dominated by a Reformation understanding of salvation. Given the debates represented in Section C below, it is also a rather poignant text.

We do better to adore the mysteries of Deity than to investigate them. What is more, these matters cannot be probed without great danger, and even holy men have often experienced this. The Lord God Almighty clothed his Son with flesh that he might draw us from contemplating his own majesty to a consideration of the flesh and especially of our weakness. Paul writes in 1 Cor. 1: 21 [cf. **59**] that God wishes to be known in a new way, i.e. through the foolishness of preaching, since in his wisdom he could not be known through wisdom. Therefore there is no reason why we should labour so much on those exalted topics such as 'God', 'The Unity and Trinity of God', 'The Mystery of Creation' and 'The Manner of the Incarnation'. What, I ask you, did the Scholastics accomplish during the many ages they were examining only these points? Have they not, as Paul says, become vain in their disputations, always trifling about universals, formalities, connotations, and various other foolish words? Their stupidity could be left unnoticed if those stupid discussions had not in the meantime covered up for us the gospel and the benefits of Christ.

Now, if I wanted to be clever in an unnecessary pursuit I could easily overthrow all their arguments for the doctrines of the faith. Actually they seem to argue more accurately for certain heresies than they do for the Catholic doctrines.

But as for the one who is ignorant of the other fundamentals, namely, 'The Power of Sin', 'The Law', and 'Grace', I do not see how I can call him a Christian. For from these things Christ is known, since to know Christ means to know his benefits, and not as *they* teach, to reflect upon his natures and the modes of his incarnation. For unless you know why Christ put on flesh and was nailed to the cross, what good will it do you to know merely the history about him? Would you say that it is enough for a physician to know the shapes, colours, and contours of plants, and that it makes no difference whether he knows their innate power? Christ was given us as a remedy and, to use the language of Scripture, a saving remedy. It is therefore proper that we know Christ in another way than that which the Scholastics have set forth.

This, then, is Christian knowledge: to know what the law demands, where you may seek power for doing the law and grace to cover sin, how you may strengthen a quaking spirit against the devil, the flesh, and the world, and how you may console an afflicted conscience. Do the Scholastics teach those things? In his letter to the Romans when he was writing a compendium of Christian doctrine, did Paul philosophise about the mysteries of the Trinity, the mode of incarnation, or active and passive creation? No! But what does he discuss? He takes up the law, sin, grace; fundamentals on which the knowledge of Christ exclusively rests. How often Paul states that he wishes for the faithful a rich knowledge of Christ! For he foresaw that when we had left the saving topics, we would turn our minds to disputations that are cold and foreign to Christ.

Philip Melanchthon, *Loci Communes Theologici*, extract (1521)

164   Sin, Grace, and Salvation

The Augsburg Confession was written by Melanchthon (cf. **163**) as a statement of the Lutheran case to the Roman hierarchy. Afterwards it became (in a revised form) one of the basic documents of Lutheranism. This extract shows how the doctrines of Christology were firmly set within a story about sin, the Fall, grace, and salvation which provides the primary frame of reference for Reformation theology. (Cf. **163**, **217**.)

It is taught among us that since the fall of Adam all men who are born according to the course of nature are conceived and born in sin. That is, all men are full of evil lust and inclinations from their mothers' wombs and are unable by nature to have true fear of God and true faith in God. Moreover, this inborn sickness and hereditary sin is truly sin and condemns to the eternal wrath of God all those who are not born again through Baptism and the Holy Spirit.

Rejected in this connection are the Pelagians and others who deny that original sin is sin, for they hold that natural man is made righteous by his own powers, thus disparaging the sufferings and merit of Christ.

It is also taught among us that God the Son became man, born of the virgin Mary, and that the two natures, divine and human, are so inseparably united in one person that there is one Christ, true God and true man, who was truly born, suffered, was crucified, died, and was buried in order to be a sacrifice not only for original sin but also for all other sins and to propitiate God's wrath. The same Christ also descended into hell, truly rose from the dead on the third day, ascended into heaven, and sits on the right hand of God, that he may eternally rule and have dominion over all creatures, that through the Holy Spirit he may sanctify, purify, strengthen, and comfort all who believe in him, that he may bestow on them life and every grace and blessing, and that he may protect and defend them against the devil and against sin. The same Lord Christ will return openly to judge the living and the dead, as stated in the Apostles' Creed.

It is also taught among us that we cannot obtain forgiveness of sin and righteousness before God by our own merits, works, or satisfactions, but that we receive forgiveness of sin and become righteous before God by grace, for Christ's sake, through faith, when we believe that Christ suffered for us and that for his sake our sin is forgiven and righteousness and eternal life are given to us. For God will regard and reckon this faith as righteousness, as Paul says in Romans 3: 21–26 and 4: 5.

The Augsburg Confession, Articles II–IV (1530)

165 Salvation and the Creed

The Heidelberg Catechism was written by two Calvinist theologians, Zacharias Ursinus (1534–83) and Gaspar Olevian (1536–87). Here it shows the typical Reformation dominance of soteriology: every phrase of the creed concerning Jesus is interpreted by reference to the basic Reformation framework of sin, grace, and salvation. (Cf. **164**, **217**.)

Question 29. *Why is the Son of God called Jesus, which means 'Saviour'?*
Because he saves us from our sins, and because salvation is to be sought or found in no other.

Question 30. *Do those who seek their salvation and well-being from saints, by their own efforts, or by other means really believe in the only Saviour Jesus?*

No. Rather, by such actions they deny Jesus, the only Saviour and Redeemer, even though they boast of belonging to him. It therefore follows that either Jesus is not a perfect Saviour, or those who receive this Saviour with true faith must possess in him all that is necessary for their salvation.

Question 31. *Why is he called 'Christ', that is, the 'Anointed One'?*
Because he is ordained by God the Father and anointed with the Holy Spirit to be our chief Prophet and Teacher, fully revealing to us the secret purpose and will of God concerning our redemption; to be our only High Priest, having redeemed us by the one sacrifice of his body and ever interceding for us with the Father; and to be our eternal King, governing us by his Word and Spirit, and defending and sustaining us in the redemption he has won for us.

Question 32. *But why are you called a Christian?*
Because through faith I share in Christ and thus in his anointing, so that I may confess his name, offer myself a living sacrifice of gratitude to him, and fight against sin and the devil with a free and good conscience throughout this life and hereafter rule with him in eternity over all creatures.

Question 33. *Why is he called 'God's only-begotten Son', since we also are God's children?*
Because Christ alone is God's own eternal Son, whereas we are accepted for his sake as children of God by grace.

Question 34. *Why do you call him 'Our Lord'?*
Because, not with gold or silver but at the cost of his blood, he has redeemed us body and soul from sin and all the dominion of the devil, and has bought us for his very own.

Question 35. *What is the meaning of 'Conceived by the Holy Spirit, born of the virgin Mary'?*
That the eternal Son of God, who is and remains true and eternal God, took upon himself our true manhood from the flesh and blood of the virgin Mary through the action of the Holy Spirit, so that he might also be the true seed of David, like his fellow men in all things, except for sin.

Question 36. *What benefit do you receive from the holy conception and birth of Christ?*
That he is our Mediator, and that, in God's sight, he covers over with his innocence and perfect holiness the sinfulness in which I have been conceived.

Question 37. *What do you understand by the word 'suffered'?*
That throughout his life on earth, but especially at the end of it, he bore in body and soul the wrath of God against the sin of the whole human race, so that by his suffering, as the only expiatory sacrifice, he might redeem our body and soul from everlasting damnation, and might obtain for us God's grace, righteousness, and eternal life.

Question 38. *Why did he suffer 'under Pontius Pilate' as his judge?*
That he, being innocent, might be condemned by an earthly judge, and thereby set us free from the judgment of God which, in all its severity, ought to fall upon us.

Question 39. *Is there something more in his having been crucified than if he had died some other death?*
Yes, for by this I am assured that he took upon himself the curse which lay upon me, because the death of the cross was cursed by God.

Question 40. *Why did Christ have to suffer 'death'?*
Because the righteousness and truth of God are such that nothing else could make reparation for our sins except the death of the Son of God.

Question 41. *Why was he 'buried'?*
To confirm the fact that he was really dead.

Question 42. *Since, then, Christ died for us, why must we also die?*
Our death is not a reparation for our sins, but only a dying to sin and an entering into eternal life.

Question 43. *What further benefit do we receive from the sacrifice and death of Christ on the cross?*
That by his power our old self is crucified, put to death, and buried with him, so that the evil passions of our mortal bodies may reign in us no more, but that we may offer ourselves to him as a sacrifice of thanksgiving.

Question 44. *Why is there added: 'He descended into hell'?*
That in my severest tribulations I may be assured that Christ my Lord has redeemed me from hellish anxieties and torment by the unspeakable anguish, pains, and terrors which he suffered in his soul both on the cross and before.

Question 45. *What benefit do we receive from 'the resurrection' of Christ?*
First, by his resurrection he has overcome death that he might make us share in the righteousness which he has obtained for us through his death. Second, we too are now raised by his power to a new life. Third, the resurrection of Christ is a sure pledge to us of our blessed resurrection.

Question 46. *How do you understand the words: 'He ascended into heaven'?*
That Christ was taken up from the earth into heaven before the eyes of his disciples and remains there on our behalf until he comes again to judge the living and the dead.

Question 47. *Then, is not Christ with us unto the end of the world, as he has promised us?*
Christ is true man and true God. As a man he is no longer on earth, but in his divinity, majesty, grace, and Spirit, he is never absent from us.

Ursinus and Olevian, *The Heidelberg Catechism*, Questions 29–47 (1562)

166 Only Faith

Ursula of Münsterburg (*c.* 1495–after 1534) was a noble Bohemian woman who was placed while still a girl in the convent of Mary Magdalene the Penitent. Unhappy there from the start, she was influenced by a chaplain with Lutheran ideas who convinced her that, since only faith matters, and good works have no merit for salvation, life in the cloister is unnecessary. The security at the convent was lax enough for Ursula and two others to escape in 1528. Later that same year Ursula published an 'Apology' with a preface by Luther. (Cf. **176**.)

Our defence will not impress those who take offence at the crucified Christ, whom we confess to be the power and the wisdom of God. [. . .] You see that our salvation rests only on faith. Our consciences have been greatly troubled and our flesh corrupted. The only hope lies in faith. By baptism we have been received into the kingdom of Christ. To say that the monastic vow is a second baptism and washes away sins, as we have heard from the pulpit, is blasphemy against God, as if the blood of Christ were not enough to wash away all sins. We are married to Christ and to seek to be saved through another is adultery. The three monastic vows are the work of men's hands. There is only one way to relieve our consciences and that is to make a clean break. [. . .] We are as sheep without pasture save through Christ the Shepherd. Our salvation is not so light a thing that we should sell it for human favour, for we know that we have here no abiding place. We must go out to him who was crucified before the gate and bear his shame. We await the time when the same crucified and rejected Christ will come again in the glory of his Father and we trust we shall not be among those to whom he will say, 'I know you not.' Dear friends, brothers and sisters in Christ, these are the reasons we are ready to let go body, life, honour, and goods.

Ursula of Münsterburg, *Apology*, extracts (1528)

167 Victim and Victor

Martin Luther (1483–1546) (cf. **168, 177**) was one of the chief catalysts of the European Reformation; his 1517 protest against the penitential practices of the Church can be taken to mark the public eruption of that Reformation. Luther's own thundering emphasis was on the need for God's free gift of salvation as the only medicine for a humanity incapable of improving or saving itself; a salvation strangely wrought by God through the horror of the Cross. Here, in a 1535 commentary on Galatians 3: 13, Luther explains what took place on the Cross.

All the prophets saw this, that Christ was to become the greatest thief, murderer, adulterer, robber, desecrator, blasphemer, etc., there has ever been anywhere in the world. He is not acting in his own person now. Now he is not the Son of God, born of the Virgin. But he is a sinner, who has and bears the sin of Paul, the former blasphemer, persecutor, and assaulter; of Peter, who denied Christ; of David, who was an adulterer and a murderer, and who caused the Gentiles to blaspheme the name of the Lord. In short, he has and bears all the sins of all men in his body not in the sense that he has committed them but in the sense that he took these sins committed by us upon his own body in order to make satisfaction [cf. **158**] for them with his own blood. Therefore this general Law of Moses included him although he was innocent so far as his own person was concerned, for it found him among sinners and thieves. Thus a magistrate regards someone as a criminal and punishes him if he catches him among thieves, even though the man has never committed anything evil or worthy of death. Christ was not only found among sinners; but of his own free will and by the will of the Father he wanted to be an associate of sinners, having assumed the flesh and blood of those who were sinners and thieves and who were immersed in all sorts of sin. Therefore when the Law found him among thieves, it condemned and executed him as a thief.

This knowledge of Christ and most delightful comfort, that Christ became a curse for us to set us free from the curse of the Law—of this the sophists deprive us when they segregate Christ from sins and from sinners and set him forth to us only as an example to be imitated [cf. **148, 185**]. In this way they make Christ not only useless to us but also a judge and a tyrant who is angry because of our sins and who damns sinners. But just as Christ is wrapped up in our flesh and blood, so we must wrap him and know him to be wrapped up in our sins, our curse, our death, and everything evil. [. . .]

Not only my sins and yours, but the sins of the entire world, past, present, and future, attack him, try to damn him, and do in fact damn him. But because in the same person, who is the highest, the greatest, and the only sinner, there is also eternal and invincible righteousness, therefore these two converge: the highest, the greatest, and the only sin; and the highest, the greatest, and the only righteousness. Here one of them must yield and be conquered, since they come together and collide with such a powerful impact. Thus the sin of the entire world attacks righteousness with the greatest possible impact and fury. What happens? Righteousness is eternal, immortal, and invincible. Sin, too, is a very powerful and cruel tyrant, dominating and ruling over the whole world, capturing and enslaving all men. In short, sin is a great and powerful god who devours the whole human race, all the learned, holy, powerful, wise, and unlearned men. He, I say, attacks Christ and wants to devour him as he has devoured all the rest. But he does not see that he is a person of invincible and eternal righteousness. In this duel, therefore, it is necessary for sin to be conquered and killed, and for righteousness to prevail and live. Thus in Christ all sin is conquered, killed, and buried; and righteousness remains the victor and the ruler eternally.

Martin Luther, *Lectures on Galatians*, on 3: 13, extracts (1535)

168   Theology of the Cross

As the storm broke around Luther (cf. **167**, **177**) after 1517, he was drawn into fierce debates to explain and defend himself. At Heidelberg in 1518 he conducted a 'Disputation' which won several new adherents to his cause. The central part of the Disputation is Luther's contrast between a theology of glory and a theology of the Cross. (Cf. **169**, **141**, **281**.)

That person does not deserve to be called a theologian who looks upon the invisible things of God as though they were clearly perceptible in those things which have actually happened.

This is apparent in the example of those who were 'theologians' and still were called fools by the Apostle in Romans 1: 22. Furthermore, the invisible things of God are virtue, godliness, wisdom, justice, goodness, and so forth. The recognition of all these things does not make one worthy or wise.

He deserves to be called a theologian, however, who comprehends the visible and manifest things of God seen through suffering and the cross.

The manifest and visible things of God are placed in opposition to the invisible, namely, his human nature, weakness, foolishness. The Apostle in 1 Corinthians 1: 25 (**59**) calls them the weakness and folly of God. Because men misused the knowledge of God through works, God wished again to be recognised in suffering, and to condemn wisdom concerning invisible things by means of wisdom concerning visible things, so that those who did not honour God as manifested in his works should honour him as he is hidden in his suffering. As the Apostle says in 1 Corinthians 1, 'For since, in the wisdom of God, the world did not know God through wisdom, it pleased God through the folly of what we preach to save those who believe.' Now it is not sufficient for anyone, and it does him no good, to recognise God in his glory and majesty, unless he recognises him in the humility and shame of the cross. Thus God destroys the wisdom of the wise, as Isaiah says, 'Truly, thou art a God who hidest thyself' [Isa. 45: 15].

So, also, in John 14: 8, where Philip spoke according to the theology of glory, 'Show us the Father.' Christ forthwith set aside his flighty thought about seeing God elsewhere and led him to himself, saying, 'Philip, he who has seen me has seen the Father' [John 14: 9]. For this reason true theology and recognition of God are in the crucified Christ, as it is also stated in John 10 [actually 14: 6]: 'No one comes to the Father, but by me;' 'I am the door' [John 10: 9]; and so forth.

A theology of glory calls evil good and good evil. A theology of the cross calls the thing what it actually is.

This is clear: He who does not know Christ does not know God hidden in suffering. Therefore he prefers works to suffering, glory to the cross, strength to weakness, wisdom to folly, and, in general, good to evil. These are the people whom the apostle calls 'enemies of the cross of Christ' [Phil. 3: 18], for they hate the cross and suffering and love works and the glory of works. Thus they call the good of the cross evil and the evil of a deed good. God can be found only in suffering and the cross, as has already been said. Therefore the friends of the cross say that the cross is good and works are evil, for through the cross works are dethroned and the old Adam, who is especially edified by works, is crucified. It is impossible for a person not to be puffed up by his good works unless he has first been deflated and destroyed by suffering and evil until he knows that he is worthless and that his works are not his but God's.

Martin Luther, *Heidelberg Disputation* 19–21 (1518)

169 The Bitter Christ

Thomas Müntzer (*c.* 1490–1525) was a preacher on the radical wing of the Reformation. He demanded root and branch reforms of the Church (including the end of infant baptism), the formation of a truly Spirit-led Church, and social revolution; he was captured and executed after taking a leading role in the failed Peasants' Revolt. His fervour, as well as the similarity of his Christology to that of Luther, are evident in this extract from a 1523 tract. (Cf. **168**, **141**.)

Sheep are poisoned by bad pastures, but nourished by salt. To preach a sweet

Christ to the fleshly world is the most potent poison that has been given to the dear sheep of Christ from the very beginning. For a man who accepts this wants to be God-formed, but has not the least desire, indeed is totally disinclined, to become Christ-formed. Further—and at the most basic level—he is not even true to himself but changes his appearance in all he sets his hand to like a salamander or a leopard. Hence the insistence of Christ: 'My sheep hear my voice and pay no heed to the voice of the stranger' [John 10: 27] The stranger is anyone who neglects the way to eternal life, leaves the thorns and thistles standing, and proclaims: 'Believe! believe! Be firm, be firm with a strong, strong faith, one which will drive piles into the ground' [Prov. 9: 1].

There is no other basis of faith than the whole Christ; half will not do; for one does not sneak into a house by the window. Any one who rejects the bitter Christ will gorge himself to death on honey. Christ is a corner-stone. Just as he had to be shaped, so we have to be knocked into shape by the master-mason if we are to grow into a true living building. Not a cent must go missing at any time of our lives; every Christian must stand up to scrutiny from top to toe, and must strain his utmost, according to his talent or gift, to measure up to Christ. Only he who dies with Christ can rise with him. How can anyone be living the true life if he has not once taken off his old garment? Therefore those who console before they sadden are thieves and murderers; they want to spring into action before Christ comes; they have no idea what it is to which they say 'Yes' or 'No'.

Thomas Müntzer, On Counterfeit Faith 10–11 (1523)

170   Free Election

Jean Calvin (1509–64) was another of the great Reformers, but unlike Luther his peculiar strengths were in organization, institutional and intellectual. He created a Protestant government in Geneva, and, in his *Institutes of the Christian Religion* (the first edition of which was published in 1536), produced one of the major intellectual achievements of the era. Here he treats the topic of election, which he saw as implied by any talk of truly free grace, and relates it to his Christology. (Cf. **178**.)

Many persons dispute all these positions, which we have set forth, especially the free election of believers; nevertheless, this cannot be shaken. For generally these persons consider that God distinguishes among men according as he foresees what the merits of each will be. Therefore, he adopts as sons those whom he foreknows will not be unworthy of his grace; he appoints to the damnation of death those whose dispositions he discerns will be inclined to evil intentions and ungodliness. [. . .]

They ought at least so to tremble at the example of Christ as not to prate so irresponsibly about this lofty mystery. He is conceived a mortal man of the seed of David. By what virtues will they say that he deserved in the womb itself to be made head of the angels, only-begotten Son of God, image and glory of the Father, light, righteousness, and salvation of the world? Augustine [cf. 38] wisely notes this: namely, that we have in the very head of the church the clearest mirror of free election that we who are among the members may not be troubled about it; and that he was not made Son of God by righteous living but was freely given such honour so that he might afterwards share his gift with others. If here anyone should ask why others were not as he was—or why all of us are corrupt, while he is purity itself, such a questioner would display not only his madness but with it also his shamelessness. But if they wilfully strive to strip God of his free power to choose or reject, let them at the same time also take away what has been given to Christ.

Now it behooves us to pay attention to what Scripture proclaims of every person. When Paul teaches that we were chosen in Christ 'before the creation of the world' [Eph. 1: 14], he takes away all consideration of real worth on our part, for it is just as if he said: since among all the offspring of Adam, the heavenly Father found nothing worthy of his election, he turned his eyes upon his Christ, to choose from his body as members those whom he was to take into the fellowship of life. Let this reasoning, then, prevail among believers: we were adopted in Christ into the eternal inheritance because in ourselves we were not capable of such great excellence.

Jean Calvin, Institutes of the Christian Religion III. 22, extracts (1559)

Section B

Christm in Word and Sacrament

Christ in Word and Sacrament

The Reformation was as much about a reshaping of Church practice as it was about a change in soteriology. Word and Sacrament provided two foci for this process of reformation. On the one hand, new attitudes to the Bible were fostered during the Reformation: attitudes concerning the desirability of its translation into various vernaculars, its wide popular availability, and the importance of expository preaching as the heart of Church life. On the other hand, many of the Reformers protested against the late medieval abuses of the Mass, and of what they saw to be the confusing and obscuring theology of eucharistic transubstantiation (cf. **156**) and sacrifice. However, although there was considerable agreement about the place of the Bible, there was little agreement among the reformers on the theology or practice which should replace the medieval Mass, and the Eucharist became one of the more obvious flashpoints of controversy which prevented the unification of the various reforming Churches.

171 Christ and the Word

Thomas More (1478–1535) was a man of the Renaissance: a classical scholar and a statesman, a political philosopher and devotional writer. He opposed Lutheran theology and, fatally, the English throne's break with Rome. In this dialogue he vigorously opposes a strict biblicism which would make the Bible the only curb which Christ places on his Church, effectively the only means by which Christ's presence within the Church is felt.

[The messenger said,] 'God is and shall be until the world's end with his church in his holy scripture. As Abraham answered the rich man in hell saying, "they have Moses and the prophets" [Luke 16: 29] not meaning that they had *them* all at that time present with them, but only that they had their *books*, so [it is with] Christ forasmuch as the scripture hath his faith comprehended therein according to his own words: "Search you the scriptures for they bear witness of me" [John 5: 39]. Therefore he said, "I am with you to the end of the world," because his holy scripture shall never fail as long as the word endureth: "Heaven and earth," saith he, "shall pass away, but my words shall never pass away" [Matt. 24: 35]. And therefore in his holy writing is he with us still and therein he keepeth and teacheth us his right faith, if we list to look for it, and else [. . .] our own fault and folly it is.'

'If God,' quoth I, 'be none otherwise with us but in holy scripture, then be those words of Christ, "I am with you to the world's end" some-what strangely spoken, and unlike the words of Abraham whereunto ye resemble them. For Christ left never a book behind him of his own making [. . .]

'Christ also said, "I *am* with you till the end of the world," not, "I *shall be*"; but, "I *am*", which is the word appropriated to his godhead. And therefore that word "am" is the name by which our Lord would as he told Moses be named unto Pharaoh, as a name which from all creatures (sith they be all subject to time) clearly discerneth his godhead, which is ever being and present without difference of time past or to come. In which wise he was not in his holy scripture, for that had beginning. And at those words spoken was not yet all written. For of the chief part which is the New Testament there was yet at that time never one word written.

'And also we be not sure by any promise made that the scripture shall endure to the world's end, albeit I think verily the substance shall. But yet, as I say, promise have we none thereof. For where our lord saith that his words shall not pass away, nor one iota thereof be lost, he spake of his promises made in deed as his faith and doctrine taught by mouth and inspiration. He meant not that of his holy scripture in writing there should never a iota be lost, of which some parts be *already* lost; more, peradventure, than we can tell of. And of that we have, the books in some part corrupted with mis-writing. [. . .]

'Christ is also present among us bodily in the holy sacrament. And is he there present with us for nothing? [. . .]

'Our saviour also said unto his apostles that when they should be accused and brought in judgment, they should not need to care for answer; it should even then be put in their minds. And that he meant not only the remembrance of holy scripture which before the paynim judges were but a cold and bare alleging, but such words new given them by God inspired in their hearts so effectual and confirmed with miracles that their adversaries, though they were angry thereat, yet should not be able to resist it. And thus with secret help and inspiration is Christ with his church, and will be to the world's end, present and assistant, not only spoken of in writing.'

Thomas More, A Dialogue concerning Heresies 20, extract (1531)

172 Christ's Absence

Huldreich Zwingli (1484–1531) was the key figure in the Swiss Reformation, whose work and impact developed to some extent independently from Luther. Zwingli's insistence against Luther that no form of Christ's bodily presence in the eucharistic elements must be denied kept the two movements from uniting, despite attempts to broker peace at a Colloquy in

Marburg in 1529. The Christological implications of the debate (cf. **177–81**) are very clear in this extract. (Cf. **14, 176**.)

Note well, good Christian, that in Christ there are two different natures, the divine and the human: and yet the two are only the one Christ. According to his divine nature Christ never left the right hand of the Father, for he is one God with the Father, and that is why he says: 'I and the Father are one' [John 10: 30], and again, 'No man hath ascended up to heaven, but the Son of man which is in heaven' [John 3: 13]. According to his divine nature he did not need to ascend up to heaven: for he is omnipresent. Even where two or three gather together in his name, he is there in the midst. Again, according to this nature he is always at the right hand of the Father, for he says that he is in heaven even when in the body he is upon earth. That was possible only according to his divine nature.

The other nature is Christ's human nature. For our sakes he took this upon him in the pure body of Mary by the receiving and fructifying of the Holy Spirit, and he carried it truly in this present time. According to this nature he increased and grew both in wisdom and stature. According to it he suffered hunger and thirst and cold and heat and all other infirmities, sin only excepted. According to it he was lifted up on the cross, and with it he ascended up into heaven. This nature was a guest in heaven, for no flesh had ever previously ascended up into it. Therefore when we read in Mark 16: 19 that Christ was received up into heaven and sat on the right hand of God we have to refer this to his human nature, for according to his divine nature he is eternally omnipresent, etc. But the saying in Matthew 28: 20 'Lo, I am with you alway, even unto the end of the world' [**19**], can refer only to his divine nature, for it is according to that nature that he is everywhere present to believers with his special gifts and comfort.

If without distinction we were to apply to his human nature everything that refers to the divine, and conversely, if without distinction we were to apply to the divine nature everything that refers to the human, we should over-throw all Scripture and indeed the whole of our faith. For what can we make of a saying like: 'My God, my God, why hast thou forsaken me?' [**16**] if we try to refer it to his divine nature? And the same is true of countless other Scriptures, although I know that by virtue of the fact that the two natures are one Christ, things which are said of only the one nature are often ascribed to the other. Nevertheless, the proper character of each nature must be left intact, and we ought to refer to it only those things which are proper to it. For instance, it is often said that God suffered on our behalf. This saying is tolerated by Christians and I myself do not object to it: not that the Godhead can suffer, but because he who suffered according to his human nature is very God as well as very man. Yet strictly speaking, the suffering appertains only to the humanity. [. . .]

That which is said concerning the Ascension must be referred specifically to the human nature, as, for example, in Mark 16: 'He was received up into heaven, and sat on the right hand of God.' And that which is proper to his divine nature must be referred specifically to that nature, as for example, his omnipresence, his abiding fellowship with us, his presence in all our hearts, and that all things consist in him, etc. In our reading of Scripture this distinction must always be made.

But if Christ is now seated at the right hand of God, and will sit there until he comes at the last day, how can he be literally eaten in the sacrament? You say: 'He is God. He can be everywhere.' But note with what circumspection you say this. First you say: He is God. You give it to be understood that it is the property of God to be everywhere. But it is not the property of the body. I will elucidate. In John 16: 28 Christ says: 'I came forth from the Father, and am come into the world: again, I leave the world, and go to the Father.' Note that these words contradict his saying: 'Lo, I am with you alway, even unto the end of the world,' for here he says: 'Again, I leave the world.' How then does he leave the world? With his divine presence and protection and grace and goodness and loving-kindness? God forbid: it is not for any creature to say that. But necessarily he has left us, for he said so himself, and he cannot lie. It follows, then, that he has departed from us at any rate in the body, he has left us in the body.

And there is nothing singular in that, for in Matthew 26: 11 he said even more plainly: 'You have the poor always with you; but me you have not always.' Now if the saying: 'Lo, I am with you alway, even unto the end of the world,' refers to the body of Christ, it follows that he is with us in the body, but not with divine grace and power, for he said: 'Me you have not always.' But that saying is incredible and misleading if we refer it to his divine nature. Therefore we have conclusive proof that the two sayings: 'Again, I leave the world,' and: 'Me you have not always,' both refer to the departure and absence of his human nature. But if he has gone away, if he has left the world, if he is no longer with us, then either the Creed is unfaithful to the words of Christ, which is impossible, or else the body and blood of Christ cannot be present in the sacrament.

Zwingli, *On the Lord's Supper*, extract (1526)

173   Exhibiting without Containing Grace

Richard Hooker (*c.* 1554–1600) was the greatest theologian of the Anglican Church, as created by the settlement under Elizabeth I. Standing against Roman Catholicism on the one hand and the Puritans on the other, he tried to define a moderate Protestant position. (Cf. **14, 156**.)

Seeing that by opening the several opinions which have been held they are grown (for ought I can see) on all sides at the length to a general agreement concerning that which alone is material, namely the *real participation* of Christ and of life in his body and blood *by means of this sacrament*, wherefore should the world continue still distracted and rent with so manifold contentions when there remaineth now no controversy saving only about the subject *where* Christ is? Yea even in this point no side denieth but that the soul of man is the receptacle of Christ's presence. Whereby the question is yet driven to a narrower issue, nor doth anything rest doubtful but this: whether, when the sacrament is administered, Christ be whole *within man only* or else his body and blood be also externally seated in the very consecrated elements themselves, which opinion, they that defend, are driven either to *consubstantiate* and incorporate Christ with elements sacramental or to *transubstantiate* and change their substance into his, and so the one to hold him really, but invisibly moulded up with the substance of those elements, the other to hide him under the only visible show of bread and wine, the substance whereof (as they imagine) is abolished and his succeeded in the same room.

All things considered and compared with that success, which truth hath hitherto had, by so bitter conflicts with errors in this point, shall I wish that men would more give themselves to meditate with silence what we have by the sacrament, and less to dispute of the manner how? [. . .]

Is there anything more expedite, clear and easy than that as Christ is termed our life because through him we obtain life, so the parts of this sacrament are his body and blood for that they are so to us who receiving them receive that by them which they are termed? The bread and cup are his body and blood because they are causes instrumental upon the receipt whereof the participation of his body and blood ensueth. For that which produceth any certain effect is not vainly nor improperly said to be that very effect whereunto it tendeth. Every cause is in the effect which groweth from it. Our souls and bodies quickened to eternal life are effects the cause whereof is the person of Christ; his body and his blood are the true wellspring out of which this life floweth. So that his body and blood are in that very subject whereunto they minister life, not only by effect or operation (even as the influence of the heavens is in plants, beasts, men, and in every thing which they quicken), but also by a far more divine and mystical kind of union which maketh us one with him even as he and the father are one.

The real presence of Christ's most blessed body and blood is not therefore to be sought for in the sacrament, but in the worthy receiver of the sacrament. And with this the very order of our Saviour's words agreeth: first 'Take and eat'; then 'This is my body which was broken for you'; first

'Drink ye all of this,' then followeth 'This is my blood of the new testament which is shed for many for the remission of sins' [Mark 14: 22–4.]

I see not which way it should be gathered by the words of Christ when and where the bread is his body or the cup his blood but only in the very heart and soul of him which receiveth them. As for the sacraments they really exhibit, but for ought we can gather out of that which is written of them they are not really nor do really contain in themselves that grace which with them or by them it pleaseth God to bestow. [. . .]

The fruit of the Eucharist is the participation of the body and blood of Christ. There is no sentence of holy scripture which saith that we cannot by this sacrament be made partakers of his body and blood except they be first contained in the sacrament or the sacrament converted into them. 'This is my body,' and 'This is my blood,' being words of promise, sith we all agree that by the sacrament Christ doth really and truly in us perform his promise, why do we vainly trouble ourselves with so fierce contentions whether by consubstantiation or else by transubstantiation the sacrament itself be first possessed with Christ or no?—a thing which no way can either further or hinder us howsoever it stand, because our participation of Christ in this sacrament dependeth on the co-operation of his omnipotent power which maketh it his body and blood to us, whether with change or without alteration of the element such as they imagine we need not greatly to care nor inquire.

Take therefore that wherein all agree and then consider by itself what cause why the rest in question should not rather be left as superfluous than urged as necessary. It is on all sides plainly confessed:

— first that this sacrament is a true and a real participation of Christ, who thereby imparteth himself, even his whole entire person, *as a mystical head* unto every soul that receiveth him, and that every such receiver doth thereby incorporate or unite himself unto Christ *as a mystical member* of him, yea of them also whom he acknowledgeth to be his own;
— secondly that to whom *the person of Christ* is thus communicated to them he giveth by the same sacrament his holy spirit to sanctify them as it sanctifieth him which is their head;
— thirdly that what *merit, force or virtue soever there is in his sacrificed body and blood*, we freely, fully and wholly have it by this sacrament;
— fourthly that *the effect thereof in us is a real transmutation of our souls and bodies* from sin to righteousness, from death and corruption to immortality and life;
— fifthly that because the sacrament, being of itself but a corruptible and earthly creature, must needs be thought an unlikely instrument to work so admirable effects in man, we are therefore to rest ourselves altogether

upon *the strength of his glorious power* who is able and will bring to pass that the bread and cup which he giveth us shall be truly the thing he promiseth.

Richard Hooker, Of the Laws of Ecclesiastical Polity v. 67. 2–3, 5–7, extracts (1597)

174 Eating, Dwelling, and Washing

> In 1548 an English supplement to the Latin Prayer Book was drawn up, containing a set of prayers for Communion. This, the Prayer of Humble Access was composed for the book; like the rest it was intended as an English interlude in an otherwise Latin Mass. Although it leans in a fairly Catholic direction theologically, it survived in all later versions of the English Prayer Book. (Cf. **42**.)

We do not presume to come to this thy table, O merciful Lord, trusting in our own righteousness, but in thy manifold and great mercies; we be not worthy so much as to gather up the crumbs under the table. But thou art the same Lord, whose property is always to have mercy: Grant us therefore gracious Lord so to eat the flesh of thy dear son Jesus Christ, and to drink his blood in these holy mysteries, that we may continually dwell in him, and he in us, that our sinful bodies may be made clean by his body, and our souls washed through his most precious blood. Amen.

The body of our Lord Jesus Christ, which was given for thee, preserve thy body unto everlasting life.

The blood of our Lord Jesus Christ, which was shed for thee, preserve thy soul unto everlasting life.

'The Order of Communion', extract (1548)

175 The Sacrifice of the Mass

> The Council of Trent, which sat between 1545 and 1563, was the seal of the Counter-Reformation. In reaction against the Reformation, but also in response to many of the calls for reform which had fed the Reformation, the council undertook a thorough examination of dogma and discipline in the Church. In 1562 the Eucharist was discussed, and a doctrine of transubstantiation affirmed against all varieties of Reformation eucharistic theology. (Cf. **156**.)

Since under the former Testament, according to the testimony of the apostle Paul, there was no perfection because of the weakness of the Levitical priesthood, there was need, God the Father of mercies so ordaining, that another priest should rise according to the order of Melchisedech, our Lord Jesus Christ, who might perfect and lead to perfection as many as were to be sanctified. He, therefore, our God and Lord, although he was by his death about to offer himself once upon the altar of the cross to God the Father that he might there accomplish an eternal redemption, nevertheless, that his priesthood might not come to an end with his death, at the last supper, on the night he was betrayed, that he might leave to his beloved spouse the church a visible sacrifice, such as the nature of man requires, whereby that bloody sacrifice once to be accomplished on the cross might be represented, the memory thereof remain even to the end of the world, and its salutary effects applied to the remission of those sins which we daily commit, declaring himself constituted a priest forever according to the order of Melchisedech, offered up to God the Father his own body and blood under the form of bread and wine, and under the forms of those same things gave to the apostles, whom he then made priests of the New Testament, that they might partake, commanding them and their successors in the priesthood by these words to do likewise ('Do this in commemoration of me' [14]), as the Catholic Church has always understood and taught.

For having celebrated the ancient passover which the multitude of the children of Israel sacrificed in memory of their departure from Egypt, he instituted a new passover, namely, himself, to be immolated under visible signs by the church through the priests in memory of his own passage from this world to the Father, when by the shedding of his blood he redeemed and delivered us from the power of darkness and translated us into his kingdom. And this is indeed that clean oblation which cannot be defiled by any unworthiness or malice on the part of those who offer it; which the Lord foretold by Malachias was to be great among the Gentiles, and which the apostle Paul has clearly indicated when he says, that they who are defiled by partaking of the table of devils cannot be partakers of the table of the Lord, understanding by table in each case the altar. It is, finally, that sacrifice which was prefigured by various types of sacrifices during the period of nature and of the law, which, namely, comprises all the good things signified by them, as being the consummation and perfection of them all.

And inasmuch as this divine sacrifice which is celebrated in the Mass is contained and immolated in an unbloody manner the same Christ who once offered himself in a bloody manner on the altar of the cross, the holy council teaches that this is truly propitiatory and has this effect, that if we, contrite and penitent, with sincere heart and upright faith, with fear and reverence, draw nigh to God, we obtain mercy and find grace in seasonable aid. For, appeased by this sacrifice, the Lord grants the grace and gift of penitence and pardons even the gravest crimes and sins. For the victim is one and the same, the same now offering by the ministry of priests who then offered himself on the cross, the manner alone of offering being different. The fruits of that bloody sacrifice, it is well understood, are received most abundantly through this unbloody one, so far is the latter from derogating in any way from the former. Wherefore, according to the tradition of the apostles, it is rightly offered not only for the sins, punishments, satisfactions, and other necessities of the faithful who are living, but also for those departed in Christ but not yet fully purified.

Canons and Decrees of the Council of Trent, Session 22, 1–2 (1562)

176   Torture and the Eucharist

> Elizabeth Dirks (d. 1549) was a Dutch Anabaptist. An escaped nun like Ursula of Münsterburg (cf. 166), she was arrested while fleeing. She was interrogated about her beliefs, tortured with thumb- and leg-screws in a vain attempt to make her recant or incriminate her friends, and finally drowned in a sack. Although other issues arose, to do with baptism, the Church, and confession, her views on the Eucharist loom large in the accounts of her interrogation.

EXAMINERS: What do you think of our Mass?

ELIZABETH: My Lords, I have no faith in your Mass but only in that which is in the Word of God.

EXAMINERS: What do you believe about the Holy Sacrament?

ELIZABETH: I have never in my life read in Scripture about a Holy Sacrament, but only of the Supper of the Lord.

EXAMINERS: Shut your mouth. The devil speaks through it.

ELIZABETH: Yes, my Lords, this is a little matter, for the servant is not greater than his Lord.

EXAMINERS: You speak with a haughty tongue.

ELIZABETH: No, my Lords, I speak with a free tongue.

EXAMINERS: What did the Lord say when he gave the supper to his disciples?

ELIZABETH: What did he give them, flesh or bread?

EXAMINERS: He gave them bread.

ELIZABETH: Did not the Lord continue to sit there? How then could they eat his flesh? [. . .]

EXAMINERS: You say that you accept everything in accord with Holy Scripture. Do you not then hold to the word of James?

ELIZABETH: How can I not hold to it?

EXAMINERS: Did he not say, 'Go to the elders of the congregation that they should anoint you and pray for you' [Jas. 5: 13]?

ELIZABETH: Yes, but would you say, my Lords, that you are such a congregation?

EXAMINERS: The Holy Ghost has made you so holy that you don't need penance or the sacrament?

ELIZABETH: No, my Lords. I freely confess that I have transgressed the ordinances of the pope which the emperor has confirmed with placards. But if you can show me that in any articles I have transgressed against the Lord, my God, I will wail over myself as a miserable sinner.

'Account of the examination of Elizabeth Dirks', extracts (1549)

Section C

Christ in Two Natures

Despite Melanchthon's belief that the vanity of medieval scholasticism had been shown in nothing more than its disputations 'upon Christ's natures and the modes of his incarnation' (163), the bitter disagreements over the Eucharist among the Reformers inevitably developed into deep-seated differences in Christology. Far from leaving Christological debates behind, the period immediately after the Reformation saw some of the most hard-fought debates in technical Christology ever to be pursued in the West.

177   The Unity of the Natures

At the heart of the Christological debates of the Reformation period was a disagreement between Luther and Calvin over what might properly be said of the human nature of Christ. The debate was tied to the eucharistic debates: what might be said of the bodily presence of Christ in the Eucharist was determined by what might in general be said of the body of Christ due to its assumption by the divine Word. Luther (cf. 167) here explains some of the basic grammar which he sees governing talk of the two natures. (Cf. 181.)

When speaking of Christ here one must teach clearly that he is one Person, but that there are two distinct natures, the divine and the human [86]. Again, just as there the nature or the divine essence remains unmingled in the Father and in Christ, so also the Person of Christ remains undivided here. Therefore the attributes of each nature, the human and the divine, are ascribed to the entire Person, and we say of Christ: 'The man Christ, born of the Virgin, is omnipotent and does all that we ask—not, however, according to the human but according to the divine nature, not by reason of his birth from his mother but because he is God's Son.' And again, 'Christ, God's Son, prays to the Father, not according to his divine nature and essence, according to which he is coequal with the Father, but because he is true man and Mary's Son.' Thus the words must he brought together and compared according to the unity of the Person. The natures must always be differentiated, but the Person must remain undivided.

And now since he is believed as one Person, God and man, it is also proper for us to speak of him as each nature requires. Some words reflect his human, others his divine nature. Therefore we should consider what Christ says according to his human nature and what he says according to his divine nature. For where this is not observed and properly distinguished, many types of heresy must result, as happened in times gone by, when some people asserted that Christ was not true God and others that he was not true man. They were unable to follow the principle of differentiating between the two types of discourse on the basis of the two natures [cf. **82, 83, 172**].

Christ often spoke as the lowliest man on earth should hardly speak. For example, when he says: 'I have not come to be served, but to serve' [Matt. 20: 28]. With these words he really makes himself a servant among all men, although he is true God and Lord over all creatures, whom all must serve and worship. And in Psalm 41: 4 he makes himself a sinner and says that he is being punished because of sin. This, of course, is out of the question accord-ing to the divine nature. And again, he employs the speech of exalted majesty, such as no angel or creature should use, even though he was in the lowliest form and figure of his sojourn on earth. We read, for instance, in John 6: 62: 'Then what if you were to see the Son of Man ascending where he was before?'

Yes, all that Scripture says of Christ covers the whole Person, just as though both God and man were one essence. Often it uses expressions inter-changeably and assigns the attributes of both to each nature. This is done for the sake of the personal union, which we call the 'communication of proper-ties'. Thus we can say: 'The Man Christ is God's eternal Son, by whom all creatures were created, Lord of heaven and earth.' And by the same token we say: 'Christ, God's Son (that is, the Person who is true God), was con-ceived and born of the Virgin Mary, suffered under Pontius Pilate, crucified and dead.' Furthermore: 'God's Son sits at meat with tax collectors and sinners, and washes the feet of the disciples.' He does not do this, of course, according to the divine nature. But since this is done by one and the same Person, it is correct to say that God's Son is doing it. Thus St. Paul declares in 1 Corinthians 2: 8: 'If they had understood this, they would not have crucified the Lord of glory.' And Christ himself states in John 6: 62: 'What if you were to see the Son of Man ascending where he was before?' This is really spoken of the divine nature, which alone was with the Father from eternity; yet it is also said of the person who is true man.

In brief, whatever this person, Christ, says and does, is said and done by both, true God and true man, so that all his words and works must always be attributed to the whole Person and are not divided, as though he were not true God or not true man. But this must be done in such a way as to identify and recognise each nature properly. If we want to speak correctly and dis-tinctly of each, then we must say: 'God's nature is different from man's. The human nature is not from eternity as the divine nature is; and the divine nature was not born temporally, nor did it die temporally, etc., like the human nature. And yet the two are united in one Person. Therefore there is but one Christ, and we may say of him: "This man is God; this man created all things." '

Martin Luther, *Sermons on the Gospel of John*, on 14: 16 (1537–8)

178   The Immeasurable and the Measurable

> Calvin (cf. **170**) for his part was concerned that talk of Christ's human nature should not deny the limitations of humanity—including its natural susceptibility to sin. He was led therefore to speak in the following way, which Lutherans took as dangerously close to a denial of the unity of the person.[1]

They thrust upon as something absurd the fact that if the Word of God became flesh, then he was confined within the narrow prison of an earthly body. This is mere impudence! For even if the Word in his immeasurable essence united with the nature of man into one person, we do not imagine that he was confined therein. Here is something marvellous: the Son of God descended from heaven in such a way that, without leaving heaven, he willed to be born in the virgin's womb, to go about the earth, and to hang upon the cross; yet he continuously filled the world even as he had done from the beginning!

Institutes II. 13, extract

For we make Christ free of all stain not just because he was begotten of his mother without copulation with man, but because he was sanctified by the Spirit that the generation might be pure and undefiled as would have been true before Adam's fall—i.e. Christ's holiness is not something natural to an unfallen human nature, but a work of the Spirit. [Cf. **254**.]

Institutes II. 13. 4, extract

We do not doubt that Christ's body is limited by the general characteristics common to all human bodies, and is contained in heaven.

Institutes IV. 17. 12, extract

We must establish such a presence of Christ in the Supper as may not take from him his own stature, or parcel him out to many places at once, or invest him with boundless magnitude to be spread through heaven and earth. For these things are plainly in conflict with a nature truly human.

Jean Calvin, *Institutes of the Christian Religion* II. 17. 19, extract (1559)

179   Ubiquitous Humanity?

The debate between the Lutheran and Calvinist understandings of the limitations of Christ's humanity is clearly set out in this dialogue by Pietro Martire Vermigli (1499–1562), an Augustinian abbot turned Reformer. In the dialogue Pantachus represents the Lutheran position, Orothetes Vermigli's own Calvinist position. (Cf. **181**.)

P: Answer me this. Since you grant to the humanity of Christ because of the hypostatic union the power of vivifying, healing and sanctifying, why are you later so difficult and grudging that you are unwilling to concede that it is everywhere and fills all things when this property is much inferior in dignity and excellence to those just mentioned? There is a popular saying: Why does he who grants the big things deny the little ones?

O: I have a ready answer. Because the powers and faculties you listed do not destroy human nature but perfect it. But it's impossible to make the humanity coextensive with the Godhead without making the humanity also infinite which is the same thing as destroying it.

Let's not argue for now which of the two sets of the gifts or properties, which you just compared with each other, is better than the other. I say that I don't accept that doctrine of yours which you enunciated with complete confidence: that we should give lesser powers to the nature to which we have granted greater ones. For man is made to the image of God, which condition is undoubtedly most excellent. But he was not given the strength of lions nor the sharp eyesight of eagles. Arguments of this kind are probable, but they do not prove the question at issue firmly and solidly or, as the Greeks say, apodictically.

P: Whatever the outcome of our previous discussions back and forth, there now comes to my mind something I often used to think about: you shrink away from our teaching because you don't really grasp it. You of course think that we believe that the humanity is everywhere and fills all things by its own nature—which is not at all our position since we say it does not have that power from itself. Neither do we think that this power should be attributed to the humanity if it is considered in isolation. The Word communicates that property to it. That prerogative is attributed to it because of the hypostatic union which it has with the Word. In conclusion we say that the body of Christ does not fill all things insofar as it is a human body but insofar as it is an assumed body.

O: Neither case is acceptable. For a body as human can't fill all things, as you yourself just admitted; nor can it do so as conjoined to the divine nature in the same person. Certainly the divine hypostasis does not rob the body it assumes of being a real human body, and it belongs to its definition to be organic, as the philosophers call it. In fact instruments are defined and embraced by the limits of their activity. Hence they can't at the very same time fill all places, and since they are limited and defined, they can't be coextensive with the infinite.

P: But we do not stretch out the body of Christ by spatial diffusion, just as the divinity itself is not spatially diffused.

O: Just look at what you're doing. We know this for sure, that any sort of human body at all, united to any sort of nature, by any sort of union that pleases you, simply can't fill a place except spatially. And that is restricted to the Godhead, which is a spirit so that it can be present nonspatially. And since it is a Spirit, indeed an infinite one, it can't be limited by any places or boundaries. [. . .]

P: If we have accounted for the divine way in which we assert how God fills all things, then if you were to grant the hypostatic union of the two natures in Christ, you either have to admit that the humanity of Christ fills all things or you affirm the unity of the divine person in words but you dissolve in reality that union by establishing two persons: one someplace with the humanity and the other someplace without the humanity. Each nature in Christ, the human and the divine, retains its own property but in a way so that the person of Christ is not divided and that wherever the divine nature exists, it has there the human nature united to it, lest if these two natures are separated by different places, different persons come into existence.

O: We indeed grant that God fills all things by his infinite essence, and we do not deny the hypostatic union of the two natures in Christ, as you have heard often enough. But that does not force us to profess that the humanity of Christ fills all things. As to your contention that it follows that we only verbally assert the unity of his person but really dissolve it—that's a barefaced lie. For the union of the humanity with the divinity should be appraised in such wise that no more of the divine properties are transferred over to the humanity than the humanity has capacity for. And as the infinity of the Godhead can't be restricted to the limits of the humanity or of man's little body, so the finite humanity and the limited substance of the human body can't be coextensive with the limitless divinity. Certainly the human head is united to the rest of the body and does not have a different hypostasis from it, but it nevertheless does not occupy as much space as the rest of the body. But if this is true when we compare body with body, and both are finite, how should it not be admitted all the more when the creature is compared with the creator and the finite with the infinite? Because of the screeching sound that you so often emit, I am also forced to keep coming back to my comparison.

Pietro Martire Vermigli, *Dialogue on the Two Natures in Christ* iii, extracts (1561)

180   Errors Concerning the Union

The 1577 Formula of Concord (incorporated three years later with other foundational documents in *The Book of Concord*) definitively sets out the basic Lutheran position on (among other issues) divinity and humanity in Christ—although some non-German Lutherans never accepted the book's authority. (Cf. **177, 181**.)

We unanimously reject and condemn with mouth and heart all errors which are inconsistent with the doctrine here set forth as contrary to the prophetic and apostolic writings, the orthodox Creeds, and our Christian Augsburg Confession:

1. If anyone were to believe or teach that because of the personal union the human nature has allegedly been blended with the divine or has been transformed into it.
2. Likewise, that the human nature in Christ is everywhere present in the same way as the Deity, as an infinite essence, through an essential power or property of its nature.
3. Likewise, that the human nature in Christ has been equalised with and has become equal to the divine nature in its substance and essence or in its essential properties.
4. Likewise, that the humanity of Christ is locally extended into every place in heaven and earth, something which ought not be attributed to the deity. Without transforming or destroying his true human nature, Christ's omnipotence and wisdom can readily provide that through his divine omnipotence Christ can be present with his body, which he has placed at the right hand of the majesty and power of God, wherever he desires and especially where he has promised his presence in his Word, as in the Holy Communion. [Cf. **179**.]
5. Likewise, that the mere human nature of Christ alone, with which the Son of God had no communion whatever in the passion, suffered for us and redeemed us.
6. Likewise, that in the preached Word and in the right use of the holy sacraments Christ is present with us on earth only according to his deity, and that this presence does not involve his assumed human nature in any way whatever.
7. Likewise, that the assumed human nature in Christ does not share in deed and truth in the divine power, might, wisdom, majesty, and glory, but has only the bare title and name in common with it.
8. We reject and condemn these errors and all others that contradict and contravene the above doctrine as being contrary to the pure Word of God, the writings of the holy prophets and apostles, and our Christian Creed

and Confession. Since the Holy Scriptures call Christ a mystery over which all heretics break their heads, we admonish all Christians not to pry presumptuously into this mystery with their reason, but with the holy apostles simply to believe, close the eyes of reason, take their intellect captive to obey Christ, comfort themselves therewith, and rejoice constantly that our flesh and blood have in Christ been made to sit so high at the right hand of the majesty and almighty power of God. In this way they will be certain to find abiding comfort in all adversities and will be well protected against pernicious errors.

The Formula of Concord, Solid Declaration VIII, extract (1577)

181 Communication Between the Natures

Martin Chemnitz (1522–86) was one of the greatest codifiers of Lutheran theology, and one of his most important contributions was the following analysis (an extract from a much longer discussion) of the ways in which the attributes of one nature in Christ relate to the attributes of another, the so-called *communicatio idiomatum*. (Cf. **177**.)

As Luther rightly says, the hypostatic union of the two natures in the one person of Christ does not permit the kind of division whereby I can properly say that the divine nature of Christ does this or the human nature does that. For such a division of works would be followed by a division of the person, for the actions, as Damascenus says, are not of the natures but of the person [cf. **85**, **107**]. Hence the property which is characteristic of one nature is communicated or attributed to the person in the concrete or through a concrete term, as when we say that God died or that the Son of Man descended from heaven.[2] For there is one person who subsists in both natures or who consists of two natures. Therefore, this is the first degree or first category of the communication of attributes, namely, when that which is proper to one nature is predicated of the person concretely. It is customary in this predication to add the statement that something is attributed to the person *according to a particular nature* [cf. **177**].

Second, it is abundantly clear that this is not the only kind of communication which results from the hypostatic union of the two natures in the one person of Christ. For this wondrous union of his two natures took place in such a way that those things which pertain to the office of the Messiah, the Son of God was unwilling to accomplish only in one nature, either the divine or the human, but rather in, with, and through each. Therefore the descriptions and the works of the offices of Christ are attributed to his person, not according to only one nature but *according to both*. And the person in these offices carries on activities in and according to both natures at the same time.

Furthermore, because of the hypostatic union, each nature in Christ, although it has its own properties, yet does not have its own separate actions whereby the divine nature would carry out its activities separately from the humanity or the humanity from the deity. But according to the definition of the Council of Chalcedon each nature in Christ 'performs in communion with the other that which is proper to each' [86]. [. . .]

In the first category the properties either of the individual nature or of both natures are considered in themselves and separately, and nothing is attributed to the person [as a whole], but only to that particular nature whose properties they are, as Luther says in his *Major Confessio de Coena Domini*: 'The person of Christ acts now according to this and now according to that nature.' But in the second degree or category we turn our attention to the work to which the actions of each nature apply, or the work which one nature performs in communion with the other according to its properties. In this genus the things which are attributed to the person are appropriate to it not only according to one nature but according to both. This is the plain difference between the first and second genera.

Third, in addition to this it is certain and manifest that there is something which results from and follows the hypostatic union of Christ's natures. For in the divine nature of Christ, because it is perfect and immutable, there certainly can be no change, either diminution or addition. But the assumed human nature in Christ not only has and retains its own natural properties, but above, beyond, and in addition to its essential properties, because of the hypostatic union with the divine nature of the Logos (while the substance of the humanity remains intact and also keeps its essential attributes unimpaired), it also is adorned and enriched with and increased and exalted by innumerable and excellent prerogatives, pre-eminences, dignities, and excellencies (or whatever you may wish to call them) which are above every name that is named not only in this life but in the life to come. Christ's humanity does not possess these prerogatives by virtue of its own nature, but receives and possesses them as gifts which have been communicated by the intimate hypostatic union with the divine nature, through interpenetration (perichoresis), beyond and above the condition of all men and even the angels themselves.

[. . .] For it is a sure and undeniable fact that his human nature, as a result of the hypostatic union, has received and still possesses, in addition to its own natural properties or essential attributes, also innumerable gifts which are above and beyond nature. It is also a fact that this assumed nature co-operates in the offices of the kingship and the high priesthood of Christ and receives its efficacy not only from its own natural properties but particularly from and according to those pre-eminent and excellent dignities and prerogatives which it has received and possesses because of the hypostatic union with Christ's divine nature. [. . .]

It is clear that this genus is different and distinct from the two preceding ones. In the first degree or genus the property of one nature is not attributed to the other nature so that it becomes also an essential property of it, but it is attributed to the person according to that nature of which it is an essential property. And in the first genus, although the properties of the natures are actually attributed to the person, yet only those things are attributed to the natures themselves which are naturally and essentially theirs. In the first genus this communication to the one person is reciprocal and mutual among the properties of both the divine and the human natures. [. . .]

Further, this third genus is manifestly different and distinct from the second. For in the second genus each nature in Christ acts in communication with the other, but we must add the words 'that which belongs to each.' But in this third genus the person of Christ in his function as King and High Priest performs and carries on at the same time both in, with, and through the human nature. It does this not only according to and through the attributes which belong to the human nature in itself and are considered according to its principles, but [. . .] particularly according to those attributes which his human nature has received and possesses above, beyond, and outside its natural properties. All this is a result of the hypostatic union with the Logos and because of the interpenetration (perichoresis).

Martin Chemnitz, *The Two Natures in Christ* xii, extract (1578)

182   King amid the Kine

Moving away from the debates of Reformation or Counter-Reformation theology, we can turn to Vittoria Colonna (1490–1547), best known as a friend and inspiration to Michelangelo. After the death of her husband she became an admired poet. Dissatisfied with the violence and worldliness of Italian society, she became attracted by the message of the Capuchin[3] preacher Bernardino Ochino[4] and adopted an ascetic, Christ-centred piety. (Cf. **1, 99, 244**.)

> What joy, oh star and blessed sign
> Twinkling on the cattle stall,
> From the fabled east you call
> Wise men to the birth divine.
> Behold the King amid the kine
> Swaddled in no lordly hall.
> Above, what love surpassing all
> Lifts our hearts and makes them thine!
> The place, the beasts, the cold, the hay,
> The lowly coverlet and bed
> Of thy love what more could say?

Then, for the star which hither led
And gave such proof of thy design
To joyful praise our hearts incline.

Vittoria Colonna, 'The Star' (before 1547)

Section D

Pursuing Christ

So far, we have concentrated on the main Christological emphases and debates of the major Reformers, and on Catholic thought only in so far as it responds to or parallels those debates. It is true that, beyond this, there are in this short period not many other notable contributions to Christology narrowly defined. Nevertheless, Christians continued to pay other kinds of attention to Jesus of Nazareth, and to pursue themes which were to an extent submerged in the turmoil of Reformation debates. We will look particularly at contemplation of or meditation on Christ and at the imitation of Christ, and at the use of striking metaphors and similes in expounding the life of Christ.

183   Filling up Christ

Sebastian Franck (*c.* 1499–*c.* 1542), having been for some time a Renaissance humanist and then a Lutheran, left the bounds of both Lutheranism and Catholicism behind, proclaiming a Christianity something like that of later Pietists, including a rejection of dogma and a concentration on religious experience. Here, he expounds a strong view of the mystical participation of the Christian in Christ. (Cf. **214**.)

To regard Christ with spiritual eyes, contemplate his motivation, what God does in the flesh and why he became incarnate, to contemplate why we cling to him and are drawn to him, why we are resigned in faithfulness and faith, so that it is no longer we who live, but we deny all things, and allow Christ to live and work in us who have been rescued from Adam—that is our righteousness, salvation, wisdom and everything. For thus we stand under God who takes possession of us as his dominion and property through his Holy Spirit (who then pours love into our heart), rules, indwells, teaches, loves and leads us into all wisdom, into the peace and joy of the heart, into the life and righteousness, so that by the nature of rebirth we now fulfil the entire law and will and are incapable of doing anything other than what God wills who is our nature and our life.

Note here, Christ is in us, not outside of us; he is our righteousness, salvation and life so that we, having been ingrafted into him from Adam, might become in all things like his image and might be guided by the model, he has set before us, yes, which he himself lives out within us. For since Christ is our flesh so he must also be born in us, live, die, rise and ascend to heaven—his life, suffering and resurrection must be realised in all his members so that we might live and suffer with him and that we all might be Christ who alone can enter heaven.

Christ must accept you and me, become our flesh and blood; the word also must become flesh within us, it must be born, suffer, die, rise and ascend to heaven in Christ. The effect of this vine must reach all branches. Whoever does not eat Christ must die. Christ is sent by the Father to gather together the scattered Israel, bring them before God and subject all things to him. Now where Christ who has suffered in Abel is born in you and me and in all his members, becomes flesh, lives, drives out Adam, enters in, teaches, suffers, dies, rises, ascends to heaven, presents and subjects all of us to the Father, there only is his task, course, suffering and dying fully accomplished.

Therefore, everyone must suffer Christ in his own body, die, ascend to heaven, etc., and no one can suffer, die, believe or become a Christian for another. [. . .] He prepared a way and allowed us to see his to be the way since he too has come into his own glory with the Father by this very way of the cross and apart from him no one else [can come]. Therefore, the suffering of Christ is not yet accomplished and perfected and is of no avail to anyone until it enters into him. Yes, though Christ should accomplish and suffer his suffering in all his members except one, the suffering of Christ would not yet be perfected until he has suffered in this particular member too and entered into his glory, for he cannot carry in his body a member that has not died. The total Christ [cf. **38**] must suffer and die, even the lowliest toe, and thus enter his glory. This is what Paul means in Colossians 1: 24: 'I make up in my body what is lacking in the suffering of Christ, etc.' In other words, what is lacking still in Christ within me, I complement in my suffering and death so that Christ's power, death, life, resurrection and ascension become perfected in me. For even though no one other than Christ ascends to heaven, Christ must, nonetheless, take hold of all of us and put us on. The word of Christ must be born in us, live, suffer, die, rise and ascend to heaven. We must decrease, Christ must increase. We must not be ourselves anymore, but Christ must be all in all; we must no longer live, but Christ must live in us.

Sebastian Franck, *280 Paradoxes or Wondrous Sayings* 109–14, extract (1534)

184   Hunting Christ

John of the Cross (1542–91) was a Spanish mystic, a member of the Carmelite order and co-founder of a reformed, more rigorous order of 'Discalced Carmelites'. Trained in the tradition of theology springing from Thomas Aquinas (cf. **158**), yet a poet of great sensitivity, he wrote complex, powerful works of mystical theology framed as commentaries on his own poems. 'The Spiritual Canticle' describes the arduous pursuit of Christ by the soul enraptured by him (cf. **48**, **210**).

Bride

> Where have you hidden,
> Beloved, and left me moaning?
> You fled like the stag
> After wounding me;
> I went out calling you, and you were gone.
>
> Shepherds, you that go
> Up through the sheepfolds to the hill,
> If by chance you see
> Him I love most,
> Tell him that I sicken, suffer, and die.
>
> Seeking my love
> I will head for the mountains and for watersides,
> I will not gather flowers,
> Nor fear wild beasts;
> I will go beyond strong men and frontiers.
>
> O woods and thickets
> Planted by the hand of my beloved!
> O green meadow,
> Coated, bright with flowers.
> Tell me, has he passed by you?
>
> 'Pouring out a thousand graces,
> He passed these groves in haste;
> And having looked at them,
> With his image alone,
> Clothed them in beauty.'
>
> Ah, who has the power to heal me?
> Now wholly surrender yourself!
> Do not send me
> Any more messengers,
> They cannot tell me what I must hear.
>
> All who are free
> Tell me a thousand graceful things of you;
> All wound me more
> And leave me dying
> Of, ah, I-don't-know-what behind their stammering.
>
> How do you endure
> O life, not living where you live?
> And being brought near death
> By the arrows you receive
> From that which you conceive of your beloved.

Why, since you wounded
This heart, don't you heal it?
And why, since you stole it from me,
Do you leave it so,
And fail to carry off what you have stolen?

Extinguish these miseries,
Since no one else can stamp them out;
And may the vision of your beauty be my death;
For the sickness of love
Is not cured
Except by your very presence and image.

O spring like crystal!
If only, on your silvered-over face,
You would suddenly form
The eyes I have desired,
Which I bear sketched deep within my heart.

Withdraw them, beloved,
I am taking flight!

Bridegroom

Return, dove,
The wounded stag
Is in sight on the hill,
Cooled by the breeze of your flight.

John of the Cross, 'The Spiritual Canticle', stanzas 1–13 (1578)

185   Imitating Christ

In the 1570s Jeremias II (1536–1595), Patriarch of Constantinople at various points between 1572 and 1595, was contacted by Lutherans wondering if the Orthodox Church would prove an ally against the Catholics. Nothing came of the overtures at the time, and Jeremias's reply shows why: he speaks a different language about Christ and the following of Christ from that spoken by a Lutheran. For Jeremias, the life of Christ is the school of human virtue, and virtue is that which joins human beings to the life of the Trinity. (Cf. **148**, **150**.)

These Articles of faith [i.e. Trinity, Incarnation, Resurrection], which seem to he included in the Creed, lead us not only to the true philosophy and vision of Christ, but also to a more spiritual and moral practice, which finally leads us to salvation. Because it is said that the Lord came down to earth for our salvation, in order for us to imitate his life and be saved. And even his suffering and his death were made for us, and even his resurrection was in order to strengthen our hope that he will come again to judge the living and the dead. All this was done for our preparation. Through all this, the three parts of our soul are purified, that is to say, the reason is purified by the pious confession of the Holy Trinity, our emotion is purified by the remembrance of the incarnation, and our will is purified by the proclamation of the resurrection.

By longing for all this, let us live according to the commandments; and since there are seven cardinal virtues: humility, lack of vanity, poverty, temperance, chastity, patience and generous tolerance, and since there are seven vices: pride, vanity, greed, gluttony, fornication, negligence and intolerance, the sacred Creed also teaches us to avoid these vices and urges us to follow these virtues.

Concerning humility [cf. **94–8**], and in order to make us desirous of humility, it teaches that the divine Logos came down from heaven: in order to urge us to give up vanity, and in order to encourage us not to have any private property and to fast and to be chaste, it teaches the incarnation of Christ; in order to encourage us to be patient and tolerant, it teaches that Christ, despite the fact that he possessed everything, suffered the cross and death. Moreover, the Saviour abolished all vices: by his humility, he conquered pride, from which derives infidelity and blasphemy of God; by simplicity or self-sufficiency he conquered vainglory, from which derives madness, envy and murder; by not possessing personal property he abolished greed, from which stealing, trickery, lying, betrayal of God and brothers derive; by fasting he conquered gluttony, from which drunkenness, profligacy, disorder and all passions come; by chastity he conquered fornication, from which all impurity, sinfulness and separation from Holy God derives; by patience he conquered negligence and narrow-mindedness, from which hopelessness, ingratitude and darkness of mind and despair of soul derive; and finally, by tolerance he conquered anger and the satanic madness against brothers, from which all hatred, corruption and killing derive, and also from which derives the overthrow of the three basic and highest virtues, that is to say, hope, faith and love. These three basic virtues entirely unite the person who holds them with the Holy Trinity, and these three virtues transform a man to God by grace.

Therefore let us also, brothers, purify our mind with right faith, and by purifying ourselves with these virtues as well as with all other virtues, that is to say, generosity, prudence, justice and self-control, in which all other major virtues are included, let us realise, as much as possible, integrity, and let us all live in Christ, carrying with ourselves the true faith of Christ and his practical paradigm. Furthermore, let us love Christ and let us follow his commandments and become Christ's temples and his odour and his sanctified members so that we may be members of his immortal life and glory and kingdom, eternally, by his grace, and not solely by our works of justice, according to his unfaulty promise.

Jeremias II, *First Reply to the Lutherans*, extract (1576)

186 Imagining Christ

Ignatius Loyola (C. 1491–1556) was in his own way a reformer who, although very different in emphases and methods from the Protestant Reformers, had an impact upon the Church almost as great. He was founder of the Society of Jesus (the Jesuits), which, by means of education, concentration on the Eucharist, and missionary activity, was instrumental in transforming the Counter-Reformation Church. His *Spiritual Exercises*, for use by all members of the order, inculcate a distinctive use of the imagination in prayer, bringing the crucified and risen Christ vividly before the mind as a model for life. Remember that the following is from a manual for meditation, rather than itself a description of the results of meditation.

The preparatory prayer is to ask our Lord God for grace that all my intentions, actions, and operations may be ordained purely to the service and praise of his divine majesty.

The first prelude is a composition of place, seeing the spot. Here it is to be observed that in contemplation or meditation on visible matters, such as the contemplation of Christ our Lord, who is visible, the composition will be to see with the eyes of the imagination the corporeal place where the thing I wish to contemplate is found. I say the corporeal place, such as the Temple or the mountain, where Jesus Christ or our Lady is found, according to what I desire to contemplate. In meditation on invisible things, such as the [. . .] meditation on sins, the composition will be to see with the eyes of the imagination and to consider that my soul is imprisoned in this corruptible body, and my whole self in this vale of misery, as it were in exile among brute beasts; I say my whole self, that is, soul and body.

The second prelude is to ask of God our Lord that which I wish and desire. The petition ought to be according to the subject-matter, i.e., if the contemplation is on the resurrection, the petition ought to be to ask for joy with Christ rejoicing; if it be on the passion, to ask for grief, tears, and pain in union with Christ in torment. [. . .]

Third Week: The first contemplation, made at midnight, is how Christ our Lord proceeded from Bethany to Jerusalem, including the Last Supper [cf. 14]. It contains the preparatory prayer, three preludes, six points, and a colloquy.

The usual preparatory prayer.

The first prelude is to call to mind the history, which is here how Christ our Lord sent from Bethany two disciples to Jerusalem to prepare the supper, and how afterwards he himself went thither with the other disciples, and how, after having eaten the paschal lamb, and after having supped, he washed their feet and gave to his disciples his most holy body and precious blood, and made them a discourse, after Judas had gone to sell his Lord.

The second prelude is a composition of place, seeing the spot: it will be here to view the way from Bethany to Jerusalem, whether broad, or narrow, or level, etc., and likewise the supper-room, whether great or small, whether of this shape or some other.

The third prelude is to ask for that which I want: here it will be to feel sorrow, affliction, and confusion, because for my sins our Lord is going to his passion.

The first point is to see the persons at the Supper, and, by reflecting on myself, to take care to derive some fruit from them.

The second is to hear what they say, and likewise derive some fruit from it.

The third point is to see what they are doing, and derive some fruit.

The fourth is to consider what Christ our Lord suffers, or wishes to suffer in his humanity, according to the portion of his passion which is being contemplated; and here to begin with great force to strive to grieve, and bewail, and lament, and in the same way continue labouring through the other points which follow.

The fifth point is to consider how the divinity hides itself, that is to say, how it could destroy its enemies, and does not, and how it allows the most holy humanity to suffer so cruelly.

The sixth is to consider that he suffers all these things for my sins, etc., and what I ought to do and to suffer for him.

To finish with a colloquy to Christ our Lord, and finally a *paternoster* [5].

Ignatius Loyola, *Spiritual Exercises* 46–8, 190–8 (1521–3)

187   Awakened by Christ

Lorenzo Scupoli (1530–1610) was a leading light in the Theatine order, a reformist movement founded in Rome in 1524. The order developed a distinctive spirituality, illustrated here by Scupoli's meditation on the Crucifixion. Such meditation is presented as the doorway to a wide repertoire of feelings, which provide the affective world within which Christian devotional life can flourish. (Cf. **16, 134**.)

If you intend [. . .] to meditate on the crucifixion, then among other points to consider within that mystery are the following.

First. How the Lord, on the hill of Calvary, was brutally stripped by those enraged folk, tearing to pieces the flesh that adhered to the clothing because of the recent scouring.

Second. How the crown of thorns was raised from his head, and then replaced, causing new wounds.

Third. How he was cruelly affixed to the cross with nails and the blows of a hammer.

Fourth. How his holy limbs, failing to reach the width required, were pulled from their sockets with such violence that all the dislocated bones could be counted one by one.

Fifth. How his most holy wounds were enlarged and worsened with indescribable pain, because of the weight of the body, since the Lord was hanging from that rough wood with no other support than the nails.

When desiring to rouse feelings of *love* in yourself, study these or other points through meditation, and pass from mere acquaintance to greater knowledge of the infinite love and goodness of your Lord, who chose to suffer this way for you. The more this knowledge increases in you, the more love will equally increase.

From the same knowledge of the infinite goodness and love that the Lord has shown to you, you will easily draw *contrition* and pain for so often and ungratefully having offended your God who was maltreated and torn in such ways for your iniquities.

In order to move yourself to *hope*, consider that so great a Lord fell into this state of calamity to extinguish sin, to free you from the snares of the devil and from all your personal guilt, to render you right before the eternal Father, and to give you confidence to resort to him in all your needs.

You will feel *happiness* in passing from his pains to their effect. Through them he purges the sins of the whole world, satisfies the wrath of the Father, confounds the prince of darkness, kills death and refills the chairs of the angels.

Move yourself to *joy* even more by the contentment that the most holy Trinity, along with the Virgin Mary and all the Church triumphant and militant, receives from this.

In order to incite yourself to *hatred* of all your sins, apply all the points on which you must meditate to this end only: as if the Lord had suffered for no other reason than to lead you to hatred of your evil inclinations and of the fault that dominates you and very seriously offends his divine goodness.

In order to move yourself to *wonder*, consider whether anything could be greater than this—seeing the Creator of the universe who gave life to all things being persecuted, even to death, by his creatures; seeing the supreme majesty oppressed and reviled, justice condemned, the beauty of God spat upon, the love of the celestial Father despised, that inner and inaccessible light given over to the power of darkness. For glory and felicity itself was deemed a dishonour and disgrace by the human race and buried in unbelievable misery.

In order to *pity* your suffering Lord even beyond the meditation on his physical tortures, mentally penetrate to the unequalled internal pain that tormented him. For if you are distressed by the former physical tortures it would be strange if the latter did not break your heart with pain. The soul of Christ saw the divine essence then just as that soul sees God now in heaven. The soul of Christ knew that essence to be most worthy, above all, of every honour and service. The soul desired that all creatures direct themselves to this through the ineffable love of God and with all their strength. Seeing the contrary—God so unimaginably offended and dishonoured through the infinite guilt and abominable wickedness of the world—the soul of Christ was then pierced by unbearable pains. The more his creatures crucified him the greater was his soul's love and desire that the most high majesty be honoured and served by all.

Lorenzo Scupoli, *The Spiritual Combat* 51, extract (*c.* 1585)

188   Dancing with Christ

The popular Christian life in its annual liturgical cycle was a life punctuated by feasts, vigils, fasts, and celebrations. This carol, which may come from the sixteenth century and from just such a popular context, interprets life in Christ and the life of Christ through the image of a dance.

Tomorrow shall be my dancing day:
I would my true love did so chance
To see the legend of my play,
To call my true love to my dance:
Sing *O my love, O my love, my love, my love;*
This have I done for my true love.

Then was I born of a virgin pure,
Of her I took fleshly substánce;
Thus was I knit to man's natúre,
To call my true love to my dance:

In a manger laid and wrapped I was,
So very poor, this was my chance,
Betwixt an ox and a silly poor ass,
To call my true love to my dance:

Then afterwards baptised I was;
The Holy Ghost on me did glance,
My Father's voice heard from above,
To call my true love to my dance:

Into the desert I was led,
Where I fasted without substánce;
The devil bade me make stones my bread,
To have me break my true love's dance:

The Jews on me they made great suit,
And with me made great variance,
Because they loved darkness rather than light,
To call my true love to my dance:

For thirty pence Judas me sold,
His covetousness for to advance;
'Mark whom I kiss, the same do hold,'
The same is he shall lead the dance:

Before Pilate the Jews me brought,
Where Barabbas had deliveránce;
They scourged me and set me at nought,
Judged me to die to lead the dance:

Then on the cross hanged I was,
Where a spear to my heart did glance;
There issued forth both water and blood,
To call my true love to my dance:

Then down to hell I took my way
For my true love's deliveránce,
And rose again on the third day,
Up to my true love and the dance:

Then up to heaven I did ascend,
Where now I dwell in sure substánce,
On the right hand of God, that man
May come unto the general dance:
    Sing O my love, O my love, my love, my love;
    This have I done for my true love.

Traditional, 'My Dancing Day' (date unknown)

189   Reading Christ

John Fisher (1469–1535) was an English bishop who fought for Catholic
doctrines (particularly concerning the Eucharist) in the face of Protestant
innovations. He was eventually executed for refusing to accept Henry VIII's
definition of the king's supremacy over the Church in England. Fisher was a
fine scholar and a powerful preacher, as the following extract demonstrates.
(Cf. 16.)

You marvel, peradventure, why I call the crucifix a book? I will now tell you
the consideration why. A book hath boards, leaves, lines, writings, letters,
both small and great. First, I say, that a book hath two boards: the two boards
of this book are the two parts of the cross, for when the book is opened and
spread, the leaves be couched upon the boards. And so the blessed body of
Christ was spread upon the cross.

The leaves of this book be the arms, the hands, legs and feet, with the other members of his most precious and blessed body.

Never any parchment skin was more straightly stretched by strength upon the tentors than was this blessed body upon the cross. These lorels that crucified him drew by violence his most precious arms with ropes unto either branch of the cross, that the sinews burst asunder, and so nailed his hands fast with spiking nails of iron unto the cross. After they stretched his feet likewise unto another hole beneath in the cross, and there nailed them with the third nail through both his feet. And so they reared up this body aloft against the sun, even as a parchment skin is set forth before the heat of the sun to dry. It was set up aloft to the intent that all the world might look upon this book.

This book was written within and without. First, within was written but one word; nevertheless this one word compriseth in it, as saith St Paul, the whole treasure of all cunning and wisdom pertaining unto God, 'In whom are all the treasures of the wisdom of God' [Col. 2: 3]. Of this word St John speaketh, saying: 'The Word was in the beginning, before all creatures' [66]. This Word is the second person in the Godhead, the Son of God, which by the Holy Ghost was written in the inward side of this parchment. For the Godhead of Christ was covered and hidden under the likeness of man. The Holy Ghost was the pen of Almighty God the Father; he set his most mighty word unto the body of Christ within the womb of the Virgin Mary, and so this book was written within.

For as St Paul sayeth, 'If they had known the Son of God, which was and is the Lord of everlasting glory, they would never have crucified him' [1 Cor. 2: 8]. They saw his manhood which was in outward sight, but they saw not his Godhead, which was covered within the same. The Godhead was the inward side, and the manhood was the outward side. Furthermore, when a book is spread, you see that in the leaves are many lines drawn. And many letters, some red, some black and some blue; so in this book (the most blessed body of Christ) were drawn many lines, for it was all scourged with whips, so that everywhere the print of the cords of the scourges was left behind, and that in every place, from the neck downward unto the soles of his feet, so that there was no margin left in all this book, there was no void place, but everywhere it was either drawn with lines or else written with letters; for these scourges filled not only his most precious body with lines drawn everywhere, but also left many small letters, some black, some blue, some red. For the blood, by the violence of the scourges, sprung out in every place. And for because no part of this book should be unwritten, his head also was pierced with sharp thorns.

These cruel Jews put upon his head a crown of thorns, and pressed it down upon the same as hard as they might press it by violence, beating it down with a strong reed. And his blessed head so crowned, they did beat it down with a gadde or a hard reed.

Thus you perceive that this book was full of lines and small letters (which were of divers colours, as I said), some black, some blue, some red, some bluish, that is to say, full of strokes and lashes, whereby the skin was torn and rent in a thousand places. Besides these small letters yet was there also great capital letters preciously illumined with roset colour; roset is a red colour like unto the colour of a rose, which colour that most precious blood which issued out of his hands and feet doth represent unto us; with this most precious blood was illumined the five great capital letters in this wonderful book. I mean by these capital letters the great wounds of his body, in his hands, and in his feet, and in his side.

These five great wounds were engraved with sharp and violent pens, that is to say, the sharp nails and the spear. And they do represent unto us the five capital letters of this book. Thus then you may perceive what be the boards of this book, and what be the leaves; how it is written within and without; how it is lined and leathered, and what be the letters, as well the small as the great. Now we shall hear what manner of writing is contained in this book. But first here let us make our prayer for grace, beseeching Almighty God to give unto our hearts the gracious light of his beams, whereby we may the more clearly perceive the writings of this book, and that they may bring forth some good fruit to our souls' health.

Now you shall hear what writings be contained in this book. In the book which Ezechiel did see, were written three manner of things: lamentations, songs and woe [Ezek. 2: 10]. And the same three things in like manner are written in this book of the crucifix. First is lamentation, and this very conveniently is written in this book of the crucifix. For whosoever will joy with Christ must first sorrow with him. And by sorrow and lamentation he may come unto joy; but he that will not sorrow and lament with Christ here in this life, he shall come finally to the place where is everlasting woe, I say woe that shall never have end. Here therefore is written all these three, lamentation, song and woe.

John Fisher, 'A Sermon Verie Fruitfull, Godly, and Learned upon . . . the Passion of Christ', extract (1535)

PART 5

Early Modernity: 1601–1789

The fragmentation of Europe continued in the seventeenth century. From 1618 to 1648 the Thirty Years' War raged in German lands; Protestants and Catholics fought each other for religious, political, and economic advantage. Protestantism was effectively banned in the Holy Roman Empire in 1629; but by 1648 the fragmented states of the empire won the right to choose their own religious practice. Along the way, Swedish, Spanish, and French forces had been drawn into a general bloody mêlée. The revulsion which these wars of religion caused was one of the driving forces in the development of early modern theology.

A good deal of the material from the seventeenth century in this chapter comes from England, which, although it had its own Civil War in the middle of the century, escaped the worst ravages of the European wars of religion. The Renaissance had reached England at the end of the previous century, under Elizabeth I, and many English representations of Jesus in this period demonstrate the new vitality of English literature (e.g. **190**, **193**, **198**). The Elizabethan settlement in the Church of England, which had aimed to steer a line between Protestant and Catholic extremes, did not, however, prove stable in the seventeenth century. The victors in the Civil War were on the side of the Puritans (e.g. **210**, **211**), those who felt that the Elizabethan settlement had not been Protestant enough; the Restoration of the English monarchy in 1660 put their episcopal opponents back in charge.

On the Continent, once the wars of religion had ended, the now divided denominations went their separate ways. The flourishing of Catholic spirituality continued, with such figures as Pierre de Bérulle (cf. **207**, **220**) and Jean-Jacques Olier (cf. **199**) spearheading movements of great vitality. Lutheranism developed in two different directions, somewhat antagonistic to one another. On the one hand, there was the development of a rigorous Lutheran orthodoxy, almost a new scholasticism (e.g. **219**); on the other the emergence of Pietism (e.g. **201–5**; cf. **196**) which sought for a more personally involving and emotionally rich experience of Christ. The latter had a strong influence on the rise of Methodism in England in the eighteenth century: John Wesley found his heart strangely warmed, and then found the doors of much of the Church of England closed against this enthusiasm (cf. **196**). Alongside these movements, Reformed theology on the Continent developed its own orthodoxy, with parallels in the work of English Puritan divines (e.g. **218**). Despite all this diversity, however, there was a surprising amount in common between many of these strands when it came to devotion to Christ and desire for Christ, even if there was much that separated them in technical Christology (cf. **201–15**).

The seventeenth and, particularly, the eighteenth centuries also saw the rise of what is commonly called the Enlightenment. In England, the seventeenth and eighteenth centuries saw the development of philosophical empiricism, accompanying the growth of modern scientific practice and institutions and, later, the beginnings of the Industrial Revolution; in theology various forms of deism (cf. **223**) emerged, denying what were seen as the obscurantist, incomprehensible, and immoral doctrines of the Trinity, the Incarnation, miracles, and Atonement. Polemical pamphlets and essays, and some extraordinarily dull polemical books, poured from the presses. French intellectuals soon joined the fray, and freethinkers and radicals flourished there, often daring to attack Christ rather more directly than their English cousins (cf. **226**). German scholars and writers took up the baton (cf. **224, 227**), and what we can in retrospect see as the beginnings of modern biblical criticism emerged.

Europe was in ferment—but the ferment was not just intellectual. Philosophical and theological radicalism often went hand in glove with political radicalism (cf. **215**). American independence in 1783 and then the French Revolution in 1789 (cf. **228**) set the seal on the Enlightenment, marking the triumph of a thoroughly secular politics from which the face of Christ had apparently been erased.

Section A

The Drama of Christ

In England the end of the sixteenth and the beginning of the seventeenth century saw a flowering of dramatic and poetic literature, from Jonson and Shakespeare to the metaphysical poets and beyond. We find new dramatic forms, a love of audacious metaphors and similes, and the beginnings of modern literature and language. These developments left their mark on the period's writings about Christ, as we shall see in this section and the next—although we shall also look beyond England to the continuing impact of the Reformation and Counter-Reformation elsewhere.

190 Christ's Stage

Robert Herrick (1591–1674), a Devon priest except when exiled in London during the Puritan Commonwealth, was a man of the English Renaissance. A follower of Ben Jonson, he loved classical literature and forms and tried to emulate them in his own work. This poem, 'Good Friday: *Rex Tragicus*; or, Christ Going to His Cross' (1648), uses to great effect the imagery of the stage a generation after Shakespeare.

> Put off thy robe of purple, then go on
> To the sad place of execution:
> Thine hour is come, and the tormentor stands
> Ready to pierce thy tender feet and hands.
> Long before this, the base, the dull, the rude,
> The inconstant and unpurged multitude
> Yawn for thy coming: some ere this time cry
> 'How he defers, how loath he is to die!'
> Amongst this scum, the soldier with his spear,
> And that sour fellow with his vinegar,
> His sponge, and stick, do ask why thou dost stay.
> So do the scurf and bran too: go thy way,
> Thy way, thou guiltless man, and satisfy
> By thine approach each their beholding eye.
> Not as a thief shalt thou ascend the mount,
> But like a person of some high account:
> The cross shall be thy stage, and thou shalt there
> The spacious field have for thy theatre.
> Thou art that Roscius,[1] and that marked-out man,
> That must this day act the tragedian,
> To wonder and affrightment: thou art he

Whom all the flux of nations comes to see;
Not those poor thieves that act their parts with thee:
Those act without regard, when once a king,
And God, as thou art, comes to suffering.
No, no, this scene from thee takes life and sense,
And soul and spirit, plot and excellence.
Why then begin, great king! Ascend thy throne,
And thence proceed to act thy passïon
To such a height, to such a period[2] raised,
As hell, and Earth, and heaven may stand amazed.
God and good angels guide thee; and so bless
Thee in thy several parts of bitterness
That those who see thee nailed unto the tree
May, though they scorn thee, praise and pity thee.
And we, thy lovers, while we see thee keep
The laws of action,[3] will both sigh and weep,
And bring our spices to embalm thee dead:
That done, we'll see thee sweetly burièd.

Robert Herrick, 'Good Friday: *Rex Tragicus*; or, Christ Going to his Cross' (1648)

191   Dialogue with the Devil

John Milton (1608–74) was a controversial man. Breaking first with the
Church of England, and then with the Presbyterians, supporter then critic
of Cromwell's regime, opponent of the restored monarchy, he was a man
of fiercely independent political and theological opinions—with an unparal-
lelled gift for setting them out in poetry and prose. *Paradise Regained* was the
sequel to his famous epic description of the Fall in *Paradise Lost*, and
describes the reversal of Adam's fall in Christ's overcoming of the temptations (cf. **2, 51, 52**). These are the final lines of the poem. The devil speaks.

'Hear, O Son of David, virgin-born!
For Son of God to me is yet in doubt.
Of the Messiah I have heard foretold
By all the prophets; of thy birth, at length
Announced by Gabriel, with the first I knew,
And of the angelic song in Bethlehem field,
On thy birth-night, that sung thee Saviour born.
From that time seldom have I ceased to eye
Thy infancy, thy childhood, and thy youth,
Thy manhood last, though yet in private bred;
Till, at the ford of Jordan, whither all
Flocked to the Baptist, I among the rest
(Though not to be baptised), by voice from Heaven
Heard thee pronounced the Son of God beloved.
Thenceforth I thought thee worth my nearer view

And narrower scrutiny, that I might learn
In what degree or meaning thou art called
The Son of God, which bears no single sense.
The Son of God I also am, or was;
And, if I was, I am; relation stands:
All men are Sons of God; yet thee I thought
In some respect far higher so declared.
Therefore I watched thy footsteps from that hour,
And followed thee still on to this waste wild,
Where, by all best conjectures, I collect
Thou art to be my fatal enemy.
Good reason, then, if I beforehand seek
To understand my adversary, who
And what he is; his wisdom, power, intent;
By parle or composition, truce or league,
To win him, or win from him what I can.
And opportunity I here have had
To try thee, sift thee, and confess have found thee
Proof against all temptation, as a rock
Of adamant and as a centre, firm
To the utmost of mere man both wise and good,
Not more; for honours, riches, kingdoms, glory,
Have been before contemned, and may again.
Therefore, to know what more thou art than man,
Worth naming the Son of God by voice from heaven,
Another method I must now begin.'
   So saying, he caught him up, and, without wing
Of hippogrif, bore through the air sublime,
Over the wilderness and o'er the plain,
Till underneath them fair Jerusalem,
The holy city, lifted high her towers,
And higher yet the glorious Temple reared
Her pile, far off appearing like a mount
Of alabaster, topt with golden spires:
There, on the highest pinnacle, he set
The Son of God, and added thus in scorn: —
   'There stand, if thou wilt stand; to stand upright
Will ask thee skill. I to thy Father's house
Have brought thee, and highest placed: highest is best.
Now shew thy progeny; if not to stand,
Cast thyself down. Safely, if Son of God;
For it is written, "He will give command
Concerning thee to his angels; in their hands
They shall uplift thee, lest at any time
Thou chance to dash thy foot against a stone." '
   To whom thus Jesus: 'Also it is written,
"Tempt not the Lord thy God." ' He said, and stood;

But Satan, smitten with amazement, fell.
[. . .]
So, strook with dread and anguish, fell the Fiend,
And to his crew, that sat consulting, brought
Joyless triumphals of his hoped success,
Ruin, and desperation, and dismay,
Who durst so proudly tempt the Son of God.
So Satan fell; and straight a fiery globe
Of angels on full sail of wing flew nigh,
Who on their plumy vans received him⁴ soft
From his uneasy station, and upbore,
As on a floating couch, through the blithe air;
Then, in a flowery valley, set him down
On a green bank, and set before him spread
A table of celestial food, divine
Ambrosial fruits fetched from the tree of life,
And from the fount of life ambrosial drink,
That soon refreshed him wearied, and repaired
What hunger, if aught hunger, had impaired,
Or thirst; and, as he fed, angelic quires
Sung heavenly anthems of his victory
Over temptation and the tempter proud: —
    'True image of the Father, whether throned
In the bosom of bliss, and light of light
Conceiving, or, remote from heaven, enshrined
In fleshly tabernacle and human form,
Wandering the wilderness—whatever place,
Habit, or state, or motion, still expressing
The Son of God, with Godlike force endued
Against the attempter of thy Father's throne
And thief of paradise! Him long of old
Thou didst debel, and down from heaven cast
With all his army; now thou hast avenged
Supplanted Adam, and, by vanquishing
Temptation, hast regained lost paradise,
And frustrated the conquest fraudulent.
He never more henceforth will dare set foot
In paradise to tempt; his snares are broke.
For, though that seat of earthly bliss be failed,
A fairer paradise is founded now
For Adam and his chosen sons, whom thou,
A Saviour, art come down to reinstall;
Where they shall dwell secure, when time shall be,
Of tempter and temptation without fear.
But thou, infernal serpent! shalt not long
Rule in the clouds. Like an autumnal star,
Or lightning, thou shalt fall from heaven, trod down

Under his feet. For proof, ere this thou feel'st
Thy wound (yet not thy last and deadliest wound)
By this repulse received, and hold'st in Hell
No triumph; in all her gates Abaddon rues
Thy bold attempt. Hereafter learn with awe
To dread the Son of God. He, all unarmed,
Shall chase thee, with the terror of his voice,
From thy demoniac holds, possession foul—
Thee and thy legions; yelling they shall fly,
And beg to hide them in a herd of swine (7),
Lest he command them down into the deep,
Bound, and to torment sent before their time.
Hail, Son of the Most High, heir of both worlds,
Queller of Satan! On thy glorious work
Now enter, and begin to save mankind.'
    Thus they the Son of God, our Saviour meek,
Sung victor, and, from heavenly feast refreshed,
Brought on his way with joy. He, unobserved,
Home to his mother's house private returned.

John Milton, *Paradise Regained* IV. 500–62, 576–639 (1671)

---

192   Christ Narcissus

Juana Inés de la Cruz (1651–95) was an independently minded sister of a convent in Mexico, who drew criticism from the ecclesiastical hierarchy for the supposedly unwomanly nature of her celebrated poetry. In her extraordinary poem *The Divine Narcissus* she uses the classical story of self-obsessed Narcissus as a template for the story of Christ dying for love of his own image—that is, for humanity. (Cf. **64**.)

Narcissus:

    Pain now conquers me. For my Belovèd's sake
I have reached the fated point in time.
How far the matter of a life falls short
of a fire's form as vast as this of mine!
    To death my spirit I deliver now
with leave to sever it from flesh,
although my deity yet will cleave to both,
conjoining them afresh.
    I thirst, for my heart remains unsated,
despite the heavy pain I have to bear,
by the flames my love has fanned.
O Father, why, in my frightful hour of care,
hast thou forsaken me? It is finished now [**16**].
My spirit I commend into thy hand.

Human Nature:

    Nymphs, all you who dwell
in this sylvan setting,
some in clear waters,
in green trunks others;
    Shepherds, you who roam
these happy meadows,
keeping, with your flocks,
your simple rustic ways:
    those two heavenly lights
of my fair Narcissus,
glory of your retreat,
are quenched by early death.
    Oh, come and share my sorrow,
lament, lament his death!

Music

Lament, lament his death!

Human Nature:

    It was his love that killed him,
for nothing else beside
the very love of his own
could ever overcome him.
    Through gazing at his likeness,
he falls in love and dies,
for his image, even copied,
wields almighty power.
    Oh, come and share my sorrow,
lament, lament his death!

Music

Lament, lament his death!

Human Nature:

    The universe entire grieves
beholding his sad end:
rocks are rent asunder,
mountains melt with pain;
    the moon puts on mourning,
the poles are shaken,
the sun hides his light,
the heavens are darkened.
    Oh, come and share my sorrow,
lament, lament his death!

Music

> Lament, lament his death!

Human Nature:

> Air is hung with cloud,
> Earth's depths are stirred,
> Fire leaps about,
> Waters boil and swirl.
> Graves open wide
> their gaping mouths,
> making plain to all
> the distress of the dead.
> Oh, come and share my sorrow,
> lament, lament his death!

Music

> Lament, lament his death!

Human Nature:

> The veil of the temple
> is rent in twain,
> that all may behold
> the breaking of its laws.
> The universe entire,
> grieving for his beauty,
> trails a cloak of mourning,
> hangs black baize in grief.
> Oh, come and share my sorrow,
> lament, lament his death!

Music

> Lament, lament his death!

> Sor Juana Inés de la Cruz, *The Divine Narcissus* IV. 12, V. 14,
> extracts (between 1676 and 1691)

Section B

....

Crucified for Me

....

In earlier periods we have seen many forms of meditation upon Christ's Passion, much of it highly charged and deeply felt. In the early modern period, however, we find a new emphasis emerging, an emphasis coloured by Reformation theology. The Cross is seen as a transaction for our salvation, and meditation upon its horror or brutality is not so much directed towards tracing of the ideal humility to which we are called, or awakening penitential grief at our complicity in the crime, but towards nurturing grateful love at the extreme price which was paid for our salvation—in many cases *my* salvation, given the thoroughly personal nature of many of these texts.

193 Christs Blood
....

Richard Crashaw (1612–49) was a High Church priest in the Church of England who, when the Puritan revolution came, fled to Europe; there he eventually joined the Roman Catholic Church. He wrote much devotional poetry, seeking to awaken the emotions in the service of faith.

> They've left thee naked, Lord—oh that they had!
>   This garment too I would they had denied.
> Thee with thyself they have too richly clad,
>   Opening the purple wardrobe in thy side.
> Oh never could there be garment too good
> For thee to wear, but this of thine own blood.

Richard Crashaw, 'Upon the Body of Our Blessed Lord, Naked and Bloody' (1646)

I. The School of Love

Love is the keynote of many of the texts written about the Passion at this time: here, they say, is love, shown at its most powerful, that Christ should willingly pay even this price for unworthy sinners; let it awaken you to responding love.

194 Love Defined

George Herbert (1593–1633) was a poet and priest in the Church of England, and the first great poet of Anglicanism, a proponent of an ideal of sober and moderate churchmanship and devout religion. His poems read the world and the things of faith through the spectacles provided by the celebration of the Liturgy. (Cf. **117, 118.**)

> Philosophers have measur'd mountains
> Fathom'd the depths of seas, of states, and kings,
> Walk'd with a staff to heaven, and traced fountains:
>   But there are two vast, spacious things,
> The which to measure it doth more behove
> Yet few there are, that sound them: sin, and love.
>
> Who would know sin, let him repair
> Unto Mount Olivet, there shall he see
> A man so wrung with pains, that all his hair,
>   His skin, his garments bloody be.
> Sin is that press and vice, which forceth pain
> To hunt his cruel food through ev'ry vein.
>
> Who knows not love, let him assay
> And taste that juice, which on the cross a pike
> Did set again a-broach; then let him say,
>   If ever he did taste the like.
> Love is that liquor sweet and most divine,
> Which my God feels as blood, but I, as wine.

George Herbert, 'The Agony' (posthumously pub., 1633)

195 Love so Amazing

Isaac Watts (1674–1748) was, as well as being the learned author of works on geography, astronomy, and on sundials, one of the greatest Nonconformist hymn-writers, and this is one of his most famous hymns. The words are emotive enough, but to realize its true impact one has to remember that it has over the years been fervently and repeatedly sung many thousands of times, shaping the sensibilities of countless congregations. (Cf. **96.**)

> When I survey the wondrous cross
> On which the prince of glory dy'd,
> My richest gain I count but loss,
> And pour contempt on all my pride.
>
> Forbid it, Lord, that I should boast,
> Save in the death of Christ, my God;
> All the vain things that charm me most,
> I sacrifice them to his blood.

See! from his head his hands his feet,
Sorrow and love flow mingled down;
Did e'er such love and sorrow meet,
Or thorns compose so rich a crown?

His dying crimson, like a robe
Spreads, o'er his body on the tree [cf. **193**.]
Then am I dead to all the globe
And all the globe is dead to me.

Were the whole realm of nature mine,
That were a present far too small;
Love so amazing, so divine,
Demands my soul, my life, my all.

Isaac Watts, 'When I Survey the Wondrous Cross' (1707)

196   Love Christ's Name and Nature

Charles Wesley (1707–88) was brother of John, the founder of the Methodist
movement. Like his brother he was an Anglican influenced by continental
Pietism (cf. **201–5**), and like his brother he became an itinerant preacher, as
well as finding time to write 5,500 hymns. Charles remained more clearly
within the structures of the Church of England, and many of his hymns
have had a tremendous effect on Methodists, Anglicans, and others. The
whole hymn is a commentary on Genesis 32: 24–32.

Come, O thou Traveller unknown,
    Whom still I hold, but cannot see,
My company before is gone,
    And I am left alone with thee;
With thee all night I mean to stay,
And wrestle till the break of day.

I need not tell thee who I am,
    My misery or sin declare;
Thyself hast called me by my name,
    Look on thy hands, and read it there
But who, I ask thee, who art thou?
Tell me thy name, and tell me now.

In vain thou strugglest to get free,
    I never will unloose my hold:
Art thou the man that died for me?
    The secret of thy love unfold.
Wrestling I will not let thee go,
Till I thy name, thy nature know.

Wilt thou not yet to me reveal
    Thy new, unutterable name.

Tell me, I still beseech thee, tell;
  To know it now resolved I am.
Wrestling I will not let thee go,
Till I thy name, thy nature know.

'Tis all in vain to hold thy tongue,
  Or touch the hollow of my thigh:
Though every sinew be unstrung,
  Out of my arms thou shalt not fly.
Wrestling I will not let thee go,
Till I thy name, thy nature know.

What though my shrinking flesh complain,
  And murmur to contend so long,
I rise superior to my pain,
  When I am weak then I am strong;
And when my all of strength shall fail,
I shall with the God-Man prevail.

My strength is gone, my nature dies,
  I sink beneath thy weighty hand,
Faint to revive, and fall to rise;
  I fall, and yet by faith I stand,
I stand, and will not let thee go,
Till I thy name, thy nature know.

Yield to me now—for I am weak,
  But confident in self-despair:
Speak to my heart, in blessings speak,
  Be conquered by my instant prayer,
Speak, or thou never hence shalt move,
And tell me, if thy name is Love.

'Tis Love, 'tis Love! Thou died'st for me,
  I hear thy whisper in my heart.
The morning breaks, the shadows flee:
  Pure universal Love thou art;
To me, to all, thy bowels move,[5]
Thy nature and thy name is Love.

My prayer hath power with God; the grace
  Unspeakable I now receive,
Through faith I see thee face to face,
  I see thee face to face, and live:
In vain I have not wept and strove,
Thy nature and thy name is Love.

I know thee, Saviour, who thou art,
  Jesus, the feeble sinner's friend;
Nor wilt thou with the night depart,
  But stay, and love me to the end;
Thy mercies never shall remove,
Thy nature and thy name is Love.

The Sun of Righteousness on me
   Hath rose with healing in his wings,
Withered my nature's strength; from thee
   My soul its life and succour brings,
My help is all laid up above;
Thy nature and thy name is Love.

Contented now upon my thigh
   I halt, till life's short journey end;
All helplessness, all weakness I,
   On thee alone for strength depend,
Nor have I power, from thee, to move;
Thy nature and thy name is Love.

Lame as I am, I take the prey,
   Hell, earth, and sin with ease o'ercome;
I leap for joy, pursue my way,
   And as a bounding hart fly home,
Through all eternity to prove
Thy nature and thy name is Love.

        Charles Wesley, 'Wrestling Jacob' (18th century)

197   Love Unknown

Samuel Crossman (1624–83) was a priest in Bristol, and at his death dean of that city's cathedral. He published several sermons and one small book of hymns, *The Young Man's Meditation.*

My song is love unknown,
   My Saviour's love to me,
Love to the loveless shown,
   That they might lovely be.
     O, who am I,
       That for my sake
       My Lord should take
     Frail flesh, and die?

He came from his blest throne,
   Salvation to bestow:
But men made strange, and none
   The longed-for Christ would know.
     But O, my friend
       My friend indeed,
       Who at my need
     His life did spend!

Sometimes they strew his way,
   And his sweet praises sing;

Resounding all the day
   Hosannas to their King.
     Then 'Crucify!'
      Is all their breath
      And for his death
     They thirst and cry.

They rise, and needs will have
   My dear Lord made away;
A murderer they save,
   The prince of life they slay
     Yet cheerful he
      To suffering goes,
      That he his foes
     From thence might free.

In life, no house, no home,
   My Lord on earth might have;
In death no friendly tomb
   But what a stranger gave.
     What may I say?
      Heav'n was his home;
      But mine his tomb
     Wherein he lay.

Here might I stay and sing,
   No story so divine;
Never was love, dear King,
   Never was grief like thine.
     This is my friend,
      In whose sweet praise
      I all my days
     Could gladly spend.

Samuel Crossman, 'My Song is Love Unknown' (1664)

II. The Power of the Cross

We finish this section with three texts which present different ways in which Christ's Crucifixion impinges upon the believer, illustrating something of the diversity of models of salvation which can be found in the West in this period, yet confirming the centrality of the Cross in all of them.

John Donne (1571–1631) became, after a Catholic upbringing and a controversial writing career, Dean of St Paul's Cathedral in London, and a brilliant preacher. He is best known for his complex and powerful poetry, in much of which he explores the fierce mercy of a loving God who loves sinners enough to knead them violently back into shape. (Cf. **308**, **169**.)

Let man's soul be a sphere,[6] and then, in this,
The intelligence that moves, devotion is;
And as the other spheres, by being grown
Subject to foreign motions, lose their own,
And being by others hurried every day,
Scarce in a year their natural form obey:
Pleasure or business, so, our souls admit
For their first mover, and are whirled by it.
Hence is't that I am carried towards the west
This day, when my soul's form bends to the east.
There I should see a sun by rising set,
And by that setting endless day beget;
But that Christ on this cross did rise and fall,
Sin had eternally benighted all.
Yet dare I almost be glad I do not see
That spectacle of too much weight for me.
Who sees God's face, that is self life, must die;
What a death were it then to see God die?
It made his own lieutenant nature shrink,
It made his footstool crack, and the sun wink.
Could I behold those hands which span the poles,
And turn all spheres at once, pierced with those holes?
Could I behold that endless height which is
Zenith to us, and our antipodes,
Humbled below us? or that blood which is
The seat of all our souls, if not of his,
Made dirt of dust, or that flesh which was worn
By God, for his apparel, ragged and torn?
If on these things I durst not look, durst I
Upon his miserable mother cast mine eye,
Who was God's partner here, and furnished thus
Half of that sacrifice which ransomed us?
Though these things, as I ride, be from mine eye,
They are present yet unto my memory,
For that looks towards them; and thou lookst towards me,
O Saviour, as thou hangst upon the tree;
I turn my back to thee but to receive
Corrections, till thy mercies bid thee leave.
Oh think me worth thine anger, punish me,
Burn off my rusts and my deformity,

Restore thine image so much, by thy grace,
That thou mayst know me, and I'll turn my face.

John Donne, 'Good Friday, 1613: Riding Westward' (1613)

199   Crucified with Christ

Jean-Jacques Olier (1608–57) was a Catholic priest and educator. He founded a seminary and several catechetical schools in the parish of Saint-Sulpice in Paris, developing a model which was widely used elsewhere. He was a follower of John Eudes (cf. **206**). The approach to the Cross illustrated here, related more closely to a theology of the Church and the spirit, is a good example of a Counter-Reformation Catholic spirituality in greater continuity with late medieval traditions than the Protestant texts we have presented.

We must all be conformed to Jesus Christ. Saint Paul teaches us this when he says that God predestined us to be conformed to the image of his Son. This conformity consists in being like him; first in his exterior mysteries, which were like sacraments of the interior mysteries he was to bring about in souls. Therefore, just as our Lord was exteriorly crucified we are called to be interiorly crucified. As he died in exterior reality we must die interiorly. As he was buried exteriorly we must be buried interiorly. Everyone should have within him the interior life that the exterior mysteries represent as well as the grace acquired by these same mysteries because they have been merited for everyone. That is why Saint Paul speaking about all of us said, 'You have died' [Col 3: 3].

It is true that God has chosen certain souls to express through them these very mysteries even in an exterior way. We see this in certain holy religious whom he sent to earth in order to renew the life of Jesus Christ. They were so thoroughly filled with his Spirit and the grace of these mysteries that they expressed visibly his external state. Such was Saint Francis [cf. **127**], to whom the Spirit of our Lord Jesus Christ crucified was so fully given that it overflowed into his flesh, thus manifesting externally the mystery of the crucifix through the wounds of his body. He allows this to continue in his children who mortify their flesh continually. Such was the case of Saint Benedict, who symbolised the burial of Jesus Christ by hiding himself in a cave and leaving his children in tombs. In a similar way several other saints, who have appeared in the holy church, have borne certain exterior manifestations of these mysteries. But the remainder of Christians, to whom they left the example of their devotion by placing these mysteries in a concrete form before their eyes, must have within themselves these graces and this spirit even if they do not conform externally to these same mysteries.

The spirit of these holy mysteries is given to us through baptism, which activates within us graces and sentiments that are in relation and conformity to the mysteries of Jesus Christ. We have only to allow him to operate in us, and through the power of his graces and lights, to work on us and others in conformity to these holy mysteries.

For example, we have in us the Spirit of Jesus Christ crucified, which offers us the light and grace to crucify us interiorly and to mortify us at those times when our flesh seeks its own pleasure and satisfaction. Thus, through this Spirit we will be conformed interiorly to Jesus Christ crucified. [. . .]

The second way in which we should conform to Jesus Christ is to his interior through his mysteries. In this way our souls, in their interior senti-ments and dispositions, will become conformed not only to the outer aspects of the mysteries, as we have seen, but also to the interior dispositions and sentiments that our Lord had in these mysteries.

Christian life strictly speaking is the Christian person living interiorly, through the operation of the Spirit, in the same way Jesus Christ lived. Without this there can be neither the unity nor the perfect conformity to which our Lord does call us. He wishes that, through the operation of the Holy Spirit, we live with him a life that is truly one, just as the Father and Son live with one another. For they have only one life, one sentiment, one desire, one love, one light, because they are but one God living in the two persons.

This is why the Spirit of God is poured forth in Christians, as in the members of the same body, to enliven them with the same life and to have in them the same operations he produced in Jesus Christ, thus dilating his occupations, dispositions, loves and movements. It is like a drop of oil on a piece of white satin, which at first covers only a small corner of the material, but spreads out quickly over the whole piece. In the same way the Spirit of God, who lived in the heart of Jesus Christ, with time and the passage of the years during which the faithful have been united to Jesus Christ, has spread out in all, guaranteeing that everyone is made to share in the same taste and the same smell and finally in the same sentiments.

It is the same Spirit in all, producing the same effects in everyone. Having been transformed and reformed in this way by the Spirit in Jesus Christ at the depth of their souls, they are no longer distinct by the individual sentiments of their flesh and their self-love, which normally rule in everyone differently according to their various temperaments and distinct caprices. Rather, they are all one through the unity of the same Spirit, who rules in them and penetrates their hearts. They are no longer distinct through the diversity of religions [. . .] nor through the distinction of climates, nations, nor the oppos-ition of temperaments and barbaric customs [. . .] nor through the distinction of social condition [. . .] nor through sexual distinction [. . .] because they are all the same in Jesus Christ: 'You are all the same in Christ Jesus' [Gal 3: 28]; and Jesus Christ is all things in all.

Jean-Jacques Olier, *Introduction to the Christian Life and Virtues* 2–3, extract (17th century)

200 Blest Cross

John Bunyan (1628–88) was a Nonconformist preacher. A proponent of the Parliamentary cause in the English Civil War, he was imprisoned upon the Restoration of the monarchy. During one of his imprisonments he wrote a startlingly original allegorical book which was to become one of the most popular books ever written: *The Pilgrim's Progress* (1678) (cf. **154**.). In the following passage the pilgrim Christian reaches the Cross. (Cf. **268, 280**.)

I saw in my dream, that the highway up which Christian was to go, was fenced on either side with a wall, and that wall was called Salvation. Up this way, therefore, did burdened Christian run, but not without great difficulty, because of the load on his back.

He ran thus till he came at a place somewhat ascending, and upon that place stood a cross, and a little below, in the bottom, a sepulchre. So I saw in my dream, that just as Christian came up with the cross, his burden loosed from off his shoulders, and fell from off his back, and began to tumble, and so continued to do, till it came to the mouth of the sepulchre, where it fell in, and I saw it no more. Then was Christian glad and lightsome, and said, with a merry heart, 'He hath given me rest by his sorrow, and life by his death.' Then he stood still awhile to look and wonder; for it was very surprising to him, that the sight of the cross should thus ease him of his burden. He looked therefore, and looked again, even till the springs that were in his head sent the waters down his cheeks. Now, as he stood looking and weeping, behold three Shining Ones came to him and saluted him with 'Peace be unto thee.' So the first said to him, 'Thy sins be forgiven thee'; the second stripped him of his rags, and clothed him with change of raiment; the third also set a mark on his forehead, and gave him a roll with a seal upon it, which he bade him look on as he ran, and that he should give it in at the Celestial Gate. So they went their way.

> 'Who's this? the Pilgrim. How! 'tis very true,
> Old things are past away, all's become new.
> Strange! he's another man, upon my word,
> They be fine feathers that make a fine bird.'

Then Christian gave three leaps for joy, and went on singing —

> 'Thus far I did come laden with my sin;
> Nor could aught ease the grief that I was in
> Till I came hither: What a place is this!
> Must here be the beginning of my bliss?
> Must here the burden fall from off my back?
> Must here the strings that bound it to me crack?
> Blest cross! blest sepulchre! blest rather be
> The man that there was put to shame for me!'

John Bunyan, *The Pilgrim's Progress*, extract (1678)

Section C

Union with Christ

Desire for intimate union with Christ, spoken of with the language of marriage and sexual love, is a theme that unites several strands of early modern theology which are otherwise disparate: it can be found among Puritans as well as in the Catholicism of the Counter-Reformation; among the Quakers and among political radicals as well as among Anglicans and Continental Pietists. (Cf. **38**, **48**, **112**, **272**.)

I. Pietist

Pietism began as a movement for reform within the Lutheran Church. Philipp Jakob Spener (1635–1705) wrote a passionate plea for a return to true, warm-hearted religion in his 1675 *Pia Desideria*. It spread throughout Protestant Germany, taking on a different character in different locations, notably the emphasis on individual commitment to the Redeemer which developed among those Pietists gathered round von Zinzendorf (cf. **203**).

201 The Bridegroom's Arrival

Johann Arndt (1555–1621) was a follower of Philip Melanchthon (cf. **163**), who set himself against what he saw as the dryness of emerging Protestant orthodoxy (see e.g. **219**). His work was a strong influence on later Pietism (**202–5**), and he might be considered the forefather of German Pietism.

If the bridegroom comes, the holy soul rejoices and looks closely and eagerly toward his presence. By his joyous, enlivening, and holy arrival he drives out darkness and night and the heart has sweet joy, the waters of meditation flow in upon it, the soul melts for love, the spirit rejoices, the affections and the desires become fervid, love is ignited, the mind rejoices, the mouth gives praise and honour, man takes vows, and all the powers of the soul rejoice in and because of the bridegroom. It rejoices, I say, because it has found what it loves and because he whom it loves has taken it up to himself as his bride. Oh what a love! Oh what a fiery desire! Oh what a loving conversation! Oh how chaste a kiss! If the Holy Spirit comes, if the consoler overshadows the soul, if the highest enlightens it, if the Word of the Father is there, wisdom speaks and loves and receives it in joy.

At the same time, the soul is made into a temple of God, into a seat of wisdom, into a dwelling place of chastity, into a receiver of the covenant, into a tabernacle of holiness, into a chamber of the bridegroom, into a spiritual heaven, into a blessed land, into a house of mysteries, into a dear bride, into a dear garden, into a room and chamber of the marriage, and into a paradise garden sweet-smelling and strewn with many beautiful flowers of virtue to which the Lord of all angels and the King of honour goes, so that he might marry the deeply beloved bride who is sick with love, adorn her with the flower of holy desire, bedeck her with the apples of virtue, and wait upon his dearly beloved when he comes in his adornment. Since she shines with the crown of a pure conscience, with the snow-white cloak of chastity that she has put on, and with the precious, noble pearl of good works that adorns her, she is no way afraid before him as before the sight of a harsh judge, but her only and deepest desire is that she might see and contemplate the presence of the Lord bridegroom for which she has carried her desire (which also the blessed hosts and the heavenly spirits of joy, the angels in heaven consider as the highest glory).

After the soul enjoys his chaste association, no creature can know how great a joy it has from this and how it feels in its heart, how fervent it is internally, how it rejoices and shouts for joy because of love, how lovely and heartfelt words and conversations come to it. No one, I say, can know this except the person who has experienced it. To feel and to experience this is possible for a man but to express it is impossible, for it is a spiritual mystery and divine matter concerning which man dare not speak so that he carry no fault against the bridegroom who loves to dwell in the mystery and in the stillness of the heart.

Above all things and in particular, this bridegroom has his greatest pleasure to dwell in the lowly and humble heart whose honour is a treasure of many and great graces, a daily growth and development of gifts, the peace of the conscience, the light of understanding, a spiritual exultation, a pure prayer, a justified heart and mind, a continuing faith, the power of compassion, a firm hope, a burning love, a taste of divine sweetness, a desire to learn, a thirst for virtue. This is the greatest treasure of the humble one, which no thief can take away or steal. It is his precious, noble stone, his unceasing wealth, his highest honour, his chief glory, his secret pleasure, the bridegroom's gift, the highest adornment and the spiritual wine cellar of the bride into which the proud cannot enter, nor are the lazy and impure allowed in. Indeed, through this as through the spiritual gates the bridegroom comes to the bride, teaches and instructs it and shares his presence with it, not through the bodily form but through the light of faith, through the beam of understanding, through the taste of meditation, through the joyous cry of exultation, through the gracious leaping of love, through the kiss of peace, through the embrace of faithfulness.

Johann Arndt, *True Christianity* 7, extract (1605)

202 All for Sinner's Gain

Paul Gerhardt (*c.* 1607–76) was one of the greatest Protestant hymn-writers. A staunch Lutheran, he was nevertheless influenced by earlier Catholic spiritual writers, and his warmly emotional, often intimate hymns became anthems of the Pietist movement, a reform movement which grew in the Lutheran Church at the very end of his life (cf. 203). This hymn is based on words probably by Bernard of Clairvaux (cf. 97), *Salve caput cruentatum.* (Cf. 141.)

O sacred head, now wounded,
With grief and shame weighed down,
Now scornfully surrounded
With thorns, thine only crown.
O sacred head, what glory,
What bliss, till now was thine!
Yet, though despised and gory,
I joy to call thee mine.

Men mock and taunt and jeer thee,
Thou noble countenance,
Though mighty worlds shall fear thee
And flee before thy glance.
How art thou pale with anguish,
With sore abuse and scorn!
How doth thy visage languish
That once was bright as morn!

Now from thy cheeks has vanished
Their colour, once so fair;
From thy red lips is banished
The splendour that was there.
Grim death, with cruel rigour,
Hath robbed thee of thy life;
Thus thou has lost thy vigour,
Thy strength, in this sad strife.

My burden in thy Passion,
Lord, thou hast borne for me,
For it was my transgression
Which brought this woe on thee.
I cast me down before thee,
Wrath were my rightful lot;
Have mercy, I implore thee;
Redeemer, spurn me not!

My shepherd, now receive me;
My guardian, own me thine.
Great blessings thou didst give me,
O source of gifts divine!
Thy lips have often fed me
With words of truth and love,
Thy Spirit oft hath led me
To heavenly joys above.

Here I will stand beside thee,
From thee I will not part;
O Saviour, do not chide me!
When breaks thy loving heart,
When soul and body languish
In death's cold, cruel grasp,
Then, in thy deepest anguish,
Thee in mine arms I'll clasp.

The joy can ne'er be spoken,
Above all joys beside,
When in thy body broken
I thus with safety hide.
O Lord of life, desiring
Thy glory now to see,
Beside thy cross expiring,
I'd breathe my soul to thee.

What language shall I borrow
To thank thee, dearest friend,
For this, thy dying sorrow,
Thy pity without end?
Oh, make me thine forever!
And should I fainting be,
Lord, let me never, never,
Outlive my love for thee.

My Saviour, be thou near me
When death is at my door;
Then let thy presence cheer me,
Forsake me nevermore!
When soul and body languish,
Oh, leave me not alone,
But take away mine anguish
By virtue of thine own!

Be thou my consolation,
My shield when I must die;
Remind me of thy passion
When my last hour draws nigh.
Mine eyes shall then behold thee,

Upon thy cross shall dwell,
My heart by faith enfold thee.
Who dieth thus dies well!

Paul Gerhardt, 'O Sacred Head Now Wounded' (1656)

203   Hearts Submitting to Christ

Nikolaus Ludwig Graf von Zinzendorf (1700–60) was one of the key figures in the second generation of Pietism, and godson of the key first-generation figure Philipp Jakob Spener (1635–1705) (cf. **202**). He founded the Herrnhuter Brethren movement, devoted to the cultivation of an intimate, emotional, and personal relationship to the Christ the Redeemer. His ideas later influenced Friedrich Schleiermacher (cf. **255, 256**).

LEADER: Christ came here in the flesh from the Father. He is God above all, praised in eternity. He left us an image which we are to follow in his footsteps. He was like to his brothers in all ways, because he was merciful and a true High Priest before God. He was tempted in all ways like us, but without sin. Because he suffered and was tempted, he can help those who are tempted.

CONGREGATION: Lamb of God, holy Lord God, hear our prayer of need; have mercy upon us.

LEADER: From the sin of not believing in you,
From all sins of the flesh and the spirit,
From all self-righteousness,
From all lukewarmness and drunkenness,
From all indifference to your wounds and death.

CONGREGATION: Defend us, dear Lord God. There is nothing in us but poverty. By your blood, death, and suffering give us a warm, completely submissive heart.

LEADER: O Immanuel,[7] Saviour of the World
CONGREGATION: Make yourself known to us!
LEADER: By your holy incarnation and birth
CONGREGATION: Make us love our humanity!
LEADER: By your poverty and servanthood
CONGREGATION: Teach us to be lowly in this world!
LEADER: By your powerlessness and weakness
CONGREGATION: Strengthen our weakness!
LEADER: By your gracious childlikeness
CONGREGATION: Help us reach the joy of children!
LEADER: By your correct understanding of the Scripture
CONGREGATION: Make firm the word of truth in us!

LEADER: By your holy simplicity
CONGREGATION: Make our hearts and minds simple!
LEADER: By your obedience and servanthood
CONGREGATION: Help us to be obedient in heart
> Make me like in mind to you, as an obedient child, meek and still.
> Jesus, now, help me that I might be obedient as you.

LEADER: By your holy life on earth
CONGREGATION: Teach us to walk peacefully!
LEADER: By your endurance and industry
CONGREGATION: Help us patiently endure!
LEADER: By your faithfulness
CONGREGATION: Make us faithful on our part!
LEADER: By your pilgrim life on earth
CONGREGATION: Teach us to be at home everywhere!
LEADER: By your watching and praying
CONGREGATION: Teach us to be wakeful in prayer!
LEADER: By your humility, meekness, and patience
CONGREGATION: Make us proud to bear your yoke!
LEADER: By your mildness and mercy
CONGREGATION: Teach us to be merciful!
LEADER: By your zeal for your Father's house
CONGREGATION: Make us zealous for your kingdom!
> Now, our King, you have our heart and mind!
> We are able to do little but we bring ourselves to you, so that each of us in our whole person might read your holy image.

LEADER: Christ, Lamb of God, you who take away the sins of the world
CONGREGATION: Give us your peace!
LEADER: By your willingness to die
CONGREGATION: Give us the mystery of your love!
LEADER: By your holy baptism of blood
CONGREGATION: Set us forth upon God's earth!
LEADER: By your tears and cry of dread
CONGREGATION: Console us in dread and pain!
> You shed so many tears for us,
> So many drops of blood flowed out from you,
> So many are the voices which pray for us and plead for us.

LEADER: By your head crowned with thorns
CONGREGATION: Teach us the nature of the kingdom of the cross!
LEADER: By your outstretched hands on the cross
CONGREGATION: Be open to us at all times!

LEADER: By your nail-pierced hands
CONGREGATION: Show us where our names stand written!
LEADER: By your wounded feet
CONGREGATION: Make our path certain!
LEADER: By your pale beautiful lips
CONGREGATION: Speak to us consolation and peace!
LEADER: By the last look of your breaking eyes
CONGREGATION: Lead us into the Father's hands!

> Holy Lord God,
> Holy strong God,
> Holy merciful Saviour,
> You eternal God.
> Never let us fall
> From the consolation in your death!
> *Kyrie eleison.*

LEADER: By the form of your suffering and death
CONGREGATION: Remain continually before our eyes!
LEADER: May the impression of your passing
CONGREGATION: Be before us always.
LEADER: May your martyrdom and blood
CONGREGATION: Nourish us to eternal life!
LEADER: May the permanent testament of death
CONGREGATION: Be a rule for your heirs!
LEADER: May the Word of your Cross
CONGREGATION: Remain our confession of faith!

> We wish to remain by the Cross, and to follow your martyrdom until we see you face to face.

LEADER: Worthy is the Lamb who was slain to receive power and wealth and wisdom and might and honour and glory and blessing.
CONGREGATION: From eternity to eternity. Amen.

> Nikolaus Ludwig, Graf von Zinzendorf, *The Litany of the Life, Suffering and Death of Jesus Christ*, extract (18th century)

204 Nothing but Jesus

> Gerhard Tersteegen (1697–1796) was an independently minded Pietist, who by means of spiritual direction and devotional meetings had a wide influence in Germany and beyond.

Dearly Beloved Friend and Brother in the Grace of God,

Jesus Christ, the true book of life, wishes to imprint himself in the ground of our soul so that through his spirit we might become the written, living copy, and letters of him, which cannot be read by all men. To this end let us study eagerly in this book. There is no danger in reading much in this book. By doing so, one cannot damage the understanding and where this happens it is only seen to so happen in the eyes of the world whose greatest wisdom is foolishness with God [59]. I hope, then, and I wish from the ground of the soul, that the Father of our Lord Jesus will daily more and more transfigure his tongue in us and make us great, so that everything else might become small and nothing, and our heart might be able to say with truth: Jesus, Jesus, nothing but Jesus, be my wish and my goal.

Gerhard Tersteegen, Spiritual Letters, extract (18th century)

205 Christ in Me

> Friedrich Christoph Oetinger (1702–82) was a Pietist mystical writer, influenced by the German mysticism of Jacob Boehme. Here, every element of Christianity is re-established on the basis of a Christ-formed inner life. (Cf. 97.)

I was dead, but now I live; yet not I but Christ in me. Thus, I have died to the law and its ceremonies, living alone for him who freed me from all except the commandment of love.

He declared me of age and has entrusted my spiritual inheritance to the protection of my care; therefore, I need no guardian.

Spirit and truth are the essential elements of my saving religion; the narrow and specific fulfilment of all aspects of a proper and unselfish love is my unending worship.

My church is the temple of my body, purified externally as well as internally and prepared as a dwelling place for the trinity. Jesus alone is preacher in it; he chose and designated my conscience as his pulpit. Heart, senses, and all desires are the listeners who attend and maintain in inward morality and industry what proceeds from his gracious mouth.

When he mounts the chancel and proclaims his loving gospel, it is Sunday; a feast day if he stirs in my soul living and weighty thoughts of his good deeds or of those of a true friend and martyr. If, however, because of my errors and sins he speaks to me and punishes me, it is for me a day of repentance, prayer, and silence.

Oftentimes my teacher is completely silent; at such times I consider what I have previously heard, reach to meditate in my Bible as the best sermon for change, or if neither of these is available, I read in the great book of nature. Moreover, I remain completely submissive to him who wishes to make me a new creature.

If at times he grants me the pleasure of having a glimpse of his friends and travellers on his journey, members of my head and branches of my true vine, my heart rejoices with them in him and binds as a community of suffering those who are able to meet us on the way toward the goal before us; in this order I hold with them, according to the mind of the lamb, a love feast.

My baptism is that true burial after the complete mortification of all that which can be reckoned in me as the image of the first Adam.

If Christ, the second Adam, appears in essence in me, and if there is sensed in my activities and surrenderings the mind of his child, then I celebrate Christmas. It is Easter if my spirit proceeds triumphant through all suffering, death, and hell. I celebrate Ascension if I receive meanwhile the freedom to sweep myself up to God, my source. I celebrate Pentecost if grace is poured out from the heights into my heart through the Holy Spirit.

If pleasing beams of light are seen from afar it is day, and morning if the sun shines actively on my horizon; it is noon if it reveals itself in its most beautiful clarity in the firmament, but evening if grace, for a time, hides itself and sets. Yes, it is truly night, and midnight, if loneliness and temptation storm over me and darken my mind so that I am not even capable of catching a glimpse of my sun of grace. But if finally all that I am is increasingly renewed by the great restorer, then the New Year beams forth. After many harsh, cold winters follows a pleasant spring which grants me experience of beautiful sensations of the glorious might and power of my heavenly gardener. In summer the full fruit of the scattered seed first manifests itself. In autumn, among manifold changes, everything matures and is gathered in with joy by him who scattered seed and planted it. In winter my tree of life is often robbed of all its ornament and form; it seems as if completely withered. But this is only so that in new fruitfulness, it might be ready and strong where constancy is inconstancy. And this will continue until finally the tree after many misdirections will finally be planted by the unseen hand of the Lord in the heavenly paradise.

What will then be revealed will be those things which carnal eye has not seen nor mortal ear heard and taken up; indeed those who are least capable of seeing are best prepared to experience it more than to speak of it.

Lord, help me to this by grace—and what delight would that be if I saw you and stood there before your throne! Ah, teach me more of this that I might continually seek you with a prudent heart! Amen!

Friedrich Christoph Oetinger, 'A Confession of Faith' (18th century)

II. Catholic

There was a wide revival of Catholic theology and devotion in the sixteenth and seventeenth centuries, which has become known, misleadingly, as the Counter-

Reformation. It was marked not only by the emergence of various new orders, such as the Jesuits, but also by the growth of several new schools of devotion, such as those associated with Pierre de Bérulle (cf. **207**, **220**) and John Eudes (cf. **199**, **206**).

206   Christ's Second Body

John Eudes (1601–80) was a French Catholic devotional writer and evangelist, and one of the early practitioners of devotion to Jesus' Sacred Heart (cf. **159**). Jean-Jacques Olier (cf. **199**) was one of his followers. The following extract shows the importance to Eudes' theology of Christian participation in Christ. (Cf. **34**, **38**, **112**.)

So that you might understand more clearly and establish more firmly in your soul this basic truth of Christian life, religion and devotion, please pay attention and realise that our Lord Jesus Christ possesses two types of bodies and two types of lives. His first body is his own body, which he received from the blessed Virgin. His first life is the life that he lived in this same body while he was on earth. His second body is his mystical body, that is, the church, which Saint Paul calls *corpus christi*, the body of Jesus Christ. His second life is the life that he has in this body and in those authentic Christians who are members of this body.

The temporal, vulnerable life, which Jesus lived in his personal body, was fulfilled and came to an end with his death. But he wishes to continue this same life in his mystical body until the end of time so that he might glorify his Father by the actions and sufferings of a life, which is mortal, laborious and painful, not only for thirty-four years, but until the end of the world. So much so that the temporal, vulnerable life that Jesus has in his mystical body has not yet reached its fulfilment, but is fulfilled day by day in every true Christian. It will not have been completely fulfilled until the end of time. This is why Saint Paul says that he fills up what is lacking in the sufferings of Jesus Christ for the sake of his body the church. What Saint Paul says about himself can be said of every true Christian, whenever he suffers something in a spirit of submission and love for God. What Saint Paul says about suffering can be said about all the other actions of a Christian on earth. For just as Saint Paul assures us that he fills up what is lacking in the sufferings of Jesus Christ, in the same way we can say that any true Christian, who is a member of Jesus Christ, and who is united to him by his grace, continues and completes, through all the actions that he carries out in the spirit of Christ, the actions that Jesus Christ accomplished during the time of his temporary life on earth.

So that when a Christian prays, he continues and fulfils the prayer that Jesus Christ offered on earth. Whenever he works, he continues and fulfils the laborious life of Jesus Christ. Whenever he relates to his neighbour in a spirit of charity, then he continues and fulfils the relational life of Jesus Christ. Whenever he eats or rests in a Christian manner, he continues and fulfils the subjection that Jesus Christ wished to have to these necessities. The same can be said of any other action that is carried out in a Christian manner.

It is thus that Saint Paul tells us that the church is the fulfilment of Jesus Christ and that Jesus Christ, who is the head of the church, is fulfilled in all things in all people. In another place, he teaches that all of us are co-operating in the perfection of Jesus Christ and in the age of his fulfilment, that is, his mystical age in his church, which will never be fulfilled until the day of judgment.

Now you see what the Christian life is. It is a continuation and fulfilment of the life of Jesus. All our actions must be the continuation of the actions of Jesus. We should be like other Jesus Christs on earth, so as to continue his life and works and to accomplish and suffer all that we accomplish and suffer in a holy and divine manner, in the spirit of Jesus, that is, with the holy and divine dispositions and intentions with which this same Jesus accomplished all his actions and sufferings. This divine Jesus is our head and we are his members, united with him in a way that is incomparably more intimate, more noble and more exalted than the union between the head and members of a natural body. Therefore it follows logically that we must be enlivened by his spirit and his life more closely and more perfectly than the members of a natural body are enlivened by the spirit and life of their head.

John Eudes, *The Life and Kingdom of Jesus in Christian Souls* II, extract (17th century)

207 Christt the Door

Madeleine de Saint-Joseph (1578–1637) was a member of the French School of Counter-Reformation Catholic spirituality. She was prioress of the first reformed Carmelite convent in France, and spread the teachings of the founder of the French School, Pierre de Bérulle (cf. **220**), through the movement.

My good Mother,

May the love of Jesus Christ fill your soul.

Since you wish to know the explanation of the words by which the Son of God teaches us that he is the door, and the others which follow them, I am satisfied that you are not in any way interested in leaving him. This is a leave-taking I would wish on no one. I fear it for myself and for those whom I love in our Lord, not simply as I would fear death, but rather eternal death. For Jesus is life and life eternal.

Previously, good Mother, I experienced at times the same difficulty with these words of the gospel ['I am the gate; whoever enters through me will be saved. He will come in *and go out*, and find pasture'; [John 10: 9]. I asked for an interpretation from our blessed Father Cardinal Bérulle. He helped me understand it and I was overjoyed. He said to me that it was not a question here of leaving Jesus Christ, which he could not approve. Also let us note that when he asks his apostles if they wish to leave him, Saint Peter answers: 'Lord, to whom shall we go? You have the words of eternal life' [John 6: 68]. Rather, it is a manner of speaking which means that whoever unites himself perfectly to our Lord Jesus Christ as the way by which we go to God and the only way to get there, placing all his confidence in him alone without relying on himself or even other creatures, this person will live in perfect freedom. He will go and come freely and nothing will prevent him, as the same Son of God says in Saint John: 'You will see heavens open and the angels ascending and descending on the Son of Man' [John 1: 51]; that is, serving him in his every command and accomplishing perfectly his every will. Scripture teaches us that because of this they are powerful.

To enter then and leave through this door who is Jesus Christ is a manner of speaking that means to accomplish freely everything God asks of us, entering into the divinity and going out into the humanity of Jesus Christ. We enter into his interior life where he is occupied with his Father. We go out into his exterior life where he lives familiarly with men [cf. **199**]. We ascend in imitation of the angels through attention and contemplation of his grandeurs, in which 'he is in all things equal to his Father' [John 10: 30]. We descend through love and the imitation of his humiliation, by which he says through his prophet 'that he is a worm, not a man, a disgrace among men and the scorn of the people' [Ps. 22: 7]. We enter with Mary and go out with Martha. At times we remain recollected within ourselves and occupied solely in adoring him in spirit and truth, listening in silence to the words of life he speaks to our heart. At other times we go out through the practice of charity and all the exterior virtues of which he gave us such a perfect example.

Without doubt, my dear Mother, in these holy reflections we will find a pasture quite capable of nourishing our souls, capable of sustaining them and causing them to grow in this holy union with Jesus Christ and with God, which his own Son wished for us, asked for us and acquired for us at such a great price. I beg him to make us worthy of it and believe me that I am yours in him . . .

Madeleine de Saint-Joseph, Letter 139 (early 17th century)

III. Anglican

In the seventeenth century several impressive voices emerged in the Anglican Church, following the lead of Richard Hooker (**173**) and accompanied by the poetry of such men as George Herbert (**194**). The 'Caroline divines' (a term not restricted to those who flourished under Charles I or Charles II) took patristic theology as their inspiration, and expounded a High Church theology and ecclesiology which were distinct both from Roman Catholicism and from the Puritanism of many in the English Church.

208 Keeping Close to the Union

Thomas Traherne (1636–74) was an Anglican priest and theologian and, like John Donne (**198**) and George Herbert (**194**), a metaphysical poet, but most of his works were not published in his lifetime. Many came to light during the twentieth century, and some are still unpublished. His four 'centuries' of meditations were published in 1908.

When we hear or read of the hypostatical union, divine love, or the passion of our Lord, these objects appear as diverse as the eyes are several that behold the same. The things are open and obvious to all, but the right apprehension of them inaccessible. To some eyes they seem false, to some dubious and uncertain, to others dim and to others light and of little value, to all the world distant and sublime, to the most of all, cold and uneffectual; only to the wise and holy they appear what they ought. To me they appear infinitely less, weaker and inferior than what they are. Others see them as things afar off, out of their houses and concerns. I see them in my house, my infinite concern, singly and solely pertaining to me, true, real, near, certain, infallible. I see them also as my joys invaluable, divine, and celestial. But O that I could see them with a sad yet great and serious eye, fain would I have a stable, sound, and venerable esteem, a profound and reverend apprehension of them, as they are indeed infinitely deep, true and serious. Is not his blood deep and serious! are his agonies, sighs and wounds things to be jested at! O the deep and dreadful abyss of his humiliation! Let me, my God, see the serious profoundness of thine eternal care, and while I lament my levity, let me attain that fixed and heavenly frame that may keep my heart close unto thee. O make me weighty in all my deeds! and let me be as serious in enjoying my treasures, as Jesus Christ was in redeeming sinners! It is my tedious shame that I am not answerable to the powerful bloodiness of his most serious passion.

Thomas Traherne, *Select Meditations*, The Third Century 97

209   No Union So Knitteth

> Lancelot Andrewes (1555–1626) was Bishop of Winchester, a friend of Rich-
> ard Hooker (173) and George Herbert (194) and one of the seminal figures
> of seventeenth-century Anglicanism. In his day he was best known for his
> verbally riddling, theologically profound sermons.

It is very agreeable to reason [. . .], if we may by any means, to apprehend
him in *his*, by whom we are thus in *our* nature apprehended, or comprehended, even Christ Jesus, and be united to him this day as he was to us this
day, by a mutual and reciprocal apprehension. We may so, and we are bound
so. And we do so, so oft as we do lay hold of, apprehend, or receive the *word*
which is daily grafted into us. But that is not the proper of this day unless
there be another joined unto it. This day the *Word* became *flesh*, and so must
be apprehended in both, but specially in his *flesh*, as this day giveth it, as this
day would have us.

   Now the bread which we break, is it not the partaking of the body, of the
flesh, of Jesus Christ? It is surely, and by it (and by nothing more) are we made
partakers of this blessed union. [Heb. 2: 14 says] 'Because the children were
partakers of flesh and blood, he also would take part with them'; may we not
say the same? Because he hath so done, taken ours of us, we also, ensuing his
steps, will participate with him, and with his flesh which he has taken of us. It
is most kindly, to take part with him in that which he took part in with us,
and that to no other end but that he might make the receiving of it by us a
means whereby he might dwell in us, and we in him. He taking our flesh, and
we receiving his spirit; by his flesh which he took of us receiving his spirit
which he imparteth to us; that, as he by ours became a partaker of human
nature, so we by his might become partakers of the divine nature.

   Verily, it is the most straight and perfect 'taking hold' that is. No union so
knitteth, as it. Not consanguinity: brethren fall out. Not marriage: man and
wife are severed. But that which is nourished and the nourishment
wherewith—they never are, never can be severed but remain one for ever.
With this act, then, of mutual taking, taking of his flesh, as he has taken ours,
let us seal our duty to him, this day, for taking [. . .] the seed of Abraham.

Lancelot Andrewes, 'Sermon 1 of the Nativitie: Christmas 1605', extract

IV. Puritan

The Puritans were the more radical English Protestants, those who felt that the
Protestant settlement under Elizabeth I did not go nearly far enough in the purification of the Church and the State. The term does not refer to one single movement,
however: in the seventeenth century it could be used of the more Protestant

among the clergy of the Church of England, as well as of various Presbyterian and Congregationalist groups and sects.

210   Christ's Kisses

Richard Sibbes (1577–1635) was a respected Puritan preacher, who taught at Holy Trinity, Cambridge, and at Gray's Inn, London. His works were instrumental in the conversion of Richard Baxter (cf. **48**, **211**).

If Christ be strange to us, it is from ourselves, not from Christ; for he is all love. It is either because our loose hearts run after some carnal contents; and then no marvel though Christ shew himself strange unto us, and we go mourning all the day long, without a sense of his love.

Or else, second, it is when we will not seek for his kisses, a further taste of his love, as we should, in his ordinances, nor exercise those graces that we have as we should, in attending upon the ordinance, resting by faith upon God's promise for a blessing.

Or else, third, we are so negligent, that we do not stir up those graces of God in us by private duties.

Or else, fourth, we join ourselves to evil company, or to persons led with an evil spirit. These are the causes why Christ is strange to us.

Or else, fifth, it is to exercise and try our faith, and to let us see ourselves and our own weakness. Thus he left Peter. Otherwise, it is Christ, his nature, to manifest himself and his love by familiar kisses of his mouth. Search into your hearts, and you shall find that these and such like are the causes why Christ is strange unto you, and why you are senseless of your communion with him.

Consider, again, when it is, at what time is it that we have the sweetest kisses, and are most refreshed with Christ's love. Is it not when we put our strength to good means, as when we strive with God in prayer, and labour in humility, rightly and profitably to use all his ordinances? Mark these two well as a means to preserve and increase the assurance of Christ's love in you:

First, how you fall into deadness, and the causes of it.

Secondly, how you come to have most communion with Christ. and at what time, and after what performances. Canst thou say, I was thus and thus dead and senseless of Christ's love, but now I am thus and thus comforted and refreshed? either when thou deniedst anything to thyself, which thy heart stood strongly for, or when thou hadst been most careful in holy duties. If we deny ourselves in anything, that our hearts stand strongly for, because it hinders us in holy courses, God will be sure to recompense us in spiritual things abundantly, yea, and in temporal things many times.

Consider, again, when I was afflicted and had none else to comfort me, then the Lord was most sweet unto me, then he refreshed my soul with a sense of his love.

These may help us much in getting a further assurance of Christ's love. Be stirred up, then, to desire to be where Christ is, and to have the kisses of his love in his ordinances, as further testimonies of his favour, and never rest from having a desire to increase in grace and communion with Christ. So shall you never want assurance of a good estate, nor comfort in any good estate. Cast such a man into a dungeon, he hath paradise there. Why? Because Christ comes to him. And if we have this communion with Christ, then though we are compassed about with death, yet it cannot affright us, because the great God is with us. Do with such a one what you will; cast him into hell, if it were possible; he having a sweet communion with Christ, will be joyful still; and the more sense we have of the love of Christ, the less we shall regard the pleasures or riches of the world. For what joy can be compared with this, that the soul hath communion with Christ? All the world is nothing in comparison.

Now, then, seeing you cannot requite this love of Christ again, yet shew your love to Christ in manifesting love to his members, to the poor, to such poor especially as have the church of God in their families. As the woman poured oil on the head of Christ, so shall we do well to pour some oil upon the feet of Christ. That which we would do to him, if he were here, let us do to his members, that thereby we may further our communion with Christ.

Richard Sibbes, *The Spouse, her Earnest Desire after Christ*, extract (1638)

211   The Bridegroom's Departure

Richard Baxter (1615–91) was a moderate and irenic man: an Anglican who disliked episcopacy; a Puritan who fought puritan extremism and welcomed the Restoration of the monarchy; and a careful pastor who worked with Anglicans and Nonconformists alike. *The Saints' Everlasting Rest* is his most famous work, and has become a classic. (Cf. **48**, **210**)

The bridegroom's departure was not upon divorce. He did not leave us with a purpose to return no more. He hath left pledges enough to assure us to the contrary. We have his word, his many promises, his ordinances, which show forth his death till he come; and his Spirit, to direct, sanctify, and comfort till he return. We have frequent tokens of love from him, to show us he forgets not his promise, nor us. We daily behold the forerunners of his coming, foretold by himself. We see the fig-tree putteth forth leaves, and therefore know that summer is nigh. Though the riotous world say, 'My Lord delayeth his coming', yet let the saints lift up their heads, for their redemption draweth nigh.

Alas! fellow Christians, what should we do if our Lord should not return? What a case are we here left in! What! leave us in the midst of wolves, and among lions, a generation of vipers, and here forget us! Did he buy us so dear, and then leave us sinning, suffering, groaning, dying daily; and will he come no more to us? It cannot be. This is like our unkind dealing with Christ, who, when we feel ourselves warm in the world, care not for coming to him; but this is not like Christ's dealing with us. He that would come to suffer, will surely come to triumph. He that would come to purchase, will surely come to possess. Where else were all our hopes? What were become of our faith, our prayers, our tears and our waiting? What were all the patience of the saints worth to them? Were we not left of all men the most miserable? Christians, hath Christ made us forsake all the world, and to be forsaken of all the world? to hate all, and be hated of all? and all this for him, that we might have him instead of all? And will he, think you, after all this, forget us and forsake us himself? Far be such a thought from our hearts!

But why staid he not with his people while he was here? Why? Was not the work on earth done? Must he not take possession of glory in our behalf? Must he not intercede with the Father, plead his sufferings, be filled with the Spirit to send forth, receive authority, and subdue his enemies? Our abode here is short. If he had staid on earth, what would it have been to enjoy him for a few days and then die? He hath more in heaven to dwell among; even the spirits of many generations. He will have us live by faith, and not by sight.

O fellow Christians, what a day will that be, when we, who have been kept prisoners by sin, by sinners, by the grave, shall be brought out by the Lord himself! It will not be such a coming as his first was, in poverty and contempt, to be spit upon, and buffeted, and crucified again. He will not come, O careless world! to be slighted and neglected by you any more. Yet that coming wanted not its glory. If the heavenly host, for the celebration of his nativity, must praise God; with what shoutings will angels and saints at that day proclaim glory to God, peace and good-will toward men! If a star must lead men from remote parts, to come to worship the child in the manger; how will the glory of his next appearing constrain all the world to acknowledge his sovereignty! If, riding on an ass, he enter Jerusalem with hosannas; with what peace and glory will he come toward the New Jerusalem! If, when he was in the form of a servant, they cry out, 'What manner of man is this, that even the winds and the sea obey him?' [10] what will they say when they shall see him coming in his glory, and the heavens and the earth obey him? 'Then shall all the tribes of the earth mourn' [Matt. 24: 30]. To think and speak of that day with horror doth well become the impenitent sinner, but ill the believing saint. Shall the wicked behold him, and cry, 'Yonder is he whose blood we neglected, whose grace we resisted, whose counsel we refused, whose government we cast off!' and shall not the saints, with inconceivable gladness, cry, 'Yonder is he whose blood redeemed us, whose Spirit cleansed us, whose law governed us; in whom we trusted, and he hath not deceived our trust; for whom we long waited, and now we see we have not waited in vain! O cursed corruption! that would have had us turn to the world and present things, and say, "Why should we wait for the Lord any longer?" Now we see, Blessed are all they that wait for him.'

And now, Christians, should we not put up that petition heartily, 'Thy kingdom come?' 'The Spirit and the bride say, Come: and let him that heareth (and readeth) say, Come.' Our Lord himself says, 'Surely I come quickly. Amen: even so, come! Lord Jesus' [Rev. 22: 17, 20].

Richard Baxter, The Saints' Everlasting Rest 2, extract (1650)

212   One with Christ

> Between 1643 and 1653 a synod of the Church of England was convened by Parliament, and boycotted by most of the episcopalians loyal to the king—and so was dominated by Presbyterians. This Westminster Assembly suggested many Puritan reforms, some of which were enacted during the Commonwealth before being repressed on the Restoration of the monarchy. The Assembly developed a Directory of Public Worship, or Westminster Directory, to replace the Prayer Book, including this from the eucharistic prayer. (Cf. **29**, **174**.)

Let the prayer, thanksgiving, or blessing of the bread and wine, be to this effect: [. . .] Earnestly to pray to God, the Father of all mercies, and God of all consolation, to vouchsafe his gracious presence, and the effectual working of his Spirit in us, and to sanctify these elements both of bread and wine, and to bless his own ordinance, that we may receive by faith the body and blood of Jesus Christ, crucified for us, and so to feed upon him, that he may be one with us, and we with him; that he may live in us, and we in him, and to him who hath loved us, and given himself for us.

The Westminster Directory, extract (1645)

V. Radical

If 'Puritan' is a title which covers very disparate ground, we are using 'radical' in an even wider-ranging sense, to cover those individuals and groups who rejected the structures and trappings of the established Churches in favour of a root-and-branch reform, a return to purity and simplicity going beyond that of the Puritans. We look here at the Quakers, a hugely influential movement inspired by the preaching of George Fox (1624–91) in the late seventeenth century, and the Levellers, a seventeenth-century group who advocated democracy, widened suffrage, and religious freedom.

213 **Christ Born in the Soul**

Quaker teaching has frequently emphasized the inner working of Christ in the believer's soul, the 'inner light' which guides and illuminates the devout life. Susanna Bateman (fl. 1656) was an English Quaker writer who used poetry to communicate a powerful vision of this radical union with Christ. (Cf. **59**.)

> Thinks human wisdom I can eas'ly see
> The Scripture can this thing declare to me;
> But it's not known by pleasure, ease or sleep,
> Who finds this Pearly must dig both low and deep.
> And whoso finds before it be his own,
> He must sell all to purchase that alone,
> And cast up all his stock and look within,
> Before to build this house he doth begin.
> Remember Babel, do not build too high,
> Nor make a Tower to reach unto the Sky,
> Nor look without, but turn thy eye within,
> See Christ be laid, then build thy house on him.
> Who builds not on this rock, shall surely fall,
> For he's the Corner-stone uniteth all.
> Cease then a while, you human learned men,
> And know your wisdom cannot find out him.
> Thou willing and obedient, know it's thee
> Whose veil is rent to see this mystery:
> It's not the prudent, learned, wife, that shall
> Him comprehend, who is the light of all.
> Follow the light, for surely 'twill thee bring
> Where he is born, then bow and worship him.
> No sooner is he born, but thou shalt see,
> That Herod's nature by its cruelty,
> Works to destroy that New-born-babe in thee.

Susanna Bateman, untitled poem, (1656)

214 The Birth of Christ in the Believer

Job Scott (1751–93) was a New England Quaker minister who left behind him, when he died, a controversial set of theological manuscripts, including *Salvation by Christ: Remarks upon the Nature of Salvation by Christ; Showing that it is a Birth of Divine Life in Man*. It was not published until 1824, when it provoked a flurry of controversy. (Cf. **97**, **271**.)

Full reconciliation to God is not consistent with a state of opposition to his holy law, his divine will, and working in us. While filth and opposition to divine influence remain in man, there remains fuel for the fiery baptism of Jesus, nor can the floor of the heart be thoroughly cleansed till all defilement is removed. God and evil are in eternal contrariety, and as God cannot change, he cannot at one time be unreconciled, and at another time reconciled to the same state. 'Imputation' of Christ's righteousness to sinners, so as to reconcile them to God in a state of actual sin, or alienation from him, is as impossible as to reconcile light and darkness, or Christ and Belial. It is a phantom that has risen up in the fogs and mists of benighted minds. It is attempting to climb up to heaven some other way than by Christ, the door. And yet such is the power of darkness, that this is called magnifying the merits of a crucified saviour, who never saves his people but as he saves them from their sins!

He is the eternal Word, and as such is God. To us he is the emanation, or son of God's love. When he lives and reigns complete in us; when he is our life, and has in all things the pre-eminence with us, and so is our complete justification, as such he must have been begotten and formed in us; strictly and truly so; for it is thus, and thus only, that we are or can be complete in him.

He is one in all the only begotten of God forever. God alone is his Father. Every true believer is his mother. Hence he assures us, 'Whosoever shall do the will of my Father which is in heaven, the same is my brother, and sister, and mother' [Matt. 12: 50]. [. . .] It was and is necessary, in order to [procure] our restoration and union with God, that the life of the Deity, the holy word, should so operate as to bring forth in us a conception and birth of his own divine nature; a real birth of the incorruptible seed and word of God. As in this holy offspring a real union of life, human and divine, is formed and brought forth, and as man herein becomes the mother of this heavenly offspring, this is really the seed of the woman, the seed of the church and spouse of Christ; for it is not only as the seed of Mary or of Eve, that the only begotten is the seed of the woman. The souls in whom he is begotten and brought forth, are all in the relation of parent to him, as well as brethren and sisters; and according to the nature of the work which forms this relation, it is strikingly represented by the parent in the female line; 'Whosoever shall do the will of my Father which is in heaven, the same is my brother, and sister, and mother.'

Job Scott, *Salvation by Christ*, extract (1790s)

215   The Spiritual Dispensation

Gerrard Winstanley (1609–c.1660) was a founder of the Diggers, a subgroup of the Levellers, who emphasized common ownership and manual labour on shared land. This radical political practice was grounded in an equally radical theology. (Cf. **34, 38, 112, 241, 271**.)

The Lord takes up all into himself, even into that Spirit that governs the creation; for he is in all, and acts through all. And all power of righteousness that appears in any subject is still but the Lord, in such or such a discovery.

For as the man Christ Jesus swallowed up *Moses*; and so the Spirit dwelt bodily in that lamb, which was spread abroad in the types; and mankind is to behold the Law of Righteousness in none but in that his well-beloved Son; even so that single body is a type: that the same Spirit that filled every member of that one body, should in these last days be sent into whole mankind, and every branch shall be a joint or member of the mystical body, or several spreadings forth of the vine, being all filled with the one Spirit, Christ the anointing, who fills all with himself, and so he becomes the alone King of righteousness and peace that rules in man.

And the powers of the flesh which is the serpent or curse, shall be subdued under him, and mankind shall be made only subject to this one Spirit, which shall dwell bodily in every one, as he dwelt bodily in the man Christ Jesus, who was the Son of Man [34].

Now as Moses declared, that the Lamb Jesus Christ should be that great prophet to whom every one should give ear, and delivered it in general terms, leaving the particular discoveries of his new doctrine to the Lamb himself when he came; and so did not go about to imagine matters that were above his circle; and we see the doctrine of Jesus Christ, when he came, far exceeded the doctrine of Moses; the one being the substance of the other, and so more spiritual makings forth than the other; even so, the man Christ Jesus, the great prophet, declared in general terms what should be in later times; leaving it to every son and daughter, to declare their particular experiences, when the Spirit doth rise up in them, and manifests himself to them. 'For they that believe,' saith he, 'out of their bellies shall flow rivers (or plentiful discoveries) of the water of life' [John 7: 38]

Therefore as Moses gave way to Christ; for when Christ appeared in flesh, Moses' administration began to be silent and drew back, and set Jesus Christ in the chair to be the great prophet that should be the teacher in types after him, and the ministration of these discoveries were to reign in the world, their appointed times; even so the Lamb Christ Jesus, or that single body, gives way to the holy Ghost, or spreading Spirit; 'If I go not away, the Comforter cannot come to you; for he that dwells bodily in me, is to spread himself in you, that as the Father in me, and I in him are one: even so I in you, and you in me, may become one with the Father' [John 17: 21]. [. . .]

The Son of Man declares, that both outward forms, customs and types of Moses' worship under that ministration at Jerusalem, likewise all forms and customs, and types of this ministration of himself, as the Lamb held forth at a distance to be our Mediator, should all cease and give way to the spiritual worship of the Father in the latter days; or to the spreading of the divine power in men, the one Law of Righteousness, being the teacher of all.

So that upon the rising up of Christ in sons and daughters, which is his second coming, the ministration of Christ in one single person is to be silent and draw back, and set the spreading power of Righteousness and wisdom in the chair, of whose Kingdom there shall be no end. So as all things were gone out from the Spirit, and were gone astray and corrupted, the Spirit in this great mystery of truth being manifested in flesh, burns up that dross out of the Creation, and draws in all things back again into himself, and declares himself to be the alone wisdom and power of Righteousness, that rules, dwells, that governs and preserves both in and over the whole Creation. And now the Son delivers up the Kingdom unto the Father; and he that is the spreading power, not one single person, become all in all in every person; that is the one King of Righteousness in every one.

Gerrard Winstanley, The New Law of Righteousness, extract (1649)

Section D

Discussing Doctrine

Histories of theology sometimes treat the seventeenth and eighteenth centuries as if the only interesting story to be told was that of the birth of a characteristically modern theology through the fires of English empiricism and deism, French philosophy, and German criticism. However, various strands of robust and energetic dogmatic theology flourished in the period, and should in no way be dismissed simply as an old-fashioned backdrop to apparently more radical developments. Much of the most interesting Christology of the period is to be found in these little-visited treasure houses.

216 The Father's Self-Knowledge

Francis de Sales (1567–1622) was one of the greatest of Counter-Reformation theologians, fighting Calvinism on its home territory around Geneva. In this extract from his *Treatise on the Love of God*, originally intended as instruction for a particular individual, he develops Christological themes within an analysis of the 'beatific vision', the vision of God which late medieval theology had seen as the end of Christian life, and which captivated Counter-Reformation thought.

Our minds, Theotimus, will see God. They will see him [. . .], 'as he is, face to face' [1 Cor. 13: 12; 1 John 3: 2]. They will gaze on the vision of his very essence through the actuality and reality of his presence. They will have sight of his infinite perfections: all-powerful, all-good, all-wise, all-just . . . and so on through that inexhaustible mine.

The human mind will then have clear sight of the Father's infinite knowledge from all eternity of his own beauty, to which he gives expression within himself by uttering the Word [cf. **66**]—an expression, an utterance, that is unique, infinite. Since it includes and portrays the complete perfection of the Father, it can but be one identical God with him, in nature numerically single and indivisible. In this way, we shall see the eternal wonderful generation of God's Word, God's Son, by which he was eternally begotten as the Father's image and likeness. This living, natural image is no accidental or external thing: in God everything is substantial, nothing accidental;[8] all his activity immanent, nothing transient. This image is so living, so natural, such an essential, substantial reflection of the Father, that it can but be the same God with no distinction or difference of essence or substance—the only distinction, that of personality.[9] How could God's Son be the true, living, natural image, likeness, 'radiance of his Father's splendour, and the full expression of his being' [Heb. 1: 3], if he did not infinitely reflect, to the life and in his nature, the Father's infinite perfections? How could he infinitely reflect those infinite perfections, unless he too were infinitely perfect? How could he be infinitely perfect, if he were not God; and how could he be God, if he were not the same one God as the Father?

The Son, therefore, the express image, the exact expression of the Father, is one, single, infinite God, equal to the Father, undivided from him in substance, but distinct in personality. Not only is this distinction of persons necessary, it is all that is required for the Father to utter and for the Son to be the Word uttered, for the Father to speak and the Son to be the Word spoken, for the Father to express himself and the Son to be the image, likeness, radiance expressed—all that is needed, after all, for the Father to be Father, the Son to be Son, two distinct persons, but one single divine nature. In this way God is one; but, for all that, he is not alone in the godhead. He is one in his single and simple divinity; yet he is not alone, since he is Father and Son in two persons. The joy we shall know, Theotimus, the bliss of celebrating this eternal birth 'amid the splendour of the holy places';[10] of celebrating it, I repeat, in the vision of it—a vision that is itself a celebration!

Gentle St Bernard [cf. 97], when still a little boy at Châtillon-sur-Seine, was waiting in a church late one Christmas Eve for the divine office to begin. As he waited, poor child, he dropped off into a light slumber. Dear God, the charm of it! —while he slept, he had a clear vision of the way in which the Son of God wedded human nature, became a little Child in the pure womb of his Mother, was born virginally of her in a combination of humility and majesty, and 'came forth like a bridegroom coming from his tent' [Ps. 19: 6]. This vision so filled little Bernard's soul with gladness, joyfulness and spiritual delight, he felt the effects of it strongly all his life. Although he used to gather spiritual honey from each of the divine mysteries, Christmas always charmed him most of all, and he would speak with special relish of his Master's birth [cf. 1, 127].

For pity's sake, Theotimus! . . . if a mystical imaginative vision of the human birth of God's Son in time, when he was born as man from a virgin, so utterly captivated and satisfied a child's heart—how will it be for us in heaven, when eternal light floods our souls, when we shall have sight of that eternal birth by which the Son proceeds 'God from God, light from light, true God from true God' [76], divinely, everlastingly? There, in union with so delightful an object, our minds will be satiated beyond our present capacity to understand—riveted to God for ever by an attentiveness that knows no distraction.

Francis de Sales, *Treatise on the Love of God* 12 (1616)

The Westminster Assembly (cf. **212**) compiled two Catechisms in 1647–8; the shorter became one of the charter documents of Presbyterianism. It has also been used by many Baptist and Congregationalist groups. In this extract we see the basic framework of Presbyterian Christology: fall and covenant; Christ's threefold office; Christ's two states; and the components of salvation. (Cf. **164–5**.)

Q. *What is the misery of that estate whereinto man fell?*

A. All mankind by their fall lost communion with God, are under his wrath and curse, and so, made liable to all miseries in this life, to death itself, and to the pains of hell for ever.

Q. *Did God leave all mankind to perish in the estate of sin and misery?*

A. God having, out of his mere good pleasure, from all eternity, elected some to everlasting life, did enter into a covenant of grace, to deliver them out of the estate of sin and misery, and to bring them into an estate of salvation by a redeemer.

Q. *Who is the redeemer of God's elect?*

A. The only redeemer of God's elect is the Lord Jesus Christ, who, being the eternal Son of God, became man, and so was, and continueth to be, God and man in two distinct natures, and one person, for ever.

Q. *How did Christ, being the Son of God, become man?*

A. Christ, the Son of God, became man, by taking to himself a true body, and a reasonable soul, being conceived by the power of the Holy Ghost, in the womb of the Virgin Mary, and born of her, yet without sin.

Q. *What offices doth Christ execute as our redeemer?*

A. Christ, as our Redeemer, executeth the offices of a prophet, of a priest, and of a king, both in his estate of humiliation and exaltation.

Q. *How doth Christ execute the office of a prophet?*

A. Christ executeth the office of a prophet, in revealing to us, by his Word and Spirit, the will of God for our salvation.

Q. *How doth Christ execute the office of a priest?*

A. Christ executeth the office of a Priest, in his once offering up of himself a sacrifice to satisfy divine justice, and reconcile us to God; and in making continual intercession for us.

Q. *How doth Christ execute the office of a king?*

A. Christ executeth the office of a king, in subduing us to himself, in ruling and defending us, and in restraining and conquering all his and our enemies.

Q. *Wherein did Christ's humiliation consist?*

A. Christ's humiliation consisted in his being born, and that in a low condition, made under the law, undergoing the miseries of this life, the wrath of

God, and the cursed death of the cross in being buried, and continuing under the power of death for a time.

Q. *Wherein consisteth Christ's exaltation?*

A. Christ's exaltation consisteth in his rising again from the dead on the third day, in ascending up into heaven, in sitting at the right hand of God the Father, and in coming to judge the world at the last day.

Q. *How are we made partakers of the redemption purchased by Christ?*

A. We are made partakers of the redemption purchased by Christ, by the effectual application of it to us by his Holy Spirit.

Q. *How doth the Spirit apply to us the redemption purchased by Christ?*

A. The Spirit applieth to us the redemption purchased by Christ, by working faith in us, and thereby uniting us to Christ in our effectual calling.

Q. *What is effectual calling?*

A. Effectual calling is the work of God's Spirit, whereby, convincing us of our sin and misery, enlightening our minds in the knowledge of Christ, and renewing our wills, he doth persuade and enable us to embrace Jesus Christ, freely offered to us in the Gospel.

Q. *What benefits do they that are effectually called partake of in this life?*

A. They that are effectually called do in this life partake of justification, adoption, and sanctification, and the several benefits which, in this life, do either accompany or flow from them.

Q. *What is justification?*

A. Justification is an act of God's free grace, wherein he pardoneth all our sins, and accepteth us as righteous in his sight, only for the righteousness of Christ imputed to us, and received by faith alone.

Q. *What is adoption?*

A. Adoption is an act of God's free grace, whereby we are received into the number, and have a right to all the privileges, of the Sons of God.

Q. *What is sanctification?*

A. Sanctification is the work of God's free grace, whereby we are renewed in the whole man after the image of God, and are enabled more and more to die unto sin, and live unto righteousness.

Q. *What are the benefits which, in this life, do accompany or flow from justification, adoption, and sanctification?*

A. The benefits which, in this life, do accompany or flow from justification, adoption, and sanctification, are, assurance of God's love, peace of conscience, joy in the Holy Ghost, increase of grace, and perseverance therein to the end.

Q. *What benefits do believers receive from Christ at death?*

A. The souls of believers are at their death made perfect in holiness, and do immediately pass into glory; and their bodies, being still united to Christ, do rest in their graves till the resurrection.

Q. *What benefits do believers receive from Christ at the resurrection?*

A. At the resurrection, believers being raised up in glory, shall be openly acknowledged and acquitted in the day of judgment, and made perfectly blessed in the full enjoying of God to all eternity.

The Shorter [Westminster] Catechism 19–38 (1647–8)

218 Humiliation and Exaltation

Jonathan Edwards (1703–58), Congregationalist minister and catalyst of the revival known as the Great Awakening, was the greatest of American theologians. Combining strict Calvinist theology with philosophical interests stimulated by his reading of Locke, he did important theological work on grace and human freedom. The following is from a sermon on Revelation 5: 5–6: 'See, the Lion of the tribe of Judah, the Root of David, has triumphed . . . . Then I saw a Lamb.' (Cf. **217**.)

Christ was in the greatest degree of his humiliation, and yet by that, above all other things, his divine glory appears.

Christ's humiliation[II] was great, in being born in such a low condition, of a poor virgin, and in a stable. His humiliation was great, in being subject to Joseph the carpenter, and Mary his mother, and afterwards living in poverty, so as not to have where to lay his head; and in suffering such manifold and bitter reproaches as he suffered, while he went about preaching and working miracles. But his humiliation was never so great as it was, in his last sufferings, beginning with his agony in the garden, till he expired on the cross. Never was he subject to such ignominy as then, never did he suffer so much pain in his body, or so much sorrow in his soul; never was he in so great an exercise of his condescension, humility, meekness, and patience, as he was in these last sufferings; never was his divine glory and majesty covered with so thick and dark a veil; never did he so empty himself and make himself of no reputation, as at this time.

And yet, never was his divine glory so manifested, by any act of his, as in yielding himself up to these sufferings. When the fruit of it came to appear, and the mystery and ends of it to be unfolded in its issue, then did the glory of it appear, then did it appear as the most glorious act of Christ that ever he exercised towards the creature. [. . .]

Christ never so eminently appeared for divine justice, and yet never suffered so much from divine Justice, as when he offered up himself a sacrifice for our sins.

In Christ's great sufferings did his infinite regard to the honour of God's justice distinguishingly appear, for it was from regard to that that he thus humbled himself. And yet in these sufferings, Christ was the target of the vindictive expressions of that very justice of God. Revenging justice then spent all its force upon him, on account of our guilt; which made him sweat blood, and cry out upon the cross, and probably rent his vitals—broke his heart, the fountain of blood, or some other blood vessels—and by the violent fermentation turned his blood to water. [. . .] And this was the way and means by which Christ stood up for the honour of God's justice, namely, by thus suffering its terrible executions. For when he had under-taken for sinners, and had substituted himself in their room, divine justice could have its due honour no other way than by his suffering its revenges. [. . .]

Christ's holiness never so illustriously shone forth as it did in his last sufferings, and yet he never was to such a degree treated as guilty.
Christ's holiness never had such a trial as it had then, and therefore never had so great a manifestation. When it was tried in this furnace it came forth as gold, or as silver purified seven times. His holiness then above all appeared in his steadfast pursuit of the honour of God, and in his obedience to him. For his yielding himself unto death was transcendently the greatest act of obedience that ever was paid to God by any one since the foundation of the world.

And yet then Christ was in the greatest degree treated as a wicked person would have been. He was apprehended and bound as a malefactor. His accusers represented him as a most wicked wretch. In his sufferings before his crucifixion, he was treated as if he had been the worst and vilest of mankind, and then, he was put to a kind of death, that none but the worst sort of malefactors were wont to suffer, those that were most abject in their persons, and guilty of the blackest crimes. And he suffered as though guilty from God himself, by reason of our guilt imputed to him; for he who knew no sin, was made sin for us; he was made subject to wrath, as if he had been sinful himself. He was made a curse for us.

Christ never so greatly manifested his hatred of sin, as against God, as in his dying to take away the dishonour that sin had done to God; and yet never was he to such a degree subject to the terrible effects of God's hatred of sin, and wrath against it, as he was then. In this appears those diverse excellencies meeting in Christ, namely, love to God, and grace to sinners. [. . .]

It was in Christ's last sufferings, above all, that he was delivered up to the power of his enemies; and yet by these, above all, he obtained victory over his enemies.
Christ never was so in his enemies' hands, as in the time of his last sufferings. They sought his life before; but from time to time they were restrained, and Christ escaped out of their hands, and this reason is given for it, that his time was not yet come [John 8: 20]. But now they were suffered to work their will

upon him, he was in a great degree delivered up to the malice and cruelty of both wicked men and devils. [. . .]

And yet it was principally by means of those sufferings that he conquered and overthrew his enemies. Christ never so effectually bruised Satan's head, as when Satan bruised his heel. The weapon with which Christ warred against the devil, and obtained a most complete victory and glorious triumph over him, was the cross, the instrument and weapon with which he thought he had overthrown Christ, and brought on him shameful destruction. [. . .]

Thus Christ appeared at the same time, and in the same act, as both a lion and a lamb. He appeared as a lamb in the hands of his cruel enemies; as a lamb in the paws, and between the devouring jaws, of a roaring lion; yea, he was a lamb actually slain by this lion: and yet at the same time, as the lion of the tribe of Judah, he conquers and triumphs over Satan; destroying his own destroyer; as Samson did the lion that roared upon him, when he rent him as he would a kid. And in nothing has Christ appeared so much as a lion, in glorious strength destroying his enemies, as when he was brought as a lamb to the slaughter. In his greatest weakness he was most strong; and when he suffered most from his enemies, he brought the greatest confusion on his enemies.

Jonathan Edwards, The Excellency of Christ 2. c. 1, 3, 4, 7, extracts (1736)

219 The Limitations of Atonement

Johannes Wollebius (1586–1629) was another Reformed dogmatician. In this piece he first combats the kind of Atonement theories associated with Fausto Paulo Socinus (1539–1604), an early Unitarian (cf. **251**, **260**, **266**), and then argues that Christ cannot have died for everyone in any strict sense.

The purpose of the passion of Christ is the revelation of the glory of God, and especially of his wrath against sin, and of his righteousness and mercy; also, revelation of divine and human nature. The special and distinctive purpose is satisfaction for our sins. [. . .]

Those who teach that Christ's passion was merely to give us an example destroy the purpose and result of this passion. It is of course true that Christ, by his suffering, gave us an example, but the primary result of his passion is satisfaction for our sins. The Socinians acknowledge Christ as saviour only in the following senses (1) that he proclaimed heavenly truth, (2) that he confirmed it, (3) that he gave the example of his passion and resurrection, (4) that he conferred life eternal. When the words of Scripture, which declare that Christ died for us, are brought forward against them, they try to evade their force by explaining the preposition 'for' as meaning 'on behalf of'; that is, that

Christ died on our behalf or for our welfare, but not instead of us. The following arguments refute this most pestilential heresy:

(1) Christ died for us in such a way as to give his life as the price of redemption for many. He gave himself as 'a ransom for all' [1 Tim. 2: 6]. He is said to have redeemed us with his most precious blood. Now, who does not know that it is one thing to give an example, and another to pay the price of redemption for someone? How can one ransom someone for a price unless he satisfies by legal purchase, and stands in the very place of that one?

(2) Because he so died for us as to be made sin for us, so that he could take our sins upon himself and bear the punishment that was due to us [53]. But is taking the transgression of another upon oneself and bearing the punishment which he deserves merely giving an example? Is it not rather a case of being punished and making satisfaction in his place [cf. 158]?

(3) If the sacrifices of the Old Testament were offered by the priests in place of the people, then also the sacrifice of Christ is performed in our place. The first premise is true; therefore the second is true. The Socinians declare boldly that there is no place in Scripture where the preposition 'for' is the equivalent of 'in place of another.' But who can fail to see this meaning in the following: 'The good shepherd gives his life for his sheep' [John 10: 11]; that is, fighting even to death in place of the sheep; 'Scarcely for a righteous man will anyone die' [Rom. 5: 7]; 'The Spirit intercedes for us' [Rom. 8: 26]; 'If God be for us, who can be against us?' [Rom. 8: 31]; 'I could wish that I were cursed for my brethren' [Rom 9: 3]? Nor can it be argued that Christ's passion is inadequate as ransom price, on the ground that the punishment we deserve for our sins is eternal, whereas the sufferings of Christ are not eternal. Although these sufferings are in time, they have the same value as an eternal punishment, both because of the infinite majesty and worthiness of the person of Christ, and because of the infinite weight and magnitude of the suffering and the burden of the divine anger, to the bearing of which the entire world and all created things were inadequate.

[. . .] While Christ's passion is minimised by the foregoing errors, those who teach that he died for all human beings broaden the object of his passion more than is allowable. Of course, if we take into consideration the magnitude and worthiness of the merit, we admit that it would suffice for the redemption of ten worlds; but if we take the plan of God and the intention of Christ into consideration, then it is false to say that Christ died for every person. For this reason others say that his death was sufficient for all, but not effective for all; that is, the merit of Christ, because of his worthiness, is sufficient for all, but it is not effective for all in its application, because Christ did not die with the intention that his death be applied to all. Why should he die for those for whom he would not pray? But he told us that he did not pray for the world. Those who oppose us argue from passages in which there is reference to the whole world, or to all men, in which all men in general are named.

But in I John 2: 2 the meaning of 'the whole world' is, by metonymy, 'the elect scattered throughout the whole world,' and in I Timothy 2: 4 'all men' means men of every sort, whether gentiles or Jews, kings or private citizens, and so not individuals in a class, but classes of individuals, as the words that follow make plain.

Johannes Wollebius, *Compendium of Christian Theology* XVII, extracts (1626)

Section E

The Enlightenment

Theology, like so much else in the Western world, has been decisively shaped for good or ill by a complex movement of thinkers and writers who set themselves, in the name of reason, in conscious opposition to the authorities and traditions of the past. For our purposes, we can trace the beginnings of the movement in English deism and political philosophy, and see its transformation among the French *philosophes*, and its maturity among German theologians and philosophers in the eighteenth and through into the nineteenth centuries. Deeply affected by the rise of modern science, by new understandings of human identity, by the theology of the radical fringe of the Reformation, the Enlightenment transformed the intellectual landscape of the West.

220 · Copernican Christ

Pierre de Bérulle (1575–1629) was not an Enlightenment theologian. A Roman Catholic cardinal prominent in the Counter-Reformation, he was a celebrated spiritual director, and a theologian deeply concerned with the Incarnation. In this extract from a swirling symphony of reflections on the Incarnation, however, we with hindsight can hear in passing the rumour of approaching revolution. (Cf. **49, 65, 207, 274**.)

An excellent mind of this age[12] claimed that the sun and not the earth is at the centre of the world. He maintained that it is stationary and that the earth, in conformity with its round shape, moves in relation to the sun. This position goes against all appearances, which constrain our senses to believe that the sun is in continuous movement around the earth. This new opinion, which has little following in the science of the stars, is useful and should be followed in the science of salvation.

For Jesus is the sun that is immovable in his greatness and that moves all other things. Jesus is like his Father. Seated at his right hand, he is immovable like him and moves all things. Jesus is the true centre of the world and the world should be in continuous movement toward him. Jesus is the Sun of our souls and from him we receive every grace, every light and every effect of his power. The earth of our hearts should be in continuous movement toward him, so that we might welcome, with all its powers and components, the favourable aspects and benign influences of this great star. Let us bring, then, the movements and affections of our soul to Jesus. Let us raise our spirits and praise God for his only begotten Son and for the mystery of his incarnation.

Pierre de Bérulle, *Elevations upon the Incarnation* 2. 2, extract (early 17th century)

221   Christ Simplified

Thomas Hobbes (1588–1679) was a key figure at the birth of secular political philosophy, dismissing God from the governance of human affairs. In this theological parenthesis in his major political work, *Leviathan*, he makes a characteristically modern move: heightening the purity and simplicity of the gospel in order to confine it to its 'proper place' so that it will not interfere with his new, thoroughly secular politics. (Cf. **262**.)

The only article of faith, which the scripture maketh simply necessary to salvation, is this, that Jesus is the Christ. By the name of Christ, is understood the King, which God had before promised by the prophets of the Old Testament, to send into the world, to reign (over the Jews, and over such of other nations as should believe in him) under himself eternally; and to give them that eternal life, which was lost by the sin of Adam. [. . .] For proof that the belief of this article, 'Jesus is the Christ,' is all the faith required to salvation, my first argument shall be from the scope of the evangelists; which was by the description of the life of our saviour, to establish that one article, 'Jesus is the Christ.' The sum of St. Matthew's gospel is this, that Jesus was of the stock of David; born of a Virgin; which are the marks of the true Christ; that the magi came to worship him as King of the Jews; that Herod for the same cause sought to kill him; that John Baptist proclaimed him; that he preached by himself, and his Apostles that he was that King; that he taught the law, not as a scribe, but as a man of authority; that he cured diseases by his word only, and did many other miracles, which were foretold the Christ should do; that he was saluted king when he entered into Jerusalem; that he forewarned them to beware of all others that should pretend to be Christ; that he was taken, accused, and put to death, for saying, he was King; that the cause of his condemnation written on the cross, was 'Jesus of Nazareth, King of the Jews'. All which tend to no other end than this, that men should believe, that Jesus is the Christ. Such therefore was the scope of St. Matthew's Gospel. But the scope of all the evangelists (as may appear by reading them) was the same. Therefore the scope of the whole gospel, was the establishing of that only article. And St. John expressly makes it his conclusion. 'These things are written, that you may know that Jesus is the Christ, the Son of the living God' [John 20: 31] [. . .]

The third argument is, from those places of scripture, by which all the faith required to salvation is declared to be easy. For if an inward assent of the mind to all the doctrines concerning Christian faith now taught (whereof the greatest part are disputed) were necessary to salvation, there would be nothing in the world so hard, as to be a Christian. The thief upon the cross, though repenting, could not have been saved for saying, 'Lord remember me when thou comest into thy Kingdom' [Luke 23: 42]; by which he testified no belief of any other article, but this, that Jesus was the King. Nor could it be said that Christ's yoke is easy, and his burthen light. Nor that little children believe in him. Nor could St. Paul have said, 'It pleased God by the foolishness of preaching, to save them that believe' [1 Cor. 1: 21]; nor could St. Paul himself have been saved, much less have been so great a Doctor of the Church so suddenly, that never perhaps thought of transubstantiation, nor purgatory, nor many other articles now obtruded. [. . .]

But a man may here ask, whether it be not as necessary to salvation, to believe, that God is omnipotent; creator of the world; that Jesus Christ is risen; and that all men else shall rise again from the dead at the last day; as to believe, that Jesus is the Christ. To which I answer, they are; and so are many more articles: but they are such, as are contained in this one, and may be deduced from it, with more or less difficulty. For who is there that does not see, that they who believe Jesus to be the Son of the God of Israel, and that the Israelites had for God the omnipotent creator of all things, do therein also believe, that God is the omnipotent creator of all things? Or how can a man believe, that Jesus is the King that shall reign eternally, unless he believe him also risen again from the dead? For a dead man cannot exercise the office of a king. In sum, he that holdeth this foundation, 'Jesus is the Christ,' holdeth expressly all that he seeth rightly deduced from it, and implicitly all that is consequent thereunto, though he have not skill enough to discern the consequence. And therefore it holdeth still good, that the belief of this one article is sufficient faith to obtain remission of sins to the penitent, and consequently to bring them into the Kingdom of Heaven. [. . .]

Having thus shewn what is necessary to salvation; it is not hard to reconcile our obedience to God, with our obedience to the civil sovereign . . . .

Thomas Hobbes, *Leviathan* 43, extracts (1651)

 222   **Christl and Archimedes**

Blaise Pascal (1623–62) was a French scientist and mathematician who in 1654 had a dramatic conversion experience. He became a champion of a rigorously moral theology and a defender of the absolute priority of God's grace, without which we can do nothing. His *Pensées* were collected thoughts from his notebooks published posthumously; in this extract he presents Christ's excellence to his age, seeking to lure his readers to faith.

I consider Jesus Christ in all persons and in ourselves: Jesus Christ as a Father in his Father, Jesus Christ as a brother in his brethren, Jesus Christ as poor in the poor, Jesus Christ as rich in the rich, Jesus Christ as doctor and priest in priests, Jesus Christ as sovereign in princes, etc. For by his glory he is all that is great, being God; and by his mortal life he is all that is poor and abject. Therefore he has taken this unhappy condition, so that he could be in all persons and the model of all conditions. [. . .]

What man ever had more renown? The whole Jewish people foretell him before his coming. The Gentile people worship him after his coming. The two peoples, Gentile and Jewish, regard him as their centre.

And yet what man enjoys this renown less? Of thirty-three years, he lives thirty without appearing. For three years he passes as an impostor; the priests and the chief people reject him; his friends and his nearest relatives despise him. Finally, he dies, betrayed by one of his own disciples, denied by another, and abandoned by all.

What part, then, has he in this renown? Never had man so much renown; never had man more ignominy. All that renown has served only for us, to render us capable of recognising him; and he had none of it for himself.

The infinite distance between body and mind is a symbol of the infinitely more infinite distance between mind and charity; for charity is supernatural.

All the glory of greatness has no lustre for people who are in search of understanding; the greatness of clever men is invisible to kings, to the rich, to chiefs, and to all the worldly great. The greatness of wisdom, which is nothing if not of God, is invisible to the carnal-minded and to the clever. These are three orders differing in kind.

Great geniuses have their power, their glory, their greatness, their victory, their lustre, and have no need of worldly greatness, with which they are not in keeping. They are seen, not by the eye, but by the mind; this is sufficient. The saints have their power, their glory, their victory, their lustre, and need no worldly or intellectual greatness, with which they have no affinity; for these neither add anything to them, nor take away anything from them. They are seen of God and the angels, and not of the body, nor of the curious mind. God is enough for them.

Archimedes, apart from his rank, would have the same veneration. He fought no battles for the eyes to feast upon; but he has given his discoveries to all men. Oh! how brilliant he was to the mind! Jesus Christ, without riches and without any external exhibition of knowledge, is in his own order of holiness. He did not invent; he did not reign. But he was humble, patient, holy, holy to God, terrible to devils, without any sin. Oh! in what great pomp and in what wonderful splendour he is come to the eyes of the heart, which perceive wisdom!

It would have been useless for Archimedes to have acted the prince in his books on geometry, although he was a prince. It would have been useless for our Lord Jesus Christ to come like a king, in order to shine forth in his kingdom of holiness. But he came there appropriately in the glory of his own order.

It is most absurd to take offence at the lowliness of Jesus Christ, as if his lowliness were in the same order as the greatness which he came to manifest. If we consider this greatness in his life, in his passion, in his obscurity, in his death, in the choice of his disciples, in their desertion, in his secret resurrection, and the rest, we shall see it to be so immense that we shall have no reason for being offended at a lowliness which is not of that order. But there are some who can only admire worldly greatness, as though there were no intellectual greatness; and others who only admire intellectual greatness, as though there were not infinitely higher things in wisdom.

All bodies, the firmament, the stars, the earth and its kingdoms, are not equal to the lowest mind; for mind knows all these and itself; and these bodies nothing. All bodies together, and all minds together, and all their products, are not equal to the least feeling of charity. This is of an order infinitely more exalted. From all bodies together, we cannot obtain one little thought; this is impossible and of another order. From all bodies and minds, we cannot produce a feeling of true charity; this is impossible and of another and supernatural order.

Blaise Pascal, Pensées 785, 792–3 (1660)

223 Against Atonement

Thomas Morgan (1719–99) was a deist thinker. In the name of a philosophical belief which removed God from messy involvement with the world, he attacked traditional Christianity. Unwilling to attack Christ directly, he sought to show that the true, simple, pre-Christian Christ had been submerged beneath such moral barbarisms as a theory of Atonement, and such absurdities as a belief in miracles.

That the righteousness of Christ, or the redundancy of his merit, could not be placed to our account, so as to make any Part of our justifying righteousness in the sight of God, seems farther evident from hence, that all that was done or suffered by him was necessary to himself; and upon his *own account* [cf. 114, 158]. For having, in submission to the will of God, freely undertaken the work he was sent about, he was as much bound to obedience herein, as we are in our proper sphere and capacity. As Christ was under a law from God, and acted with the prospect of a glorious personal reward, he could not have failed, in any part of his obedience, without losing that reward, and forfeiting the divine favour. It is true, he obeyed perfectly this law of God, and finished everything that was given him to do; but herein he did no more than what he was bound to, and nothing less could have been accepted from him. And, however free and voluntary the obedience of Christ was, yet it was a necessary obligation laid upon him by the will and law of God, and from which he would gladly have been excused, had his heavenly Father thought fit [cf. **15**]. He therefore obeyed, in the point of martyrdom, from the same principle which every wise and good man must always act upon, by choosing the greatest sufferings in this world rather than disobey God, and lose the hopes and prospects of futurity. Now here certainly could be no such thing as supererogation, or redundant merit,[13] where nothing was done or suffered, but under an indispensable, personal obligation.

Christ himself seems to have had no such notion of the necessity of his death, as a propitiation and atonement for the sins of the world, and an indispensable condition of the salvation of mankind, when he prayed so often and earnestly not to be put upon any such Trial, and that if possible this cup of sorrow might pass from him. No man can imagine, that Christ would have spent a whole night in such passionate prayers and supplications to God, in order to prevent a thing which he certainly knew must happen, and which had been previously agreed on between the Father and him. Would the common saviour and friend of mankind have thus declined a few hours bodily pain, in a way that many thousands had suffered before him, had he thought it necessary to destroy the power of the devil, and to open the gates of heaven to a whole world of lost, undone creatures?

In short, since personal merit and demerit have a necessary, immutable relation to the individual persons themselves, and cannot possibly be communicated from one person to another, it must be an eternal contradiction in the nature and reason of things, to suppose or say, that Christ was ever punished for our sins, or that we are rewarded for his righteousness; because this would be rewarding and punishing men without any regard to the natural individuality, or moral characters of the persons thus rewarded or punished. They who have founded this doctrine of imputed righteousness and merit, upon some metaphorical expressions of St. Paul, have not well considered how little this can serve their purpose, when they come to apply it literally to the Christian scheme.

Thomas Morgan, The Moral Philosopher, extract (1738)

224   Christ Falsified

Hermann Samuel Reimarus (1694–1768) was Professor of Hebrew and Oriental Languages at Hamburg—and a German deist (cf. **223**). In secret, he wrote an analysis of the Gospels in which he rejected miracles and revelation, and condemned the authors as fabricators. When parts of the work were published posthumously by Gotthold Ephraim Lessing (cf. **227**) in 1774–8, they created a major outcry. Some regard them as the beginning of modern biblical criticism.

When John, Jesus, and Jesus' messengers or apostles preached everywhere, 'The Kingdom of Heaven has come near; believe the gospel,' people knew that the pleasing message of the immediate coming of the expected Messiah would be brought to them, but we nowhere read that John, Jesus, or the disciples by this proclamation ever said anything further of what the Kingdom of God consisted, and of what kind and nature it would be. Therefore the Jews must necessarily have attached such words of the approaching Kingdom of Heaven to the concepts that ruled among them. The ruling concept of the Messiah and his kingdom, however, was that he would be a great worldly king and would establish a mighty kingdom at Jerusalem through which he would rescue them from all servitude and even more, making them rule over other nations.[14] [. . .]

The evangelists also belong to the number of disciples and apostles of Jesus and therefore attributed the hope in Jesus to themselves as well as to all the disciples. Therefore they also hoped in Jesus as a *secular* saviour of the nation of Israel up until his death, and after the failure of this hope, only after his death, did they build the system of a *spiritual* suffering saviour for the whole human race. It also follows that their previous system of the goal, teaching, and actions of Jesus changed.

Now all of the gospel writers wrote their stories of Jesus' teaching and actions long after his death. Consequently the evangelists wrote their narrative of the teaching and actions of Jesus *after* they had changed their system and opinion of the purpose of the teaching and actions of Jesus. [. . .]

The reading of the gospels by itself indicates that these conclusions which I have reached are fully justified. For there, on the one hand, is the new system of a suffering *spiritual* saviour presented very clearly and succinctly in Jesus' own words, but on the other hand, there are so few and such vague traces in Jesus' speeches and actions of his purpose to become a *secular* saviour of Israel that, according to the current report of the story, one cannot understand at all how all disciples throughout all that time could have reached the conclusions of the old system, or still more have persisted in the belief if Jesus really said nothing other than that which they tell and said or did nothing else directed more toward secular deliverance.

It is particularly impossible to understand if we consider that before his death, Jesus had spoken so clearly of his death and of his resurrection after three days, why, after he had really died and was buried, did this recent promise come to the mind of no single disciple, apostle, evangelist, or woman? But they speak and act as if they heard nothing about it during their lifetime. They wrap up the corpse and try to preserve it with many spices to protect it from foulness and decomposition. In fact, they were still trying to do this on the third day after his death, now that the promised time of his resurrection had arrived. They apparently also knew nothing of such a promise. They think of nothing other than that Jesus is dead and will remain dead and like other men will decompose and stink. They completely give up all hope of a deliverance through him, and they do not leave the slightest trace of another hope, a resurrection, or a spiritual deliverance. They are amazed and startled when they find the stone moved away from the door of the tomb; they still think the gardener might have taken away the corpse, since they could no more see it, and when the women even bring the message of Jesus' resurrection to the disciples, they are shocked as if over something unexpected and do not want to believe it. Is it really possible that each and every disciple would have behaved in this way if the last sayings of their Master as he was going to his death had so clearly contained the promise of the resurrection, on a definite day as they now tell it? [. . .]

Now since the narrative of Jesus according to his disciples after the system changed differs in important points from that which it originally would have said—since they told as having happened things on which the new system principally depends, of which they did not know the slightest bit before the change of their system; and since they would have left out of the story other things which they must have held to be essential before the change of their system—so the new system is not in agreement with history but history must be made to conform to their new system. Because so long as they really had the sayings and actions of Jesus during his lifetime before their eyes, they hoped that he would deliver Israel *temporally*, and their system was based simply on *facta*, but now after their hope had vanished, they change the whole system in a few days and make him a suffering saviour of all men.

After that even their *facta* change, and [they imagine] Jesus must have said and promised things during his lifetime [. . .] according to [their new ideas] of which they previously had not the slightest idea. In all points where the system is not established according to the history but the history [is] established according to the system, then both history and system are to that degree unfounded: the history, because it was not taken from fact, and from experience and recollection which originate from these facts, but is simply told to have happened, so that it agrees with the new and changed hypothesis or the new system; the system, however, because it refers to the *facta* which first began after the system had been composed in the thoughts of the author, and are therefore simply *fabricated and false*.

As much as we can conclude by the ambiguous and completely changed conduct of Jesus' disciples and particularly of the evangelists about the true purpose which Jesus held in his sayings and actions, we can only think that their first system of a previously-held *secular* salvation of Israel was well grounded and true, and that they fabricated a different system of his purpose, namely that he would be a suffering *spiritual* saviour of mankind, only because of the unfulfilled hope after his death, and that they wrote down the narration of his speeches and actions, in a way that was according to their system, and that accordingly, this account and system is to that degree invalid and false.

Hermann Samuel Reimarus, The Goal of Jesus and his Disciples 1. 30–3, extracts
(posthumously pub., 1774–8)

225   Jesus the Jew

> Rabbi Jacob Emdem (1697–1776) was a Jewish theologian and philosopher who had a deep impact upon Jewish life in Germany and Poland, and developed an extraordinarily generous Jewish theology of Christianity and Islam. Although the relationship between Enlightenment thinkers and Judaism was extremely mixed, views like that of Emdem did have a definite impact upon Enlightenment accounts of the religions, and of Jesus. (Cf. 242, 340.)

Christian scholars have assumed from certain passages in the Gospels that [Jesus] wished to give a new Torah to take the place of the Torah of Moses. How could he then have said explicitly that he comes only to fulfil it? But it is as I have said earlier—that the writers of the Gospels never meant to say that the Nazarene came to abolish Judaism, but only that he came to establish a religion for the Gentiles from that time onward. Nor was it new, but actually ancient; they being the seven commandments of the sons of Noah, which were forgotten. The apostles of the Nazarene then established them anew. However, those born as Jews, or circumcised as converts to Judaism (Exodus 12: 49: 'One law shall be to him that is home-born, and unto the stranger') are obligated to observe all commandments of the Torah without exception.

But for the Gentiles he reserved the seven commandments which they have always been obligated to fulfil. It is for that reason that they were forbidden pollutions of idols, fornication, blood, and things strangled. They also forbade them circumcision and the Sabbath. All of this was in accord with the law and custom of our Torah, as expounded by our sages, the true transmitters from Moses at Sinai. It was they who sat upon his seat (as the Nazarene himself attested). It was they (the sages or Pharisees) who said that it is forbidden to circumcise a Gentile who does not accept upon himself the yoke of (all) the commandments. The sages likewise said that the Gentile is enjoined not (fully) to observe the Sabbath. The apostles of the Nazarene therefore chose for those Gentiles who do not enter the Jewish faith that instead of circumcision they should practice immersion (for truly immersion is also a condition of full conversion), and a commemoration of the Sabbath was made for them on Sunday.

But the Nazarene and his apostles observed the Sabbath and circumcision as mentioned earlier, for they were born as Jews. They observed the Torah fully, until after a period of time a few of them decided to give up the Torah among themselves completely. They said that its observance was too difficult for them and agreed to remove its yoke from their necks. But even here they did correctly as far as the Gentiles were concerned, for they were not commanded to observe it. Nor is it proper to make it difficult for them, since they did not receive the Torah and are not enjoined to observe the 613 commandments. However, it is completely different as far as the Jews are concerned, for they became obligated to fulfil the Torah because God delivered them from the iron furnace (Egypt) to be the people of his possession. Therefore they and their children became subject to it forever. This, their covenant, will not be forgotten from their mouths, nor be discontinued from their children. For it they have given their lives throughout the generations, as the Psalmist has recorded. All this is come upon us; yet have we not forgotten thee, neither have we been false to thy covenant.

Certainly, therefore, there is no doubt that one who seeks truth will agree with our thesis, that the Nazarene and his Apostles never meant to abolish the Torah of Moses from one who was born a Jew. Likewise did Paul write in his letter to the Corinthians that each should adhere to the faith in which each was called. They therefore acted in accordance with the Torah by forbidding circumcision to Gentiles, according to the Halakha, as it is forbidden to one who does not accept the yoke of the commandments. They knew that it would be too difficult for the Gentiles to observe the Torah of Moses. They therefore forbade them to circumcise, and it would suffice that they observe the seven Noahide Commandments, as commanded upon them through the Halakha from Moses at Sinai.

It is therefore a habitual saying of mine (not as a hypocritical flatterer, God forbid, for I am of the faithful believers of Israel, and I know well that the remnant of Israel will not speak falsehood, nor will their mouths contain a deceitful tongue) that the Nazarene brought about a double kindness in world. On the one hand, he strengthened the Torah of Moses majestically, as mentioned earlier, and not one of our Sages spoke out more emphatically concerning the immutability of the Torah. And on the other hand, he did much good for the Gentiles [. . .] by doing away with idolatry and removing the images from their midst. He obligated them with the seven commandments so that they should not be as the beasts of the field. He also bestowed upon them ethical ways, and in this respect he was much more stringent with them than the Torah of Moses, as is well known.

Jacob Emdem, Letter to the Polish Council, extract (1757)

226 Christ the Charlatan

Paul-Henri Thiry, Baron d'Holbach (1723–89), an aristocratic French atheist, philosopher, and contributor to the famous *Encyclopaedia*, took much of his book *Ecce Homo!* from an earlier, anonymous writing, *Critical History of Jesus Son of Mary*, supposedly by 'Salvador, a Jew'. He added various materials, including this summary of his own verdict on Christ. (Cf. **224**.)

In the midst of an ignorant and superstitious nation, perpetually fed with oracles and pompous promises; miserable at that time and discontented with the Roman yoke; continually cajoled with the expectation of a deliverer, who was to restore them with honour, our enthusiast had no difficulty finding an audience and, by degrees, followers. People are naturally disposed to listen to, and believe those who make them hope for an end to their miseries. Misfortunes render them timorous and credulous, and lead them to superstition. A fanatic easily makes conquests among a wretched people. No wonder, then, that Jesus should soon acquire partisans, especially among the populace who in any country are easily seduced.

Our hero knew the weakness of his fellow-citizens; they wanted prodigies, and he, in their eyes, performed them. Stupid people, totally ignorant of natural sciences, medicine, or to the resources of trickery, easily mistook very simple operations for miracles, and attributed to the finger of God results possibly due to the knowledge Jesus had acquired during the long interval that preceded his mission. Nothing in the world is more common than a combination of enthusiasm and deceit; the most sincere devotees, seeking to advance what they believe to be the work of God, or to make religion prosper, often countenance fraud which they style pious. Some very recent examples will suffice to persuade us that piety and knavery are incompatible. All Paris has been observed flocking to see miracles, cures, convulsions, and to hear predictions that were obviously fraudulent, dreamed up by certain good souls in order to gain support for their group which they called God's cause. There are but few zealots who do not think crimes permissible even where the interests of religion are concerned. In religion, as in gambling, one begins by being a dupe, and ends being a knave.

Thus, considering things attentively, and weighing up the various circumstances in the life of Jesus, we remain convinced that the man could have been a fanatic, who really thought himself inspired, favoured by heaven, sent to his nation, in short a Messiah; and that in order to support his divine mission, he did not scruple to employ such deceptions as were best calculated for a people to whom miracles were absolutely necessary; and whom, without miracles, the most eloquent harangues, the wisest precepts, the most intelligent counsels, and the truest principles could never have convinced. In short, it seems the character of Jesus was a fairly constant combination of zeal and trickery; it is the same with all spiritual adventurers who assume the name of reformer, or become the leaders of sects.

For throughout his mission, we always find Jesus preaching the kingdom of his Father, and supporting his preaching with wonders. At first he only spoke in a very reserved manner of his status as Messiah, son of God, and son of David. He had the foresight not to proclaim himself as such; but he suffered the secret to be revealed by the mouth of the devil, to impose silence on whom he commonly took great care; not, however, until after the devil had spoken in a manner sufficiently intelligible to make an impression on the spectators. So with the assistance of his possessed, his demoniacs, or his convulsionaries, he procured testimonies which, from his own mouth, would have been too suspicious, and might have caused him hatred.

Our clever operator also took care to choose his ground for performing miracles; he constantly refused to operate before those whom he supposed inclined to criticise his wonders. He may sometimes have performed them in the synagogues, and in presence of the doctors, but it was in the certainty that the less exacting populace, who believed in his miracles, would take his part, and defend him against the evil designs of the more acute spectators.

The apostles of Jesus appear to have been men of their master's temper, which is to say credulous or misled enthusiasts, dextrous cheats, or often both together. There is reason to believe that Jesus, who knew what human beings are like, admitted into his intimate confidence those only in whom he remarked the most submissive credulity or the greatest ability. On important occasions such as the miracle of multiplying the loaves, the transfiguration etc., we find that he used always the ministry of Peter, James and John.

It is easy to understand why his disciples were attached to him either for personal gain, or from credulity. The most crafty perceived that their fortune could only improve under the guidance of a man who knew how to impress common folk, and to make his followers live at the expense of charitable devotees. Fishermen, formerly obliged to subsist by hard and often unsuccessful labour, saw that it was more advantageous to attach themselves to one who made them live quite comfortably without exertion. The most credulous expected to make a brilliant fortune, and to fill high office in the new kingdom their leader intended to establish.

The hopes and comforts of both vanished with the death of Jesus. The more cowardly completely lost courage, but the more able and subtle did not think it necessary to give up. They contrived therefore, as we have seen, the tale of the resurrection, by the aid of which the reputation of their master and their own fortune were secured.

Paul-Henri Thiry, Baron d'Holbach, Ecce Homo! 17, extract (1770)

227   Christ's Distance

Gotthold Ephraim Lessing (1729–81) was one of the major figures of the German Enlightenment. A playwright and art critic, he was also a phil-osopher and religious controversialist. It was he who published Reimarus's critique of the Gospels (cf. **224**). He believed that the various major reli-gions needed to be purified until their true heart (a rational humanitarian-ism) emerged, and rejected what he took to be the miraculous and meta-physical claims that have obscured this as, to a modern mind, meaningless.

If I had lived at the time of Christ, then of course the prophecies fulfilled in his person would have made me pay great attention to him. If I had actually seen him do miracles; if I had had no cause to doubt that these were true miracles; then in a worker of miracles who had been marked out so long before, I would have gained so much confidence that I would willingly have submitted my intellect to his, and I would have believed him in all things in which equally indisputable experiences did not tell against him.

Or: if I even now experienced that prophecies referring to Christ or the Christian religion, of whose priority in time I have long been certain, were fulfilled in a manner admitting no dispute; if even now miracles were done by believing Christians which I had to recognise as true miracles: what could prevent me from accepting this proof of the spirit and of power, as the apostle calls it [1 Cor. 2: 4]? [. . .]

But [. . .] I live in the eighteenth century, in which miracles no longer happen. If I even now hesitate to believe anything on the proof of the spirit and of power, which I can believe on other arguments more appropriate to my age: what is the problem?

The problem is that this proof of the spirit and of power no longer has any spirit or power, but has sunk to the level of human testimonies of spirit and power. The problem is that reports of fulfilled prophecies are not fulfilled prophecies; that reports of miracles are not miracles. These, the prophecies fulfilled before my eyes, the miracles that occur before my eyes, are immedi-ate in their effect. But those—the reports of fulfilled prophecies and miracles, have to work through a medium which takes away all their force. [. . .]

If then this proof of the proof has now entirely lapsed; if then all historical certainty is much too weak to replace this apparent proof of the proof which has lapsed: how is it to be expected of me that the same inconceivable truths which sixteen to eighteen hundred years ago people believed on the strongest inducement, should be believed by me to be equally valid on an infinitely lesser inducement?

Or is it invariably the case, that what I read in reputable historians is just as certain for me as what I myself experience?

I do not know that anyone has ever asserted this. What is asserted is only that the reports which we have of these prophecies and miracles are as reliable as historical truths ever can be. And then it is added that historical truths cannot be demonstrated: nevertheless we must believe them as firmly as truths that have been demonstrated.

To this I answer: [. . .] who will deny (not I) that the reports of these miracles and prophecies are as reliable as historical truths ever can be? But if they are only as reliable as this, why are they treated as if they were infinitely more reliable?

And in what way? In this way, that something quite different and much greater is founded upon them than it is legitimate to found upon truths historically proved. If no historical truth can be demonstrated, then nothing can be demonstrated by means of historical truths.

That is: *accidental truths of history can never become the proof of necessary truths of reason.* [. . .]

If on historical grounds I have no objection to the statement that Christ raised to life a dead man; must I therefore accept it as true that God has a Son who is of the same essence as himself? What is the connection between my inability to raise any significant objection to the evidence of the former and my obligation to believe something against which my reason rebels?

If on historical grounds I have no objection to the statement that this Christ himself rose from the dead, must I therefore accept it as true that this risen Christ was the Son of God?

That the Christ, against whose resurrection I can raise no important historical objection, therefore declared himself to be the Son of God; that his disciples therefore believed him to be such; this I gladly believe from my heart. For these truths, as truths of one and the same class, follow quite naturally on one another.

But to jump with that historical truth to a quite different class of truths, and to demand of me that I should form all my metaphysical and moral ideas accordingly; to expect me to alter all my fundamental ideas of the nature of the Godhead because I cannot set any credible testimony against the resurrection of Christ: if that is not a 'metabasis eis allo genos',[15] then I do not know what Aristotle meant by this phrase.

It is said: 'The Christ of whom on historical grounds you must allow that he raised the dead, that he himself rose from the dead, said himself that God had a Son of the same essence as himself and that he is this Son.' This would be quite excellent! if only it were not the case that it is not more than historically certain that Christ said this.

If you press me still further and say: 'Oh yes! this is more than historically certain. For it is asserted by inspired historians who cannot make a mistake.'

But, unfortunately, that also is only historically certain, that these historians were inspired and could not err.

That, then, is the ugly, broad ditch which I cannot get across, however often and however earnestly I have tried to make the leap.

Gotthold Ephraim Lessing, On the Proof of the Spirit and of Power, extracts (1777)

228 The Revolutionary Christ

> The French Revolution was, on the whole, not kind to Christianity, but not all political radicals rejected the Christian faith; Claude Fauchet (d. 1793), a radical bishop of Caen who preached social equality and supported the revolution, but fatally opposed the execution of the King, wrote this on the eve of the revolution, enlisting Jesus on the side of the poor. (Cf. **296**.)

The false doctors of despotism triumph because it is written, 'Render unto Caesar that which is Caesar's.' Yet should that which is not Caesar's also be rendered to him? For *freedom* in no way belongs to Caesar: it is part of human nature. The *right to oppress* in no way belongs to Caesar, and the *right to protection* belongs to the people. Tributes only belong to a prince when the people consent to them. Kings only have those rights in society which are accorded to them by law, and nothing is given to them except by the will of the people, which is the voice of God.

Jesus Christ died for humanity by dying for his people, and it was as an enemy of Caesar that he was sacrificed [. . .] He set himself against the aristocrats of his nation: think on this important truth, my brothers. He did not cease to subject to public indignation the tyrants of the people, the unjust exacters of taxes, the thought police: all oppressors. The aristocrats, indignant, deceived the crowd who grovelled before their pride; they insinuated in the base souls of their slaves the rage which stirred them against the liberator of humanity.

Finally, my brothers, I will die content after having said this one thing: *It is the aristocracy which crucified the Son of God!*

Claude Fauchet, Discours sur la liberté françoise, extract (1789)

PART 6

The Nineteenth Century: 1790–1913

The beginning of the nineteenth century saw Europe dominated by French armies commanded by Napoleon Bonaparte, whose rise seemed inexorable until his massive miscalculation in Russia in 1812. For Western academic theologians and philosophers, however, the years at the end of the eighteenth and the beginning of the nineteenth century were dominated by German-speaking figures; in fact, they can seem like the beginning of a wholly German-dominated century. The start of the period saw the ground-breaking systems of Kant (cf. **229**), Hegel (cf. **230**) and Schleiermacher (cf. **255**), each of whom probed the nature and limits of knowledge and understanding. New claims about what constituted intellectual rigour emerged, and, in tandem with the growth in the slowly unifying German bloc of a new sense of academic professionalism, forced theologians to justify their status as genuine intellectuals, truly able to contribute methodically to the sum of human knowledge. One of the new intellectual disciplines that rose to great heights in nineteenth-century Germany was biblical criticism (cf. **237**), a development which sent shock waves around the Christian world as more and more traditional belief was subjected to the acid tests of historical investigation. The nineteenth century also saw the triumph of a theology which sought to accommodate itself to the stark results of the new historical criticism, and the tight boundaries of the new philosophy: German liberal Protestantism (cf. **256, 262**), which cast a temporarily less vigorous orthodoxy (Lutheran or Reformed) into the shade (although cf. **249**, for example). The German-speaking lands seemed to be the intellectual engine house of Europe, combining huge cultural confidence and intellectual optimism with massive scholarly industriousness. Both in questing for the historical Jesus, and in attempting to build a liberal Protestant Christology or alternative to Christology, Germany was at the forefront of scholarly grappling with Jesus Christ.

Britain, meanwhile, was at the forefront of the continuing Industrial and Scientific Revolutions—but sometimes seemed left behind in the theological turmoils of the time, playing catch-up to the radical thinking arriving from across the North Sea. (George Eliot's novel *Middlemarch* is as good an introduction to this as any.) Much interesting theology was done by Quakers, Methodists, Anglicans, Unitarians, Independents, and others (e.g. **254**), but it was only with the rise of the Oxford Movement in the 1830s that a distinctive British voice was heard further afield (**258**). Yet, for our purposes, one of the most noticeable factors in the latter years of the nineteenth century in Britain is not the aftermath of a specific movement within the Anglican Church, but the way in which the somewhat sentimental tints of Victorian culture made their way far more generally into religious devotion (cf. **244–7**), and coloured the images of Jesus which generations of twentieth-century children have inherited.

America, despite the Civil War, grew immensely in strength and vibrancy over the nineteenth century, but its vigour showed itself not in the rise to dominance of any one noticeably American form of Christianity, but in the development of immense diversity. Numerous denominations and sects sprang into existence along the American frontier or in the established centres, Unitarianism in particular rising to great prominence; the Mormon Church was founded and began to spread; various forms of what is now called fundamentalism emerged. The permutations and variations of American religion were multiple, the ingredients poured into the melting pot by successive waves of immigration endless, the visions of Jesus claimed and propagated uncountable.

The nineteenth century was above all an age of empires and of missionary societies. While the Ottoman Empire, once such a threat on the south-eastern edge of Europe, collapsed, other empires, spanning wider stretches of the globe than any seen before, were still expanding. Russia expanded eastwards and southwards, taking the Russian Orthodox Church—and a revival of a distinctively Orthodox tradition of contemplative prayer—with it (cf. **273**); Britain, France, Belgium, and other European nations increased their holdings in Africa, Asia, and beyond, colouring maps with vast swathes of their own tint, spreading Western culture, commerce, and Christianity wherever they could; Protestant missionary societies flourished and took this faith and culture further even than the limits of empire.

In South America the long arm of the older Catholic empires faltered, Brazil achieving independence in 1822 and other Spanish and Portuguese colonies struggling for independence from then on. The Church was caught up in that struggle, and so was the image of Christ which the Church had brought with it—but although the Latin American situation made particularly clear the contested nature of the interpretation of Jesus, and its inextricable involvement with the power politics of the day, the same was true wherever Western empires went. Christ was brought by the soldiers, the traders, the teachers, and the missionaries into ever deeper contact with Hindus, Buddhists, and various indigenous religions—and the Hindus, the Buddhists, and the others looked at him long and hard, sometimes discerning beneath the white man's Christ a figure of a different colour, imperfectly disguised (e.g. **277**). The age of European dominance, the nineteenth century nevertheless saw the beginnings of the movement by which Western domination of Christianity, and of the images of Christ it used, began to fragment.

Section A

The Historical Jesus

The nineteenth century saw the height of the endeavour to brush away the long tradition of Christian interpretation so as to uncover the 'real' Jesus. We saw the beginnings of this quest in the Churches of the Reformation, with the attempt to go behind the supposed corruptions of scholasticism to the pure gospel behind (cf. **163**); we saw it taking on new form in the learned societies and coffee houses of the seventeenth and eighteenth centuries as deists and *philosophes* attacked all the priest-craft which stood between them and the truth (cf. **223**, **226**). In the nineteenth century it finds its home in the modern university, as the disciplined criticism of history bars entry to all claims that cannot present satisfactory empirical credentials.

I. The Invention of Christ?

As the long years between Christ's time and our own were no longer seen as the period of God's mysterious mercy, in which the riches of Christ could be unfolded, explored, and broadcast, but as a great gulf separating us from the foundational events of the Christian faith (cf. **227**), it became more tempting to deny that faith had any necessary connection to a particular historical figure standing on the far side of that gulf. One way or another, it was claimed by many in the nineteenth century that the 'Jesus' recognized by faith is more the invention of Christianity than its source and head.

229 | The Idea of the Son of God

The Prussian philosopher Immanuel Kant (1724–1804) defined the field in which much European philosophy of the nineteenth and twentieth centuries would stand. Taking the German rationalism and British empiricism of the Enlightenment, he produced a synthesis which highlighted the human mind's construction of knowledge from the perceptions it receives. Stressing the limitation of human knowing, he argued that most religious ideas (including ideas about Christ) fall irrevocably outside those limits, but can nevertheless have a place within a stern morality which requires them for its full and persuasive elaboration. (Cf. **233**, **266**.)

Now it is our universal human duty to *elevate* ourselves to [the] ideal of moral perfection, i.e. to the prototype of moral disposition in its entire purity; and for this the very idea, which is presented to us by reason for emulation, can give us force. But, precisely because we are not its authors, the idea having rather established itself in the human being without our comprehending how human nature could have even been receptive of it, it is better to say that that *prototype* has *come down* to us from heaven, that it has taken up humanity [. . .]. This union with us may therefore be regarded as a state of abasement of the Son of God if we represent to ourselves this God-like human being, our prototype, in such a way that, though himself holy and hence not bound to submit to sufferings, he nonetheless takes these upon himself in the fullest measure for the sake of promoting the world's greatest good [cf. **249**]. [. . .]

We cannot think the ideal of a humanity pleasing to God (hence of such moral perfection as is possible to a being pertaining to this world and dependent on needs and inclinations) except in the idea of a human being willing not only to execute in person all human duties, and at the same time to spread goodness about him as far and wide as possible through teaching and example, but also, though tempted by the greatest temptation, to take upon himself all sufferings, up to the most ignominious death, for the good of the world and even for his enemies. For human beings cannot form for themselves any concept of the degree and the strength of a force like that of a moral disposition except by representing it surrounded by obstacles and yet—in the midst of the greatest possible temptations—victorious [cf. **191**].

In the *practical faith in this Son of God* (so far as he is represented as having taken up human nature) the human being can thus hope to become pleasing to God (and thereby blessed); that is, only a human being conscious of such a moral disposition in himself as enables him to *believe* and self-assuredly trust that he, under similar temptations and afflictions (so far as these are made the touchstone of that idea), would steadfastly cling to the prototype of human-ity and follow this prototype's example in loyal emulation—only such a human being, and he alone, is entitled to consider himself not an unworthy object of divine pleasure.

From the practical point of view this idea has complete reality within itself. For it resides in our morally legislative reason. We *ought* to conform to it, and therefore we must also *be able* to. [. . .] There is no need, therefore, of any example from experience to make the idea of a human being morally pleas-ing to God a model to us; the idea is present as model already in our reason. If anyone, in order to accept for imitation a human being as such an example of conformity to that idea, asks for more than what he sees, i.e. more than a course of life entirely blameless and as meritorious as indeed one may ever wish; and if, in addition, he also asks for miracles as credentials, to be brought about either through that human being or on his behalf—he who asks for this thereby confesses to his own moral unbelief, to a lack of faith in virtue which no faith based on miracles (and thus only historical) can remedy [cf. **227**], for only faith in the practical validity of the idea that lies in our reason has moral worth. [. . .]

Now if a human being of such a truly divine disposition had descended, as it were, from heaven to earth at a specific time, and had he exhibited in his self, through teaching, conduct, and suffering, the *example* of a human being well-pleasing to God, to the extent that such an example can at all be expected from outer experience (for, in fact, the *prototype* of any such human being is nowhere to be sought except in our reason); had he brought about, through all this, an incalculably great moral good in the world, through a revolution in the human race: even then we would have no cause to assume in him anything else except a naturally begotten human being (because he too feels to be under the obligation to exhibit such an example in himself). Not that we would thereby absolutely deny that he might indeed also be a supernaturally begotten human being. But, from a practical point of view any such presupposition is of no benefit to us, since the prototype which we see embedded in this apparition must be sought in us as well (though natural human beings), and its presence in the human soul is itself incomprehensible enough that we should also assume, besides its supernatural origin, its hypostasization in a particular human being. On the contrary, the elevation of such a Holy One above every frailty of human nature would rather, from all that we can see, stand in the way of the practical adoption of the idea of such a being for our imitation. For let the nature of this human being well-pleasing to God be thought as human, inasmuch as he is afflicted by just the same needs and hence also the same sufferings, by just the same natural inclinations and hence also the same temptations to transgression, as we are. Let it also be thought as superhuman, however, inasmuch as his unchanging purity of will, not gained through effort but innate, would render any transgression on his part absolutely impossible. The consequent distance from the natural human being would then again become so infinitely great that the divine human being could no longer be held forth to the natural human being as *example*. [. . .]

To be sure, the thought that this divine human being had actual possession of his eminence and blessedness from eternity (and did not need to earn them first through such sorrows), and that he willingly divested himself of them for the sake of plainly unworthy individuals, even for the sake of his enemies, to deliver them from eternal damnation—this thought must attune our mind to admiration, love and thankfulness toward him. Likewise the idea of a conduct in accordance with so perfect a rule of morality could no doubt also be valid for us, as a precept to be followed. Yet he himself could not be presented to us as an example to be emulated, hence also not as proof that so pure and exalted a moral goodness can be practised and attained by us.

Yet such a divinely disposed teacher, though in fact totally human, would nonetheless be able to speak truly of himself as if the ideal of goodness were displayed incarnate in him (in his teaching and conduct). For he would be speaking only of the disposition which he makes the rule of his actions but which, since he cannot make it visible as an example to others in and of itself, he places before their eyes externally through teachings and actions.

Immanuel Kant, *Religion within the Bounds of Reason Alone*, book II, 1. A–C, extracts (1793)

230   Christ in the Unfolding of Spirit

In the wake of Kant and his immediate followers, Georg Wilhelm Friedrich Hegel (1770–1831) produced an immensely complex system in which the knowing subjects and ineffable objects of Kant's philosophy were seen as parts of a more comprehensive whole: the unfolding of 'Spirit' in and as history. The history of human knowledge is the history of Spirit coming to know itself, and of the complex detours and stages through which it must pass on the way. Hegel here relates a decisive moment in the story of Spirit in which humanity, having moved away from a divinizing of the finite towards a recognition of the infinite, is enabled to overcome the apparent absolute distinction between that infinite and the radically limited finitude of human life, and to see instead finitude as caught up in the unfolding process of the infinite. (Cf. **231**, **237**.)

Among those friends and acquaintances who were taught by Christ, there was present this presentiment, this representation, this desire for a new kingdom, a new heaven and a new earth, a new world. This hope and certainty penetrated the actuality of their hearts and became entrenched there. [. . .] In the hearts and souls of believers is the firm belief that the issue is not a moral teaching, nor in general the thinking and willing of the subject within itself and from itself; rather what is of interest is an infinite relationship to God, to the present God, the certainty of the kingdom of God—finding satisfaction not in morality, ethics, or conscience, but rather in that than which nothing is higher, the relationship to God himself. [. . .]

The defining characteristic of this kingdom of God is the *presence of God*, which means that the members of this kingdom are expected to have not only a love for humanity but also the consciousness that God is love [. . .] The kingdom of God, God's presentness, *is* this determination of one's feeling, so the certainty of God's presentness belongs to it. [. . .] This certainty can here occur only in the mode of sensible appearance. [. . .]

We have seen God [. . .] at first in the subjective, limited forms of the folk-spirits and in the contingent shapes of phantasy; next we saw the anguish of the world following the suppression of the folk-spirits. The anguish was the birthplace of a new spirit, the impulse to know God as spiritual, in universal form and stripped of finitude. This need [i.e. for the certainty of God's presentness, through a sensible appearance] was engendered by the progress of history and the progressive formation of the world-spirit.[1] This immediate impulse, this longing which wants and desires something determinate—this is the witness of the Spirit and the subjective side of faith. This need and longing demanded such an appearance, the manifestation of God as infinite spirit in the shape of an actual human being. [. . .]

The words of Christ are truly grasped and understood only by faith. The history of Christ is also narrated by those on whom the Spirit has already been poured out. The miracles are grasped and narrated in this Spirit, and the death of Christ has been truly understood through the Spirit to mean that in Christ God is revealed together with the unity of divine and human nature.

The death of Christ is the touchstone, so to speak, by which faith is verified, since it is here, essentially, that its understanding of the appearance of Christ is set forth. This death means principally that Christ was the God-man, the God who at the same time had human nature, even unto death. It is the lot of human finitude to die. Death is the most complete proof of humanity, of absolute finitude; and indeed Christ has died the aggravated death of the evildoer: not merely a natural death, but rather a death of shame and humiliation on the cross. In him, humanity was carried to its furthest point.

[. . .] *God has died, God is dead*—this is the most frightful of all thoughts, that everything eternal and true *is not*, that negation itself is found in God. The deepest anguish, the feeling of complete irretrievability, the annulling of everything that is elevated, are bound up with this thought. However, the process does not come to a halt at this point; rather, a reversal takes place: God, that is to say, maintains himself in this process, and the latter is only the death of death. God rises again to life, and thus things are reversed. The resurrection is something that belongs just as essentially to faith as the crucifixion.

After his resurrection, Christ appeared only to his friends. This is not an external history for unbelievers; on the contrary, this appearance occurs only for faith. The resurrection is followed by the glorification of Christ, and the triumph of his ascension to the right hand of God concludes this history, which, as understood by believing consciousness, is the explication of God. This history is the explication of the divine nature itself. [. . .]

Concerning Christ's death, we have still particularly to emphasise the aspect that it is God who has put death to death, since he comes out of the state of death. In this way, finitude, human nature, and humiliation are posited of Christ—as of him who is strictly God—as something alien. It is evident that finitude is alien to him and has been taken over from an other; this other is the human being who stands over against the divine process. It is their finitude that Christ has taken upon himself, this finitude in all its forms, which at its furthest extreme is evil. This humanity, which is itself a moment in the divine life, is now characterised as something alien, not belonging to God. This finitude, however, on its own account (as against God), is evil, is something alien to God. But he has taken it upon himself, in order to put it to death by his death. As the monstrous unification of these absolute extremes, this shameful death is at the same time infinite love.

It is out of infinite love that God has made himself identical with what is alien to him in order to put it to death. This is the meaning of the death of Christ. It means that Christ has borne the sins of the world and has reconciled God with the world [cf. 330]. [. . .]

For the true consciousness of spirit, the finitude of humanity has been put to death in the death of Christ. This death of the natural has in this way a universal significance: finitude and evil are altogether destroyed. Thus the world has been reconciled; by this death it has been implicitly delivered from its evil. In the true understanding of death, the relation of the subject as such to death comes into view in this way. Here any merely historical view comes to an end; the subject itself is drawn into the process. The subject feels the anguish of evil and of its own estrangement, which Christ has taken upon himself by putting on humanity, while at the same time destroying it by his death.

Georg Wilhelm Friedrich Hegel, Lectures on the Philosophy of Religion III. B. C, extracts
(1827–31)

231   The Last Wish of Religion

Ludwig Feuerbach (1804–72), a follower of Hegel, stepped away from his teacher's heady theories of Spirit to a philosophy focused squarely on humanity's realization of concrete human nature. Christianity is not, for Feuerbach, about a transcendent God, nor about a problematic historical person; it is about humanity's first, indirect, and externalized grasp of its own internal nature—a grasp which fastens on an image of an incarnate saviour. (Cf. **232**.)

The fundamental dogmas of Christianity are realised wishes of the heart—the essence of Christianity is the essence of human feeling. It is pleasanter to be passive than to act, to be redeemed and made free by another than to free oneself; pleasanter to make one's salvation dependent on a person than on the force of one's own spontaneity; pleasanter to set before oneself an object of love than an object of effort; pleasanter to know oneself beloved by God than merely to have that simple, natural self-love which is innate in all beings; pleasanter to see oneself imaged in the love-beaming eyes of another personal being, than to look into the concave mirror of self or into the cold depths of the ocean of Nature; pleasanter, in short, to allow oneself to be acted on by one's own feeling, as by another, but yet fundamentally identical being, than to regulate oneself by reason. [. . .]

To see God is the highest wish, the highest triumph of the heart [cf. **216**]. Christ is this wish, this triumph, fulfilled. God, as an object of thought only, i.e., God as God, is always a remote being; the relation to him is an abstract one, like that relation of friendship in which we stand to a man who is distant from us, and personally unknown to us. However his works, the proofs of love which he gives us, may make his nature present to us, there always remains an unfilled void—the heart is unsatisfied, we long to see him. So long as we have not met a being face to face, we are always in doubt whether he be really such as we imagine him; actual presence alone gives final confidence, perfect repose. Christ is God known personally; Christ, therefore, is the blessed certainty that God is what the soul desires and needs him to be. God, as the object of prayer, is indeed already a human being, since he sympathises with human misery, grants human wishes; but still he is not yet an object to the religious consciousness as a real man. Hence, only in Christ is the last wish of religion realised, the mystery of religious feeling solved:—solved, however, in the language of imagery proper to religion, for what God is in essence, that Christ is in actual appearance. So far the Christian religion may justly be called the absolute religion. That God who in himself is nothing else than the nature of man, should also have a real existence as such, should be as man an object to the consciousness—this is the goal of religion, and this the Christian religion has attained in the incarnation of God, which is by no means a transitory act, for Christ remains man even after his ascension—man in heart and man in form, only that his body is no longer an earthly one, liable to suffering.

Ludwig Andreas Feuerbach, *The Essence of Christianity* xv, extracts (2nd edn. 1843)

232   The Heart's Invention

Louisa Sarah Bevington (1845–95) was a radical thinker, a self-avowed anarchist who considered all property to be theft, property being simply another way in which human beings try to exercise domination over one another. Unsurprisingly, she had controversial opinions concerning religion. (Cf. **231**.)

> What blesses yet is difficult,
> This—goodness: worship, the result.

> What man doth worship man doth love,
> And what he loveth he would prove.

> And if proof fail he'll place it high,
> And claim a god's authority.

What man can pray for, man can share,
His boon foreshadowed in his prayer.

Were man of all his needs bereft
There would not be a bible left.

Were needy man to lose his creed
To-morrow one would spring at need.

Because men are by life enticed
They love their murdered Jesus Christ.

Because their god is still their good,
Kind Christ was God in flesh and blood.

Because they feel the hurt of sin
His mother was a maiden clean.

Because men long for purity
He, born of her security.

Because so many women fail
Therefore his Magdalen was frail.

Because lone women need to love,
One Christ was set all change above.

Some heart whose will could weakness be
Invented his Gethsemane;

Some soul in passion's sore distress
Temptation in the wilderness.

Since notions are not deep as needs,
Religion deeper is than creeds.

If e'er the Christ be quite forgot,
'Twill be that love is needed not!

Or else that love has found a way
To every heart of every day.

The very truth is set at nought
If there be nothing lovely taught;

And any solemn lie will do,
So it be sweet and solemn too.

In all of which 'tis clear to scan,
Religion bindeth social man.

What blesses, yet is difficult,
This—goodness: worship—the result.

Louisa Sarah Bevington, 'Religion: An Essay in Couplets' (1882)

233   **A Translation of the Rule of Virtue**

John Stuart Mill (1806–73) was, with Jeremy Bentham, the foremost proponent of Utilitarianism, a philosophy directing human action towards the greatest happiness for the greatest number. Explicitly taking his stand on what will survive the fires of historical criticism, Mill's Christ is a man stripped of theological claims: a useful exemplar chosen by the propagators of an austere rational virtue. (Cf. **229**, **266**.)

The most valuable part of the effect on the character which Christianity has produced by holding up in a divine person a standard of excellence and a model for imitation, is available even to the absolute unbeliever and can never more be lost to humanity. For it is Christ, rather than God, whom Christianity has held up to believers as the pattern of perfection for humanity. It is the God incarnate, more than the God of the Jews or of nature, who being idealised has taken so great and salutary a hold on the modern mind. And whatever else may be taken away from us by rational criticism, Christ is still left; a unique figure, not more unlike all his precursors than all his followers, even those who had the direct benefit of his personal teaching. [. . .]

About the life and sayings of Jesus there is a stamp of personal originality combined with profundity of insight, which if we abandon the idle expectation of finding scientific precision where something very different was aimed at, must place the prophet of Nazareth, even in the estimation of those who have no belief in his inspiration, in the very first rank of the men of sublime genius of whom our species can boast. When this pre-eminent genius is combined with the qualities of probably the greatest moral reformer, and martyr to that mission, who ever existed upon earth, religion cannot be said to have made a bad choice in pitching on this man as the ideal representative and guide of humanity; nor, even now, would it be easy, even for an unbeliever, to find a better translation of the rule of virtue [cf. **185**] from the abstract into the concrete, than to endeavour so to live that Christ would approve our life. When to this we add that, to the conception of the rational sceptic, it remains a possibility that Christ actually was what he supposed himself to be—not God, for he never made the smallest pretension to that character and would probably have thought such a pretension as blasphemous as it seemed to the men who condemned him—but a man charged with a special, express and unique commission from God to lead mankind to truth and virtue; we may well conclude that the influences of religion on the character which will remain after rational criticism has done its utmost against the evidences of religion, are well worth preserving, and that what they lack in direct strength as compared with those of a firmer belief, is more than compensated by the greater truth and rectitude of the morality they sanction.

John Stuart Mill, *Theism*, 'General Result', extract (1874)

Arthur Drews (1865–1935) was a German thinker who took to its extreme the turn away from the increasingly problematic historical Jesus, and towards the community in which the story of Jesus was developed. It is not so much that he denies the existence of a man called Jesus from Nazareth; rather that the 'Jesus' of Christianity is simply a fictional projection backwards of the early Church's distinctive ideals, a foundational myth—and the quest for the 'historical Jesus' a wild-goose chase.

In the opinion of liberal theologians, not the God but rather the man Jesus forms the valuable religious essence of Christianity. In saying this it says nothing less than that the whole of Christendom up to the present day—that is, till the appearance of a Harnack, Bousset, Wernle,[2] and others of like mind—was in error about itself, and did not recognise its own essence. For Christianity, as the present account shows, from the very first conceived the God Jesus, or rather the God-man, the Incarnate, the God-redeemer, suffering with man and sacrificing himself for humanity, as the central point of its doctrine. The declaration of the real manhood of Jesus appears, on the other hand, but as an after-concession of this religion to outer circumstances, wrung from it only later by its opponents [cf. **67**, **70**], and so expressly championed by it only because of its forming the unavoidable condition of its permanence in history and of its practical success. Only the God, therefore, not the man Jesus, can be termed the 'founder' of the Christian religion.

It is in fact the fundamental error of the liberal theology to think that the development of the Christian Church took its rise from an historical individual, from the man Jesus. The view is becoming more common that the original Christian movement under the name of Jesus would have remained an insignificant and transient movement within Judaism but for Paul, who first gave it a religious view of the world by his metaphysics of redemption, and who by his break with the Jewish Law really founded the new religion. It will not be long before the further concession is found necessary, that an historical Jesus, as the Gospels portray him, and as he lives in the minds of the liberal theologians of to-day, never existed at all; so that he never founded the insignificant and diminutive community of the Messiah at Jerusalem. It will be necessary to concede that the Christ-faith arose quite independently of any historical personality known to us; that indeed Jesus was in this sense a product of the religious 'social soul' and was made by Paul, with the required amount of reinterpretation and reconstruction, the chief interest of those communities founded by him. The 'historical' Jesus is not earlier but later than Paul; and as such he has always existed merely as an idea, as a pious fiction in the minds of members of the community. The New Testament with its four Gospels is not previous to the Church, but the latter is antecedent to them; and the Gospels are the derivatives, consequently forming a support for the propaganda of the Church, and being without any claim to historical significance.

Arthur Drews, *The Christ Myth*, 'The Religious Problem of the Present', extract (1909)

235   Christ's Unavoidable Historicity

Ernst Troeltsch (1865–1923) was a thinker who in the early years of the twentieth century seemed to many to represent one extreme of the development of historical thinking within German theology. He was radically committed to tracing the historical development of religious traditions as concrete social phenomena. Here his focus on the possibilities of actual social life in history lead him to question any attempt to bypass historical-critical attention to Jesus of Nazareth. (Cf. **282, 284**.)

There is no possibility of a sure and powerful redeeming knowledge of God without community and cult. A cult illuminated by the Christian idea must therefore always centre upon gathering the congregation around its head, nourishing and strengthening it by immersion in the revelation of God contained in the image of Christ, spreading it not by dogmas, doctrines and philosophies but by handing on and keeping alive the image of Christ, the adoration of God in Christ. So long as Christianity survives in any form it will always be connected with the central position of Christ in the cult. It will either exist in this form or not at all. That rests on social-psychological laws which have produced exactly the same phenomena in other religious areas and recur a thousand times over on a smaller scale up to the present. They render utopian the whole idea of a piety that simply springs from every man's heart and nevertheless forms a harmony, that does not need reciprocity and yet remains a living power.

Social psychology therefore provides the main aspect under which our problem must be seen. The connexion of the Christian idea with Christ's central position in cult and doctrine is not a conceptual necessity inherent in the notion of salvation. Even if we are right to point out the need which ordinary piety has for support and strengthening it does not absolutely require the person of Jesus. In fact a real personal relationship with him is not possible. But neither is this person a purely historical fact simply clarifying the origins and then no longer essential. For social-psychological reasons he is indispensable for cult, power, efficacy and expansion, and that should be sufficient to justify and assert the connexion. Without it a further development of the Christian idea is unthinkable. A new religion would have to be a new cult of a historical prophet. All hope of a non-cultic, purely personal and individual religion of conviction and knowledge is mere illusion. If on the other hand we need a cult and community then we need Christ as the head and rallying-point of the congregation too. The Christian knowledge of God has no other mode of union and visibility. Lectures on religious philosophy will never produce or replace a real religion.

If this is how things stand it is of course not possible to be really and completely indifferent to historical-critical questions either. Admittedly Jesus is here the symbol of Christian faith generally. But those who think that it does not matter whether such a symbol is rooted in historical factuality and that the great achievement of religion in history is precisely the embodiment of ideas in myth [cf. **237**], are themselves not in the least inclined to enter a religious group. They personally do not wish to surrender themselves enthusiastically and through practical work to a group whose idea is embodied in this mythical symbol. They only expect that believers can tighten their belts and be fully satisfied with a mythical symbol. Examples of this like Samuel Lublinski are merely cases of that aesthetic playing with realities which is so common today. The aesthete expects believers to satisfy their existential hunger on a mythical symbol because he himself never thinks of stilling a real hunger for certainty and conviction but only the unreal needs of imagination. Someone who really belongs in his heart to the world of Christian experience will never be able to see in the centre and head of the congregation, the focal point for all cult and vision of God, a mere myth—no matter how beautiful. For him, God is not an idea or possibility but a holy reality. He will therefore insist upon standing with this symbol of his on the solid ground of real life. It is for him a truly significant fact that a real man thus lived, struggled, believed and conquered, and that from this real life a stream of strength and certainty flows down to him. The symbol is only a real symbol for him in that behind it stands the greatness of a superior and real religious prophet. Not only is God made visible by reference to this; he can also find here support and strength in his own uncertainty, just as elsewhere he needs to hold on to superior personal religious authority, and experiences it in life in many ways. [. . .]

Granted these circumstances it is of course impossible to ignore historical critical research. The 'fact', like all other historical facts, given first only in the form of reports, can only be established by historical research. Faith can interpret facts; it cannot establish them. There should be no need to waste time arguing about this, though even here theology frequently works with most confused methods. It is not a question of individual details but of the actuality of the total historical phenomenon of Jesus and the basic outline of his teaching and his religious personality. This must be capable of being established by means of historical criticism as historical reality if the 'symbol of Christ' is to have a firm and strong inner basis in the 'fact' of Jesus. This was of course unnecessary for a world that did not think historically, so the problem did not arise until the eighteenth century. But given a fundamentally historical mode of thought like that of the present then faith cannot escape this admixture of the historical and scientific way of thinking. It must face this and secure the historical basis of its community and cult as far as the historical questions have any significance for these. There is no ducking or ignoring this. The struggle must be fought out and if it were decided against the historicity of Jesus or against any possibility of knowing about him, that would in fact be the beginning of the end of the Christ symbol amongst scientifically educated people. From there doubt and dissolution would soon percolate down to the lower classes, so far as it had not reached there already as a result of their social reforms and anti-ecclesiastical inclinations. It is a mere playing with words to hold on to the Christian principle and yet want to leave the historical questions on one side. That is a practical way out for individuals in difficulties and confusion; it is impossible for a religious and cultic community.

Ernst Troeltsch, *The Significance of the Historical Existence of Jesus for Faith* 3, extract (1911)

II. Reconstructing Jesus

As in all the earlier periods we have explored, many attempts were made in the nineteenth century to retell the story of Jesus. Dominant among them were those which sought to turn the newly critical eye of historical enquiry on Jesus' life; not just those who in the footsteps of Reimarus (cf. **224**) and Holbach (cf. **226**) were intent upon a sceptical reconstruction, but many who thought they could discern a Jesus fit for faith, albeit a chastened and purified faith, behind the New Testament writings.

236 Another Testament of Christ

The historical critics were, of course, not the only ones to tell Jesus' story. Another kind of telling entirely was produced, for example, by Joseph Smith (1805–44), the founder of the Church of Jesus Christ of the Latter-Day Saints, known as the Mormons. He claimed to have been led by angels to the rediscovery and miraculous translation of the ancient Book of Mormon, in which is described (among much else) the post-Resurrection appearance of Jesus to ancient American peoples. (Cf. **18**.)

It came to pass that there were a great multitude gathered together, of the people of Nephi, round about the temple which was in the land Bountiful; and they were marvelling and wondering one with another, and were showing one to another the great and marvellous change which had taken place. And they were also conversing about this Jesus Christ, of whom the sign had been given concerning his death. And it came to pass that while they were thus conversing one with another, they heard a voice as if it came out of heaven; and they cast their eyes round about, for they understood not the voice which they heard; and it was not a harsh voice, neither was it a loud voice; nevertheless, and notwithstanding it being a small voice it did pierce them that did hear to the centre, insomuch that there was no part of their frame that it did not cause to quake; yea, it did pierce them to the very soul, and did cause their hearts to burn.

And it came to pass that again they heard the voice, and they understood it not. And again the third time they did hear the voice, and did open their ears to hear it; and their eyes were towards the sound thereof; and they did look steadfastly towards heaven, from whence the sound came. And behold, the third time they did understand the voice which they heard; and it said unto them: 'Behold my beloved Son, in whom I am well pleased, in whom I have glorified my name—hear ye him' [cf. 2].

And it came to pass, as they understood they cast their eyes up again towards heaven; and behold, they saw a man descending out of heaven; and he was clothed in a white robe; and he came down and stood in the midst of them; and the eyes of the whole multitude were turned upon him, and they durst not open their mouths, even one to another, and wist not what it meant, for they thought it was an angel that had appeared unto them.

And it came to pass that he stretched forth his hand and spake unto the people, saying: 'Behold, I am Jesus Christ whom the prophets testified shall come into the world. And behold, I am the light and the life of the world; and I have drunk out of that bitter cup which the Father hath given me, and have glorified the Father in taking upon me the sins of the world, in the which I have suffered the will of the Father in all things from the beginning.'

And it came to pass that when Jesus had spoken these words the whole multitude fell to the earth; for they remembered that it had been prophesied among them that Christ should show himself unto them after his ascension into heaven.

And it came to pass that the Lord spake unto them saying, 'Arise and come forth unto me, that ye may thrust your hands into my side, and also that ye may feel the prints of the nails in my hands and in my feet, that ye may know that I am the God of Israel, and the God of the whole earth, and have been slain for the sins of the world.'

And it came to pass that the multitude went forth, and thrust their hands into his side, and did feel the prints of the nails in his hands and in his feet; and this they did do, going forth one by one until they had all gone forth, and did see with their eyes and did feel with their hands, and did know of a surety and did bear record, that it was he, of whom it was written by the prophets, that should come.

And when they had all gone forth and had witnessed for themselves, they did cry out with one accord, saying: 'Hosanna! Blessed be the name of the Most High God!' And they did fall down at the feet of Jesus, and did worship him.

And it came to pass that he spake unto Nephi (for Nephi was among the multitude) and he commanded him that he should come forth. And Nephi arose and went forth, and bowed himself before the Lord and did kiss his feet. And the Lord commanded him that he should arise. And he arose and stood before him. And the Lord said unto him, 'I give unto you power that ye shall baptise this people when I am again ascended into heaven.' And again the Lord called others, and said unto them likewise; and he gave unto them power to baptise. And he said unto them, 'On this wise shall ye baptise; and there shall be no disputations among you. Verily I say unto you, that whoso repenteth of his sins through your words, and desireth to be baptised in my name, on this wise shall ye baptise them—Behold, ye shall go down and stand in the water, and in my name shall ye baptise them. And now behold, these are the words which ye shall say, calling them by name; saying, "Having authority given me of Jesus Christ, I baptise you in the name of the Father, and of the Son, and of the Holy Ghost. Amen" [cf. **19**]. And then shall ye immerse them in the water, and come forth again out of the water. And after this manner shall ye baptise in my name; for behold, verily I say unto you, that the Father, and the Son, and the Holy Ghost are one; and I am in the Father, and the Father in me, and the Father and I are one. And according as I have commanded you thus shall ye baptise. And there shall be no disputations among you, as there have hitherto been; neither shall there be disputations among you concerning the points of my doctrine, as there have hitherto been.'

The Book of Mormon, 3 Nephi 11: 1–28 (1830)

237 A Mythical Transfiguration

David Friedrich Strauss (1808–74) was a German theologian, influenced first by Schleiermacher (cf. **255**) and then by Hegel (cf. **230**), who in 1835–6 produced the most controversial, and arguably the most important, *Life of Jesus* to be written in the nineteenth century. Rejecting the kinds of views represented by August Neander (cf. **238**), he explained the supernatural elements in the gospel as 'myth'; not, that is, as simple fabrication, but as the expression in primitive narrative terms of spiritual ideas. (Cf. **12**.)

To the oriental, and more particularly to the Hebrew imagination, the beautiful, the majestic, is the luminous [cf. **27**, **45**, **65**, **87**, **89**, **220**]; the poet of the Song of Songs compares his beloved to the hues of morning, to the moon, to the sun; the holy man supported by the blessing of God, is compared to the sun going forth in his might; and above all the future lot of the righteous is likened to the splendour of the sun and the stars. Hence, not only does God appear clothed in light, and angels with resplendent countenances and shining garments, but also the pious of Hebrew antiquity, as Adam before the fall, and among subsequent instances, more particularly Moses and Joshua, are represented as being distinguished by such a splendour; and the later Jewish tradition ascribes celestial splendour even to eminent rabbins in exalted moments. But the most celebrated example of this kind is the luminous countenance of Moses, which is mentioned in Exodus 34: 29 ff., and as in other points, so in this, a conclusion was drawn from him in relation to the Messiah, *a minori ad majus*.[3] Such a mode of arguing is indicated by the Apostle Paul, though he opposes to Moses, the minister of the letter, not Jesus, but, in accordance with the occasion of his epistle, the apostles and Christian teachers, ministers of the spirit, and the glory of the latter, which surpassed the glory of Moses, is an object of hope, to be attained only in the future life. But especially in the Messiah himself, it was expected that there would be a splendour which would correspond to that of Moses, nay, outshine it; and a Jewish writing which takes no notice of our history of the transfiguration argues quite in the spirit of the Jews of the first Christian period, when it urges that Jesus cannot have been the Messiah, because his countenance had not the splendour of the countenance of Moses, to say nothing of a higher splendour.[4] Such objections, doubtless heard by the early Christians from the Jews, and partly suggested by their own minds, could not but generate in the early church a tendency to introduce into the life of Jesus an imitation of that trait in the life of Moses, nay, in one respect to surpass it, and instead of a shining countenance that might be covered with a veil, to ascribe to him a radiance, though but transitory, which was diffused even over his garments. [. . .]

By the transfiguration on the mount Jesus was brought into contact with his type Moses, and as it had entered into the anticipation of the Jews that the messianic time, according to Isaiah 52: 6 ff., would have not merely one but several forerunners, and that among others the ancient lawgiver especially would appear in the time of the Messiah: so no moment was more appropriate for his appearance than that in which the Messiah was being glorified on a mountain, as he had himself once been. With him was then naturally associated the prophet, who, on the strength of Malachi 3: 23, was the most decidedly expected to be a messianic forerunner, and, indeed, according to the rabbins, to appear contemporaneously with Moses. If these two men appeared to the Messiah, it followed as a matter of course that they conversed with him; and if it were asked what was the tenor of their conversation nothing would suggest itself so soon as the approaching sufferings and death of Jesus, which had been announced in the foregoing passage, and which besides, as constituting emphatically the messianic mystery of the New Testament, were best adapted for the subject of such a conversation with beings of another world: whence one cannot but wonder how Olshausen can maintain that the mythus would never have fallen upon this theme of conversation. According to this, we have here a mythus, the tendency of which is twofold: first, to exhibit in the life of Jesus an enhanced repetition of the glorification of Moses; and secondly, to bring Jesus as the Messiah into contact with his two forerunners,—by this appearance of the lawgiver and the prophet, of the founder and the reformer of the theocracy, to represent Jesus as the perfector of the kingdom of God, and the fulfilment of the law and the prophets; and besides this, to show a confirmation of his messianic dignity by a heavenly voice.

Before we part with our subject, this example may serve to show us with peculiar clearness, how the natural system of interpretation [cf. **238**], while it seeks to preserve the historical certainty of the narratives, loses their ideal truth—sacrifices the essence to the form: whereas the mythical interpretation, by renouncing the historical body of such narratives, rescues and preserves the idea which resides in them [cf. **56**], and which alone constitutes their vitality and spirit. Thus if, as the natural explanation would have it, the splendour around Jesus was an accidental, optical phenomenon, and the two appearances either images of a dream or unknown men, where is the significance of the incident? where the motive for preserving in the memory of the church an anecdote so void of ideas, and so barren of inference, resting on a common delusion and superstition? On the contrary, while according to the mythical interpretation, I do not, it is true, see in the evangelical narrative any real event,—I yet retain a sense, a purpose in the narrative, know to what sentiments and thoughts of the first Christian community it owes its origin, and why the authors of the gospels included so important a passage in their memoirs.

David Friedrich Strauss, *The Life of Jesus Critically Examined*, ii. x. 107, extract (1835–6)

238   A Rational Transfiguration

Johann August Wilhelm Neander (1789–1850) was a Jewish convert to Christianity and a follower of Friedrich Schleiermacher (cf. **255**). In 1837 he wrote a *Life of Jesus* in response to David Friedrich Strauss (cf. **237**). In its combination of a sentimental devotion and naturalistic explanation of the gospel story, it well illustrates the combination of Pietism and rationalism which characterized many German theologians of the time. (Cf. **12**.)

By following the indications given in Luke, we may arrive at the following view of the narrative: Jesus retired in the evening with three of his dearest disciples, apart, into a mountain to pray in their presence. We may readily imagine that his prayer referred to the subjects on which he had spoken so largely with the disciples on the preceding days, viz. the coming development of his kingdom, and the conflicts he was to enter into at Jerusalem in its behalf. They were deeply impressed by his prayer; his countenance beamed with radiance, and he appeared to them glorified and transfigured with celestial light. At last, worn out with fatigue, they fell asleep; and the impressions of the Saviour's prayer, and of their conversation with him, were reflected in a vision thus: Beside him, who was the end of the law and the prophets, appeared Moses and Elias in celestial splendour; for the glory that streamed forth from him was reflected back upon the law, and the prophets foretold the fate that awaited him at Jerusalem. In the mean time they awoke, and in a half-waking condition, saw and heard what followed. Viewed in this light, the most striking feature of the event is the impression which Christ's words had made upon them, and the conflict between the new views thus received and their old ideas, showing itself thus while they were in a state of unconsciousness.

Still the difficulty remains, that the phenomena, if simply psychological, should have appeared to all the three Apostles precisely in the same form. It is, perhaps, not improbable, that the account came from the lips of Peter, who is the prominent figure in the narrative.

The disciples did not, at first, dwell upon this phenomenon. The turn of Christ's conversations with them, and the pressure of events, withdrew their attention from it until after the resurrection, when, as the several traits of their later intercourse with Christ were brought to mind, this transfiguration was vividly recalled, and assigned to its proper connexion in the epoch which preceded and prepared the way for the sufferings of the Saviour.

Johann August Wilhelm Neander, The Life of Jesus Christ in its Historical Connexion and
Historical Development 185, extract (1845)

239   The Historical Kernel

In its day as sensational as Strauss's Life of Jesus (cf. 237), Wally the Sceptic, a novel by Karl Gutzkow (1811–78), told the story of a man whose questing intelligence brought him to, among other things, irregular marital relations and a historical-critical assessment of the Jesus story. Gutzkow was eventually briefly imprisoned for his inflammatory novel. In this extract Wally explains his new view of Jesus.

In Judea, a very baroque land, there appeared a young man by the name of Jesus who, as a result of a serious confusion of his ideas, came to believe that his coming as the liberator of the nation to which he belonged had already been announced to his ancestors. Jesus was born in Nazareth, an illegitimate child, the stepson of a good carpenter by the name of Joseph. Jesus steeped himself in the writings of Jewish literature, travelled, educated himself, and strove by noble self-denial to achieve a stoic kind of chastity. Jesus felt a sense of mission throbbing within him. It seemed to him that he must fulfil a mandate that he was never clear about for the whole course of his life. He adopted the belief in a promised king who would make his vain nation the ruler of the world [cf. 224] but he himself quailed at this presumptuous promise that was quite unworthy of a true idea of God. Jesus himself did not know where it was all going to lead when he took his first rash steps, when he had sent forth his friend John to feel out and test the masses; he became a rabbi, a sanctioned teacher of the people, he acquired students, he preached repentance and pious living, he preached the pure, basic Jewry of Moses, he called himself messiah and never fought against the false interpretation of his intention nor against the conceptions that were bound up with the messiah in Judea. Jesus did not even mention the Roman yoke; he seems to have felt that the messiah could only have a theological significance, and yet he aimed his invectives at the political constitution in Jerusalem, at the high court, and at priests whom he accused of falsely interpreting the old books to further their own interests. Meanwhile the unrest spread, Jesus travelled in the company of thousands through the land, he made a powerful entry into Jerusalem, actively attacked the temple, the national shrine of the Jews, and fell as a sacrifice to his own false calculations and inner confusion. He had credited the lazy people with energy; they abandoned him, as they did Thomas Müntzer [cf. 169], when he could no longer perform miracles, as they have abandoned countless revolutionaries of past and recent ages when they did not produce the help they had promised. Jesus was crucified. 'My God, why hast thou forsaken me?' he cried and died [16]. Jesus was not the greatest being but nevertheless the most noble person whose name history has preserved.

This is the historical kernel of an event out of which later ages made an epic poem replete with miracles and a fabulous machinery of gods. A minor anecdote became significant to history. [. . .] And so it also came about that the abortive revolution of the dreamer Jesus [cf. 243] left something behind that in the end became a religion.

Karl Ferdinand Gutzkow, Wally the Sceptic, book 3: 'Wally's Diary', 'Confessions concerning Religion and Christianity', extract (1835)

If Strauss (cf. **237**) and Gutzkow (cf. **239**) produced the most controversial *Lives of Jesus* in the nineteenth century, the most widely influential was probably the lively adventure story produced by the French orientalist scholar Ernest Rénan (1823–92). Jesus appears without supernatural trappings, but also without any stern morality; he is a quixotic itinerant preacher in a colourful landscape, an amiable man made noble by suffering. The book was extraordinarily popular, and ran through many editions and translations, long after its initial publication. (Cf. **15**.)

During these last days a deep sadness appears to have filled the soul of Jesus, which was generally so joyous and serene. All the narratives agree in relating that before his arrest he went through a brief phase of misgiving and trouble, a kind of agony in anticipation. According to some, he suddenly exclaimed, 'Now is my soul troubled . . . Father, save me from this hour' [John 12: 27]. It was believed that a voice from heaven was heard at that moment: others said that an angel came to console him. According to one widely spread version, the incident occurred in the garden of Gethsemane. Jesus, it was said, went about a stone's-throw from his sleeping disciples, taking with him only Cephas and the two sons of Zebedee. Then he fell on his face and prayed. His soul was sick even unto death; a terrible anguish weighed him down; but resignation to the divine will sustained him. This scene, by reason of the instinctive art which regulated the compilation of the Synoptics, and often led them to follow rules of adaptability and effect in the arrangement of the narrative, is stated as having happened on the last night of the life of Jesus, and at the moment of his arrest. Were this version the true one, we should scarcely understand why John, who had been the immediate witness of so touching an episode, should not have spoken of it to his disciples, and that the author of the fourth Gospel, in the very circumstantial narrative which he gives of the evening of the Thursday, should have omitted mention of it. All that one can safely say is, that, during his last days, the enormous weight of the mission he had accepted bore cruelly upon Jesus. For a moment human nature asserted itself. It may be that he began to have doubts about his work. Terror and hesitation seized him and cast him into a state of exhaustion worse than death itself. He who has sacrificed his repose and the legitimate rewards of life to a great idea ever experiences a feeling of revulsion when the image of death presents itself for the first time to him, and seeks to persuade him that all has been in vain. Perhaps some of those touching memories preserved by the strongest souls, and at times sharp as a sword, came to him at this moment. Did he remember the clear fountains of Galilee, where he might have found refreshment; the vine and the fig-tree under which he might have rested, the young maidens who perhaps might have consented to love him? Did he curse the cruel destiny which had denied him the joys granted to all others? Did he regret his too lofty nature, and, victim of his greatness, mourn that he had not remained a simple workman in Nazareth? We know not. For all these inward troubles were evidently a sealed chapter to his disciples. They understood nothing of them, and by simple conjectures supplied what in their Master's great soul was obscure to them. It is at least certain that his divine nature soon regained the supremacy. He might still have escaped death; but he would not. Love of his work sustained him. He was willing to drink the cup to its dregs. Henceforth we behold Jesus entirely himself and with his character unclouded. The subtleties of the controversial-ist, the credulity of the thaumaturgist and exorcist are forgotten. There remains but the incomparable hero of the passion [cf. **253**], the founder of the rights of free conscience, the complete exemplar whom all suffering souls will contemplate to fortify and to console themselves.

Ernest Rénan, *Life of Jesus*, extract (1863)

241 Christ the Communist

Eliza Lynn Linton (1822–98) was a vicar's daughter who became a radical novelist, producing among other more acceptable works an anonymous novel-cum-communist-tract, in which a thinly disguised Christ figure, Joshua Davidson, propounds and is martyred to the communist cause. Here Joshua explains his understanding of his forebear and namesake. (Cf. **239, 215**.)

'Friends,' he said, 'I have at last cleared my mind and come to a belief. I have proved to myself the sole meaning of Christ: it is humanity. I relinquish the miracles, the doctrine of the atonement, the doctrine of the divinity of Jesus, and the unelastic finality of his knowledge. He was the product of his time; and if he went beyond it in some things, he was only abreast of it in others. His views of human life were oriental; his images are drawn from the auto-cratic despotism of the great and the slavish submission of the humble, and there is never a word of reprobation of these conditions, as conditions, only of the individuals according to their desert. He did his best to remedy that injustice, so far as there might be solace in thought, by proclaiming the spiritual equality of all men, and the greater value of worth than status; but he left the social question where he found it—paying tribute even to Caesar without reluctance—his mind not being ripe to accept the idea of a radical revolution, and his hands not strong enough to accomplish it, if even he had imagined it. But neither he nor his disciples imagined more than the com-munism of their own sect; they did not touch the throne of Caesar, or the power of the hereditary irresponsible Lord. Their communism never aimed at the equalisation of classes throughout all society. Hence, I cannot accept the beginning of Christian politics as final, but hold that we have to carry on the work under different forms. The modern Christ would be a politician. His aim would be to raise the whole platform of society, he would not try to make the poor contented with a lot in which they cannot be much better than savages or brutes. He would work at the destruction of caste, which is the vice at the root of all our creeds and institutions. He would not content himself with denouncing sin as merely spiritual evil; he would go into its economic causes, and destroy the flower by cutting at the roots—poverty and ignorance. He would accept the truths of science, and he would teach that a man saves his own soul best by helping his neighbour. That, indeed, he did teach; and that is the one solid foothold I have. Friends, Christianity according to Christ is the creed of human progress, not that of resignation to the avoidable miseries of class; it is the confession that society is elastic, and that no social arrangements are final; that morals themselves are only experimental, and that no laws are divine—that is, absolute and unchangeable by circumstance. It is the doctrine of evolution, of growth; and just as Christ was the starting-point of a new era of theological thought, so is the present the starting-point of a new era of social fact. Let us then strip our Christianity of all the mythology, the fetishism that has grown about it. Let us abandon the idolatry with which we have obscured the meaning of the Life; let us go back to the *man* and carry on his work in its essential spirit in the direction suited to our times and social condition. Those of you who still cling to the mystical aspect of the creed, and who prefer to worship the God rather than imitate the man, must here part company with me. You know that, as a youth, I went deep into the life of prayer and faith; as a man, I have come out into the upper air of action; into the understanding that Christianity is not a creed as dogmatised by churches, but an organisation having politics for its means and the equalisation of classes as its end. It is Communism. Friends! the doctrine I have chosen for myself is Christian Communism—and my aim will be, the life after Christ in the service of humanity, without distinction of persons or morals. The man Jesus is my master, and by his example I will walk.

Eliza Lynn Linton, *The True History of Joshua Davidson* IV, extract (1872)

242   Jesus the Jew

Despite its frequent anti-Judaism, one of the important but frequently overlooked factors in nineteenth-century historical investigation of Jesus is precisely the influence of Jewish thinkers and writers. Heinrich Grätz (1817–91) was a Jewish historian. Here, in anticipation of themes which were to become prominent in Christian scholarship only a century later (cf. **225**, **340**), Jesus is presented as a character in the history of Judaism, firmly a part of the religion which he sought to reform.

Jesus made no attack upon Judaism itself, he had no idea of becoming the reformer of Judaean doctrine or the propounder of a new law; he sought merely to redeem the sinner, to call him to a good and holy life, to teach him that he is a child of God, and to prepare him for the approaching Messianic time. He insisted upon the unity of God, and was far from attempting to change in the slightest degree the Judaean conception of the deity. To the question once put to him by an expounder of the law, 'What is the essence of Judaism?' he replied, ' "Hear, O Israel, our God is one;" and "Thou shalt love thy neighbour like thyself." These are the chief commandments' [Mark 12: 28]. His disciples who had remained true to Judaism promulgated the declaration of their Master—'I am not come to destroy, but to fulfil; till heaven and earth pass, one jot or one tittle shall in nowise pass from the law till all be fulfilled' [Matt. 5: 17]. Jesus made no objection to the existing custom of sacrifice, he merely demanded—and in this the Pharisees agreed with him—that reconciliation with his fellow-man should precede any act of religious atonement. Even fasting found no opponent in him, so far as it was practised without ostentation or hypocrisy. He wore on his garments the fringes ordered by the law [Luke 8: 44], and he belonged so thoroughly to Judaism that he shared the narrow views held by the Judaeans at that period, and thoroughly despised the heathen world. He was animated by that feeling when he said, 'Give not that which is holy unto the dogs, neither cast ye your pearls before swine, lest they trample them under their feet and turn again and rend you' [Matt. 7: 6].

The merit of Jesus consisted principally in his efforts to impart greater force to the precepts of Judaism, in the enthusiasm with which he followed them out himself in his ardour to make the Judaeans turn to God with filial love as children to their father, in his fervent upholding of the brotherhood of men, in his insistence that moral laws be placed in the foreground, and in his endeavours to make them accepted by those who had been hitherto regarded as the lowest and most degraded of human beings.

It was not to be expected, however, that through his teaching alone Jesus could attract such devoted followers, or have achieved such great results; something more was required—something strange and wonderful to startle and inflame. His appearance, his mystical character, his earnest zeal produced, doubtless, a powerful effect, but to awaken in the dull and cold a lasting enthusiasm, to gain the confidence of the masses, and to kindle their faith, it was necessary to appeal to their imagination by strange circumstances and marvellous surroundings. The Christian chronicles abound in extraordinary events and descriptions of miraculous cures performed by

Jesus. Though these stories may in part be due to an inclination to exaggerate and idealise, they must doubtless have had some foundation in fact. Miraculous cures—such, for example, as the exorcism of those possessed by demons—belonged so completely to the personality of Jesus that his followers boasted more of the exercise of that power than of the purity and holiness of their conduct. If we are to credit the historical accounts of that period, the people also admired Jesus more for the command he displayed over demons and Satan than for his moral greatness. It was indeed first through the possession of such influence that he appeared to the uncultured masses as a supernatural being.

Heinrich Grätz, History of the Jews, from the Earliest Times to the
Present Day II. vi, extract (1891)

243   One Unknown

> Albert Schweitzer (1875–1965) was an extraordinary figure. A prominent theologian, he abandoned his academic career (as well as his second career as a virtuoso organist) to become a medical missionary in West Africa, for which work he eventually received the 1952 Nobel Peace Prize. He came to academic prominence with a 1906 book in which he traced the history of *Lives of Jesus* in the nineteenth century, arguing that such attempts to domesticate Jesus must be abandoned. (Cf. **238, 239**.)

The Jesus of Nazareth who came forward publicly as the Messiah, who preached the ethic of the Kingdom of God, who founded the Kingdom of Heaven upon earth, and died to give his work its final consecration, never had any existence [cf. **234**]. He is a figure designed by rationalism, endowed with life by liberalism, and clothed by modern theology in an historical garb.

This image has not been destroyed from without, it has fallen to pieces, cleft and disintegrated by the concrete historical problems which came to the surface one after another, and in spite of all the artifice, art, artificiality, and violence which was applied to them, refused to be planed down to fit the design on which the Jesus of the theology of the last hundred and thirty years had been constructed, and were no sooner covered over than they appeared again in a new form. [. . .]

The study of the Life of Jesus has had a curious history. It set out in quest of the historical Jesus, believing that when it had found him it could bring him straight into our time as a teacher and saviour. It loosed the bands by which he had been riveted for centuries to the stony rocks of ecclesiastical doctrine, and rejoiced to see life and movement coming into the figure once more, and the historical Jesus advancing, as it seemed, to meet it. But he does not stay; he passes by our time and returns to his own. What surprised and dismayed the theology of the last forty years was that, despite all forced and arbitrary interpretations, it could not keep him in our time, but had to let him go. He returned to his own time, not owing to the application of any historical ingenuity, but by the same inevitable necessity by which the liberated pendulum returns to its original position. [. . .]

We modern theologians are too proud of our historical method, too proud of our historical Jesus, too confident in our belief in the spiritual gains which our historical theology can bring to the world. The thought that we could build up by the increase of historical knowledge a new and vigorous Christianity and set free new spiritual forces, rules us like a fixed idea, and prevents us from seeing that the task which we have grappled with and in some measure discharged is only one of the intellectual preliminaries of the great religious task. [. . .]

There was a danger of our thrusting ourselves between men and the gospels, and refusing to leave the individual man alone with the sayings of Jesus.

There was a danger that we should offer them a Jesus who was too small, because we had forced him into conformity with our human standards and human psychology. To see that, one need only read the Lives of Jesus written since the 'sixties, and notice what they have made of the great imperious sayings of the Lord, how they have weakened down his imperative world-contemning demands upon individuals, that he might not come into conflict with our ethical ideals, and might tune his denial of the world to our acceptance of it. Many of the greatest sayings are found lying in a corner like explosive shells from which the charges have been removed. No small portion of elemental religious power needed to be drawn off from his sayings to prevent them from conflicting with our system of religious world-acceptance. We have made Jesus hold another language with our time from that which he really held. [. . .]

But the truth is, it is not Jesus as historically known, but Jesus as spiritually arisen within men, who is significant for our time and can help it. Not the historical Jesus, but the spirit which goes forth from him and in the spirits of men strives for new influence and rule, is that which overcomes the world.

It is not given to history to disengage that which is abiding and eternal in the being of Jesus from the historical forms in which it worked itself out, and to introduce it into our world as a living influence. It has toiled in vain at this undertaking. As a water-plant is beautiful so long as it is growing in the water, but once torn from its roots, withers and becomes unrecognisable, so it is with the historical Jesus when he is wrenched loose from the soil of eschatology,[5] and the attempt is made to conceive him 'historically' as a being not subject to temporal conditions. The abiding and eternal in Jesus is absolutely independent of historical knowledge and can only be understood by contact with his spirit which is still at work in the world. In proportion as we have the spirit of Jesus we have the true knowledge of Jesus.

Jesus as a concrete historical personality remains a stranger to our time, but his spirit, which lies hidden in his words, is known in simplicity, and its influence is direct. Every saying contains in its own way the whole Jesus. The very strangeness and unconditionedness in which he stands before us makes it easier for individuals to find their own personal standpoint in regard to him.

Men feared that to admit the claims of eschatology would abolish the significance of his words for our time; and hence there was a feverish eagerness to discover in them any elements that might be considered not eschatologically conditioned. When any sayings were found of which the wording did not absolutely imply an eschatological connexion there was great jubilation—these at least had been saved uninjured from the coming *débâcle*.

But in reality that which is eternal in the words of Jesus is due to the very fact that they are based on an eschatological world-view, and contain the expression of a mind for which the contemporary world with its historical and social circumstances no longer had any existence. They are appropriate, therefore, to any world, for in every world they raise the man who dares to meet their challenge, and does not turn and twist them into meaninglessness, above his world and his time, making him inwardly free, so that he is fitted to be, in his own world and in his own time, a simple channel of the power of Jesus. [. . .]

It is a good thing that the true historical Jesus should overthrow the modern Jesus, should rise up against the modern spirit and send upon earth, not peace, but a sword. He was not teacher, not a casuist; he was an imperious ruler. It was because he was so in his inmost being that he could think of himself as the Son of Man. That was only the temporally conditioned expression of the fact that he was an authoritative ruler. The names in which men expressed their recognition of him as such, Messiah, Son of Man, Son of God, have become for us historical parables. We can find no designation which expresses what he is for us.

He comes to us as one unknown, without a name, as of old, by the lakeside, he came to those men who knew him not. He speaks to us the same word: 'Follow thou me!' and sets us to the tasks which he has to fulfil for our time. He commands. And to those who obey him, whether they be wise or simple, he will reveal himself in the toils, the conflicts, the sufferings which they shall pass through in his fellowship, and, as an ineffable mystery, they shall learn in their own experience who he is.

Albert Schweitzer, *The Quest of the Historical Jesus: A Critical Study of its Progress from Reimarus to Wrede* xx, extracts (1906)

Section B

Humility

In several different but complementary ways, the nineteenth century saw a concentration upon the humility of Jesus Christ in Western Europe, yet it was a humility which looks strangely different from that emphasized in the medieval world. In part, it is a response to the historical critics' demand for a Jesus fully subject to the constraints of history; in part it is the natural child of the Lutheran solution to the post-Reformation Christological debates (cf. **181**); in part it is a further development of Pietistic spirituality (cf. **202–5**); and in part it is the appropriate theology for an age in which Romanticism and sentimentality are often difficult to distinguish.

I. Jesus the Child

Jesus' childhood has frequently been the subject of conjecture and devotion in Christian history (cf. **23**), but in the nineteenth century a new portrayal emerges: the curly-locked, sweet-tempered Christ-child with an angelic face and winning ways.

244 The Creator in the Cradle

It is clear from this poem by Irish poet and convert to Catholicism Aubrey Thomas de Vere (1814–1902) that the concentration on the child Jesus need not simply be sentimentality. The first two verses demonstrate the place of this imagery in a consideration of Christ's Incarnation and obedience, and recalls earlier Christological debates (cf. **249**); the second half of the poem points in the direction of a thoroughly modern sensibility. (Cf. **99, 247, 326**.)

> He willed to lack; he willed to bear;
>   He willed by suffering to be schooled;
> He willed the chains of flesh to wear:
>   Yet from her arms the worlds he ruled.
>
> As tapers 'mid the noontide glow
>   With merged yet separate radiance burn,
> With human taste and touch, even so,
>   The things he knew he willed to learn.
>
> He sat beside the lowly door;
>   His homeless eyes appeared to trace
> In evening skies remembered lore,
>   And shadows of his Father's face.

One only knew him. She alone
　　Who nightly to his cradle crept,
And lying like the moonbeams prone,
　　Worshipped her maker as he slept.

Aubrey Thomas de Vere, 'Mater Christi' (1857)

245   The Wounded Child

Oscar Wilde (1854–1900) is best known for the flashing brilliance of his wit, for his hedonistic aestheticism, and for his tragic fall from grace. In 1888 he published a book of children's stories, *The Happy Prince and Other Stories*, including the elegant parable from which this extract comes. Never accused of being a theologian, Wilde here demonstrates a sure hand in touching the religious sentiments of his day. Behind high walls, a misanthropic and child-hating Giant lives in a perpetual winter . . . (Cf. **316**.)

The Spring never came, nor the Summer. The Autumn gave golden fruit to every garden, but to the Giant's garden she gave none. 'He is too selfish,' she said. So it was always Winter there, and the North Wind, and the Hail, and the Frost, and the Snow danced about through the trees.

One morning the Giant was lying awake in bed when he heard some lovely music. It sounded so sweet to his ears that he thought it must be the King's musicians passing by. It was really only a little linnet singing outside his window, but it was so long since he had heard a bird sing in his garden that it seemed to him to be the most beautiful music in the world. Then the Hail stopped dancing over his head, and the North Wind ceased roaring, and a delicious perfume came to him through the open casement. 'I believe the Spring has come at last,' said the Giant; and he jumped out of bed and looked out.

What did he see?

He saw a most wonderful sight. Through a little hole in the wall the children had crept in, and they were sitting in the branches of the trees. In every tree that he could see there was a little child. And the trees were so glad to have the children back again that they had covered themselves with blossoms, and were waving their arms gently above the children's heads. The birds were flying about and twittering with delight, and the flowers were looking up through the green grass and laughing. It was a lovely scene, only in one corner it was still Winter. It was the farthest corner of the garden, and in it was standing a little boy. He was so small that he could not reach up to the branches of the tree, and he was wandering all round it, crying bitterly. The poor tree was still quite covered with frost and snow, and the North Wind was blowing and roaring above it. 'Climb up! little boy,' said the Tree, and it bent its branches down as low as it could; but the boy was too tiny.

And the Giant's heart melted as he looked out. 'How selfish I have been!' he said; 'now I know why the Spring would not come here. I will put that poor little boy on the top of the tree, and then I will knock down the wall, and my garden shall be the children's playground for ever and ever.' He was really very sorry for what he had done.

So he crept downstairs and opened the front door quite softly, and went out into the garden. But when the children saw him they were so frightened that they all ran away, and the garden became Winter again. Only the little boy did not run, for his eyes were so full of tears that he did not see the Giant coming. And the Giant stole up behind him and took him gently in his hand, and put him up into the tree. And the tree broke at once into blossom, and the birds came and sang on it, and the little boy stretched out his two arms and flung them round the Giant's neck, and kissed him. And the other children, when they saw that the Giant was not wicked any longer, came running back, and with them came the Spring. 'It is your garden now, little children,' said the Giant, and he took a great axe and knocked down the wall. And when the people were going to market at twelve o'clock they found the Giant playing with the children in the most beautiful garden they had ever seen.

All day long they played, and in the evening they came to the Giant to bid him good-bye.

'But where is your little companion?' he said: 'the boy I put into the tree.' The Giant loved him the best because he had kissed him.

'We don't know,' answered the children; 'he has gone away.'

'You must tell him to be sure and come here to-morrow,' said the Giant. But the children said they did not know where he lived, and had never seen him before; and the Giant felt very sad.

Every afternoon, when school was over, the children came and played with the Giant. But the little boy whom the Giant loved was never seen again. The Giant was very kind to all the children, yet he longed for his first little friend, and often spoke of him. 'How I would like to see him!' he used to say.

Years went over, and the Giant grew very old and feeble. He could not play about any more, so he sat in a huge armchair, and watched the children at their games, and admired his garden. 'I have many beautiful flowers,' he said, 'but the children are the most beautiful flowers of all.'

One winter morning he looked out of his window as he was dressing. He did not hate the Winter now, for he knew that it was merely the Spring asleep, and that the flowers were resting.

Suddenly he rubbed his eyes in wonder, and looked and looked. It certainly was a marvellous sight. In the farthest corner of the garden was a tree quite covered with lovely white blossoms. Its branches were all golden, and silver fruit hung down from them, and underneath it stood the little boy he had loved.

Downstairs ran the Giant in great joy, and out into the garden. He hastened across the grass, and came near to the child. And when he came quite close his face grew red with anger, and he said, 'Who hath dared to wound thee?' For on the palms of the child's hands were the prints of two nails, and the prints of two nails were on the little feet.

'Who hath dared to wound thee?' cried the Giant; 'tell me, that I may take my big sword and slay him.'

'Nay!' answered the child; 'but these are the wounds of Love.'

'Who art thou?' said the Giant, and a strange awe fell on him, and he knelt before the little child.

And the child smiled on the Giant, and said to him, 'You let me play once in your garden; to-day you shall come with me to my garden, which is Paradise.'

And when the children ran in that afternoon, they found the Giant lying dead under the tree, all covered with white blossoms.

Oscar Fingall O'Flahertie Wills Wilde, 'The Selfish Giant', extract (1888)

246   The Crown of Roses

This poem started life in Russian,[6] before being translated into German (by Hans Schmidt) and thence into English (by Geoffrey Dearmer). It is best known from an 1883 choral setting by Tchaikovsky. (Cf. **23**.)

> When Jesus Christ was yet a child
> He had a garden small and wild,
> Wherein he cherished roses fair,
> And wove them into garlands there.
>
> Now once, as summer-time drew nigh,
> There came a troop of children by,
> And seeing roses on the tree,
> With shouts they plucked them merrily.
>
> 'Do you bind roses in your hair?'
> They cried, in scorn, to Jesus there.
> The boy said humbly: 'Take, I pray,
> All but the naked thorns away.'
>
> Then of the thorns they made a crown,
> And with rough fingers pressed it down,
> Till on his forehead fair and young
> Red drops of blood like roses sprung.

Plechtchéev, 'The Crown of Roses' (date unknown)

247   Little Jesus

Francis Thompson (1859–1907) was a Catholic poet of unaffected innocence, a man incapable of looking after himself who was rescued from destitution by another Catholic poet, Alice Christiana Meynell (1847–1922). If de Vere's poem (cf. 244) shows the theological roots of reflection on the child Jesus, Thompson's shows its sentimental fruit.

Little Jesus, wast thou shy
Once, and just so small as I?
And what did it feel like to be
Out of heaven, and just like me?
Didst thou sometimes think of *there*,
And ask where all the angels were?

I should think that I would cry
For my house all made of sky;
I would look about the air,
And wonder where my angels were;
And at waking 'twould distress me—
Not an angel there to dress me!

Hadst thou ever any toys,
Like us little girls and boys?
And didst thou play in heaven with all
The angels, that were not too tall,
With stars for marbles? Did the things
Play *Can you see me?* through their wings?

Didst thou kneel at night to pray,
And didst thou join thy hands, this way?
And did they tire sometimes, being young,
And make the prayer seem very long?
And dost thou like it best, that we
Should join our hands to pray to thee?
I used to think, before I knew,
The prayer not said unless we do
And did thy mother at the night
Kiss thee, and fold the clothes in right?
And didst thou feel quite good in bed,
Kissed, and sweet, and thy prayers said?

Thou canst not have forgotten all
That it feels like to be small;
And thou know'st I cannot pray
To thee in my father's way—
When thou wast so little, say,
Couldst thou talk thy Father's way?

So, a little child, come down
And hear a child's tongue like thy own;

Take me by the hand and walk,
And listen to my baby-talk.
To thy Father show my prayer
(He will look, thou art so fair),
And say: 'O Father, I, thy Son,
Bring the prayer of a little one.'

And he will smile, that children's tongue
Has not changed since thou wast young!

Francis Thompson, 'Little Jesus' (1893)

II. Divinity and the Limitations of Humanity

The apparent incompatibility of divinity with human nature animated various theologies in the nineteenth century. Some found in the contrast simply cause for renewed wonder and worship; others denied that there could be any personal union of divine and human natures, and became Unitarians. Most prominent among the theologians who felt the same tension that drove the Unitarians, but who remained within the bounds of orthodox Christology, were the Lutherans. Before the nineteenth century Lutheran Christology had been dominated by the attempt to demonstrate against Calvinist theologians the 'communication of attributes' from Christ's divinity to his humanity (cf. **181**). In the nineteenth century some Lutheran theologians turned the question on its head, and stressed the limitation of Christ's divine nature by virtue of union with the human; others found that changing understandings of human nature to which these attributes were to be ascribed led them to rethink the personal union which held the natures together.

248   Lowly Majesty

Henry Hart Milman (1791–1868) was Professor of Poetry at the University of Oxford, and then Dean of St Paul's Cathedral. In the former post he produced a controversial study of Old Testament history; in the latter, a famous history of the Latin Church. He was also a poet and playwright of some note.

Ride on! ride on in majesty!
Hark! all the tribes 'Hosanna!' cry;
O Saviour meek, pursue thy road
With palms and scattered garments strowed.

Ride on! ride on in majesty
In lowly pomp ride on to die;
O Christ, thy triumphs now begin
O'er captive death and conquered sin.

Ride on! ride on in majesty!
The wingèd squadrons of the sky

Look down with sad and wondering eyes
To see the approaching sacrifice.

Ride on! ride on in majesty!
Thy last and fiercest strife is nigh;
The Father on his sapphire throne
Awaits his own anointed Son [cf. **136**].

Ride on! ride on in majesty!
In lowly pomp ride on to die;
Bow thy meek head to mortal pain,
Then take, O God, thy power, and reign.

Henry Hart Milman, 'Ride on! ride on in majesty!' (1827)

249   The Self-Limitation of the Divine

Gottfried Thomasius (1802–75) was the German Lutheran theologian who first seriously proposed a kenotic theory of the Incarnation—a view which became very popular in Lutheran circles and later (in modified form) in Anglican circles. (Cf. **86, 105, 107**.)

The incarnation comes under a twofold point of view:

(a) It appears first as the assumption of human nature on the part of the second person of the Godhead. The incarnation must be *assumption* because the question is not one of the production of an utterly new person but rather one of the origin of an historical person who, standing in organic connection with us, belongs to the living tree of the race whose members we are. It must be assumption of human *nature*, not of a human individual, because only in this way can a divine-human person come to be. But the nature which the Son of God appropriates must be a completely human one, fully homogeneous with ours, because only as true man can he mediate our communion with God; and it is complete only when it has in common with us the whole creaturely essential existence of man, i.e. the totality of bodily and spiritual powers and thus the real possibility of all the physical and moral relations for which man is structured. [. . .]

(b) Nevertheless, the concept of an assumption still does not reach all the way in explaining the historical person of the God-man. We must go yet one step further, to the supposition of a self-limitation of the divine.

That is to say, if he, the eternal Son of God, remains in his divine mode of being and action in the finite human nature assumed by him, if he persists in his trans-worldly position, in the unlimitedness of his world-ruling and world-embracing governance, then the mutual relation of the two also remains always afflicted by a certain duplication. The divine then, so to speak, surpasses the human as a broader circle does a smaller one;[7] in its knowledge, life and action the divine extends infinitely far over and above the human, as the extra-historical over the temporal, as that which is perfect in itself over that which becomes, as the all-permeating and all-determining over the conditioned, over that which is bound to the limits and laws of earthly existence. The consciousness that the Son has of himself and of his universal governance does not come together as one with the consciousness of the historical Christ—it hovers, as it were, above him; the universal activity which the Son continuously exercises does not coincide with his divine-human action in the state of humiliation—it lies beyond or behind the latter; 'while the Logos in all-permeating presence rules throughout the creation, Christ is restricted to the sphere of redemption, at least temporarily to a definite space.' Thus here is a twofold mode of being, a double life, a doubled consciousness: the Logos still is or has something which is not merged into his historical appearance, which is not also the man Jesus, and all this seems to destroy the unity of the person, the identity of the ego; thus there occurs no living and complete penetration of both sides, no proper being-man of God. *One* subject, as we postulate it, in which it is God in his totality, the fullness of deity as it subsists in the Son, that has become man—such a subject will not result from this mode of thinking; the great practical interests that we have precisely at this point are not satisfied.

Conversely, however, if the Son of God in assuming human nature had at once imparted to it the unlimited fullness of his divine lordship and transfigured it into his divine mode of being and action, then it would thereby have been stripped of the earthly limitation naturally inherent in it, withdrawn from homogeneity with our present state of life and suffering, and from the outset raised to a perfection from which point on no history, at any rate, would any longer have been possible. In particular, a gradual, naturally human development of life and a naturally human suffering seem incompatible with such a divinization of the human, and a life-movement of the redeemer in the flesh, a conflict with the powers of the world and of wickedness, would be hardly more conceivable. Justice would not be done precisely to the side of his condition and activity to which justifying faith especially clings, the suffering in the body of flesh, the real participation in our 'poor flesh', in our weakness, in our desolation, in our death and in our trespasses. And thus from the act of incarnation there would never result that person of the historical Christ which is the postulate of our communion with God mediated through him, and which corresponds to the picture we have of him from the gospel accounts.

This divine-human person can only have originated through God's determining of himself to actual participation in the human mode of being, i.e. in the human form of life and consciousness, and indeed in that form which is peculiar to the present state of our race. And thus we shall have to posit the incarnation itself precisely in the fact that he, the eternal Son of God, the second person of the deity, gave himself over into the form of human limitation, and thereby to the limits of a spatio-temporal existence, under the conditions of a human development, in the bounds of an historical concrete being, in order to live in and through our nature the life of our race in the fullest sense of the word, without on that account ceasing to be God. Only so does there occur an actual entrance into humanity, an actual becoming-one with it, a becoming-man of God; and only so does there result that historical person of the mediator which we know to be the God-man.

The transition into this condition is manifestly a self-limitation for the eternal Son of God. It is certainly not a divesting of that which is essential to deity in order to be God, but it is a divesting of the divine mode of being in favour of the humanly creaturely form of existence, and *eo ipso* a renunciation of the divine glory which he had from the beginning with the Father and exercised vis-à-vis the world governing and ruling it throughout.

Gottfried Thomasius, Christ's Person and Work II. 1. 39–40, extracts (2nd edn. 1857)

250 The Development of God-Humanity

> Isaak August Dorner (1809–84) was a German Lutheran theologian who worked to integrate Lutheranism with Kant's philosophy (cf. **229**). Here the combination of a modern view of historical humanity and a Lutheran insistence on the communication of attributes (cf. **181**) leads to a developmental Christology.

Since development is proper to humanity, and Christ presents true humanity in an actual human life, a truly human development pertains to him. Since on the other hand God can be perfectly manifest in Christ only when the whole fullness of the divine Logos has become this man's own fullness in knowledge and will, and has thus become divine-human, a development of God-manhood is also necessarily given in him along with the development of the human side. The incarnation is not to be conceived as finished at one moment, but as continuing, even as growing, since God as Logos constantly grasps and appropriates each of the new facets that are formed out of the true human unfolding, just as conversely the growing actual receptivity of the humanity joins consciously and willingly with ever new facets of the Logos. But in spite of this development within the *unio*, the Logos is from the beginning united with Jesus in the deepest ground of being, and Jesus' life was always a divine-human one since an existent receptivity for deity never remained without its fulfilment. Human development and the immutability of deity are congruous in that God as Logos can enter history without loss of self, for the purpose of a progressive self-revelation in humanity, and humanity is capable of being set increasingly in immutability, again without alteration of its essence. [. . .]

God can wed his being and life, his nature, with the nature of this man in a unique way, different from the being of God in the world generally. God's essence can work and rule even in the beginnings of this human child, can even be mysteriously united with his soul, that he may become the consecrated place in which God as Logos, the divine world-centre, will sometime find his adequate actuality in the world. As we can conceive no moment in which the humanity is nothing but an empty form [cf. 105], so the loving will of the incarnating God withholds no impartation for which receptivity exists. And if even the plant longs for the light, why should not the humanity of Jesus gravitate toward its innate life-ground in unconscious inclination and impulse, being not merely passively appropriated by it but already in some way participant in the life of the Logos? But if so, there is at no time a humanness in Christ that the deity did not assume, in order to satisfy the receptivity to the degree that it existed; thus there is no moment in Jesus' life that does not bear divine-human character. And conversely as well, after the *unio* of the Logos with humanity, God never knows himself apart from the assumed man, but knows himself as having become man—even if neither in such a way that the relative separability of the elements of this person (and thereby a true development) is excluded by a process that puts the movable into immutability nor in such a way that the one absolute divine personality becomes man (rather, God knows and wills himself as incarnate only in the Logos).

Isaak August Dorner, *System of Christian Doctrine* II. 104, extracts (2nd edn. 1886–7)

251 Christt Only Human

William Ellery Channing (1780–1842) was a leader among those liberal Congregationalists who split from their conservative fellows in the early nineteenth century, proclaiming a non-Trinitarian gospel without a doctrine of Atonement (cf. 223). He believed that by freeing Christ's human nature from the complex theories and speculations that attend any attempt to see it in unity with the divine, a 'vastly more affecting' theology resulted. (Cf. 260, 266.)

We believe that Jesus is one mind, one soul, one being, as truly one as we are, and equally distinct from the one God. We complain of the doctrine of the Trinity that, not satisfied with making God three beings, it makes Jesus Christ two beings, and thus introduces infinite confusion into our conceptions of his character [cf. 106]. This corruption of Christianity, alike repugnant to common sense and to the general strain of Scripture, is a remarkable proof of the power of a false philosophy in disfiguring the simple truth of Jesus. [. . .]

Surely, if Jesus Christ felt that he consisted of two minds, and that this was a leading feature of his religion, his phraseology respecting himself would have been coloured by this peculiarity. The universal language of men is framed upon the idea that one person is one person, is one mind and one soul; and when the multitude heard this language from the lips of Jesus, they must have taken it in its usual sense, and must have referred to a single soul all which he spoke, unless expressly instructed to interpret it differently. But where do we find this instruction? Where do you meet, in the New Testament, the phraseology which abounds in Trinitarian books and which necessarily grows from the doctrine of two natures in Jesus? Where does this divine teacher say, 'This I speak as God, and this as man; this is true only of my human mind, this only of my divine' [cf. **82, 83**]? Where do we find in the Epistles a trace of this strange phraseology? Nowhere. It was not needed in that day. It was demanded by the errors of a later age.

We believe, then, that Christ is one mind, one being, and, I add, a being distinct from the one God. [. . .] We wish that those from whom we differ would weigh one striking fact. Jesus, in his preaching, continually spoke of God. The word was always in his mouth. We ask, does he by this word ever mean himself? We say, never. On the contrary, he most plainly distinguishes between God and himself, and so do his disciples. How this is to be reconciled with the idea that the manifestation of Christ as God was a primary object of Christianity, our adversaries must determine. [. . .]

Trinitarians profess to derive some important advantages from their mode of viewing Christ. It furnishes them, they tell us, with an infinite atonement [cf. **114**], for it shows them an infinite being suffering for their sins. The confidence with which this fallacy is repeated astonishes us. When pressed with the question whether they really believe that the infinite and unchangeable God suffered and died on the cross, they acknowledge that this is not true, but that Christ's human mind alone sustained the pains of death. How have we, then, an infinite sufferer? This language seems to us an imposition on common minds, and very derogatory to God's justice, as if this attribute could be satisfied by a sophism and a fiction.

We are also told that Christ is a more interesting object, that his love and mercy are more felt, when he is viewed as the Supreme God who left his glory to take humanity and to suffer for men. That Trinitarians are strongly moved by this representation we do not mean to deny; but we think their emotions altogether founded on a misapprehension of their own doctrines. They talk of the second person of the Trinity's leaving his glory and his Father's bosom to visit and save the world. But this second person, being the unchangeable and infinite God, was evidently incapable of parting with the least degree of his perfection and felicity [cf. **178, 249**]. At the moment of his taking flesh, he was as intimately present with his Father as before, and equally with his Father filled heaven, and earth, and immensity. This

Trinitarians acknowledge; and still they profess to be touched and over-whelmed by the amazing humiliation of this immutable being! But not only does their doctrine, when fully explained, reduce Christ's humiliation to a fiction, it almost wholly destroys the impressions with which his cross ought to be viewed. According to their doctrine, Christ was comparatively no suf-ferer at all. It is true, his human mind suffered; but this, they tell us, was an infinitely small part of Jesus, bearing no more proportion to his whole nature than a single hair of our heads to the whole body, or than a drop to the ocean. The divine mind of Christ, that which was most properly himself, was infin-itely happy at the very moment of the suffering of his humanity. While hanging on the cross, he was the happiest being in the universe, as happy as the infinite Father; so that his pains, compared with his felicity, were nothing. This Trinitarians do, and must, acknowledge. It follows necessarily from the immutableness of the divine nature which they ascribe to Christ; so that their system, justly viewed, robs his death of interest, weakens our sympathy with his sufferings, and is, of all others, most unfavourable to a love of Christ founded on a sense of his sacrifices for mankind.

We esteem our own views to be vastly more affecting. It is our belief that Christ's humiliation was real and entire, that the whole Saviour, and not a part of him, suffered, that his crucifixion was a scene of deep and unmixed agony. As we stand round his cross, our minds are not distracted, nor our sensibility weakened, by contemplating him as composed of incongruous and infinitely differing minds, and as having a balance of infinite felicity. We recognise in the dying Jesus but one mind. This, we think, renders his sufferings, and his patience and love in bearing them, incomparably more impressive and affecting than the system we oppose.

William Ellery Channing, *Unitarian Christianity*, extract (1819)

III. Against Humility

Not every writer of the nineteenth century found the near-pervasive concentration on Jesus' humility bearable. The two thinkers represented here each produced stinging criticisms of it from positions at the edges of the century's intellectual life.

252   Was Jesus Gentle?

William Blake (1757–1827) was an artist and poet, famous for the luminous visionary engravings with which he illustrated his own unconventional writings. His theological views were equally unusual, as this striking attack on gentle Jesus shows. (Cf. 247.)

Was Jesus gentle or did he
Give any marks of gentility?
When twelve years old he ran away,
And left his parents in dismay;
When after three days sorrow found,
Loud as Sinai's trumpet sound:
'No earthly parents I confess,
My heavenly Father's business.
Ye understand not what I say,
And angry force me to obey.'
Obedience is a duty then,
And favour gains with God and men.
John from the wilderness loud cried;
Satan gloried in his pride.
'Come!' said Satan, 'come away!
I'll soon see if you'll obey;
John for disobedience bled,
But you can turn the stones to bread.
God's high king and God's high priest
Shall plant their glories in your breast—
If Caiaphas you will obey,
If Herod you with bloody prey
Feed with the sacrifice and be
Obedient, fall down, worship me.'
Thunders and lightnings broke around
And Jesus' voice in thunders sound,
'Thus I seize the spiritual prey;
Ye smiters with disease make way!
I come your king and God to seize.
Is God a smiter with disease?'
The God of this world raged in vain;
He bound old Satan in his chain,
And bursting forth his furious ire
Became a chariot of fire.
Throughout the land he took his course,
And traced diseases to their source;
He curs'd the scribe and pharisee,
Trampling down hypocrisy.
Where e'er his chariot took its way,
There gates of death let in the day,
Broke down from every chain and bar.
And Satan in his spiritual war
Dragg'd at his chariot wheels; loud howl'd
The God of this world; louder roll'd
The chariot wheels, and louder still
His voice was heard from Zion's hill.
And in his hand the scourge shone bright;

He scourg'd the merchant Canaanite
From out the temple of his mind;
And in his body tight does bind
Satan and all his hellish crew.
And thus with wrath he did subdue
The serpent bulk of nature's dross,
Till he had nail'd it to the cross;
He took on sin in the Virgin's womb,
And put it off on the cross and tomb,
To be worshipp'd by the church of Rome.
The vision of Christ that thou dost see
Is *my* vision's greatest enemy;
Thine has a great hook nose like thine,
Mine has a snub nose like to mine;
Thine is the friend of all mankind,
Mine speaks in parables to the blind;
Thine loves the same world that mine hates;
Thy heaven doors are my hell gates.
Socrates taught what Melitus
Loath'd as a nation's bitterest curse,
And Caiaphas was in his own mind
A benefactor to mankind;
Both read the bible day and night—
But thou readst black where I read white.

William Blake, 'The Everlasting Gospel', extracts (*c.* 1818)

253 The Anti-Christ

Friedrich Wilhelm Nietzsche (1844–1900), a German Professor of Philology who retired to devote himself to philosophical writing, was a man of passionate brilliance. Struggling above all to grasp unflinchingly the violent and power-driven nature of human existence without comfort or dissembling, he regarded Christianity as a great deceit, an instrument by which the weak and those who hate life overcome the strong and those who enjoy life; but he regarded Jesus of Nazareth as something completely different: the unfollowed exemplar of the only alternative to power; his only worthy opponent.

What concerns me is the psychological type of the Saviour. This type might be depicted in the Gospels, in however mutilated a form and however much overladen with extraneous characters—that is, in *spite* of the Gospels; just as the figure of Francis of Assisi shows itself in his legends in spite of his legends. It is *not* a question of mere truthful evidence as to what he did, what he said and how he actually died; the question is, whether his type is still conceivable, whether it has been handed down to us.—All the attempts that I know of to read the *history* of a 'soul' in the Gospels seem to me to reveal only a lamentable psychological levity. M. Renan [cf. 240], that mountebank *in psychologicus*, has contributed the two most *unseemly* notions to this business of explaining the type of Jesus: the notion of the *genius* and that of the *hero* ('*héros*'). But if there is anything essentially unevangelical, it is surely the concept of the hero. What the Gospels make instinctive is precisely the reverse of all heroic struggle, of all taste for conflict: the very incapacity for resistance is here converted into something moral: ('resist not evil!'—the most profound sentence in the Gospels, perhaps the true key to them), to wit, the blessedness of peace, of gentleness, the *inability* to be an enemy. What is the meaning of 'glad tidings'? —The true life, the life eternal has been found—it is not merely promised, it is here, it is in *you*; it is the life that lies in love free from all retreats and exclusions, from all keeping of distances. Every one is the child of God—Jesus claims nothing for himself alone—as the child of God each man is the equal of every other man. . . . Imagine making Jesus a *hero*!

And what a tremendous misunderstanding appears in the word 'genius'! Our whole conception of the 'spiritual', the whole conception of our civilisation, could have had no meaning in the world that Jesus lived in. In the strict sense of the physiologist, a quite different word ought to be used here. . . . We all know that there is a morbid sensibility of the tactile nerves which causes those suffering from it to recoil from every touch, and from every effort to grasp a solid object. Brought to its logical conclusion, such a physiological *habitus* becomes an instinctive hatred of all reality, a flight into the 'intangible', into the 'incomprehensible'; a distaste for all formulae, for all conceptions of time and space, for everything established—customs, institutions, the church—; a feeling of being at home in a world in which no sort of reality survives, a merely 'inner' world, a 'true' world, an 'eternal' world. . . . 'The Kingdom of God is within *you*'. . . .

The instinctive hatred of reality: the consequence of an extreme susceptibility to pain and irritation—so great that merely to be 'touched' becomes unendurable, for every sensation is too profound.

The instinctive exclusion of all aversion, all hostility, all bounds and distances in feeling: the consequence of an extreme susceptibility to pain and irritation— so great that it senses all resistance, all compulsion to resistance, as unbearable *anguish* (—that is to say, as *harmful*, as *prohibited* by the instinct of self-preservation), and regards blessedness (joy) as possible only when it is no longer necessary to offer resistance to anybody or anything, however evil or dangerous—love, as the only, as the *ultimate* possibility of life. . . . [. . .]

I can only repeat that I set myself against all efforts to intrude the fanatic into the figure of the Saviour: the very word *impérieux*, used by Renan, is alone enough to *annul* the type. What the 'glad tidings' tell us is simply that there are no more contradictions; the kingdom of heaven belongs to *children*; the faith that is voiced here is no more an embattled faith—it is at hand, it has been from the beginning, it is a sort of recrudescent childishness of the spirit. The physiologists, at all events, are familiar with such a delayed and incomplete puberty in the living organism, the result of degeneration. A faith of this sort is not furious, it does not denounce, it does not defend itself: it does not come with 'the sword' [Matt. 10: 34]—it does not realise how it will one day set man against man. It does not manifest itself either by miracles, or by rewards and promises, or by 'scripture': it is itself, first and last, its own miracle, its own reward, its own promise, its own 'kingdom of God.' This faith does not formulate itself—it simply *lives*, and so guards itself against formulae. To be sure, the accident of environment, of educational background gives prominence to concepts of a certain sort: in primitive Christianity one finds *only* concepts of a Judaeo-Semitic character (—that of eating and drinking at the last supper belongs to this category—an idea which, like everything else Jewish, has been badly mauled by the church). But let us be careful not to see in all this anything more than symbolical language, semantics, an opportunity to speak in parables. It is only on the theory that no work is to be taken literally that this anti-realist is able to speak at all. Set down among Hindus he would have made use of the concepts of Sankhya, and among Chinese he would have employed those of Lao-tse—and in neither case would it have made any difference to him.—With a little freedom in the use of words, one might actually call Jesus a 'free spirit'—he cares nothing for what is established: the word *killeth*, whatever is established *killeth*. The idea of 'life' as an *experience*, as he alone conceives it, stands opposed to his mind to every sort of word, formula, law, belief and dogma. He speaks only of inner things: 'life' or 'truth' or 'light' is his word for the innermost—in his sight everything else, the whole of reality, all nature, even language, has significance only as sign, as allegory.—Here it is of paramount importance to be led into no error by the temptations lying in Christian, or rather *ecclesiastical* prejudices: such a symbolism *par excellence* stands outside all religion, all notions of worship, all history, all natural science, all worldly experience, all knowledge, all politics, all psychology, all books, all art—his 'wisdom' is precisely a *pure ignorance* of all such things. He has never heard of *culture*; he doesn't have to make war on it—he doesn't even deny it. . . . The same thing may be said of the *state*, of the whole bourgeois social order, of labour, of war—he has no ground for denying 'the world', for he knows nothing of the ecclesiastical concept of 'the world'. . . . *Denial* is precisely the thing that is impossible to him.—In the same way he lacks argumentative capacity, and has no belief that an article of faith, a 'truth,' may be established by proofs (—*his* proofs are inner 'lights,' subjective sensations of happiness and self-approval, simple 'proofs of power'—.) Such a doctrine *cannot* contradict: it doesn't know that other doctrines exist, or can exist, and is wholly incapable of imagining anything opposed to it. . . . If anything of the sort is ever encountered, it laments the 'blindness' with sincere sympathy—for it alone has 'light'—but it does not offer objections. . . . [. . .]

This 'bearer of glad tidings' died as he lived and *taught*—not to 'save mankind', but to show mankind how to live. It was a *way of life* that he bequeathed to man: his demeanour before the judges, before the officers, before his accusers—his demeanour on the cross. He does not resist; he does not defend his rights; he makes no effort to ward off the most extreme penalty—more, *he invites it.* . . . And he prays, suffers and loves *with* those, *in* those, who do him evil. . . . *Not* to defend one's self, *not* to show anger, *not* to lay blames. . . . On the contrary, to submit even to the Evil One—to *love* him. . . .

Friedrich Nietzsche, *The Antichrist* 29, 30 (extract), 32, 35 (1888)

Section C

....

Christ and the Spirit

....

One theological concomitant of the triumph of historical consciousness in the nineteenth century was a new attention to the doctrine of the Spirit. This concentration could take two conflicting forms. On the one hand, the doctrine might be cited in support of concentration upon God's work in and through the radical finitude and contingency of historical existence; on the other hand, it was taken to allow an escape route from the uncertainty and irrelevancy to which critical methods seemed to consign the bare and messy facts of history.

I. The Spirit of Christ

Both of these strategies can be found in nineteenth-century Christological reflection, although in this sphere it was the latter which was by far the most influential. Against the Lutheran theology of the *communicatio idiomatum* (cf. **181**) and the kenotic Christologies which emerged from it (cf. **249**), Reformed theologians continued to refine Calvin's insistence on the ineradicable finitude of Christ's human nature, and to explore the doctrine of the Spirit which made sense of that insistence (cf. **178**). However, although this Reformed theology contained all the ingredients for a genuine dialogue with the developing historical consciousness, it was the other strategy which was by far the most prominent: the attempt to use a doctrine of the Spirit to immunize the connection between Christ and believers from the virulence of historical criticism.

254   *Christ's Fallen Nature*

The Reformed insistence upon the limitations of Christ's human nature was taken up and taken further by a Church of Scotland minister, Edward Irving (1792–1834). An innovative Trinitarian theologian, firebrand preacher, millenarian, and proponent of such 'gifts of the spirit' as prophecy and speaking in tongues, he was excommunicated in 1830 for this statement about Christ's humanity. (Cf. **178**.)

That Christ took our fallen nature is most manifest, because there was no other in existence to take. The fine dust of Adam's being was changed, and the divine goodness of his will was oppressed by the mastery of sin; so that, unless God had created the Virgin in Adam's first estate . . . it was impossible to find in existence any human nature *but* human nature fallen, whereof Christ might partake with the brethren. I believe, therefore, in opposition to all who say the contrary, that Christ took unto himself a true body and a reasonable soul; and that the flesh of Christ, like my flesh, was in its proper nature mortal and corruptible; that he was of the seed of David; that he was of the seed of Abraham, as well as of the seed of the woman; yea, that he was of the seed of the woman after she fell, and not before she fell. Even the time for making known the truth that Christ in human nature was to come did not arrive till after the fall, because it was determined in the counsel of God that he who was to come should come in the fallen state of the creature, and therein be cut off—yet not for himself—to the end it might be proved that the creature substance which he took, and for ever united to the God-head, was not of the Godhead a part, though by the Godhead sustained.

If he had come in the unfallen manhood and had not truly been subject unto death, but, for some lesser end and minor object, and as it were by intent, had laid aside the mantle of the flesh for a season, who would have been able to say that the manhood of Christ had not become deified, that is, become a part of the Godhead? And if so, then not only he, but all his members likewise, who are to be brought into the very self-same estate with himself, must also be deified, or pass into the Godhead; the creature become an object of worship; the creator be mingled with the creature; the doctrine of God in the soul of the world brought in . . . in the room of the most fruitful, most holy mystery of a personal God, separated from the creature, yet supporting the creature by eternal union with, though in perfect distinction from, himself, in the person of the Son, and through the indwelling of the divine nature in the person of the Holy Ghost; to the end of worshipping the invisible Godhead of Father, Son and Holy Ghost, remaining hidden, and for ever to remain hidden, in the person of the Father. [. . .]

When a spiritual world had been created, and by its fall demonstrated that it was not an end in itself; and when a visible work had been superadded thereunto, and by its fall shown that neither was this the end of the purpose; the fullness of the time being come, forth proceedeth the Holy Ghost to lay the foundation-stone of that temple of the divinity, to bring into being that right-hand man of God, to form that body . . . which had been the great end of God in coming forth at all by creation to give existence beside himself. And the instant that act of the Holy Ghost began, in the very beginning of it, in the instant of life quickened before the sight of God, did the Son, in his independent personality, once and forever join himself to the holy thing, which by that conjunction became properly named the Son of God [cf. **105**]. And such I conceive to be the mystery of this conception of the child whose name is Wonderful, Counsellor, the Everlasting Father, the Mighty God, the Prince of Peace. . . . And is this all? No: this is not all. With humility be it spoken that the fallen humanity could not have been sanctified and redeemed by the union of the Son alone; which directly leadeth unto an inmixing and confusing of the Divine with the human nature. . . . The human nature is thoroughly fallen; and without a thorough communication, inhabitation, and empowering of a divine substance, it cannot again be brought up pure and holy. The mere apprehension of it by the Son doth not make it holy. Such a union leads directly to the apotheosis or deification of the creature, and this does away with the mystery of the Trinity in the Godhead. Yet do I not hesitate to assert, that this is the idea of the person of Christ generally set forth [cf. **249**]: and the effect has been to withdraw from the eye of the Church the work of the Holy Spirit in the incarnation, which is as truly the great demonstration of the Spirit's power and manner of working, as the incarnation itself is of the Father's goodness, and the Son's surpassing love. This comes from the omission of the third part in the composition of Christ, which is, the substance of the Godhead in the person of the Holy Ghost: to whose Divine presence and power it is given, the mighty works which Christ did ascribed, and the spotlessness of his sacrifice attributed, in the Holy Scripture. The Holy Ghost sanctifying and empowering the manhood of Christ even from his mother's womb, is the manifestation both of the Father and of the Son in his manhood, because the Holy Ghost testifieth of the Father and the Son, and of them only: so that in the manhood of Christ was exhibited all of the Godhead that shall ever be exhibited, Father, Son, and Spirit; according as it is written, 'In him dwelt all the fullness of the Godhead bodily' [Col. 2: 9], or in a body. The time was not come for manifesting it gloriously, because the heat of battle was then going forward, when the warrior is all soiled with sweat, and dust, and blood. He was wrestling with sin, in sin's own obscure dwelling-place; against the powers of darkness, in their dark abode: he was overcoming sin in the flesh. And therefore was it that he appeared not in the glorious raiment of a conqueror, or in the full majesty of a possessor, as he shall appear when he cometh the second time.

Edward Irving, *The Orthodox and Catholic Doctrine of Our Lord's Human Nature*, 'The Method is by Taking up the Fallen Humanity', extracts (1830)

255   Christ's Spiritual Presence

Friedrich Schleiermacher (1772–1829) was the greatest proponent of the alternative strategy, and the founder of liberal theology in Germany. Brought up in the Pietist air of the Herrnhutter Brethren (cf. **203**) and deeply influenced by the philosophy of Kant (cf. **229**), he became champion of theology's status in the new University of Berlin, and a Reformed preacher. This sermon illustrates well the heart of Schleiermacher's theology: the Pietist insistence on the 'joyous, immediate recognition' of the divine power in Christ, constantly in dialogue with the 'original testimony' which evokes and shapes that recognition, and which can be the object of sustained critical enquiry.

We are all aware of the glorious treasure we have in God's Word, and we as members of the evangelical church are especially called to be the guardians and keepers of the Word for all Christendom. Indeed, the right way of contending for the truth and integrity of our evangelical Christianity is and always will be what it was when our church began: to prove our good cause from scripture, just as Paul, and Stephen before him, did for the cause of Christianity in general, even in the schools. If this were all, however, would we be certain that we had and held true and vital Christianity among us? Or does not each of us admit that there are many people who share this good fight with us; many who, like us, strive against all works-righteousness and all power of human authority, and do so from the scripture, but of whom we cannot say that the love of Christ constrains them? Yes, I have more to say. There are many people who, when they behold from a distance the commandments Christ gave to his own, the ordinances he established in the early church, the exemplary nature of his life, and the characteristic features of the way he acted as a person, also feel something special there, so that their heart likewise burns within them [cf. **18**]. But their eyes remain closed, and they do not come to that joyous, immediate recognition that this is the Lord, that here is manifested the glory of the only-begotten Son of the Father, that here alone are the words of life.

True and vital Christianity rests on this recognition alone; we must admit that Christianity cannot be preserved or spread among us unless the effects that come from the living memory and spiritual presence of Christ and are based upon the whole of his nature and manifestation are added to what is, in the narrowest and most particular sense, the effect of word and doctrine. I do not mean to argue that if we truly take the redeemer's teaching from the words of scripture but separate it from his personal influence, then it must necessarily degenerate again into a dead letter. But this has indeed happened. Often enough in our own church we have been—perhaps still are—content with the mere letter of orthodox doctrine, without giving effective evidence of a true Christian disposition. We all know this from our own experience. But we do not usually find this problem in those who are susceptible to the personal influences of Christ.

Besides, consider how many difficulties one finds in interpreting the word of scripture. It comes from a remote time [cf. **227**], deals with strange customs, and was written in a language only slightly related to our own. What risky scope for human caprice opens up there! How many sad examples do we see in which caprice actually has been exerted on scripture to make dead and dull what reflects the true essence of Christianity most brightly, or to read into scripture something not in accord with the original spirit of Christian faith. But every attempt, however well-intentioned, to restrain this caprice by external means has proved to be in vain! How necessary it is, then, that scripture be complemented by something that works from the inside. And what else is there but that continuing work of the redeemer himself, those living impressions he creates even now immediately in the human soul? This is what must ever come to the aid of the Word in the Christian church, just as in the redeemer's own life the two were always united and supported each other [cf. **171**].

But if we wanted to give ourselves solely to these immediate influences, despising the clear and precious treasure of God's Word in comparison with them, we would without a doubt be exposed to dangers just as great, if not greater. One cannot deny that from time immemorial much that betrays the unruliness, fanaticism, and excesses of the human heart has often crept into what is supposed to be the Lord's immediate effects in the soul. God's Word must ever remain the standard for measuring and judging everything else if we are to avoid deceiving ourselves into unintentionally confusing the human and the divine, or falling into the danger of becoming prey to those who intentionally substitute or pass off the human for the divine. The Lord cannot be different in his effects in believers' souls than he reveals himself to be in his Word. And if we wanted to claim as Christ's work in us anything that is in conflict with this rule of God's Word, we would make him a liar and thus wantonly separate ourselves from him, since in fact we would be doing it to put ourselves in his place and to claim for ourselves his position. Then instead of believers being pointed to Christ, we would much rather point them to ourselves and have them hold fast to us, all because of the perverse pride of our heart.

It may be said that there is a light sparked immediately in the human soul by the Son of God—regardless of when or how it happens—so that we can easily dispense with God's Word if we have this illumination, since this is how Christ glorifies and reveals himself immediately in the soul with greater clarity and certainty. But in that case, we must always put to use without the slightest hesitation these words of Christ: 'If any one says to you, "Lo, here is the Christ!" or "There he is!" do not believe it' [Matt. 24: 22]. Otherwise we might be tempted, through the most perverse pride, to a totally destructive separation from the proper unity of faith. As the apostle wrote, God is not a God of disorder, but of order in all Christian communities. Nothing in them that stands in contradiction to the divine Word of scripture can be thought to come from God. The Word contains above all the original testimony about the life and existence of the redeemer, and it is by this testimony alone that we must judge whether something is taken from what is his.

Friedrich Schleiermacher, 'The Effects of Scripture and the Immediate Effects of the
Redeemer', 2, extract (before 1826)

256   The Power of God in Christ

Wilhelm Herrmann (1846–1922), Professor of Systematic Theology at the University of Marburg and teacher of Karl Barth (cf. **281**), was an ardent admirer of Schleiermacher's theology (cf. **255**). His whole theology revolved around the awakening of communion with God through encounter with the effective personality of Christ. Although the Spirit is not mentioned, this is effectively a pneumatology: a theology of the work of God's Spirit upon us through Christ.

When once he has attracted us by the beauty of his person, and made us bow before him by its exalted character, then even amid our deepest doubts the person of Jesus will remain present with us as a thing incomparable, the most precious fact in history, and the most precious fact our life contains [cf. **92**] . If we then yield to his attraction and come to feel with deep reverence how his strength and purity disclose to us the impurity and weakness of our souls, then his mighty claim comes home to us. We learn to share his invincible confidence that he can uplift and bless perfectly those who do not turn away from him. In this confidence in the person and cause of Jesus is implied the idea of a power greater than all things, which will see to it that Jesus, who lost his life in this world, shall be none the less victorious over the world. The thought of such a Power lays hold of us as firmly as did the impression of the person of Jesus by which we were overwhelmed. It is the beginning of the consciousness within us that there is a living God [cf. **230**]. This is the only real beginning of an inward submission to him. As soon as trust in Jesus awakens this thought within us, we connect the thought at once with our experience of the inner life of Jesus as a present fact in our own life. The startled sense we felt at the disclosure of actual, living goodness in his person, and the sense of condemnation that we felt, are at once attributed by our souls to the power of God, of which we have now become conscious. The man who has felt these simple experiences cannot possibly attribute them to any other source. The God in whom he now believes for Jesus' sake, is as real and living to him as the man Jesus is in his marvellous sublimity of character. [. . .]

As soon as the law of duty is set forth and expounded to us as Jesus does it, we recognise its unassailable right. But unless our existence in the world bore some sure sign that the good is not essentially foreign to human nature, we should never be certain that our knowledge of moral law could lift *us* to a higher life, or that *we* could attain to the blessed liberty of a moral life. Jesus Christ is that sign. His attitude towards us uplifts us and makes it possible for us to trust that the divine power, which must be with him and with his work, cares for us and makes us fellow workmen with him in his work which aims at nothing less than the actual realisation of the good, and a coming of the

Kingdom of God. Hence, by the conviction that in Christ God communes with us, we are placed inwardly in a position to overcome the opposition between our natural life and the law of duty. It thus becomes possible for us to believe that those very things in our surroundings which are hostile to the good, are by God's power being made of service for what is good. For although our moral striving seems to exhaust itself in vain attempts, yet we have still the consolation that we stand in and belong to a historical movement in which the good wields ever greater sway, for Christ's work must reach its goal, and we know through God's communion with us that we are assisting in that work.

> Wilhelm Herrmann, *The Communion of the Christian with God Described on the Basis of*
> *Luther's Statements* ii, extracts (4th edn. 1903)

257 The Impact of Christ's Spirit

It was Martin Kähler (1835–1912) who spelled out most forcefully the implications of the liberal approach to theology (cf. **255**, **256**) for historical criticism. He was Professor of Systematic Theology at the University of Halle, and, as a lifelong Lutheran, took justification as the central theme in his theology. The views he describes here had a strong impact on such twentieth-century figures as Rudolf Bultmann (cf. **282**).

One cannot make the figure of Jesus the mere object of historical research, as one can other figures belonging to the past. The figure of Jesus has in every age exerted too powerful and too direct an influence on all sorts of people and still makes too strong a claim on everyone to allow a person to suppose that a decisive stand with respect to Jesus is not implicit in a negative attitude to the claim made by the apostolic 'recollection' of him, a recollection with which 'none of the records of mankind can even remotely be compared.'[8] [. . .] The way in which the figure of Jesus today confronts men with his claim to be of unique significance for the religion and morality of every person is precisely the way the Gospel accounts portray his encounter with his own contemporaries. It is through these accounts alone that we are able to come into contact with him. They are not the reports of impartial observers who have been alerted to his presence, but, rather, the *testimonies* and *confessions* of believers in Christ.

What is it then that they were able, or deemed wise, to report to us? It was only the activity of Jesus as a grown man. From the sources we know his personality for a period of only about thirty months, at the most, of his public ministry. We know the prophet whose initial as well as final preachings make it understandable that his forerunner should have humbled himself so profoundly before him. We know the master teacher who, through what he taught and did, carefully nurtured his wider and narrower circle of acquaintances and brought them, finally, to a decision. We know the resolute Messiah who by interpreting the signs on his life's horizon adhered firmly to his mission and advanced toward the goal he so clearly perceived. We know the royal sufferer whose brief public conflicts show us a man at all times the absolute master of himself, as hardly anyone else has ever been. We know him who rose from the dead, a stranger to his table and travel companions, and yet, at the same time, familiar to them beyond all doubt [cf. **18**]. [. . .] It is obvious that those lovingly devoted to him were in a position to preserve many fascinating and winsome details about him, inasmuch as, like ourselves, he lived a busy and active life subject to the routine tasks of the day. However, the recollections preserved by his community give us no information on such matters. Every detail of the apostolic recollection of Jesus can be shown to have been preserved for the sake of its religious significance. [. . .]

How many a person has not read the Gospels for devotions and discovered, at first to his annoyance, how reticent and reserved they are in their reporting of Jesus' words and deeds. Without a doubt the Gospels are the complete opposite of the embellishing, rationalising, and psychologizing rhetoric of the recent biographies of Jesus. The 'Counsellor' has guided the evangelists 'into all the truth,' which is Jesus himself [cf. **13**]. Under the Spirit's guidance they remembered Jesus, his words, his deeds, his life. All the chaff of what is purely and simply historical was sifted by the winnowing fan of this pneumatic hypomnesia,[9] and only the ripened grain of the words and works of the Father in and through Christ was garnered into the granary. [. . .]

This is [. . .] sufficient for preaching and dogmatics, at least for the kind of dogmatics which is willing to leave behind the thorny problems of Christology and instead develop a clear and living soteriology, the knowledge of faith concerning the person of the Saviour [cf. **163**].

Martin Kähler, *The So-Called Historical Jesus and the Historic, Biblical Christ* 2, extracts

(1896)

II. The Development of Doctrine

If the influence of the Spirit upon Christ's historical humanity, or the Spirit's communication of Christ's personality across history, were two of the ways in which pneumatology shaped nineteenth-century theology, another was in the understanding of the nature of the Church. The century saw a widespread emphasis upon the Church as a community the development of which was guided and led by the Spirit of Christ, or the constancy of which despite all historical development was guaranteed by the Spirit of Christ.

John Henry Newman (1801–90) was the leading light in the Oxford Movement, an attempt to revive High Church worship and theology in the Church of England; he was eventually received into the Roman Catholic Church. A theologian and patristic scholar, he pondered deeply the nature of the development of doctrine and the establishment of orthodoxy—as in this Christmas sermon on John 1: 14 (**66**).

He [i.e. John], who had seen the Lord Jesus with a pure mind, attending him from the Lake of Gennesareth to Calvary, and from the sepulchre to Mount Olivet, where he left this scene of his humiliation; he who had been put in charge with his virgin mother, and heard from her what she alone could tell of the mystery to which she had ministered; and they who had heard it from his mouth, and those again whom these had taught, the first generations of the church, needed no explicit declarations concerning his sacred person. Sight and hearing superseded the multitude of words; faith dispensed with the aid of lengthened creeds and confessions. There was silence. 'The Word was made flesh'; 'I believe in Jesus Christ his only Son our Lord'; sentences such as these conveyed everything, yet were officious in nothing. But when the light of his advent faded and love waxed cold, then there was an opening for objection and discussion, and a difficulty in answering. Then misconceptions had to be explained, doubts allayed, questions set at rest, innovators silenced. Christians were forced to speak against their will, lest heretics should speak instead of them.

Such is the difference between our own state and that of the early church. [. . .] In the New Testament we find the doctrine of the incarnation announced clearly indeed, but with a reverent brevity. 'The Word was made flesh.' 'God was manifest in the flesh.' 'God was in Christ.' 'Unto us a Child is born—the mighty God.' 'Christ, over all, God, blessed for ever.' 'My Lord and my God.' 'I am alpha and omega, the beginning and the ending—the Almighty.' 'The Son of God, the brightness of his glory, and the express image of his person' [**66**; 1 Tim. 3: 16; 2 Cor. 5: 19; Isa. 9: 6; Rom. 9: 5; John 20: 28; Rev. 1: 8; Heb. 1: 2, 3]. But we are obliged to speak more at length in the creeds and in our teaching, to meet the perverse ingenuity of those who, when the apostles were removed, could with impunity insult and misinterpret the letter of their writings. [. . .]

Time having proceeded, and the true traditions of our Lord's ministry being lost to us, the object of our faith is but faintly reflected on our minds, compared with the vivid picture which his presence impressed upon the early Christians. True is it the Gospels will do very much by way of realising for us the incarnation of the Son of God, if studied in faith and love. But the creeds are an additional help this way. The declarations made in them, the distinctions, cautions, and the like, supported and illuminated by scripture, draw down, as it were, from heaven, the image of him who is on God's right hand, preserve us from an indolent use of words without apprehending them, and rouse in us those mingled feelings of fear and confidence, affection and devotion towards him, which are implied in the belief of a personal advent of God in our nature, and which were originally derived to the Church from the very sight of him. [. . .]

[The credal formulas] are the terms in which we are constrained to speak of our Lord and Saviour, by the craftiness of his enemies and our own infirmity; and we intreat his leave to do so. We intreat his leave, not as if forgetting that a reverent silence is best on so sacred a subject; but, when evil men and seducers abound on every side, and our own apprehensions of the truth are dull, using zealous David's argument, 'Is there not a cause' for words? We intreat his leave, and we humbly pray that what was first our defence against pride and indolence, may become an outlet of devotion, a service of worship. Nay, we surely trust that he will accept mercifully what we offer in faith, 'doing what we can'; though the ointment of spikenard which we pour out is nothing to that true divine glory which manifested itself in him, when the Holy Ghost singled him out from other men, and the Father's voice acknowledged him as his dearly beloved Son. Surely he will mercifully accept it, if faith offers what the intellect provides; if love kindles the sacrifice, zeal fans it, and reverence guards it. He will illuminate our earthly words from his own divine holiness, till they become saving truths to the souls which trust in him. He who turned water into wine, and (did he so choose) could make bread of the hard stone, will sustain us for a brief season on this mortal fare. And we, while we make use of it, will never so forget its imperfection, as not to look out constantly for the true beatific vision [cf. **216**]; never so perversely remember that imperfection as to reject what is necessary for our present need. The time will come, if we be found worthy, when we, who now see in a glass darkly, shall see our Lord and Saviour face to face; shall behold his countenance beaming with the fullness of divine perfections, and bearing its own witness that he is the Son of God. We shall see him as he is.

John Henry Newman, 'Sermon III on the Incarnation', extracts (1835)

259 Christ Advancing

Charles Augustus Briggs (1841–1913) was the first prominent historical critic of the Old Testament in the United States. Professor of Hebrew at Union Seminary, he was suspended from ministering in the Presbyterian Church for his controversial views, although an action against him for heresy was unsuccessful. Here he shows that he combined his historical criticism with a remarkably positive view of the development of doctrine.

That which underlies the biblical statements of the Christ, that which envelops them on all sides, that which logically, both by induction and deduction, is involved in the biblical doctrine, that which in religious experience is the necessary consequence of the vital union and communion with him [cf. **256**], involved in regeneration, in the indwelling divine Spirit, and in the realisation of the real presence of the Christ in accordance with his promise, in the consciousness of the individual and of the church: all these make it certain that the Christ of the church is much more than the Christ of the apostles [cf. **257**]. As the church advances toward the realisation of her ideal, she learns more and more in her experience that all things are summed up in Jesus Christ, that her task is to christianise the world, christologise all knowledge, and crown him Lord of all.

When one begins to realise what the church is and comprehends, according to the experience and teaching of the biblical writers, he sees, to some extent at least, that it was not possible for any one biblical writer, even though it was a St. Peter, a St. Paul, or a St. John, to comprehend the whole Christ, still less for the church at any period of history to give full expression to all that Christ is to her. What St. Paul tells us of the pious individual is true of the church in all ages: 'Now we know in part, now we see in a mirror darkly' [1 Cor. 13: 12]. And not until the church has been perfected at the second advent of our Lord, shall we see 'face to face'. So St. John tells us that when 'he shall be manifested, we shall be like him; for we shall see him even as he is' [1 John 3: 2].

The Christ is 'the same yesterday and to-day and forever' [Heb. 13: 8]; but the church's experience of him is not the same; it varies from time to time [*pace* **266**] in the apprehension of those specific characteristics of the person, life, and work of Christ that her experience in other matters leads her to emphasise at the time. On the whole the church advances steadily and firmly toward her ideal, notwithstanding reactionary movements that occasionally arise, as human knowledge extends its area and human activity enlarges its scope. Those who, at any time, emphasise the importance of this new knowledge and these new achievements, often in the pride of their possession are disposed to challenge the Christ of the church, who does not seem to agree altogether with them, and obstinately to resist his supremacy over them. This could hardly be otherwise, human nature being what it is. It is an inevitable result of the development of the world and man as the environment of the kingdom of Christ, as our Lord is gradually, surely, and irresistibly bringing all things under his gracious rule. 'He must reign, till he hath put all his enemies under his feet' [1 Cor. 15: 25].

The Christ of the church advances through the ages of history, in the religious experience of his people, the doctrinal definitions of the church, and the institutions of worship and discipline that further union and communion with him. So far as her apprehension of Christ is concerned the church always advances. Whatever her faults and failures may be in other respects, she never retreats from him. Individuals may and do fall away into serious error and sin. Her scholars are sometimes unfaithful, and, in their pride of the knowledge of other things, forget their Lord. Her people sometimes are recreant and negligent of their exalted privileges. But the church as a body has never retracted her Christology, has never withdrawn the Christ of her experience from her faith and worship.

It is indeed one of the most remarkable things in history that the church has always maintained the Christological definition that her experience of Christ has impelled her to make. There have been numerous errors and heresies which required long and severe struggles to overcome; but once overcome, the church has maintained her Christology as an impregnable fortress.

The ancient heresies revive from time to time in those who find it difficult to reconcile the Christ of the church with their speculations in philosophy or science; but these speculators have never made any important or lasting impression upon the world. They have been thrown off by the church without hesitation and at little cost. Whatever has been discovered by science or philosophy that had any validity, has fitted into the Christology of the church with the utmost nicety and exactness; for all truth is harmonious, and our Christ is the eternal Logos, the King of Truth.

Charles Augustus Briggs, 'The Christ of the Church', extract (1912)

260 Christ's Enduring Words

Theodore Parker (1810–60) was a moderate Unitarian preacher (cf. **251**, **266**) and prominent social campaigner (cf. **265**). He emphasizes the constant, unchanging influence of Christ's powerful words which, although itself apparently immune from development, has nevertheless shaped so much of what is good in the historical development of the last two thousand years.

Christ says, his Word shall never pass away. Yet, at first sight, nothing seems more fleeting than a word. It is an evanescent impulse of the most fickle element. It leaves no track where it went through the air. Yet to this, and this only, did Jesus entrust the truth wherewith he came laden to the earth; truth for the salvation of the world. He took no pains to perpetuate his thoughts: they were poured forth where occasion found him an audience—by the side of the lake, or a well; in a cottage, or the temple; in a fisher's boat, or the synagogue of the Jews. He founds no institution as a monument of his words. He appoints no order of men to preserve his bright and glad relations. He only bids his friends give freely the truth they had freely received. He did not even write his words in a book. With a noble confidence, the result of his abiding faith, he scattered them broadcast on the world, leaving the seed to its own vitality. He knew that what is of God cannot fail, for God keeps his own. He sowed his seed in the heart, and left it there, to be watered and warmed by the dew and the sun which heaven sends. He felt his words were for eternity. So he trusted them to the uncertain air; and for eighteen hundred years that faithful element has held them good—distinct as when first warm from his lips.

Now they are translated into every human speech, and murmured in all earth's thousand tongues, from the pine forests of the North to the palm groves of eastern Ind. They mingle as it were, with the roar of a populous city, and join the chime of the desert sea. Of a Sabbath morn they are repeated from church to church, from isle to isle, and land to land, till their music goes round the world. These words have become the breath of the good, the hope of the wise, the joy of the pious, and that for many millions of hearts. They are the prayers of our churches; our better devotion by fireside and fieldside; the enchantment of our hearts. It is these words that still work wonders, to which the first recorded miracles were nothing in grandeur and utility. It is these which build our temples and beautify our homes. They raise our thoughts of sublimity; they purify our ideal of purity; they hallow our prayer for truth and love. They make beauteous and divine the life which plain men lead. They give wings to our aspirations. What charmers they are! Sorrow is lulled at their bidding. They take the sting out of disease, and rob adversity of his power to disappoint. They give health and wings to the pious soul, broken-hearted and shipwrecked in his voyage through life, and encourage him to tempt the perilous way once more. They make all things ours: Christ our brother; time our servant; death our ally, and the witness of our triumph. They reveal to us the presence of God, which else we might not have seen so clearly, in the first windflower of spring, in the falling of a sparrow, in the distress of a nation, in the sorrow or the rapture of the world. Silence the voice of Christianity, and the world is well-nigh dumb, for gone is that sweet music which kept in awe the rulers and the people, which cheers the poor widow in her lonely toil, and comes like light through the windows of morning, to men who sit stooping and feeble with failing eyes and a hungering heart. It is gone—all gone! only the cold, bleak world left before them.

Such is the life of these words; such the empire they have won for themselves over men's minds since they were spoken first. In the meantime, the words of great men and mighty, whose name shook whole continents, though graven in metal, and stone, though stamped in institutions, and defended by whole tribes of priests and troops of followers—their words have gone to the ground, and the world gives back no echo of their voice. Meanwhile, the great works, also, of old times, castle, and tower, and town, their cities and their empires, have perished, and left scarce a mark on the bosom of the earth to show they once have been. The philosophy of the wise, the art of the accomplished, the song of the poet, the ritual of the priest, though honoured as divine in their day, have gone down a prey to oblivion. Silence has closed over them; only their spectres now haunt the earth. A deluge of blood has swept over the nations; a night of darkness, more deep than the fabled darkness of Egypt, has lowered down upon that flood, to destroy or to hide what the deluge had spared. But through all this the words of Christianity have come down to us from the lips of that Hebrew youth, gentle and beautiful as the light of a star, not spent by their journey through time and through space. They have built up a new civilisation, which the wisest Gentile never hoped for, which the most pious Hebrew never foretold. Through centuries of wasting these words have flown on, like a dove in the storm, and now wait to descend on hearts pure and earnest, as the Father's spirit, we are told, came down on his lowly Son [cf. 2]. The old heavens and the old earth are indeed passed away, but the Word stands. Nothing shows clearer than this how fleeting is what man calls great, how lasting what God pronounces true.

Theodore Parker, A Discourse of the Transient and the Permanent in Christianity,
extract (19th century)

261 The Gospel's Embodiment

Alfred Loisy (1857–1940) was a French Catholic, a biblical scholar, and a prominent Modernist, working for the reform of the theology of the Catholic Church in line with recent intellectual developments. *L'Évangile et l'église* was written in response to Adolf von Harnack (cf. 262), the prominent liberal Protestant; in it Loisy sought to mark out a thoroughly Catholic liberalism. He broke with the Catholic Church after the papal condemnation of Modernism in 1907.

Jesus, on the earth, was the great representative of faith. Now, the religious faith of humanity always has been and always will be supported by symbols more or less imperfect: its aspirations, which have infinity as their object, can only become definite in human thought in a finite form. The concrete symbol, the living image, not the pure idea, is the normal expression of faith, and the condition of its moral efficacy in man and in the world. The choice and the quality of the symbols are necessarily related to the stage of evolution of faith and of religion. The conceptions of the kingdom and of the Messiah are not merely the features that made it possible for Christianity to come forward beside Judaism, they are the necessary form in which Christianity had to be born in Judaism before spreading out into the world.

Nothing could make Jesus other than a Jew. He was only man under condition of belonging to one branch of humanity. In that in which he was born, the branch that may well be said to have carried in it the religious future of the world, this future was known in quite a precise manner, by the hope of the reign of God, by the symbol of the Messiah [cf. **243**]. He who was to be the Saviour of the world could only enter on his office by assuming the position of Messiah, and by presenting himself as the founder of the kingdom come to accomplish the hope of Israel. The Gospel, appearing in Judaea and unable to appear elsewhere, was bound to be conditioned by Judaism. Its Jewish exterior is the human body, whose divine soul is the spirit of Jesus. But take away the body, and the soul will vanish in the air like the lightest breath. Without the idea of the Messiah, the gospel would have been but a metaphysical possibility, an invisible, intangible essence, even unintelligible, for want of a definition appropriate to the means of knowledge, not a living and conquering reality. The gospel will always need a body to be human. Having become the hope of Christian people, it has corrected in the interpretation certain parts of its Israelitish symbolism. None the less, it remains the shadowy representation of the great mystery, God and the providential destiny of man and of humanity, because it is a representation always striving after perfection, inadequate and insufficient.

This is the mystery that Jesus revealed, as far as it could be revealed, and under the conditions which made revelation possible. It may be said that Christ lived it as much as he made it manifest. If he had only had in view the propagation of a doctrine, the organisation of an earthly society, or even the foundation of a particular religion, Christ must have been judged not only less wise than Socrates, but much less able than Mahomet. He sought no such object, and it was for no deceiving dream that he turned aside from it. His dream was his project, the realisation of perfect happiness in perfect justice, of immortality in holiness. This realisation was already complete in him, by his union with God, his faith in the heavenly Father, the inner certainty of the eternal future guaranteed to humanity in his person and by his agency. The historian, as such, cannot appreciate the objective value of this persuasion: the Christian will not doubt it, and, beyond any question, no one is Christian who does not admit it.

Alfred Loisy, *The Gospel and the Church* III. iii, extract (1902)

262   Freeing the Kernel

Adolf von Harnack (1851–1930) was a devoted and formidable historian of doctrine in the early Church, yet was no champion of doctrine. The wealth of detail which he accumulated in his massive histories only served to convince him that doctrine was an accretion, an accidental husk gathered around the pure heart of the gospel. In 1899 and 1900 he gave a course of lectures in which he expounded that pure heart: the religion *of* Jesus rather than the religion *about* Jesus. (Cf. 243.)

Jesus was convinced that God does, and will do, justice. [. . .] Further, he demanded of his disciples that they should be able to renounce their rights. In giving expression to this demand, far from having all the circumstances of his own time in mind, still less the more complex conditions of a later age, he has one and one only present to his soul, namely, the relation of every man to the kingdom of God. Because a man is to sell all that he has in order to buy the pearl of great price, so he must also be able to abandon his earthly rights and subordinate everything to that highest relation. But in connexion with this message of his, Jesus opens up to us the prospect of a union among men, which is held together, not by any legal ordinance, but by the rule of love, and where a man conquers his enemy by gentleness. It is a high and glorious ideal, and we have received it from the very foundation of our religion. It ought to float before our eyes as the goal and guiding star of our historical development. Whether mankind will ever attain to it, who can say? but we can and ought to approximate to it, and in these days—otherwise than two or three hundred years ago—we feel a moral obligation in this direction. Those of us who possess more delicate and therefore more prophetic perceptions no longer regard the kingdom of love and peace as a mere utopia. [. . .]

What position did Jesus himself take up towards the Gospel while he was proclaiming it, and how did he wish himself to be accepted? We are not yet dealing with the way in which his disciples accepted him, or the place which they gave him in their hearts, and the opinion which they formed of him; we are now speaking only of his own testimony of himself. But the question is one which lands us in the great sphere of controverted questions which cover the history of the Church from the first century up to our own time. In the course of this controversy men put an end to brotherly fellowship for the sake of a nuance [cf. 76, 77, 78]; and thousands were cast out, condemned, loaded with chains and done to death. It is a gruesome story. On the question of 'Christology' men beat their religious doctrines into terrible weapons, and spread fear and intimidation everywhere. This attitude still continues; Christology is treated as though the Gospel had no other problem to offer, and the accompanying fanaticism is still rampant in our own day. Who can wonder at the difficulty of the problem, weighed down as it is with such a burden of history and made the sport of parties? Yet anyone who will look at our Gospels with unprejudiced eyes will not find that the question of Jesus' own testimony is insoluble. So much of it, however, as remains obscure and mysterious to our minds ought to remain so; as Jesus meant it to be, and as in the very nature of the problem it is. It is only in pictures that we can give it expression. 'There are phenomena which cannot, without the aid of symbols, be brought within the range of the understanding.' [. . .]

Let us first of all consider the designation, 'Son of God'. Jesus in one of his discourses made it specially clear why and in what sense he gave himself this name. The saying is to be found in Matthew, and not, as might perhaps have been expected, in John: 'No man knoweth the Son but the Father; neither knoweth any man the Father, save the Son, and he to whomsoever the Son will reveal him' [Matt. 11: 27]. It is 'knowledge of God' that makes the sphere of the divine Sonship. It is in this knowledge that he came to know the sacred being who rules heaven and earth as Father, as *his* Father. The consciousness which he possessed of being *the Son of God* is, therefore, nothing but the practical consequence of knowing God as the Father and as his Father. Rightly understood, the name of Son means nothing but the knowledge of God.

Here, however, two observations are to be made: Jesus is convinced that he knows God in a way in which no one ever knew him before, and he knows that it is his vocation to communicate this knowledge of God to others by word and by deed—and with it the knowledge that men are God's children. In this consciousness he knows himself to be the Son called and instituted of God, to be *the* Son of God, and hence he can say: *my* God and *my* Father, and into this invocation he puts something which belongs to no one but himself.

How he came to this consciousness of the unique character of his relation to God as a Son; how he came to the consciousness of his power, and to the consciousness of the obligation and the mission which this power carries with it, is his secret, and no psychology will ever fathom it. The confidence with which John makes him address the Father: 'Thou lovedst me before the foundation of the world,' is undoubtedly the direct reflection of the certainty with which Jesus himself spoke. No research can carry us further. We are not even able to say when it was that he first knew himself as the Son, and whether he at once completely identified himself with this idea and let his individuality be absorbed in it, or whether it formed an inner problem which kept him in constant suspense. Only a man who had had a similar experience himself could do anything to fathom this mystery. Let a prophet try, if he chooses, to raise the veil, but, for our part, we must be content with the fact that this Jesus who preached humility and knowledge of self nevertheless named himself and himself alone as *the Son of God*.

He is certain that he knows the Father, that he is to bring this knowledge to all men, and that thereby he is doing the work of God. Among all the works of God this is the greatest; it is the aim and end of all creation. The work is given to him to do, and in God's strength he will accomplish it. It was out of this feeling of power and in the prospect of victory that he uttered the words: 'The Father hath committed all things unto me' [John 3: 35].

Again and again in the history of mankind men of God have come forward in the sure consciousness of possessing a divine message, and of being compelled, whether they will or not, to deliver it. But the message has always happened to be imperfect; in this spot or that, defective; bound up with political or particularistic elements; designed to meet the circumstances of the moment; and very often the prophet did not stand the test of being himself an example of his message. But in this case the message brought was of the profoundest and most comprehensive character; it went to the very root of mankind and, although set in the framework of the Jewish nation, it addressed itself to the whole of humanity—the message from God the Father. Defective it is not, and its real kernel may be readily freed from the inevitable husk of contemporary form. Antiquated it is not, and in life and strength it still triumphs today over all the past. He who delivered it has as yet yielded his place to no man, and to human life he still today gives a meaning and an aim—he *the Son of God*.

Adolf von Harnack, What is Christianity? 7.4–5, extracts (1899–1900)

263 Christ Betrayed

Josephine Butler (1828–1906) involved herself in charity work after the death of her 6-year-old daughter in 1863; she began to campaign for women's education, and later campaigned on other issues affecting women. This extract is from an address given at the Committee of the Social Purity Alliance in Cambridge, 1879.

I will ask you the question of to-day, therefore, in this connection, 'What think ye of Christ?' Come with me into his presence. Let us go with him into the temple; let us look at him on the occasion when men rudely thrust into his presence a woman, who with loud-tongued accusation they condemned as an impure and hateful thing. 'He that is without sin among you, let him first cast a stone at her.' At the close of that interview, he asked, 'Woman, where are those thine accusers?' [John 8: 10.] It was a significant question; and we ask it again to-day. Where, and who, are they? In what state are their consciences? Beginning from the eldest even to the youngest, they went out, scared by the searching presence of him who admitted not for one moment that God's law of purity should be relaxed for the stronger, while imposed in its utmost severity on the weaker.

Almost as soon as that holy teacher had ascended into the heavens, Christian society and the Church itself began to be unfaithful to his teaching; and man has too generally continued up to this day to assert, by speech, by customs, by institutions, and by laws, that, in regard to this evil, the woman who errs is irrevocably blighted, while the man is at least excusable.

Josephine Butler, Social Purity, extract (1879)

264   Jesus' Simple Teaching

> Leo Tolstoy (1828–1910) is best known as a novelist, author of *War and Peace*, and *Anna Karenina* among others. In 1877, however, he turned away from literary fame and adopted a simple, ascetic lifestyle. He followed a simple moral gospel, from which—as he saw it—all miraculous and speculative obscurities had been removed. (Cf. 4.)

Jesus had pity on men because they knew not true happiness, and he taught them. He said:

Blessed are those who have no goods, no fame, and no care for these things, but wretched are they who seek wealth and honours; for the poor and the oppressed obey the will of the Father, which the rich and the honoured seek only from men in this life. In order to fulfil the will of the Father, we must not fear to be poor and despised; we must be glad of it, and thus show men in what true happiness consists.

In order to fulfil the will of the Father, which gives life and happiness to all men, we must fulfil five commandments.

The first commandment—To offend no one, and by no act to excite evil in others, for out of evil comes evil.

The second commandment—To be in all things chaste, and not to quit the wife whom we have taken; for the abandoning of wives and the changing of them is the cause of all loose living in the world.

The third commandment—Never to take an oath, because we can promise nothing, for man is altogether in the hands of the Father, and oaths are imposed for wicked ends.

The fourth commandment—Not to resist evil, to bear with offences, and to do yet more than is demanded of us; neither to judge, nor to go to law, for every man is himself full of faults, and cannot teach. By seeking revenge men only teach others to do the same.

The fifth commandment—To make no distinction between our own countrymen and foreigners, for all men are the children of one Father.

These five commandments should be observed, not to gain praise from man, but for our own sakes, for our own happiness, and therefore neither prayer nor fasting in the sight of man is necessary. The Father knows all we need. So we have nothing to ask him for, but only to strive to do his will. The will of the Father is this, that we should have no malice in our hearts to anyone.

To fast is unnecessary, because men only fast to obtain the praise of others, and the praise of man is what we should avoid. We have only to care for one thing—to live according to the will of the Father, and the rest will all come of itself. If we take care for the things of the flesh, we cannot take care for the things which are of the kingdom of Heaven. A man may live without care for food or dress. The Father will give life. We only need to take care that we are living at the present moment after the will of the Father. The Father gives even to children what they need. We have only to desire the strength of the spirit, which is given by the Father. The five commandments show the way to the kingdom of Heaven. This narrow path alone leads to eternal hope. False teachers, wolves in sheep's clothing, always try to drive men from this road. We must beware of them. It is always easy to recognise these false teachers, because they teach evil in the name of good. If they teach violence and slaughter, they are false teachers. By what they teach they may be known.

It is not he who calls upon the name of God, but he who does good work, that fulfils the will of the Father. Thus, whoever fulfils these five commandments will have the absolute certainty of a true life which nothing can deprive him of; but whoever does not fulfil them will not have any certainty of life, but a life which he will soon lose, so that nothing will remain to him.

The teaching of Jesus astonished and delighted all the people, because it promised liberty to all. The teaching of Jesus was the fulfilment of the prophecies of Isaiah, that the chosen of God should bring light unto men, should defeat evil, and should establish truth, not by violence, but by mildness, humility, and goodness.

Leo Tolstoy, *The Spirit of Christ's Teaching* IV (1880s)

265 Deeds not Doctrine

Lucretia Mott (1793–1880) was a controversial Quaker preacher and a social reformer who enraged some of her contemporaries by campaigning for the abolition of slavery and equal rights for women. She too (cf. **264**) finds the heart of the gospel in the Sermon on the Mount, and finds doctrinal development a distraction from its moral message.

It is time that Christians were judged more by their likeness to Christ than their notions of Christ. Were this sentiment generally admitted we should not see such tenacious adherence to what men deem the opinions and doctrines of Christ while at the same time in every day practice is exhibited anything but a likeness to Christ. My reflections in this meeting have been upon the origin, parentage, and character of Jesus. I have thought we might profitably dwell upon the facts connected with his life, his precepts, and his practice in his walks among men. Humble as was his birth, obscure as was his parentage, little known as he seemed to be in his neighbourhood and country, he has astonished the world and brought a response from all mankind by the purity of his precepts, the excellence of his example. Wherever that inimitable sermon on the mount is read, let it be translated into any language and spread before the people, there as an acknowledgement of its truth. When we come to judge the sectarian professors of his name by the true test, how widely do their lives differ from his?

Instead of going about doing good as was his wont, instead of being constantly in the exercise of benevolence and love as was his practice, we find the disposition too generally to measure the Christian by his assent to a creed which had not its sign with him nor indeed in his day. Instead of engaging in the exercise of peace, justice and mercy, how many of the professors are arrayed against him in opposition to those great principles even as were his opposers in his day. Instead of being the bold nonconformist (if I may so speak) that he was, they are adhering to old church usages, and worn-out forms and exhibiting little of a Christ-like disposition and character. Instead of uttering the earnest protests against wickedness in high places, against the spirit of proselytism and sectarianism as did the blessed Jesus—the divine, the holy, the born of God—there is the servile accommodation to this sectarian spirit and an observance of those forms even long after there is any claim of virtue in them; a disposition to use language which shall convey belief that in the inmost heart of many they reject. [. . .]

Jesus' spirit is now going up and down among men seeking their good, and endeavouring to promote the benign and holy principles of peace, justice, and love. And blessing to the merciful, to the peace maker, to the pure in heart, and the poor in spirit, to the just, the upright, to those who desire righteousness [cf. 4] is earnestly proclaimed, by these messengers of the highest who are now in our midst. These the preachers of righteousness are no more acknowledged by the same class of people than was the messiah to the Jews. They are the anointed of God, the inspired preachers and writers and believers of the present time. In the pure example which they exhibit to the nations, they are emphatically the beloved sons of God.

Lucretia Mott, 'Likeness to Christ', extracts (1849)

266   The Teacher of True Morality

Ralph Waldo Emerson (1803–82) was a Unitarian philosopher, preacher, and poet (cf. **251**, **260**), an American friend of Coleridge and Wordsworth. He had a high view of the nature of humanity, believing that the divine was present in every human being, and that salvation could be found within. In his preaching and his essay-writing he turned his considerable literary and oratorical skill to the inculcation of a universal morality, of which he believed Christ was a great exemplar—a fact which had been hidden under the defects of historical Christianity. (cf. **233**.)

Jesus taught as one having authority. How was he able to give this dignity to his instructions?

He was not like Paul learned. For all that we know the carpenter's shop and his mother's humble house were his only academy. And never in his discourses does he refer to any other books than those of the Jewish Scriptures.

He was not a subtile reasoner. It is the fame of a few men that they have analysed every action and every thought of man into its first elements; that they have received nothing until it was proved, and have shaken the evidence of the best authenticated facts and have introduced doubt under the foundations of every opinion. Others there are who have applied the same ingenuity to better purpose, and have done what they could, to fortify with impregnable reason every useful custom, every important truth. Neither of these sorts of skill was the merit of Jesus of whose instructions it is one of the most remarkable features, that he does not reason at all. He proves nothing by argument. He simply asserts, and appeals to his divine commission. Christianity could not be defended if it looked to its author for a systematic account of its pretensions arranged by the rules of logic.

Nor was it by powerful declamation nor insinuating arts of address that he attained this end. Nothing can be more simple than the style of his discourses. It is the style of conversation. Nor by the charm of a great name nor the stateliness of manners of a sage; the story of his life shows us how free were his habits of intercourse with men. Many passages seem to show the wonderful deference with which he was approached, yet so entirely did this spring from other causes than physical accomplishments, that no pen has transmitted one syllable respecting the personal appearance, or the manners, or the voice of so remarkable a personage [cf. **129**].

How then was it, if he was not learned, or subtile, or dogmatical, or eloquent, like many of his later disciples, that he spoke with an authority which they have never obtained?

I conceive it was because he taught truth and the supreme kind of truth, that which relates to morals, to a greater extent than any other, because he taught what man recognised as true the moment it was declared, because speaking on his own convictions he expressed with unexampled force the great moral laws to which the human understanding must always bow, whilst it retains its own constitution; for the great laws of the gospel, my brethren, are they which after all our doubts, after running the round of scepticism, we return to acknowledge with new conviction. He spoke of God in a new tongue. He spoke of him not as the philosophers had done, as an intellectual principle, but in terms of earnest affection, as the grand object of all human thought; that a connexion with him was the home and beatitude of the soul.

He spoke of sin as the disease of man, as an evil of unknown consequence, full of danger and leading to death.

He opened the great doctrine of benevolence to the human race, showing them that glory did not exist in selfish seeking, but in bearing one another's burdens, in meekness, in returning good for evil, in doing good to all men.

He spoke of heaven, as the natural felicity of a good mind resulting to it from the harmony of its affections with truth and God. He spoke of it, of the spiritual good, as the only good worth seeking for.

He spoke of the immortality of the soul as the law of moral nature, as the effectual consideration to bind us to virtue and warn us of vice.

He was a preacher of righteousness, temperance and judgment to come.

There are many faculties in the mind but the highest faculty is the con- science. And there are many parts of truth but moral truth is the greatest. It was his full understanding of this superiority that distinguished Jesus as a teacher. It was the value of this truth that gave him his spiritual empire. Do not think that he owed to the curiosity and reverence that followed one possessed of miraculous power the weight of his lesson. The same truth will have the same effect from whatever lips. Doubtless a mind so pure and so great as his will succeed in giving to all its utterance the expression of its own grandeur. His character was consistent, part with part, and the mighty work of his hand was justified by the mighty word of his mouth. His miraculous powers were not separate but harmonised into his character. But believe rather that the hand was strong because the soul was filled with heavenly knowledge. [. . .]

Brethren, does Jesus speak to us with authority? Do we receive his doctrine with joy? Or as each sentiment falls from his lips do we feel that it condemns us and so feel towards him as an enemy? Let us beware of being found fighting against the truth. We cannot contend against spiritual truth and be innocent for our own consciences bear witness to him within us. Let us not be slower than the multitude who first heard him, but let us pluck out from ourselves the only enemies his words can find in the human heart, our own sins, our false estimates of earthly good, our sensual, our selfish, our uncharitable thoughts, and we shall find that as we do this the voice of our

Saviour becomes the voice of a friend, sounds to us full of consolation, of promise, of praise. At last, when truth has had its whole effect on our minds, it will gain its fullness of authority by becoming to us simply the echo of our own thought. We shall find we think as Christ thought. Thus we shall be one with him and with him one in the Father.

Ralph Waldo Emerson, Sermon LXXVI, extracts (1830)

Section D

Life in Christ

I. Conversion

The nineteenth century saw the growth to dominance of the Pietist emphasis upon heartfelt conversion as the keystone of Christian life (cf. **201–5**), now in an Evangelical form shaped by strong currents from the Puritan Reformed heritage (**210**, **211**). Many of the conversion-centred idioms familiar in popular Western Christianity today first became pervasive towards the end of the nineteenth century.

267 Personal Saviour

The Scofield Reference Bible was a runaway success. A Bible packed with study aids (glosses, cross-referencing apparatus, introductions, and supplementary materials), it expounded a powerfully coherent Evangelical theology covering world history (which could be seen to fall into distinct Dispensations, episodes in God's plan) and individual faith. The latter is described concisely in this extract by the American evangelist Reuben Archer Torrey (1856–1928) on becoming a Christian, which was part of a longer tract bound at the back of the Bible. (Cf. **268**.)

Definition of What it Means to be a Christian
A Christian is any man, woman or child, who comes to God as a lost sinner, accepts the Lord Jesus Christ as their personal Saviour, surrenders to him as their Lord and Master, confesses him as such before the world and strives to please him in everything day by day.

A Suggested Form for Personal Decision in the Acceptance of Jesus Christ as Saviour and Lord
'As many as received him (that is, Jesus Christ), to them gave he power to become the sons of God, even to them that believe on his name' [John 1: 12].

> I believe God's testimony concerning Jesus Christ, namely that God laid all my iniquity upon him and that he bore my sins in his own body on the cross, and that he has thus redeemed me from the curse of the law of God (which I had broken) by becoming a curse for me, and

I do now accept Jesus as my Sin-bearer and Saviour and believe what God tells me in his Word, namely, that all my sins are forgiven because Jesus died in my place.

I also believe God's further testimony concerning Jesus Christ that he is both Lord and Christ (anointed King); and I do now receive him to be my Lord and King.

I therefore yield to him the control of all I am and all I have, my thoughts, my words, my actions. Lord Jesus, thou art my Lord; I belong to thee; I surrender all to thee.

I purpose to confess Jesus as my Lord before the world, as I shall have opportunity, and to live to please him in all that I do each day.

I will take no man for my example, but Jesus only.

Having thus received Jesus Christ I know on the authority of God's sure word of promise that I am a child of God and that I have everlasting life.

Thanks be unto God for his unspeakable gift.

Reuben Archer Torrey, How to Study the Bible, extracts (1909)

268 Jesus Taking Possession

In the eighteenth century John Wesley (cf. **196**) had described the conversion experience in terms of finding his 'heart strangely warmed'. A similar, more exuberant description is provided over a century later by Amanda Berry Smith (1837–1915), a freed Maryland slave who became an evangelist and social reformer with an international ministry.

[The preacher, Brother Inskip, said:] 'You don't need to fix any way for God to live in you; get God in you in all his fullness and he will live himself.'

'Oh!' I said, 'I see it.' And somehow I seemed to sink down out of sight of myself, and then rise; it was all in a moment. I seemed to go two ways at once, down and up. Just then such a wave came over me, and such a welling up in my heart, and these words rang through me like a bell: 'God in you, God in you,' and I thought doing what? Ruling every ambition and desire, and bringing every thought unto captivity and obedience to his will. How I have lived through it I cannot tell, but the blessedness of the love and the peace and power I can never describe. O, what glory filled my soul! The great vacuum in my soul began to fill up; it was like a pleasant draught of cool water, and I felt it.

I wanted to shout, 'Glory to Jesus!' but Satan said, 'Now, if you make a noise they will put you out.' I was the only coloured person there and I had a very keen sense of propriety; I had been taught so, and Satan knew it. I wonder how he ever did know all these little points in me, but in spite of all my Jesus came out best. As we coloured folks used to sing in the gone by years:

> 'Jesus is a mighty captain
> Jesus is a mighty captain
> Jesus is a mighty captain
>   Soldier of the cross.
> 'Jesus never lost a battle,
> Jesus never lost a battle,
> Jesus never lost a battle,
>   Soldier of the cross.'

Hallelujah! Hallelujah! Amen.

I did not shout, and by-and-by Brother Inskip came to another illustration. He said, speaking on faith: 'Now, this blessing of purity like pardon is received by faith, and if by faith why not now?'

'Yes,' I said.

'It is instantaneous,' he continued. 'To illustrate, how long is a dark room dark when you take a lighted lamp into it?'

'O,' I said 'I see it!' And again a great wave of glory swept over my soul— another cooling draught of water—I seemed to swallow it, and then the welling up at my heart seemed to come still a little fuller. Praise the Lord forever, for that day!

Speaking of God's power, he went on still with another illustration. He said: 'If God in the twinkling of an eye can change these vile bodies of ours and make them look like his own most glorious body, how long will it take God to sanctify a soul?'

'God can do it,' I said, 'in the twinkling of an eye,' and as quick as the spark from smitten steel I felt the touch of God from the crown of my head to the soles of my feet, and the welling up came, and I felt I must shout: but Satan still resisted me like he did Joshua.

And when they sang these words, 'Whose blood now cleanseth,' O what a wave of glory swept over my soul! I shouted glory to Jesus. Brother Inskip answered, 'Amen, Glory to God.' O, what a triumph for our King Emmanuel. I don't know just how I looked, but I felt so wonderfully strange, yet I felt glorious. One of the good official brethren at the door said, as I was passing out, 'Well, auntie, how did you like that sermon?' but I could not speak; if I had, I should have shouted, but I simply nodded my head. Just as I put my foot on the top step I seemed to feel a hand, the touch of which I cannot describe. It seemed to press me gently on the top of my head, and I felt something part and roll down and cover me like a great cloak! I felt it distinctly; it was done in a moment, and O what a mighty peace and power took possession of me!'

Amanda Berry Smith, *An Autobiography* VII, extract (1893)

269 Ongoing Conversion

A rather different description of the ongoing conversion of the heart emerges from a thoroughly different milieu. The following extract comes from the anonymous *Candid Narrations of a Pilgrim to his Spiritual Father*, which describes the hero's adventures in a turbulent Russia, armed only with the Jesus Prayer and his copy of the *Philokalia*. (Cf. **92, 93, 151, 295**.)

I began to feel that the prayer had, so to speak, passed to my heart. In other words I felt that my heart in its natural beating began, as it were, to utter the words of the prayer. For instance, one 'Lord'; two 'Jesus'; three 'Christ,' and so forth. No longer did I say the prayer with my lips, but listened attentively to the words formed in my heart, remembering what my departed elder told me about this state of bliss. Then I began to feel a slight pain in my heart, and my whole being was glowing with so great a love for Jesus Christ that it seemed to me if only I could meet him, I would fall to his feet, embracing them and kissing them in tenderness, tears and gratitude for his love and mercy which gives such comfort in calling on his name to me, his unworthy creature. A pleasant warmth was filling my heart and spreading through my whole bosom. This urged me to a more eager reading of the *Philokalia*,[10] so as to test my emotions and to study further the effects of inner prayer. Without this test I might have fallen a victim of delusion, or might have taken natural results for the manifestation of grace, and prided myself at the quick mastering of the prayer. My late elder had warned me of this danger. I decided therefore to walk more at night and to devote my days mainly to reading the *Philokalia*, sitting under the forest trees. Ah! A wisdom so great that I had never thought it possible was revealed to me in this reading. As I went on, I felt a happiness which, until then, had been beyond my imagination. Although many passages were still incomprehensible to my dull mind, the prayer of the heart brought the understanding I wanted.

Anonymous, *The Candid Narrations of a Pilgrim to his Spiritual Father* II, extract (1884)

270 Contemporaneity with Christ

Søren Kierkegaard (1813–55) was a Danish Lutheran philosopher and theologian who from 1843 produced a series of works, many of them pseudonymous, proclaiming a gripping 'existentialism' against the tyrannies of Hegelianism (cf. **230**) and the established Church. Truth, for Kierkegaard— and above all the truth of God—is something that takes place in contemporaneity, imperiously demanding from us a response. (Cf. **281, 282**.)

There is [. . .] an infinite chasmic difference between God and man, and therefore it became clear in the situation of contemporaneity that to become a Christian (to be transformed into likeness with God) is, humanly speaking, an even greater torment and misery and pain than the greatest human torment, and in addition a crime in the eyes of one's contemporaries. And so it will always prove to be if becoming a Christian truly comes to mean becoming contemporary with Christ. And if becoming a Christian does not come to mean this, then all this talk about becoming a Christian is futility and fancy and vanity, and in part blasphemy and sin against the Second Commandment of the Law and sin against the Holy Spirit.

In relation to the absolute, there is only one time, the present; for the person who is not contemporary with the absolute, it does not exist at all. And since Christ is the absolute it is easy to see that in relation to him there is only one situation, the situation of contemporaneity; the three, the seven, the fifteen, the seventeen, the eighteen hundred years make no difference at all; they do not change him, but neither do they reveal who he was, for who he is is revealed only to faith.

Christ is no play-actor, if I may say it this soberly; neither is he a merely historical person, since as the paradox he is an extremely unhistorical person. But this is the difference between poetry and actuality: contemporaneity. The difference between poetry and history is surely this, that history is what *actually* happened, whereas poetry is the possible, the imagined, the poetised. But that which has actually happened (the past) is still not, except in a certain sense (namely, in contrast to poetry), the actual. The qualification that is lacking—which is the qualification of truth (as inwardness) and of all religiousness is—*for you*. The past is not actuality—for me. Only the contemporary is actuality for me. That with which you are living simultaneously is actuality—for you. Thus every human being is able to become contemporary only with the time in which he is living—and then with one more, with Christ's life upon earth, for Christ's life upon earth, the sacred history, stands alone by itself, outside history.

History you can read and hear about as about the past; here you can, if it so pleases you, judge by the outcome. But Christ's life on earth is not a past; it did not wait at the time, eighteen hundred years ago, and does not wait now for the assistance of any outcome. A historical Christianity is nonsense and un-Christian muddled thinking, because whatever true Christians there are in any generation are contemporary with Christ, have nothing to do with Christians in past generations but everything to do with the contemporary Christ. His life on earth accompanies the human race and accompanies each particular generation as the eternal history; his life on earth has the eternal contemporaneity. And this in turn makes all didacticizing of Christianity (didacticizing that essentially has its mask and refuge in the pastness of Christianity and in the eighteen hundred years of history) into the most un-Christian of all heresies, as anyone would perceive and therefore would abandon didacticizing if he tried to imagine the generation contemporary with Christ—didacticizing. But every generation (of believers) is indeed contemporary. [. . .]

If you cannot bear contemporaneity, if you cannot bear to see this sight in actuality, [. . .] then you are not essentially Christian. What you have to do, then, is to confess this unconditionally to yourself so that you above all maintain humility and fear and trembling in relation to what it truly means to be Christian. For it is along that way that you must go in order to learn and to practice resorting to grace in such a way that you do not take it in vain; for God's sake do not go to anyone in order to be 'reassured'. Indeed it does say, 'Blessed are the eyes that saw what you saw' [Luke 10: 23], words with which the preachers in particular have busied themselves—strangely enough, at times perhaps even to justify a worldly high style of living that precisely in the situation of contemporaneity would become somewhat incongruous—just as if these words were not said simply and solely about those contemporaries who became believers. If the glory had been directly perceptible so that everyone could see it as a matter of course, then it is surely an untruth that Christ abased himself and took the form of a servant; it is superfluous to warn against offence, for how in all the world could anyone be offended by glory attired in glory! And how in all the world can one then explain what happened to Christ, that all did not rush in admiration to see what was directly to be seen! No, there was 'nothing for the eye in him, no splendour so that we should be able to look at him, and no esteem so that we could desire him' [Isa. 53: 2]. *Directly* there was nothing to be seen except a lowly human being who by signs and wonders and by claiming to be God continually constituted the possibility of offence—a lowly human being who thus expressed (1) what God understands by compassion (including what it means to be oneself a lowly and poor person, if one is to be compassionate) and (2) what God understands by human misery, which in both cases is altogether different from what people understand thereby and is something everyone in every generation to the end of time must learn for himself from the beginning, beginning at exactly the same point as every contemporary with Christ and practising it in the situation of contemporaneity. Human irascibility and intractability are, of course, no help. Whether one will succeed in becoming essentially Christian, no one can tell him. But anxiety and fear and despair are no help, either. Honesty before God is the first and the last, honestly to confess to oneself where one is, in honesty before God continually keeping the task in sight. However slowly it goes, if one only creeps ahead, one still has one thing—one is properly situated, not led astray and deceived by the trick of recasting Christ so that instead of being God he becomes that sentimental sympathy that human beings themselves have invented, so that Christianity, instead of drawing human beings to the divine, is delayed along the way and becomes the merely human.

Anti-Climacus (Søren Aabye Kierkegaard), *Practice in Christianity* I: 'Come here all you who Labour and are Burdened', 4: 'Awakening and Inward Deepening' IV, extracts (1848)

II. Participation

Just as the motif of the turning of the heart to Christ finds its nineteenth-century home in the growth of Evangelical theology, but is also found in other habitats, so the motif of the mystical or sacramental participation in the life of Christ is found primarily in Catholic sources, but can also be found beyond that—including in the Shakers, and in Evangelicalism.

271   Christ's Second Incarnation

> The Shakers, a pacifist and communistic offshoot of the Quakers, were founded in England in the 1740s, and soon coalesced around Mother Ann Lee (1736–84), a woman whom they believed to be the Second Coming of Christ, this time united to a female form. Here, in a compendium of Shaker theology, this Second Coming is put in the context of the first Church's apostasy. (Cf. **97, 206, 214, 215**.)

Although the 'holy city', or Jewish Christian Church, was trodden down by the Roman Catholic, or fallen Gentile Christian Church (antichrist), yet God, by revelation, raised up in every age of the apostasy male and female witnesses, who, reviving the principles or testimony of the Jewish Christian Church, as already set forth, testified, or witnessed, against the beast and his image, by word and by their lives of innocence. They held no union with church or state; the took no oaths, bore no arms, held no slaves, lived a virgin life, and had all things common.

These were the holy people, whose power was continually scattered by the persecuting arm of antichrist. They were known to their enemies by the term 'heretics', and by historians as Marcionites, Therapeutics, Manicheans, Nestorians, Waldenses, Moravians, etc., and lastly, as Quakers, who, with the exception of a virgin life, embodied more of the principles of the Primitive Church than any other of the witnesses. [. . .]

Out of the last of the witnesses, the Quakers, the 'forty-and-two months' having expired, arose Ann Lee and her little company, to whom Christ appeared the second time, without sin unto salvation, and made a new revelation to her of the seven principles, and of all the truths that had been revealed, in his first appearing, to Jesus; the practice of which constituted him the first Christian Church; and the same principles being reduced to practice by Ann Lee, constituted her the second Christian Church.

The marriage of the Lamb had come, for this wife had made herself ready (thus showing that she was not born ready); and to her was given to be arrayed in fine linen, clean and white; the fine linen was the righteousness of saints, nothing more. Ann, by strictly obeying the light revealed within her, became righteous even as Jesus was righteous. She acknowledged Jesus Christ as her Head and Lord, and formed the same character as a spiritual woman that he formed as a spiritual man.

Ann followed Jesus, not as an imitator [cf. **148, 167**], but through being baptised with, and led by, the same Christ Spirit that he was baptised with and led and guided by. She became a Mother in Israel, and was thenceforth known to her followers (or children) by the endearing name of Mother. Still it was the principles (before explained) that were the foundation of the second Christian Church, and not man or woman, whether Jesus or Ann. Their importance is derived from the fact of their being the first man and first woman perfectly identified with the principles and Spirit of Christ.

F. W. Evans, *Compendium of the Origin, History . . . and Doctrines of the United Society of Believers in Christ's Second Appearing*, ch. 7: 'Rise of the Two Witnesses', 2–3, 10–13 (1859)

272   Incorporation and Unification

Johann Joseph Ignaz von Döllinger (1799–1890) was a Catholic theologian from Bavaria who, influenced by Newman (cf. **258**), became an advocate of liberal reform within the Catholic Church and a critic of the First Vatican Council. He was excommunicated in 1871. (Cf. **34, 38, 112, 206**.)

It is a truth of the utmost fruitfulness and widest application that in consuming the body of Christ we are one body with him. . . . The idea of the sacrifice of the mass is not simply that Christ was offered to God in the sacrifice, but that through the consumption of the body and blood of Christ the whole church is joined into a single body. The fathers already established that in the activity of the eucharist itself we have a symbolic representation of this joining: St Cyprian said that the addition of water to the wine symbolised the uniting of the whole church with the body and blood of Christ. A similar symbolism can also be found in the bread, in the fact that the bread is made from many grains of corn—and that the wine is made from many grapes—which shows well the unification of the church in Christ. As the many grains form one bread, so all faithful form one body with Christ, says Cyprian. This is nothing other than the infusion of one substance into another. . . .

As the church consumes the body of Christ, it becomes united with his body; as Christ is sacrificed, it is offered up with him. The consumption of the holy Lord's Supper is thus an incorporation and unification of individuals and the church with Christ. The faithful who consume the communion all become one body because they consume one and the same body—and this consumed body transforms, in its strength, all of them into one body. . . . It is literally true that we are all members of body of Christ. It is not simply a symbolic expression, it is factually so, that through the communion all are now the body of Christ.

Once this has been firmly established, it is also established that we have to regard the eucharist as a widening and an extension of the incarnation. The Word has become man and has assumed human nature and flesh, precisely in order to transform the whole church in his body and through that to sanctify them and bring them to bliss.

Through this one man, who has been united with God, the uniting of the whole human race shall take place. Christ must therefore become a meal for us, and it is therefore necessary that he change and become edible for us, so Christ gives himself to us under the forms of bread and wine as a meal. This eucharist is therefore a widening, a completion of the incarnation. In the incarnation God anointed the first-born of the human race, namely the man Jesus; now God shall anoint the human race, and this can only happen through the eucharist. Through this the whole mass of the faithful will be anointed. Through the incarnation, the divine nature has descended into a human being; through the eucharist, in turn, the deified man himself descends into all human beings. Through this, he renews, establishes and enlarges the incarnation. It is not therefore simply by the bond of the spiritual body that we all are made into the one body of Christ; it is rather through the consumption of the body of Christ itself. . . . Without this communion, Christ and the faithful are separated; through it they are fused together into one—although in such a way that the faithful take a subordinate place in the body of Christ.

There is a double fashion by which a human being is united with God: on the one hand through the indwelling of the Holy Spirit, who is not only said so to dwell, but really does dwell in human beings; on the other hand, through the consumption of the body of Christ which is a corporeal consumption. This indicates the way in which, under the tutelage of Christ, our body has attained a dignity and an honour which it had lost through sin—and is thus considered worthy of the resurrection and of eternal life. What the indwelling of the Holy Spirit is for the soul, that is the consumption of the Christ in the communion for the body. As Christ is one with the heavenly Father, so will we, through the communion, be one with him and with his Father. Jesus is the mediator between us and the Father.

Johann Joseph Ignaz von Döllinger, Dogmatics, extract (1837–8)

273   Breathing Christ

John Ilyitch Sergieff (1829–1908) was not a monk, and was not a follower of the Jesus Prayer tradition (cf. **269**), but was nevertheless widely admired as a holy man in his native Russia, and in the wider Orthodox world—although not by political radicals, who found him deeply reactionary. It was largely at his prompting that more frequent celebration of the Eucharist became prevalent in Russia. (Cf. **274**.)

In receiving the holy sacrament be as undoubtedly sure you communicate of the body and blood of Christ, as you are sure that every moment you breathe air. Say to yourself, 'As surely as I constantly breathe the air, so surely do I now receive into myself, together with the air, my Lord Jesus Christ himself, my breathing, my life, my joy, my salvation. He is my breath, before air, at every moment of my life; he is my word, before any other word; he is my thought, before any other thought; he is my light, before any other light; he is my meat and drink, before any other meat and drink; he is my raiment before any other raiment; he is my fragrance, before any other fragrance; he is my sweetness, before any other sweetness; he is my father and mother, before any other father and mother; before the earth, he is the firmest ground, that nothing can ever shake and that bears me.' As we, earthly creatures, forget that at all times we breathe, live, move, and exist in him, and have hewed out cisterns, broken cisterns for ourselves, he has opened unto us, in his holy mysteries, in his blood, the source of living water, flowing into life eternal, and gives himself to us as food and drink; in order 'that we may live by him' [Col. 2: 6].

John Ilyitch Sergieff, *My Life in Christ*, extract (early 20th century?)

274   Created for Christ

Edward Payson (1783–1827) was a Congregational minister in Portland, Maine, during the Second Great Awakening. (Cf. **218**.)

If we would view every object in its true light, and rightly estimate its nature and design, we must consider it with reference to Christ and his cross. To the cross of Christ all eternity has looked forward: to the cross of Christ all eternity will look back. The cross of Christ was, if I may so express it, the first object which existed in the divine mind; and with reference to this great object all other objects were created. With reference to the same object they are still preserved. With reference to the same object every event that takes place in heaven, earth and hell, is directed and overruled. Surely then, this object ought to engage our undivided attention. We ought to regard this world merely as a stage, on which the cross of Christ was to be erected, and the great drama of the crucifixion acted [cf. **190**]. We ought to regard all that it contains as only the scenes and draperies necessary for its exhibition. We ought to regard the celestial luminaries merely as lamps, by the light of which this stupendous spectacle may be beheld. We ought to view angels, men and devils as subordinate actors on the stage, and all the commotions and revolutions of the world as subservient to this one grand design. Separate any part of this creation, or any event that has ever taken place, from its relation to Christ, and it dwindles into insignificancy. No sufficient reason can be assigned for its existence, and it appears to have been formed in vain. But when viewed as connected with him, every thing becomes important; every thing then appears to be a part of one grand, systematic, harmonious whole; a whole worthy of him that formed it. [. . .]

From this subject, my Christian friends, you may learn what reason you have for gratitude and joy. You, as well as all other objects and beings, were created for Christ. You were created on purpose to promote his glory and execute his will. Nay more, you were created on purpose to be his servants, his friends, his members; you were created that he might redeem you by his blood, sanctify you by his grace, dwell in you by his spirit, form in you his image, raise you to heaven by his power, and show forth the unsearchable riches of his glory in you as vessels of mercy, through eternity. You were created that at the last day, Christ, your exalted redeemer and Lord may be glorified in you as his work, and admired, as he will be, in all them that believe. You were created, that like so many planets, you may revolve around Christ the Sun of Righteousness [cf. **220**], drink in light, and love, and glory, from his beams, and reflect those beams to the admiring eyes of fellow saints and angels forever and ever. Yes, these are the great and benevolent purposes for which you were created and destined; you were beloved with an everlasting love; and with loving kindness you were drawn to Christ, that these purposes might be fulfilled. And they shall be all fulfilled. They are the purposes of him with whom designs and actions are the same; who never changes, and who will not, cannot, be disappointed.

Edward Payson, 'Sermon III: All Things Created for Christ' (early 19th century)

275   Representing the King

Catherine Mumford Booth (1829–1890) was a devout Christian with a strong social conscience, a fierce commitment to temperance, and a gift for eloquent preaching who founded with her husband the movement which was to become the Salvation Army. This extract is from an address preached in London in 1880, taken down by a shorthand writer. (Cf. **19**.)

God needs witnesses in this world. Why? Because the whole world is in revolt against him. The world has gone away from God. The world ignores God, denies and contradicts his testimony, misunderstands his character, government, and purposes, and is gone off into utter and universal revolt and rebellion. Now if God is to keep any hold upon man at all, and have any influence with him, he must be represented down here. There was no other way of doing it. If a province of this realm were in anarchy and rebellion, unless there be some persons in the province whose duty it is to represent the King and his Government, it will lapse altogether and be lost to the kingdom for ever. So God must be represented, and, praise his name, he has had his faithful witnesses from the beginning until now. As the apostle says—He left not himself without witness. Down from the days of Enoch, who walked with God, to this present hour, God has always had his true and faithful witnesses. In the worst times there have been some burning and shining lights. Sometimes few and far between, sometimes, like Noah, one solitary man in a whole generation of men, witnessing for God—but one, at least, there has been. God has not left himself without witness.

But Jesus Christ the Son—the well-beloved of the Father—he was the great witness. He came especially to manifest, to testify of, and to reveal the Father to men. This was his great work. He came not to testify of himself, but of his Father; not to speak his own words, but the words his Father gave him to speak. He came to reveal God to men. He was the 'faithful and true witness' [Rev. 3: 14]. And when he had to leave the world and go back to his Father, then he commissioned his disciples to take his place, and to be God's witnesses on earth. And Oh! friends, God's real people are his only witnesses. He will not allow angels—we do not know why—to witness for him here. He has called man to witness for him—his people—'Ye shall be witnesses unto me' [19].

Jesus witnessed a good confession, did he not? He witnessed nobly, consistently, bravely of his Father, and sealed his testimony with his blood. The world treated him as it has treated most of God's faithful witnesses from the beginning: it persecuted him; it slew him, as it would every faithful witness for God—if God allowed it—and would leave itself without a single spiritual light: for the spirit that worketh in the children of disobedience hath an eternal and devilish hatred of every real, living, spiritual child of God. It hates him as it hates the Son himself, and it is not the Devil's fault if he does not extinguish and exterminate every such witness. It is because God will not allow him, but holds us, keeps us, saves us, in spite of him.

The Lord commissioned, then, his disciples to be his witnesses, and he said—oh! beautiful words, and yet, how much they involve which few understand—'As thou hast sent me into the world, even so send I them into the world' [John 17: 18]. Even so: as thou hast sent me to be thy representative in the world, to spend and be spent for thee, and shed my blood for thee; if necessary, so send I them; and so he did send them, and they had just the same fare as their Master, and many of them just the same end. But they were faithful witnesses, and they went forward and testified everywhere, to the Jews and to the Gentiles, in the Temple and in the Market Place, by the wayside and in the highways and hedges—they went and testified of this Saviour, and charged the wicked Jews with his crucifixion, and God accompanied their testimony by the Spirit, and thousands upon thousands were converted—turned from their rebellion to God.

Catherine Mumford Booth, *Papers on Aggressive Christianity*, 'Witnessing for Christ',
extract (1880)

276 A Vocation of Love

Thérèse of Lisieux (1873–97) entered a Carmelite convent when only 15, and remained with them until dying of tuberculosis nine years later. In that time, she deeply impressed those around her with her devotion, and was asked to write her autobiography describing a life of constant, joyful small-scale renunciations. She was canonized in 1925, and has become extraordinarily popular, particularly in France.

To be thy spouse, O my Jesus, to be a daughter of Carmel, and by my union with thee to be the mother of souls, should not all this content me? Yet other vocations make themselves felt, and I would wield the sword, I would be a priest, an apostle, a martyr, a doctor of the church, I would accomplish the most heroic deeds—the spirit of the crusader burns within me and I would gladly die on the battlefield in defence of the church.

The vocation of the priesthood! With what love, my Jesus, would I bear thee in my hand when my words brought thee down from heaven! With what love, too, would I give thee to the faithful! And yet, with all my longing to be a priest, I admire and envy the humility of St Francis of Assisi [cf. **127**] and feel myself drawn to imitate him by refusing that sublime dignity. How can these opposite desires be reconciled?

Like the prophets and doctors, I would be a light unto souls. I would travel the world over to preach thy name, O my Beloved, and raise on heathen soil the glorious standard of the cross. One mission alone would not satisfy my longings. I would spread the gospel in all parts of the earth, even to the farthest isles. I would be a missionary, but not for a few years only. Were it possible, I should wish to have been one from the world's creation and to remain one till the end of time.

But the greatest of all my desires is to win the martyr's palm. Martyrdom was the dream of my youth, and the dream has only grown more vivid in

Carmel's narrow cell. Yet this too is folly, since to slake my thirst for suffering, not one but every kind of torture would be needful. Like thee, O my adorable Spouse, I would be scourged, I would be crucified! I would be flayed like St Bartholomew, plunged into boiling oil like St John, or, like St Ignatius of Antioch [cf. **67**], ground by the teeth of wild beasts into a bread worthy of God. [. . .] With St Agnes and St Cecilia I would offer my neck to the sword of the executioner, and like Joan of Arc murmur the name of Jesus at the burning stake. When I think of the fearful torments awaiting Christians at the time of antichrist, my heart thrills within me and I wish those torments could be reserved for me. Open, O Jesus, the book of life, in which are written the deeds of all thy saints: each one of those deeds I long to accomplish for thee. [. . .]

As I meditated on the mystical body of the church I could not recognise myself among any of its members described by St Paul [cf. **34**], or was it not rather that I wished to recognise myself in all? Charity gave me the key to *my vocation*. I understood that since the church is a body composed of different members, she could not lack the most necessary and most nobly endowed of all the bodily organs. I understood, therefore, that the church has a *heart*—and a heart on fire with love. I saw, too, that love alone imparts life to all the members, so that should love ever fail, apostles would no longer preach the gospel and martyrs would refuse to shed their blood. Finally, I realised that love includes every vocation, that love is all things, that love is eternal, reaching down through the ages and stretching to the uttermost limits of the earth.

Beside myself with joy, I cried out: 'O Jesus, my love, my vocation is found at last—my vocation is love!' I have found my place in the heart of the church, and this place, O my God, thou hast thyself given to me: in the heart of the church, my mother, *I will be love!* Thus shall I be all things and my dream will be fulfilled.

Thérèse of Lisieux, *Autobiography* ch. 13: 'A Canticle of Love', extracts (posthumously pub. 1899)

Section E

Looking Eastwards

The extension of Western empires in the East led to an ever greater encounter between Christianity and Eastern religions and cultures. The encounter could take many forms from the irenic to the violent, from liberation to imposition. In order to illustrate the range of possibilities, we have chosen to focus upon India, and on the encounter between Christ and Hinduism which was fostered there.

277 Returning Christ Eastwards

> Keshub Chunder Sen (1838–84) was a leader of the reformist Brahmo-Samaj movement within Hinduism. Influenced by Christian missionaries, and by the writings of Theodore Parker (cf. 260), he proposed a return to a purer, more universal Hinduism, open to Jesus of Nazareth. (Cf. 337.)

England has sent unto us, after all, a Western Christ. This is indeed to be regretted. Our countrymen find that in this Christ, sent by England, there is something that is not quite congenial to the native mind, not quite acceptable to the genius of the nation. It seems that the Christ that has come to us is an Englishman, with English manners and customs about him, and with the temper and spirit of an Englishman in him. Hence is it that the Hindu people shrink back and say: who is this revolutionary reformer who is trying to sap the very foundations of native society, and establish here an outlandish faith and civilisation quite incompatible with oriental instincts and ideas? Why must we submit to one who is of a different nationality? Why must we bow before a foreign prophet? It is a fact which cannot be gainsaid that hundreds upon hundreds, thousands upon thousands, even among the most intelligent in the land, stand back in moral recoil from this picture of a foreign Christianity trying to invade and subvert Hindu society; and this repugnance unquestionably hinders the progress of the true spirit of Christianity in this country. When they feel that Christ means nothing but the worst form of denationalisation, the whole nation must certainly as one man stand up to repudiate and banish this acknowledgement of evil. But why should you Hindus go to England to learn Jesus Christ? Is not his native land nearer to India than England? Is he not, and are not his apostles and immediate followers more akin to Indian nationality than Englishmen? Are not the scenes enacted in the drama of the Christian dispensation altogether homely to us

Indians? When we hear of the lily, and the sparrow, and the well, and a hundred other things of Eastern countries, do we not feel we are quite at home in the Holy Land? Why should we then travel to a distant country like England, in order to gather truths, which are to be found much nearer our homes? Gentlemen, go to the rising sun in the East, not to the setting sun in the West, if you wish to see Christ in the plenitude of his glory and in the fullness and freshness of his divine life. Why do I speak of Christ in the West as the setting sun? Because there we find apostolical Christianity almost gone; there we find the life of Christ formulated into lifeless dogmas and antiquated symbols. But if you go to the true Christ in the East and his apostles, you are at once seized with inspiration. You find the truths of Christianity all fresh and resplendent. Recall to your minds, gentlemen, the true Asiatic Christ, divested of all western appendages, carrying on the work of redemption among his own people. Behold, he cometh to us in his loose flowing garment, his dress and features altogether oriental, a perfect Asiatic in every-thing. Watch his movements, and you will find genuine orientalism in all his habits and manners,—in his uprising and down-sitting, his going forth and his coming in, his preaching and ministry, his very language and style and tone. Indeed, while reading the Gospel, we cannot but feel that we are quite at home when we are with Jesus and that he is altogether one of us. Surely Jesus is *our* Jesus. [. . .]

It appears to me that Christ held earnestly and consistently what I should, in the absence of a better expression, call the doctrine of divine humanity. He not only believed this, but he carried it, theoretically and practically, to its uttermost logical sequence. I am satisfied that in Christ Jesus there was an abundance of philosophy and logic, before which even the proudest philosophy of modern times must hide her face in the very shame. From his very early life he seized this great and philosophical idea of divine humanity, and throughout his career he carried it out, with wonderful logical consist-ency, in all its bearings, speculative and practical. This doctrine he realised in its fullest measure in his own consciousness, and therefore he never made a secret of it, but fearlessly proclaimed it in the streets, and tried to make converts to the new doctrine wherever he went. How did he enunciate this principle? Christ struck the key-note of his doctrine when he announced his divinity before an astonished and amazed world in these words 'I and my Father are one' [John 10: 30]. [. . .]

When I come to analyse this doctrine, I find in it nothing but the philo-sophical principle underlying the popular doctrine of self-abnegation—self-abnegation in a very lofty spiritual sense. 'I and my Father are one.' These words clearly mean—if you would only exercise the smallest amount of reflection, they would clearly appear to you to mean—nothing more than the highest form of self-denial. Christ ignored and denied his self altogether; we, on the contrary, have each our hard selfishness, and it is our desire and interests to serve and gratify it heartily. All the pursuits of our lives, our affections, our associations, our daily thoughts, and feelings, our hopes and aspirations gather round this central self. *I* think, *I* preach, *I* am a true man and a right man. This is *my* virtue, that is *my* holiness, this is *my* charity, that is *my* prayer. You have given this unto *me*. You cannot take it away from *me*. These are selfish ideas which prevail universally among mankind, and constitute the real danger of society and the root of our sins and wickednesses. Upon these shoals many a life has been wrecked, and many a life is being wrecked every day. Self must be extinguished and eradicated completely. Christ said so, and Christ did so. He destroyed self. And as self ebbed away, heaven came pouring into the soul. For, as you all know, nature abhors a vacuum, and hence as soon as the soul is emptied of self divinity fills the void. So it was with Christ. The Spirit of the Lord filled him, and everything was thus divine within him.

Keshub Chunder Sen, *India Asks: Who is Christ?*, extracts (1879)

278 Translating Christ

Brahmabandhab Upadhyay (1861–1907) was a fiery Indian holy man who mixed Christianity and Hinduism, and who played a vital role in India's struggle for independence. (Cf. **279**.)

We Christians believe that the Logos [cf. **66**], the eternal image of the Father, became incarnate, that is, united himself to a human nature created and so adapted as to be wedded to divinity.

The Christian doctrine of incarnation needs elucidation to be properly appreciated. I shall try to make it explicit in a way familiar to the Hindu mind.

According to the Vedanta, human nature is composed of five sheaths or divisions (*kosha*). They are: (1) physical (*annamaya*), which grows by assimilation; (2) vital (*pranamaya*); (3) mental (*mano-maya*), through which are perceived relations of things: (4) intellectual (*vijnanamaya*), through which is apprehended the origin of being; and (5) spiritual (*anandamaya*), through which is felt the delight of the supreme reality. These five sheaths are presided over by a personality (*ahampratyayin*) which knows itself. This self-knowing individual (*jivacaitanya*) is but a reflected spark of the supreme reason (*kutastha-caitanya*), who abides in every man as the prime source of life and light. The time-incarnate divinity is also composed of five sheaths; but it is presided over by the Person of the Logos himself and not by any created personality (*aham*). The five sheaths and the individual agent, enlivened and illuminated by divine reason, who resides in a special manner in the temple of humanity, make up man. But in the God-man the five sheaths are acted upon direct by the Logos-God and not through the medium of any individuality. The Incarnation was thus accomplished by uniting humanity with divinity in the person of the Logos. This incarnate God in man we call Jesus Christ. He took flesh from the womb of a spotless, immaculate Virgin for the formation of his body. As the first man (*adi-purusa*) was produced by divine *samkalpa* (will) so was the body of Jesus Christ, whom we hold to be the *adi-purusa* of the spiritual world, formed by the power of the Spirit of God and not by the usual process of procreation. Jesus Christ is God by the necessity of his being, but he became man of his own free choice. His birth did not depend upon man's will. It was compassion for us which made him our brother, like us in sorrow and suffering, but without sin. Jesus Christ is perfectly divine and perfectly human. He is the incarnate Logos.

I beg to present readers [...] with the following Sanskrit hymn I have composed in praise of the incarnate Logos:

The transcendent Image of Brahman blossomed and mirrored in the full-to--
    overflowing (*upacita*), eternal knowledge (*ciracit*): Victory be to God, the God-man.
Child of the pure Virgin, director of the universe, absolute, yet charming with
    relations: Victory be to God, the God-man.
Ornament of the assembly of the learned, destroyer of fear, chastiser of the spirit of
    wickedness: Victory be to God, the God-man.
Dispeller of spiritual and physical infirmities, ministering unto others, one whose
    actions and doings are sanctifying: Victory be to God, the God-man.
One who has offered up his agony, whose life is sacrifice, destroyer of the poison of
    sin: Victory be to God, the God-man.
Tender, beloved, charmer of the heart, soothing pigment of the eye, crusher of fierce
    death; Victory be to God, the God-man.

Brahmabandhab Upadhyay, 'The Incarnate Logos' (1901)

279   Incorporating Christ

Swami Vivekananda (1803–1902) was a disciple of Sri Ramakrishna. On his master's death he took up his mission on a national and international stage. Internationally, he rose to fame after addressing the Parliament of Religions in Chicago in 1893; nationally, he was a tireless worker for the renewal of India. (Cf. 335–7.)

What you see in the life of Christ is the life of all the past. The life of every man is, in a manner, the life of the past. It comes to him through heredity, through surroundings, through education, through his own reincarnation—the past of the race. In a manner, the past of the earth, the past of the whole world is there, upon every soul. What are we, in the present, but a result, an effect, in the hands of that infinite past? What are we but floating wavelets in the eternal current of events, irresistibly moved forward and onward and incapable of rest? But you and I are only little things, bubbles. There are always some giant waves in the ocean of affairs, and in you and me the life of the past race has been embodied only a little; but there are giants who embody, as it were, almost the whole of the past and who stretch out their hands for the future. These are the sign-posts here and there which point to the march of humanity; these are verily gigantic, their shadows covering the earth—they stand undying, eternal! As it has been said by the Messenger, 'No man hath seen God at any time, but through the Son' [John 6: 46]. And that is true. And where shall we see God but in the Son? It is true that you and I, and the poorest of us, the meanest even, embody that God, even reflect that God. The vibration of light is everywhere, omnipresent; but we have to strike the light of the lamp before we can see the light. The omnipresent God of the universe cannot he seen until he is reflected by these giant lamps of the earth—the prophets, the man-Gods, the incarnations, the embodiments of God.

We all know that God exists, and yet we do not see him, we do not understand him. Take one of these great Messengers of light, compare his character with the highest ideal of God that you ever formed, and you will find that your God falls short of the ideal, and that the character of the prophet exceeds your conceptions. You cannot even form a higher ideal of God than what the actually embodied have practically realised and set before us as an example. Is it wrong, therefore, to worship these as God? Is it a sin to fall at the feet of these man-Gods and worship them as the only divine beings in the world? If they are really, actually, higher than all our conceptions of God, what harm is there in worshipping them? Not only is there no harm, but it is the possible and positive way of worship. However much you may try by struggle, by abstraction, by whatsoever method you like, still so long as you are a man in the world of men, your world is human, your religion is human, your God is human. And that must be so. Who is not practical enough to take up an actually existing thing and give up an idea which is only an abstraction, which he cannot grasp, and is difficult of approach except through a concrete medium? Therefore, these incarnations of God have been worshipped in all ages and in all countries. [. . .]

Let us, therefore, find God not only in Jesus of Nazareth but in all the great ones that have preceded him, in all that came after him, and all that are yet to come. Our worship is unbounded and free. They are all manifestations of the same infinite God. They are all pure and unselfish; they struggled and gave up their lives for us, poor human beings. They each and all suffer vicarious atonement for every one of us, and also for all that are to come hereafter.

In a sense you are all prophets; every one of you is a prophet, bearing the burden of the world on your own shoulders. Have you ever seen a man, have you ever seen a woman, who is not quietly, patiently, bearing his or her little burden of life? The great prophets were giants—they bore a gigantic world on their shoulders. Compared with them we are pygmies, no doubt, yet we are doing the same task in our little circles, in our little homes, we are bearing our little crosses. There is no one so evil, no one so worthless, but he has to bear his own cross. But with all our mistakes, with all our evil thoughts and evil deeds, there is a bright spot somewhere, there is still somewhere the golden thread through which we are always in touch with the divine. For, know for certain, that the moment the touch of the divine is lost there would be annihilation. And because none can be annihilated, there is always somewhere in our heart of hearts, however low and degraded we may be, a little circle of light which is in constant touch with the divine.

Swami Vivekananda, Christ the Messenger, extracts (1900)

280   Embracing Christ

Pandita Ramabai (1838–1922) was born in a Hindu family and, exceptionally for a girl, was taught to read and write. A widowed single mother by the age of 22, she travelled to England and found a refuge with the Sisters of Wantage. Baptized under their influence, she returned to India and established an educational and reforming mission to women in 1889. (Cf. **268**.)

I do not know if any one of my readers has ever had the experience of being shut up in a room where there was nothing but thick darkness and then groping in it to find something of which he or she was in dire need. I can think of no one but the blind man, whose story is given in St. John chapter nine. He was born blind and remained so for forty years of his life; and then suddenly he found the mighty one, who could give him eyesight. Who could have described his joy at seeing the daylight, when there had not been a particle of hope of his ever seeing it? Even the inspired evangelist has not attempted to do it. I can give only a faint idea of what I felt when my mental eyes were opened, and when I, who was 'sitting in darkness saw great light,' and when I felt sure that to me, who but a few moments ago 'sat in the region and shadow of death, light *had* sprung up' [Isa. 9: 2]. I was very like the man who was told, 'In the name of Jesus Christ of Nazareth rise up and walk. . . . And he leaping up stood, and walked, and entered with them into the temple, walking and leaping and praising God' [Acts 3: 8].

I looked to the blessed Son of God who was lifted up on the cross and there suffered death, even the death of the cross, in my stead, that I might be made free from the bondage of sin, and from the fear of death, and I received life. O the love, the unspeakable love of the Father for me, a lost sinner, which gave his only Son to die for me! I had not merited this love, but that was the very reason why he showed it to me.

How very different the truth of God was from the false idea that I had entertained from my earliest childhood. That was that I must have merit to earn present or future happiness, the pleasure of Svarga, or face the utterly inconceivable loss of Moksha [. . .]. This I could never hope for, since a woman, as a woman, has no hope of Moksha according to Hindu religion. The Brahman priests have tried to deceive the women and the Shudras and other low-caste people into the belief that they have some hope. But when we study for ourselves the books of the religious law and enquire from the higher authorities we find that there is nothing, no nothing whatever for us.

They say that women and Shudras and other low-caste people can gain Svarga by serving the husband and the Brahman. But the happiness of Svarga does not last long. The final blessed state to which the Brahman is entitled is not for women and low-caste people. But here this blessed nook, the Christians' Bible says, 'When we were yet without strength, in due time Christ died for the ungodly. For scarcely for a righteous man will one die: yet peradventure for a good man some would even dare to die. But God commendeth his love toward us, in that, while we were yet sinners Christ died for us. . . . For . . . when we were enemies, we were reconciled to God by the death of his Son' [Rom. 5: 8–10]. 'In this was manifested the love of God toward us, because that God sent his only begotten Son into the world, that we might live through him. Herein is love, not that we loved God, but that he loved us, and sent his Son to be the propitiation for our sins' [1 John 4: 9–10].

How good, how indescribably good! What good news for me a woman, a woman born in India, among Brahmans who hold out no hope for me and the like of me! The Bible declares that Christ did not reserve this great salvation for a particular caste or sex. 'But as many as received him, to them gave he power to become the sons of God, even to them that believe on his name: which were born, not of blood, nor of the will of the flesh, nor of the will of man, but of God' [66]. 'For the grace of God that bringeth salvation hath appeared to all men' [Titus 2: 11]. 'The kindness and love of God our Saviour toward man appeared, not by works of righteousness which we have done, but according to his mercy he saved us' [Titus 3: 4].

No caste, no sex, no work, and no man was to be depended upon to get salvation, this everlasting life, but God gave it freely to any one and every one who believed on his Son whom he sent to be the 'propitiation for our sins.' And there was not a particle of doubt left as to whether this salvation was a present one or not. I had not to wait till after undergoing births and deaths for countless millions of times, when I should become a Brahman man, in order to get to know the Brahma. And then, was there any joy and happiness to be hoped for? No, there is nothing but to be amalgamated into Nothingness-Shunya, Brahma.

Pandita Ramabai, A Testimony, extract (1907)

PART 7

The Twentieth Century: 1914–2000

The twentieth century was a dark century, born in the trenches of the First World War and coming of age in the concentration camps of the Holocaust. It saw, on a greater scale than ever before, genocide, the use of weapons of mass destruction, ethnic cleansing, and the spread of state-sponsored torture. The twentieth century was also a turbulent century, witnessing revolutions in Russia, China, Iran, and elsewhere; the rise and collapse of Soviet communism; the inexorable spread of the multinationals and global capitalism; the proliferation of nationalisms. Where was Jesus of Nazareth in the twentieth century?

In Europe the First World War signalled the death of nineteenth-century cultural confidence; the assurance of men like Herrmann (cf. **256**) and Harnack (cf. **262**) was swept away as their culture—which seemed in their theology almost coterminous with the influence of Christ—descended into barbarism. Men like Karl Barth (cf. **281**), with a starker, more uncomfortable vision, took their place; and the judgement pronounced by Christ on human confidence, the demands that he made on human life, moved to centre-stage. There was a shift away from what seemed to many to be the idle and unsatisfiable curiosity of the quest for the historical Jesus, and a turn to examine the perennially challenging proclamation of early Christianity, a message which called across the centuries for human beings to repent.

Intermingled with this shift, another development shaped mainstream European theology. The Russian Revolution sent a wave of émigrés across Europe and America, bringing Orthodox and Western theology into dialogue again. Among other benefits, this dialogue brought the Orthodox theology of the patristic and early Byzantine period into renewed prominence in theological debates. This renewal went along with a return to the dogmatic theology of Protestant orthodoxy insti-gated by Karl Barth (cf. **318**), and a return to the riches of medieval theology sealed by the Second Vatican Council in Roman Catholic theology (cf. **296**). The Trinitarian Christology of many earlier ages, all but abandoned by Enlightenment and nineteenth-century theologians, has once again begun to be heard (cf. **329–333**).

The same Russian Revolution made the demand for an alternative to Western capitalism difficult to ignore. When Vatican II (**296**) was called to reform the Roman Catholic Church further, one of its aims was to attempt a Christian response to Marxism; to attempt to show again how Christianity had its own proper concern for the poor and disfranchised, its own guidelines for the reformation of society. In its wake, in South America and beyond, liberation theologies sprang up as Catholic priests and theologians put the solidarity of Christ with the poor at the heart of their projects (cf. 300–1).

Images of Christ were also found on both sides of other struggles for liberation. Feminist theologians debated the significance of a male Saviour (e.g. 326–8); black theologians pushed at the idol of the 'white Christ' which had been imposed on them (e.g. 306); theologians in the countries newly independent from the European empires rediscovered the oppressed Eastern Jesus under the Western Christ they had been taught (e.g. 293, 304, 303).

In terms of sheer numbers, and in terms of energy, the centre of gravity of Christianity shifted ever further from Western Europe. The diverse vitality of Christianity in the United States (most noticeably, but not exclusively, in the strength of conservative and fundamentalist Protestant denominations) pulled the centre of gravity towards North America, but it is Africa which has seen the most dynamic growth of Christianity (as well as of Islam), with South America and Asia close behind. At the end of the century Western Christians were hardly even beginning to come to terms with their steady relegation to backwater status in global Christianity. The changing colour of the face of Christ is only just becoming visible in the West.

Various forms of Pentecostalism, Evangelicalism, and 'fundamentalism' (e.g. 291–2, 302, 325) spread with enormous vitality, dwarfing most of the older Protestant denominations—and not just in the developing world. If, for instance, one searches for representations of Jesus on the Internet, the overwhelming majority of sites that one finds come from individuals and groups in these growing churches.

In all this diversity, as the feminist Christ, the black Christ, the poor Christ, the Pentecostal Christ, the evangelical Christ vie with older representations in a seething mix which is almost impossible to map, one other development has emerged which may well be the most significant of them all. In the century which opened with casual anti-Semitism ingrained across the West, the century which saw at its heart the most violent and wholesale explosion of anti-Semitism yet perpetrated, Jesus the Jew has begun to reappear from under centuries of disguise (e.g. 287, 288, 340). The executed healer and preacher with whom this whole tale began has looked at us again with Jewish eyes, demanding that we take account of him.

Section A

Crisis

281 Christ the Crisis

Twentieth-century theology began with a rejection, powered by the horrors of the First World War, of all that mainstream nineteenth-century theology had valued as it flowed from the confident pens of men like Harnack (cf. **262**), Herrmann (cf. **256**), and Schleiermacher (cf. **255**). Karl Barth, one of the greatest of twentieth century theologians (cf. **318**), insisted in his epoch-making commentary on Paul's Letter to the Romans that the 'Yes' pronounced to humanity in salvation was inseparable from God's shattering 'No', God's judgement on all confidence human beings might have in progress, in human culture, in moral development, in all religiosity.

Romans 3: 22a: The righteousness of God is manifested through his faithfulness in Jesus Christ.[1]

The faithfulness of God is the divine patience according to which he provides, at sundry times and at many divers points in human history, occasions and possibilities and witnesses of the knowledge of his righteousness. *Jesus* of Nazareth is the point at which it can be seen that all the other points form one line of supreme significance. He is the point at which is perceived the crimson thread which runs through all history. *Christ*—the righteousness of God himself—is the theme of this perception.

The faithfulness of God and Jesus the Christ confirm one another. The faithfulness of God is established when we meet the Christ in Jesus. Consequently, in spite of all our inadequacy, we are able to recognise the veritable possibility of the action of God in all his divers witnesses in history; consequently also, we are able to discover in the traces of the righteousness of God in the world more than mere chance occurrences, and are in a position to see that our own position in time is pregnant with eternal promise, if—nay, because! —we meet truth of another order at one point in time, at one place in that time which is illuminated throughout by reality and by the answer of God. The Day of Jesus Christ is the Day of all days; the brilliant and visible light of this one point is the hidden invisible light of all points; to perceive the righteousness of God once and for all here is the hope of righteousness everywhere and at all times. By the knowledge of Jesus Christ all human waiting is guaranteed, authorised, and established; for he makes it known that it is not men who wait, but God—in his faithfulness. Our discovery of the Christ in Jesus of Nazareth is authorised by the fact that every manifestation of the faithfulness of God points and bears witness to what we have actually encountered in Jesus. The hidden authority of the Law and the Prophets is the Christ who meets us in Jesus.

Redemption and resurrection, the invisibility of God and a new order, constitute the meaning of every religion; and it is precisely this that compels us to stand still in the presence of Jesus. All human activity is a cry for forgiveness; and it is precisely this that is proclaimed by Jesus and that appears concretely in him. The objection that this hidden power of forgiveness and, in fact, the whole subject-matter of religion, is found elsewhere, is wholly wide of the mark, since it is precisely we who have been enabled to make this claim. In Jesus we have discovered and recognised the truth that God is found everywhere and that, both before and after Jesus, men have been discovered by him. In him we have found the standard by which all discovery of God and all being discovered by him is made known as such; in him we recognise that this finding and being found is the truth of the order of eternity. Many live their lives in the light of redemption and forgiveness and resurrection; but that we have eyes to see their manner of life we owe to the One. In his light we see light. That it is the Christ whom we have encountered in Jesus is guaranteed by our finding in him the sharply defined, final interpretation of the Word of the faithfulness of God to which the Law and the Prophets bore witness.

His entering within the deepest darkness of human ambiguity and abiding within it is *the* faithfulness. The life of Jesus is perfected obedience to the will of the faithful God. Jesus stands among sinners as a sinner; he sets himself wholly under the judgement under which the world is set; he takes his place where God can be present only in questioning about him; he takes the form of a slave; he moves to the cross and to death; his greatest achievement is a negative achievement. He is not a genius, endowed with manifest or even with occult powers; he is not a hero or leader of men; he is neither poet nor thinker—*My God, my God, why hast thou forsaken me?* Nevertheless, precisely in this negation, he is the fulfilment of every possibility of human progress, as the Prophets and the Law conceive of progress and evolution, because he sacrifices to the incomparably Greater and to the invisibly Other every claim to genius and every human heroic or aesthetic or psychic possibility, because there is no conceivable human possibility of which he did not rid himself. Herein he is recognised as the Christ; for this reason God hath exalted him; and consequently he is the light of the Last Things by which all men and all things are illuminated. In him we behold the faithfulness of God in the depths of Hell. The Messiah is the end of mankind, and here also God is found faithful. On the day when mankind is dissolved the new era of the righteousness of God will be inaugurated.

Romans 3: 22b: Unto all them that believe.

Here is the necessary qualification. The vision of the New Day remains an indirect vision; in Jesus revelation is a paradox, however objective and universal it may be. That the promises of the faithfulness of God have been fulfilled in Jesus the Christ is not, and never will be, a self-evident truth, since in him it appears in its final hiddenness and its most profound secrecy. The truth, in fact, can never be self-evident, because it is a matter neither of historical nor of psychological experience, and because it is neither a cosmic happening within the natural order, nor even the most supreme event of our imaginings. Therefore it is not accessible to our perception: it can neither be dug out of what is unconsciously within us, nor apprehended by devout contemplation, nor made known by the manipulation of occult psychic powers. These exercises, indeed, render it the more inaccessible. It can neither be taught nor handed down by tradition, nor is it a subject of research. Were it capable of such treatment, it would not be universally significant, it would not be the righteousness of God for the whole world, salvation for all men.

Faith is conversion: it is the radically new disposition of the man who stands naked before God and has been wholly impoverished that he may procure the one pearl of great price; it is the attitude of the man who for the sake of Jesus has lost his own soul. Faith is the faithfulness of God, ever secreted in and beyond all human ideas and affirmations about him, and beyond every positive religious achievement. There is no such thing as mature and assured possession of faith: regarded psychologically, it is always a leap into the darkness of the unknown, a flight into empty air. Faith is not revealed to us by flesh and blood: no one can communicate it to himself or to any one else. What I heard yesterday I must hear again to-day; and if I am to hear it afresh tomorrow, it must be revealed by the Father of Jesus, who is in heaven, and by him only.

The revelation which is in Jesus, because it is the revelation of the righteousness of God, must be the most complete veiling of his incomprehensibility. In Jesus, God becomes veritably a secret: he is made known as the Unknown, speaking in eternal silence; he protects himself from every intimate companionship and from all the impertinence of religion. He becomes a scandal to the Jews and to the Greeks foolishness. In Jesus the communication of God begins with a rebuff, with the exposure of a vast chasm, with the clear revelation of a great stumbling-block. 'Remove from the Christian Religion, as Christendom has done, its ability to shock, and Christianity, by becoming a direct communication, is altogether destroyed. It then becomes a tiny superficial thing, capable neither of inflicting deep wounds nor of healing them; by discovering an unreal and merely human compassion, it forgets the qualitative distinction between man and God' [270].

Faith in Jesus, like its theme, the righteousness of God, is the radical 'Nevertheless'. Faith in Jesus is to feel and comprehend the unheard of 'loveless' love of God, to do the ever scandalous and outrageous will of God, to call upon God in his incomprehensibility and hiddenness. To believe in Jesus is the most hazardous of all hazards. This 'Nevertheless', this unheard of action, this hazard, is the road to which we direct men. We demand faith, no more and no less; and we make this demand, not in our own name, but in the name of Jesus, in whom we have encountered it irresistibly. We do not demand belief in our faith; for we are aware that, in so far as faith originates in us, it is unbelievable. We do not demand from others our faith; if others are to believe, they must do so, as we do, entirely at their own risk and because of the promise. We demand faith in Jesus; and we make this demand here and now upon all, whatever may be the condition of life in which they find themselves. There are, however, no preliminaries necessary to faith, no required standard of education or intelligence, no peculiar temper of mind or heart, no special economic status. There are no human avenues of approach, no 'way of salvation'; to faith there is no ladder which must be first scaled. Faith is its own initiation, its own presupposition. Upon whatever rung of the ladder of human life men may happen to be standing—whether they be Jews or Greeks, old or young, educated or uneducated, complex or simple—in tribulation or in repose they are capable of faith. The demand of faith passes diagonally across every type of religious or moral temperament, across every experience of life, through every department of intellectual activity, and through every social class. For all faith is both simple and difficult; for all alike it is a scandal, a hazard, a 'Nevertheless'; to all it presents the same embarrassment and the same promise; for all it is a leap into the void. And it is possible for all, only because for all it is equally impossible.

Karl Barth, The Epistle to the Romans, ch. 3: 'The Righteousness of God', on 3: 22 (1921)

Section B

The Historical Jesus?

The quest for the historical Jesus, pursued so vigorously in the nineteenth century and dissected so mercilessly by Albert Schweitzer (cf. **243**) at the beginning of the twentieth, has had a chequered history since 1914. For much of the first half of the century it seemed as if the champions of academic theology had declared the quest over, its grail unattainable. Yet in the second half of the century there were repeated calls to take up arms again on the quest and pursue it on a new basis, or with a new sophistication. A 'second' quest was proclaimed, and then a 'third'—and life of Jesus research at the turn to the twenty-first century appeared as lively as at any time during the nineteenth.

I. Against History?

By the early twentieth century many theologians had become convinced that little or nothing of the Gospel depiction of Jesus of Nazareth could survive the fires of historical criticism with certainty. The attempts to peel back the teaching and the preaching of the early Church to find the original Jesus underneath had failed, leaving us simply with an enigma (cf. **243**). In New Testament scholarship the most prominent version of this claim was made by those who, following Martin Kähler (cf. **257**), said that, in any case, the quest had been wrong-headed; the teaching and preaching of the early Church conveys the *impact* that Jesus had upon his time and upon subsequent generations, and it is the spreading and passing on of that impact in which we should be interested, for Christians believe it was the work of God. As we shall see, however, this sceptical solution did not gain everyone's support.

282   The Message not the Man

Rudolf Bultmann (1884–1976) was the most influential New Testament scholar of the twentieth century. He drew upon form-critical techniques[2] to uncover the basic message of early Christianity: the call to existential decision for or against Christ crucified. He elaborated this call, and translated it from the 'mythological' language of the Bible (cf. **237**) into terms relevant to 'modern man', with the help of Martin Heidegger's philosophy.

However good the reasons for being interested in the personalities of significant historical figures, Plato or Jesus, Dante or Luther, Napoleon or Goethe, it still remains true that this interest does not touch that which such men had at heart; for *their* interest was not in their personality but in their *work*. And their work was to them not the expression of their personality, nor something through which their personality achieved its 'form', but the cause to which they surrendered their lives. Moreover, their work does not mean the sum of the historical effects of their acts; for to this their view could not be directed. Rather, the 'work' from *their* standpoint is the end they really sought, and it is in connection with their purpose that they are the proper objects of historical investigation. This is certainly true if the examination of history is no neutral orientation about objectively determined past events, but is motivated by the question how we ourselves, standing in the current of history, can succeed in comprehending our own existence, can gain clear insight into the contingencies and necessities of our own life purpose.

In the case of those who like Jesus have worked through the medium of word, what they purposed can be reproduced only as a group of sayings, of ideas—as teaching. Whoever tries, according to the modern fashion, to penetrate behind the teaching to the psychology or to the personality of Jesus, inevitably, for the reasons already given, misses what Jesus purposed. For his purpose can be comprehended only as teaching.

But in studying the teaching there is again danger of misunderstanding, of supposing such teaching to be a system of general truths, a system of propositions which have validity apart from the concrete life situation of the speaker. In that case it would follow that the truth of such statements would necessarily be measured by an ideal universal system of truths, of eternally valid propositions. In so far as the thought of Jesus agreed with this ideal system, one could speak of the super-historical element in his message. But here it would again become clear that one has missed the essential of history, has not met with anything really new in history. For this ideal system would not be learned from history, it implies rather a standard beyond history by which the particular historical phenomena are measured. The study of history would then at best consist in bringing this pre-existent ideal system to clearer recognition through the observation of concrete 'cases'. Historical research would be a work of 'recollection' in the Platonic sense, a clarifying of knowledge which man already possesses. Such a view would be essentially rationalistic; history as event in time would be excluded.

Therefore, when I speak of the teaching or thought of Jesus, I base the discussion on no underlying conception of a universally valid system of thought which through this study can be made enlightening to all. Rather the ideas are understood in the light of the concrete situation of a man living in time; as his interpretation of his own existence in the midst of change, uncertainty, decision; as the expression of a possibility of comprehending this life; as the effort to gain clear insight into the contingencies and necessities of his own existence. When we encounter the words of Jesus in history, *we* do not judge *them* by a philosophical system with reference to their rational validity; *they* meet *us* with the question of how we are to interpret our own existence. That we be ourselves deeply disturbed by the problem of our own life is therefore the indispensable condition of our inquiry. Then the examination of history will lead not to the enrichment of timeless wisdom, but to an encounter with history which itself is an event in time. This is dialogue with history.[3]

[. . .] The subject of this book is, as I have said, not the life or the personality of Jesus, but only his teaching, his message. Little as we know of his life and personality, we know enough of his message to make for ourselves a consistent picture. Here, too, great caution is demanded by the nature of our sources. What the sources offer us is first of all the message of the early Christian community, which for the most part the church freely attributed to Jesus. This naturally gives no proof that all the words which are put into his mouth were actually spoken by him. As can be easily proved, many sayings originated in the church itself; others were modified by the church. [. . .]

Of course the doubt as to whether Jesus really existed is unfounded and not worth refutation. No sane person can doubt that Jesus stands as founder behind the historical movement whose first distinct stage is represented by the oldest Palestinian community [cf. **234**]. But how far that community preserved an objectively true picture of him and his message is another question. For those whose interest is in the personality of Jesus, this situation is depressing or destructive; for our purpose it has no particular significance. It is precisely this complex of ideas in the oldest layer of the synoptic tradition which is the object of our consideration. It meets us as a fragment of tradition coming to us from the past, and in the examination of it we seek the encounter with history. By the tradition Jesus is named as bearer of the message; according to overwhelming probability he really was. Should it prove otherwise, that does not change in any way what is said in the record. I see then no objection to naming Jesus throughout as the speaker. Whoever prefers to put the name of 'Jesus' always in quotation marks and let it stand as an abbreviation for the historical phenomenon with which we are concerned, is free to do so.

Rudolf Bultmann, *Jesus*, Introduction, extracts (1926)

283   The Earthly Jesus and the Exalted Lord

In the generation after Bultmann (cf. **282**), various New Testament scholars began to re-evaluate the possibility of a quest for the historical Jesus. They attempted not so much to reconstruct Jesus' biography (as in the first quest) but to push Bultmann's quest for the potent message of early Christianity back in a search for Jesus' transformative teaching. Ernst Käsemann (1906–98) was one of the key figures in this 'second quest' for the historical Jesus, and should perhaps be considered its founder. A student of Bultmann, he became unhappy with Bultmann's refusal to concern himself with the historical Jesus; the following extract is from a famous article in which he championed an alternative.

In writing a life of Jesus, we could not dispense with some account of his exterior and interior development. But we know nothing at all about the latter and next to nothing about the former, save only the way which led from Galilee to Jerusalem, from the preaching of the God who is near to us to the hatred of official Judaism and execution by the Romans. Only an uncontrolled imagination could have the self-confidence to weave out of these pitiful threads the fabric of a history in which cause and effect could be determined in detail.

But conversely, neither am I prepared to concede that, in the face of these facts, defeatism and scepticism must have the last word and lead us on to a complete disengagement of interest from the earthly Jesus. If this were to happen, we should either be failing to grasp the nature of the primitive Christian concern with the identity between the exalted and the humiliated Lord; or else we should be emptying that concern of any real content, as did the docetists. We should also be overlooking the fact that there are still pieces of the Synoptic tradition which the historian has to acknowledge as authentic if he wishes to remain an historian at all. My own concern is to show that, out of the obscurity of the life story of Jesus, certain characteristic traits in his preaching stand out in relatively sharp relief, and that primitive Christianity united its own message with these. The heart of our problem lies here: the exalted Lord has almost entirely swallowed up the image of the earthly Lord and yet the community maintains the identity of the exalted Lord with the earthly. The solution of this problem cannot, however, if our findings are right, be approached with any hope of success along the line of supposed historical *bruta facta* but only along the line of the connection and tension between the preaching of Jesus and that of his community. The question of the historical Jesus is, in its legitimate form, the question of the continuity of the Gospel within the discontinuity of the times and within the variation of the kerygma. We have to put this question to ourselves and to see within it the element of rightness in the liberal Life of Jesus movement, the presuppositions of whose questioning we no longer share. The preaching of the Church may be carried on anonymously; the important thing is not the person, but the message. But the Gospel itself cannot be anonymous, otherwise it leads to moralism and mysticism. The Gospel is tied to him, who, both before and after Easter, revealed himself to his own as the Lord, by setting them before the God who is near to them and thus translating them into the freedom and responsibility of faith. This he did once without any demonstrable credentials, even without claiming to be the Messiah, and yet he did it as having the authority of him whom the Fourth Gospel calls the only-begotten Son. He cannot be classified according to the categories either of psychology or of the comparative study of religion or, finally, of general history. If he can be placed at all, it must be in terms of historical particularity. To this extent the problem of the historical Jesus is not our invention, but the riddle which he himself sets us.

The historian may establish the existence of this riddle, but he is unable to solve it. It is only solved by those who since the Cross and the Resurrection confess him as that which, in the days of his flesh, he never claimed to be and yet was—their Lord, and the bringer of the liberty of the children of God, which is the correlate of the kingdom of God. For to his particularity there corresponds the particularity of faith, for which the real history of Jesus is always happening afresh; it is now the history of the exalted Lord, but it does not cease to be the earthly history it once was, in which the call and the claim of the Gospel are encountered.

Ernst Käsemann, 'The Problem of the Historical Jesus', extract (1953)

284   Faith-Image and History

Norman Perrin (1920–76) was an American exponent of the second quest. Here he explains why he finds some such quest necessary.

As a product of an Anglo-Saxon liberal Baptist tradition we have been taught to 'believe in Jesus', and all the various forms of proclamation to which we have been subject have served to produce for us what we would call a 'faith-image' of this Jesus. Part of this faith-image is certainly made up of traits of the liberal historical Jesus, but then the writings of the liberal 'questers' were in their own way kerygmatic;[4] the mistake is to claim them as historical. Again, part of the faith-image could be the result of the existential impact of knowledge of Jesus mediated by a modern historiography, historic knowledge, for to a believer brought up in this tradition almost anything that talks about Jesus can become kerygma, that is, it can contribute to the faith-image. This faith-image is, so far as the individual believer is concerned, the kerygmatic Christ, since it is an image mediated to him by the multiple forms of Christian proclamation, and it has to be distinguished from the historical Jesus even though historical knowledge of Jesus may have been a constituent factor in its creation. It has to be distinguished from the historical Jesus because its ultimate origin is not historical research, but Christian proclamation, even if it may have been historical research which has unwittingly become proclamation, as in the case of much liberal life of Christ research. It also has to be distinguished from the historical Jesus because the results of historical research are not a *determining* factor in the constituence of this figure; like the Christ of the gospels, the Jesus of one's faith-image is a mixture of historical reminiscence, at a somewhat distant remove, and myth, legend and idealism. What gives this faith-image validity is the fact that it grows out of religious experience and is capable of mediating religious experience; that it develops in the context of the complex mixture of needs, etc., which originally created, and continues to create, an openness towards the kerygma; and that it can continue to develop to meet those needs.

Historical knowledge of Jesus, then, is significant to faith in that it can contribute to the formation of the faith-image. In a tradition which 'believes in Jesus', historical knowledge can be a source for the necessary content of faith. After all, in the Christian use, faith is necessarily faith *in* something, a believer believes in something, and in so far as that 'something' is 'Jesus', historical knowledge can help to provide the content, without thereby becoming the main source of that content. The main source will always be the proclamation of the Church, a proclamation arising out of a Christian experience of the risen Lord.

Now there arises immediately the obvious question: If there are so many different forms of proclamation, and, in effect, as many faith-images as there are believers, how do we distinguish true from false? This is a question of peculiar force in America, where the tradition is to 'believe in Jesus' and where there are a multitude of conflicting and competing kerygmata; where everything from radical right racism to revolutionary Christian humanism is proclaimed as kerygma, and as Christian. It is also a question of peculiar force to us, because we must fully admit the highly individualistic character of a believer's faith-image, and yet, at the same time, face the question of which, if any, are to be called 'Christian', and so face the necessity of distinguishing true from false. In this situation we introduce the second aspect of our own position: We believe we have the right to appeal to our limited, but real, historical knowledge of Jesus. The true kerygmatic Christ, the justifiable faith-image, is that consistent with the historical Jesus. The significance of the historical Jesus for Christian faith is that knowledge of this Jesus may be used as a means of testing the claims of the Christs presented in the competing kerygmata to be Jesus Christ. To this limited extent our historical knowledge of Jesus validates the Christian kerygma; it does not validate it as *kerygma*, but it validates it as *Christian*.

Norman Perrin, *Rediscovering the Teaching of Jesus*, ch. 5, extract (1967)

II. Questing for the Historical Jesus

The 'third quest' for the historical Jesus is a catch-all term used to refer to a diverse crop of writers from the last third of the twentieth century who have set about the task of reconstructing Jesus' life and message with a new confidence, drawing upon a wealth of new sources such as the Dead Sea Scrolls, and relying on the positive possibilities of refined historical methods. The extract from E. P. Sanders below gives a relatively uncontroversial outline; the next three extracts illustrate something of the variety and commonality found among the third questers; the final extract in the section demonstrates just why it is that absolute certainty in these matters is unavailable.

285   A Framework

E. P. Sanders (1937–), a Professor at Duke University, is chiefly known for his revolutionary work on the nature of first-century Judaism, which has helped recent scholarship to see beyond the polemics of the Reformation and the anti-Judaistic nature of so much Christian theology, and to begin to appreciate the richness and diversity of the religion in which early Christianity took root. Here he summarizes what he thinks can be known about Jesus with reasonable confidence. (Cf. 1–20, 234.)

The year of Jesus' birth is not entirely certain. [. . .] Most scholars, I among them, think that the decisive fact is that Matthew dates Jesus' birth at about the time Herod the Great died. This was in the year 4 BCE, and so Jesus was born in that year or shortly before it; some scholars prefer 5, 6 or even 7 BCE. [. . .]

Jesus lived with his parents in Nazareth, a Galilean village. One of Herod the Great's heirs, Antipas, was the ruler of Galilee for the entirety of Jesus' life (except for the very earliest period, when Herod the Great was still alive). It is a strong possibility that virtually all of Jesus' active ministry, except the last two or three weeks, was carried out in Antipas' Galilee. Jesus was not an urbanite. The cities of Galilee—Sepphoris, Tiberias and Scythopolis (Hebrew: Beth-Shean)—do not figure in the accounts of his activities. He doubtless knew Sepphoris, which was only a few miles from Nazareth, but he nevertheless seems to have regarded his mission as being best directed to the Jews in the villages and small towns of Galilee. Nazareth itself was quite a small village. It was in the hill country, away from the Sea of Galilee, but Jesus taught principally in the villages and towns on the sea. Some of his followers were fishermen. Rural images are fairly frequent in the teaching that is ascribed to him.

When Jesus was a young man, probably in his late twenties, John the

Baptist began preaching in or near Galilee. He proclaimed the urgent need to repent in view of the coming judgement. Jesus heard John and felt called to accept his baptism. All four gospels point to this as an event that transformed Jesus' life. According to Mark's account, Jesus 'saw the heavens opened and the Spirit descending upon him like a dove'; he also heard a voice saying, 'You are my beloved son' [2].

Antipas arrested John because he had criticised his marriage to Herodias (the gospels) or because he feared that the Baptist's preaching would lead to insurrection (Josephus) or both. At about that time Jesus began his public ministry. Whereas John had worked outside settled areas, Jesus went from town to town, village to village, usually preaching in synagogues on the sabbath. He called a small number of people to be his disciples, and they joined him in his travels. Unlike John, Jesus not only preached but also healed the sick. He developed a reputation, and people thronged to see him. Soon he too had to preach in open areas because of the crowds.

We do not know just how long this itinerant ministry continued, but apparently it lasted only one or possibly two years. After preaching and healing for this period of time in Galilee, Jesus, with his disciples and some other followers, went to Jerusalem for Passover. Jerusalem was in Judaea, which, unlike Galilee, was a Roman province. Jerusalem itself was governed by the Jewish high priest, who was responsible to a Roman prefect. Jesus rode into the city on an ass, and some people hailed him as 'son of David'. When he went to the Temple, he attacked the money-changers and dove-sellers. The high priest and his advisers determined that Jesus was dangerous and had to die. After the Passover meal with his disciples, Jesus went apart to pray. One of his followers had betrayed him, and the high priest's guards arrested him. He was tried, after a fashion, and turned over to the Roman prefect, with the recommendation that he be executed. After a brief hearing, the prefect ordered his execution. He was crucified as an insurgent, along with two others.

He died after a relatively brief period of suffering. A few of his followers placed him in a tomb. According to some reports, when they returned two days later to anoint his body, they found the tomb empty. Thereafter his followers saw him. These resurrection experiences convinced them that Jesus would return and that in Jesus' life and death God had acted to save humanity. The disciples began to persuade others to put their faith in Jesus. They gave him various titles, including 'Anointed' (which is 'Messiah' in Hebrew and 'Christ' in Greek), 'Lord' and 'Son of God'. These titles reveal that, as the decades passed, Jesus' disciples and their converts developed various views of Jesus' relation to God and of his significance in God's plan for Israel and the world. Their movement finally separated from Judaism and became the Christian church. When the gospels were written, however,

Christology (theological explanations of the person and work of Jesus) was at an early stage, and the separation of Christianity from Judaism not yet complete.

E. P. Sanders, *The Historical Figure of Jesus*, ch. 2, extracts (1993)

286   A Mediterranean Jewish Peasant

> John Dominic Crossan is a Professor at DePaul University in Chicago. Going beyond the bare-bones approach provided in the previous extract, Crossan risks a coherent but controversial picture of the message of Jesus in his historical context. He focuses his presentation around the idea of a life which breaks the rules of present political and social reality: a 'brokerless kingdom'. (Cf. 3, 5, 7, 8, 287, 288.)

In the beginning was the performance; not the word alone, not the deed alone, but both, each indelibly marked with the other forever. He comes as yet unknown into a hamlet of Lower Galilee. He is watched by the cold, hard eyes of peasants living long enough at subsistence level to know exactly where the line is drawn between poverty and destitution. He looks like a beggar, yet his eyes lack the proper cringe, his voice the proper whine, his walk the proper shuffle. He speaks about the rule of God, and they listen as much from curiosity as anything else. They know all about rule and power, about kingdom and empire, but they know it in terms of tax and debt, malnutrition and sickness, agrarian oppression and demonic possession. What, they really want to know, can this kingdom of God do for a lame child, a blind parent, a demented soul screaming its tortured isolation among the graves that mark the edges of the village? Jesus walks with them to the tombs, and, in the silence after the exorcism, the villagers listen once more, but now with curiosity giving way to cupidity, fear, and embarrassment. He is invited, as honour demands, to the home of the village leader. He goes, instead, to stay in the home of the dispossessed woman. Not quite proper, to be sure, but it would be unwise to censure an exorcist, to criticise a magician. The village could yet broker this power to its surroundings, could give this kingdom of God a localisation, a place to which others would come for healing, a centre with honour and patronage enough for all, even, maybe, for that dispossessed woman herself. But the next day he leaves them, and now they wonder aloud about a divine kingdom with no respect for proper protocols, a kingdom, as he had said, not just for the poor, like themselves, but for the destitute. [. . .]

Jesus himself had not always seen things that way. Earlier he had received John's baptism and accepted his message of God as the imminent apocalyptic judge. But the Jordan was not just water, and to be baptised in it was to recapitulate the ancient and archetypal passage from imperial bondage to national freedom. Herod Antipas moved swiftly to execute John, there was no apocalyptic consummation, and Jesus, finding his own voice, began to speak of God not as imminent apocalypse but as present healing. To those first followers from the peasant villages of Lower Galilee who asked how to repay his exorcisms and cures, he gave a simple answer, simple, that is, to understand but hard as death itself to undertake. You are healed healers, he said, so take the Kingdom to others, for I am not its patron and you are not its brokers. It is, was, and always will be available to any who want it. Dress as I do, like a beggar, but do not beg. Bring a miracle and request a table. Those you heal must accept you into their homes.

That ecstatic vision and social programme sought to rebuild a society upward from its grass roots but on principles of religious and economic egalitarianism, with free healing brought directly to the peasant homes and free sharing of whatever they had in return. The deliberate conjunction of magic and meal, miracle and table, free compassion and open commensality, was a challenge launched not just at Judaism's strictest purity regulations, or even at the Mediterranean's patriarchal combination of honour and shame, patronage and clientage, but at civilisation's eternal inclination to draw lines, invoke boundaries, establish hierarchies, and maintain discriminations. It did not invite a political revolution but envisaged a social one at the imagination's most dangerous depths. No importance was given to distinctions of Gentile and Jew, female and male, slave and free, poor and rich. Those distinctions were hardly even attacked in theory; they were simply ignored in practice.

What would happen to Jesus was probably as predictable as what had happened already to John. Some form of religiopolitical execution could surely have been expected. What he was saying and doing was as unacceptable in the first as in the twentieth century, there, here, or anywhere. Still, the exact sequence of what happened at the end lacks multiple independent accounts, and the death is surer in its connection to the life than it is in its connection to the preceding few days. It seems clear that Jesus, confronted, possibly for the first and only time, with the Temple's rich magnificence, symbolically destroyed its perfectly legitimate brokerage function in the name of the unbrokered kingdom of God. Such an act, if performed in the volatile atmosphere of Passover, a feast that celebrated Jewish liberation from inaugural imperial oppression, would have been quite enough to entail crucifixion by religiopolitical agreement. And it is now impossible for us to imagine the offhand brutality, anonymity, and indifference with which a peasant nobody like Jesus would have been disposed of.

What could not have been predicted and might not have been expected was that the end was not the end. Those who had originally experienced divine power through his vision and his example still continued to do so after his death—in fact, even more so, because now it was no longer confined by time or place. [. . .] Jesus' own followers, who had initially fled from the danger and horror of the crucifixion, talked eventually not just of continued affection or spreading superstition but of resurrection. They tried to express what they meant by telling, for example, about the journey to Emmaus undertaken by two Jesus followers, one named and clearly male, one unnamed and probably female [cf. 18]. The couple were leaving Jerusalem in disappointed and dejected sorrow. Jesus joined them on the road and, unknown and unrecognised, explained how the Hebrew Scriptures should have prepared them for his fate. Later that evening they invited him to join them for their evening meal, and finally they recognised him when once again he served the meal to them as of old beside the lake. And then, only then, they started back to Jerusalem in high spirits. The symbolism is obvious, as is the metaphoric condensation of the first years of Christian thought and practice into one parabolic afternoon. Emmaus never happened. Emmaus always happens.

> John Dominic Crossan, *The Historical Jesus: The Life of a Mediterranean Jewish Peasant*,
> Overture, extracts (1991)

287   A Marginal Jew

John P. Meier, a Professor at Notre Dame University, Indiana, is a Catholic proponent of the third quest. A less controversial figure than Crossan (cf. 286), and somewhat less prone to dramatizing his findings, he nevertheless provides a similar picture of Jesus' message, focusing his presentation on the idea of God's future triumphant rule being made real in present experience. (Cf. 3, 5, 7, 8)

In using the multifaceted, multilayered symbol of 'the kingdom of God', Jesus conjured up in his audience's imagination the whole biblical drama of God's kingly rule over his creation and over his people Israel. It was God the King who in the beginning had called order out of chaos, who had saved a ragtag group of refugees from the slavery of Egypt and chosen them as his people Israel, who had exiled and scattered his people for their sins, and who now in this last hour was gathering, healing, and forgiving his people in preparation for final judgment and final salvation. It was this dynamic, multivalent, 'salvation-history-in-a-nutshell' quality of 'kingdom of God' that allowed Jesus to use it both of his pivotal ministry in the present moment and of the denouement of his ministry, soon to come.

On the one hand, the kingdom of God meant for Jesus the full appearance of God's victorious rule over the world in the near future. It was with a sober awareness that all was not yet perfect in Israel that Jesus taught his disciples to pray to the Father: 'Your kingdom come' [5]. It was with anguish and yet trust that Jesus told his disciples at his last fellowship meal that he would not drink wine again until he drank it in the kingdom of God. One is tempted to stretch a point here by saying that Jesus went to his death promising himself the kingdom of God he had promised others. To be sure, though, the banquet in the kingdom was not meant for Jesus alone. He had promised that many others would come from the east and the west to recline with the patriarchs of Israel at the final banquet in the kingdom. Then and then alone would the hungry be fully fed, the mourners be finally comforted, the inequities of this world be reversed, and all the promises listed in Jesus' beatitudes be kept—kept for him as well as for those who heard him.

On the other hand, the kingdom was not just a future reality. If Jesus had simply prophesied an imminent coming of God to rule Israel with a full and definitive display of power, the Nazarene would not have differed all that much from some of the Old Testament prophets, the writers of Jewish apocalypses or John the Baptist. Jesus proved to be a more complicated and puzzling figure because the kingdom he proclaimed as coming was the kingdom he also proclaimed as present in his ministry: 'The kingdom of God is in your midst' [Luke 17: 21]. In some sense this was true of Jesus' powerful preaching and teaching, especially of his riddle-like parables, which confronted listeners with a kingdom of God that challenged and threatened their present ways of thinking and living. To hear these parables of the kingdom properly was to experience the coming of the kingdom into one's own existence. But the experience of the kingdom Jesus gave was not simply a modern, existentialistic 'word event'.[5] Jesus wanted his fellow Jews to experience the kingdom present in action in their everyday lives. Hence he made the final banquet of the kingdom present and palpable in his table fellowship, which he shared most strikingly with social and religious outcasts.

While all this is true, Jesus himself emphasised that the presence of God's rule was especially experienced in the exorcisms and healings he performed. With an allusion to the absence of miracles in the Baptist's ministry, Jesus pointed out to John's inquiring envoys the stunning difference in his own ministry. Now at last Isaiah's prophecies of Israel's healing in the end time were being fulfilled: 'The blind see, the lame walk, lepers are cleansed, the deaf hear, the dead are raised' [Matt. 11: 5]—all as part of Jesus' larger programme of proclaiming the good news of salvation to Israel's poor. In particular, Jesus saw his exorcisms as a striking sign that even now, in the lives of individual Israelites, Satan's hold over God's people was being broken. Even now, on the limited turf of concrete Israelite lives, God's rule was triumphant: 'If by the finger of God I cast out demons, then the kingdom of God has come upon you.' [Luke 11: 20]. Thus, in both word and deed, Jesus made God's future kingdom a present experience, at least in some partial or proleptic sense. Jesus was not just another prophet uttering more prophecies about the future. He was the prophet who was accomplishing what the prophets had foretold: 'Happy the eyes that see what you see, and the ears that hear what you hear. For I say to you that many prophets and kings longed to see what you see and did not see it, and to hear what you hear and did not hear it.' [Matt. 13: 16–17].

For the crowds that followed Jesus, his supposed miracles were no doubt the most striking and attractive element of his ministry, the one that gave his mysterious talk about the kingdom of God palpable impact and meaning for ordinary Jews. For all his rejection of crass faith based on 'miracles-on-demand', Jesus obviously appreciated the value of miracles as pedagogy, as propaganda, and especially as the present enactment of the powerful rule of God that he promised for the future. Miracles loom large in the four gospels because they first loomed large in the ministry of the historical Jesus. A good deal of the popular excitement over Jesus was fed by reports of his exorcisms, his healings of the infirm (especially people suffering from paralysed limbs or from blindness), and even of his raising the dead.

> John P. Meier, *A Marginal Jew: Rethinking the Historical Jesus, ii: Mentor, Message and Miracles*, Conclusion 11, extract (1994)

288 The Jesus Revolution

N. T. Wright, now Canon Theologian of Westminster Abbey, is a major English contributor to the third quest and one rather more open than usual to traditional theological claims about Jesus. He has combined lengthy and detailed works on the historical Jesus and Christian origins with a large number of popular books. In this extract from one of his popular presentations, he emphasizes Jesus' proclamation of a universal kingdom, which breaks down the wall between Jews and Gentiles. (Cf. **3, 5, 7, 8, 286, 287**.)

'No King but God' was the revolutionary slogan of the day. If you had been a Galilean peasant, working in your smallholding, your impression of Jesus would have been that he was a prophet who was announcing that God was now at last becoming King. This could only mean one thing: Israel was at last going to be redeemed, rescued from oppression. God's 'Kingdom' wasn't a state of mind, or a sense of inward peace. It was concrete, historical, real.

Twentieth-century Western Christians need to shed a few ideas at this point. When people downed tools for a while and trudged off up a hillside to hear this Jesus talking, we can be sure they weren't going to hear someone tell them to be nice to each other; or that if they behaved themselves (or got their minds round the right theological scheme) there would be a rosy future waiting for them when they got to 'heaven'; or that God had decided at last to do something about forgiving them for their sins. First-century Jews knew that they ought to be nice to each other. In so far as they thought at all about life after death, they believed that their God would look after them, and eventually give them new physical bodies in his renewed world. (The phrase 'Kingdom of Heaven', which we find in Matthew's gospel, does *not* mean 'a Kingdom-place called "heaven".' It is a reverent way of saying 'the King*ship* of God'.) There is no sign that first-century Jews were walking around gloomily wondering how their sins were ever going to be forgiven. They had the Temple and the sacrificial system, which took care of all that. If Jesus had only said what a lot of Western Christians seem to think he said, he would have been just a big yawn-maker.

What he in fact said was so revolutionary that it woke everybody up. It was so dramatic that Jesus seems to have adopted a deliberate policy of keeping to the villages, always moving quickly on, never getting into the big Galilean towns like Sepphoris, just over the hill from Nazareth, or Tiberias, down by the sea of Galilee, just south of Magdala. Why? What was so different?

The strange thing about Jesus' announcement of the Kingdom of God was that he managed *both* to claim that he was fulfilling the old prophecies, the old hopes, of Israel *and* to do so in a way which radically subverted them. The Kingdom of God is here, he seemed to be saying, *but it's not like you thought it was going to be.*

How so? When Israel's God acts, the Gentiles will benefit as well! When Israel's God brings in his new world, some of Israel's cherished traditions (like the food laws) will be swept away, no longer needed in the new world-wide family! Abraham, Isaac and Jacob will sit down in the Kingdom and welcome people from all over the world, while some of the sons of the Kingdom will be cast out. It's no wonder Jesus needed to use parables to say all this. If too many people realised the doubly revolutionary implications, he wouldn't have lasted five minutes.

Doubly revolutionary: first, anyone saying that Israel's God was becoming King was raising a standard for revolution, and, as Jesus himself wryly noted, all and sundry, particularly those bent on violence, would try to get in on the act. Second, to claim to be announcing the Kingdom while at the same time subverting Israel's national institutions, and/or the fiercely held agendas of certain pressure groups, was asking for trouble. It would be like announcing in a Moslem country that one was fulfilling the will of Allah—while apparently vilifying Mohammed and burning a copy of the Koran.

In particular, Jesus' characteristic behaviour spoke as many volumes as his characteristic teaching. Wherever he went, there was a party. After all, if God is becoming King at last, who wouldn't want to celebrate? But he celebrated with all the wrong people. He went into low dives and back alleys. He knocked back the wine with the shady and disrespectable. He allowed women of the street to come and fawn over him. And all the time he seemed to be indicating that, as far as he was concerned, they were in the process being welcomed into the new day that was dawning, the day of God's becoming King. That was the significance of his remarkable healings (which, incidentally, most serious scholars today are prepared to admit as historical).

What had happened to all the old taboos, to Israel's standards of holiness? They seemed to have gone by the board. Jesus was saying—in his actions as much as in his words—that you didn't have to observe every last bit of the Torah before you would count as a real member of Israel. He was saying that you didn't have to make the journey to Jerusalem, offer sacrifice, and go through purity rituals, in order to be regarded as clean, forgiven, restored as a member of Israel. You could be healed, restored, and forgiven right here, where Jesus was, at this party, just by being there with him and welcoming his way of bringing in the Kingdom. No wonder his family said he was out of his mind.

N. T. Wright, *Who was Jesus?*, ch. 5: 'Jesus Revisited', extract (1992)

289 The Sacred Mushroom

The authors of the other extracts in this section could be said to fall in the current academic 'mainstream', and their works have a certain clear commonality. But there are many others working and writing on the historical Jesus, and every point which is accepted or argued among those in the mainstream can be found questioned or denied elsewhere. Perhaps the most striking example in existence of an interpretation which starts from a fundamentally different set of assumptions is that provided by John Allegro (1923–88), a scholar of the Dead Sea Scrolls, who provides an alternative explanation of first-century religion and Jesus' place within it.

The way to God and the fleeting view of heaven was through plants more plentifully endued with the sperm of God than any other.[6] These were the drug-herbs, the science of whose cultivation and use had been accumulated over centuries of observation and dangerous experiment. Those who had this secret wisdom of the plants were the chosen of their god; to them alone had he vouchsafed the privilege of access to the heavenly throne. And if he was jealous of his power, no less were those who served him in the cultic mysteries.

Theirs was no gospel to be shouted from the rooftops: Paradise was for none but the favoured few. The incantations and rites by which they conjured forth their drug plants, and the details of the bodily and mental preparations undergone before they could ingest their god, were the secrets of the cult to which none but the initiate, bound by fearful oaths, had access.

Very rarely, and then only for urgent practical purposes, were those secrets ever committed to writing. Normally they would be passed from the priest to the initiate by word of mouth; dependent for their accurate transmission on the trained memories of men dedicated to the learning and recitation of their 'scriptures'. But if, for some drastic reason like the disruption of their cultic centres by war or persecution, it became necessary to write down the precious names of the herbs and the manner of their use and accompanying incantations, it would be in some esoteric form comprehensible only to those within their dispersed communities.

Such an occasion, we believe, was the Jewish Revolt of AD 66. Instigated probably by members of the cult, swayed by their drug-induced madness to believe God had called them to master the world in his name, they provoked the mighty power of Rome to swift and terrible action. Jerusalem was ravaged, her temple destroyed. Judaism was disrupted, and her people driven to seek refuge with communities already established around the Mediterranean coastlands. The mystery cults found themselves without their central fount of authority, with many of their priests killed in the abortive rebellion or driven into the desert. The secrets, if they were not to be lost for ever, had to be committed to writing, and yet, if found, the documents must give nothing away or betray those who still dared defy the Roman authorities and continue their religious practices.

The means of conveying the information were at hand, and had been for thousands of years. The folk-tales of the ancients had from the earliest times contained myths based upon the personification of plants and trees. They were invested with human faculties and qualities and their names and physical characteristics were applied to the heroes and heroines of the stories. Some of these were just tales spun for entertainment, others were political parables like Jotham's fable about the trees in the Old Testament (Judg. 9: 7–15), while others were means of remembering and transmitting therapeutic folklore. The names of the plants were spun out to make the basis of the stories, whereby the creatures of fantasy were identified, dressed, and made to enact their parts. Here, then, was the literary device to spread occult knowledge to the faithful. To tell the story of a rabbi called Jesus, and invest him with the power and names of the magic drug. To have him live before the terrible events that had disrupted their lives, to preach a love between men, extending even to the hated Romans. Thus, reading such a tale, should it fall into Roman hands, even their mortal enemies might be deceived and not probe farther into the activities of the cells of the mystery cults within their territories.

The ruse failed. Christians, hated and despised, were hauled forth and slain in their thousands. The cult well nigh perished. What eventually took its place was a travesty of the real thing, a mockery of the power that could raise men to heaven and give them the glimpse of God for which they gladly died. The story of the rabbi crucified at the instigation of the Jews became an historical peg upon which the new cult's authority was founded. What began as a hoax, became a trap even to those who believed themselves to be the spiritual heirs of the mystery religion and took to themselves the name of 'Christian'. Above all they forgot, or purged from the cult and their memories, the one supreme secret on which their whole religious and ecstatic experience depended: the names and identity of the source of the drug, the key to heaven—the sacred mushroom.

John M. Allegro, *The Sacred Mushroom and the Cross*, Introduction, extract (1970)

Section C

Christ and Salvation

Much twentieth-century theology was driven by a re-evaluation of soteriology: the question of how the salvation produced or initiated by Christ is to be understood. The assumption of many earlier theologians that the work of Christ was patent in the inexorable progress of Christian civilization was demolished by the violence poured out in two world wars and the oppression recognized in the imperial projects of precisely those nations supposed in the previous century to be most cultured. Many theologians found themselves forced to rethink the change which Christ brought about in human life, finding solutions in the recognition of Christ's radical judgement upon all the securities established by human effort (cf. **281**), or in the rediscovery of a transformative political vision in the gospel. (cf. **286**, **288**.)

I. Justification and Sanctification

Some twentieth-century soteriologies have drawn upon new philosophical resources in a self-conscious attempt to provide a modern answer to the old question; others have tried to repristinate the answers given in the Reformation; still others have tried to give answers which respond to the rhythms of the many different cultures in which Christianity flourishes.

290 Christ and New Being

Paul Tillich (1886–1965) was a German Lutheran theologian who was compelled by the rise of National Socialism to leave for America in 1933 and who there exercised an extraordinary influence on a whole generation of theologians. He sought to produce a theology which would show how the Christian tradition could provide an answer to the demands of our contemporary situation, drawing upon the vocabulary of existential philosophy as a mediator between the situation and the tradition.

According to eschatological symbolism, the Christ is the one who brings the new eon. When Peter called Jesus 'the Christ', he expected the coming of a new state of things through him. This expectation is implicit in the title 'Christ'.[7] But it was not fulfilled in accordance with the expectations of the disciples. The state of things, of nature as well as of history, remained unchanged, and he who was supposed to bring the new eon was destroyed by the powers of the old eon. This meant that the disciples either had to accept the breakdown of their hope or radically transform its content [cf. **224**]. They were able to choose the second way by identifying the New Being with the being of Jesus, the sacrificed. In the Synoptic records Jesus himself reconciled the messianic claim with the acceptance of a violent death. The same records show that the disciples resisted this combination. Only the experiences which are described as Easter and Pentecost created their faith in the paradoxical character of the messianic claim. It was Paul who gave the theological frame in which the paradox could be understood and justified. One approach to the solution of the problem was to state the distinction between the first and the second coming of the Christ. The new state of things will be created with the second coming, the return of the Christ in glory. In the period between the first and the second coming the New Being is present in him. He is the Kingdom of God. In him the eschatological expectation is fulfilled in principle. Those who participate in him participate in the New Being, though under the condition of man's existential predicament and, therefore, only fragmentarily and by anticipation.

New Being is essential being under the conditions of existence, conquering the gap between essence and existence.[8] For the same idea Paul uses the term 'new creature', calling those who are 'in' Christ 'new creatures'. 'In' is the preposition of participation; he who participates in the newness of being which is in Christ has become a new creature. It is a creative act by which this happens. Inasmuch as Jesus as the Christ is a creation of the divine Spirit, according to Synoptic theology, so is he who participates in the Christ made into a new creature by the Spirit. The estrangement of his existential from his essential being is conquered in principle, i.e., in power and as a beginning. The term 'New Being', as used here, points directly to the cleavage between essential and existential being—and is the restorative principle of the whole of this theological system. The New Being is new in so far as it is the undistorted manifestation of essential being within and under the conditions of existence. It is new in two respects: it is new in contrast to the merely potential character of essential being; and it is new over against the estranged character of existential being. It is actual, conquering the estrangement of actual existence.

There are other ways of expressing the same idea. The New Being is new in so far as it is the conquest of the situation under the law—which is the old situation. The law is man's essential being standing against his existence, commanding and judging it. In so far as his essential being is taken into his existence and actualised in it, the law has ceased to be law for him. Where there is New Being, there is no commandment and no judgment. If, therefore, we call Jesus as the Christ the New Being, we say with Paul that the Christ is the end of the law.

In terms of the eschatological symbolism it can also be said that Christ is the end of existence. He is the end of existence lived in estrangement, conflicts, and self-destruction. The biblical idea that the hope of mankind for a new reality is fulfilled in Jesus as the Christ is an immediate consequence of the assertion that in him the New Being is present.

Paul Tillich, *Systematic Theology*, part III: 'Existence and the Christ' II. B. I, extract (1957)

291 Substitutionary Atonement

In a very different vein from Tillich, many Evangelical theologians sought to understand the nature of salvation as the atoning result of Christ's substitution for sinful humanity on the Cross. Such writers as John Stott (1921–), one of the strongest voices in English Evangelicalism, draw upon a tradition which started with Anselm (cf. **114**), and was strongly influenced by Luther (cf. **167**), to explain how it is that Christ's death is efficacious.

God must 'satisfy himself', responding to the realities of human rebellion in a way that is perfectly consonant with his character. This internal necessity is our fixed starting-point. In consequence, it would be impossible for us sinners to remain eternally the sole objects of his holy love, since he cannot both punish and pardon us at the same time. Hence the second necessity, namely substitution. The only way for God's holy love to be satisfied is for his holiness to be directed in judgment upon his appointed substitute, in order that his love may be directed towards us in forgiveness. The substitute bears the penalty, that we sinners may receive the pardon. Who, then, is the substitute? Certainly not Christ, if he is seen as a third party. Any notion of penal substitution in which three independent actors play a role—the guilty party, the punitive judge and the innocent victim—is to be repudiated with the utmost vehemence. It would not only be unjust in itself but would also reflect a defective Christology. For Christ is not an independent third person, but the eternal Son of the Father, who is one with the Father in his essential being.

What we see, then, in the drama of the cross is not three actors but two, ourselves on the one hand and God on the other. Not God as he is in himself (the Father), but God nevertheless, God-made-man-in-Christ (the Son). Hence the importance of those New Testament passages which speak of the death of Christ as the death of God's Son: for example, 'God so loved the world that he gave his one and only Son' [John 3: 16], 'he . . . did not spare his own Son' [Rom. 8: 22], and 'we were reconciled to God through the death of his Son' [Rom. 5: 10]. For in giving his Son he was giving himself. This being so, it is the Judge himself who in holy love assumed the role of the innocent victim, for in and through the person of his Son he himself bore the penalty which he himself inflicted. As Dale put it, 'the mysterious unity of the Father and the Son rendered it possible for God at once to endure and to inflict penal suffering.'[9] There is neither harsh injustice nor unprincipled love nor Christological heresy in that; there is only unfathomable mercy. For in order to save us in such a way as to satisfy himself, God through Christ substituted himself for us. Divine love triumphed over divine wrath by divine self-sacrifice. The cross was an act simultaneously of punishment and amnesty, severity and grace, justice and mercy.

Seen thus, the objections to a substitutionary atonement evaporate. There is nothing even remotely immoral here, since the substitute for the law-breakers is none other than the divine Lawmaker himself. There is no mechanical transaction either, since the self-sacrifice of love is the most personal of all actions. And what is achieved through the cross is no merely external change of legal status, since those who see God's love there, and are united to Christ by his Spirit, become radically transformed in outlook and character.

We strongly reject, therefore, every explanation of the death of Christ which does not have at its centre the principle of 'satisfaction through substitution', indeed divine self-satisfaction through divine self-substitution. The cross was not a commercial bargain with the devil, let alone one which tricked and trapped him; nor an exact equivalent, a quid pro quo to satisfy a code of honour or technical point of law; nor a compulsory submission by God to some moral authority above him from which he could not otherwise escape; nor a punishment of a meek Christ by a harsh and punitive Father; nor a procurement of salvation by a loving Christ from a mean and reluctant Father; nor an action of the Father which bypassed Christ as Mediator. Instead, the righteous, loving Father humbled himself to become in and through his only Son flesh, sin and a curse for us, in order to redeem us without compromising his own character. The theological words 'satisfaction' (cf. 158) and 'substitution' need to be carefully defined and safeguarded, but they cannot in any circumstances be given up. The biblical gospel of atonement is of God satisfying himself by substituting himself for us.

John R. W. Stott, *The Cross of Christ*, ch. 6: 'The Self-Substitution of God', extract (1986)

292 Jesus as Lord

Martin Lloyd Jones (1899–1981) was a prominent English Evangelical whose sermons at Westminster Chapel drew large, eager congregations. Here he fills out the Evangelical picture of salvation (cf. 267), the groundwork of which is presented in the extract from Stott (cf. 291).

Probably you have often heard people say, 'You can take Christ as your Saviour, but perhaps you will not take him as your Lord for years, or perhaps you will not believe in him as your Lord for years.' For a long time, they say, you may be a Christian; yes, you have believed in him as your Saviour; but then, after all these years of struggling and so on, at long last you surrender to him and you take him as your Lord. As I understand the matter, this teaching is not only wrong, it is impossible. You cannot divide the person; this one and the self-same person is always Jesus Christ our Lord. You cannot say he is only Jesus, or only Christ, or only Lord. No, no! The one person is the Lord Jesus Christ, or Jesus Christ the Lord. Now the apostle himself, of course, in writing to the Colossians, puts it quite specifically. Here is a text which you very rarely hear, and which is so sadly forgotten: 'As ye have therefore received Christ Jesus the Lord, so walk ye in him' [Col. 2: 6]. There is nowhere in the Scripture where you will find that you can accept him or take him, or believe in him or receive him, as Jesus only, Saviour only, or Christ only. No! The person is one and indivisible. And if you think that you believe in the Lord Jesus Christ without realising that he is your Lord, I would not hesitate to say that your belief is of no value. You cannot take him as Saviour only, because he saves you by buying you with his precious blood. And if you believe that, you must know at once that he is your Lord.

That is where the whole danger comes in, doesn't it?—the danger which we have already seen of saying that you can be justified without being sanctified. You cannot. You cannot be in relationship to the Lord Jesus Christ unless he is your Lord. Our realisation of this, of course, may vary from time to time, but to teach specifically that you can take him as Saviour without taking him as Lord is nothing but sheer heresy. It is a dividing of the person in a way that this one little word 'our' alone completely prohibits.

Therefore I say, let us be careful; let us examine ourselves. Have I perhaps until now only thought of him as someone who has purchased for me forgiveness of sins and deliverance from hell, and no more? If so, I had better go back again and make sure that I really do believe in him, because if I really believe in the New Testament teaching about sin it means this—that I am condemned and I am hopeless. Christ is Saviour. What does it mean? Well, not simply that he saves me from hell, but that 'he will save his people from their sins' [Matt. 1: 21]. Why did he die for us? Well, ask the apostle Paul. In writing to Titus, he says, 'Who gave himself for us that he might separate unto himself a peculiar people, zealous of good works' [Titus 2: 4]. There is the Lordship. You cannot truly believe in him unless he is your Lord, as well as the Jesus who saves you, and as the Christ who has done this work for you. Let us, then, follow the apostolic example; let us not get into the habit of speaking about him as either Jesus, or Christ, or even Lord alone, although if you must have one word only, then choose the last—the Lord. But let us, I say, follow the apostolic pattern and example, and let us, when we speak of him and when we think of him, do so in these terms: The Lord Jesus Christ— Jesus Christ my Lord. Let us give him the full title; let us ascribe to him the whole designation; let us stand before him and think of him in all his fullness, his completeness, and in all his glory.

Martin Lloyd Jones, *Romans: An Exposition of Chapter 1: The Gospel of God*, ch. 10, extract
(1955)

293   Becoming Lesser Christs

Toyohiko Kagawa (1888–1960) was a convert to Christianity from Buddhism who devoted himself to work in the slums of Japan, and who eventually became a democratic leader in that country after the Second World War. This prayer illustrates the way in which talk of Christ's Lordship, as seen in the previous extract, avoids becoming a 'theology of glory' in Luther's terms (cf. **168**), and becomes a theology of the Cross.

Father God: Even to-day we are still absorbed in the contemplation of the figure of Christ, as he suffered and agonised from the peak of popularity during the Galilean ministry to the time of his elevation on the cross. But we ourselves, we confess it with shame, are always choosing things which are selfish, comfortable, too much according to our own preferences and tastes. Show us, we beseech thee, the way of the cross that we must follow, the way of Jesus. Show to me, I pray thee, the cross in my daily occupation, the cross in my intellectual life, the cross connected with my economic status, the cross in my social life, the cross in my family life, and the cross that I must bear for Jesus sake. Even though I shrink back from the cross and say as Jesus said, 'If possible do not put this cross upon me; if possible take this cup away from me' [**15**], yet if this cross and this cup be mine to bear and drink, enable me to accept them gladly. In ever deeper meditation on the cross, enable each one of us to become a lesser Christ and to bring his truth into active and effective operation in this present-day world. In his holy name, we pray. Amen.

Toyohiko Kagawa, *Meditations on the Cross* III: 'The Cross in the Mind of Christ',
Prayer (1930s)

Kosuke Koyama (1924–) was born in Tokyo and has worked in Thailand and Singapore as well as in New Zealand and the United States. In *Water-buffalo Theology* he developed a theology immersed in the realities of Asian Christianity.

When I meet missionaries from the West in the varieties of localities in South East Asia, what I call the Johannine principle, 'He must increase, but I must decrease' [John 3: 30], comes to my mind. John the Baptist introduced Jesus in these moving terms. He must increase! Missionaries must decrease *if* their decrease points to the increase of Jesus Christ. Increase of Jesus Christ? Yes! Increase of Jesus Christ in the given South East Asian locality. How is Jesus Christ to be increased in Hong Kong? He is increased when the local people are increased in the knowledge of Jesus Christ in whom the dead–alive, lost–found history came to its final substance and expression. Missionaries must decrease, then, in order to make the local people increase. However, as soon as the given local people are increased, *they* must decrease for the sake of the increase of other local people. Chain reaction of increase and decrease must continue. This continuity of increase and decrease is the wave of salvation-history, the beginning and end of which is Jesus Christ.

The Johannine principle of increase and decrease goes through a tremendous upheaval when the 'he' decreases in order to make 'us' increase. 'For you know the grace of our Lord Jesus Christ, that though he was rich, yet for your sake he became poor, so that by his poverty you might become rich' (2 Cor. 8. 9). He is the author of reconciliation. In decreasing himself to an incomprehensible degree, he becomes the foundation of reconciliation. At this point the Johannine principle is, as it were, swallowed up by the Christ principle. If missionaries decrease themselves, they are doing so not only in the light of the Johannine principle, but also in the revolutionary principle of Christ. Here lies the secret of the dynamic identity of the Christian missionary.

What does this 'decrease' mean? Decrease in number? In influence? In prestige? I understand it in the framework of the history of 'reviled (decrease)–bless (increase); persecuted (decrease)–endure (increase); slandered (decrease)–conciliate (increase)'. It is the mind open to give. It is the mind that does not seek profit for itself. It is the mind which is happy in becoming refuse (decrease) of humanity since it will bring increase to others. It is a crucified mind, the mind of Jesus Christ. 'Have this mind among yourselves, which you have in Christ Jesus, who, . . . ' (Phil. 2. 5–11). It is a mind of self-denial based on Christ's self-denial. 'Love does not insist on its way' (1 Cor. 13. 5). The crucified mind is not a pathological or neurotic mind. It is love seeking the benefit of others. This mind sees man 'as he is seen' (I John 4. 20). This mind creates the communicator's mind. This mind appreciates the complexity of man and history. It participates in the dead–alive/lost–found history in the way Christ participated. This must be the mind of the missionary. This mind is radically different from the crusading mind which bulldozes man and history without appreciation of their complexities. The crusading mind is not the mind of the biblical communicators. It must not be the mind of the missionary. The crucified mind, not the crusading mind, must it not be the mind of all missionaries, indeed of all Christians? Does not the Crucified One create the crucified mind within us and nurture it? Is it not true that only the crucified mind can respond joyously to the call of the Father reclaiming his lost Son to 'dance, music and feast' in the event of dead–alive/lost–found?

Kosuke Koyama, *Waterbuffalo Theology*, 'Towards a Crucified Mind' extract (1974)

295 Christ's Mercy

An Orthodox understanding of humanity's plight and salvation is provided by Anthony Bloom, Metropolitan Archbishop of the Russian Orthodox diocese covering Great Britain, in his exegesis of the Jesus Prayer. (Cf. **92**, **93**, **269**.)

[The Jesus Prayer] is profoundly rooted in the spirit of the gospel, and it is not in vain that the great teachers of Orthodoxy have always insisted on the fact that the Jesus Prayer sums up the whole of the gospel. This is why the Jesus Prayer can only be used in its fullest sense if the person who uses it belongs to the gospel, is a member of the church of Christ.

All the messages of the gospel, and more than the messages, the reality of the gospel, is contained in the name, in the person of Jesus. If you take the first half of the prayer you will see how it expresses our faith in the Lord: 'Lord Jesus Christ, Son of God.' At the heart we find the name of Jesus; it is the name before whom every knee shall bow, and when we pronounce it we affirm the historical event of the incarnation. We affirm that God, the Word of God, co-eternal with the Father, became man, and that the fullness of the godhead dwelt in our midst bodily in his person.

To see in the man of Galilee, in the prophet of Israel, the incarnate Word of God, God become man, we must be guided by the Spirit, because it is the Spirit of God who reveals to us both the incarnation and the lordship of Christ. We call him Christ, and we affirm thereby that in him were fulfilled the prophecies of the Old Testament [cf. **1**, **56**]. To affirm that Jesus is the Christ implies that the whole history of the Old Testament is ours, that we accept it as the truth of God. We call him son of God, because we know that the Messiah expected by the Jews,[10] the man who was called 'son of David' by Bartimaeus, is the incarnate son of God. These words sum up all we know, all we believe about Jesus Christ, from the Old Testament to the New, and from the experience of the church through the ages. In these few words we make a complete and perfect profession of faith.

But it is not enough to make this profession of faith; it is not enough to believe. The devils also believe and tremble. Faith is not sufficient to work salvation, it must lead to the right relationship with God; and so, having professed, in its integrity, sharply and clearly, our faith in the lordship and in the person, in the historicity and in the divinity of Christ, we put ourselves face to face with him, in the right state of mind: 'Have mercy on me, a sinner.'

These words 'have mercy' are used in all the Christian churches and, in Orthodoxy, they are the response of the people to all the petitions suggested by the priest. Our modern translation 'have mercy' is a limited and insufficient one. The Greek word which we find in the gospel and in the early liturgies is *eleison*. *Eleison* is of the same root as *elaion*, which means olive tree and the oil from it. [. . .] We find the image of the olive tree in Genesis. After the flood Noah sends birds, one after the other, to find out whether there is any dry land or not, and one of them, a dove—and it is significant that it is a dove—brings back a small twig of olive. This twig conveys to Noah and to all with him in the ark the news that the wrath of God has ceased, that God is now offering man a fresh opportunity. All those who are in the ark will be able to settle again on firm ground and make an attempt to live, and never more perhaps, if they can help it, undergo the wrath of God.

In the New Testament, in the parable of the good Samaritan, olive oil is poured to soothe and to heal. In the anointing of kings and priests in the Old Testament, it is again oil that is poured on the head as an image of the grace of God that comes down and flows on them giving them new power to fulfil what is beyond human capabilities. The king is to stand on the threshold, between the will of men and the will of God, and he is called to lead his people to the fulfilment of God's will; the priest also stands on that threshold, to proclaim the will of God and to do even more: to act for God, to pronounce God's decrees and to apply God's decision.

The oil speaks first of all of the end of the wrath of God, of the peace which God offers to the people who have offended against him; further it speaks of God healing us in order that we should be able to live and become what we are called to be; and as he knows that we are not capable with our own strength of fulfilling either his will or the laws of our own created nature, he pours his grace abundantly on us. He gives us power to do what we could not otherwise do.

The words *milost* and *pomiluy* in Slavonic have the same root as those which express tenderness, endearing, and when we use the words *eleison*, 'have mercy on us', *pomiluy*, we are not just asking God to save us from his wrath—we are asking for love.

If we turn back to the words of the Jesus Prayer, 'Lord Jesus Christ, Son of God, have mercy on me, a sinner,' we see that the first words express with exactness and integrity the gospel faith in Christ, the historical incarnation of the Word of God; and the end of the prayer expresses all the complex rich relationships of love that exist between God and his creatures.

Anthony Bloom, *Living Prayer*, ch. 6: 'The Jesus Prayer', extract (1966)

II. Liberation

The twentieth century saw a resurgence of a theology according to which the gospel entailed a view of the world that called into question many established social, political, and cultural structures. The memory of Jesus has been found to be a disruptive, disquieting, disturbing memory—a memory which challenges the Church and undermines the oppressive societies within which the Church finds itself.

296   Recognizing the Poor

The Second Vatican Council (1962–5) was called by Pope John XXIII to renew and reform the life of the Catholic church. It proved to be a decisive moment not just for Catholics, but for Christians worldwide, and many of its implications are still being worked out and fought over. The Dogmatic Constitution on the Church, *Lumen Gentium*, was promulgated in 1964, and opened a door for Catholic liberation theology. (Cf. **300, 332**.)

Christ, the one mediator, established and ceaselessly sustains here on earth his holy church, the community of faith, hope and charity, as a visible structure. Through her he communicates truth and grace to all. But, the society furnished with hierarchical agencies and the mystical body of Christ [34] are not to be considered as two realities, nor are the visible assembly and the spiritual community, nor the earthly church and the church endowed with heavenly riches. Rather they form one interlocked reality which is comprised of a divine and a human element. For this reason, by an excellent analogy, this reality is compared to the mystery of the incarnate Word [cf. **112, 272**]. Just as the assumed nature inseparably united to the divine Word serves him as a living instrument of salvation [cf. **71**], so, in a similar way, does the communal structure of the church serve the Christ's Spirit, who vivifies it by way of building up the body. [. . .]

Just as Christ carried out the work of redemption in poverty and under oppression, so the church is called to follow the same path in communicating to men the fruits of salvation. Christ Jesus, 'though he was by nature God . . . emptied himself, taking the poor nature of a slave' [**39**] and 'being rich, he became poor' [2 Cor. 8: 9] for our sakes. Thus, although the church needs human resources to carry out her mission, she is not set up to seek earthly glory, but to proclaim humility and self-sacrifice, even by her own example.

Christ was sent by the Father 'to bring good news to the poor, and to heal the contrite of heart' [Luke 4: 18], 'to seek and to save what was lost' [Luke 19: 10]. Similarly, the church encompasses with love all those who are afflicted with human weakness. Indeed, she recognises in the poor and the suffering the likeness of her poor and suffering founder [cf. **37**]. She does all she can to relieve their need and in them she strives to serve Christ. While Christ, 'holy, innocent, undefiled' [Heb. 7: 20], knew nothing of sin, but came to expiate only the sins of the people, the church, embracing sinners in her bosom, is at the same time holy and always in need of being purified, and incessantly pursues the path of penance and renewal.

The church, 'like a pilgrim in a foreign land, presses forward amid the persecutions of the world and the consolations of God,'[III] announcing the cross and death of the Lord until he comes [cf. **14**]. By the power of the risen Lord, she is given strength to overcome patiently and lovingly the afflictions and hardships which assail her from within and without, and to show forth in the world the mystery of the Lord in a faithful though shadowed way, until at last it will be revealed in total splendour.

Vatican II, *Dogmatic Constitution of the Church*, ch. 1, §8, extracts (1964)

297 Liberating Jesus

Kim Chi Ha (1941–) is a Korean Catholic poet and playwright who through the 1970s and 1980s was repeatedly imprisoned and tortured by the Seoul authorities for his subversive work. The leper, a sorry outcast, has just been addressed by a statue of Jesus standing behind him, adorned with a golden crown. (Cf. **298**.)

JESUS: Don't be surprised. I am only Jesus. Why are you surprised? Now listen carefully to what I say.

LEPER: Jesus, you are Jesus? I must be going crazy! There's something wrong with my hearing. (*Pauses. Looks again at statue.*) Did I just hear Jesus speak?

JESUS: There is nothing wrong with your hearing. Because you are an honest and poor man you have drawn me close to you. That is why you can now hear my words.

LEPER: Oh, you are truly Jesus. (*He kneels down, crosses himself, without being aware of it, and clasps his hands, prayer-like.*)

JESUS: Come closer to me. Forget your fear and listen carefully to what I tell you. Remember these words.

LEPER: (*He stands up and moves closer to Jesus, as if he cannot resist.*) Yes, Jesus. (*When he comes close to the figure, he again kneels down.*)

JESUS: I have been closed up in this stone for a long, long time, . . . entombed in this dark, lonely, suffocating prison. I have longed to talk with you, the kind and poor people like yourself, and share your sufferings. I can't begin to tell you how long I have waited for this day, . . . this day when I would be freed from my prison, this day of liberation when I would live and burn again as a flame inside you, inside the very depths of your misery. But now you have finally come. And because you have come close to me I can speak now. You are my rescuer.

LEPER: Who put you in prison? Tell me who they are.

JESUS: You know them well. They are like the Pharisees. They locked me in a shrine for their own gain. They pray using my name in a way that prevents my reaching out to poor people like yourself. In my own name, they nailed me down to the cross again. They boast about being my disciples, but they are egotistical, they cannot trust each other, they do not suffer loneliness, and they are without wisdom, like those who first crucified me. They shun the poor and hungry, ignore the cries of the suffering, and dwell only on the acquisition of material gain, wealth, power, and glory. And this stops up their ears so they do not hear my words of warning or the laments of people like you. It is for these reasons that they imprisoned me.

LEPER: What can be done to free you, Jesus, make you live again so that you can come to us?

JESUS: My power alone is not enough. People like you must help to liberate me. Those who seek only the comforts, wealth, honour, and power of this world, who wish entry to the kingdom of heaven for themselves only and ignore the poor and less fortunate, cannot give me life again. Neither can those who have never suffered loneliness, who remain silent while injustice is done and so acquiesce to it, who are without courage. It is the same with those without courage who are unwilling to resist such evildoers as dictators and other tyrants who inflict great suffering on the weak and poor. Prayer alone is not enough; it is necessary also to act. Only those, though very poor and suffering like yourself, who are generous in spirit and seek to help the poor and the wretched can give me life again. You have helped give me life again. You removed the gold crown from my head and so freed my lips to speak. People like you will be my liberators.

LEPER: Jesus, as you can see, I am helpless (*points to his crippled body*). I cannot even take care of myself. How then can I help you?

JESUS: It is for that exact reason you can help me. You are the only one who can do it. And through your deeds, and with the help of your people,

I will establish the kingdom of heaven on earth for all. It is your poverty, your wisdom, your generous spirit, and, even more, your courageous resistance against injustice that makes all this possible. Come closer, come closer and liberate now my body as you freed my lips. Remove this prison of cement. It is sufficient that I keep the crown of thorns. The crown of gold is merely the insignia of those ignorant, greedy, and corrupt people who value only displays of external pomp and showy decorations. Wearing it, I was tarnished, and neither free nor able to speak until you came along.

Kim Chi Ha, *The Gold-Crowned Jesus*, Act III, extract (*c.* 1971)

298   Hiding Jesus

Steve Turner (1944–) is a British pop journalist who has written on, among others, the Beatles, Cliff Richard, and Jack Kerouac. He is also a poet. This is from his 1980 collection *Nice and Nasty*. (Cf. **297**.)

There are people after Jesus.
They have seen the signs.
Quick, let's hide him.
Let's think; carpenter,
                fisherman's friend,
                disturber of religious comfort.
Let's award him a degree in theology,
a purple cassock
and a position of respect.
They'll never think of looking here.
Let's think;
his dialect may betray him,
his tongue is of the masses.
Let's teach him Latin
and seventeenth-century English,
they'll never think of listening in.
Let's think;
humble,
man of sorrows,
nowhere to lay his head.
We'll build a house for him,
somewhere away from the poor.
We'll fill it with brass and silence.
It's sure to throw them off.
There are people after Jesus.
Quick, let's hide him.

Steve Turner, 'How to Hide Jesus' (before 1980)

299   The Refusal of Tyranny

Conrad Noel (1864–1942) was the so-called 'red vicar' of Thaxted, Essex—a radical political thinker and liturgical innovator. This extract is a retelling of the story of Jesus' temptation in the wilderness, and has a wide eye open to the political implications of Jesus' refusal to be swayed. (Cf. **2, 191**.)

It was inevitable that once Jesus had seen the hollowness of the programme suggested by the second temptation he should sooner or later abandon the whole idea of nationalist dominion with which it was essentially bound up. But the mind in rejecting a certain policy does not for the moment perceive all its implications. His struggle in the wilderness had already brought him to the certainty that liberty is more important than provender, and that the liberty preached by the Jewish revolutionary party was the Puritans' liberty—that is, liberty to impose on others a 'rigorist culture'. Must he not then abandon the conventional role of the 'Son of God', the programme expected of a Messiah by his nationalist contemporaries?

Here in the rank swamps of the desert both mind and body are oppressed and circumscribed. The Galileans loved the heights. Jesus had been brought up in a hill country and in after life, faced with tremendous issues, a climb in the mountains brings him vigour and assurance; there he could walk and talk with God; they seemed to transfigure him. 'I will lift up mine eyes unto the hills, from whence cometh my help' [Ps. 121: 1].

As he climbs into that free world of the hills he seems to be climbing out of the small world of Palestinian politics, with its attempt to force God's hand, its bargainings, its parochial self-satisfaction, its Pharisaic sneer at all that is not Israel. Moses from the summit, that now loomed above him, must have had a great outlook on things, and a national poet had sung: 'Ask of me and I shall give thee the heathen for thine inheritance, and the uttermost parts of the earth for thy possessions' [Ps. 2: 8]. But Moses, after all, had wanted to annex these lands for the benefit of his own folk. Surely God's scheme of things is larger than this? The winds from far lands that beat about him as he climbed, and the mountain earth beneath his feet warmed by the universal sun, proclaimed a bigger world than Palestine. And suddenly, from the top of that exceeding high mountain, there bursts upon him a vision of the kingdoms of the world and the glory of them. He sees one at least of the great trade routes that cut through Palestine, linking up Europe with the desert people of the East, and perhaps the route that connects Egypt with Asia. He sees the caravans of many nations crawling along the roads beneath him—a Roman legion or the troops of Herod, that Edomite servant of Rome. [. . .]

The horizon widens. He has cast aside the nationalist dream. [. . .] Is he not called by God to the lordship of existing kingdoms and empires, welding them into a mighty whole and dominating them for their good?

By capturing the existing governmental machineries would he not also capture the allegiance of the peoples? If Rome had succeeded, to some extent, in mingling the peoples of the Mediterranean world, destroying frontiers, removing barriers of race and speech, and overcoming those prejudices of the mind and spirit which divide mankind—if Rome had done this in spite of her but thinly concealed object of exploitation, how much better would he be able to weld the world together for the purpose of bringing mankind that peace it so much needed? Could not a benevolent overlord, rejecting the greed and avarice of both Gentile and Jewish imperialism, secure for the nations the freedom and plenty which were their God-given right?

Would not the capture of existing machineries secure for him the allegiance of the common man, who only longed for peace and security? After all, why make too great a demand on human nature at the first? Why not win the world by satisfying its age-long needs? Were they not anxious about what they should eat and what they should drink and wherewithal they should be clothed? After all these things the nations were seeking, and surely with reason after ages of internecine wars. Why not satisfy their immediate needs, and once having won their loyalty begin to teach them those deeper principles which the cares of hunger and bondage must for the present obscure? [. . .]

At all costs one must worship God and do him service, but what is the nature of God? If God be the thundering Jupiter of the pagans, or the alien Jehovah of current Jewish thought, then he is truly represented by the divine emperor exercising lordship over all the kingdoms; but Jesus was convinced that God was not like that. He called him the father of the human family, and his Messiah the servant of mankind.

To rule mankind as benevolent tyrant was now clearly seen by our Lord to be a rejection of the will of God who does not impose his sway upon unwilling peoples or force them into submission for their good. If Jesus were truly the Son of God, his Messiahship must not be a benevolent despotism; he must not rule men in majestic aloofness, but must become their commander through having learned to be their minister.

And even if a good despotism had been the divine method of governing mankind, what method had to be used if one were to climb to such a world-leadership? Political cunning, crafty alliances, callousness to human suffering, lying subterfuges—the leaven of the Herods.

Not only the long and mudstained climb to the summit, the Herodian way, by which one might gain the whole world, but lose one's own soul and find oneself a soulless despot, possessing all power, but with the will to use it benevolently for ever gone—not only this sinister method of obtaining power, but the power itself when obtained is seen by Jesus to be a falling down and a worshipping of Satan. With vehemence he rejects it with the words: 'Get thee hence, Satan; for it is written, "Thou shalt worship the Lord thy God, and him only shalt thou serve." '

Conrad Noel, *The Life of Jesus*, ch. XII, extracts (1937)

300 Liberation Christology

Leonardo Boff (1938–) is a Brazilian Franciscan theologian. He studied under Karl Rahner (cf. **321**) in Germany, and has been one of the key voices in Latin American Liberation Theology, a movement emerging from post-Vatican II (cf. **296**) Catholicism seeking to resituate theology within practical solidarity with the poor and disfranchised and their struggle for liberation. (Cf. **332**.)

The liberation Christology elaborated from the stand-point of Latin America stresses the historical Jesus over the Christ of faith:

— Because it sees a structural similarity between the situations in Jesus' day and those in our own time. In other words, it sees objective oppression and dependence lived out subjectively as contrary to God's historical design.

— Because the historical Jesus puts us in direct contact with his liberative program and the practices with which he implements it.

— Because the historical Jesus makes clear the conflict that any liberative praxis will provoke and points up the probable destiny of any prophetic bearer of a liberation project.

— Because the historical Jesus sheds clear light on the chief elements of christological faith: i.e., following his life and his cause in one's own life. It is in this following that the truth of Jesus surfaces; and it is truth insofar as it enables people to transform this sinful world into the kingdom of God while also being able to vindicate itself before the demands of human reason insofar as reason is open to the infinite. Jesus does not present himself as the explanation of reality. He presents himself as an urgent demand for the transformation of that reality.[12] It is in that sense that he constitutes its definitive explanation.

— Because the historical Jesus reveals the Father to us insofar as he shows us how to journey to that Father. Only in and through the process of conversion and practical change do we have access to the God of Jesus Christ. Abstract reflection (theory) does not provide us with that access.

— Because the historical Jesus fosters a critique of humanity and society as they appear historically. Only through conversion can they anticipate and

concretise God's kingdom, which is God's ultimate intention for humanity and the world. The historical Jesus signifies a crisis, not a justification,
for the world [cf. **281**]. He calls for a transformation rather than an
explanation of it. [. . .]

The advent of the eschatological kingdom as the full embodiment of
liberation has been delayed. In this context human life possesses a paschal[10]
structure. This translates into following the crucified and risen Jesus Christ.

The first and primary aspect of following Jesus is proclaiming the utopia of
the kingdom as the real and complete meaning of the world that is offered to
all by God.

Second, the following of Jesus means translating that utopia into practice.
We must try to change the world on the personal, social, and cosmic level.
This utopia is not an ideology, but it does give rise to functional ideologies
that will guide liberative practices. The following of Jesus is not mere imitation. We must take due account of the differences between Jesus' situation
and our own. In his day there was an apocalyptic atmosphere and people
were looking for the immediate breakthrough of the kingdom. In our eyes
the parousia has been held up and history still has a future. Hence there must
be differences in the way we organise love and justice in society.

To be sure, for both Jesus and us God is the future and his kingdom has not
yet fully arrived; but our way of shouldering history will vary from his. Jesus
did not prescribe any concrete model. Instead he offered a way of being
present in every concrete embodiment of the kingdom, though such
embodiments will obviously depend on the details of a given situation. What
he offers us by way of example is an option on behalf of those who are
treated unjustly, a refusal to succumb to the will for power and domination,
and solidarity with everything that suggests greater participation in societal
living and fraternal openness to God.

Third, God's liberation translates into a process that will entail conflict and
struggle. These conflicts must be taken on and understood in the light of
Jesus' own burdensome journey. It is a journey of love that sometimes must
sacrifice itself. It is a journey of eschatological hope that must go by way of
political hopes. It is a journey of faith that must move ahead gropingly; the
fact that we are Christians does not provide us with a key to decipher political
and economic problems. Cross and resurrection are paradigms of Christian
existence.

To follow Jesus means to follow through with his work and attain his
fulfilment.

Leonardo Boff, *Jesus Christ Liberator: A Critical Christology for our Time*, Epilogue, extracts
(1972)

301 Christ and the Crowd

Byung Mu Ahn is a Korean Professor of New Testament and a campaigner for social justice. He was a key figure in the development of Minjung theology, a theology which works from the point of view of the people (*minjung*), the masses, the crowd, rather than the elite.

Because we have been enslaved by the Christology of the Kerygma,[14] even when we read the Synoptics, we focused our attention on Jesus as the Christ and considered him to be the centre of the Gospel. In this way we used to identify Jesus with the Christ and were quite content with this identification. However, as we began to read the Synoptics again with more sceptical eyes, the features of Jesus turned out to be quite different.

First, we found out that Jesus is in incessant action. Unlike the Christ of the Kerygma, Jesus is not holding fast to his unshakeable seat (throne) within the Church. By no means is he ruling as an original perfect being, but acts freely without being bound to religious norms. This image of Jesus is quite different from such images as the Son of God, the Messiah, the pre-existent Being, the exalted Christ sitting on a throne, and the coming Christ who will be the Judge on the last day, etc.

Secondly, Jesus associates and lives with the Minjung. On no account is he an aloof, lofty person, but instead he eats and drinks with the Minjung, sometimes asking favours from them or vice versa, granting their requests. So we can say: 'Where there is Jesus, there is the Minjung. And where there is the Minjung, there is Jesus.' [. . .]

Traditional Christology has been consistent in its explanation of seeing Jesus' role within the frame of God's drama. That is to say, Jesus is the true Messiah in the sense that he obeyed and fulfilled God's will. In the Gospels, of course, similar ideas can be found. In the Passion-history, for example, Jesus' agony at Gethsemane and his cry on the cross reflect such an image of Jesus. But we do have another tradition, which conveys an absolutely different image of Jesus, who identifies himself with the cries and wishes of the suffering Minjung. It is particularly the healing-stories that expose this image of Jesus. The Jesus who heals the sick people is by no means described as someone who fulfils a pre-established programme. Jesus never seeks for the sick persons voluntarily, nor does he follow an earlier intention (plan) for helping them. On the contrary, the request always comes from the Minjung's side first. And accordingly, Jesus' healing activities appear as him being obedient to the wishes of the patients. In other words, it is the sick who take the initiative for such events to happen. Jesus' healing power, which has a functional relation to the suffering of the Minjung, can be realised only when it is met by the will of the Minjung. It is from this aspect that Mark reports, without hesitation, that Jesus could do no mighty works in his native town, because they did not believe in him.

Jesus, sharing the living realities of the sick, the poor, the alienated, and the women, speaks to God on behalf of the Minjung, as if he was their spokesman. [. . .]

[I]n order to correctly interpret Jesus as the Christ we must endow *ochlos*[15] in the Gospels with the proper esteem with regard to their relationship with Jesus. This Jesus is not the Christ who is facing man from God's side, but the Christ who is facing God from man's side. So in this case it means that man is not an abstract being but the concrete Minjung who are suffering. Therefore the Jesus who is one with the Minjung, facing God from their direction—*he is Christ*. He identifies himself with the Minjung. He exists for no other than for the Minjung.

Now, is Jesus as the Christ the Saviour of mankind? If so, salvation is not a manufactured product given to man from heaven to possess. On the contrary, it means the salvation that Jesus realised in the action of transforming himself, by listening to and responding to the cry of Minjung.

Byung Mu Ahn, 'Jesus and the People', extract (1987)

302   Soulful Christianity

The relationship of Christians to revolutionary politics has been complex. In the late 1960s the Christian World Liberation Front (CWLF) emerged as one of the groups making up the Jesus People, or Jesus Freaks, a Christian component of or alternative to the radical subcultures of the time. They produced their own 'Liberation Programme' as a response to the radical left-wing manifesto published by the Berkeley Liberation Movement. Whether the CWLF manifesto is politically radical or radically apolitical is open to debate.

Christian World Liberation Front, *New Berkeley Liberation Program* (c.1970)

Berkeley Liberation Programme	*New Berkeley Liberation Programme*
1. We will make Telegraph Avenue and the South Campus a strategic free territory for revolution.	1. He will free all who come to him from bondage to the crippled self, the maimed world, and the scheming devil.
2. We will create our revolutionary culture everywhere.	2. He will enable all who come to him to develop their inner talents, abilities and resources to the fullest.

3. We will turn the schools into training grounds for liberators.

3. He will turn the schools into training grounds for liberation of the inner self.

4. We will destroy the university unless it serves the people.

4. He will destroy the powers that bind us as we turn to him, the only one who truly serves the people.

5. We will struggle for the full liberation of women as a necessary part of the revolutionary process.

5. He will provide for the full liberation of men and women as a necessary part of the revolutionary process of building his family.

6. We will take command responsibility for basic human needs.

6. He will take responsibility for basic human needs.

7. We will protect and expand our drug culture.

7. He will make drugs obsolete.

8. We will break the power of the landlords and provide beautiful housing for everyone.

8. He will bring a new spirit of concern and co-operation among people who turn to him and trust him for moment by moment direction.

9. We will tax the corporations, not the working people.

9. He will continue to show his concern for the poor and oppressed people of the world.

10. We will defend ourselves against law and order.

10. He will eliminate fear of tyrannical forces and powers.

11. We will create a soulful socialism in Berkeley

11. He will create a soulful Christianity in Berkeley.

12. We will create a people's government.

12. He will govern perfectly.

13. We will unite with other movements throughout the world to destroy this racist-capitalist-imperialist system.

13. He will unite Berkeley Christians with others throughout the world to demonstrate his alternative to the present world system in all of its manifold manifestations.

Christian World Liberation Front, *New Berkeley Liberation Program* (c.1970)

Kofi Appiah-Kubi was a Ghanaian sociologist who was involved in the Ecumenical Association of Third World Theologians. Here he explores what contribution a specifically African context can make to the elucidation of Christology. (Cf. **304**.)

Jesus is a liberator. Liberation here must be understood in its totality, as removal of all that which keeps the African in bondage, all that makes him less than what God intended him to be. It connotes the total idea of liberation from fear, uncertainty, sickness, evil powers, foreign domination and oppression, distortion of his humanity, poverty and want. In brief, it embraces religious, political, socio-economic, spiritual and mystical, personal and societal concerns of the African convert. Jesus Christ therefore, by implication, liberates the African Christian from disease, human and natural disasters, from tribalism, racism and any monstrous and inhuman political domination. Liberation therefore is central in the contemporary oral African Theology. [. . .] Jesus' own self-identification with the poor and needy makes his proclamation—'I have come that they may have life and have it more abundantly' [John 10: 10]—more meaningful to the African Christian. This ties in neatly with his traditional idea of religion, which strongly repudiates the complacent Euro-American doctrine of 'Pie-in-the-sky-when-you-die', which is a distortion of the message and person of Christ. [. . .]

Illness in African society is often attributed to the breaking of a taboo or machinations of malicious or sometimes displeased ancestral spirits. Other causes may be 'the evil eye', witchcraft, possession by an evil spirit, or a curse by a sorcerer or an offended neighbour. It is generally believed that the victim himself may not be the offender, but may suffer from the mistake or offence of a kinsman, or relative. Most African societies regard illness as a misfortune which involves the whole person. This has direct bearing on the relationship of the patient with the spiritual or supernatural world and with the members of the society.

[. . .] Even though most Africans recognise the natural causes of certain illnesses, this does not preclude the simultaneous role of the supernatural causes. Every misfortune, like any piece of good fortune, involves two questions: The first is how it happened, and the second is why. The 'How' is answered by common-sense empirical observation, but the 'Why' is not easily explicable. Belief in witchcraft and other supernatural powers explains why particular persons at particular times and places suffer particular misfortunes—death, accident, disease, barrenness, or crop failure. It is the 'Why me?' question that the Africans ask to which they seek an answer; an answer in which they link social problems to divine actions. The belief in evil forces as a cause of misfortune and disease is part of the African answer to the general problem of misfortune and the existence of evil in the world. Natural events and the morality of social relations are interrelated. To the African, society, its natural environment and its members, form a single system or morally inter-dependent relationship. As far as African people are concerned, disease, misfortune, etc. have a mystical causation. To combat these therefore, the cause must be found and uprooted.

For common people, however, religion is largely the means of reinforcing life, of proper precautions against powers which might destroy them. Africans do not make a clear distinction between religion and medicine. Health to most Africans is symptomatic of a correct relationship between people and their environment. Health therefore, is not an isolated phenomenon, but part of the entire magico-religious fabric [. . .]. Salvation therefore to the African is a matter of here and now. Eschatology as understood in the western world does not form part of the African thought-form. For many, the experience of salvation is a sign that with the coming of Jesus, suffering and death are eliminated, and these will have no room in the Kingdom of God established here on earth.

Jesus Christ is thus conceived by many African Christians as the great physician, healer and victor over worldly powers *par excellence*. To many, Jesus came that we might have life and have it more abundantly. [. . .]

It is precisely at this point that Indigenous African Christian Churches have made a break-through. They believe that total personal healing of spiritual, psychological and physical man is the gift of God, which he pours on his believing community through Jesus Christ. Christ is seen as being more powerful than any evil power, even though they recognise the existence of such evil powers.

These Churches' approach to healing does not aim at supplanting medical treatment, but at supplementing it. Their healing message through prayers, vision, dreams, use of consecrated water, olive oil, and ashes in the name of Jesus aims at dealing with practical problems of life. For them God or Jesus is the power by which they can overcome their daily worries, concerns and fears; and the source of their entire life. The commonest reply one gets to the question, 'Why did you join this or that Indigenous African Church?' is, 'I was ill for a long time. I tried all forms of treatment, but to no avail. I was advised by a friend to go to prophet so-and-so. I did and now I am better. Praise the Lord!'

Jesus said, 'Heal the sick, cleanse the lepers, raise the dead, cast out demons. Freely ye received; freely give' [Matt. 10: 8]. And the indigenous African Christian Churches answer: in the name of Jesus the great healer, our churches are not only churches but hospitals. Therefore bring all your worries of unemployment, poverty, witch troubles, ill-luck, enemy, barrenness, sorrow, blindness, etc. Jesus is ready to save all who come to him in belief and faith. We treat, and God or Jesus heals.

Kofi Appiah-Kubi, 'Christology', extracts (1976)

304   Jesus, Master of Initiation

> Anselme T. Sanon is the Catholic Bishop of Bobo-Dioulasso in Burkino Faso. Here he explores how African culture can provide new resources for us to understand the nature of salvation in Christ. (Cf. 303.)

Salvation stands for the final state of things and persons. To lead them to this final perfection, and bring to a good end what is already begun, a master is needed, a teacher, a chief who will set those who are to be saved gradually and dynamically upon this path. The initiatory dynamic can be conceptualised as the beginning of a journey, as a gradual undertaking, and as the acquisition of the perfection that constitutes the goal. At each step, so to speak, the master of initiation is present.

On this score, to say that Jesus is Chief of initiation is to recognise in him, in our particular cultural tonality, the eldest sibling who guides to perfection those who have undergone their initiation—that is, those who, with him, have started down the road to the experience of the invisible through what is visible, to the encounter with God through the human being, to touch eternity through the symbol of the present life. [. . .]

According to the initiation tradition, Jesus cannot be promoted to master without having himself been subjected to the initiatory experience. The chief who presides as initiation master must himself have undergone initiation.

If we examine the matter attentively, we see that, from his birth to his burial, Jesus lived after the fashion of his people, according to the tradition that had been given him. That tradition, while availing itself of the mediation of the book, was above all contoured to the fundamental rhythms of biological and social life. It is very often through this received tradition that Jesus introduces surprising novelties—for example, the eucharistic meal, whose setting is the traditional Passover meal. Thus was Jesus initiated according to the tradition of his people, in their manner, and from out of their tradition. He was for us an initiation chief who introduces into every cultural initiation a radical novelty that does not pass. [. . .]

According to the letter to the Hebrews Jesus is the one who leads saved humanity to its perfection, and this in a definitive manner. The initiatory rhythm that he inaugurates is that of his entire life. To be born, to grow, to suffer, to die, and to be buried with the desire for an endless happiness—here is an experience found inscribed on the horizon of all human beings. In Jesus' experience, these stages assume the sorrowful aspect of the cross, but proclaim the glorious resurrection.

When Jesus says, 'It is consummated,' we recognise that he has completed his human initiation. All has come to the final term designated by the Father.

The same letter plunges us to the heart of our undertaking, when it declares: 'By a single oblation, he has perfected forever those whom he sanctifies' [Heb. 10: 14]. Christ's oblation, his total gift by the sacrifice on the cross, is the act of initiation for himself definitively, and it is valid with regard to all human beings. It is the visibly foundational act of the redemption.

A more careful reading of this passage clearly reveals not only a vocabulary of initiation, but also the stages of the initiation experience. Jesus enters upon these stages of his own free will as eldest child. In the footsteps of this initiation master so full of constancy and perseverance, the disciples race to the fore, catching what he says word for word, desirous of beholding what he delineates in draft, hoping to arrive where he leads. [. . .]

Initiation, established by the ancestors and proceeding according to the spirit of their tradition, is the deed of a subsequent generation. The candidacy of the initiated is regarded as that of children born of one and the same life, albeit in a hierarchy of siblingship.

We strongly feel this bond of siblingship with Christ. He is the child in the house of his Father. He chose the path of initiation as a child seeking to obey a Father. He who has not known the sin of rebellion in solidarity with his siblings, will know what it costs to obey on behalf of the one who has deserted the Father's house.

We find here one of the functions of siblingship in initiation: that of mediation. According to this tradition, one of the sibling candidates, most likely the eldest, the chief candidate, represents the group. He is the group— for better or for worse. We readily understand that he would be regarded as 'intercessor as God himself would do.' After all, 'he intercedes for the poorest.'

Christ plays this role as elder brother, acknowledging a multitude of siblings. He is the first elder brother of human beings. In solidarity with them he accepts all of the trials of human existence, accomplishing, first on their behalf, and then with them, the dolorous path of return to the house of the Father. He does so as master and sovereign.

Here he exercises a type of authority proper to initiatory societies. He is indeed chief, but as a brother. He is master, but as servant. He exercises an authority of siblingship.

Anselme T. Sanon, 'Jesus, Master of Initiation', extracts (1992)

Elizabeth Amoah is a theologian at the University of Ghana who has written extensively on the experience of African women and its implications for theology. Here she surveys some of the ways in which Christology has become indigenous in Africa. (Cf. **304**.)

Throughout Africa unifying elements of emerging Christologies include a strong reliance on the Bible and church traditions; an emphasis on African traditional teachings and the use of indigenous African symbolism and imagery; and significant consideration of the socio-cultural context, the real situations in which Africans live. Widely accepted images or understandings of Jesus are Christ as the Greatest Ancestor [. . .], the Proto-Ancestor [. . .], and Christ the Brother-Ancestor [. . .]. Jesus is also understood as healer, liberator, chief, or elder brother. Use of these images is often dependent on the historical, cultural, or social context and responds directly to the needs of Christians for relief from hunger, suffering, injustice, or oppression. In Ghana, for example, certain features of the religio-cultural heritage of the people influence the development of both formal and informal Christologies. These include the pervasive presence and power of the Spirit and the constant need to equip oneself spiritually for life's contingencies; the tendency to emphasize the spiritual dimension of social experiences and the belief that spiritual powers can intervene in all aspects of human life; and the tendency to view religion as a means for survival and for enhancing all of life.

These resilient features of our cultural heritage have immensely coloured and influenced the formulation of Christological statements, particularly by the 'new' or 'popular' churches, otherwise known as charismatic, African instituted, or independent churches. Members of these churches have interpreted the gospel in ways relevant to African realities through popular 'gospel' music and other creative forms of expression. In these churches, an all-embracing Being, Jesus, helps people cope with concrete situations, ranging from hunger, barrenness, broken relationships, unemployment, fear of evil spirits and diseases, to death.

African women express their relationship with Jesus in particular Christological images. Christ becomes truly friend and companion, liberating women from the burden of disease, and from the ostracism of a society riddled with taboos and patriarchal assumptions about women. Women are honoured, accepted, and sanctified, whether single or married, mothers, or without children. A pregnant woman without primary health care available might see Jesus as the great and efficient midwife who helps ease the pain of childbirth. African widows, whose lives are often characterized by misery and poverty, might perceive Jesus as husband.

African Christians affirm a strong belief that Jesus enhances their entire life, which includes prosperity, fertility, virility, good health, and total protection from any evil spirit or source of fear. One might arguably conclude that the main emphasis of African Christologies is what Jesus can do to effect positive change in people's lives. This is not to say, however, that Africans ignore the Being of Jesus Christ, for one cannot separate the Being from his actions. The pragmatic attitude to religion and the holistic view of life clearly underscore the perception of Jesus Christ as a Being who cannot be limited to a particular model. Jesus Christ is the miraculous, all-embracing, wonderful Being who builds people up, particularly the excluded and those at the fringes of society, and leads them to experience the love of God.

Such varying bases of Christologies raise certain issues, such as how African Christological models, based on the use of African symbolism and imagery with their multiple interpretations and meanings in specific African contexts, can benefit the universal community of Christians. The image of Christ as ancestor is a good example. Some have argued that because the meaning of the word 'ancestor' is culturally specific, Jesus Christ cannot be an ancestor to all Africans and to the entire Christian community or to all humanity. Yet, the concept of Jesus Christ as ancestor can enrich the church's universal understanding of Christ if the ancestor is seen as a symbol of perfection and of relationships that are eternal, that extend beyond death. African ancestors, whose exemplary lives are worthy of emulation, are believed to be very concerned with the well-being of the members of the community. Jesus Christ as ancestor, then, is another way of saying that Jesus continues to live, to influence the lives of people, and to give them abundant life, according to his promises.

Elizabeth Amoah, 'African Christologies', extract (2000)

306 Black Jesus

Jaramogi Abebe Agyeman (Albert B. Cleagle Jr.) was founder and Holy Patriarch of the Pan-African Orthodox Christian Church, started in America in 1953. He was one of the early proponents of Black Theology. (Cf. **277**.)

For nearly 500 years the illusion that Jesus was white dominated the world only because white Europeans dominated the world. Now, with the emergence of the nationalist movements of the world's coloured majority, the historic truth is finally beginning to emerge—that Jesus was the non-white leader of a non-white people struggling for national liberation against the rule of a white nation, Rome. The intermingling of the races in Africa and the Mediterranean area is an established fact. The Nation Israel was a mixture of Chaldeans, Egyptians, Midianites, Ethiopians, Kushites, Babylonians and other dark peoples, all of whom were already mixed with the black people of Central Africa.

That white Americans continue to insist upon a white Christ in the face of all historical evidence to the contrary and despite the hundreds of shrines to Black Madonnas all over the world, is the crowning demonstration of their white supremacist conviction that all things good and valuable must be white. On the other hand, until black Christians are ready to challenge this lie, they have not freed themselves from their spiritual bondage to the white man nor established in their own minds their right to first-class citizenship in Christ's kingdom on earth. Black people cannot build dignity on their knees worshipping a white Christ. We must put down this white Jesus which the white man gave us in slavery and which has been tearing us to pieces.

Black Americans need to know that the historic Jesus was a leader who went about among the people of Israel, seeking to root out the individualism and the identification with their oppressor which had corrupted them, and to give them faith in their own power to rebuild the Nation. This was the real Jesus whose life is most accurately reported in the first three gospels of the New Testament. On the other hand, there is the spiritualised Jesus, reconstructed many years later by the Apostle Paul who never knew Jesus and who modified his teachings to conform to the pagan philosophies of the white gentiles. Considering himself an apostle to the gentiles, Paul preached individual salvation and life after death. We, as black Christians suffering oppression in a white man's land, do not need the individualistic and other-worldly doctrines of Paul and the white man. We need to recapture the faith in our power as a *people* and the concept of Nation, which are the foundations of the Old Testament and the prophets, and upon which Jesus built all of his teachings 2,000 years ago.

Jesus was a revolutionary black leader, a Zealot, seeking to lead a Black Nation to freedom.

Albert B. Cleagle, Jr., 'The Black Messiah', extracts (1968)

307   Christ for the Enslaved

> Kelly Brown Douglas is an African American theologian who has, with other womanist writers, taken mainstream feminism to task for its lack of attention to the specificity of black women's experience. Here she indicates how a Christology sensitive to that experience might look. (Cf. **306**.)

Each generation of Christians must answer the question: 'What does it mean for Jesus, a first-century Palestinian Jew, to be Christ (the Messiah, the incarnate one)?' The answer is inevitably shaped by a particular community's social, historical, cultural, and political context. Instead of a singular or universal Christological understanding, various Christologies emerge from diverse communities of people who attempt to understand fully the significance of God's revelation in Jesus.

Black Christology reflects a long tradition of black Christians probing the meaning of Jesus Christ in their struggle for life and freedom in a society that would deny them both because of their blackness. This Christology begins with the notion that Jesus brings God down to earth and is God's intimate presence in human history. The central symbol, the black Christ, signifies black people's witness to a Christ who walks with them, talks with them, and understands their tears and pain.

Black Christology is not grounded in the Nicaea/Chalcedon tradition but rather in the experience of slavery. While the Nicaea/Chalcedon tradition tends to minimize the significance of Jesus' earthly ministry, enslaved Africans highlighted this ministry in their attempts to reconcile their Christian faith with their enslavement. Relying on the gospels' witness to Jesus as opting for the downtrodden and oppressed, and recognizing the poignant similarities between their condition as chattel and Jesus' crucifixion, enslaved Christians testified in diverse ways that Jesus Christ was black.

Blackness in enslaved Christianity was not a statement about Jesus' ethnicity or skin colour but a testimony to his existential commitment to the life and freedom of the black enslaved. Jesus was a trusted friend who understood their agony, grief, and struggles. Grounded in the resurrection, the enslaved also believed that Jesus would deliver them from the tyranny of slavery. A Christology emerged that defined Jesus Christ as one who opposed white racism and affirmed black humanity.

Kelly Brown Douglas, 'African American Christologies', extract (2000)

308   Captivity

Dorothy L. Sayers (1893–1957) is best known as a writer of detective stories and creator of Lord Peter Wimsey. She turned to more theological themes later in life, translating Dante's *Divine Comedy* for instance, but already in 1918 she had published a strange book of poems about Christ, from which this piece comes.

Go, bitter Christ, grim Christ! haul if thou wilt
Thy bloody cross to thine own bleak Calvary!
When did I bind thee suffer for my guilt
To bind intolerable claims on me?
I loathe thy sacrifice; I am sick of thee.
They say thou reignest from the Cross. Thou dost,

And like a tyrant. Thou dost rule by tears,
Thou womanish Son of woman. Cease to thrust
Thy sordid tale of sorrows in my ears,
Jarring the music of my few, short years.
Silence! I say it is a sordid tale,
And thou with glamour hast bewitched us all;
We straggle forth to gape upon a graal,[16]
Sink into a stinking mire, are lost and fall . . .
The cup is wormwood and the drink is gall.
I am battered and broken and weary and out of heart,
I will not listen to talk of heroic things,
But be content to play some simple part,
Freed from preposterous, wild imaginings . . .
Men were not made to walk as priests and kings.
Thou liest, Christ, thou liest; take it hence,
That mirror of strange glories; I am I;
What wouldst thou make of me? O cruel pretence,
Drive me not mad with the mockery
Of that most lovely, unattainable lie!
I hear thy trumpets in the breaking morn,
I hear them restless in the resonant night,
Or sounding down the long winds over the corn
Before thee riding in the world's despite,
Insolent with adventure, laughter-light.
They blow aloud between love's lips and mine,
Sing to my feasting in the minstrel's stead,
Ring from the cup where I would pour the wine,
Rouse the uneasy echoes about my bed . . .
They will blow through my grave when I am dead.
O King, O Captain, wasted, wan with scourging,
Strong beyond speech and wonderful with woe,
Whither, relentless, wilt thou still be urging
Thy maimed and halt that have not strength to go? . . .
Peace, peace, I follow. Why must we love thee so?

Dorothy L. Sayers, 'Pantas Elkyso' (1918)

III. Ethics

In the twentieth century many theologians asked with renewed force just how acknowledging Jesus Christ should shape Christian action. The question has been posed and answered in endless forms, but we concentrate here on one central European figure, Dietrich Bonhoeffer (309), and one major American conversation, started by H. Richard Niebuhr (310). Niebuhr's ideas were taken in two different directions by subsequent generations—represented here by James Gustafson (311) and Stanley Hauerwas (312).

309   Life with Christ

Dietrich Bonhoeffer (1906–45) (cf. **320**) was one of the most attractive figures of twentieth century Western theology. He wove his impressive theological writing around involvement in the anti-Nazi Confessing Church, experiments in Christian community at Finkenwalde, involvement in a plot against Hitler, and finally imprisonment and execution by the Gestapo. In his unfinished *Ethics* he presents a powerful vision of life confronted by the word of God; life with Christ incarnate, crucified, and risen.

Radicalism hates time, and compromise hates eternity. Radicalism hates patience, and compromise hates decision. Radicalism hates wisdom, and compromise hates simplicity. Radicalism hates moderation and measure, and compromise hates the immeasurable. Radicalism hates the real, and compromise hates the word. To contrast the two attitudes in this way is to make it sufficiently clear that both alike are opposed to Christ. For in Jesus Christ those things which are here ranged in mutual hostility are one. The question of the Christian life will not, therefore, be decided and answered either by radicalism or by compromise, but only by reference to Jesus Christ himself. In him alone lies the solution for the problem of the relation between the ultimate and the penultimate.

In Jesus Christ we have faith in the incarnate, crucified and risen God. In the incarnation we learn of the love of God for his creation; in the crucifixion we learn of the judgement of God upon all flesh; and in the resurrection we learn of God's will for a new world. There could be no greater error than to tear these three elements apart; for each of them comprises the whole. It is quite wrong to establish a separate theology of the incarnation, a theology of the cross, or a theology of the resurrection, each in opposition to the others, by a misconceived absolutization of one of these parts; it is equally wrong to apply the same procedure to a consideration of the Christian life. A Christian ethic constructed solely on the basis of the incarnation would lead directly to the compromise solution. An ethic which was based solely on the cross or the resurrection of Jesus would fall victim to radicalism and enthusiasm. Only in the unity is the conflict resolved.

Jesus Christ the man—this means that God enters into created reality. It means that we have the right and the obligation to be men before God. The destruction of manhood, of man's quality as man, is sin, and is therefore a hindrance to God's redemption of man. Yet the manhood of Jesus Christ does not mean simply the corroboration of the established world and of the human character as it is. Jesus was man 'without sin' (Heb. 4.15); that is what is decisive. Yet among men Jesus lived in the most utter poverty, unmarried, and he died as a criminal. Thus the manhood of Jesus implies already a twofold condemnation of man, the absolute condemnation of sin and the relative condemnation of the established human orders. But even under this condemnation Jesus is really man, and it is his will that we shall be men. He neither renders the human reality independent nor destroys it, but he allows it to remain as that which is before the last, as a penultimate which requires to be taken seriously in its own way, and yet not to be taken seriously, a penultimate which has become the outer covering of the ultimate.

Jesus Christ the crucified—this means that God pronounces its final condemnation on the fallen creation. The rejection of God on the cross of Jesus Christ contains within itself the rejection of the whole human race without exception The cross of Jesus is the death sentence upon the world. Man cannot glory now in his humanity, nor the world in its divine orders. The glory of men has come now to its last end in the face of the Crucified, bruised and bloody and spat upon. Yet the crucifixion of Jesus does not simply mean the annihilation of the created world, but under this sign of death, the cross, men are now to continue to live, to their own condemnation if they despise it, but to their own salvation if they give it its due. The ultimate has become real in the cross, as the judgement upon all that is penultimate, yet also as mercy towards that penultimate which bows before the judgement of the ultimate.

Jesus Christ who rose again—this means that God out of his love and omnipotence sets an end to death and calls a new creation into life, imparts new life. 'Old things are passed away' (2 Cor. 5.17). 'Behold, I make all things new' (Rev. 21.5). Already in the midst of the old world, resurrection has dawned, as a last sign of its end and of its future, and at the same time as a living reality. Jesus rose again as a man, and by so doing he gave men the gift of the resurrection. Thus man remains man, even though he is a new, a risen man, who in no way resembles the old man. Until he crosses the frontier of his death, even though he has already risen again with Christ, be remains in the world of the penultimate, the world into which Jesus entered and the world in which the cross stands. Thus, so long as the earth continues, even the resurrection does not annul the penultimate, but the eternal life, the new life, breaks in with ever greater power into the earthly life and wins its space for itself within it.

We have tried to make clear the unity and the diversity of the incarnation, the cross and the resurrection. Christian life is life with the incarnate, crucified and risen Christ, whose word confronts us in its entirety in the message of the justification of the sinner by grace alone. Christian life means being a man through the efficacy of the incarnation; it means being sentenced and pardoned through the efficacy of the cross; and it means living a new life through the efficacy of the resurrection. There cannot be one of these without the rest. As for the question of the things before the last, it follows from what has been said so far that the Christian life means neither a destruction nor a sanctioning of the penultimate. In Christ the reality of God meets the reality of the world and allows us to share in this real encounter. It is an encounter beyond all radicalism and beyond all compromise. Christian life is participation in the encounter of Christ with the world.

Dietrich Bonhoeffer, *Ethics*, 'Last and Penultimate Things', extract (1943)

310 Virtue and Obedience

H. Richard Niebuhr (1894–1962), a Professor at Yale Divinity School influenced by Karl Barth (cf. **281**) and Ernst Troeltsch (cf. **235**), was the younger brother of the better-known Reinhold (1892–1971), yet may turn out to have had the more lasting influence on American theology. *Christ and Culture* is one of the seminal texts in theological ethics this century; here Niebuhr tries to provide a Chalcedonian (cf. **86**) interpretation of Christ's love, in order to ensure that Christian virtue is seen firmly in the context of radical obedience to God.

Jesus nowhere commands love for its own sake, and nowhere exhibits that complete dominance of the kindly over the aggressive sentiments and emotions which seems indicated by the idea that in him and for him love 'must completely fill the soul', or that his ethics is characterised by 'the ideal of love'. The virtue of love in Jesus' character and demand is the virtue of the *love of God and of the neighbour in God*, not the virtue of the love of love. The unity of this person lies in the simplicity and completeness of his direction toward God, whether the relation be one of love or of faith or of fear. Love, to be sure, is characterised by a certain extremism in Jesus, but its extremism is not that of a passion unmodified by any other passions; it is the extremism of devotion to the one God, uncompromised by love of any other absolute good. [. . .] For Jesus there is no other finally love-worthy being, no other ultimate object of devotion, than God; he is the Father; there is none good save God; he alone is to be thanked; his kingdom alone is to be sought. Hence the love of God in Jesus' character and teaching is not only compatible with anger but can be a motive to it, as when he sees the Father's house made into a den of thieves or the Father's children outraged. Hence also it is right and possible to underscore the significance of this virtue in Jesus, while at the same time one recognises that according to the Synoptic Gospels he emphasised in conduct and in teaching the virtues of faith in God and humility before him much more than love. [. . .]

To this interpretation of the unique nature of the virtue of love in Jesus as based on the single-mindedness of his devotion to God it will be objected that he practises and teaches a double love, of the neighbour as well as of God, and that his ethics has two foci, 'God, the Father, and the infinite value of the human soul' [cf. 262]. Such statements forget that the double commandment, whether originally stated or merely confirmed by Jesus, by no means places God and neighbour on a level, as though complete devotion were due to each. It is only God who is to be loved with heart, soul, mind and strength; the neighbour is put on the same level of value that the self occupies. Moreover, the idea of ascribing 'infinite' or 'intrinsic' value to the human soul seems wholly foreign to Jesus. He does not speak of worth apart from God. The value of man, like the value of sparrow and flower, is his value to God; the measure of true joy in value is the joy in heaven. Because worth is worth in relation to God, therefore Jesus finds sacredness in all creation, and not in humanity alone—though his disciples are to take special comfort from the fact that they are of more value to God than are the also valued birds. The virtue of neighbour-love in Jesus' conduct and teaching can never be adequately described if it is in any way abstracted from the primary love of God. Christ loves his neighbour not as he loves himself but as God loves him. Hence the Fourth Gospel, discerning that the Jewish statement 'Love thy neighbour as thyself' fitted adequately neither Jesus' actions nor his requirements, changed the commandment to read, 'Love one another as I have loved you.' Beyond that it became clear to the disciples that Jesus Christ's love of men was not merely an illustration of universal benevolence but a decisive act of divine Agape.[17] For we must face the recognition that what the early Christians saw in Jesus Christ, and what we must accept if we look at him rather than at our imaginations about him, was not a person characterised by universal benignity, loving God and man. His love of God and his love of neighbour are two distinct virtues that have no common quality but only a common source. Love of God is adoration of the only true good; it is gratitude to the bestower of all gifts; it is joy in holiness; it is 'consent to Being'. But the love of man is pitiful rather than adoring; it is giving and forgiving rather than grateful; it suffers for and in their viciousness and profaneness; it does not consent to accept them as they are, but calls them to repentance. The love of God is non-possessive eros; the love of man pure agape; the love of God is passion; the love of man, compassion. There is duality here, but not of like-minded interest in two great values, God and man. It is rather the duality of the Son of Man and Son of God, who loves God as man should love him, and loves man as only God can love, with powerful pity for those who are foundering.

H. Richard Niebuhr, *Christ and Culture*, ch. 1, §2: 'Toward a Definition of Christ', extracts (1949)

311 Christle Norm

James Gustafson, a student of H. Richard Niebuhr's, here presents a careful description of Christ's influence on Christian ethics: the Christian's image of Christ (described in terms very like those of Perrin; **284**), influences the factors brought to bear in the calculus of responsible moral decision-making. Gustafson has been highly critical of Stanley Hauerwas's alternative position (cf. **312**).

First, Christ provides for the Christian the normative point for the theological interpretation of what God is willing in the time and place of his life. He becomes the content-filled symbol for man's efforts to discern what God is enabling and requiring in the world. Second, the figure of Christ as given in the New Testament, with all of its descriptive and theological diversity, and the teachings attributed to him are normative in the sense of being the specific instance in which trust in God, and words and deeds directed toward men, find their most perfect correlation. Thus Christ is a particular paradigm to be turned to in order to shed light on what those who would follow him ought to be and do in particular instances as they seek to express their faith in words and deeds. Third, insofar as one's discipleship to Christ is to be the point around which the being and words and deeds of a person find their integrity, the Christian is obliged to consider Christ as the most important norm among others that are brought to bear in his judgments and actions. [. . .]

The Christian finds Christ to be a norm that illuminates his options and, insofar as he is loyal to Christ, deeply conditions his choice. Note that this is neither a claim that Christ prescribes what the options are, nor a claim that he dictates the choice. The latter, stronger affirmations are wrong, in my judgment, for several reasons. As has been reiterated again and again in this chapter, the analyses and choices are human, made by finite creatures with various biases and perspectives, and as the effects of human agency they can never claim divine sanction unambiguously. Agency, the capacity to decide, to act, to initiate and respond, is not only our human condition, but it is such by creation, and I believe it necessarily is respected by the providential power of God. Further, there is in most instances of serious moral choice no final happy resolution in which a single loyalty to Christ, or indeed to self or nation or any other object, simply and harmoniously makes all things fall together for the good of all concerned, or for the happiness and well-being of all concerned. Too often men seek and use Christ as the resolution for a secure decision in which all elements of tragedy and suffering are supposedly eliminated. Also there are many factors in most moral choices that have their own stubborn autonomy, and are not readily subsumed under an exclusive source of insight, whether this source be Christ, or love, or anything else. It is neither Christ nor love alone that tells the conscientious youth what his vocation ought to be; it is also his aptitudes, his opportunities, his desire to achieve, his awareness of various purposes, and many more. Neither Christ nor love alone tells the conscientious physician when to cease prolonging life; his medical knowledge, his obligations to the law and his patient, and many other factors are involved. Christ does not prescribe the options and dictate the choice of the Christian.

Christ, as a norm brought to bear, does, can, and ought to illuminate the options, and deeply condition the choice of the Christian. The figure of Christ given in the New Testament with all of its descriptions and theological diversity and the teachings attributed to him provide Christians with a source of illumination and a criterion of judgment, for in him there is an integrity of trust in, and loyalty to, God, and words and deeds directed toward men.

Certainly it must be admitted that conscientious Christians have somewhat different configurations of the meaning of Christ, are attracted by different 'portraits' of Christ. Part of the life of the Church is the formation of such a portrait, the judgment of excessively inadequate ones, the enrichment of those that suffer a poverty of appreciation. This task of the Church and of the Christian is not without some objectivity, however, since it is done in recognition of the place of Scripture as the document that provides the charter for faith and life.

To remember Christ, and the significance of his work, is part of making moral judgments in the Christian life.

James M. Gustafson, Christ and the Moral Life, ch. VIII: 'A Constructive Statement', extracts (1968)

312   Christ's Community

Stanley Hauerwas, Professor of Theological Ethics at Duke University, North Carolina, is a controversial theological ethicist who has taken an approach that differs significantly from Gustafson's (cf. **311**). Rather than focusing on moral decision-making as such, he describes the ways in which Christians are trained in Christian virtues in the Christ-shaped Church; focusing on the life-forming community rather than the morally responsible individual.

To be a disciple is to be part of a new community, a new polity, which is formed on Jesus' obedience to the cross. The constitutions of this new polity are the Gospels. The Gospels are not just the depiction of a man, but they are manuals for the training necessary to be part of the new community. To be a disciple means to share Christ's story, to participate in the reality of God's rule.

[. . .] Such a rule is more than the claim that God is Lord of this world. It is the creation of a 'world' through a story that teaches us how such a rule is constituted. Christians learn the power of this rule by loving as God has loved, through Jesus' life. That is, they love their 'enemies, and do good and lend without expecting return' for, if they do, their 'reward will be great, and you will be sons of the Most High; for he is kind to the ungrateful and the selfish. Be merciful, even as your Father is merciful' [Luke 6: 35–6].

It is through such love that Christians learn that they are to serve as he served. Such service is not an end in itself, but reflects the Kingdom into which Christians have been drawn. This means that Christians insist on service which may appear ineffective to the world. For the service that Christians are called upon to provide does not have as its aim to make the world better, but to demonstrate that Jesus has made possible a new world, a new social order.

It is a new world because no longer does the threat of death force us into desperate measures to ensure our safety or significance. A people freed from the threat of death must form a polity, because they can afford to face the truth of their existence without fear and defensiveness. They can even take the risk of having the story of a crucified Lord as their central reality. He is a strange Lord, appears powerless, but his powerlessness turns out to be the power of truth against the violence of falsehood.

The power that comes from trusting in truth is but a correlative of our learning through Jesus to accept our life as a gift. In Jesus we have met the one who has the authority and power to forgive our fevered search to gain security through deception, coercion, and violence. To learn to follow Jesus means we must learn to accept such forgiveness, and it is no easy thing to accept, as acceptance requires recognition of our sin as well as vulnerability. But by learning to be forgiven we are enabled to view other lives not as threats but as gifts. Thus in contrast to all societies built on shared resentments and fears, Christian community is formed by a story that enables its members to trust the otherness of the other as the very sign of the forgiving character of God's Kingdom.

By making the story of such a Lord central to their lives, Christians are enabled to see the world accurately and without illusion. Because they have the confidence that Jesus' cross and resurrection are the final words concerning God's rule, they have the courage to see the world for what it is: The world is ruled by powers and forces that we hardly know how to name, much less defend against. These powers derive their strength from our fear of destruction, cloaking their falsehood with the appearance of convention, offering us security in exchange for truth. By being trained through Jesus' story we have the means to name and prevent these powers from claiming our lives as their own.

From this perspective the church is the organised form of Jesus' story. The church provides the conditions we need to describe what is going on in our lives. That does not mean that all other descriptions are rendered irrelevant, but rather that we learn how to negotiate the limits and possibilities of those descriptions. We test them against the cross. It is in his cross that we learn we live in a world that is based on the presupposition that man, not God, rules.

Jesus is the story that forms the church. This means that the church first serves the world by helping the world to know what it means to be the world. For without a 'contrast model' the world has no way to know or feel the oddness of its dependence on power for survival. Because of the church the world can feel the strangeness of trying to build a politics that is inherently untruthful; the world lacks the basis to demand truth from its people. Because of a community formed by the story of Christ the world can know what it means to be a society committed to the growth of individual gifts and differences. In a community that has no fear of the truth, the otherness of the other can be welcomed as a gift rather than a threat.

All politics should be judged by the character of the people it produces. The depth and variety of character which a polity sustains is a correlative of the narrative that provides its identity and purpose. The contention and witness of the church is that the story of Jesus provides a flourishing of gifts which other politics cannot know. It does so because Christians have been nourished on the story of a saviour who insisted on being nothing else than what he was. By being the son of God he provided us with the confidence that insofar as we become his disciples our particularity and our regard for the particularity of our brothers and sisters in Christ contribute to his Kingdom. Our stories become part of the story of the Kingdom.

Stanley Hauerwas, A Community of Character: Toward a Constructive Christian Social Ethic,
ch. 2: 'Jesus: The Story of the Kingdom', §2.2, extract (1981)

Section D

Retelling the Story

As in every previous period, Jesus' story was told and retold many times in the twentieth century. This Reader is not able to provide extracts from all those retellings on the radio, in television, or in film, which have had such an impact upon the way in which the memory of Jesus is preserved and reimagined, but tellings in print, and in poetry and prose, have continued to pour out.

I. In Literature

Many twentieth-century poets and novelists have taken up the story of Jesus of Nazareth, or some part of it. Literary approaches to the story matured in the twentieth century, with many authors able to take a step back from the debates which had led their nineteenth-century forebears to produce works which were often either sentimentally devotional or harshly polemical.

313   Journey of the Magi

> T. S. Eliot (1888–1965) was an American-English poet and critic most famous for his groundbreaking works *The Wasteland* and *Four Quartets*. Eliot loved to draw on a rich and sometimes obscure treasury of symbol and allusion, and this poem is, like many others of his, at times puzzling; nevertheless, the reimagination of the Magi's quest (Matt. 2: 1–12) is potent. (Cf. **128**.)

> A cold coming we had of it,
> Just the worst time of the year
> For a journey, and such a long journey:
> The ways deep and the weather sharp,
> The very dead of winter.
> And the camels galled, sore-footed, refractory,
> Lying down in the melting snow.
> There were times we regretted
> The summer palaces on slopes, the terraces,
> And the silken girls bringing sherbet.
> Then the camel men cursing and grumbling
> And running away, and wanting their liquor and women,
> And the night-fires going out, and the lack of shelters,
> And the cities hostile and the towns unfriendly

And the villages dirty and charging high prices:
A hard time we had of it.
At the end we preferred to travel all night,
Sleeping in snatches,
With the voices singing in our ears, saying
That this was all folly.

Then at dawn we came down to a temperate valley,
Wet, below the snow line, smelling of vegetation,
With a running stream and a water-mill beating the darkness,
And three trees on the low sky.
And an old white horse galloped away in the meadow.
Then we came to a tavern with vine-leaves over the lintel,
Six hands at an open door dicing for pieces of silver,
And feet kicking the empty wine-skins.
But there was no information, and so we continued
And arrived at evening, not a moment too soon
Finding the place; it was (you may say) satisfactory.

All this was a long time ago, I remember,
And I would do it again, but set down
This set down
This: were we led all that way for
Birth or Death? There was a Birth, certainly,
We had evidence and no doubt. I had seen birth and death,
But had thought they were different; this Birth was
Hard and bitter agony for us, like Death, our death.
We returned to our places, these Kingdoms,
But no longer at ease here, in the old dispensation,
With an alien people clutching their gods.
I should be glad of another death.

Thomas Stearns Eliot, 'Journey of the Magi' (1927)

314 The Gospel according to the Son

Norman Mailer (1923–) is an American novelist, essayist, and journalist. He here creates a strange, unexpected voice for Jesus: a quicksilver intelligence dominated by the Father's image, running in fragments and snatches through the remembered Crucifixion from the vantage point of a mysterious Resurrection. (Cf. **16**.)

It was still morning, but darkness had come over the land; it was dark. Within myself, I recited a verse from the Psalms: 'My bones are burned with heat; my bowels boil; my skin is black.'

Yet as Job had passed from fever into that chill which is worse than fever, so I shivered in my loincloth. From out of my nakedness, I said aloud: 'The face of the deep is frozen.' I could not hear God's reply. When I said, 'I thirst,' one of the soldiers came forward to offer me vinegar. When I refused, for vinegar is worse than thirst, he said: 'King of the Jews, why don't you come down from the cross?'

And I remembered what was written in the Second Book of Kings: 'Hath he not sent me to the men who sit on the wall, that they may eat their own dung and drink of their own piss?'

I cried out to my Father, 'Will you allow not one miracle in this hour?'

When my Father replied, it was like a voice from the whirlwind. He said in my ear; and he was louder than my pain: 'Would you annul my judgment?'

I said: 'Not while breath is in me.'

But my torment remained. Agony was written on the sky. And pain came down to me like lightning. Pain surged up to me like lava. I prayed again to my Father:

'One miracle,' I asked.

If my Father did not hear me, then I was no longer the Son of God. How awful to be no more than a man. I cried out, 'My Lord, hast thou forsaken me?'

There was no answer. Only the echo of my cry. I saw the Garden of Eden and remembered the Lord's words to Adam: 'Of every tree in the Garden you may eat freely, but from the Tree of the Knowledge of Good and Evil, you shall not eat.'

Let my Father's voice strike Golgotha and his thunder become as loud as his voice, but pain had driven me to believe what one must not believe.

God was my Father, but I had to ask: Is he possessed of all powers? Or is he not? Like Eve, I wanted knowledge of good and evil. Even as I asked if the Lord was all-powerful, I heard my own answer: God, my father, was one god. But there were others. If I had failed him, so had he failed me. Such was now my knowledge of good and evil. Was it for that reason that I was on the cross?

One of the soldiers took a sponge, filled it with vinegar, and forced it between my lips. He jeered at me.

The taste was so vile that I cried out with the last of the heavenly rage left to me, and I looked upon the face of the Roman soldier who had squeezed this vinegar into my mouth. 'I have a prayer,' he said. 'I wish you were Barabbas. I would torture you. I would wipe my filth upon your face.'

At that moment the Devil spoke. 'Join me,' he said, and his voice was in my ear. 'I will introduce this bully of a Roman to a few humiliations I can lay upon men. There is no pleasure greater than revenge itself. And,' said the Devil, 'I will bring you down from the cross.'

It was a temptation. Only one thought kept me from assent. Tears hot as fire stood in my eyes at this thought, for it told me that I must say no to Satan. Yet I knew. By these hours I had lived on the cross, I knew. My Father was only doing what he could do. Even as I had done what I could do. So he was truly my Father. Like all Fathers he had many sore troubles, and some had little to do with his son. Had his efforts for me been so great that now he was exhausted? Even as I had been too heavy to walk in the Garden of Gethsemane.

By the aid of such a thought, as sobering as the presence of death itself, so did the Devil's voice withdraw from my ear. And I returned to the world where I lay on the cross.

Yet now I felt less pain. For I had learned that I did not wish to die with a curse in my heart. I had told my disciples: 'He who kills you will believe he is performing service for God,' and those words came back to me—a comfort in this extremity. I said, 'My Lord, they do not see. They came into the world empty and they will depart from the world empty. Meanwhile, they are drunk. Forgive them. They know not what they do.'

The strength of my life passed from me and entered the Spirit. I had time only to say, 'It is finished.' Then I died. And it is true that I died before they put the spear in my side. Blood and water ran out of my side to mark the end of morning. I saw a white light that shone like the brilliance of heaven, but it was far away. My last thought was of the faces of the poor and how they were beautiful to me, and I hoped it would be true, as all my followers would soon begin to say, that I had died for them on the cross.

Norman Mailer, *The Gospel according to the Son*, ch. 48, extract (1997)

315   The Man who Died

D. H. Lawrence (1885–1930) was an English novelist, playwright, and essayist. His Jesus, the victim of a failed crucifixion, is a thoroughly embodied Jesus; a Jesus for whom the basic facts of physical existence and vulnerability have been driven under his fingernails by the agony he has undergone, and the rest he has been denied. (Cf. 17.)

A man awoke from a long sleep in which he was tied up. He woke numb and cold, inside a carved hole in the rock. Through all the long sleep his body had been full of hurt, and it was still full of hurt. He did not open his eyes. Yet he knew that he was awake, and numb, and cold, and rigid, and full of hurt, and tied up. His face was banded with cold bands, his legs were bandaged together. Only his hands were loose.

He could move if he wanted: he knew that. But he had no want. Who would want to come back from the dead? A deep, deep nausea stirred in him, at the premonition of movement. He resented already the fact of the strange, incalculable moving that had already taken place in him: the moving back into consciousness. He had not wished it. He had wanted to stay outside, in the place where even memory is stone dead.

But now, something had returned to him, like a returned letter, and in that return he lay overcome with a sense of nausea. Yet suddenly his hands moved. They lifted up, cold, heavy and sore. Yet they lifted up, to drag away the cloth from his face, and push at the shoulder bands. Then they fell again, cold, heavy, numb, and sick with having moved even so much, unspeakably unwilling to move further.

With his face cleared, and his shoulders free, he lapsed again, and lay dead, resting on the cold nullity of being dead. It was the most desirable. And almost, he had it complete: the utter cold nullity of being outside.

Yet when he was most nearly gone, suddenly, driven by an ache at the wrists, his hands rose and began pushing at the bandages of his knees, his feet began to stir, even while his breast lay cold and dead still.

And at last the eyes opened. On to the dark. The same dark! yet perhaps there was a pale chink of the all-disturbing light, prising open the pure dark. He could not lift his head. The eyes closed. And again it was finished.

Then suddenly he leaned up, and the great world reeled. Bandages fell away. And narrow walls of rock closed upon him, and gave the new anguish of imprisonment. There were chinks of light. With a wave of strength that came from revulsion, he leaned forward, in that narrow well of rock, and leaned frail hands on the rock near the chinks of light.

Strength came from somewhere, from revulsion; there was a crash and a wave of light, and the dead man was crouching in his lair, facing the animal onrush of light. Yet it was hardly dawn. And the strange, piercing keenness of daybreak's sharp breath was on him. It meant full awakening.

Slowly, slowly he crept down from the cell of rock, with the caution of the bitterly wounded. Bandages and linen and perfume fell away, and he crouched on the ground against the wall of rock, to recover oblivion. But he saw his hurt feet touching the earth again, with unspeakable pain, the earth they had meant to touch no more, and he saw his thin legs that had died, and pain unknowable, pain like utter bodily disillusion, filled him so full that he stood up, with one torn hand on the ledge of the tomb.

To be back! To be back again, after all that! He saw the linen swathing-bands fallen round his dead feet, and stooping, he picked them up, folded them, and laid them back in the rocky cavity from which he had emerged. Then he took the perfumed linen sheet, wrapped it round him as a mantle, and turned away, to the wanness of the chill dawn.

He was alone; and having died, was even beyond loneliness.

Filled still with the sickness of unspeakable disillusion, the man stepped with wincing feet down the rocky slope, past the sleeping soldiers, who lay wrapped in their woollen mantles under the wild laurels. Silent, on naked, scarred feet, wrapped in a white linen shroud, he glanced down for a moment on the inert, heap-like bodies of the soldiers. They were repulsive, a slow squalor of limbs, yet he felt a certain compassion. He passed on towards the road, lest they should wake.

Having nowhere to go, he turned from the city that stood on her hills. He slowly followed the road away from the town, past the olives, under which purple anemones were drooping in the chill of dawn, and rich-green herbage was pressing thick. The world, the same as ever, the natural world, thronging with greenness, a nightingale winsomely, wistfully, coaxingly calling from the bushes beside a runnel of water, in the world, the natural world of morning and evening, forever undying, from which he had died.

D. H. Lawrence, The Man who Died, ch. 1, extract (1929)

316 The Lion, the Witch, and the Wardrobe

C. S. Lewis (1898–1963) was a firmly confident Oxford don, a popular apologist for Christianity, and a story-writer. His Chronicles of Narnia tell of various children's adventures in a fantastic world, from its creation to its eschaton—and in the process explore many Christian themes and ideas. Sometimes Lewis treads lightly and indirectly; sometimes his Christian message is present with audacious directness. Here, in the most famous of the books, the Lion Aslan has been slain on the Stone Table by the White Witch, and two girls who were his followers and friends— Lucy and Susan, visitors from our world—have witnessed the event. (Cf. **17**.)

'I'm so cold,' said Lucy.

'So am I,' said Susan. 'Let's walk about a bit.'

They walked to the eastern edge of the hill and looked down. The one big star had almost disappeared. The country all looked dark grey, but beyond, at the very end of the world, the sea showed pale. The sky began to turn red. They walked to and fro more times than they could count between the dead Aslan and the eastern ridge, trying to keep warm; and oh, how tired their legs felt. Then at last, as they stood for a moment looking out towards the sea and Cair Paravel (which they could now make out) the red turned to gold along the line where the sea and the sky met and very slowly up came the edge of the sun. At that moment they heard from behind them a loud noise—a great cracking, deafening noise as if a giant had broken a giant's plate.

'What's that?' said Lucy, clutching Susan's arm.

'I—I feel afraid to turn round,' said Susan; 'something awful is happening.'

'They're doing something worse to him,' said Lucy. 'Come on!' And she turned, pulling Susan round with her.

The rising of the sun had made everything look so different—all colours and shadows were changed—that for a moment they didn't see the important thing. Then they did. The Stone Table was broken into two pieces by a great crack that ran down it from end to end; and there was no Aslan.

'Oh, oh, oh!' cried the two girls, rushing back to the Table.

'Oh, it's too bad,' sobbed Lucy; 'they might have left the body alone.'

'Who's done it?' cried Susan. 'What does it mean? Is it magic?'

'Yes!' said a great voice behind their backs. 'It is more magic.' They looked round. There, shining in the sunrise, larger than they had seen him before, shaking his mane (for it had apparently grown again) stood Aslan himself.

'Oh, Aslan!' cried both the children, staring up at him, almost as much frightened as they were glad.

'Aren't you dead then, dear Aslan?' said Lucy.

'Not now,' said Aslan.

'You're not—not a—?' asked Susan in a shaky voice. She couldn't bring herself to say the word *ghost*. Aslan stooped his golden head and licked her forehead. The warmth of his breath and a rich sort of smell that seemed to hang about his hair came all over her.

'Do I look it?' he said.

'Oh, you're real, you're real! Oh, Aslan!' cried Lucy, and both girls flung themselves upon him and covered him with kisses.

'But what does it all mean?' asked Susan when they were somewhat calmer.

'It means,' said Aslan, 'that though the Witch knew the Deep Magic, there is a magic deeper still which she did not know. Her knowledge goes back only to the dawn of time. But if she could have looked a little further back, into the stillness and the darkness before Time dawned, she would have read there a different incantation. She would have known that when a willing victim who had committed no treachery was killed in a traitor's stead, the Table would crack and Death itself would start working backwards. And now—'

'Oh yes. Now?' said Lucy, jumping up and clapping her hands.

'Oh, children,' said the Lion, 'I feel my strength coming back to me. Oh, children, catch me if you can!' He stood for a second, his eyes very bright, his limbs quivering, lashing himself with his tail. Then he made a leap high over their heads and landed on the other side of the Table. Laughing, though she didn't know why, Lucy scrambled over it to reach him. Aslan leaped again. A mad chase began. Round and round the hill-top he led them, now hopelessly out of their reach, now letting them almost catch his tail, now diving between them, now tossing them in the air with his huge and beautifully velveted paws and catching them again, and now stopping unexpectedly so that all three of them rolled over together in a happy laughing heap of fur and arms and legs. It was such a romp as no one has ever had except in Narnia; and whether it was more like playing with a thunderstorm or playing with a kitten Lucy could never make up her mind. And the funny thing was that when all three finally lay together panting in the sun the girls no longer felt in the least tired or hungry or thirsty.

'And now,' said Aslan presently, 'to business. I feel I am going to roar. You had better put your fingers in your ears.'

And they did. And Aslan stood up and when he opened his mouth to roar his face became so terrible that they did not dare to look at it. And they saw all the trees in front of him bend before the blast of his roaring as grass bends in a meadow before the wind. Then he said, 'We have a long journey to go. You must ride on me.' And he crouched down and the children climbed on to his warm, golden back, and Susan sat first, holding on tightly to his mane and Lucy sat behind holding on tightly to Susan. And with a great heave he rose underneath them and then shot off, faster than any horse could go, down hill and into the thick of the forest.

That ride was perhaps the most wonderful thing that happened to them in Narnia.

Clive Staples Lewis, *The Lion, the Witch, and the Wardrobe*, ch. 15: 'Deeper Magic' (1950)

II. In Theology

It was, of course, not only novelists, poets, and storytellers who revisited the story of Jesus in the twentieth century. It continued to provide fuel for the fires of theologians and spiritual writers of all kinds. The two extracts which follow illustrate respectively a relatively familiar and a relatively novel way in which that process was carried out in the twentieth century: a devotional writer who uses a story about Jesus to great effect to illuminate the Christian life, and a theologian who seeks to allow all the themes of dogmatic theology to be shaped afresh by the particularities of the Gospel stories.

317　Emmaus and Us

The story of Jesus has, over the centuries, infiltrated and shaped numberless sermons, meditations, devotional writings of all kinds; it has been mined for materials to build a thousand shapes of Christian life; it has been constantly revisited and put to work by new generations of preachers and writers. We have chosen just one example, a retelling of the Emmaus story (cf. **18**) from a century in which more devotional and spiritual books than ever before have come rolling off the presses. Henri Nouwen (1932–66) was a Dutch

Roman Catholic priest who gave up his academic career to work in a L'Arche community dedicated to people with severe learning disabilities.

As the two travellers walk home mourning their loss, Jesus comes up and walks by their side, but their eyes are prevented from recognising him. Suddenly there are no longer two but three people walking, and everything becomes different. The two friends no longer look down at the ground in front of them but into the eyes of the stranger who has joined them and asked, 'What are all these things you are discussing as you walk along?' There is some astonishment, even agitation: 'You must be the only person who does not know the things that have been happening!' Then there follows a long story: the story of loss, the story of puzzling news about an empty tomb. Here at least is someone to listen, someone who is willing to hear the words of disillusionment, sadness, and utter confusion. Nothing seems to make sense. But it is better to tell a stranger than to repeat the known facts to each other.

Then something happens! Something shifts. The stranger begins to speak, and his words ask for serious attention. He had listened to them; now they listened to him. His words are very clear and straightforward. He speaks of things they already knew: their long past with all that had happened during the centuries before they were born, the story of Moses who led their people to freedom, and the story of the prophets who challenged their people never to let go of their dearly acquired freedom. It was an all-too-familiar story. Still it sounded as if they were hearing it for the first time.

The difference lay in the storyteller! A stranger appearing from nowhere yet one who, somehow, seems closer than anyone who had ever told that story. The loss, the grief, the guilt, the fear, the glimpses of hope, and the many unanswered questions that battled for attention in their restless minds, all of these were lifted up by this stranger and placed in the context of a story much larger than their own. What had seemed so confusing began to offer new horizons; what had seemed so oppressive began to feel liberating; what had seemed so extremely sad began to take on the quality of joy! As he talked to them, they gradually came to know that their little lives weren't as little as they had thought, but part of a great mystery that not only embraced many generations, but stretched itself out from eternity to eternity.

The stranger didn't say that there was no reason for sadness, but that their sadness was part of a larger sadness in which joy was hidden. The stranger didn't say that the death they were mourning wasn't real, but that it was a death that inaugurated even more life—real life. The stranger didn't say that they hadn't lost a friend who had given them new courage and new hope, but that this loss would create the way to a relationship far beyond any friendship they had ever experienced. Never did the stranger deny what they told him.

To the contrary, he affirmed it as part of a much larger event in which they were allowed to play a unique role.

Still, this was not a soothing conversation. The stranger was strong, direct, unsentimental. There were no easy consolations. It even seemed that he pierced their complaints with a truth they might have preferred not to know. After all, continual complaining is more attractive than facing reality. But the stranger was not the least bit afraid to break through their defences and to call them far beyond their own narrowness of mind and heart.

'Foolish people,' he said. 'So slow to believe.' These words go straight to the hearts of the two men. 'Foolish' is a hard word, a word that offends us and makes us defensive. But it can also crack open a cover of fear and self-consciousness and lead to a whole new knowledge of being human. It is a wake-up call, a ripping off of blindfolds, a tearing down of useless protective devices. You foolish people, don't you see—don't you hear—don't you know? You have been looking at a little bush not realising that you are on the top of a mountain that offers you a world-wide view. You have been staring at an obstacle not willing to consider that the obstacle was put there to show you the right path. You have been complaining about your losses, not realising that these losses are there to enable you to receive the gift of life.

The stranger had to call them 'foolish' to make them see. And what is the challenge? To trust. They didn't trust that their experience was more than the experience of an irretrievable loss. They didn't trust that there was anything else to do than to go home and take up their old way of living again. 'Foolish people . . . so slow to believe.' Slow to believe; slow to trust in the larger scheme of things; slow to jump over their complaints and discover the wide spectrum of new opportunities; slow to move beyond the pains of the moment and see them as part of a much larger healing process.

This slowness is not an innocent slowness because it can entrap us in our complaints and narrow-mindedness. It is the slowness that can prevent us from discovering the landscape in which we live. It is quite possible to come to the end of our lives without ever having known who we are and what we are meant to become. Life is short. We cannot simply expect that the little we see, hear, and experience will reveal to us the whole of our existence. We are too near-sighted and too hard of hearing for that. Someone has to open our eyes and ears and help us to discover what lies beyond our own perception. Someone has to make our hearts burn!

Jesus joins us as we walk in sadness and explains the scriptures to us. But we do not know that it is Jesus. We think of him as a stranger who knows less than we do of what is happening in our lives. And still—we know something, we sense something, we intuit something: our hearts begin to burn. At the very moment that he is with us we can't fully understand what is happening. We can't speak about it to each other. Later, yes later, when it is all over, we might be able to say, 'Did not our hearts burn within us as he talked to us on the road and explained the scriptures to us?'

Henri J. M. Nouwen, *With Burning Hearts: A Meditation on the Eucharistic Life*, ii: 'Discerning the Presence', extract (1994)

318 Jesus in Gethsemane

Almost single-handedly Karl Barth (cf. **281**) retrieved dogmatics for the mainstream of academic theology after its marginalization in the eighteenth and nineteenth centuries. His retrieval was distinctive, however, for the unprecedented degree to which every theme, every doctrine, was rethought through the lens provided by the biblical story of what God had done in Jesus of Nazareth. Vast sections of Barth's immense *Church Dogmatics* re-envisage the world and its relation to God simply by patiently telling the story of Jesus, and exploring its implications. Here, he explores the significance of Gethsemane (cf. **15**).

It is now shown where the victory which Jesus won in the temptation in the wilderness leads, that the end will involve the death of the victor. The penitence and the fulfilment of righteousness which Jesus has undertaken is now approaching its climax. The reversal in which the Judge becomes the judged is now about to take place. The story closes with the present: 'The hour is come; behold, the Son of man is betrayed (*paradidotai*) into the hands of sinners.'

But it brings out once again the whole absolutely inconceivable difficulty of the matter: the Son of man come down from heaven, the King and Judge sent by God, in the hands of sinners, betrayed, delivered up, surrendered to them. 'The hour is come,' and in a moment there will appear, and with him the first of those *hamartoloi* (sinners), the little *paradidous* (betrayer) Judas, a chosen apostle, who with his kiss sets the whole event in train. Does all this have to happen? In this solemn moment, quite naturally but unexpectedly and disruptively in view of all that has gone before, there is a pause. Jesus himself—in prayer to God—raises the whole question afresh. He prays that 'if it were possible, the hour might pass from him.' This is repeated in direct speech: 'Abba, Father, all things are possible unto thee; take away this cup from me.'

But had not his whole way from Jordan been a single march—which Satan could not arrest, not even in the form of Peter—to this very hour, a single and determined grasping of the divine wrath? But now there is a stumbling, although only for a—repeated—moment: a moment in which there is a pause and trembling not only on earth and in time, not only in the soul of Jesus which is 'sorrowful even unto death', but in a sense in heaven, in the bosom of God himself, in the relationship between the Father and the Son; a moment in which the question is raised of another possibility than that which will in fact be realised relentlessly and by divine necessity in view of all that has gone before. [. . .]

For a moment it holds out before the reader another possible form of the coming event: not in any clear outline, only vaguely—for Jesus is not proposing to God any alternative plan—defined only in a negative way; not this event, the frightful event which now impends. Jesus prays that this hour, this cup of wrath, might pass from him, might be spared him. He prays therefore that the good will and the sacred work and the true word of God should not coincide with the evil will and the corrupt work and the deceitful word of the tempter and of the world controlled by him, the *hamartoloi*. He prays that God should not give him up to the power the temptation of which he had resisted and willed to resist in all circumstances. He prays that God will so order things that the triumph of evil will be prevented, that the claim of Satan to world dominion will not be affirmed but given the lie, that a limit will be set to him, and with him to the evil course of the world and the evil movement of men. He prays that, directed by God's providence, the facts might speak a different language from that which they are about to speak, that in their end and consequence they should not be against him, just as he had decided for God and not against him in the wilderness. He prays that for the sake of God's own cause and glory the evil determination of world-occurrence should not finally rage against himself, the sent one of God and the divine Son. Surely this is something which God cannot will and allow. Such is the prayer of Jesus as prayed once in Luke, twice in Mark, and as many as three times in Matthew. [. . .]

But he only prays. He does not demand. He does not advance any claims. He does not lay upon God any conditions. He does not reserve his future obedience. He does not abandon his status as a penitent. He does not cease to allow that God is in the right even against himself. He does not try to anticipate his justification by him in any form, or to determine it himself. He does not think of trying to be judge in his own cause and in God's cause. He prays only as a child to the Father knowing that he can and should pray, that his need is known to the Father, is on the heart of the Father, but knowing also that the Father disposes what is possible and will therefore be, and that what he allows to be will be the only thing that is possible and right.

If we understand the beginning of Jesus' prayer to God in this way—and how else can we understand it in view of what the texts say and in the context of the Gospels—then the meaning of what follows is clear: 'But, or nevertheless, not what I will, but what (as) thou wilt.' [Mark 14: 36; Matt. 26: 39]. Or more explicitly: 'Nevertheless, not my will, but thine, be done.' [Luke 22: 42].

Or even more explicitly: 'O my Father, if this cup may not pass away from me except I drink it, thy will be done.' [Matt. 26: 42]. [. . .] This is not a kind of return of willingness to obey, which was finally forced upon Jesus and fulfilled by him in the last hour; it is rather a readiness for the act of obedience which he had never compromised in his prayer. The proviso 'if it be possible' which was an integral part of the prayer now comes into force. The prayer reckoned on the possibility of quite a different answer. This is what had made it a genuine prayer to God. But now this possibility fades from view. Jesus does not change his mind when he says, 'Thy will be done.' After pausing with very good reason, he now proceeds all the more determinedly along the way which he had never left.

But we must be careful how we praise the humility which Jesus displayed in the second form of his prayer. Naturally, it is the prayer of humility of the Son of God made man. But we must also see that in the 'Thy will be done' he emerges from the serious and inevitable astonishment and oppression in which he had prayed that the cup should pass from him. He stands upright in what we might almost call a supreme pride. He faces the reality the avoidance of which he had so earnestly desired. Because it is the reality of the will of God he grasps it as that which is better, which alone is good. He does not do so in sad resignation, therefore, but because he will and can affirm this reality and this alone. In the last analysis, therefore, we can describe what Jesus does as renunciation only if we explain it more closely. He does renounce the content of that wish which he had spread before God, and therefore the prospect of a different future from that which actually came to him, and therefore the fixing of a different will to correspond to this different future. But what Jesus did is ill adapted to be used, as we love to use it, as an example of that renunciation of all kinds of hopes and fears which is demanded of man. For, according to the sense of the texts, we cannot speak of any intention which was opposed to that of God and which he then renounced. Above all, the emphasis of the prayer is not at all upon that which might not happen, as in all kinds of mysticism both new and old, both higher and lower. It is upon that which might happen. It is positive prayer and not a negative. The statement—and in this it goes far beyond the answers of Jesus to the tempter in the wilderness—is at its open core a radiant Yes to the actual will of God. It is radiant because the decision which it expresses and fulfils ceases to regard any other divine possibilities which there might be and fixes itself on the one actual will of God—'what thou wilt'—and unreservedly accepts it. This is not a withdrawal on the part of Jesus, but a great and irresistible advance. It is not a resignation before God. It is an expression of the supreme and only praise which God expects of man and which is rendered to him only by this one man in place of all, the praise which comes from the knowledge that he does not make any mistakes, that his way, the way which he whose thoughts are higher than our thoughts actually treads himself, is holy and just and gracious.

But in all this we do not forget what it was all about, what Jesus was affirming and accepting and taking on himself with this 'Thy will be done.' It was not simply that he had to suffer and die, and that in contrast to others who have gone a similar way he accepted it rather painfully and tardily, as the moralists have easily been able to hold against him. It was not a matter of his suffering and dying in itself and as such, but of the dreadful thing that he saw coming upon him in and with his suffering and dying. He saw it clearly and correctly. It was the coming of the night in which no man can work [John 9: 4], in which the good will of God will be indistinguishably one with the evil will of men and the world and Satan. It was a matter of the triumph of God being concealed under that of his adversary, of that which is not, of that which supremely is not. It was a matter of God himself obviously making a tryst with death and about to keep it. It was a matter of the divine judgment being taken out of the hands of Jesus and placed in those of his supremely unrighteous judges and executed by them upon him. It was a matter of the enemy who had been repulsed as the tempter having and exercising by divine permission and appointment the right, the irresistible right of might. It was a matter of the obedience and penitence in which Jesus had persisted coming to fruition in his own rejection and condemnation—not by chance, but according to the plan of God himself, not superficially, but in serious earnest. That was what came upon him in his suffering and dying, as God's answer to his appeal. Jesus saw this cup. He tasted its bitterness. He had not made any mistake. He had not been needlessly afraid. There was every reason to ask that it might pass from him. [. . .]

But what happened when Jesus prayed in this way in Gethsemane? How was this prayer heard, which no other ever could pray or ever has prayed before or since, but which was in fact heard as no other prayer was heard when it received the answer which it requested?

One thing is clear. In the power of this prayer Jesus received, i.e., he renewed, confirmed and put into effect, his freedom to finish his work, to execute the divine judgment by undergoing it himself, to punish the sin of the world by bearing it himself, by taking it away from the world in his own person, in his death. The sin of the world was now laid upon him. It was now true that in the series of many sinners, he was the only one singled out by God to be its bearer and representative, the only one that it could really touch and oppress and terrify. That the deceiver of men is their destroyer, that his power is that of death, is something that had to be proved true in the one who was not deceived, in order that it might not be true for all those who were deceived, that their enmity against God might be taken away from them, that their curse might not rest upon them. This was the will of God in the dreadful thing which Jesus saw approaching—in that conjunction of the will and work and word of God with those of evil. The power of evil had to break on Jesus, its work of death had to be done on him, so that being done on him it might be done once and for all, for all men, for the liberation of all men. This is what happened when Jesus took the cup and drank it to the last bitter drops. 'For this cause came I unto this hour' is what he says in John 12: 27 when he had just prayed on this occasion too: 'Father, save me from this hour.' If the Father was the Father of Jesus, and Jesus his Son, he could not save him from this hour. That would have been not to hear his prayer. For Jesus had come to this hour in order that the will of God should be done in this hour as it actually was done.

And Satan, the evil one, and the world ruled by him, and the *hamartoloi* as his agents and instruments? Is it not clear that in the prayer prayed by Jesus in this hour the 'prince of the world' is judged, 'cast out'? 'He hath nothing in me.' Satan does him every possible injury, but he cannot injure that which Jesus does when he allows this to happen. In relation to him Satan makes his supreme and final effort. He has his supreme *kairos*. For the world must 'know that I love the Father, and as the Father gave me commandment, even so I do.' [John 14: 31]. Satan uses his power to overwhelm Jesus, and he succeeds, but his power loses its subjects, for the whole world and men escape him once and for all, and it ceases to be power over them, an impassable gulf being opened between him and the world ruled by him, between him and the *hamartoloi* deceived by him. He himself is impressed into the service of the will of God as fulfilled in the suffering and death of Jesus. His act of violence on this one man can achieve only what God has determined to his own glory and the salvation of all. A limit is therefore set to his lordship and its end is already in sight. That is what happened to him when Jesus prayed that not his will but God's will should be done.

Karl Barth, *Church Dogmatics*, IV: *The Doctrine of Reconciliation* 1, §59. 2, extracts (1953)

Section E

God Incarnate

The wrangles and debates of modern theology have repeatedly stumbled around the doctrine of the Incarnation. From the footsoldiers of Protestant orthodoxy debating the *communicatio idiomatum* (cf. **181**) to deists decrying the mystifications of hair-splitting theologians (cf. **223**); from liberals looking for the supreme God-consciousness of Christ (cf. **256**) to Lutherans explaining the self-emptying of the Son (cf. **249**); the doctrine time and time again comes in for clarifications or explanations, speculations, or rejections. The twentieth century was, in this, no exception, but simply carried on the unfinished business of the nineteenth.

I. Debating Incarnation

It can sometimes seem that the doctrine of the Incarnation is no more than an intellectual puzzle designed to hone the skills of theologians, and certainly the twentieth century saw its fair share of dry debates about the possibility or probability of Incarnation, and about the proper explanation of incarnational claims. Many of those who reject the doctrine argue in consequence that they are doing nothing which should cause the heart of living faith to miss a beat. Yet although there are those who respond simply with the dry currency of speculative analysis, the most vigorous defence of the doctrine comes from those who see it as vital to Christian communal and individual life—or from those who simply live in a world shaped for them by belief in the divine assumption of human flesh.

319   Incarnation Unnecessary

In the 1970s in England a conflagration was sparked by the publication of a collection of essays entitled *The Myth of God Incarnate*. Many responses have followed, and theological shelves bend under books called *The Truth of God Incarnate, The Logic of God Incarnate, The Metaphor of God Incarnate, The Saga of God Incarnate*, and so on. This essay from the original collection, by Maurice Wiles (1923–), helps to explain what the controversy was about.

The primary importance of Jesus for Christians has never been as a model for human living; it has resided rather in the conviction that he is the one in whom we meet God, the one through whom God has acted decisively for the salvation of the world. How, apart from a full doctrine of the incarnation, could Jesus be the saviour of the world? Would not any change of the kind suggested imply that the worship of Christ, traditional throughout the whole of Christian history, was idolatrous in character? It is at this point that the greatest difficulties are likely to be felt. Can they be met? It is important to remember that in the strictest sense it is never simply Jesus who saves nor is Christ by himself the object of man's worship. Jesus as Second Person of the Trinity incarnate is the one through whom we come to the Trinitarian God, the one through whom the whole Trinity acts towards us. And, as the liturgy so carefully expresses it, the norm of Christian worship is an offering to God through Jesus Christ as Lord.

The absence of incarnational belief would not simply destroy this mediatorial function altogether. It would still be possible to see Jesus not only as one who embodies a full response of man to God but also as one who expresses and embodies the way of God towards men. For it is always through the lives of men that God comes to us and we are enabled to meet him and respond to him. It was through the personality and leadership of Moses in their escape from Egypt that the Israelites experienced the redemptive power of Yahweh. It was through the experience and prophetic ministry of Hosea that they grasped the inexhaustible depth of his demanding but forgiving love. So, it may be claimed, it is supremely through Jesus that the self-giving love of God is most fully expressed and men can be caught up into the fullest response to him. For Jesus was not merely a teacher about God; the power of God was set at work in the world in a new way through his life, ministry, death and resurrection. On such a basis it is reasonable to suggest that the stories about Jesus and the figure of Jesus himself could remain a personal focus of the transforming power of God in the world. They could still properly fulfil that role, even without the concept of 'incarnation', though they would not impinge upon us in precisely the same way. But as we have seen already the precise way in which Jesus is understood and impinges upon the life of the church has been a constantly changing phenomenon in the history of the church and has undergone particularly great change in recent years, even where the concept of incarnation has been strenuously preserved. The particular direction of change which would result from the abandonment of the incarnation model cannot easily be predicted in advance, for religious development is not simply a matter of logical deduction but of an evolving life. The most likely change would be towards a less exclusive insistence on Jesus as the way for all peoples and all culture. [. . .]

So we come back at the end to the point with which I began the complex interweaving of ideas that are associated with 'incarnation'. I have been arguing that its abandonment as a metaphysical claim about the person of Jesus (for which there seems to me to be a strong case) would not involve the abandonment of all the religious claims normally associated with it. Of course it would make a difference. But the truth of God's self-giving love and the role of Jesus in bringing that vision to life in the world would remain.

Maurice Wiles, 'Christianity without Incarnation?' 3(c), extracts (1977)

320   Anti-Logos

In his lectures on Christology, Dietrich Bonhoeffer (cf. 309), sought to quench the feverish desire which we have, when faced with Jesus Christ, to busy ourselves with misdirected explanations and conjectures. (Cf. 63; 66.)

An unknown subject becomes known through the possibility of finding a place for it in [an] already existing pattern. How does the subject *x* fit into the order which is already there? The question is directed towards the potentialities of the subject, towards its 'How?' The subject is defined, grasped, known by this 'How?' In other words, man's immanent Logos answers the question 'How?' posed by the need for classification. That is important in the case of Christology. How can this subject be classified?

Man's ultimate presupposition lies in his human Logos, which engages in this process of classification. What happens if doubt is cast on this presupposition of his scientific activity? What if somewhere the claim is raised that this human Logos is superseded, judged, dead? What happens if an Anti-Logos appears which refuses to be classified? A Logos which annihilates the first? What if the proclamation goes out that the old order has been dissolved, that it is out of date, and that the counterpart of a new world has already begun? What answer does man's Logos give when it is addressed like this? [. . .]

What if the Anti-Logos raises his claim in a completely new form? If he is no longer an idea, but a Word, which challenges the supremacy of the Logos? If he appears at some time and in some place in history as a person? If he declares himself to be a judgment on the human Logos and points to himself: 'I am the Way, the Truth and the Life' [John 14: 6]; I am the death of the human Logos, I am the life of God's Logos; man with his Logos must die, he falls into my hands; I am the first and the last?

If the Anti-Logos no longer appears in history as an idea, but as the Word incarnate, there is no longer any possibility of incorporating him into the order of man's own Logos. There is in fact only one question left: 'Who are you? Speak!' The question 'Who are you?' is the question of deposed, distraught reason. But it is equally the question of faith: Who are you? Are you God himself? This is the question with which Christology is concerned. Christ is the Anti-Logos. There is no longer any possibility of classification because the existence of this Logos means the end of the human Logos. The question 'Who are you?' is the only appropriate question. To this question the phenomenon discloses itself. Christ gives an answer to the question 'Who?'

The question 'Who?' is the question of transcendence. The question 'How?' is the question of immanence. Because the one who is questioned here is the Son, the immanent question cannot grasp him. Not, 'How are you possible?'—that is the godless question, the serpent's question—but 'Who are you?' The question 'Who?' expresses the strangeness and otherness of the encounter and at the same time reveals itself as the question of the very existence of the enquirer himself. He enquires about the being which is alien to his own being, about the boundaries of his own existence. Transcendence puts his own being in question. With the answer that his Logos has found its limit man comes up against the boundaries of his existence. So the question of transcendence is the question of existence and the question of existence is the question of transcendence. In theological terms: man only knows who he is in the light of God. [. . .]

Even today the Unknown One meets men on the road [cf. **18**] in such a way that they can only ask the question 'Who are you?', however often they try to parry it. They must come to grips with him. We must also come to grips with Goethe and Socrates. On this our education and our ethos depend. But on our coming to grips with Christ depend life and death, salvation and damnation. This cannot be appreciated from outside. But in the church it is the principle on which everything rests. 'And there is salvation in no one else' [Acts 4: 12]. The cause of the encounter with Jesus is not the same as that of the encounter with Socrates and Goethe. It is impossible to avoid the person of Jesus because he is alive. If need be, Goethe can be avoided because he is dead. [. . .]

The question 'Who are you?' remains ambiguous. It can be the question of the one who knows that he has been encountered and can hear already the counter-question, 'And who are you?' But it can also be the question of the person who, when he asks, means, 'How can I deal with you?' In that case, the question is simply a disguised form of the question 'How?' The question 'Who?' can be put to Jesus only when the counter-question has been heard. In that case it is not man who has dealt with Jesus, but Jesus who has dealt with man. So the question 'Who?' is to be spoken only in faith.

As long as the christological question is the question of the human Logos, it remains stuck in the ambivalence of the question 'How?' But if it is asked in the act of faith, it has the possibility of putting the question 'Who?'

Dietrich Bonhoeffer, *Christology*, Introduction 1, extracts (1933)

Karl Rahner (1904–84) was an important Catholic theologian who strongly influenced the Second Vatican Council (cf. **296**). In his *Foundations of the Christian Faith* (1976) he (among other things) developed an account of the nature of human existence in the world's evolution in tandem with an account of the Incarnation, shaping both towards each other so that his Christology capped and confirmed his vision of human existence, and his vision of the world explained and supported his Christology. The following is an extract from an earlier magazine article in which he canvassed the central idea of this theology.

We human beings are of such a kind that we are always beyond and above ourselves. It is our burden and our dignity. We are free and responsible for ourselves; we are those who hope. We are always already beyond and above what can be mentioned, designated and specified. We live the tangible on the basis of the intangible. We are grounded in the abyss of what cannot be named or expressed. We can certainly, of course, shut ourselves off and say we can make nothing of it. We can try to stick to what is commonplace and within range, to inspect what light falls on and refuse to turn to the unfathomable light which alone makes visible for us what it shines on. Yet even so mystery permeates our human existence and compels us again and again to turn our eyes towards it: in the joy which has no longer an object, in the anguish which ends the obvious matter-of-factness of our existence, in the love which knows itself unconditional and eternally binding, in the question which takes fright at its own unconditionality and unlimited scope.

In this way we are always finding ourselves facing a mystery which is, which is without limit, which grounds without itself having a ground, which is always there and always withdraws, intangible. We call it God. We point to mystery as such when we say God. When we do not overlook thought because of what is thought of, joy because of what gives joy, responsibility because of what we take responsibility for, unending future because of the present, immeasurable hope because of the object of striving here and now, we are already concerned with God, whether we give to this namelessness this or that name or no name at all.

And if in the depth of our being we have accepted this thinking, loving, hoping human reality despite all the overhasty, impatient smarts and protests on the surface of our existence, then we have by that very fact entered into relations with God, given ourselves over to him. Many will do this even if they think that they do not know God (he must of course always be known as incomprehensible, otherwise something else has been mistaken for him), even if in their mute reverence they do not venture to name him.

In such acceptance of human existence, obediently entrusting itself to mystery, it is possible for what in Christian terminology is called grace to occur: God is mystery, and remains so. But he is the abyss in which the existence of man is accepted, he is presence and not simply remoteness, forgiveness and not simply judgment. He fills the unending question of thought, the immeasurable scope of hope and the infinite demand of love with himself, silent still and in that ground of our being which only opens out to us if we obediently allow ourselves to be encompassed by this mystery, without seeking to master it. If this happens, however, Christmas is already within us, that coming of God which Christianity acknowledges always to occur by the grace of God in every human being who does not refuse it by that guilt which is both terror of God and proud self-sufficiency.

But we are men of history, of the tangible here and now. And this coming of God, his action in us, was intended to be tangible and irrevocable, irrevocably and tangibly historical both as God's self-giving and as God's coming definitively accepted by man. Consequently mankind has experienced in human history this coming of God as definitive, unsurpassable and irrevocable. In Jesus of Nazareth. In him surrender to the infinite mystery as such is present as man's action. And this itself, like everything that involves freedom and decision, is grace. In him, God as ineffable mystery (and remaining so) has expressed himself as Word wholly and irrevocably. In him that Word is 'there' as spoken to all of us, as the God of inexpressibly close presence and forgiveness.

Here question and answer, unmixed and inseparable, have become one. The one person is there in whom God and man are one, without detriment to one or the other.

Even when someone who is still far from any explicit and verbally formulated revelation accepts his human reality in silent patience, or rather in faith, hope and love (however he may name these), as a mystery which loses itself in the mystery of eternal love and bears life in the very midst of death, that person says Yes to Jesus Christ even if he does not realize it. For if someone lets go and jumps, he falls into the depth which is actually there, not merely the depth he has measured. Anyone who accepts his human reality—that is indescribably difficult and it remains uncertain whether we really do so—has accepted the Son of man, because in him God accepted man. [. . .]

If in this way some have courage explicitly to believe in the truth of Christmas, if the others silently accept the unfathomable depth of their human reality which is namelessly filled with joyful hope and are themselves accepted by the first as 'anonymous' Christians, then all can celebrate Christmas together. The apparently superficial and conventional business of Christmas then acquires truth and depth after all. The apparent falsehood of the whole business is then not the ultimate truth about it. Behind it stands the holy and silent truth that God has in fact come and celebrates Christmas with us.

Karl Rahner, 'Grace in the Abysses of Man' (1962), extract

322   Grace and Incarnation

D. M. Baillie (1887–1954) was a Scottish Free Church minister who became Professor of Systematic Theology at the University of St Andrews. In focusing the question of Incarnation on the question of Jesus' perfection, Baillie is able to demonstrate that the paradox of the Incarnation is the same as the paradox of grace—that to refuse the difficulties of the doctrine of the Incarnation is also to refuse the working of God's grace in the world.

The whole problem of the incarnation is contained in the old question, which can be asked in so many ways: Was Jesus divine because he lived a perfect life, or was he able to live a perfect life because he was divine? To put it otherwise: Did the incarnation depend upon the daily human choices made by Jesus, or did he always choose aright because he was God incarnate? [. . .] This question does not present us with a genuine dilemma. It must, of course, be true that his choices were genuine human choices, and that in a sense everything depended upon them. 'He that sent me is with me; he hath not left me alone; for (or because) I do always the things that are pleasing to him' [John 8: 29]. All depended on those human choices from moment to moment. And yet as soon as we have said that, we must inevitably turn round and say something apparently opposite, remembering that in the last analysis such human choice is never prevenient or even co-operative, but wholly dependent on the divine prevenience. We must say that in the perfect life of him who was 'always doing the things that are pleasing to God', this divine prevenience was nothing short of incarnation, and he lived as he did because he was God incarnate. Thus the dilemma disappears when we frankly recognise that in the doctrine of the incarnation there is a paradox which cannot be rationalised but which can in some small measure be understood in the light of the 'paradox of grace'.

Somebody may wish to press the question in another form: Would any man who lived a perfect life be therefore and thereby God incarnate? But such a questioner would indeed be a Pelagian, showing by his very question that he regarded the human side of the achievement as the prevenient, the conditioning, the determinative. When we really accept the paradox of grace, when we really believe that every good thing in a man is wrought by God, when we have really understood the confession: 'I . . . yet not I, but God', and have taken that divine priority in earnest, the question loses its meaning, and, like the proposed dilemma, fades away into the paradox of the incarnation. And if we take these things in earnest, we have, as it appears to me, at least an approach to the *mysterium Christi* which will enable us to combine the most transcendent claims of a full and high Christology with the frankest recognition of the humanity of the historical Jesus.

D. M. Baillie, *God was in Christ: An Essay on Incarnation and Atonement*, ch. IV, extract (1948)

323 Alpha and Omega

Pierre Teilhard de Chardin (1881–1955) was a scientist and a theologian. A Jesuit, he worked in his native France, in China, and in the United States, as both a palaeontologist and a theological speaker and writer. He drew upon evolutionary ideas to develop a distinctive theology in which the world in all its growing complexity was seen, in the light of the Incarnation, as sacramental. (Cf. **220**, **274**.)

Christ is not something added to the world as an extra, he is not an embellishment, a king as we now crown kings, the owner of a great estate . . . . He is the alpha and the omega, the principle and the end, the foundation stone and the keystone, the plenitude and the plenifier. He is the one who consummates all things and gives them their consistence. It is towards him and through him, the inner life and light of the world, that the universal convergence of all created spirit is effected in sweat and tears. He is the single centre, precious and consistent, who glitters at the summit that is to crown the world, at the opposite pole from those dim and eternally shrinking regions into which our science ventures when it descends the road of matter and the past.

When we consider this profound harmony that for us Christians links and subordinates the zone of the multiple and the zone of unity, the essentially analytical domain of science and the ultra-synthetic domain of religion, then, my friends, I believe that we may draw the following conclusions: and they are the moral of this over-long address.

Above all, we Christians have no need to be afraid of, or to be unreasonably shocked by, the results of scientific research, whether in physics, in biology, or in history. Some Catholics are disconcerted when it is pointed out to them— either that the laws of providence may be reduced to determinisms and chance—or that under our most spiritual powers there lie hidden most complex material structures—or that the Christian religion has roots in a natural religious development of human consciousness—or that the human body presupposes a vast series of previous organic developments. Such Catholics either deny the facts or are afraid to face them. This is a huge mistake. The analyses of science and history are very often accurate; but they detract nothing from the almighty power of God nor from the spirituality of the soul, nor from the supernatural character of Christianity, nor from man's superiority to the animals. Providence, the soul, divine life, are synthetic realities. Since their function is to 'unify', they presuppose, outside and below them, a system of elements; but those elements do not constitute them; on the contrary it is to those higher realities that the elements look for their 'animation'.

Thus science should not disturb our faith by its analyses. Rather, it should help us to know God better, to understand and appreciate him more fully. Personally, I am convinced that there is no more substantial nourishment for the religious life than contact with scientific realities, if they are properly understood. The man who habitually lives in the society of the elements of this world, who personally experiences the overwhelming immensity of things and their wretched dissociation, that man, I am certain, becomes more acutely conscious than anyone of the tremendous need for unity that continually drives the universe further ahead, and of the fantastic future that awaits it. No one understands so fully as the man who is absorbed in the study of matter, to what a degree Christ, through his incarnation, is interior to the world, rooted in the world even in the heart of the tiniest atom. We compared the structure of the universe to that of a cone: only that man can fully appreciate the richness contained in the apex of the cone, who has first gauged the width and the power of the base.

It is useless, in consequence, and it is unfair, to oppose science and Christ, or to separate them as two domains alien to one another. By itself, science cannot discover Christ—but Christ satisfies the yearnings that are born in our hearts in the school of science. The cycle that sends man down to the bowels of matter in its full multiplicity, thence to climb back to the centre of spiritual unification, *is a natural cycle*. We could say that it is a *divine cycle*, since it was first followed by him who had to 'descend into Hell' before ascending into Heaven, that he might fill all things.

Pierre Teilhard de Chardin, *Science and Christ*, ch. III, extract (1921)

324 Christ beneath All

Margaret Spufford, an English historian of the seventeenth century, suffers from osteoporosis; she has described life under its sentence in a book called *Celebration*. It contains almost in passing this testimony to the potency of incarnational thinking.

I do not remember whether it was on the return from that visit to hospital or the next, that the worst thing ever so far to happen to me, myself, happened.

Ambulance men are the most patient, and usually the most skilled, of all beings. This pair had a misadventure. As they carried me in through the door, one of them tripped on the step. As he recovered himself, he trod on his companion's foot. They stumbled. They dropped, and then caught, me. I can only have fallen a couple of inches, but the effect was terrifying. All my reflexes seemed to go berserk in the pain. I, who so much valued control, was completely out of control. I was screaming, not even able to stop in case my son could hear. My fingers were clenched in someone's hair, the world ran amok, and my husband, who was there, was utterly irrelevant through the pain. He could not reach me. Nor could anyone. 'She probably collapsed another vertebra or two,' said the hospital on the telephone, apparently. 'Just keep her quiet.'

It was months before I dared tell even my husband, who was not likely to feel that I had suddenly been afflicted with religious mania, and knew I did not go in for pious or saccharine imagery, that quite extraordinarily at that moment of unreachability, I had suddenly been aware even as I screamed, of the presence of the Crucified. He did not cancel the moment, or assuage it, but was inside it.

Margaret Spufford, Celebration, Bones I, extract (1989)

325   Meekness and Majesty

The twentieth century has seen a revolution in Christian music, with the rise almost to ubiquity of new kinds of worship song and chorus. Just as with older explosions of Christian hymn-writing, most of these songs will not survive the winnowing processes of time; some, such as this celebration of the Incarnation by English song-writer Graham Kendrick, may show greater resilience (cf. 72).

> Meekness and majesty,
> manhood and deity,
> in perfect harmony,
> the man who is God.
> Lord of eternity
> dwells in humanity,
> kneels in humility
> and washes our feet.
>
> *O what a mystery,*
> *meekness and majesty.*
> *Bow down and worship*
> *for this is your God.*
>
> Father's pure radiance,
> perfect in innocence,

yet learns obedience
to death on a cross.
Suffering to give us life,
conquering through sacrifice,
and as they crucify
prays: 'Father forgive.'

Wisdom unsearchable,
God the invisible,
love indestructible
in frailty appears.
Lord of infinity,
stooping so tenderly,
lifts our humanity
to the heights of his throne.

Graham Kendrick, 'Meekness and Majesty' (1986)

II. A Male Christ?

Some of the most serious questions for incarnational theology in the twentieth century were raised by feminist thinkers, who pointed to the presence of a male figure at the heart of Christian devotion, the heart of Christian claims about reality and truth, and asked what this could have to do with the oppression and liberation of women.

326   Beyond Christolatry

Mary Daly is an American feminist philosopher and theologian, who has stridently criticized Christianity for its perpetuation of patriarchy, and Christology for providing the ideological support for that perpetuation.

It is still not unusual for Christian priests and ministers, when confronted with the issue of women's liberation, to assert that God 'became incarnate' uniquely as a male and then to draw arguments for male supremacy from this. Indeed the Christological tradition itself tends to justify such conclusions. The underlying—and often explicit—assumption in the minds of theologians down through the centuries has been that the divinity could not have deigned to 'become incarnate' in the 'inferior' sex, and the 'fact' that 'he' did not do so of course confirms male superiority. The erosion of consent to male dominance on the part of women is undermining such assumptions of the tradition. [. . .]

I am proposing that Christian idolatry concerning the person of Jesus is not likely to be overcome except through the revolution that is going on in women's consciousness. It will, I think, become increasingly evident that exclusively masculine symbols for the ideal of 'incarnation' or for the ideal of the human search for fulfilment will not do. As a uniquely masculine image and language for divinity loses credibility, so also the idea of a single divine incarnation in a human being of the male sex may give way in the religious consciousness to an increased awareness of the power of Being in all persons.

Seeds of this awareness are already present in the traditional doctrine that all human beings are made to the image of God and in a less than adequate way in the doctrine of grace. Now it should become possible to work out with increasing realism the implications in both of these doctrines that human beings are called to self-actualisation and to the creation of a community that fosters the becoming of women and men. This means that no adequate models can be taken from the past.

It may be that we will witness a remythologising of religion. Symbolism for incarnation of the divine in human beings may continue to be needed in the future, but it is highly unlikely that women or men will continue to find plausible that symbolism which is epitomised in the image of the Virgin kneeling in adoration before her own son. Perhaps this will be replaced by the emergence of imagery that is not hierarchical. The point is not to deny that a revelatory event took place in the encounter with the person Jesus. Rather, it is to affirm that the creative presence of the Verb can be revealed at every historical moment, in every person and culture.

> Mary Daly, *Beyond God the Father: Toward a Philosophy of Women's Liberation*, ch. 3: 'Beyond Christolatry: A World without Models', extract (1973)

327 Christ beyond Jesus

Rosemary Radford Reuther (1936–) is a leading Roman Catholic feminist theologian. The article excerpted here is one of the key feminist writings to pose the question whether a male Incarnation can be liberative for women.

A Christology that identified the maleness of the historical Jesus with normative humanity and with the maleness of the divine Logos must move in an increasingly misogynist direction that not only excludes woman as representative of Christ in ministry but makes her a second-class citizen in both creation and redemption. Androgynous Christologies try to affirm the female side in the vision of a Christ that is 'neither male nor female'. But the identification of this androgynous Christ with the male Jesus continues to give an androcentric bias to the vision of redemptive humanity. Woman can represent only the 'feminine' side of a male-centred symbol the fullness of which is disclosed only in a male person.

[. . .] Where does this leave the quest for a feminist Christology? Must we not say that the very limitations of Christ as a male person must lead women to the conclusion that he cannot represent redemptive personhood for them? That they must emancipate themselves from Jesus as redeemer and seek a new redemptive disclosure of God and of human possibility in female form?

A starting point for this inquiry must be a re-encounter with the Jesus of the synoptic Gospels, not the accumulated doctrine about him but his message and praxis. Once the mythology about Jesus as Messiah or divine Logos, with its traditional masculine imagery, is stripped off, the Jesus of the synoptic Gospels can be recognised as a figure remarkably compatible with feminism. This is not to say, in an anachronistic sense, that 'Jesus was a feminist,' but rather that the criticism of religious and social hierarchy characteristic of the early portrait of Jesus is remarkably parallel to feminist criticism.

Fundamentally, Jesus renews the prophetic vision whereby the Word of God does not validate the existing social and religious hierarchy but speaks on behalf of the marginalised and despised groups of society. Jesus proclaims an iconoclastic reversal of the system of religious status: The last shall be first and the first last. The leaders of the religious establishment are blind guides and hypocrites. The outcasts of society—prostitutes, publicans, Samaritans—are able to hear the message of the prophet. This reversal of social order doesn't just turn hierarchy upside down, it aims at a new reality in which hierarchy and dominance are overcome as principles of social relations. [. . .]

Women play an important role in this Gospel vision of the vindication of the lowly in God's new order. It is the women of the oppressed and marginalised groups who are often pictured as the representatives of the lowly. The dialogue at the well takes place with a Samaritan woman. A Syro-Phoenician woman is the prophetic seeker who forces Jesus to concede redemption of the Gentiles. Among the poor it is the widows who are the most destitute. Among the ritually unclean, it is the woman with the flow of blood who extorts healing for herself contrary to the law. Among the morally outcast, it is the prostitutes who are the furthest from righteousness. The role played by women of marginalised groups is an intrinsic part of the iconoclastic, messianic vision. It means that the women are the oppressed of the oppressed. They are the bottom of the present social hierarchy and hence are seen, in a special way, as the last who will be first in the Kingdom of God. [. . .]

Jesus as liberator calls for a renunciation, a dissolution, of the web of status relationships by which societies have defined privilege and deprivation. He protests against the identification of this system with the favour or disfavour of God. His ability to speak as liberator does not reside in his maleness but in the fact that he has renounced this system of domination and seeks to embody in his person the new humanity of service and mutual empowerment. He speaks to and is responded to by low-caste women because they represent the bottom of this status network and have the least stake in its perpetuation.

Theologically speaking, then, we might say that the maleness of Jesus has no ultimate significance. It has social symbolic significance in the framework of societies of patriarchal privilege. In this sense Jesus as the Christ, the representative of liberated humanity and the liberating Word of God, manifests the *kenosis of patriarchy* [cf. **249**], the announcement of the new humanity through a lifestyle that discards hierarchical caste privilege and speaks on behalf of the lowly. In a similar way, the femaleness of the social and religiously outcast who respond to him has social symbolic significance as a witness against the same idolatrous system of patriarchal privilege. This system is unmasked and shown to have no connection with favour with God. Jesus, the homeless Jewish prophet, and the marginalised women and men who respond to him, represent the overthrow of the present world system and the sign of a dawning new age in which God's will is done on earth.

But this relation of redeeming Christ and redeemed women should not be made into ultimate theological gender symbols. Christ is not necessarily male, nor is the redeemed community only women, but a new humanity, female and male. We need to think in terms of a dynamic, rather than a static, relationship between redeemer and redeemed. The redeemer is one who has been redeemed, just as Jesus himself accepted the baptism of John. Those who have been liberated can, in turn, become paradigmatic, liberating persons for others.

Christ, as redemptive person and Word of God, is not to be encapsulated 'once-for-all' in the historical Jesus. The Christian community continues Christ's identity. As vine and branches Christic personhood continues in our sisters and brothers. In the language of early Christian prophetism, we can encounter Christ in the form of our sister. Christ, the liberated humanity, is not confined to a static perfection of one person two thousand years ago. Rather, redemptive humanity goes ahead of us, calling us to yet incompleted dimensions of human liberation.

Rosemary Radford Reuther, Sexism and God Talk, ch. 5: 'Can a Male Saviour Save Women?', extracts (1983)

328   **An Inclusive Christ**

Patricia Wilson-Kastner's book *Faith, Feminism and the Christ* is perhaps the most orthodox of the feminist theologians represented here when it comes to Christology. More than Rosemary Radford Reuther (cf. **327**), and certainly more than Mary Daly (cf. **326**), she argues that the idea of the Incarnation of God in Jesus of Nazareth is capacious enough to include and support the hopes of women.

If in the cross of Christ we celebrate the power of sacrificial love, then in the resurrection we foresee triumph for all humanity, indeed for all the world, over the forces of alienation. One of the most fundamental insights of feminism is that the various divisions of hierarchy—alienation of humanity from the animate and inanimate world about it, dualisms of body and spirit—all need to be healed and overcome in us. In the resurrected Jesus, God has assured us that such healing has entered the world through the Spirit and is at work among us, and that this is the promise which God is fulfilling among us. The cosmic vision of feminism is not an illusory dream of naive individuals, but in its most thoroughgoing and radical form is the vision of the gospel, the promise made by God to the world through Jesus Christ. The struggles of feminism find their fullest context and their strongest promise of fulfilment in the risen Christ.

The resurrection of Christ is God's pledge to the divisions and dualisms in the world. Power and insignificance, matter and spirit, activity and inertia are united through the resurrection. The life of the risen Christ that pervades all things unites the divided, and continues as an active force for reconciliation in the world. Feminism, with its strong drive to both preserve the integrity of all beings and yet nurture the interconnectedness of the world, is confirmed in the figure of the risen Christ.

Such an ecological concern, which endeavours to conserve the world and its creatures, and yet also encourages the dynamism of life to surge through the cosmos, is manifest in the resurrection. The integrity of all reality is preserved, nurtured, and sustained. Such a dynamic growth process emerges from the creation itself. The resurrection does not signify an eternal imposition of meaning or purpose on the world; the resurrection is the fulfilment of the dynamic which is most profoundly within the world. The resurrection powerfully evokes and strengthens that which constitutes the most fundamental identity of the world, the urge which is at the heart of creation. Such respect for the evolution of life from this dynamic is at the heart of feminist concerns, often emerging in a rejection of what is perceived as the oppressive power of divine transcendence. In the resurrection such labelling of the power and love of God is shown to be a misunderstanding of both God and the way in which God acts in the world. In the resurrection the false dichotomies between transcendence and immanence are shown to be foreign to the God who is present in the risen Christ, who sustains and nurtures the world as an organic unity, respecting the integrity of the individual within the context of the dynamic of the whole.

The incarnation, passion, resurrection of Christ, and the sending of the

Spirit are not acts of an exclusive or oppressive God. No one can deny that Jesus the Christ was a male person, but the significance of the incarnation has to do with his humanity, not his maleness. When it was being true to its gospel the church understood this truth, although it has often been unfaithful indeed to its own faithful vision of Christ. In the crucifixion of Christ the dualisms and negativity that feminism seeks to overcome have been conquered. Through the resurrection the whole is healed and is being healed. Through the dynamic life of the risen Christ, the varied beings of the cosmos gather into one living whole in God, in which all that is good, beautiful, and true is nurtured and grows in the unending life of God. All reality, from the remotest subatomic particle to the most comprehensive and abstract idea, is living in God and being brought to its own completion as a part of God's gift of divine life to us [cf. 323]. Any individual feminist may choose to reject this vision of Christ for any number of reasons. However, the figure of Christ remains our central symbol: one of inclusiveness, healing, and living unity, which fulfils the expectation of feminism.

If Christianity has not presented such an inclusive Christ to the world, the fault is not due to a fundamental exclusiveness or excuse for oppression and divisiveness found in Christ himself. Rather, the church's own lack of fidelity and vision has allowed it to be used by others, and itself to use Christ, as a sacred justification for social, political, economic, and religious repression. To acknowledge the reality of such evil done in Christ's name is to identify the negative effects of the human tendency to misuse freedom and to evoke the holy in the service of people's own selfish and oppressive end, rather than God's creative purpose.

Patricia Wilson-Kastner, *Faith, Feminism and the Christ*, ch. 5:
'Who is this Christ?', extract (1983)

III. Incarnation, Cross, Resurrection, Trinity

It was not an innovation when twentieth-century theologians began to consider again the Cross of Christ as the doorway to a rich Trinitarian account of God's being and ways with the world—but after the poverty of Trinitarian dogmatic themes in much Western academic theology in the nineteenth century, it felt like it. Theologians once again asked, from various different angles, what it meant for God to be in Christ who was obedient to the extent of death on the Cross; what that event unfolded of the eternal being of God for the world.

After spending his early life as a sceptical radical in pre-revolutionary Russia, Sergius Bulgakov (1871–1944) became an Orthodox priest and was expelled after the revolution. He settled in Paris, as Dean of the Orthodox Theological Academy there. In this extract he draws on some of the precision of Orthodox Trinitarian theology to address the theme of the crucified God in ways which foreshadow Protestant and Catholic accounts later in the century. (Cf. **333**.)

Christ's exhaustion on the cross shows how his divine nature humbles itself to fit human measure. His divinity is self-constrained to yield to death, and though it does not itself die, it bears the weight of his dying humanity. It is his divine hypostasis itself that thus shares in death, for it is the hypostasis of his human nature indissolubly united with the divine. Therefore it is the God-man in the integral unity of his complex being who dies, but dies differently in his respective natures: the human nature dies, and consequently its hypostasis, which is the divine hypostasis of the Logos, passes with it through the gates of death to the depths of creaturely non-being. It thus brings to the utmost diminution in death its divine nature as well. In this sense death extends to the whole God-man, both to his humanity and to his divinity, though in a different way, and therefore it is quite impossible to exclude his divinity from participation in death.

The same idea must be carried further and applied not only to the Logos himself, but to the other persons of the holy Trinity. Here we could think about the last two cries from the cross. The first is the God-forsakenness, indicating a kind of sinking of the Son out of sight of the Father, his link with whom is thus known only in the pain of yearning. Now the Son calls to him out of the depths of the creatureliness of his human nature. This forsaking the Son is an act of the Father, expressing his acceptance of the Son's death, and to that extent the Father's participation in it. To leave the Son to die on the cross is for the Father a spiritual participation in the vicarious sacrifice of love, though the Father did not die.

No less significant of this participation of the Father in the Son's exhaustion on the cross is the Son's last cry, committing his spirit unto the hands of the Father. The Son returns to the Father's bosom, though not as yet to abide there beyond all worlds and to sit on the right hand of the Father as in the glorious ascension. The incarnate Son is as it were forcibly made discarnate in death, and his divine-human spirit returns to his Father and his God, just as in human death the dust returns to the earth and the spirit unto God who gave it. This is a special depth of abasement in the self-humbling of the Son, in which the Father takes part in his own way. It is the Father who accepts the spirit of the Son and shelters it for the three days before the resurrection. The spirits of all whom God sends to the earth return to him in death, and it is, so to speak, as one of these spirits that the Father receives the spirit of the Son who has tasted death. The Son's commitment into the Father's hands signifies the deepest self-lowering of divinity. A divine mystery, inaccessible to human understanding, is hidden in the Father's acceptance of the Son in the exhaustion of death and his tending of him until the resurrection; but we touch reverently upon this mystery, since the holy gospel bears witness to it.

The Son's God-forsakenness and the exhaustion of his divinity implies that the Holy Spirit, while ever resting upon the God-man, yet somehow forsakes him also. For the Holy Spirit is, first and foremost, the perceptible nearness of the Father, abiding in his love. The Holy Spirit is the actual personal love of the Father for the Son and of the Son for the Father, their unity, itself hypostatic (this is why Christ's words 'I and the Father are one' [John 10: 30] tacitly assume 'in the Holy Spirit'). The state of God-forsakenness as sinking out of sight of the Father necessarily implies being also forsaken by the Holy Spirit, who descended upon the Son when he was plunged in the waters of Jordan, which symbolised his coming death [2]. The Holy Spirit returned, as it were, once more to the Father when death had taken place in complete God-forsakenness (and indeed apart from this God-forsakenness death could not have taken place in the God-man). Since, then, the Holy Spirit acquiesces in this way in the self-emptying of the Son, in his exhaustion on the cross, he also spends himself with him; for to refrain from manifesting oneself to the beloved is to do violence to love, a fortiori for him whose being is love. (The human image of this self-shedding of the Spirit is given by the Mother of God standing by the cross while a sword was piercing through her soul, and her Son entrusting her to the care of the beloved disciple.) The Holy Spirit is joy, he is the comforter, but the Son in his agony on the cross was left without joy and comfort; he found comfort only in obedience to the will of the Father and in prayer.

In coming down from heaven, in his nativity, the Son leaves the heavenly glory of the Holy Trinity; in going down into the bowels of the earth the Son as it were surrenders his place as God in God, and his divine hypostasis ('My Spirit') is committed to the Father's care.

Sergius Bulgakov, 'The Lamb of God', extract (1933)

330   God on the Cross

Jürgen Moltmann (1926–), a German Reformed theologian, has been one of the most influential dogmatic theologians of recent times, and has found an audience well beyond the confines of the academic world. His book *The Crucified God* drove home the implications of the Cross for our understanding of God. (Cf. **329**.)

The death of Jesus on the cross is the *centre* of all Christian theology. It is not the only theme of theology, but it is in effect the entry to its problems and answers on earth. All Christian statements about God, about creation, about sin and death have their focal point in the crucified Christ. All Christian statements about history, about the church, about faith and sanctification, about the future and about hope stem from the crucified Christ. The multiplicity of the New Testament comes together in the event of the crucifixion and resurrection of Jesus and flows out again from it. It is one event and one person. The addition of 'cross and resurrection' represents only the inevitable temporality which is a part of language; it is not a sequence of facts. For cross and resurrection are not facts on the same level; the first expression denotes a historical happening to Jesus, the second an eschatological event. Thus the centre is occupied not by 'cross and resurrection', but by *the resurrection of the crucified Christ*, which qualifies his death as something that has happened for us; and *the cross of the risen Christ*, which reveals and makes accessible to those who are dying his resurrection from the dead.

In coming to terms with this Christ event, the christological tradition closely followed the Christ hymn in Philippians 2 [**39**]. It therefore understood the incarnation of the Son of God as his course towards the humiliation on the cross. The incarnation of the Logos is completed on the cross. Jesus is born to face his passion. His mission is fulfilled once he has been abandoned on the cross. So it is impossible to speak of an incarnation of God without keeping this conclusion in view. There can be no theology of the incarnation which does not become a theology of the cross. 'As soon as you say incarnation, you say cross.' God did not become man according to the measure of our conceptions of being a man. He became the kind of man we do not want to be: an outcast, accursed, crucified. *Ecce homo!* Behold the man! is not a statement which arises from the confirmation of our humanity and is made on the basis of 'like is known by like'; it is a confession of faith which recognises God's humanity in the dehumanised Christ on the cross. At the same time the confession says *Ecce deus!* Behold God on the cross! Thus God's incarnation 'even unto the death on the cross' is not in the last resort a matter of concealment; this is his utter humiliation, in which he is completely with himself and completely with the other, the man who is dehumanised. Humiliation to the point of death on the cross corresponds to God's nature in the contradiction of abandonment. When the crucified Jesus is called the 'image of the invisible God' [**50**], the meaning is that this is God, and God is like this. God is not greater than he is in this humiliation. God is not more glorious than he is in this self-surrender. God is not more powerful than he is in this helplessness. God is not more divine than he is in this humanity [cf. **218**, **331**].

Jürgen Moltmann, The Crucified God, 'The "Crucified God"', extract (1973)

331   The Christlikeness of God

Michael Ramsey (1904–88) was Archbishop of Canterbury from 1961, having held chairs in Theology in the Universities of Cambridge and Durham some time before. A careful and attractive writer, he here provides a short overview of the heart of incarnational theology.

The importance . . . of the confession 'Jesus is Lord' is not only that Jesus is divine but that God is Christlike. 'God is Christlike and in him there is no unChristlikeness at all.'

In realising the meaning of Christ, the Church found itself thinking about God in new ways. The doctrine of the Trinity did not arise from speculation or theorising but from the experience of the first Christians. As they reflected upon their old faith in the God of the Hebrew Scriptures, together with their recognition of the deity in Jesus and of the power within them of the Holy Spirit, they believed themselves to be encountering not a mere set of passing phases in the life of God (the view which appeared in later history under the name of Sabellianism) but deity as he is eternally. Here the teaching of the fourth gospel about the love and glory of God is significant, for in the discourse and prayer of Jesus at the last supper the love and mutual glorifying of the Father and the Son in the passion is presented as the disclosure in history of God as he eternally is. The doctrine of the Trinity is the affirmation that self-giving is characteristic of Being, that mutuality of self-giving love belongs to God's perfection; and the self-giving of God toward his creatures is possible because of the glory which the Father has with the Son in the love of the Spirit eternally.

The Christlikeness of God means that his passion and resurrection are the key to the very meaning of God's own deity. Is there within and beyond the universe any coherence or meaning or pattern or sovereignty? The New Testament doctrine is that in the death and resurrection of Jesus, in the fact of living through dying, of finding life through losing it, of the saving of self through the giving of self, there is this sovereignty. And to believe it with more than a bare intellectual consent is to believe it existentially, and to believe it existentially is to follow the way of finding life through losing it. Those who make their own the living-through-dying of Jesus find purpose, sovereignty, deity, in and beyond the world.

So when God became incarnate as man his meaningfulness as God came into its own. The self-giving, the becoming-man, the suffering-love were not additions to the divine experience or mere incidents in the divine history. In becoming man, God revealed the meaning of what it is to be God. But he could do so not because he is incomplete without man or dependent upon creatures for his own existence, but because he is in itself the perfection of love. The glory is seen in the becoming-man because it is a glory 'beyond' and eternal.

So, too, in Jesus the human race finds its own true meaning. Men rejected Jesus because they preferred the glory of man to the glory of God, as St. John draws out in his gospel. But the glory they preferred, and still prefer in their folly, is not man's true glory but the false glory of self-centredness, self-assertion and pride. Man's true glory is the reflection in him of the divine glory, the self-giving love seen in Jesus.

Thus it is in Jesus that we see man becoming his true self; in that giving away of self which happens when man is possessed by God. The meaning of what it is to be man appears when man is the place where deity fulfils itself, and the glory of the one is the glory of the other. The phrase 'the Man for others' is an illuminating one, but it is not the whole story, for God created man not only for others but for God.

Arthur Michael Ramsey, *God, Christ and the World: A Study in Contemporary Theology*, extract (1969)

332 Saved by the Cross

Jon Sobrino (1938–) is a Spanish Catholic theologian working in El Salvador. Writing from the perspective of liberation theology (cf. **300**), he provides a similar account of the Trinitarian life of God on the Cross to those given above, but his focus is on God's drawing of human beings into participation in this life in history.

On the cross of Jesus God himself is crucified. The Father suffers the death of the Son and takes upon himself all the pain and suffering of history. In this ultimate solidarity with humanity he reveals himself as the God of love, who opens up a hope and a future through the most negative side of history. Thus Christian existence is nothing else but a process of participating in this same process whereby God loves the world and hence in the very life of God. [. . .]

In God's abandonment of the Son [. . .] we find not only God's criticism of the world but also his ultimate solidarity with it. On the cross God's love for humanity is expressed in truly historical terms rather than in idealistic ones. Historical love presupposes activity, but it also presupposes passivity because it is love situated in a contradictory structure that makes its force and power felt. The passivity involved here is that of letting oneself be affected by all that is negative, by injustice and death. On the cross of Jesus God was present and at the same time absent. Absent to the Son, he was present for human beings. And this dialectics of presence and absence is the way to express in human language the fact that God is love. The cross is the contradiction of humanity, but it is grounded on an ultimate solidarity with it. In the Son's passion the Father suffers the pain of abandonment. In the Son's death, death affects God himself—not because God dies but because he suffers the death of the Son. Yet God suffers so that we might live, and that is the most complete expression of love. It is in Jesus' resurrection that God will reveal himself as a promise fulfilled, but it is on the cross that love is made credible. From the standpoint of the cross we can reformulate all the important problems of theology: Who is God? What are we? What is the meaning of history? What is salvation?

The Christian belief in God as a Trinity takes on a new and dynamic meaning in the light of the cross. God is a Trinitarian 'process' on the way toward its ultimate fulfilment, but it takes all history into itself. In this process God participates in, and lets himself be affected by, history through the Son; and history is taken into God in the Spirit. What is manifest on the cross is the internal structure of God himself. The eternal love between Father and Son is seen to be historically mediated in the presence of evil, and hence it takes the paradoxical form of abandonment; but from this Trinitarian love, now historicized, there wells up the force that will ensure that external history can be a history of love rather than a history of domination. In God himself the Spirit is the fruit of the love between Father and Son, as tradition tells us. In history, however, this love takes a historical form: It becomes the Spirit of love designed to effect liberation in history.

The work of the Spirit can be described as the incorporation of the human individual and of all people into the very process of God himself. The Spirit makes us children of God, but it does not do so in any idealistic way. It does so through the structure of the Son. It introduces us into God's own attitude toward the world, which is an attitude of love. But since the world is dominated by sin and hence riddled with conflict, it makes us co-actors with God in history. Alongside the notion of God as a 'process' then, we have Christian existence as a 'way' based on the following of Jesus. When we view Christian existence as the following of Jesus, we are not simply viewing it in ethical terms that flow from a prior faith. Strictly speaking, we are viewing it as a participation in the very life of God himself. We are not made children of God by some expression of intent or by some mysterious supra-historical reality (akin to what has traditionally been called the 'supernatural'). We are made children of God by participating in the very process of God. Following Jesus means taking the love that God manifested on the cross and making it real in history.

In this light we can appreciate the deeper underlying significance of a traditional notion; namely, that we have been saved by the cross. The usual explanations assume we know who God is and what salvation is at the start, suggesting that salvation is something added to a human being who is already fully constituted as such. In my opinion, however, we are saying two things when we say that the cross brings salvation: First, we are saying that in it is revealed God's unconditional love. Salvation is both gratuitous and possible in historical existence. If God has loved us first, then there is some ultimate meaning to history. Second, we are saying that the culmination of our being loved by God is his work of preparing us to be introduced into his own historical process, to move from passive love to active love.

The cross, in other words, does not offer us any explanatory model that would make us understand what salvation is and how it itself might be salvation. Instead it invites us to participate in a process within which we can actually experience history as salvation.[18] It is the same point that we have already reiterated several times: Our knowledge of God and of Jesus as the Son is ultimately a con-natural knowledge, a knowledge based on sym-pathy within the very process of God himself rather than outside it. The Son reveals himself to us as the Son insofar as we follow his path. The Father reveals himself to us as Father insofar as we experience the following of Jesus as an open road that moves history forward, opens up a future, and nurtures a hope in spite of sin and historical injustice. It is through that experience that we sense that love is the ultimate meaning of existence and feel an unquenchable hope arise within us—a hope against hope because it wells up from suffering.

> Jon Sobrino, *Christology at the Crossroads: A Latin American Approach*, 'The Death of Jesus', Thesis 13, extract (1978)

333   The Triumphant Death

> Vladimir Lossky (1903–58) was, like Sergius Bulgakov whose ideas he challenged (cf. **329**), required to leave his native Russia after the revolution, and became an ambassador for Orthodox theology in the West. Here he brings out a rather different flavour of reflection or the place of the Passion in Trinitarian theology from that of Bulgakov on the other theologians in this section. (Cf. **12**.)

The feast of the Transfiguration, so venerated by the Orthodox Church, serves as a key to the understanding of the humanity of Christ in the Eastern tradition. This never considers the humanity of Christ in abstraction, apart from his Godhead, whose fullness dwells in him bodily. Deified by the divine energies, the humanity of the Word had to appear to the sons of the Church, after the resurrection and Pentecost, in that glorious way which before the advent of grace was hidden from human eyes. This humanity revealed the divinity which is the splendour of the three persons. The humanity of Christ provides the opportunity for the manifestation of the Trinity. That is why the Epiphany (the feast of the Baptism of Christ according to the liturgical tradition of the East) and the Transfiguration are celebrated so solemnly: it is the revelation of the Trinity that is being celebrated—for the voice of the Father was made heard and the Holy Spirit was present the first time in the form of a dove, and the second time as the luminous cloud which covered the Apostles. This royal aspect of Christ—'the one of the Holy Trinity'—who came into the world to conquer death is characteristic of Orthodox spirituality in every epoch and in every country. Even the passion, the death on the cross, and the laying in the tomb become triumphant acts by which the divine majesty of Christ illuminates the images of the fall and abandonment whilst accomplishing the mystery of our salvation.

Vladimir Lossky, *Mystical Theology of the Eastern Church*, ch. VII: 'The Economy of the Son', extract (1944)

Section F

Jesus beyond Christianity

Perhaps more than at any time since the patristic period, twentieth-century Christianity found itself one among many religious traditions and communities. The ongoing encounter with Judaism was brought to a new prominence by the horrific events of mid-century; migration and globalization made day-by-day encounter with Eastern religions a reality in many countries; and Islam was once more a powerful voice on the world stage. The place of Jesus in the world of religions became again an urgent issue.

I. The Uniqueness of Christ

Evaluations of the place of Jesus of Nazareth between Christians and other religions were, in the twentieth century, dominated by the question of uniqueness or particularity. Could the claim that Jesus was *the* Saviour survive in a world of religious plurality, and in what form? We have chosen to focus on the way the question has been posed and faced in the encounter with Buddhism and Hinduism.

334 No Un-Christlikeness at All

William Temple (1881–1944) was Archbishop of Canterbury from 1942, and a man passionately concerned with issues of social justice and with ecumenism. Here he draws out the other side of the claim that God is Christlike—and in him there is no un-Christlikeness at all. (Cf. **279, 331, 335, 336**.)

The one thing we are bound to require, as it seems to me, is that men shall say that this Christ is very God, not for the sake of doing honour to Jesus of Nazareth—he did not claim honour for himself—but because every thought of God which is not in accord with the character of Jesus Christ is idolatry, a false image of God; and the more we dwell upon it, the worse it will be for us. 'This is the true God and Eternal Life. My little children, keep yourself from idols' [1 John 5: 20–1]. These are perhaps the last words written in the New Testament, and they certainly sum it all up. We cannot ever have truce with the suggestion that Jesus of Nazareth was divinely inspired as others have been divinely inspired, and that God appears in certain aspects of his being in him and in certain other aspects elsewhere; the moment that line is taken, you destroy conviction at the central point, namely that God is one whose character we know and know in perfect definiteness of outline, because it is the character of Jesus Christ. That is the Christian claim. We are, of course, very far from denying that men may learn abundantly from Christ without accepting the whole of that claim; and we are only too glad that they should do so. His treasures are for all mankind, and that all men should enter into them as they may and will must be a matter of happiness to his disciples. But nothing else than this is acceptance of the Christian religion. This is the Christian faith. This, we believe, is the power that can save the world.

William Temple, *The Universality of Christ: A Course of Lectures*, III: 'Christ the Complete Revelation', extract (1921)

335   Jesus and Buddha

Sarvepalli Radhakrishnan (1888–1975) was a Hindu philosopher and proponent of a universalist, pluralist religion, who became President of India from 1962 to 1967. (Cf. **279, 336**.)

The Gospel story bears striking resemblance to the life and teaching of Gautama the Buddha.

Nearly five hundred years before Jesus, Buddha went round the Ganges valley proclaiming a way of life which would deliver men from the bondage of ignorance and sin. In a hundred and fifty years after his death, tradition of his life and passing away became systematised. He was miraculously conceived and wondrously born.[19] His father was informed by angels about it, and, according to *Lalitavistara*, 'the queen was permitted to lead the life of a virgin for thirty-two months.' On the day of his birth a Brahmin priest predicts his future greatness. Asita is the Buddhist Simeon:[20] he comes through air to visit the infant Gautama. Simeon 'came by the Spirit into the Temple.' When he asks the angels why they rejoice, they answer that they are 'joyful and exceeding glad' as the Buddha to be is 'born for the weal and welfare in the world of men'. He steadily grew in wisdom and stature. In spite of great efforts to protect him from the sights of sorrow, Buddha found no satisfaction in the life by which he was surrounded. He resolved to flee from the joys of his home. When the tidings reached him that a son was born to him, he observed: 'This is a new and a strong tie that I shall have to break,' and he left his home without delay. Early in his career, after a fast of forty-nine days, he was tempted by Mara to give up his quest for truth, with promises of world dominion. The Evil One said unto Buddha: 'So, Lord, if the Lord desired, he could turn the Himalayas, the king of mountains, into very gold, and gold would the mountain be.' Buddha replies: 'He who hath seen pain and the source of pain, how could such a one bow to lusts?' The Evil One vanished unhappy and disconsolate. Buddha overcomes the temptations, persists in his search, meditates for days, and wins enlightenment. Like his conception and birth, Buddha's enlightenment is marked by the thirty-two great miracles. The blind receive their sight, the deaf hear, and the lame walk freely. Buddha himself is transfigured, and his body shines with matchless brightness. With a tender compassion for all beings he sets forth 'to establish the kingdom of righteousness, to give light to those enshrouded in darkness and open the gate of immortality to men.'[21] His mission begins. He has twelve disciples whom he sends forth, to carry his message among all classes of men.[22] Buddha heals the sick, is the incomparable physician [cf. 8].[23] In the striking story of the sick brother neglected by the other inmates of the monastery, whom the Buddha washed and tended with his own hands, saying afterwards to the careless monks, who would have been eager enough to serve him, 'Whosoever would wait upon me, let him wait upon the sick,'[24] he claims his oneness with humanity so that services to the sick or the destitute are in reality rendered to himself. We have the golden rule in the maxim: 'Doing as one would be done by, kill not nor cause to kill.'[25] 'As a mother would guard the life of her own and only son at the risk of her own, even so let each one practise infinite sympathy toward all beings in all the world.' 'Let goodwill without measure, impartial, unmixed, without enmity, prevail throughout the world, above, beneath, around.' Good conduct and good belief are insisted on. When once we accept Buddha's teaching all other distinctions of caste and status are lost.[26] He converts the robber Angulimala, has dinner with Ambapali the harlot,[27] and is accused of living in abundance.[28] [. . .]

Buddha has his triumphal entry into his native city of Kapilavastu. As he approaches, marvellous rays proceed from him, lighting up the gates and walls, towers and monuments. The city, like the New Jerusalem illumined by the lamp, is full of light, and all the citizens go forth to meet him. But Buddha remains unmoved. When Buddha is taken to the temple for baptism, he points out that it is unnecessary, as he is superior to the gods, though he conforms to the practice of the world. When a merchant who became his disciple proposed to return to his native town and preach to his people, Buddha said: 'The people of Sunaparanta are exceedingly violent; if they revile you, what will you do?' 'I will make no reply,' said the disciple. 'And if they strike you?' 'I will not strike in return.' 'And if they try to kill you?' 'Death', said the disciple, 'is no evil in itself. Many even desire it, to escape from the vanities of this life; but I shall take no steps either to hasten or delay the time of my departure.' Buddha was satisfied, and the merchant departed. Buddha had his troubles with his disciples. Devadatta, Buddha's cousin, was the Judas among his followers. He once hired thirty bowmen to kill him. But when these came into his presence they were awed by his majesty and fell down at his feet, like the soldiers in the garden of Gethsemane. When all his attempts failed, the faithless disciple entreated Buddha for his forgiveness. Buddha frankly forgave him. On the last day before his death, Buddha's body was again transfigured, and when he died a tremendous earthquake was felt throughout the world.[29] [. . .]

While Jesus is angry with the world which will not hear him, Buddha meets opposition with calm and confidence. He thought of the world as ignorant rather than wicked, as unsatisfactory rather than rebellious. There is therefore no nervous irritability or fierce anger about him. His behaviour is a perfect expression of courtesy and good feeling with a spice of irony in it. Three months after his death Buddha is transfigured. He is identified with the self-existent Supreme. Four centuries after his death he is declared to be a temporary manifestation in an earthly form of the Infinite, accessible at all times to his disciples and promising to make them partakers of his divine nature. By prayer and meditation the pious Buddhist enters into living communion with the heavenly Lord.

> Sarvepalli Radhakrishnan, *Eastern Religions and Western Christian Thought*,
> 'Christendom I', extracts (1939)

---

336 Christ and Ramakrishna

Swami Satprakashananda was an apostle of Hinduism in the West, bringing Hindu ideas and practices to America from the 1940s. He was a follower of the mystic and proponent of the harmony of religions Sri Ramakrishna (1836–86). (Cf. **279**, **335**.)

In the teachings of Sri Ramakrishna and Jesus Christ we find very striking similarities. Both condemned lust and greed, emphasised love of God, devotion to him; and his grace and love in return. Both stressed prayer to God in solitude, and both declare that God can be seen—that seeing God is the supreme goal of life. Like Jesus Christ, Sri Ramakrishna always emphasised purification of the heart, for it is the pure hearted that see God.

The differences in their messages are mainly due to the fact that they dealt with people of varied tendencies and capacities, living in different environments. When you want to teach the same truth to different types of people, you have to accommodate or adapt your teaching to the mental conditions of these different groups. To a child you teach geography or history in one way, but to a more mature person you must present the same geographic and historical facts in a different way.

The teachings of Jesus Christ deal particularly with the way of life, and emphasise ethical principles. Sri Ramakrishna dealt more with spiritual disciplines and the goal of God-realisation. Their handling of spiritual precepts differs but there is no essential difference in the inner spirit of their words and actions. [. . .]

Sri Ramakrishna and Jesus Christ came to turn people's minds from the transitory to the eternal. But in spite of constant cares, worries, and sufferings, people cling to their worldly desires, content to ignore the great saviours who would bring them peace. [. . .]

Jesus Christ and Sri Ramakrishna both came for the removal of all suffering, sins and bondages; the removal of all darkness and delusion. They came to lead human beings to eternal life and blessedness. [. . .]

If a person can realise God in one particular aspect, for example as Jesus Christ, he can know the true nature of God. If you take several pictures of your house from different angles, each picture will be different. No picture gives you a full view of the house; still every picture represents the entire house.

Similarly, according to one's inner development a man can conceive of God in many different ways. But each conception of God is capable of leading to God himself.

You may worship God as the divine Mother, divine Father, through Jesus Christ, Sri Ramakrishna, or countless other forms and aspects. But through any of these ways you can realise God himself, God as he is. This is the one great truth that Sri Ramakrishna taught in his life.

We find in the lives of Jesus Christ and Sri Ramakrishna many striking similarities. Though Sri Ramakrishna emphasised particularly the goal of life, and Jesus Christ the way of life, there is no fundamental difference between them. The inner spirit of their words and deeds is the same. They came in different ages to minister to the needs of different peoples. They both came to lead human beings to the one supreme goal.

Swami Satprakashananda, *Hinduism and Christianity: Jesus Christ and his Teachings in the Light of Vedanta*, ch. IV: 'Sri Ramakrishna and Jesus Christ', extracts (1975)

337   Hinduism and Christ

Raymond Panikkar (1918–) is the son of a Hindu father and a Roman Catholic mother. He is Professor Emeritus of Religious Studies at the University of California at Santa Barbara, and has done important work in promoting understanding of the interface between Hinduism and Christianity. (Cf. 277, 278.)

The strong attraction that Christ exercises at present on Hinduism can be summed up under the following headings:

A suffering god. In many Hindu homes one sees an image of Christ. The most popular is that of Christ kneeling in prayer in Gethsemane. Hinduism attempts to go beyond the great scandal of pain and suffering by denying the existence of this pain and this suffering. Then they see that in Christianity pain and suffering have entered into the very heart of this God who came down to earth. (India has no difficulty in admitting that Jesus is God, but in a sense that might not be acceptable to Christians.) Indians see that Christianity has the courage to admit the existence of suffering and even to give it a place in the life of the one they consider as saviour. This idea they find immensely attractive and they are moved to see Christians admitting the idea of a suffering God, whom they nevertheless continue to recognise as God.

A divine man. I say 'a *man*' because India has always been in danger of falling into what Westerners would call 'angelism' or even 'divinism'. The more a 'guru' or spiritual teacher abstains from food and laughter, the more he rises above human weaknesses and the accidents of life, the more a master and superior he is considered to be. Both traditional and modern India are greatly drawn to the idea of a divine man who laughs, eats, is no ascetic—for Christ is no ascetic in Indian eyes—who is truly a man and does not deny his humanity.

A human god. What surprises and delights Indians is a god who is not mythological, but who is an historical god, a god involved in the life of mankind, who lives that life with all simplicity. Indians have always had an intuitive knowledge of the mysterious union between the human and divine.

Raymond Panikkar, 'Confrontation Between Hinduism and Christ' 1(c), extract (1969)

II. Jesus and Judaism

Jesus was Jewish, but this fact has not always featured prominently in the reflections of Christians upon him, or seriously shaped their portrayals of him. In the twentieth century this has begun to change, in limited but important ways. Four things have happened: first, there have been some prominent re-evaluations of Jesus' life and message among Jewish theologians and writers, building on the work of their nineteenth-century forebears (e.g. **225**, **242**); second, the horror of the Holocaust has called into question any too-easy reconciliation, any papering-over of centuries of Christian anti-Judaism; third (and to a certain extent in consequence) there has been a retrieval among those questing for the historical Jesus of the thoroughly Jewish nature of Jesus and the movement which sprang up around him; last, the final years of the twentieth century saw the emergence of a vibrant and mutually enriching dialogue between Jewish and Christian theologians and philosophers.

Joseph Klausner (1874–1958) was a Lithuanian Jew who became Professor of Hebrew Literature and History at the Hebrew University in Palestine in 1919.

What is Jesus to the *Jewish nation* at the present day?

To the Jewish nation he can be neither God nor the Son of God, in the sense conveyed by belief in the Trinity. Either conception is to the Jew not only impious and blasphemous, but incomprehensible. Neither can he, to the Jewish nation, be the Messiah: the kingdom of heaven (the 'Days of the Messiah') is not yet come. Neither can they regard him as a Prophet: he lacks the Prophet's political perception and the Prophet's spirit of national consolation in the political-national sense.

Neither can they regard him as a lawgiver or the founder of a new religion: he did not even desire to be such. Neither is he a 'Tanna', or Pharisaic rabbi: he nearly always ranged himself in opposition to the Pharisees and did not apprehend the positive side in their work, the endeavour to take within their scope the entire national life and to strengthen the national existence.

But Jesus is, for the Jewish nation, a great teacher of morality and an artist in parable. He is the moralist for whom, in the religious life, morality counts as everything. Indeed, as a consequence of this extremist standpoint his ethical code has become simply an ideal for the isolated few, a 'Zukunfts-Musik', an ideal for 'the days of the Messiah', when an 'end' shall have been made of this 'old world', this present social order. It is no ethical code for the nations and the social order of today, when men are still trying to find the way to that future of the Messiah and the Prophets, and to the 'kingdom of the Almighty' spoken of by the Talmud, an ideal which is of 'this world' and which, gradually and in the course of generations, is to take shape in this world.

But in his ethical code there is a sublimity, distinctiveness and originality in form unparalleled in any other Hebrew ethical code; neither is there any parallel to the remarkable art of his parables. The shrewdness and sharpness of his proverbs and his forceful epigrams serve, in an exceptional degree, to make ethical ideas a popular possession. If ever the day should come and this ethical code be stripped of its wrappings of miracles and mysticism, the Book of the Ethics of Jesus will be one of the choicest treasures in the literature of Israel for all time.

Joseph Gedaliah Klausner, *Jesus of Nazareth: His Life, Times and Teaching*, ch. VIII: 'Conclusion: What is Jesus to the Jews?', extract (1922)

339   Who Killed Christ?

Samuel Sandmel (1911–79) was a Jewish rabbi and a scholar at the Jewish Institute of Religion at Hebrew Union College, Cincinnati. The claim that the Jews, all Jews, were Christ-killers has echoed all too frequently in the spaces where Jews have lived among Christians, and has fed the hatred which made Sandmel's final plea urgent—particularly for the twentieth century. (Cf. **162**.)

The events of the last week of Jesus' life contain both implicit and explicit allegations that Jews were responsible for the death of Jesus. The epithet 'Christ killer' has pursued Jews relentlessly in Christian lands, and sticks and stones and more lethal instruments have accentuated the name-calling [cf. **162**].

What shall a Jew say to himself and his children about this age-old Christian charge that the Jews, we Jews and not our ancestors alone, are 'Christ killers'? What we might say to ourselves would involve several steps. We might say, first, that the accounts in the Gospels on the one hand are so replete with legend and tendentiousness and Old Testament paraphrases as to reduce almost to the vanishing point any substantial historical value. What, for example, happened to the abundance of people resurrected with Jesus as Matthew alone related it? How reliable is an account in which the incident occurs of a severed ear miraculously restored? How authentic are accounts of a trial which contain so many contradictions and differences, such as two trials by the Sanhedrin in Mark, against one in Matthew and Luke, and none in John? [. . .] Cannot one discern the palpable shift of responsibility from Pilate to the Jews, through the patent devices by which Pilate is portrayed as reluctantly giving in to Jewish malevolence? Can the fact that the crucifixion was a Roman punishment, not a Jewish one, be so glossed over as to exculpate the Romans entirely, as Christian literature does, and not absolve the Jews at all? What shall we make of the circumstance that the Gospel accounts clarify to us why Romans would will the death of Jesus, but leave someone like me uninformed, even mystified, as to why Jews would have willed it? The Gospels show me no persuasive basis on which Jews as Jews would have levelled an accusation against a fellow-Jew; all that I read in the Gospels is a vague charge of 'blasphemy', a charge unaccompanied by any broad effort to adduce relevant particulars. I can see in the Gospels what Jews could have rejected, and what they could have, as Jews, disliked. I cannot see in the Gospels themselves, as I can see in Paul's Epistles with his scorn of Moses' laws, what Jews as Jews would have resented so bitterly. I can understand the Roman motives; from the Gospels I detect no convincing Jewish motive. I believe that the shift of responsibility is patent, is motivated, and that we Jews have been made to pay for what Romans did.

Yet what have we Jews really accomplished by such a scrutiny of the Gospels as historical sources? Perhaps we have thereby persuaded ourselves of our innocence; perhaps, if we are willing to read modern Christian commentators, we can learn, happily, that some Christians on their own have achieved this same persuasion; but many, perhaps most, Christians will never be persuaded either of our ancestors' innocence or of ours. [. . .]

Perhaps we might be willing to say to ourselves that it is not at all impossible that some Jews, even leading Jews, recommended the death of Jesus to Pilate. We are averse to saying this to ourselves, for so total has the charge been against us that we have been constrained to make a total denial. Yet if we admit—admit, not confess—that some Jews were involved, then why blame us all, both then and now? And since Jesus was a Jew, is it not more reasonable to say that people killed Jesus, than to put the statement as though Jesus were not a Jew, but his opponents were? Is it not equally unfair to say the Americans killed Lincoln and Kennedy?

These are the kinds of things we might say to ourselves. To Christians we can say very little. Do they charge us with responsibility for the death of Jesus? Or do they perchance mean that our stubborn abstention from sharing their theology is what really makes them regard us as Christ-killers? Is it consistent with Christian love and forgiveness to maintain an unforgiving hatred of Jews? Or does Christianity lessen itself, indeed, cheapen itself, by harbouring hatred for anyone? As a Jew, I openly disavow and reject the occasional minor motifs recurrent in Judaism of hatred of Gentiles; these motifs lessen and cheapen Judaism. The anti-Jewish motif in Christianity appears to me to be greater in scope and deeper in intensity than the comparable motifs in Judaism which I find abhorrent.

My parents fled Eastern Europe to escape pogroms which began with the ringing of church bells. My mother used to say that even after decades in America the ringing of church bells could still occasionally frighten her. When I was a boy, I was more than once described as Christ-killer, especially by gangs of boys. I recall a few occasions when such gangs chased me; I don't recall if they ever caught me. Most Jews my age have had at least the former experience.

My two oldest boys belong to a Boy Scout troop which has its headquarters at the near-by Episcopal Church. Not one of my sons has ever spoken to my wife or me about 'Christ-killers.' Apparently none of them has experienced what for me was no unusual occurrence. Will they some day experience it? And if they have children, will those children experience it?

This is in the hands of Christians, not of us Jews.

Samuel Sandmel, *We Jews and Jesus*, ch. 6: 'Toward a Jewish Attitude to Christianity',
extracts (1965)

Geza Vermes (1924–), Professor Emeritus of Jewish Studies at the University of Oxford, is one of those who has brought the Jewishness of Jesus into prominent relief in historical research. (Cf. **287, 288**.)

Whereas none of the claims and aspirations of Jesus can be said definitely to associate him with the role of Messiah, not to speak of that of *son of man*, the strange creation of the modern myth-makers, everything combines, when approached from the viewpoint of a study of first-century AD Galilee, or of charismatic Judaism, or of his titles and their development, to place him in the venerable company of the Devout, the ancient Hasidim. Indeed, if the present research has any value at all, it is in this conclusion that it is most likely to reside, since it means that any new enquiry may accept as its point of departure the safe assumption that Jesus did not belong among the Pharisees, Essenes, Zealots or Gnostics, but was one of the holy miracle-workers of Galilee. [. . .]

The uncovering of Jesus' real background and true Jewishness is [. . .] meant to be no more than an endeavour to clear away misunderstandings which for so long have been responsible for an unreal image of Jesus, a first step in what appears to be the direction of the real man. For it has emerged in these pages that from the beginning his followers have had the greatest difficulty in accepting his expressed opinions regarding himself. Whereas he explicitly avoided the title 'Messiah', he was very soon invested with it, and in the Christian mind has since become inseparable from it. By contrast, although he approved the designation 'prophet', this was one of the first of his appellations to be discarded by the Church, one that has never since been readopted. The result has been that, unable or unwilling to establish and admit the historical meaning of words recorded by the evangelists, orthodox Christianity has opted for a doctrinal structure erected on the basis of an arbitrary interpretation of the Gospel sayings, a structure which must by nature be vulnerable to reasoned criticism. This explains why Christian New Testament scholars of today display an agnostic tendency in regard to the historical authenticity of most of these words. Indeed, they even go so far as to reject the possibility of knowing anything historical about Jesus himself.

Certainly, unless by some fortunate chance new evidence is unfolded in the future, not a great deal can be said of him at this distance of time that can be historically authenticated. Nevertheless, this much at least can be asserted with some fair measure of conviction. The positive and constant testimony of the earliest Gospel tradition, considered against its natural background of first-century Galilean charismatic religion, leads not to a Jesus as unrecognisable within the framework of Judaism as by the standard of his own verifiable words and intentions, but to another figure: Jesus the just man, the *zaddik*, Jesus the helper and healer, Jesus the teacher and leader, venerated by his intimates and less committed admirers alike as prophet, lord and *son of God*.

Geza Vermes, *Jesus the Jew: A Historian's Reading of the Gospels*, Postscript, extracts (1973)

341   Judaism and Incarnation

....

Elliot R. Wolfson is an American theologian who specializes in Jewish mysticism and philosophy. In the article from which the following is an extract he explores the place which the concept of 'incarnation' can have and has had in Judaism.

The impression one gets from historians of religion is that Judaism has officially rejected incarnation as a legitimate theological position. As the historian of early Christianity Hans Joachim Schoeps observed: 'Christological doctrine in itself—the belief that God has become man and has allowed his only-begotten son to suffer sacrificial death as a propitiation for the sins of mankind—has remained, as Paul rightly says, a "stumbling block" to the Jews. It is an impossible article of belief, which detracts from God's sovereignty and absolute otherness—an article which, in fact, destroys the world.' [. . .]

From the Jewish perspective (at least as it may be reconstructed from classical sources), God may be spatially present in a holy place or even in the congregation of the holy people, but he is not embodied in any particular human being. It may be valid to conclude (and even this is by no means beyond critical assessment) that the particular expression of incarnation in Christianity, the union of the divine and the human in the body of Jesus, is an idea that has neither precedent in the ancient Israelite religion nor parallel in any of the varieties of Judaism in late antiquity that were contemporaneous with the emerging religion. This does not mean that the doctrine of incarnation in general is antithetical to Judaism. On the contrary, the idea of incarnation unique to Christianity should be viewed as a 'particular framing' of the conception of incarnation that was idiomatic to a variety of Judaic authors who represented God as a person. The evolution of the Christological doctrine of the incarnation of the Son is undoubtedly indebted to the scriptural tradition regarding the corporeality of God, a legacy that clashed with the Greek philosophical emphasis on the incorporeality and transcendence of ultimate reality. By reclaiming the significance of incarnation in the history of Judaism, therefore, one can simultaneously acknowledge the common ground between Judaism and Christianity and the uniqueness of this doctrine in each religious culture. [. . .] Simply stated, my thesis is that classical Jewish sources yield a philosophical conception of incarnation [. . .] that refers spe-cifically to the imaginal body of God, a symbolic construct that allows human consciousness to access the transcendent reality as a concrete form manifest primarily (if not exclusively) in the sacred space of the two major forms of worship of the heart: prayer and study. [. . .]

In the history of Judaism, unlike Christianity, belief in incarnation never attained the status of dogma. On the contrary, in rabbinic texts there are clear polemical statements rejecting the Christological doctrine, and in medieval philosophical literature one of the recurring tenets viewed as basic to Judaism was the claim that God is not a body. However, in rabbinic Judaism of the formative and medieval periods, based on biblical precedent, an anthropo-morphic conception of God is affirmed. These anthropomorphic character-izations are not to be taken simply as figurative or metaphorical. Underlying the rhetoric of representation is the eidetic presumption that God can be experienced in a tangible and concrete manner. Prayer and study, according to the rabbis, are key ways that God is so experienced. Proper intentionality in these two acts of piety is predicated on the iconic visualization of the divine within the imagination. In the physical space circumscribed by words of prayer and study, the imaginal body of God assumes incarnate form. This is the intent of the statement attributed to R. Abbahu, ' "Seek the Lord while he can be found" [Isa. 55: 6]. Where is he found? In the houses of worship and the houses of study.' The rabbinic notion of incarnation embraces the para-dox that God's body is real only to the extent that it is imagined, but it is imagined only to the extent that it is real. The conception of God's imaginal body evident in different phases of Jewish thought can contribute signifi-cantly to Christian reflection on the doctrine of incarnation. Indeed, the Judaic perspective should induce us to alter our views regarding corporeality in general. Proper attunement to the idea of the divine body in ancient Israel (and subsequent periods of Jewish history) may lead one to appreciate that the body is a complex construct of the imagination rather than a material artifact that can be measured by the dimensions of three-dimensional space. The phenomenological parameters of embodiment must be significantly expanded if we are to comprehend the enigma of incarnation, the limitless delimitation of the delimited limitlessness. To place YHWH before one con-stantly is to confront the holiness of the Holy One in the otherness of his being, a confrontation that is both encounter and resistance. Facing the face that cannot be faced in hearing the name that cannot be pronounced— therein lies the secret of incarnation in Judaism, a mystery of transcendence that the imagination alone is capable of rendering imminent. As Gaston Bachelard put it, 'To enter into the domain of the superlative, we must leave the positive for the imaginary. We must listen to the poets.' In the end, the Christological doctrine of incarnation is not, as Paul surmised, a stumbling block particularly to the Jews, but rather to anyone whose religious sensibility has not been properly nourished by the wellspring of poetic imagination.

Elliot R. Wolfson, 'Judaism and Incarnation: The Imaginal Body of God', extract (1996)

Section G

The Face of Christ

At the beginning of the twenty-first century the question arises again: who will Jesus be? What will we make of him and what will he make of us? Who will we say that he is? Of one thing, and perhaps one thing only, we can be certain: in this century as in the centuries before it, many millions will encounter the face of Christ, and will find themselves compelled to come to terms with it.

342 Christ's Beauty

> François Mauriac (1885–1970) was a French Roman Catholic author of novels, plays, essays, and journalism, who was awarded the 1952 Nobel Prize for literature. (Cf. **129, 141, 343**.)

In [the] apparent opposition between a Christ who, merely by drawing near, captured hearts and a Nazarene agitator despised by the rulers and priests and who could not be distinguished from his disciples by the soldiers charged with his arrest, in this contradictory vision we must try to discover what the human appearance of Christ really was.

Undoubtedly he was like many people whose beauty, at once very secret and very striking, dazzles some and escapes others; this is especially true when beauty is of the spiritual order. The august light on this face could be perceived only by an interior disposition. When we are in love, we are often surprised by the indifference others show to the face which, for us, sums up all the splendour of the world. Many do not even think of looking at those characteristics which reflect heaven, the mere sight of which makes us wild with delight and anguish. The least moment spent with the loved one is of inestimable value to us; yet it often makes little difference to his companions or his parents to live under the same roof with him or to share in the same work and breathe the air which he breathes.

Like all creatures, Christ is transformed by the person who is attracted to him. To this very natural phenomenon grace adds its unpredictable action. We cannot appear to another person as we would like him to see us, but the God-Man is not only the master of hearts but also the master of grace that is at work in hearts. He cured many more men born blind than the Gospel recounts. Each time a creature called him his Lord and his God and confessed that he was the Christ, the Messiah come into this world, he did so because

Christ had opened the interior eye whose vision is not limited simply to appearances.

For this reason, Rembrandt, of all the painters, seems to me to have given Christ an image most in conformity with the account in the Gospels. I am thinking especially of the oil painting in the Louvre where a tired and almost anaemic God is recognised by the two disciples with whom he breaks bread in the inn at Emmaus. Nothing could be more ordinary than that suffering face. One might dare say that there is nothing more common-place. Yet this humble countenance is resplendent with a light whose source is the Father: Love itself. No one could be more a man than this poor Nazarene whom the priests mocked so terribly and who, even before the scourging disfigured him, appeared so unimposing before the bodyguards and hirelings that even one of the high priest's servants gave him a blow. Yet in this miserable flesh looming out of an abyss of humiliation and torture, God shines forth with mild and terrible grandeur. Everything seems to happen as though the miracle of the transfiguration (cf. 12) was not accomplished once on Thabor but was renewed as many times as it pleased the Lord to make himself known to one of his creatures.

François Mauriac, *The Son of Man*, §III: 'The Mystery of the Cross', extract (1931)

343   The Overwhelming Face

Dmitri Merezhovsky (1865–1941) was a Russian biographer and novelist who, after the revolution, lived in exile in Paris and elsewhere. In his strange digressive and allusive biography of Christ he presents him as the incarnation of the overwhelming mystery of God.

I cannot remember when or where I bought an old and very poor copy of the *achiropoiite* icon of our Lord which is in the Cathedral of the Assumption of the Virgin in Moscow—an icon not made by human hands representing the face of our Lord, which he is said to have impressed on the linen cloth himself, and which was sent to King Abgarus of Edessa. It had hung on my wall for years and years, so that familiarity had blinded my eyes to it, and I no longer saw it. But one day, when thinking of the face of the man Jesus, I went up to the copy, and suddenly saw it, and I was overwhelmed.

'Depart from me; for I am a sinful man, O Lord.'

The look in those eyes which were not human eyes, which seemed to be gazing down from another world, was slightly oblique; my soul would have turned to ashes had those eyes looked straight into mine: it seemed as though they were sparing me, waiting for my hour to come.

The hair was parted with geometrical accuracy as though drawn with compasses, and fell in two symmetrical, wavy lines. But on the forehead, just by the parting, a lock had escaped from the smooth bands, an obstinate forelock like the badly cut hair of a village boy, and the lips were slightly parted, long-suffering, childlike lips, which seemed to whisper 'My soul within me was as a child reft from its mother's breast.'

'King of terrible majesty,' and yet so simple, so childlike, so pitiful.

Two Beings in one—contrastingly harmonious—that is what we have in this picture emanating from him himself, imprinted on the linen without the use of human hands.

Dmitri Merezhovsky, *Jesus the Unknown*, ch. IX: 'His Face (In History)' 3, extract (1931)

Notes

PART I

1. 'Messiah' is Hebrew for 'anointed one' and a reference to Jewish expectations that God would send an anointed king to save Israel from her oppressors; the Greek translation is 'Christ'.
2. 'Jesus' is a Greek form of the Hebrew name Joshua, which means 'Yahweh [God] Saves'.
3. See n. 1.
4. A docetic Christology is one which calls into question the reality of Christ's humanity, and makes it *seeming* humanity only; a Jesus who floats above the necessities of ordinary human life—here, a child who needs no growth in wisdom, unlike the Jesus of Luke 2: 40.
5. See n. 4.
6. See n. 4.
7. These lines may speak of Christ's pre-existence and incarnation, or may refer to Christ's obedient reversal of Adam's grasping sin—or both.
8. Here virginity does not mean simple abstention; rather it is used to denote a complete way of life focused on purity and continence. (Cf. **271**.)
9. i.e. those already catechized and baptized.
10. i.e. Christmas.
11. 'Pasch' is Aramaic for 'Passover'; the Greek transliteration 'Pascha' was often used to refer to Easter.
12. The ideas of Plato were revived in the 3rd century AD by such men as Plotinus (205–70) and Porphyry (cf. **60**), organized around the idea of an intellectual ascent away from the shifting diversity of matter to the vision of the unchanging source of all being.
13. *Hypostasis* was a term about which there was much confusion in the 4th century; only late on did it settle down to mean, roughly, individual existent, some individual thing or person to which attributes can be applied. Here it seems to mean something closer to *ousia*, the term which eventually settled down to mean, roughly, that essence or definition of divinity which is shared by Father and Son. Cf. Part 2, n. 6.
14. See previous note.
15. This refers to an extra-canonical tradition that all the idols in Egypt toppled when Jesus arrived.

PART 2

1. The phrase is used by Simon Barrington-Ward in *The Jesus Prayer* (Oxford: Bible Reading Fellowship, 1996), by analogy with Brother Lawrence's phrase 'the practice of the presence of God'.
2. Bernard's text is taken from the *Martyrology*.
3. *Phusis* is Greek for 'nature', *monophusite* for 'of one nature'.

4. The metousiasts are those Sergius believes simply blend together divinity and humanity.

5. Monophysites accept, of course, that two natures were involved in the Incarnation, but they do not accept that the two natures persist as distinct natures once Christ has been formed from them. (Cf. **110**.)

6. 'Hypostasis' refers, roughly, to a particular existent that can have a nature, or a subject that can have properties attributed to it. A particular individual is always a hypostasis-with-a-nature (or, in this case, more than one nature). Leontius says that the Logos assumes a 'somewhat particular' human nature here because he wants to hold together two claims. He wants to say that the human nature which Christ assumes is the same human nature which we meet in all other human individuals; and he wants to say that this generic human nature became properly existent, became an actual individual, Jesus, by being made the humanity-of-this-hypostasis, the Logos' hypostasis, rather than by having a hypostasis of its own already: the humanity assumed was therefore not particular, and did not become particular in exactly the same way that other human beings are particular, but nevertheless did become particular (enhypostatic) in a special way.

7. Apparently a reference to a lost tract on the text 'Now my spirit is troubled'.

8. The belief that there are good and evil principles (God and matter) at war with one another, rather than one God who makes a good creation out of nothing.

9. That is, there is no independently existing human being who gets adopted into this relationship.

10. That is, if the previous paragraph argued that Christ is Son of Man by grace, this paragraph argues that it is nevertheless not the grace of adoption but the grace of union.

11. Cf. previous Part, n. 15.

PART 3

1. This is, apparently, an aside to Angela from the amanuensis who took down her dictation.

2. Hills within the city of Rome.

3. 'Church triumphant'—'church militant': traditional terminology for the distinction between the Church of the saints at rest with God and the labouring Church on earth.

4. Terentius Culleo marched in the triumphal procession of Scipio after the Second Punic War, having been rescued from captivity by him.

5. These two men were the first Roman generals to defeat an enemy leader in single combat; they dedicated the first spoils at the altar of Jupiter Feretrius.

6. In 390 BC, after the defeat of a Gallic army.

7. Wounds on the hands, the feet, and the side, corresponding to Christ's scars.

8. We have included the articles on Christ's passion as merit and as satisfaction; the *quaestio* also contains sections on the Passion as sacrifice, redemption, and efficient cause of salvation.

9. One can't be contrite on someone else's behalf—that is interior; one can pay satisfaction on someone else's behalf—that is exterior.

10. Some Christians held that the Jews were particularly responsible for the death of

Christ, and that, Christ being divine, this meant that the Jews were in a sense guilty of the crime of murdering God: deicide.

PART 4

1. The so-called *extra Calvinisticum*.
2. That is, although we appear to be saying that the divine nature suffered or that the human nature came down from heaven, we are in fact ascribing these things to the one *person* of Christ (cf. **85**, **86**, **105**, **107**) using a concrete term appropriate to one of the natures to refer to the whole person.
3. The Capuchins were an offshoot of the Franciscans, founded in 1529, who emphasized poverty and asceticism.
4. 1487–1564. He became a Lutheran in 1541 after contact with Peter Martyr Vermigli (cf. **179**).

PART 5

1. Roscius was a famous Roman actor.
2. 'Period' can mean acme, death, or peroration.
3. Appropriate forms of acting.
4. i.e. Christ.
5. 'Bowels': the seat of compassion; we might say 'heart'.
6. The poem begins by drawing imagery from the traditional metaphysical idea of a universe built of concentric spheres ultimately propelled in their motions by an 'unmoved mover', God.
7. Heb. Immanuel: God-with-us.
8. That is, everything characterizing God does so by definition, rather than contingently or by imposition from without: what God is is dependent only upon God, not upon any other cause or constraint.
9. Not in our sense of 'personality', but in the sense of *persona* or *hypostasis* (cf. **86**, **105**, **112**); cf. Part 2, n. 6.
10. The phrase comes from the Catholic Liturgy, Communion antiphon, first Chrismas Mass.
11. For 'humiliation' and 'exaltation', see **217**.
12. i.e. Copernicus.
13. i.e. Christ doing more than was required of him, thus acquiring merit which he could distribute to others.
14. Cf. Part 1, n. 1.
15. 'Metabasis eis allo genos' (Greek): an (invalid) jump from one topic to another

PART 6

1. Hegel here situates what he has been saying about faith in Christ within the grand sweep of his history of Spirit.
2. For Harnack, see **262**; Wilhelm Bousset was a 19th-century New Testament scholar, Paul Wernle a Church historian.
3. Arguing from a lesser case to a greater.
4. See the *Nizzahon Vetus*, ad Exod. 34: 33; cf. **161**.

5. 'Eschatology': the doctrine of the last things or end times; here referring to Jesus' expectation that God was about to bring about the end of the corrupt world and the final establishment of his kingdom. Cf. **6**.

6. It is by 'Plechtchéev', but we have been unable to discover more about the author.

7. This is the Lutheran criticism of the *extra Calvinisticum*; cf. **178**.

8. Leopold von Ranke, *Die römischen Päpiste* (1844).

9. i.e. spirit-guided selective memory.

10. The *Philokalia* is a collection of patristic and Byzantine extracts concerning the Jesus Prayer and the spiritual life. See e.g. **151**.

PART 7

1. Barth translates 'faith' in this half of the verse as meaning 'God's faithfulness'.

2. i.e. those that seek to uncover the contexts in which and the purposes for which the early Church composed and compiled the materials which we know as the Gospels.

3. To this point what Bultmann has written could be a charter for the second quest (cf. **283**–4); what follows, however, indicates why Bultmann is not on any quest for the historical Jesus.

4. *kerygma*: Christian faith-shaping proclamation.

5. This refers to the approach of such second-quest scholars as Ernst Fuchs and Gerhard Ebeling.

6. The sperm of God: God's fertilization of the world, his endowing it with spiritual power.

7. Cf. Part 1, n. 1.

8. Essence, for Tillich, denotes a balance between being an individual and part of a larger whole; between dynamism and self-consistency; between the constraints of inheritance or situation and freedom—a balance which is called 'essence' because it is proper to creaturely being. However, we experience our factual *existence* in imbalanced ways, as estranged from this balance. New being is this essential balance lived in factual existence.

9. R. W. Dale, *The Atonement* (London: Hodder & Stoughton, 1876).

10. Cf. Part 1, n. 1.

11. Augustine (cf. **38**), *City of God* 18. 51. 2

12. Cf. Karl Marx, *Theses on Feuerbach* 11 (1845): 'The philosophers have only interpreted the world in various ways; the point is to *change* it.'

13. See Part 1, n. 11.

14. Cf. n. 4.

15. Greek *ochlos* = crowd.

16. i.e. Grail.

17. See below for Niebuhr's explanation of *agape* and *eros*.

18. Cf. n. 12.

19. See *Majjhima Nikāya* 123.

20. See *Sutta Nipāta* 679–700.

21. See *Mahāvagga* I, 6, 8.

22. See *Sacred Books of the East*, xiii, ed. F. Max Müller (Oxford: Clarendon Press, 1879–1910), 112.

23. See *Itivuttaka* 100; *Sutta Nipāta*, 560.
24. See *Mahāvagga* viii. 26; *Sacred Books of the East*, xvii. 240.
25. See *Sacred Books of the East*, x 1. 36.
26. See ibid. x. 304.
27. See ibid. xvii. 105, xi. 30.
28. See *Majjhima Nikāya* 26.
29. See *Mahāparinibbāna Sutta*, 46, 62.

References

1–20, 27, 33–4, 39, 45, 50, 53–4, 59, 66. *Holy Bible*, New Revised Standard Version (Oxford: Oxford University Press, 1989).

21–4, 26. 'Isolated Sayings of the Lord' 2, 6, 9, 11, ed. J. Jeremias; 'Papyrus Fragments of Apocryphal Gospels', ed. J. Jeremias and W. Schneemelcher; 'Infancy Gospels', ed. O. Cullmann; 'The Gospel of Thomas', ed. Edgar Hennecke and Wilhelm Schneemelcher; and 'The Gospel of Peter', ed. C. Maurer; in *New Testament Apocrypha*, i: *Gospels and Related Writings*, ed. Edgar Hennecke and Wilhelm Schneemelcher, English translation ed. R. M. Wilson (London: SCM, 1963; Study Edition 1973), 88–9, 93–4, 392–4, 511–2, 514–19, 521, 185–6. Translations altered.

25, 72. 'Second and Third Century Acts of Apostles', ed. W. Schneemelcher and K. Schäferdiek; and 'The Acts of Peter'; in *New Testament Apocrypha*, ii: *Writings Relating to the Apostles*, ed. Edgar Hennecke and Wilhelm Schneemelcher, English translation ed. R. M. Wilson (London: SCM, 1965; Study Edition 1974), 225–6, 302–3.

26. See under **21** above.

27. See under **1** above.

28. *The Odes of Solomon: The Syriac Texts*, ed. James Hamilton Charlesworth, Society of Biblical Literature, Texts and Translations, 13, Pseudepigrapha Series, ed. Robert Kraft, 7 (Missoula, Mont.: Scholars Press, 1977), 116–17.

29. 'Anaphora of St. Peter', trans. Sebastian Brock from *Anaphorae Syriacae, II. 3*, ed. J.-M. Sauget (Rome: Pontifici Instituti Studiorum Orientalum, 1973), 298–30.

30, 42, 65. 'Te Deum'; Ambrose of Milan, 'Prayer for Forgiveness'; and Synesius of Cyrene, 'Hymn to Christ'; in A. Hamman (ed.), *Early Christian Prayers*, trans. Walter Mitchell (Chicago: Henry Regnery; London: Longman Green, 1961), 208, 197, 173–4.

31. Gregory of Nyssa, *Life of St. Macrina*, trans. Kevin Corrigan, Peregrina Translation Series, 10, Matrologia Graeca (Saskatoon, Sask.: Peregrina, 1987), 23–4.

32. *The Pilgrimage of Egeria*, trans. Michael Fraser, CTI Centre for Textual Studies, Oxford University Computing Services; text available online at http://users.ox.ac.uk/~mikef/durham/egetra. html

33–4. See under **1** above.

35 *The Acts of the Christian Martyrs*, trans. Herbert Musurillo, Oxford Early Christian Texts, ed. Henry Chadwick (Oxford: Clarendon Press, 1972), 27–9.

36. 'Daniel', in *The Sayings of the Desert Fathers: The Alphabetical Collection*, trans. Benedicta Ward, Cistercian Studies, 59 (London: Mowbray; Kalamazoo, Mich.: Cistercian, 1975), 44–5.

37. Sulpicius Severus, 'The Life of St. Martin', in *The Western Fathers, Being the Lives of SS Martin of Tours, Ambrose, Augustine of Hippo, Honoratus of Arles and Germanus of Auxerre*, trans. F. R. Hoare, The Makers of Christendom, ed. Christopher Dawson (London: Sheed & Ward, 1954), 14–15.

38. *St Augustine: Tractates on the Gospel of John 112–24 and Tractates on the First Epistle of St. John*, trans. John W. Rettig, The Fathers of the Church: A New Translation, ed. Thomas P. Hamilton, 92 (Washington: Catholic University of America, 1995), 265–6, 273–5.

39. See under 1 above.

40, 67. 'The Epistle to Diognetus' and 'The Letters of St. Ignatius of Antioch', trans. Gerald G. Walsh, in *The Apostolic Fathers*, The Fathers of the Church: A New Translation, ed. Roy Joseph Deferrari, 1 (Washington: Catholic University of America, 1947), 364–5.

41. Methodius of Olympus, *The Symposium: A Treatise on Chastity*, ed. Herbert Musurillo, Ancient Christian Writers, ed. Jo Quasten and Joseph C. Plumpe, 27 (Westminster: Newman; London: Longman, Green, 1958), 46–7.

42. See under 30 above.

43. Ephrem the Syrian, 'Homily on Our Lord', in *Spirituality in the Syriac Tradition*, ed. Sebastian Brock (Kottayam: SEERI, 1989), 105–8.

44, 49, 96. Paulinus of Nola, 'The Word of the Cross'; Aurelius Clemens Prudentius, 'Hymn for Morning'; and Peter Abelard, 'Good Friday: The Third Nocturn'; in *Medieval Latin Lyrics*, trans. Helen Waddell (London: Constable, 1948), 41, 81.

45. See under 1 above.

46. Gregory of Nyssa, 'On the Baptism of Christ: A Sermon for the Day of Lights', in *Gregory of Nyssa*, A Select Library of Nicene and Post-Nicene Fathers of the Christian Church, 2nd ser., ed. Henry Wace and Philip Schaff, v (Oxford: James Parker; New York: Christian Literature Company, 1892), 518–19. Translation altered.

47. Based on the translation of Athanasius of Alexandria, *On the Incarnation of the Word of God*, in *Athanasius, Select Works and Letters*, trans. Archibald Robertson, A Select Library of Nicene and Post-Nicene Fathers of the Christian Church, 2nd ser., ed. Henry Wace and Philip Schaff, iv (Oxford: James Parker; New York: Christian Literature Company, 1892), 42–4.

48. Ambrose of Milan, *Isaac; or, The Soul*, in *Saint Ambrose: Seven Exegetical Works*, trans. Michael P. McHugh, The Fathers of the Church: A New Translation, ed. Bernard M. Peebles (Washington: Catholic University of America, Consortium Press, 1972), 15–18.

49. See under 44 above.

50. See under 1 above.

51. *St Irenaeus: The Demonstration of the Apostolic Preaching*, trans. J. Armitage Robinson, Translations of Christian Literature, ser. IV: Oriental Texts, ed. W. J. Sparrow Simpson and W. K. Lowther Clarke (London: SPCK; New York: MacMillan, 1920), 97–103.

52. Paula and Julia Eustochium, Letter = Jerome, Letter 46, in *St. Jerome: Letters and Select Works*, A Select Library of Nicene and Post-Nicene Fathers of the Christian Church, 2nd ser., ed. Henry Wace and Philip Schaff, vi (Oxford: James Parker; New York: Christian Literature Company, 1893).

53–4. See under 1 above.

55. *Melito of Sardis: On Pascha and Fragments*, ed. Stuart George Hall, Oxford Early Christian Texts, ed. Henry Chadwick (Oxford: Clarendon Press, 1979), 31–3, 35–9.

56. *The Homilies of Saint Jerome*, ii: *Homilies 60–96*, ed. Mary Ligouri Ewald, The Fathers of the Church: A New Translation, ed. Roy Joseph Deferrari, 57 (Washington: Catholic University of America, 1966), 163–5, 7–8.

57. Flavius Josephus, *Antiquities of the Jews*, in *The Works of Flavius Josephus*, trans. William Whiston (London: T. Nelson, 1895), 487.

58. *Hebrew English Edition of the Babylonian Talmud: Sanhedrin*, trans. Jacob Schachter *et al.*, ed. I. Epstein, new edn. (London: Soncino, 1969).

59. See under 1 above.

60. Porphyry, *Against the Christians*, fr. 77, in *A New Eusebius: Documents Illustrating the History of the Church to AD 337*, trans. J. Stevenson and W. H. C. Frend, rev edn. (London: SPCK, 1987) 270.

61. *Pliny: Letters and Panegyricus*, ii, trans. Betty Radice, Loeb Classical Library, ed. E. H. Warmington (London: William Heinemann; Cambridge, Mass.: Harvard University Press, 1969), 285–92.

62. Translation based on the German translation of A. Kurfess, in *New Testament Apocrypha*, ii: *Writings Relating to the Apostles*, ed. Edgar Hennecke and Wilhelm Schneemelcher, English translation ed. R. M. Wilson (London: SCM, 1965; Study Edition 1974), 732–3. Rewritten to preserve the acrostic.

63. *St. Justin Martyr: The First and Second Apologies*, trans. Leslie William Barnard, Ancient Christian Writers: The Works of the Fathers in Translation, ed. Walter J. Burghardt, John J. Dillon, and Dennis D. McManus, 56 (New York: Paulist Press, 1997), 83–4.

64. 'Proba Cento', in *A Lost Tradition*, trans. Patricia Wilson-Kastner *et al.* (Lanham, NY: University Press of America, 1981), 58–9.

65. See under 30 above.

66. See under 1 above.

67. See under 40 above.

68–9. Irenaeus, 'Basilides' Teachings', and Valentinus, 'Valentinus, Fragment E: Epistle to Agathapous', in *The Gnostic Scriptures*, ed. Bentley Layton (London: SCM, 1987), 422–3, 239.

70. *Tertullian's Treatise on the Incarnation*, trans. Ernest Evans (London: SPCK, 1956), 13–21.

71. Eusebius of Caesarea, *The Proof of the Gospel, Being the Demonstratio Evangelica of Eusebius of Caesaria*, I, trans. W. J. Ferrar, Translations of Christian Literature, ser. I: Greek Texts, ed. W. J. Sparrow Simpson, and W. K. Lowther Clarke (London: SPCK; New York: MacMillan, 1920), 188–90.

72. See under 25 above.

73. *Origen on First Principles*, trans. G. W. Butterworth (London: SPCK, 1936), 109–10.

74–80. Arius, 'Thalia'; assorted creeds and confessions, trans. R. P. C. Hanson, in *The Search for the Christian Doctrine of God: The Arian Controversy, 318–381* (Edinburgh: T. & T. Clark, 1988), 14–15, 149, 163, 344–5, 593, 619–20, 816.

81–2. Gregory Nazianzus, 'Epistle to Cledonius against Apollinarius' and 'Third Theological Oration', in *S. Cyril of Jerusalem: Catechetical Letters and S. Gregory of Nazianzum: Select Orations, and Letters*, trans. Charles Gordon Browne and James Edward Swallow, A Select Library of Nicene and Post-Nicene Fathers of the Christian Church, 2nd ser., ed. Henry Wace and Philip Schaff, vii (Oxford: James Parker; New York: Christian Literature Company, 1894), 440–1, 308–9.

83. Nestorius, 'Letter 5 (Nestorius to Cyril)', in *St. Cyril of Alexandria: Letters 1–50*, trans. John I. McEnerney, The Fathers of the Church: A New Translation, ed. Thomas P. Halton, 76 (Washington: Catholic University of America, 1985), 45–7.

84. *Cyril of Alexandria: Selected Letters*, trans. Lionel R. Wickham, Oxford Early Christian Texts, ed. Henry Chadwick (Oxford: Clarendon Press, 1985).

85–6. Leo the Great, 'Tome' and Council of Chalcedon, 'Definition of Faith', in *The Seven Ecumenical Councils of the Undivided Church*, trans. Henry R. Percival, A Select Library of Nicene and Post-Nicene Fathers of the Christian Church, 2nd ser., ed. Henry Wace and Philip Schaff, xiv (Oxford: James Parker; New York: Christian Literature Company, 1900), 255–6, 264–5.

87. Pseudo-Macarius, 'First Homily', trans. Louis Bouyer, in *The Spirituality of the New Testament and the Fathers*, trans. Mary P. Ryan, History of Spirituality, ed. Louis Bouyer, Jean Leclercq, François Vandebrouche, and Louis Cognet, (London: Burns & Oates, 1963), 373–4.

88–9. Extracts from Pseudo-Dionysius the Areopagite, *The Divine Names*, and Anastasius I of Antioch, *Homily on the Transfiguration*, trans. John Anthony McGuckin, in *The Transfiguration of Christ in Scripture and Tradition*, Studies in the Bible and Early Christianity, 9 (Lewiston, NY: Edwin Mellen, 1986), 190–1, 192–3.

90. *Symeon the New Theologian: The Discourses*, trans. C. J de Cantanzaro, Classics of Western Spirituality, ed. Richard J. Payne (London: SPCK, 1980), 48–50.

91. Peter of Damaskos, *A Treasury of Divine Knowledge*, in *The Philokalia*, iii, ed. Nikodimos of the Holy Mountain, St Makarios of Corinth, ET G. E. H. Palmer *et al.* (London: Faber & Faber, 1979), 234–5.

92. Trans. for this book by T. Jenkins with M. A. Higton, from the edition in *Diadoque de Photice: Œuvres Spirituelle*, ed. and trans. Edouard des Places, Sources Chrétiennes, 5bis (Paris: Éditions du Cerf, 1955), 119–21.

93. 'A Discourse of Abba Philimon', in *The Philokalia*, ii, ed. Nikodimos of the Holy Mountain, St. Makarios of Corinth, ET G. E. H. Palmer *et al.* (London: Faber & Faber, 1979), 347–8.

94, 118. Rupert of Deutz, *Commentary on Saint John*, and Ratramnus of Corbie, *Christ's Body and Blood*, extracts in *Early Medieval Theology*, trans. George E. McCracken and Allen Cabaniss, Library of Christian Classics, ix (London: SCM, 1957), 266–8, 118, 120–1.

95. *Peter of Celle: Selected Works*, trans. Hugh Feiss, Cistercian Studies, 100 (Kalamazoo, Mich.: Cistercian Publications, 1987), 45.

96. See under **44** above.

97. Bernard of Clairvaux, 'Sixth Sermon for Christmas Eve', in *St. Bernard's Sermons on the Nativity*, trans. A Priest of Mount Melleray (1921; repr. Chulmleigh, Devon: Augustine, 1985), 110, 115, 116–18.

98. Aelred of Rievaulx, *Mirror of Charity*, extracts in *For Crist Luve: Prayers of Saint Aelred Abbot of Rievaulx*, trans. Rose de Lima, ed. D. Anselm Hoste (Den Haag: Martinus Nijhoff; Sleenbrugge: St-Pietersabdij, 1965), 20.

99. Kassia, 'Menaia, February: The Meeting of the Lord (Feb. 2) at Vespers', in *Kassia: The Legend, the Woman, and her Work*, trans. Anton'a Tripolitis, Garland Library of Medieval Literature, ser. A, 94 (New York: Garland, 1992), 39–41.

100. *Hsü-T'ing Mi-shih-ho-ching*, trans. P. Y. Saeki, in *The Nestorian Documents and Relics in China*, The Toho Bunkwa Gakuin: The Academy of Oriental Culture Tokyo Institute (Tokyo: Maruzen, 1951), 139–42.

101. Cynewulf, *Christ: Ascension*, in *The Poems of Cynewulf*, ed. Charles W. Kennedy (London: Routledge, 1910), 169–70.

102. Nicholas Bozon, 'Christ's Chivalry', in *The Anglo-Norman Lyric, An Anthology*, ed. David L. Jeffrey and Brian J. Levy, Studies and Texts, 93 (Toronto: Pontifical Institute of Mediaeval Studies, 1990), 188–9.

103–4. 'Letter I of Sergius' and 'Letter 1 of Severus', trans. Iain R. Torrance, in *Christology after Chalcedon: Severus of Antioch and Sergius the Monophysite* (Norwich: Canterbury Press, 1988), 143–4, 153–4.

105. Leontius of Jerusalem, *Adversus Nestorianos*, extracts trans. in Kenneth Paul Wesche, 'The Christology of Leontius of Jerusalem: Monophysite or Chalcedonian?', *St Vladimir's Theological Quarterly* (Faculty of St Vladimir's Orthodox Theological Seminary), 31/1 (1987), 81–2, 88–9.

106, 156. 'Third Council of Constantinople' and 'Constitutions of the Fourth Lateran Council', ed. G. Albergo *et al.*, in *Decrees of the Ecumenical Councils*, i: *Nicaea I to Lateran V*, ed. Norman P. Tanner (London: Sheed & Ward; Washington: Georgetown University Press, 1990), 127–30, 230.

107. John of Damascus, *The Orthodox Faith*, in *Saint John of Damascus: Writings*, trans. Frederic H. Chase, The Fathers of the Church: A New Translation, 37, ed. Bernard M. Peebles (Washington: Catholic University Press, 1958), 268–71, 281–4.

108. *St John of Damascus: On Divine Images, Three Apologies against those who Attack the Divine Images*, trans. David Anderson (Crestwood, NY: St Vladimir's Seminary, 1980), 23–4, 26–7, 28.

109. Adam of Eynsham, *Magna Vita Sancti Hugonis: The Life of St Hugh of Lincoln*, ii, trans. Decima L. Douie and David Hugh Farmer, Oxford Medieval Texts, ed. C. N. L. Brooke, D. E. Greenway, and M. Winterbottom (Oxford: Oxford University Press, 1985), 14–15.

110. Boethius, 'Against Eutyches and Nestorius', in *Boethius: The Theological Tractates and The Consolation of Philosophy*, trans. H. F. Stewart, E. K. Rand and S. J. Tester, Loeb Classical Library (London: William Heinemann; Cambridge, Mass.: Harvard University Press, 1973), 117–19.

111–12. Elipandus of Toledo, *Letter to the Bishops of Frankland*, and Beatus of Liebana, *Against Elipandus*, extracts trans. in John C. Cavadini, *The Last Christology of the West* (Philadelphia: University of Pennsylvania Press, 1993), 31–4, 54–6, 64–6.

113. *Hildegard of Bingen: Scivias*, trans. Mother Columba Hart and Jane Bishop, Classics of Western Spirituality, ed. Bernard McGinn (New York: Paulist Press, 1990), 425, 433–4.

114–16. Anselm of Canterbury, *Why God Became Man*, Peter Abelard, extracts from *Exposition of the Epistle to the Romans*, and Peter Lombard, extracts from *The Four Books of Sentences*, in *A Scholastic Miscellany: Anselm to Ockham*, trans. Eugene R. Fairweather, Library of Christian Classics, 10, ed. John Baillie, John T. McNeill, and Henry P. van Dusen (London: SCM, 1956), 176, 179–81, 283–4, 335–7.

117. Joseph the Visionary, 'Prayer', trans. Sebastian Brock, in *The Syriac Fathers on Prayer and the Spiritual Life*, Cistercian Studies, 101 (Kalamazoo, Mich.: Cistercian Publications, 1987), 355–8.

118. See under 94 above.

119, 269, 273. Nestor the Chronicler, *St. Theodosius*, trans. Helen Iswolsky; anonymous, *The Candid Narrations of a Pilgrim to his Spiritual Father*; and John Ilyitch Sergieff (John of Cronstadt), *My Life in Christ*; in *A Treasury of Russian Spirituality*, ed. G. P. Fedotov (London: Sheed & Ward, 1950), 19–20, 295–6, 370–1.

120. Anonymous, *Tol'doth Yeshu*, in *Jewish Views of Jesus: An Introduction and an Appreciation*, trans. Thomas Walker (London: George Allen & Unwin, 1931), 17–22.

121. Wecelin and Henry, Correspondence, trans. Anna Sapir Abulafia, in 'An Eleventh Century Exchange of Letters between a Christian and a Jew', *Journal of Medieval History*, 7 (1981), repr. in Abulafia (ed.), *Christians and Jews in Dispute: Disputational Literature and the Rise of Anti-Judaism in the West (c.1000–1150)*, Variorum Collected Studies (Aldershot: Variorum (Ashgate), 1998), III. 165–6.

122. Mardān Farukh, *Sikand-Gūmānīk Vigār*, based on the translation by E. W. West in *Pahlavi Texts*, iii: *Dīnā-ī Maīnōg-ī Khirad; Sikand-Gūmānīk Vigār; Sad Dar*, The Sacred Books of the East, ed. F. Max Müller (Oxford: Clarendon Press, 1885), 231–3.

123. *The Holy Qur'ān: Text, Translation, and Commentary*, trans. 'Abdullah Yusuf 'Ali, rev edn., (Brentwood, Md.: Amana, 1989), 235–6, 283–4, 286, 800.

124. Ed. and trans. Muhammad 'Ata ur-Rahim, in *Jesus, Prophet of Islam* (Norfolk: Diwan Press, 1977), 228.

125. Al-Hujw'r', *The Kashf al-Mahjub: The Oldest Persian Treatise on Sufism*, trans. Reynold A. Nicholson, E. J. W. Gibb Memorial Series, 17 (2nd edn. 1936; repr. London: Luzac, 1970), 39–40.

126. Ed. and trans. D. S. Margoliouth, in 'Christ in Islam: Sayings Attributed to Christ by Mohammedan Writers', *Expository Times*, 5/2 (Nov. 1893), 3 (Dec. 1893), 4 (Jan. 1894), 11 (Aug. 1894), 12 (Sept. 1894), 107, 177, 504.

127. Thomas of Celano, *First Life of St. Francis*, extracts in *Franciscan Days: Being Selections for Every Day in the Year from Ancient Franciscan Writings*, ed. and trans. A. G. Ferrers Howell (London: Methuen, 1906), 360.

128. *The Chester Mystery Cycle: A New Edition with Modernised Spelling*, ed. David Mills, Medieval Texts and Studies, 9 (East Lansing, Mich.: Colleagues Press, 1992), 169–73.

129. *The Letter of Lentulus*, in *The Apocryphal New Testament: A Collection of Apocryphal Christian Literature in an English Translation*, ed. and trans. J. K. Elliott (Oxford: Clarendon Press, 1993), 543.

130. Sa'adi, *Persian Poetry*, extract, trans. Abbas Aryanpur and William N. Wysham, in William N. Wysham, 'Jesus in the Poetry of Iran', *Muslim World*, 42/2 (Apr. 1952), 106–8.

131. *The Mathnaw' of Jalālu'dd'n Rūm'* iv: *Books 3 & 4*, trans. Reynold A. Nicholson, E. J. W. Gibbs Memorial, new ser., iv/4 (1930; repr. London: Luzac, 1972), 144–6.

132. *Meditations on the Life and Passion of Our Lord Jesus Christ*, trans. A. P. J. Cruikshank (London: Burns, Oates & Washbourne, 1925), 45–8.

133. Angela of Foligno, *The Book of Blessed Angela* in *Angela of Foligno: Complete Works*, trans. Paul Lachance, Classics of Western Spirituality, ed. Bernard McGinn (New York: Paulist, 1993), 230–3.

134. Birgitta of Sweden, *The Seventh Book of Revelations*, trans. Albert Ryle Kezel, in *Birgitta of Sweden: Life and Selected Revelations*, ed. Marguerite Tjader Harris, Classics of Western Spirituality, ed. Bernard McGinn (New York: Paulist, 1990), 188–90.

135. Al-Baydawi, *Commentary on the Quran*, extracts in *A Reader on Classical Islam*, trans. F. E. Peters (Princeton: Princeton University Press, 1994), 31–2.

136. Mechthild of Magdeburg, *The Revelations, or; The Flowing Light of the Godhead*, trans. slightly adapted from *The Revelations of Mechthild of Magdeburg*, trans. Lucy Menzies (London: Longman, Green, 1953), 153.

137. Juan Luis Vives, *The Triumph of Jesus Christ*, in *Juan Luis Vives: Early Writings*, ii, trans. Josef Ijsewijn, Angela Fritsen, and Charles Fantazzi, Selected Works of J. L. Vives, 5, ed. C. Matheeussen (Leiden: E. J. Brill, 1991), 55–9.

138, 145. *The Mirror of Perfection*, in *S. Francis of Assisi: His Life and Writings as Recorded by his Contemporaries*, ed. Leo Sherley-Price (London: A. R. Mowbray, 1959), 114–15, 113.

139. Margaret Ebner, *Revelations*, in *Margaret Ebner: Major Works*, trans. Leonard P. Hindsley, The Classics of Western Spirituality, ed. Bernard McGinn (New York: Paulist Press, 1993), 132; this extract also repr. online at Other Women's Voices: Translations of Women's Writing before 1600, http: //home. infi. net/%7Eddisse/.

140. *Meditations on the Life of Christ: An Illustrated Manuscript of the Fourteenth Century*, trans. Isa Ragusa, ed. Isa Ragusa and Rosalie P. Green (Princeton: Princeton University Press, 1961), 2–4.

141. *St Anthony of Padua: Seek First his Kingdom: An Anthology of the Sermons of the Saint*, trans. Claude Jarmak, ed. Livio Poloniato (Padua: Conventual Franciscan Friars, 1988), 47–9.

142. *Bonaventure: The Soul's Journey into God; The Tree of Life; The Life of St. Francis*, trans. Ewert Cousins, The Classics of Western Spirituality, ed. Richard J. Payne (London: SPCK, 1978).

143. Richard Rolle, 'Meditations on the Passion (Shorter Version)', in *Richard Rolle: The English Writings*, trans. Rosamund S. Allen, Classics of Western Spirituality, ed. John Farina (London: SPCK, 1989), 91–4.

144. Thomas de Cantimpré, *The Life of Lutgard of Aywières*, trans. Margot H. King, Peregrina Translation Series, 9, Matrologia Latina (Toronto: Peregrina, 1987), 21–2.

145. See under **138** above.

146. Thomas de Cantimpré, *The Life of Margaret of Ypres*, trans. Margot H. King, Peregrina Translation Series, 15, Matrologia Latina, 2nd edn. (Toronto: Peregrina, 1996).

147. Ed. and trans. James M. Clark in *Henry Suso: Little Book of Eternal Wisdom and Little Book of Truth*, Classics of the Contemplative Life (London: Faber & Faber, 1953), 55–6.

148. Geert de Groote, Letter 62, in *Devotio Moderna: Basic Writings*, trans. John van Engen, Classics of Western Spirituality, ed. John Farina (New York: Paulist Press, 1988), 88.

149. Catherine of Siena, Letter 18, in *I, Catherine: Selected Writings of Catherine of Siena*, ed. and trans. Kenelm Foster and Mary John Ronayne (London: Collins, 1980), 105–6.

150. *Theoleptos of Philadelphia: The Monastic Discourses*, ed. and trans. Robert E. Sinkewicz, Studies and Texts, 111 (Toronto: Pontifical Institute of Mediaeval Studies, 1992), 85–9.

151. Trans. G. E. H. Palmer *et al.* in *The Philokalia*, iv, ed. Nikodimos of the Holy Mountain, St Makarios of Corinth (London: Faber & Faber, 1979), 253.

152. *Julian of Norwich: Showings*, trans. Edmund Colledge and James Walsh, Classics of Western Spirituality, ed. Richard J. Payne (New York: Paulist Press, 1978), 297–9.

153. Margaret of Oingt, *Page of Meditations* in *The Writings of Margaret of Oingt: Medieval Prioress and Mystic*, trans. Renate Blumenfeld-Kosinski, Focus Library of

Medieval Women, ed. Jane Chance, 4 (Newbury Port, Mass.: Focus Information Group, 1990), 31–2.

154. Thomas à Kempis, *The Imitation of Christ: A New Reading of the 1441 Latin Autograph Manuscript*, ed. and trans. William C. Creasy (Macon, Ga.: Mercer University Press, 1989), 41–3.

155. Francis of Assisi, *Admonitions*, in *Francis and Clare: The Complete Works*, trans. Regis J. Armstrong and Ignatius C. Brady, Classics of Western Spirituality, ed. Richard J. Payne (London: SPCK, 1982), 26–7.

156. See under **106** above.

157. *The Life of Juliana of Mont-Cornillon*, trans. Barbara Newman, Peregrina Translations Series, 13, Matrologia Latina (Toronto: Peregrina, 1996), 83–4, 89–91.

158. Thomas Aquinas, *Summa Theologiae 54: The Passion of Christ (3a. 46–52)*, trans. Richard T. A. Murphy (London: Blackfriars, 1965), 75–9.

159. *Gertrude of Helfta: The Herald of Divine Love*, trans. Margaret Winkworth, Classics of Western Spirituality, ed. Bernard McGinn (New York: Paulist Press, 1993), 219.

160. *Nicholas of Cusa on Learned Ignorance*, ed. and trans. Jasper Hopkins (Minneapolis: Arthur J. Banning, 1981) 139.

161. Ed. and trans. David Berger, *The Jewish–Christian Debate in the High Middle Ages: A Critical Edition of the 'Nizzahon Vetus'*, Judaica Texts and Translations, 4 (Philadelphia: Jewish Publication Society of America, 1979), 43–4.

162. Joseph ibn Shem Tob, 'Sermon on Abot 3: 15–16' in *Jewish Preaching 1200–1800: An Anthology*, ed. and trans. Marc Saperstein, Yale Judaica Series, ed. Frank Talmage, xxvi; (New Haven: Yale University Press, 1989), 167–71.

163. Philip Melanchthon, *Loci Communes Theologici* (1521), in *Melanchthon and Bucer*, trans. Lowell J. Sartre and Wilhelm Pauck, ed. W. Pauck, Library of Christian Classics, ed. John Baillie, John T. McNeill, and Henry P. van Dusen, 19 (London: SCM, 1969), 21–2.

164, 180. 'The Augsburg Confession' and 'The Formula of Concord, Solid Declaration', in *The Book of Concord: The Confessions of the Evangelical Lutheran Church*, trans. Theodore G. Tappert (Philadelphia: Fortress Press, 1959), 23–30, 609–10.

165, 175. Ursinus and Olevian, 'The Heidelberg Catechism'; and 'Canons and Decrees of the Council of Trent', in *Confessions and Catechisms of the Reformation*, trans. Mark A. Knoll (Lancaster: Apollos, 1991), 142–5, 197–9.

166, 176, 182. Ursula von Münsterburg, 'Apology'; 'Account of the examination of Elizabeth Dirks'; and Vittoria Colonna, 'The Star', in Roland H. Bainton, *Women of the Reformation: In Germany and Italy* (Minneapolis: Augsburg, 1971), 51–2, 146, 148, 207.

167. Martin Luther, *Lectures on Galatians (1535) Chapters 1–4*, trans. Jaroslav Pelikan, Luther's Works, ed. J. Pelikan and Walter A. Hansen, 26 (St Louis: Concordia, 1963), 277–81.

168. Martin Luther, *Heidelberg Disputation*, in *Career of the Reformer*, i, trans. H. J. Grimm, Luther's Works, ed. Helmut T. Lehmann (Philadelphia: Muhlenberg Press, 1957), 52–3.

169. Ed. and trans. Peter Matheson in *The Collected Works of Thomas Müntzer* (Edinburgh: T. & T. Clark, 1988), 220–1.

170, 178. *Calvin: Institutes of the Christian Religion*, ii, trans. Ford Lewis Battles, ed. John T. McNeill, Library of Christian Classics, ed. John Baillie, John T. McNeill, and Henry P. van Dusen, 20 (London: SCM, 1960).

171. Thomas More, *A Dialogue concerning Heresies*, i: *The Text*, ed. Thomas Lawler, Germain Marc'hadour, and Richard C. Marius, The Yale Edition of the Complete Works of St. Thomas More, 6 (New Haven: Yale University Press, 1981), 113–16. Orthography modernized.

172. Zwingli, 'On the Lord's Supper', in *Zwingli and Bullinger*, trans. G. W. Bromiley, Library of Christian Classics, ed. John Baillie, John T. McNeill, and Henry P. van Dusen, 24 (London: SCM, 1953), 212–5.

173. *Richard Hooker: Of the Laws of Ecclesiastical Polity, Book V*, ed. W. Speed Hill, Folger Library Edition of the Works of Richard Hooker (London: Belknap; Cambridge, Mass.: Harvard University Press, 1977), 331–2, 334–6.

174, 212. 'The Order of Communion 1548' and 'The Westminster Directory' in *Prayers of the Eucharist: Early and Reformed*, trans. R. C. D. Jasper and G. J. Cuming, 2nd edn. (New York: Oxford University Press, 1980), 164–5, 190–1.

175. See under 165 above.

176. See under 166 above.

177. Martin Luther, *Sermons on the Gospel of John, Ch. 14–16*, trans. Martin H. Bertram, Luther's Works, ed. Jaroslav Pelikan, 24 (St Louis: Concordia, 1961), 104–6.

178. See under 170 above.

179. Pietro Martire Vermigli, *Dialogue on the Two Natures in Christ*, trans. John Patrick Donnelly, The Peter Martyr Library, ed. J. P. Donnelly and Joseph McLelland, 2, Sixteenth Century Essays and Studies, 31 (Kirksville, Mo.: Sixteenth Century Journal Publishers, 1995), 89–90, 95–6.

180. See under 164 above.

181. Martin Chemnitz, *The Two Natures in Christ*, trans. J. A. O Preiss (London: Concordia, 1971), 163–5.

182. See under 166 above.

183. *Sebastian Franck: 280 Paradoxes or Wondrous Sayings*, ed. and trans. E. J. Furcha, Texts and Studies in Religion, 26 (Lewiston, NY: Edwin Mellen, 1986), 199–201. Translation slightly altered.

184. John of the Cross, 'The Spiritual Canticle', in *John of the Cross: Selected Writings*, trans. Kieran Kavanaugh, Classics of Western Spirituality, ed. John Farina (London: SPCK, 1987).

185. Jeremias II, *First Reply to the Lutherans*, ed. and trans. Constantine N. Tsirpanlis, in *The Historical and Ecumenical Significance of Jeremias II's Correspondence with the Lutherans (1573–1581)*, i, The American Institute for Patristic and Byzantine Studies, Monograph Series in Orthodox Theology and Civilization, 5 (New York: EO Press, 1982), 33–4.

186 *The Text of the Spiritual Exercises of St. Ignatius Loyola*, trans. Henry Keane, 2nd edn. (London: Burns, Oates & Washbourne, 1952) 22–3, 67–8.

187. Lorenzo Scupoli, *The Spiritual Combat* in *Theatine Spirituality: Selected Writings*, trans. William V. Hudon, Classics of Western Spirituality, ed. Bernard McGinn (New York: Paulist Press, 1996), 186–7.

188. Traditional, 'My Dancing Day', in *The Oxford Book of Carols*, ed. Percy Dearmer, R. Vaughan Williams, and Martin Shaw (Oxford: Oxford University Press, 1928), no. 71.

189. Ed. D. O'Connor in *John Fisher: A Spiritual Consolation and Other Treatises* (London: Burns, Oates & Washbourne, 1935).

190, 193, 198. Robert Herrick, 'Good Friday: *Rex Tragicus*; or, Christ Going to his Cross'; Richard Crashaw, 'Upon the Body of Our Blessed Lord, Naked and Bloody'; John Donne, 'Good Friday, 1613: Riding Westward'; in *The New Oxford Book of Seventeenth Century Verse*, ed. Alastair Fowler (Oxford: Oxford University Press, 1992), nos. 348, 582, 136.

191. John Milton, *Paradise Regained*; text available online at The Christian Classics Ethereal Library, http://www.ccel.org.

192. Sor Juana Inés de la Cruz, *The Divine Narcissus*, in *A Sor Juana Anthology*, trans. Alan S. Trueblood (Cambridge, Mass.: Harvard University Press, 1988), 161–5.

193. See under **190** above.

194. George Herbert, 'The Agony', in *The Temple: The Bodleian Manuscript (Tanner 307)*, ed. Mario A. di Cesare, Medieval and Renaissance Texts and Studies, 54, Renaissance English Text Society, 7th ser., xvii (Binghampton, NY: Medieval and Renaissance Texts and Studies, 1995), 54.

195. Isaac Watts, 'When I Survey the Wondrous Cross', in *Hymns and Spiritual Songs* (London, 1707).

196. Charles Wesley, 'Wrestling Jacob', in *The New Oxford Book of Eighteenth Century Verse*, ed. Roger Lonsdale (Oxford: Oxford University Press, 1984), no. 226.

197. Samuel Crossman, 'My Song is Love Unknown', in *The Young Man's Meditation* (London: J. & H., 1664).

198. See under **190** above.

199, 206–7, 220. Jean-Jacques Olier, *Introduction to the Christian Life and Virtues*; John Eudes, *The Life and Kingdom of Jesus in Christian Souls*; Madeleine de Saint-Joseph, Letter 139; and Pierre de Bérulle, *Elevations upon the Incarnation*; in *Bérulle and the French School: Selected Writings*, trans. Lowell M. Glendon, ed. William M. Thompson, Classics of Western Spirituality, ed. Bernard McGinn (New York: Paulist Press, 1989), 221–4, 295–6, 197–8, 116–7.

200. John Bunyan, *The Pilgrim's Progress*; text available online at The Christian Classics Ethereal Library, http://www.ccel.org.

201. Ed. and trans. Peter Erb in *Johann Arndt: True Christianity*, Classics of Western Spirituality, ed. Richard J. Payne (London: SPCK, 1979), 255–7.

202. Paul Gerhardt, 'O Sacred Head Now Wounded', in *The Handbook to the Lutheran Hymnal*, trans. various (St Louis: Concordia, 1942), no. 172.

203–5. Nicolas Ludwig, Count von Zinzendorf, *The Litany of the Life, Suffering and Death of Jesus Christ*; Gerhard Tersteegen, *Geistliche und erbauliche Briefe uber das inwendige Leben und wahre Wesen des Christentums*, trans. as *Selected Letters*; Friedrich Christoph Oetinger, 'A Confession of Faith'; in *Pietists: Selected Writings*, trans. Peter C. Erb, Classics of Western Spirituality, ed. Richard J. Payne and John Farina (New York: Paulist Press, 1983), 243, 275–6.

206–7. See under **199** above.

208. Thomas Traherne, *Select Meditations*, ed. Julia J. Smith (Manchester: Carcanet Press, 1997), 110–1. Orthography modernized.

209. Based on the text presented in Lancelot Andrewes, *Sermons*, ed. G. M. Storey (Oxford: Clarendon Press, 1967), 20–1. Orthography modernized and other minor changes made.

210. Richard Sibbes, *The Spouse, her Earnest Desire after Christ*, in *Works of Richard Sibbes*, ed. Alexander B. Grosart, ii (Edinburgh: Banner of Truth, 1983), 207–8.

211. Richard Baxter, *The Saints' Everlasting Rest*; text available online at The Christian Classics Ethereal Library, http://www.ccel.org.

212. See under 174 above.

213. Susanna Bateman, untitled poem (1656); electronic text taken from *Quaker Women: 17th to 19th Centuries*, http://www.users.globalnet.co.uk/~helfrich/.

214. Job Scott, *Salvation by Christ*, in *The Works of that Eminent Minister of the Gospel, Job Scott, Late of Providence Rhode Island* (Philadelphia: John Comly, 1831; repr. Quaker Heritage Press, 16 Huber St., Glenside, PA 19038, 1993); electronic version at Quaker Historical Texts, http://www. voicenet.com/~kuenning/qhp/.

215. Gerrard Winstanley, *The New Law of Righteousness*, in *The Works of Gerrard Winstanley*, ed. George H. Sabine (Ithaca: Cornell University Press, 1941), 160–3.

216. *Francis de Sales: Treatise on the Love of God*, ed. and trans. Vincent Kerns (London: Burns & Oates, 1962), 140–2.

217. Ed. Alexander F. Mitchell in *Catechisms of the Second Reformation* (London: James Nisbet, 1886), 9–16.

218. Jonathan Edwards, *The Excellency of Christ*; text available online at http://www.JonathanEdwards.com/.

219. Johannes Wollebius, *Compendium Theologia Christianae* in *Reformed Dogmatics: J. Wolebius, G. Voetius, F. Turretin*, ed. and trans. John W. Beardslee III, A Library of Protestant Thought, ed. John Dillenberger *et al.* (New York: Oxford University Press, 1965), 103–6.

220. See under 199 above.

221. *Thomas Hobbes: Leviathan*, ed. Richard Tuck, Cambridge Texts in the History of Political Thought, rev. edn. (Cambridge: Cambridge University Press, 1996), 407–8, 411–13.

222. Blaise Pascal, *Pensées*, trans. W. F. Trotter; text available online at The Christian Classics Ethereal Library, http://www.ccel.org.

223. *Thomas Morgan: The Moral Philosopher*, ed. John Vladimir Price, History of British Deism (1738; repr. London: Routledge, Thoemmes, 1995), 153–6.

224. *Hermann Samuel Reimarus: The Goal of Jesus and his Disciples*, ed. George Wesley Buchanan (Leiden: E. J. Brill, 1970), 80–4.

225. Jacob Emdem, 'Rabbi Jacob Emdem's Letter (Seder Olam Rabbah Vezuta)', trans. Harvey Falk, in 'Rabbi Jacob Emdem's Views on Christianity', *Journal of Ecumenical Studies*, 19/1 (Winter 1982), 108–10.

226. *Baron Paul Thiry d'Holbach: Ecce Homo! An Eighteenth Century Life of Jesus*, trans. Andrew Hunwick, History of Religions in Translation, ed. Luther H. Martin, Jacques Waardenburg, and Donald Wiebe (Berlin: Mouton de Gruyter, 1995), 245–8.

227. Gotthold Ephraim Lessing, *On the Proof of the Spirit and of Power* in *Lessing's Theological Writings*, trans. Henry Chadwick, A Library of Modern Christian Thought (London: Adam & Charles Black, 1956), 51–5.

228. Claude Fauchet, *Discours sur la liberté françoise*, extract trans. for this book by Mike and Hester Higton from *Les Interprétations politiques de Jésus de l'Ancien Régime*, ed. Daniele Menozzi, trans. Jacqueline Touvier, Sciences Humaine et Religions (Paris: Éditions du Cerf, 1983), 136–7.

229. Immanuel Kant, *Religion within the bounds of mere reason*, trans. George di Giovanni in *Religion and Rational Theology*, trans. Allen W. Wood and George di Giovanni,

The Cambridge Edition of the Works of Immanuel Kant, ed. Paul Guyer and A. W. Wood (Cambridge: Cambridge University Press, 1996), 104–8.

230. *Georg Wilhelm Friedrich Hegel: Lectures on the Philosophy of Religion III: The Consummate Religion*, ed. Peter C. Hodgson, trans. R. F. Brown, P. C. Hodgson, and J. M. Stewart (Berkeley: University of California Press, 1985), 322–5.

231. Ludwig Andreas Feuerbach, *The Essence of Christianity*, trans. George Eliot (1854; New York: Harper & Row, 1957), 140, 144–5.

232. Louisa Sarah Bevington, 'Religion: An Essay in Couplets', in *Poems, Lyrics, and Sonnets* (London: Elliot Stock, 1882), 124–6; text transcribed for and available online at the Victorian Women Writers Project, http://www.indiana. edu/~letrs/vwwp/. Copyright 1996, The Trustees of Indiana University.

233. John Stuart Mill, *Nature, the Utility of Religion, and Theism* (London: Longman, Green, Reader & Dyer, 1874; repr. Westmead: Gregg, 1969), 253–5.

234. Arthur Drews, *The Christ Myth*, trans. C. Delisle Burns (London: T. Fisher Unwin, 1910), 285–6.

235. Ernst Troeltsch, *The Significance of the Historical Existence of Jesus for Faith*, in *Ernst Troeltsch: Writings on Theology and Religion*, ed. and trans. Robert Morgan and Michael Pye (London: Duckworth, 1977), 196–8.

236. Joseph Smith, *The Book of Mormon: Another Testament of Jesus Christ* (Salt Lake City: The Church of Jesus Christ of Latter-Day Saints, 1830; repr. 1981).

237. David Friedrich Strauss, *The Life of Jesus Critically Examined*, trans. George Eliot, new edn. (London: Swan Sonnenschein, 1898), 454–6.

238. Johann August Wilhelm Neander, *The Life of Jesus Christ in its Historical Connexion and Historical Development*, trans. John McLintock and Charles E. Blumenthal (London: Henry G. Bohn, 1851), 308–9.

239. Karl Ferdinand Gutzkow, *Wally the Sceptic*, trans. Ruth-Ellen Boetcher Joeres, German Studies in America, ed. Heinrich Meyer, 19 (Berne: Herbert Lang, 1974), 99.

240. Ernest Rénan, *Life of Jesus*, trans. William G. Hutchison (London: Walter Scott, 1897), 238–40.

241. [Eliza Lynn Linton], *The True History of Joshua Davidson*, 4th edn. (London: Strahan, 1873), 79–84.

242. H. Grätz, *History of the Jews, from the Earliest Times to the Present Day*, ii, trans. Bella Löwy (London: David Nutt, 1891), 155–7.

243. Albert Schweitzer, *The Quest of the Historical Jesus: A Critical Study of its Progress from Reimarus to Wrede*, trans. W. Montgomery (London: A. & C. Black, 1954; repr. London: Xpress Reprints, 1996), 396–401.

244, 247. Aubrey Thomas de Vere, 'Mater Christi'; and Francis Thompson, 'Little Jesus', in *Poetry of the Victorian Period*, ed. Jerome Hamilton Buckley and George Benjamin Woods, 3rd edn. (Atlanta: Scott, Foresman, 1963), 401, 855–6.

245. Oscar Wilde, 'The Selfish Giant', in *A House of Pomegranates, The Happy Prince and Other Tales*, The First Collected Edition of the Works of Oscar Wilde 1908–1922, ed. Robert Voss (London: Methuen, 1908; repr. London: Dawsons, 1969), 204–8.

246. Plechtchéev, 'The Crown of Roses', trans. Geoffrey Dearmer in *The Oxford Book of Carols*, ed. Percy Dearmer, R. Vaughan Williams, and Martin Shaw (Oxford: Oxford University Press, 1928), no. 197.

247. See under 244 above.

248. Henry Hart Milman, 'Ride on! ride on in majesty!', in *A Hymnal for Use in the English Church*, ed. F. H. Murray (London, 1852).

249–50. Gottfried Thomasius, *Christ's Person and Work*, and Isaak August Dorner, *System of Christian Doctrine*, in *God and Incarnation in Mid-Nineteenth Century German Theology*, trans. Claude Welch, A Library of Protestant Thought, ed. John Dillenberger *et al.* (New York: Oxford University Press, 1965), 46–8, 247, 254.

251. William Ellery Channing, *Unitarian Christianity*, in *Unitarian Christianity and Other Essays*, ed. Irving H. Bartlett, The American Heritage Series, ed. Oskar Piest, 21 (New York: Liberal Arts Press, 1957), 16–21.

252. William Blake, 'The Everlasting Gospel' in *The Poetry and Prose of William Blake*, ed. David V. Erdman (Garden City, NY: Doubleday, 1965), 514–6. Punctuation altered.

253. Friedrich Nietzsche, *The Antichrist*, trans. H. L. Mencken (Costa Mesa, Calif.: Noontide, 1988), 92–5, 98–101, 106.

254. Edward Irving, *The Trinitarian Face of God*, ed. Graham W. P. McFarlane, The Devotional Library, ed. James B. Torrance, and Michael Jinkins (Edinburgh: St Andrew Press, 1996), 62–3, 66–7.

255. Friedrich Schleiermacher, 'The Effects of Scripture and the Immediate Effects of the Redeemer', in *Servant of the Word: Selected Sermons of Friedrich Schleiermacher*, trans. Dawn de Vries, Fortress Texts in Modern Theology, ed. B. A. Gerrish *et al.* (Philadelphia: Fortress Press, 1987), 110–13.

256. Wilhelm Herrmann, *The Communion of the Christian with God Described on the Basis of Luther's Statements*, trans. J. Sandys Stanyon and R. W. Stewart, ed. Robert T. Voelkel, Lives of Jesus, ed. Leander E. Keck (2nd edn. London: Williams & Norgate, 1906; repr. Philadelphia: Fortress Press, 1971), 97–101.

257. Martin Kähler, *The So-Called Historical Jesus and the Historic, Biblical Christ*, trans. Carl E. Braaten, Seminar Editions, ed. Theodore G. Tappert (Philadelphia: Fortress Press, 1964), 92–7.

258. John Henry Newman, *Parochial and Plain Sermons*, ii (London: Rivingtons, 1868), 27–9, 37–8.

259. Charles A. Briggs, 'The Christ of the Church', *American Journal of Theology*, 16/2 (Apr. 1912), 197–9.

260. Theodore Parker, *A Discourse of the Transient and the Permanent in Christianity*, in Robert E. Collins, *Theodore Parker: American Transcendentalist* (Metuchen, NJ: Scarecrow Press, 1973), 77–9.

261. Alfred Loisy, *The Gospel and the Church*, trans. Bernard B. Scott, Lives of Jesus, ed. Leander E. Keck (Philadelphia: Fortress Press, 1976), 120–2.

262. Adolf von Harnack, *What is Christianity?*, trans. Thomas Bailey Saunders, 5th edn. (London: Ernest Benn, 1958) 88, 95–9.

263. Josephine Butler, *Social Purity* (London: Morgan & Scott, 1879), 6–7; text available online at the Victorian Women Writers Project, http://www.indiana.edu/~letrs/vwwp/.

264. Leo Tolstoy, *The Spirit of Christ's Teaching*, trans. Nathan Haskell Dole (London, Walter Scott, [1880s]), 184–8.

265. Lucretia Mott, 'Likeness to Christ', in *Lucretia Mott: Her Complete Speeches and Sermons*, ed. Dana Greene (New York: Edwin Mellen, 1980), repr. in Amy Oden (ed.) *In Her Words: Women's Writings in the History of Christian Thought* (London: SPCK, 1994), 293–4.

266. Ralph Waldo Emerson, Sermon LXXVI, in *The Complete Sermons of Ralph Waldo Emerson*, ii, ed. Teresa Toulouse and Andrew Delbanco (Columbia: University of Missouri, 1990), 192–5.

267. R. A. Torrey, *How to Study the Bible* (New York: Oxford University Press, 1909; bound as part of the Scofield Reference Bible), 29.

268. Amanda Berry Smith, *An Autobiography: The Story of the Lord's Dealings with Mrs. Amanda Smith, the Colored Lady Evangelist* (Chicago: Meyer, 1893; repr. New York: Garland, 1987); repr. in Amy Oden (ed.) *In Her Words: Women's Writings in the History of Christian Thought* (London: SPCK, 1994), 310–11.

269. See under **119** above.

270. Søren Kierkegaard, *Practice in Christianity*, trans. Howard V. Hong and Edna H. Hong, Kierkegaard's Writings, 20 (Princeton, NJ: Princeton University Press, 1991), 63–6.

271. F. W. Evans, *Compendium of the Origin, History . . . and Doctrines of the United Society of Believers in Christ's Second Appearing*, Shaker Manuscripts Online (Shakers, 1859), http://passtheword.org/SHAKER-MANUSCRIPTS/.

272. Trans. for this book by M. A. Higton from *Wegbereiter heutiger Theologie. Ignaz von Döllinger*, ed. Johann Finsterhölzl (Styria: Graz, 1969), 125–7.

273. See under **119** above.

274. Edward Payson, 'Sermon III: All Things Created for Christ'; text available online at http://www. intercom.net/~hisalone/index.htm.

275. Catherine Booth, *Papers on Aggressive Christianity* (London: Salvationist Publishing and Supplies, 1880), 121–3; text transcribed for and available online at the Victorian Women Writers Project, http://www. indiana.edu/~letrs/vwwp/.

276. *The Autobiography of Therese of Lisieux*, ed. Robert Blackhouse, Spiritual Lives (London: Hodder & Stoughton, 1994), 183–6.

277. Keshub Chunder Sen, *India Asks: Who is Christ?*, in *Keshub Chunder Sen: A Selection*, ed. David C. Scott, Library of Indian Christian Theology, Companion Volume Series, ed. H. S. Wilson, 1 (Bangalore: Christian Literature Society, 1979), 200–5.

278. Brahmabandhab Upadhyay, 'The Incarnate Logos', in *The Twentieth Century*, Jan. 1901, repr. in *The Writings of Brahmabandhab Upadhyay*, ed. Julius Lipner and George Gispért-Sauch, i, Library of Christian Theology, ed. J. Patmury, 6 (Bangalore: United Theological College, Division of Research and Post-Graduate Studies, 1991), 189–91.

279. Swami Vivekananda, *Christ the Messenger*, in *The Complete Works of Swami Vivekananda*, ed. Swami Mumukshananda, Mayavati Memorial Edition (Calcutta: Advaita Ashrama, 1992), 139–40, 152–3.

280. Pandita Ramabai, *A Testimony*, 9th edn. (Kadagon, Poona district: Ramabai Mukti Mission, 1968) repr. in Amy Oden (ed.) *In Her Words: Women's Writings in the History of Christian Thought* (London: SPCK, 1994), 324–6.

281. Karl Barth, *The Epistle to the Romans*, trans. Edwyn C. Hoskyns from the 2nd German edn. (Oxford: Oxford University Press, 1933), 96–9.

282. Rudolf Bultmann, *Jesus*, trans. as *Jesus and the Word* by Louise Pettibone Smith and Erminie Huntress (London: Ivor Nicholson & Watson, 1935), 9–14.

283. Ernst Käsemann, 'The Problem of the Historical Jesus', in *Essays on New Testament Themes*, trans. W. J. Montaigne, Studies in Biblical Theology, ed. C. F. D. Moule *et al.*), 41 (London: SCM, 1964), 45–7.

284. Norman Perrin, *Rediscovering the Teaching of Jesus*, New Testament Library, ed. Alan Richardson, C. F. D. Moule, and Floyd V. Filson (London: SCM, 1967), 243–4.

285. E. P. Sanders, *The Historical Figure of Jesus* (London: Allen Lane, Penguin Press, 1993), 11–14.

286. John Dominic Crossan, *The Historical Jesus: The Life of a Mediterranean Jewish Peasant* (Edinburgh: T. & T. Clark, 1991), xi–xiii.

287. John P. Meier, *A Marginal Jew: Rethinking the Historical Jesus, ii: Mentor, Message and Miracles*, The Anchor Bible Reference Library, ed. David Noel Freedman (New York: Doubleday, 1994), 1042–4.

288. N. T. Wright, *Who was Jesus?* (London: SPCK, 1992), 97–9.

289. John M. Allegro, *The Sacred Mushroom and the Cross* (London: Hodder & Stoughton, 1970), xiii–xiv.

290. Paul Tillich, *Systematic Theology, ii: Existence and the Christ* (London: SCM, 1957), 118–19.

291. John R. W. Stott, *The Cross of Christ* (Leicester: IVP, 1986), 158–61.

292. D. M. Lloyd Jones, *Romans: An Exposition of Chapter 1: The Gospel of God* (Edinburgh: Banner of Truth, 1985), 134–5.

293. Toyohiko Kagawa, *Meditations on the Cross*, trans. Helen F. Topping and Marion R. Draper (London: SCM, 1936), 55–6.

294. Kosuke Koyama, *Waterbuffalo Theology* (London: SCM, 1974), 222–4.

295. Anthony Bloom, *Living Prayer* (London: DLT (Libra), 1966), 84–7.

296. 'The Dogmatic Constitution of the Church', in *The Documents of Vatican II*, trans. Joseph Gallagher *et al.* (London: Geoffrey Chapman, 1967), 22–4.

297. Kim Chi Ha, *The Gold-Crowned Jesus and Other Writings*, trans. Chong Sun Kim and Winifred Caldwell, ed. Chong Sun Kim and Shelly Kitten (Maryknoll, NY: Orbis, 1978), 121–4.

298. Steve Turner, 'How to Hide Jesus', in *Up to Date: Poems 1968–1982* (London: Hodder & Stoughton, 1983), 95.

299. Conrad Noel, *The Life of Jesus* (London: J. M. Dent, 1937), 287–8, 290–1, 296–7.

300. Leonardo Boff, *Jesus Christ Liberator: A Critical Christology for our Time*, trans. Patrick Hughes (London: SPCK, 1980), 279–80, 291–2.

301. Byung Mu Ahn, 'Jesus and the People', *CTC Bulletin*, 7 (1987), Christian Conference on Asia, G/F, 2 Kowloon Road, Kowloon, Hong Hong; repr. in R. S. Sugirtharajah (ed.), *Asian Faces of Jesus* (London: SCM, 1993), 167–9.

302. *Berkeley Liberation Program/New Berkeley Liberation Program*, in Ronald M. Enroth and C. Breckinridge Peters, *The Story of the Jesus People: A Factual Survey* (Exeter: Paternoster, 1972), 104–5.

303. Kofi Appiah-Kubi, 'Christology', in J. Mbiti (ed.), *African and Asian Contributions to Contemporary Theology* (Geneva: Ecumenical Institute, 1976); repr. in John Parratt (ed.), *A Reader in African Theology*, International Study Guide, 23 (Advanced), new edn. (London: SPCK, 1997), 70–3.

304. Anselme T. Sanon, 'Jesus, Master of Initiation', trans. Robert R. Barr, in Robert J. Schreiter (ed.), *Faces of Jesus in Africa* (London: SCM, 1992), 93–5.

305. Elizabeth Amoah, 'Christologies: African', in *Dictionary of Third World Theologies*, ed. Virginia Fabella and R. S. Sugirtharajah (Maryknoll, NY: Orbis, 2000), 41–2.

306. Albert B. Cleage Jr., 'The Black Messiah', in James H. Cone and Gayraud S.

Wilmore (eds.), *Black Theology: A Documentary History*, i: *1966–1979*, 2nd edn. (Maryknoll, NY: Orbis, 1993), 101–2.

307. Kelly Brown Douglas, 'Christologies: African American' in *Dictionary of Third World Theologies*, ed. Virginia Fabella and R. S. Sugirtharajah (Maryknoll, NY: Orbis, 2000), 43–4.

308. Dorothy L. Sayers, 'Pantas Elkyso', in *Catholic Tales and Christian Songs* (Oxford: Blackwell, 1918); text available online at the Christian Classics Ethereal Library: http://www.ccel.org/.

309. Dietrich Bonhoeffer, *Ethics*, ed. Eberhard Bethge, trans. Neville Horton Smith, Fontana Library, Theology and Philosophy (London: Collins, 1964), 130–3.

310. H. Richard Niebuhr, *Christ and Culture* (London: Faber & Faber, 1952), 30–3.

311. James M. Gustafson, *Christ and the Moral Life* (Chicago: University of Chicago Press, 1968), 265, 268–9.

312. Stanley Hauerwas, *A Community of Character: Toward a Constructive Christian Social Ethic* (Notre Dame, Ind.: University of Notre Dame Press, 1981), 49–51.

313. T. S. Eliot, 'Journey of the Magi', in *Collected Poems, 1909–1962* (New York: Harcourt, Brace & World, 1963), 99–100.

314. Norman Mailer, *The Gospel according to the Son* (London: Little, Brown, 1997), 230–4.

315. D. H. Lawrence, *Short Novels*, ii: *St Maur, The Virgin and the Gypsy, The Man who Died* (London: Heinemann, 1956).

316. C. S. Lewis, *The Lion, the Witch, and the Wardrobe*, The Chronicles of Narnia (London: Geoffrey Bles, 1950), 146–9.

317. Henri J. M. Nouwen, *With Burning Hearts: A Meditation on the Eucharistic Life* (London: Geoffrey Chapman, 1994), 39–43.

318. Karl Barth, *Church Dogmatics, iv: The Doctrine of Reconciliation* 1, trans. G. W. Bromiley (Edinburgh: T. & T. Clark, 1956), 264–5, 267, 269–72.

319. Maurice Wiles, 'Christianity without Incarnation?', in *The Myth of God Incarnate*, ed. John Hick (London: SCM, 1977), 8–9.

320. Dietrich Bonhoeffer, *Christology*, trans. John Bowden (London: Collins, 1966), 29–31, 33–7.

321. Karl Rahner, 'Grace in the Abysses of Man', *Everyday Faith*, trans. W. J. O'Hara (New York: Herder & Herder; London: Burns & Oates, 1967), 38–41.

322. D. M. Baillie, *God was in Christ: An Essay on Incarnation and Atonement* (London: Faber & Faber, 1948), 130–1.

323. Pierre Teilhard de Chardin, *Science and Christ*, trans. René Hague (London: Collins, 1968), 34–6.

324. Margaret Spufford, *Celebration* (London: Fount Paperback, 1989), 38.

325. Graham Kendrick, 'Meekness and Majesty', in *Songs and Hymns of Fellowship* (Eastbourne: Kingsway, 1987), no. 390.

326. Mary Daly, *Beyond God the Father: Toward a Philosophy of Women's Liberation* (Boston: Beacon Press, 1973), 70–1.

327. Rosemary Radford Reuther, *Sexism and God Talk* (London: SCM, 1983), 134–8.

328. Patricia Wilson-Kastner, *Faith, Feminism and the Christ* (Philadelphia: Fortress Press, 1983), 114–16.

329. Sergius Bulgakov, 'The Lamb of God', in *A Bulgakov Anthology*, ed. James Pain and Nicholas Zernov (London: SPCK, 1976), 116–18.

330. Jürgen Moltmann, *The Crucified God: The Cross of Christ as the Foundation and Criticism of Christian Theology*, trans. R. A. Wilson and John Bowden (London: SCM, 1974), 204–5.

331. Arthur Michael Ramsey, *God, Christ and the World: A Study in Contemporary Theology* (London: SCM, 1969), 98–101.

332. Jon Sobrino, *Christology at the Crossroads: A Latin American Approach*, trans. John Drury (London: SCM, 1978), 225–7.

333. Vladimir Lossky, *Mystical Theology of the Eastern Church*, trans. The Fellowship of St Alban and St Sergius (London: James Clarke, 1957), 149–50.

334. William Temple, *The Universality of Christ: A Course of Lectures* (London: SCM, 1921), 82–3.

335. Sri Radhakrishnan, *Eastern Religions and Western Christian Thought*, 2nd edn. (Oxford: Oxford University Press; London: Humphrey Milford, 1940), 176–81, 183.

336. Swami Satprakashananda, *Hinduism and Christianity: Jesus Christ and his Teachings in the Light of Vedanta* (St Louis: Vedanta Society of St Louis, 1975), 56, 58, 60, 62.

337. Raymond Panikkar, 'Confrontation between Hinduism and Christ', *New Blackfriars*, 50/584 (Jan. 1969), 200.

338. Joseph Klausner, *Jesus of Nazareth: His Life, Times and Teaching*, trans. Herbert Danby (London: George Allen & Unwin, 1928), 413–14.

339. Samuel Sandmel, *We Jews and Jesus* (London: Victor Gollancz, 1965), 139–42.

340. Geza Vermes, *Jesus the Jew: A Historian's Reading of the Gospels* (London: Collins, 1973), 223–5.

341. Elliot R. Wolfson, 'Judaism and Incarnation: The Imaginal Body of God', in T. Frymer-Kensky, D. Novak, P. Ochs, D. F. Sandmel, and M. A. Signer (eds.), *Christianity in Jewish Terms* (Boulder, Colo.: Westview Press, 2000), 239–40, 253–4.

342. François Mauriac, *The Son of Man*, trans. Bernard Murchland (London: Burns & Oates, 1960), 52–4.

343. Dmitri Merezhovsky, *Jesus the Unknown*, trans. H. Chrouschoff Matheson (London: Jonathan Cape, 1933), 361–2.

Further Reading

Bibliographical details for all the books from which our extracts have been taken appear at the end of the book. The following list suggests some books which we have found useful in producing this *Reader*. It is restricted to books which survey a significant portion of the material covered by the *Reader*; we have not attempted the mammoth task of suggesting secondary reading for each individual extract.

GENERAL

BOUYER, LOUIS, et al., *History of Christian Spirituality* (New York: Seabury, 1963–).

FEDOTOV, G. P., *A Treasury of Russian Spirituality* (London: Sheed & Ward, 1950).

HASTINGS, ADRIAN, et al. (eds.), *The Oxford Companion to Christian Thought* (Oxford: Oxford University Press, 2000).

LIVINGSTONE, E. A., and F. L. CROSS (eds.), *The Oxford Dictionary of the Christian Church* (Oxford: Oxford University Press, 1997).

PELIKAN, JAROSLAV, *Jesus through the Centuries* (New Haven: Yale University Press, 1985).

—— *The Christian Tradition: A History of the Development of Doctrine*, 5 vols. (Chicago: University of Chicago Press, 1971–).

WISMER, DON, *The Islamic Jesus: An Annotated Bibliography of Sources in English and French* (New York: Garland, 1977).

BIBLICAL AND PATRISTIC

BARCLAY, WILLIAM, *Jesus as they Saw Him: New Testament Interpretations of Jesus* (Grand Rapids, Mich.: Eerdmans, 1978).

BAUCKHAM, RICHARD, *God Crucified: Christology and Monotheism in the New Testament* (Grand Rapids, Mich.: Eerdmans, 1999).

DI BERARDINO, ANGELO (ed.), *Encyclopedia of the Early Church*, trans. Adrian Walford (Cambridge: James Clarke, 1992).

—— and BASIL STUDER (eds.), *History of Theology*, i: *The Patristic Period*, trans. Matthew J. O'Connell (Collegeville, Minn.: Michael Glazier, 1997).

DUNN, JAMES D. G., *Christology in the Making: A New Testament Inquiry into the Origins of the Doctrine of the Incarnation* (London: SCM, 1980).

GRANT, ROBERT M., *The Earliest Lives of Jesus* (London: SPCK, 1961).

GRILLMEIER, ALOYS, *Christ in Christian Tradition*, i: *From the Apostolic Age to Chalcedon (451)*, trans. John Bowden (Louisville, Ky.: WJKP, 1975).

HANSON, R. P. C., *The Search for the Christian Doctrine of God: The Arian Controversy 318–81* (Edinburgh: T. & T. Clark, 1988).

MOULE, C. F. D., *The Origin of Christology* (Cambridge: Cambridge University Press, 1977).

STUDER, BASIL, *Trinity and Incarnation: The Faith of the Early Church*, ed. Andrew Louth, trans. Matthias Westerhoff (Edinburgh: T. & T. Clark, 1993).

BYZANTINE AND EARLY MEDIEVAL

BROWN, PETER, *The Rise of Western Christendom* (Oxford: Blackwell, 1997).

D'ONOFRIO, GIULIO (ed.), *Storia della teologia nel Medioevo* (Casale Monferrato: Piemme, 1996).

GRILLMEIER, ALOYS, et al., *Christ in Christian Tradition*, ii: *Council of Chalcedon (451) to Gregory the Great (590–604)*, vols. i. ii/1–4 (Louisville, Ky.: WJKP, 1995–).

MEYENDORFF, JOHN, *Christ in Eastern Christian Thought* (New York: St Vladimir's Seminary, 1975).

STRAYER, JOSEPH R. (ed.), *Dictionary of the Middle Ages* (New York: Scribner, 1982–).

LATER MEDIEVAL AND RENAISSANCE

BYNUM, CAROLINE WALKER, *Jesus as Mother: Studies in the Spirituality of the High Middle Ages* (Berkeley: University of California Press, 1982).

D'ONOFRIO, GIULIO (ed.), *History of Theology*, iii: *The Renaissance*, trans. Matthew J. O'Connell (Collegeville, Minn.: Michael Glazier, 1998).

RUBIN, MIRI, *Corpus Christi: The Eucharist in Late Medieval Culture* (Cambridge: Cambridge University Press, 1991).

REFORMATION AND COUNTER-REFORMATION

BLOUGH, NEAL, et al., *Jésus-Christ aux marges de la Réforme* (Paris: Desclée, 1992).

HILLERBRAND, HANS J. (ed.), *The Oxford Encyclopedia of the Reformation* (Oxford: Oxford University Press, 1996).

LIENHARD, MARC, *Luther, Witness to Jesus Christ: Stages and Themes of the Reformer's Christology*, trans. Edwin H. Robertson (Minneapolis: Augsburg, 1982).

MULLER, RICHARD A., *Christ and the Decree: Christology and Predestination in Reformed Theology from Calvin to Perkins* (Durham, NC: Labyrinth Press, 1986).

EARLY MODERNITY

BROWN, COLIN, *Jesus in European Protestant Thought, 1778–1860* (Durham, NC: Labyrinth Press, 1984).

COTTRET, BERNARD, *Le Christ des lumières: Jésus de Newton à Voltaire 1660–1760* (Paris: Éditions du Cerf, 1990).

McCARTHY, VINCENT A., *A Quest for a Philosophical Jesus: Christianity and Philosophy in Rousseau, Kant, Hegel and Schelling* (Macon, Ga.: Mercer University Press, 1986).

MENOZZI, DANIEL, *Les Interpretations politiques de Jésus de l'Ancien Régime à la Revolution* (Paris: Éditions du Cerf, 1983).

THE NINETEENTH CENTURY

ALLEN, CHARLOTTE, *The Human Christ: The Search for the Historical Jesus* (Oxford: Lion, 1998).

BOWMAN, FRANK PAUL, *Le Christ des barricades 1789–1848* (Paris: Éditions du Cerf, 1987).

HESCHEL, SUSANNAH, *Abraham Geiger and the Jewish Jesus* (Chicago: University of Chicago Press, 1998).

LAWTON, JOHN STEWART, *Conflict in Christology: A Study of British and American Christology, from 1889–1914* (London: SPCK, 1947).

SMART, NINIAN, et al. (eds.), *Nineteenth Century Religious Thought in the West* (Cambridge: Cambridge University Press, 1985–).

WELCH, CLAUDE, *Protestant Thought in the Nineteenth Century* (New Haven: Yale University Press, 1972).

ZIOLKOWSKI, THEODORE, *Fictional Transfigurations of Jesus* (Princeton: Princeton University Press, 1972).

THE TWENTIETH CENTURY

FORD, DAVID (ed.), *The Modern Theologians: An Introduction to Christian Theology in the Twentieth Century*, 2nd edn. (Oxford: Blackwell, 1997).

HEYER, C. J. DEN, *Jesus Matters: 150 Years of Jesus Research* (London: SCM, 1996).

POWELL, MARK ALLEN, *Jesus as a Figure in History: How Modern Historians View the Man from Galilee* (Louisville, Ky.: WJKP, 1998).

SCHREITER, ROBERT J., *Faces of Jesus in Africa* (London: SCM, 1991).

SUGIRTHARAJAH, R. S., *Asian Faces of Jesus* (London: SCM, 1993).

Acknowledgements

The Scripture quotations contained herein are from *The New Revised Standard Version of the Bible*, Anglicized Edition, copyright © 1989, 1995 by the Division of Christian Education of the National Council of the Churches of Christ in the United States of America and are used by permission. All rights reserved.

BANNER OF TRUTH TRUST, for D. M. Lloyd Jones, *Romans: An Exposition of Chapter I: The Gospel of God*. Published by Banner of Truth, 1985.

CATHOLIC UNIVERSITY OF AMERICA PRESS, for St Augustine, 'Tractates on the Gospel of John 112–24' and 'Tractates on the First Epistle of St John' (tr. John W. Rettig), *The Fathers of the Church: A New Translation* (ed. Roy Joseph Defarrai) 1; Catholic University of America, 1995, 1947 pp 364–5; 'The Epistle to Diognetus' and 'The Letters of St Ignatius of Antioch' 9tr. Gerald D. G. Walsh) in The Apostolic Fathers, *The Fathers of the Church: A New Translation* (ed. Roy Joseph Defarrai) 1; Catholic University of America 1947 pp 364–5; Ambrose of Milan, 'Isaac, or the Soul' in Saint Ambrose: Seven Exegetical Works (tr. Michael P. McHugh), *Fathers of the Christian Church* (ed. Bernard M. Peebles); Catholic University of America/Consortium Press, 1972 pp 15–18; Nestorius, 'Letter 5 (nestorius to Cyril)' in St Cyril of Alexandria: Letters 1–50 (tr. John I. McEnerney), *The Fathers of the Christian Church: A New Translation* (ed. Thomas P. Halton) 76; Catholic University of America, 1985 pp 45–7; John of Damascus, 'The Orthodox Faith' in Saint John of Damascus: Writings (tr. Frederic H. Chase), *The Fathers of the Church* 37 (ed. Bernard M. Peebles), Catholic University Press, 1958 pp 268–71, 281–4. The Homilies of Saint Jerome 2: Homilies 60–96 (ed. Mary Ligouri Ewald) The *Fathers of the Church: A New Translation* (ed. Roy Joseph Deferrari) 57; Catholic University of America, 1996 pp 7, 8, 163–5.

FABER AND FABER LTD., for T. S. Eliot, 'Journey of the Magi' in *Collected Poems 1909–1962*, U.S. Rights Harcourt Brace, from *Collected Poems 1909–1962* by T. S. Eliot, copyright © 1936 by Harcourt Inc., copyright © 1964, 1963 by T. S. Eliot, reprinted by permission of the publisher; Kadloubovsky and Palmer, *Philokalia II, III, IV*, published by Faber & Faber; D. M. Baillie, *God was in Christ*, published by Faber & Faber 1948; James M. Clark and John V. Skin, *Meister Eickhart: Selected Treatises and Sermons*, published by Faber and Faber, 1953.

FORTRESS PRESS, for Patricia Wilson-Kastner, *Faith, Feminism and Christ*. Published by Fortress Press, 1983.

GEORGETOWN UNIVERSITY PRESS, for 'Third Council of Constantinople' and 'Constitution of the Fourth Lateran Council' (ed. G. Albergo, et al.) in *Decrees of the Ecumenical Councils 1: Nicea I to Lateran V* (ed. Norman P. Tanner). Published by Georgetown University Press, 1990.

VICTOR GOLLANCZ, for Samuel Sandmel, *We Jews and Jesus*. Published by Victor Gollancz, 1965.

HARPERCOLLINS PUBLISHERS LTD., for Dietrich Bonhoeffer, *Christology*. From The Fontana Library, Theology and Philosophy. Published by Collins, 1964.

HARVARD UNIVERSITY PRESS, for Richard Hooker, *The Works of Richard Hooker Volume II Book V*: 'Of the Laws of Ecclesiastical Polity' edited by W. Speed Hill, Cambridge, Mass.: The Belknap Press of Harvard University Press. Copyright © 1977 by the President and Fellows of Harvard College; Sor Juana Inez de la Cruz, *A Sor Juana Anthology*, translated by Alan S. Trueblood pp 161–5, Cambridge Mass.: Harvard University Press. Copyright © 1988 by the President and Fellows of Harvard College; *Pliny: Pliny: Letters and Penegyricus II* (translated by Betty Radice), Loeb Classical Library (ed. E. H. Warmingtom). Harvard University Press, 1969 pp 285–92; Boethius, 'Against Eutyches and Nestorius' in *Boethius: The Theological Tractates* and the Consolation of Philosophy (tr. H. F. Stewart, E. K. Rand and S. J. Tester) LCL, 1973 pp 117–19. The Loeb Classical Library fi is a registered trademark of the President and Fellows of Harvard College.

HODDER & STOUGHTON, for Steve Turner, 'How to Hide Jesus' in *Up To Date: Poems 1968–1982*. Published by Hodder & Stoughton, 1983.

I.V. PRESS, for John R. W. Stott, *The Cross of Christ*. Published by IVP, 1986.

KINGSWAY'S THANKYOU MUSIC, for extract taken from the song 'I'm Special' by Graham Kendrick. Copyright © 1986 Kingsway's Thankyou Music, PO Box 75, Eastbourne, East Sussex, BN23 6NW, UK. Used by kind permission of Kingsway's Thankyou Music.

MOUTON DE GRUYTER, for Baron Paul Thierry d'Holbach, *Ecce Homo: An Eighteenth Century Life of Jesus* from *History of Religions in Translation 1*.

NORMAN MAILER, for *The Gospel According to the Son*. Published by Little Brown, 1997.

OXFORD UNIVERSITY PRESS, for *The Acts of the Christian Martyrs*, translated by Herbert Musurillo (1972) Copyright © Oxford University press 1972; *Cyril of Alexandria: Selected Letters* edited and translated by Lionel R. Wickham (1983). Copyright © Oxford University press, 1983; Adam of Eynsham, *Magna Vita Sancti Hugonis: The Life of Hugh of Lincoln* edited and translated by Decima L. Douie and David High Farmer (1985). Copyright © Decima Douie and David Hugh Farmer 1961; *The Apocryphal New Testament: A Collection of Apocryphal Christian Literature in an English Translation* edited J. K. Elliott (1993). Copyright © Oxford University press, 1993; Karl Barth, *The Epistle to the Romans* translated by Edwyn C. Hoskyns (1933); Sir Sarapalli Radhakrishnan, *Eastern Religions and Western Christian Thought* (1939) all reprinted by permission of Oxford University Press.

PAULIST PRESS, for *St Justin Martyr: The First and Second Apologies* (tr. Leslie William Barnard), *Ancient Christian Writers: The Works of the Fathers in Translation* (ed. Walter J. Burghardt, John J. Dillon, Dennis D. McManus 56) Paulist Press, 1997 pp 83–4; *Hildegard of Bingen: Scivias* (tr. Mother Columba Hart and Jane Bishop), *Classics of Western Spirituality* (ed. Bernard McGinn) Paulist Press, 1990 pp 425; 433–4; Angela of Folgino, 'The Book of Blessed Angela' in *Angela of Folgina: Complete Works* (tr. Paul

Lachance) Classics of Western Spirituality (ed. Bernard McGinn) Paulist Press, 1993 pp 230–233; Birgitta of Sweden, 'The Seventh Book of Revelations' (tr. Albert Ryle Kezel) in Birgitta of Sweden: Life and Selected Revelations (ed Marguerite Tjader Harris) Classics of Western Spirituality (ed. Bernard McGinn) Paulist 1990 pp 188–90; Geert Grote, 'Letter 62' in Devotio Moderna: Basic Writings (tr. John Van Engen), Classics of Western Spirituality (ed. John Farina) Paulist Press, 1988 p. 88; Julian of Norwich: Showings (tr. Edmund Colledge and James Walsh) Classics of Western Spirituality (ed Richard J. Payne) Paulist Press, 19878 pp 297–9; Gertruse of Helfta: The Herald of Divine Love (tr. Margaret Winkworth) Classics of Western Spirituality (ed. Bernard McGinn) Paulist Press, 1993 p. 219; Lorenzo Scupoli, 'The Spiritual Combat' in Theatine Spirituality: Selected Writings (tr. William V. Hudon). Classics of Western Spirituality (ed. Bernard McGinn). Paulist Press 1996 pp 186–7; Jean Jaques Olier, 'Introduction to the Christian Life and Virtues'; John Eudes, 'The life and Kingdom of Jesus in Christian Souls'; Madelaine de Saint Joseph, 'Letter 139' and Pierre de Berulle, 'Elevations upon the Incarnation' in Berulle and the French School: Selected Writings (tr. Lowell M. Glendon, ed. William M. Thompson) Classics of Western Spirituality (ed. Bernard McGinn). Paulist Press 1989 pp 221–4; 295–6; 197–8; 116–17; Nicholas Ludwig, Count von Zinzendorf, 'The Litany of the Life, Suffering and Death of Jesus Christ'; Gerhard Tersteegan, 'Selected Letters'; Friedrich Christoph Oetinger, 'A Confession of Faith'; in Pietists: Selected Writings (tr. Peter C. Erb) Classics of Western Spirituality (ed. Richard J. Payne and John Farina) Paulist Press, 1983 pp 243; 275–6.

PENGUIN BOOKS LTD., for E. P. Sandars, The Historical Figure of Jesus (Allen Lane The Penguin Press, 1993) copyright © E. P. Sandars, 1993.

PETERS FRASER & DUNLOP, for Jesus the Jew by Geza Vermes. Copyright © Geza Vermes. Reprinted by permission of The Peters Fraser and Dunlop Group.

LAURENCE POLLINGER LTD., for D. H. Lawrence, The Man Who Died, published by Heinemann, 1956. Used by permission of Laurence Pollinger Limited and the Estate of Frieda Lawrence Ravagli.

PRINCETON UNIVERSITY PRESS, for Soren Kierkegaard, Practice in Christianity. Copyright © by PUP; Ragusa, Meditations on the Life of Christ. Copyright © 1961 by Princeton University Press.

SCM PRESS, for Anselm of Canterbury, 'Why God Became Man', Peter Abailard, 'Exposition of the Epistle to the Romans' and Peter Lombard, extracts from 'The Four Books of Sentences' in A Scholastic Miscellany: Anselm to Ockham (tr. Eugene R. Fairweather), Library of Christian Classics 10 (ed. John Baillie, John T. McNeill and Henry P. van Dusen) SCM, 1956 pp 176; 179–81; 283–4; 335–7; Philipp Melanchthon, 'Loci Communes Theologici (1521)' in Melanchthon and Bucer (tr. Lowell J. Sartre and Wilhelm Pauck, ed. W. Pauck, Library of Christian Classics (ed. John Baillie, John T. McNeill and Henry P. van Dusen) 19; SCM 1969 pp 21–2; Calvin: Institutes of the Christian Religion 2 (tr. Ford Lewis Battles, ed. John T. McNeill), Library of Christian Classics (ed. John Baillie, John T. McNeill, and Henry P. van Dusen) 20; SCM 1960; Ernst Kasemann, 'The Problem of the Historical Jesus' in Essays on New Testament Themes (tr. W. J. Montaigne), Studies in Biblical Theology (ed. C. F. D. Moule, et al.) 41; SCM 1964 pp 45–7; Norman Perrin, Rediscovering the Teaching of Jesus, New

554   ACKNOWLEDGEMENTS

Testament Library (ed. Alan Richardson, CFD Moule, and Floyd V. Filson); SCM 1967 pp 243–4; Byung My Ahn, 'Jesus and the People', CTC Bulletin 9 (1987), in *Asian Faces of Jesus* (ed. R. S. Sugirtharajah); SCM, 1993 pp 167–9; Anselme T. Sanon, 'Jesus Master of Initiation' (tr. Robert R. Barr) in *Faces of Jesus in Africa* (ed. Robert J. Schreiter); SCM 1992 pp 93–5; Arthur Michael Ramsay, *God, Christ and the World: A Study in Contemporary Theology*; SCM 1969 pp 98–101; Rosemary Radford Reuther, *Sexism and God Talk*; SCM 1983 pp 134–8; Rupert of Deitz, 'Commentary on Saint John' and Ratramnus of Corbie, 'Christ's Body and Blood', extracts in Early Medieval Theology (tr. George E. McCracken and Allen Cabaniss), *Library of Christian Classics IX*; SCM 1957 pp 266–8; 118; 120–1; Kosuke Koyama, *Waterbuffalo Theology*; SCM 1974 pp 222–4. Maurice Wiles, 'Christianity without Incarceration' in *The Myth of God Incarnate* (ed. John Hick); SCM 1977 pp 8–9; Jon Sobrino, *Christology at the Crossroads: A Latin American Approach* (tr. John Drury); SCM 1978 pp 225–7.

SIMON & SCHUSTER, for St Ireaeus, 'The Demonstration of the Apostolic Preaching' (tr. J. Armitage Robinson), *Translations of Christian Literature, Series IV: Oriental Texts* (ed. W. J. Sparrow Simpson and W. K. Lowther Clarke), Macmillan 1920 pp 97–103; Eusebius of Caesarea, 'The Proof of the Gospel, Being the Demonstratio Evegelica of Eusebius of Cesaria, I (tr. W. J. Ferrer), *Translations of Christian Literature, Series I: Greek Texts* (ed. W. J. Sparrow Simpson. W. K. Lowther Clarke, Macmillan 1920.

UNIVERSITY OF CALIFORNIA PRESS, for G. W. F. Hegel, *Lectures on the Philosophy of Religion Vol. 3, The Consummate Religion*. Edited/translated by Peter Hodgson. Copyright © 1985 The Regents of the University of California.

UNIVERSITY OF CHICAGO PRESS, for James M. Gustafson, *Christ and the Moral Life*. University of Chicago Press, 1968.

UNIVERSITY OF PENNSYLVANIA PRESS, for John C. Cavadini, *The Last Christology of the West*. Copyright © 1993 University of Pennsylvania Press. Reprinted with permission.

WESTVIEW PRESS, for Tikva Frymer-Kensky, *Christianity in Jewish Terms*. Copyright © 2000 by Westview Press, Member of Perseus Books Group. Reprinted by permission of Westview Press, a member of Perseus Books L.L.C.

YALE UNIVERSITY PRESS, for Thomas More, 'A Dialogue Concerning Heresies, I. The Text' (ed. Thomas Lawler, Germain Marc'hadour, and Richard C. Marius), *The Yale Edition of the Complete Works of St. Thomas More, 6*; Yale University Press, 1981, pp 113–16 (orthography modernised); Joseph Ibn Shem Tob, 'Sermon on Abot 3:15–16' in *Jewish Preaching 1200–1800: An Anthology* (ed., tr. Marc Saperstein), Yale Juaica Series (ed. Frank Talmage) XXVI; Yale University press, 1989 pp 167–71.

Index

Note: Entries in **bold** indicate the author or title of an extract included in the reader. Four long entries, 'Jesus', 'benefits of Jesus', 'relationships to Jesus', and 'responses to Jesus' in the following index act as a guide to much of the content of this Reader. The entry 'Jesus' is divided into sections on Jesus' life, his characteristics, and the titles, epithets, or descriptions used of him; the entry 'benefits of Jesus' lists many descriptions used in the extracts of the salvation or help received from Jesus; the entry 'relationships to Jesus' presents some of the ways in which the relationship of a believer or follower, or of humanity in general, to Jesus has been understood, and 'responses to Jesus' lists some of the responses which Jesus has or should call forth.

Abel, son of Adam 62–3, 241
Abelard, Peter 115–16, 139–40
Abraham, patriarch 57, 59, 95, 132, 149, 153, 161, 220–1, 285, 365, 430
accommodation, of Christ to our limitations 43, 53–4, 83, 85, 106, 513
Acts, Book of 25–6, 38–9
Adam, first man 57–9, 92–3, 121–2, 161, 166, 210, 217, 219, 232, 240–1, 256, 258, 280, 304, 336, 364, 405, 473, 526; *see also* Christ, titles: second Adam
Adam of Eynsham 131–2
adoptionism 134–6, 140–2, 527
Aelred of Rievaulx 117
Aetius, neo-Arian theologian 90
Agathonicé, martyr 41
Agyeman, Jaramogi Abebe 459–60
Al-Baydawi, Islamic author 171–2
Al-Bukhari, Imam 152
Alcuin of York 134
Al-Ghazali, Sufi author 153–4
Al-Hujwiri, Sufi author 153
Allegro, John M. 431–3
Ambrose of Milan 36, 48, 49, 54–6, 141
Amoah, Elizabeth 458–9
Anabaptists 228
anamnesis 21, 35–8, 51, 115–16, 157, 174, 186, 196, 204, 227, 244–5, 268, 331, 367, 371, 443, 468, 471
anarchism 327
Anastasius I, of Antioch 49, 107–8
Andrew, apostle 18, 30
Andrewes, Lancelot 285
Angela of Foligno 166–9, 172, 527
Anglicanism 220, 223, 253, 256, 262–4, 268, 284–6, 287, 289, 319, 353, 372, 505, 510

anhypostasis, *see* incarnation, as enhypostasic
Anselm of Canterbury 104, 132, 137–9, 436
Antioch, Council of 87–8
anti-Semitism 31, 60, 81, 149–51, 171, 181, 204–5, 249–50, 313, 342, 400, 412, 423, 447–8, 517–18
Antony of Padua 177–8
apocalyptic 16, 70–1, 425–6, 428, 450
Apollinarius of Laodicea 91–3, 95–6
appearance, of Jesus 31, 84, 161–2, 284, 374; *see also* face
Appiah-Kubi, Kofi 454–6
Aquinas, Thomas 128, 178, 197–200, 201, 210, 241
Archimedes of Syracuse 306–7
Arius; Arianism 52, 82, 86–7, 88–92, 96
Arndt, Johann 272–4
Arsenius, desert father 42
Athanasius of Alexandria 52–4, 87, 127
Augsburg Confession 210–11, 235
Augustine of Hippo 36, 44–5, 49, 54, 141–2, 198, 219, 529
Augustinian Order 233, 207

Bachelard, Gaston 521
Baillie, Donald M. 492–3
Balaam, Prophet 160, 178
Baptists 296, 421
Barabbas 249, 267, 473
Barth, Karl 369, 411, 413–16, 465, 481–5, 529
Bartholomew, apostle 401
Bartimaeus, blind man 442
Basil the Great 37
Basilides, Gnostic 78–9
Bateman, Susanna 290
Baxter, Richard 287–9
Beatus of Liebana 134, 135–6

Beguine communities 172
Benedict of Nursia 269
Benedictine Order 104, 142, 182, 200
benefits of Jesus 209–10
    adoption; becoming God's children 15, 29,
        34, 44, 76, 107, 114, 131, 135–6, 140–1, 212,
        218–19, 269, 293, 297, 343, 361, 380, 382, 384,
        388–9, 399, 408, 421, 457, 465, 469, 507
    assurance 286–7, 297
    atonement 81, 138–40, 199, 254, 300, 307–8, 341,
        356–7, 406, 436–7, 529
    authority 19, 24, 197, 327, 332, 335, 433
    bearing our sins 47, 61, 84, 165, 213, 215, 246,
        334, 388–9, 484
    beauty 37, 82, 106, 108, 185, 242, 376, 474
    captivity 55, 110, 236, 295, 389, 461, 523
    cheer 94, 176, 275, 376
    comfort 15, 72, 85, 180, 211, 215, 222, 236,
        286–7, 341, 391, 428, 466
    communion with God 20, 55, 296, 443, 463,
        487–8, 496, 506, 508
    confidence 139, 176, 247, 265, 283, 327, 369, 373,
        469–70
    conversion 4, 23, 117, 200, 305, 312, 388–94,
        400, 403, 407–9, 415, 449
    death 213, 399; see also relationship: being
        crucified with Christ
    deliverance 63, 173, 181, 227, 249, 296, 310, 313,
        323, 326, 438, 461, 511
    divinization; theosis 48–50, 93, 285, 291, 365–6
    ecstasy 179, 189, 431–3
    exaltation 51, 161
    expiation 213, 444
    forgiveness 15–17, 33, 35–7, 47, 51, 55, 91, 93–4,
        139, 162–3, 177, 211–12, 227, 271, 305, 389, 414,
        430–1, 436, 438, 466, 469, 474, 491, 496, 513
    freedom; liberation 37, 50–1, 58, 63, 71, 73, 79,
        120–2, 135–6, 140, 174, 213, 215, 247, 267,
        279–80, 283, 288, 317, 326, 339, 346, 407, 421,
        447, 449–50, 452–4, 458–61, 469, 479, 484–5,
        498–9
    God's pleasure 36, 186, 322–3
    growth 196, 273, 342, 452, 470
    guidance 36, 329, 453, 456
    hallucination 431–3
    healing 61, 71–2, 83, 92, 94, 120, 166, 180, 190,
        233, 242–3, 251, 266, 376, 426, 428, 431, 442,
        444, 451, 454–6, 458, 480, 500–1; see also
        Jesus: life: healings
    heaven; paradise 37, 50–1, 94, 120, 143, 163, 175,
        179, 241, 273, 280, 288, 291, 295, 308, 350,
        386, 398, 430, 433, 454; see also kingdom
    help in temptation 173, 175, 180–1, 276, 280,
        322–3
    hope 51, 81, 120, 244, 247, 273, 324, 376, 378, 383,
        434–6, 443, 450, 479, 504, 506, 508
    imputed righteousness 212, 291, 297, 307–8
    instruction; knowledge; wisdom 35, 38, 45, 55,
        58, 72, 77, 82, 110, 112, 151, 175–6, 187, 197,
        240, 243, 247, 273, 293, 297, 331–2, 346, 371,
        380–1, 385, 391, 413, 440, 508; see also
        benefits: revelation
    judgement 34, 413, 463–4, 484–5, 488; see also
        Jesus: titles: judge
    justification 8, 47, 139, 209, 211, 273, 291, 297,
        307, 354, 370, 434, 438, 464
    life; eternal life; new life 20, 29, 33–5, 37, 47,
        50, 52, 58–9, 63, 76, 81–2, 84–5, 91, 94, 109,
        116, 118–20, 123, 127, 130–2, 172, 180, 190,
        211, 213, 218–19, 224–6, 240, 244, 258, 266,
        271, 278, 282–3, 291, 296, 300, 304, 334,
        361–2, 369, 382–3, 389, 396–7, 401, 404,
        407–8, 454–5, 459–60, 464, 479–80, 488,
        496, 501, 507, 510, 514
    mercy 15, 36, 108, 111–13, 115, 132, 154, 161, 166,
        178, 180, 200, 226–7, 265, 274, 276–7, 300,
        357, 391, 408, 437, 441–3, 464
    new being 434–6, 329
    new birth; rebirth 16, 49, 76, 188, 190–2, 211, 240
    new covenant 21, 35, 120, 273, 296
    payment of debt 49–50, 98, 138, 166, 191
    peace 29, 36, 57, 120, 187–8, 240, 273–4, 277,
        288, 292, 297, 384, 389–90, 442, 448,
    power 25, 76, 189, 265, 293, 335, 388, 390, 408,
        442, 469
    priesthood of believers 63, 227
    propitiation 199, 211, 227, 308, 408, 520
    protection, guarding 37, 47, 142, 150, 178, 181,
        211, 223, 236, 275, 459
    punishment 268, 279, 437
    purchase 50, 212, 288, 297, 301, 438
    purification, cleansing 27, 35, 37, 49, 51–2, 59,
        62–3, 73, 80, 107, 119, 142, 177–8, 189, 201,
        211, 214, 226, 228, 244, 268, 279, 289, 291,
        293, 376, 390, 428, 444, 455
    ransom 63, 268, 301
    reconciliation 36, 57, 139, 166, 291, 296, 326,
        343, 408, 436, 440, 442, 500
    redemption 24, 35–7, 47, 59, 80, 94, 114, 135,
        137, 140, 160, 165–6, 177, 180, 200, 212–13,
        227, 235, 272, 274, 276, 284, 288–9, 296–7,
        301, 326, 330–1, 343, 354, 366–8, 388, 398,
        403, 414, 429, 437, 443, 457, 463, 497–9,
        527

release of divine spark 78

responsibility 421, 490

rest, repose 37, 46, 56, 94, 185, 187–8, 271, 327

restoration 37, 48, 51–2, 80, 94, 99, 107, 138, 161, 164, 269, 280, 291, 313, 431

resurrection 37, 63, 85, 91, 189, 202, 213, 241, 297–8, 316, 396, 398, 414, 428, 464, 517

revelation 15, 20, 24, 29–30, 33–4, 42, 46–8, 50–7, 59, 71–2, 146, 181, 190, 196, 212, 296, 300, 325, 331–2, 346, 355, 368, 375–8, 380, 392, 394, 399, 413–6, 420, 449, 461, 469, 479, 497, 504–9; as veiling 49, 216–17, 246, 250, 298, 415–16, 484

reward 15, 42–3, 89, 108, 110, 308, 469

salvation 13, 16, 22, 33–59, 63, 68, 77, 79, 81, 88, 91–4, 100, 120, 122, 130, 134, 137–9, 142–3, 145, 159, 166, 173, 184, 188, 195, 197–201, 203, 210–12, 214, 217, 219, 240, 243, 259, 266, 271, 279, 283, 291, 296, 303–5, 308, 326, 331, 342, 357, 363, 375, 394, 397, 399, 408, 413, 415, 424, 427–8, 434, 437–8, 440, 442–4, 452, 455–6, 460, 464, 485–7, 489, 505, 507–9, 511

sanctification 51, 61–2, 93, 117, 211, 225, 227–8, 233, 244, 287, 297, 366, 390, 396, 398, 405, 438, 457–8

satisfaction for sins 138, 197, 199–201, 211, 215, 227–8, 247, 296, 300–1, 436–7, 527

seeing God; enjoying God 14–15, 178, 180, 294–5, 298, 327, 373, 406, 513

self-knowledge 29, 380, 479

strength 45, 47, 72, 210–11, 266, 276, 331–2, 444

substitution 61, 165, 167, 299, 301, 308, 388, 436–7, 484

transfiguration 279, 524

victory of Christ 296; over death 35–7, 53, 86, 94, 115, 213, 247, 288, 325, 352, 405, 477; over devil 37, 51, 63, 99, 161, 247, 258, 299–300, 308, 359–60, 452; over evil 326, 484; over fear 405; over the powers 453; over sin 216, 247, 352, 366, 405, 452; over the world 63, 452

wounding 242–3

Bentham, Jeremy 329

Bernard of Clairvaux 116–17, 132, 176, 274, 295, 526

Bérulle, Pierre de 253, 281–3, 303–4

Bevington, Louisa Sarah 327–8

Birgitta of Sweden 169–71

black theology 412, 459–61

Blake, William 358–60

blood, Jesus' 21, 35–6, 42–3, 57, 59, 62–3, 77, 81–2, 94, 121–2, 130, 135, 139, 142–4, 155, 170–1, 177, 180–2, 186–7, 191–2, 194–7, 200, 204, 212, 214–15, 223–7, 236, 246, 249–51, 262–4, 268, 276–8, 284–5, 289, 298–9, 301, 328, 350, 366, 390, 395, 397–400, 438, 461, 464, 474

Bloom, Anthony 10, 441–3

body of Christ; and humanity, see also humanity of Jesus: body; and passion and death 23–4, 62–3, 77, 84, 92, 142, 148, 150, 161, 165, 168–71, 185–6, 191–2, 212–13, 215, 247, 249–50, 264, 269, 275, 298, 354, 360, 388, 424, 474; resurrection body 172, 390; in the Eucharist 21, 35, 52, 95, 130, 142–5, 155, 173, 194–7, 223–7, 246, 285, 289, 292–3, 395–7 (see also Eucharist); as the Church 40, 44–5, 57, 77, 135, 219, 249, 270, 281–2, 292, 375, 395–6, 401, 443

Boehme, Jacob 279

Boethius, Anicius Manlius Torquatus Severinus 132, 133–4

Boff, Leonardo 449–50

Bonaventure 178–80

Bonhoeffer, Dietrich 4, 5, 462, 463–5, 488–9

Booth, Catherine Mumford 398–400

Bossuet, Wilhelm 330, 528

Bozon, Nicholas 121–2

Brethren of the Common Life 185

Briggs, Charles Augustus 373–5

Brigittine Order 169

Buddha; Buddhism 320, 439, 510–13

Bulgakov, Sergius 502–3, 508

Bultmann, Rudolf 370, 417–19, 529

Bunyan, John 192, 271

Butler, Josephine 381–2

Byung Mu Ahn 451–2

Caiaphas, High Priest 359–60, 424

Calvin, Jean 218–19, 230, 232, 364

Calvinism 211, 233–4, 286, 294, 298, 352

Capuchin Order 238, 528

Carmelite Order 282, 400; 'Disalced' 241

Carpus, martyr 41

Carthusian Order 191

Cathars 155

Catherine of Siena 186–7

Catholicism, Roman 143, 207–8, 223, 226–8, 240, 243, 249, 253, 262, 268–9, 272, 274, 280–4, 303, 347, 351, 372, 377, 394–5, 411, 427, 443–4, 449, 456, 479, 490, 493, 497, 502, 506, 514, 523; for earlier Catholicism see language: Latin

Cecilia, Martyr 176, 401
Chalcedon, Council of 11–12, 91, 96, 98,
    100–1, 103, 123–9, 133, 237, 461, 465
Channing, William Ellery 356–8
charismatic movement 458
Charlemagne, Emperor 104, 134
Charles I of England 284
Charles II of England 284
Chemnitz, Martin 236–8
Chester Mystery Cycle 158–61
Chief Priests 22, 23, 26
Christian World Liberation Front 452–3
Christmas 51, 116, 157–8, 204, 280, 285, 295, 372,
    491–2, 526, 528
Church 12–13, 19, 25, 40, 42, 44, 55, 57, 77, 80, 88,
    91, 130–1, 135–6, 150, 159, 172–4, 178, 183,
    190, 195–6, 198–9, 219–21, 227–8, 247,
    269–70, 279, 281–2, 287, 291, 330–2, 342,
    360–2, 366–8, 371–8, 382, 391, 394–6, 400–1,
    419, 422, 424, 441–4, 451, 455, 468, 470, 487,
    489, 501, 504–5, 519, 527
Cicero, Marcus Tullius 117
Cistercian Order 104, 113, 116–17, 182
Cleagle Jr., Albert B. 459–60
Clement of Alexandria 79
Coleridge, Samuel Taylor 385
Colonna, Vittoria 238–9
communicatio idiomatum; communication of
    attributes 83, 96–7, 100, 129, 200, 222,
    230–8, 352, 354–5, 366, 486, 508, 528
communism 341–2, 411, 452
Concord, Formula of 235–6
Confessing Church 463
Congregationalism 286, 296, 298, 356, 397, 403, 412
Constantine the Great 11, 88, 103
Constantinople, First Council of 51, 87, 91, 95
Constantinople, Third Council of 127–8
Copernicus, Nicolaus 303, 528
Corpus Christi, Feast of 195–7
Cosmic Christ 57, 422, 501
councils 103, 127, 134 see also Antioch,
    Constantinople, Lateran, Nicaea,
    Sirmium, Trent, Vatican
Counter-Reformation 9, 207, 226, 239, 245, 255,
    269, 272, 280–2, 294, 303
Crashaw, Richard 262
Creation 2, 6, 18, 27, 30, 37, 52, 57, 72, 82, 85, 88,
    91, 97, 99, 100, 113, 119, 130, 209–10, 232,
    397, 493, 504
Creed, Apostle's 211–14, 223
Creed, Athanasian 136
Creed, Nicene see Nicaea

creeds; credal formulae 11, 76, 101, 127, 134, 235,
    243–4, 342, 362, 368, 372–3, 375, 384, 442 see
    also doctrine
Cromwell, Oliver 256
Cross 22, 37–8, 49–50, 59, 130, 173, 182, 184,
    191–2, 255, 263–4, 269, 271, 277–8, 300,
    358, 360, 397–8, 439, 461, 470, 472 see also
    life: crucifixion; instruments of the
    passion
Crossan, John Dominic 425–7
Crossman, Samuel 266–7
crusades 103, 116, 155, 400, 441
Cruz, Juana Inés de la 259–61
Cynewulf 120
Cyprian of Carthage 395
Cyril of Alexandria 96–8, 126, 128

Daly, Mary 496–7, 500
Daniel, Desert Father 42–3
Daniel, prophet 150
Dante Alighieri 417, 461
David, King 13, 59, 63, 77, 94, 97, 146, 160, 212,
    215, 219, 365, 373
Dead Sea Scrolls 423, 431; see also Essenes
Dearmer, Geoffrey 350
Deism 254, 294, 303, 307–9, 486
Devil 37, 153, 210–11, 256–9, 300, 359, 389–90, 399,
    428, 437, 449, 473–4, 481–2, 484
Devotio Moderna 183–6, 189, 192
Diadochus of Photike 111–12
Digger movement 292
Diocletian, Emperor 48
Diognetus, Epistle to 46–7
Dionysius the Pseudo-Areopagite 106–7
Dirks, Elizabeth 228–9
dispensationalism 388
divinity, Jesus' 36, 82, 84–91, 95–6, 98–101, 123–8,
    133–4, 159, 178, 199, 221–3, 230–7, 246, 250,
    285, 341, 352–5, 357–8, 365, 384, 393, 396, 403,
    492, 494–5, 502, 505, 508–9, 515, 520, 526,
    528; veiled 217, 250, 298
docetism 27, 30–1, 77–8, 82–4, 86, 420, 526
doctrine; dogma 89, 115, 209–10, 221, 235, 305,
    308, 326, 330–1, 335, 341–2, 344, 356–8, 362,
    367, 371–80, 383–4, 403, 460, 478, 486, 498,
    505, 519, 520–1; development 372–5; see also
    creeds
Döllinger, Johann Joseph Ignaz von 395–6
Dominican Order 155–6, 165, 172, 175, 184, 186,
    197
Donatism 44
Donne, John 268–9, 284

Dorner, Isaak August 355–6
Douglas, Kelly Brown 460–1
Drews, Arthur 330–1

Ebner, Margaret 169, 175
Eckhart, Meister 184
Edwards, Jonathan 298–300
Egeria, pilgrim 38–9
election 37, 136–7, 167, 196, 218–19, 258, 296, 302, 383
Elijah, prophet 19, 22, 64–5, 336–8
Eliot, George 319
Eliot, Thomas Stearns 471–2
Elipandus of Toledo 134–5
Elizabeth I of England 223, 253, 285
Emdem, Rabbi Jacob 311–13
Emerson, Ralph Waldo 385–7
empiricism 254, 294, 321
Enlightenment, European 9, 254, 303–17, 321, 411, 481
Enoch, patriarch 399
Ephrem the Syrian 49
eschatology 2, 6, 14–16, 24, 345–6, 401, 414, 425, 427, 434, 436, 455, 504, 528
Essenes 519; see also Dead Sea Scrolls
Eucharist 3–5, 18, 21, 23–4, 35–6, 42, 116, 130, 142–5, 173–4, 190, 194–6, 207, 220–1, 223–9, 245, 249, 263, 285, 289, 295, 395–7, 400, 456; as sacrifice 220, 395–6; see also body of Christ
Eudes, John 269, 281–2
Eunomius, neo-Arian theologian 90
Eusebius of Caesarea 82–4, 87
Eutyches 133
Evagrius of Pontus 105
evangelicalism 388–9, 394, 412, 436–7
Evans, F. W. 394–5
Eve, first woman 41, 58, 291, 473
exaltation of Jesus 46, 296–300, 420, 451, 428; see also humiliation
exclusivism 211, 217, 487, 510–11; see also uniqueness
existentialism 391, 417–19, 421, 428, 434–6
Exodus, the 312, 426–7, 487
extra Calvinisticum 528–9
Ezekiel, prophet 105, 161

face of Jesus 7, 30, 34, 56, 106–7, 161–2, 170, 177–8, 181, 184–5, 191, 265, 268, 274, 278, 294, 327, 373, 464, 523–5; see also appearance
factuality of Jesus 326–8, 330–3, 419

Fall, the 52, 58, 210, 232, 296, 304, 365, 509
Fauchet, Claude 317
Felix of Urgel 134
feminism 10, 381–3, 407, 412, 453, 460–1, 496–501
Feodosiy of Pechersk 144–5
Feuerbach, Ludwig 326–7, 529
Fisher, John 249–51
foolishness of God 53–4, 67–8, 81, 109, 117, 209, 216–17, 279, 290, 305, 415
Fox, George 290
Francis of Assisi 9, 155, 157–8, 174–5, 176, 179, 183, 194, 269, 360, 400
Franciscan Order 121, 155–6, 166, 172, 177–8, 449, 528
Franck, Sebastian 240–1
Fuchs, Ernst 529
fulfilment of prophecy 14, 35, 39, 55, 57–8, 60–6, 89, 101, 147, 160–1, 215, 256, 292, 304, 306, 315, 334, 336–7, 339, 383, 414, 428–30, 441, 460, 479
Fulgentius of Ruspe 141
fundamentalism 320, 412

Gabriel, angel 151, 256
Gerhardt, Paul 274–5
Germinius of Sirmium 89–90
Gertrude of Helfta 200–1
Gilbert de la Porrée 133
Gnosticism 6, 28, 57, 78–80, 519
God-consciousness, Jesus' 486, 491, 503
Goethe, Johann Wolfgang von 417, 489
Gospels 13–25, 330–1, 340, 345, 354, 360–1, 370–2, 380, 417, 420, 424, 435, 451, 460–1, 465, 468, 498, 517; see also Matthew, Mark, Luke, John, Thomas, Peter
Grätz, Heinrich 342–4
Gregory Nazianzus 92–3, 93–5, 128, 131
Gregory of Nyssa 37, 51–2
Gregory of Sinai 155, 189
Gregory the Great 146
Groote, Geert de 185–6
Gustafson, James 462, 467–8
Gutzkow, Karl 338–9, 340

Harnack, Adolf von 330, 377, 379–81, 411, 413, 528
Hauerwas, Stanley 462, 467, 468–70
Hebrews, Book of 61–2
Hegel, Georg Wilhelm Friedrich 319, 324–6, 335, 391, 528
Heidegger, Martin 417
Heidelberg Catechism 211–14

Héloïse, friend of Abelard 115
Henry VIII of England 249
Henry, respondent to Wecelin 149–50
Herbert, George 263, 284
heresy 231, 236, 372–3, 375, 392, 394, 437–8
Herod Antipas 423–4, 426
Herod the Great 77, 290, 304, 359, 423, 447–8
Herrick, Robert 255–6
Herrmann, Wilhelm 369–70, 411, 413
Herrnhutter Brethren 272, 276, 366
High Chuch 262, 284, 372
Hilary of Poitiers 141
Hildegard of Bingen 136–7, 172
Hinduism 320, 362, 402–9, 510–11, 513–15
historical criticism; biblical criticism 254, 294,
 303, 309–11, 315–17, 319, 329–33, 335–9, 341–6,
 364, 370–1, 373–4, 417–33, 493–4, 517, 519–20
History, as a problem 315–17, 321, 345–6, 368, 392
Hitler, Adolf 463
Hobbes, Thomas 304–5
Holbach, Paul-Henri Thiry, Baron d' 313–15,
 333
Holocaust 9, 411, 515
homoousious; consubstantial 86–8, 91, 100,
 127–9, 134, 295, 316
Hooker, Richard 223–6, 284–5
Hosea, prophet 487
Hsü-T'ing Mi-shih-ho-ching 119–20
Hugh of Lincoln 131–2
humanity of Jesus 21, 30, 77–84, 91, 95–6,
 98–101, 117, 123–30, 132–4, 136–7, 159, 186,
 194, 199, 201, 219, 222–3, 230–7, 246, 250,
 268, 276, 285, 323–6, 330, 340–1, 352–8,
 364–6, 371, 394, 396, 404, 473, 493, 495, 502,
 504–5, 508–9, 515, 520, 526, 528; bodiliness
 53–4, 68, 77–8, 80–3, 89, 96, 100, 114, 121–2,
 124, 128–30, 134, 155, 162, 201, 222–3, 232–5,
 268, 275, 281, 296, 365–6, 405, 474, 520–1;
 excretion 79, 132; finitude 325–6; 353–5,
 364–5; growth 96, 222, 354–6, 456, 511;
 hunger and thirst 45, 82, 85, 94, 96, 114,
 222, 258–9, 473; mind 92–3, 356–8;
 particularity 421; soul 83, 92–3, 100, 128,
 130, 135, 248, 356–7, 365, 386, 481, 525;
 suffering 10, 29, 61–3, 72, 77, 79, 82, 85, 89,
 91, 95, 108, 114–15, 117, 128, 177, 216, 222,
 346, 354, 361, 363
Humble Access, Prayer of 226
humiliation of Jesus 36, 46, 50, 114, 157, 174, 177,
 183, 283–4, 288, 296, 298–300, 325, 358, 366,
 372, 420, 440, 504, 524, 528; *see also*
 exaltation

hypostasis, hypostatic union 76, 86, 88, 93, 95–8,
 100, 126–9, 133, 135, 141, 211, 230–4, 236–8,
 284, 291, 296, 352–6, 365–6, 502–3, 526–8

icons 103, 118, 129–31, 524
idolatry 52–4, 69, 94, 120, 135, 153, 311–12, 342,
 472, 496–7, 510, 526
Ignatius of Antioch 77–8, 401
incarnation 4, 6, 20, 37, 44, 48–9, 53, 58, 63, 68,
 71–2, 76–7, 85–6, 88, 97, 99–100, 105, 109,
 124, 126, 128, 131, 137, 139, 140, 150, 201,
 208–11, 230, 240, 243–4, 254, 258, 276, 288,
 296, 303–4, 324–30, 347, 351, 353–6, 366,
 372–3, 396, 404–6, 436–7, 441–3, 460, 463–4,
 483, 486–8, 490–4, 496–7, 499–500, 504–6,
 515, 520–2, 524, 526–7; as assumption of
 humanity 51, 89, 92–3, 96–9, 107–8, 126–9,
 122, 134, 138–9, 177, 203, 212, 215, 222, 230,
 233, 241, 248, 266, 295–6, 322, 325, 347,
 353–4, 360, 364–6, 396, 443, 486; as
 enhypostatic 126–9, 404, 527; *see also* two
 natures
Innocent III, pope 155, 207
instruments of the passion 173, 247, 255; nails
 169, 173, 192, 247, 250–1; crown of thorns
 121, 169–70, 181, 191, 246, 250–1, 264, 274,
 277, 350, 446; *see also* wounds of Christ
Irenaeus of Lyons 57–9, 78–9
Irving, Edward 364–6
Isaac, patriarch 63, 149, 430
Isaiah, Book of 60–1, 160, 428
Ishmael, son of Abraham 153
Islam 6, 103, 146, 151–4, 157, 162–3, 171–2, 205,
 207, 311, 412, 430, 510

Jacob, patriarch 63, 179, 430
James, apostle 19, 21, 65, 84, 314, 340
Jeremias II, Patriarch of Constantinople
 243–4
Jerome 59, 64–6, 141
Jesuit Order 208, 245, 281, 493
Jesus of Nazareth
 life
 eternal generation 35, 49, 51, 57, 73, 81, 86–93,
 95, 97, 100, 114, 129, 134, 150, 294, 323
 annunciation 511
 conception 13, 115, 128, 189, 212, 231, 511
 birth 13, 51, 153, 157, 189, 238, 241, 248, 276,
 288, 296, 323, 339, 423, 456, 472, 503; as
 virgin birth 13–14, 36, 49, 58, 63, 68, 73,
 77, 80–2, 85, 89, 91, 93, 95, 97–9, 113, 115,
 118, 122, 124, 128, 134–6, 138, 141, 150, 177,

190, 194, 203, 211–12, 215, 222, 230–2, 248, 250, 256, 281, 295–6, 298, 328, 372, 405, 511
visit of the Magi 158–61, 238, 288, 304, 471–2
presentation in the temple 114–15, 118–19, 203–4, 511
circumcision 96, 113, 115, 202
exile in Egypt 94–5
childhood 27, 30, 85, 113, 147, 152, 175, 222, 256, 298, 347–52, 356, 359, 457, 497
baptism 14, 49, 51, 72, 94, 115, 119, 189, 248, 256, 280, 373, 377, 424–5, 503, 509, 512
temptation 14, 94, 114–15, 248, 256–9, 276, 322–3, 328, 359, 447–9, 473–4, 481, 511–12
ministry 5, 14, 16–17, 19, 21, 161, 370, 372, 403, 423–4, 427–9, 439, 461, 487
wedding at Cana 114
teaching 5, 14, 25, 28–30, 55, 115, 119, 139, 165, 200, 220, 273, 296, 298, 314, 322, 324, 329, 332, 335, 338, 341–3, 345, 363, 370–1, 375–7, 379–87, 393, 403, 418, 420, 424, 427–9, 432, 457, 460, 467, 487, 512–13, 516; in parables 14–15, 64, 360, 362, 428, 430, 442, 516; Sermon on the Mount 15, 382–4; beatitudes 15, 117, 177–8, 198, 382–4, 393, 428
miracles 6, 13–14, 17–18, 20, 27, 54, 79, 94, 114–15, 124, 128, 147, 152, 162, 164, 254, 288, 298, 304, 313, 322, 325, 339, 341, 343–4, 362, 373, 376, 386, 393, 426, 429, 473, 512, 516, 519
healings 17, 63, 80, 114, 152, 162, 164, 304, 344, 359, 407, 424, 428–9, 431, 451, 517; see also benefit: healing
casting out demons 16–18, 54, 80–1, 94, 259, 314, 341, 344, 425–6, 428–9, 455
table fellowship 18, 426–8, 431, 451; see also life: Emmaus; life: last supper
fasting 154, 244, 248
praying 15, 21, 338, 351, 363, 428, 481–3
transfiguration 19, 31, 64–6, 84, 94, 105, 107, 114–15, 189, 336–8, 508–9, 512, 524
triumphal entry 266, 288, 304, 339, 352, 424, 512
cleansing of temple 339, 359–60, 424, 426
last supper 21, 35, 245–6, 362, 428, 505; see also Eucharist
foot-washing 48, 231, 245–6, 495
passion 21, 34–6, 38, 60–6, 77, 88, 92, 98, 110–11, 115–16, 121, 140, 150, 155, 161, 165–71, 174–5, 180–2, 184, 186, 190–1, 194, 196, 198–9, 201–2, 211, 213, 231, 235, 241, 243–5, 255–6, 259, 262, 267, 274, 278, 284,

296, 298, 300–1, 322, 327, 330, 332, 334, 336, 338, 340, 347, 353, 357–8, 371, 405–6, 439, 444, 456, 472–6, 484, 500, 505–6, 508–9, 515, 524–5, 527
Gethsemane 21, 165, 180, 191, 298, 308, 328, 340–1, 439, 451, 474, 481–5, 513, 515
betrayal 22, 148, 227, 249, 306, 339, 424, 481
arrest 340, 424, 513, 517
trial 67, 148, 181, 204, 249, 299, 304, 317, 329, 424, 517
mockery 181, 191
flagellation 181, 191, 249–50, 401, 463
via dolorosa 182
crucifixion 22, 46, 49–50, 57–9, 68, 80, 89, 91, 94, 96–7, 114–15, 122, 137, 148, 159, 161, 169, 178–80, 182, 186, 189, 191–2, 194, 204, 210–11, 213–17, 222, 231, 241, 244, 246, 249–51, 267–8, 274, 277, 289, 291, 297, 299, 317, 325, 339, 358, 388, 398, 400–1, 407, 414, 421, 424, 433, 436, 439, 444–5, 451, 457, 461, 463–4, 468–9, 472–4, 476, 496, 500–9; pretence 79, 81, 151–2, 171–2, 474; see also cross; instruments of the passion
cry of desolation 22, 170, 222, 259, 339, 354, 414, 473, 502, 506
death 54, 98, 171, 227, 241, 243, 259–61, 264, 275, 278, 281, 304, 306, 308–9, 314, 322, 325–6, 328, 334, 336, 339, 341, 344, 352–4, 360, 363, 365, 369, 408, 420, 426, 434–5, 481, 484, 487
deposition 171
pietà 171
burial 23, 81, 91, 115, 124, 130, 148, 161, 171, 179, 189, 211, 213, 256, 267, 271, 297, 310, 372, 424, 445, 456, 474–5, 509
descent into hell 31, 37, 71, 94, 120, 211, 213, 249, 259, 494, 503
resurrection 22, 31–2, 37, 54, 66, 77–8, 81, 86, 88–9, 91, 93, 97, 107, 114–15, 130, 148, 151, 161, 172, 189, 211, 213, 241, 243, 245, 249, 297, 305, 310, 315–16, 325, 333–4, 338, 369, 371, 414, 421, 424, 427, 435, 444, 450, 457, 461, 463–4, 472, 474–7, 487, 500, 503–5, 507, 509, 517
empty tomb 23, 310, 424, 479
Emmaus 23, 367, 427, 478–81, 489, 524
great commission 399
ascension 25, 33, 45–6, 88–9, 94, 97, 114, 124, 172, 189, 201, 211, 214, 222–3, 241, 249, 280, 297, 325, 327, 372, 399, 502
heavenly session 36, 44–5, 62, 91, 96–7, 172,

211, 222–3, 232, 235–6, 249, 297, 303, 325, 373, 451, 502

intercession 61, 194, 200, 212, 214, 241, 288, 296, 452, 457

second coming 25, 37, 88–9, 91, 94, 211, 214, 243, 287–9, 297, 366, 394, 424, 435, 444, 450–1

judgement 36, 41, 71, 88–9, 91, 94, 115, 154, 163, 211, 214, 244, 282, 297–8, 386, 424, 427, 451; see also Jesus: title: judge

characteristics:
angry 28, 215, 359–60, 513
authoritative 17–19, 20, 24, 73, 288, 304, 346, 385–7, 421, 457, 469
beautiful 61, 75, 82, 85, 106, 109, 114, 161, 164, 242–3, 247, 261, 278, 294, 332, 369, 377, 523
bitter 49, 207, 214, 217–18, 461
black 412, 459–61
chaste; pure 35, 48, 122, 173, 232, 244, 339, 369, 386, 526
cheerful 30, 162, 267
childlike 30, 42, 276, 351, 362, 482, 525; see also Jesus: life: childhood
compassionate; kind; tender 36, 47, 53, 73–4, 99, 124, 142, 162, 167–8, 181, 190–2, 312, 369, 386, 398, 405, 408, 426, 443, 465, 469, 476, 496, 512
cursed 37, 213, 215, 297–9, 388, 437, 504
dancing 248
desiring 94, 196, 270, 474–5, 483, 516
eastern; Asian 403, 412
encouraging 244, 376
enduring 34, 63, 79, 94, 110, 114, 119, 167–8, 181–2, 277
enemy of Caesar 317
faithful 191–2, 277, 399
foreign 402
free 97, 136, 138, 215, 307, 341, 362, 385, 405, 445–6, 451, 492
gentle 121, 168, 185, 358–9, 361, 377, 379
good 36, 44, 46–7, 83, 85, 109, 111, 119, 132, 166, 193, 247, 257, 322–4, 351, 364, 369, 383
grieving 21, 165–6, 267, 274
holy 35, 46–7, 53, 83, 104, 111, 116, 118, 120, 127, 142, 170, 173, 181, 191, 246–7, 272, 276–8, 282, 291, 299, 322, 384, 396, 444, 519
humble 35, 80, 104–5, 145, 157, 194, 196, 209, 217, 231, 244, 276–7, 295, 298, 306–7, 380, 383–4, 393, 437, 446, 483, 495
impassible 97, 99, 107, 129, 149, 222, 328, 357
inspired 130, 314, 329, 510

Jewish 311–13, 342–4, 362, 378, 412, 515–20
loving 31, 44–6, 50, 54, 80, 83, 89, 98, 121, 132, 140, 143, 164, 166–8, 175, 181, 184–6, 188, 190–2, 198–201, 223, 238, 247–9, 259–60, 262–7, 270, 272–3, 275, 277, 279, 282, 284, 286–7, 289, 326–7, 350, 357, 360–1, 363, 366–7, 384, 391, 398, 408, 432, 437, 465–6, 469, 485, 496, 500, 502, 505–7, 524
majestic; reigning 36, 61, 84–5, 89, 98–9, 116–17, 214, 231, 235, 247, 291, 295, 298, 301, 305–6, 312, 352–3, 366, 374, 448, 461, 495, 509, 525
male 496–9
meek 169, 176, 259, 277, 298, 352–3, 386, 437, 495
merciful 166, 226, 227, 265, 276, 277, 437, 442; see also Jesus: benefit: mercy
mild 46, 190, 277, 383, 524
naked 182, 262, 472
noble 114, 121, 164–5, 168, 184, 274, 339–40, 376
obedient 21, 46, 58, 73, 77, 114, 176, 199, 277, 299, 307–8, 347, 359, 414, 451, 457, 465, 468, 482–4, 496, 501, 503
omnipotent 151, 201, 225–6, 353–5
patient 47, 176, 244, 277, 298, 306, 358
penitent 481
perfect 89, 118, 129, 176, 204, 283, 294–5, 308, 321–2, 329, 414, 492, 495, 499
pitying 37, 121, 275, 366, 382, 466
poor 85, 117, 145, 158, 177, 244, 248, 276, 298, 306, 393, 425, 440, 443–4, 463, 524
powerful; strong 27, 37, 41, 68, 72, 79, 83–5, 89, 94, 96, 98–9, 107, 117, 161, 172–3, 201, 213, 225–6, 233, 235, 241, 257, 270, 278, 303, 353, 369–70, 380–1, 398, 414, 444–5, 448–9, 455, 469, 500, 504–5
praising 483
rich 114, 117, 306, 440, 444
righteous 29, 47, 61, 87, 215–16, 219, 240, 291–2, 297, 300, 307–8, 386, 395, 481, self-denying 345, 360–3, 403, 437, 483, 505
sensitive 168
serving; in the form of a servant 46, 96, 99, 107, 109, 134–5, 231, 288, 393, 414, 453, 457, 469
shamed 58, 81, 166, 168, 178, 201, 214, 217, 271, 274, 325–6,
silent 28, 34, 61, 94, 154, 279, 476
simple 162, 244, 277, 341, 356, 385, 426, 515, 525; metaphysically 126, 129
sinful 414, 484

sinless 99–100, 109, 111, 137–8, 199, 201, 212–13, 222, 232, 255, 276, 296, 306, 394, 405, 444, 463, 492, 495

tolerant 244

trusting 467

victorious 322, 369, 381, 405; *see also* benefit: victory

visionary 426–7

weak; powerless; helpless 81, 84, 98, 114, 117, 149, 165, 216, 276, 300, 323, 328, 354, 469, 496, 505

wise 29, 66, 83, 153, 165, 250, 276

world-denying 360–1

zealous 166, 277, 343

titles and epithets:

absolute 392

abundance 85

adviser 47

agitator 523

all 29–30

almighty 372

alpha 372, 493

ancestor 458–9

angel 29

anointed 147–8, 178, 212, 424; = Messiah 13, 19, 22–3, 164, 236, 256, 304, 309, 313–14, 330, 336–7, 339, 343–4, 346, 371, 377–8, 384, 414, 421, 424, 447–8, 460, 498, 516, 519, 523, 526; = Christ 292, 434–5, 441–2, 451–2, 499 and *passim*

anti-Logos 488–9

author of creation 120; of goodness 132; of Christianity 385; of reconciliation 440

bastard 147

beginning 57, 372

beloved 14, 20, 55, 65, 192, 242–3, 400, 405

beloved Son 46, 65, 256, 292, 334, 373, 399, 424

bishop 161

book 185, 250, 278

bread 85

breath 397

bridegroom 113, 187, 243, 272–3, 287, 295

brother 306, 376, 405, 457–8

captain 390, 462

carpenter 446

centre 303, 493

cheat 314

chevalier 121

chief 456, 458

child of the most high 36; of God 120; of the pure Virgin 405

conqueror 161, 173, 366

corner-stone 218, 290

counsellor 365

creator 74, 109

crucified 10, 495; crucified one 22, 441

director of the universe 405

door 85, 179, 217, 291

dreamer 339

Elijah 19

emanation 291

Emmanuel/Immanuel 14, 125, 161, 276, 390, 528

end 372; of mankind 414; of the law 435

enthusiast 313–14

eternal wisdom 184

everlasting father 365

example, exemplar 83, 139, 145, 183, 209, 219, 283, 300, 322–3, 329, 341–2, 360, 385, 389, 427, 450, 459, 486

faith 85

fanatic 313

father 47, 306, 397

father's beauty 75

father's seal 75

father's self-knowledge 294

first 488

first-born 35, 79, 90, 98, 142, 396; from dead 57

food 187

founder 330–1, 419

fragrance 397

friend 131, 191, 200, 266, 387, 398, 458, 461; of mankind 308; of sinners 215

genius 329, 361, 414

glory of God 219

God 36, 77, 96, 109, 127, 165, 227, 231, 256, 263, 276, 278, 291, 295, 334, 372, 405, 503, 510, 516, 523

God eternal 37

God from God 89, 295; God of God 88

God-man 168, 187, 265, 325, 330, 355, 405, 523

gold 114

good shepherd 36, 301

grace 85, 131

ground 397

guardian 47, 275

hasid 519

head 44–5, 57, 135, 159, 198–9, 219, 225, 280, 282, 331–2, 395

healer 405, 520

helm of heaven 120

helper 520

hero 361, 414, 462; of the passion 341
high priest 212, 237–8, 276, 359
holy one 46–7, 116, 120, 323
husband 458
image of Brahman 405
image of God 46, 50, 52–3, 57, 75, 87, 90, 97,
    99, 107, 131, 219, 258, 295, 372, 406, 504
image of the Father 294, 495
intellect 79
Jeremiah 19
judge 70, 215, 436, 451, 464, 481
just man 520
king 36, 59, 71, 94, 131, 164, 212, 237–8, 256,
    267, 273, 277, 293, 296, 304–6, 359, 389–90,
    463, 481; of glory 120; of Israel 22; of
    Kings 109; of Righteousness 292–3; of
    the Jews 22, 158, 160, 191, 304, 473; of
    Truth 375
knight 121
ladder 179, 186
lamb 35, 61, 63, 94, 143, 169, 276–8, 280,
    292–3, 298, 300, 394
last 488
lawmaker 437
liberator 317, 339, 454, 458, 498
life 20, 85, 96, 124, 224, 282, 397, 488
light 47, 85, 87, 96, 219, 295, 397
light from light 89, 91; light of light 88
lion 300; of Judah 298
little Jesus 351
long-awaited one 72
lord 4, 46, 65, 424, 438–9, 441, 448, 505, 520,
    523 and passim
lord of lords 109
magician 147, 425
maker 165, 348
man of sorrows 446
man-God 406
martyr 329
master 18, 65, 109, 193, 342–3, 388, 400, 457
master of initiation 456
mediator 98, 135, 179, 212, 293, 353, 355, 396,
    437, 443, 457, 487
messenger 406
midwife 458
mighty God 87
mighty one 407
mirror of grace 184
moralist 516
mother 155, 190–1, 397
mushroom 431–3
mustard-seed 85

Narcissus 259
noble one 164
nonconformist 384
norm 467
omega 372, 493
only-begotten 35–6, 87–8, 90–1, 95–8, 100,
    114, 135, 141, 212, 219, 291, 304, 367, 408,
    421, 520
ornament 405
paradigm 467
pascha 63
Passover 227
pearl 85
personal saviour 388
Pharisee 516
physician 47, 455
pilgrim 153, 277
plough 85
poet 414
poor king 158
power 96; of God 68; of the Most High 128
priest 195, 226, 296, 306
prince of life 267; of peace 365
prophet 18–19, 23, 161–2, 296, 329, 332, 370,
    406–7, 429, 441, 499, 516, 519–20
propitiation 199, 211; see also benefit:
    propitiation
prototype 322–3
rabbi 19, 339, 432–3, 516
raiment 397
reason 52
redeemer 165, 212, 272, 274, 276, 296, 330,
    354, 367–8, 398, 498–9
reformer 343, 389, 426
refreshment 85
refuge 41
rejected one 214
remedy 210
restorer 280
resurrection 85
revealer 325
revelation 331–2, 355, 394, 413–16, 420, 449,
    469, 505, 508–9; see also benefit:
    revelation
righteous one 61
righteousness 87, 219; of God 413–15
rock 34
root of David 298
ruler 346–7
sacrifice 35, 62, 115, 142, 159, 195, 211, 212, 227,
    268, 296, 330, 358, 405, 430–1, 435, 457,
    461, 496, 502, 527

salt 217
salvation 397
sanctification 396
saviour 27, 54, 71, 74, 83, 88, 92, 107, 116, 118,
    120, 125, 132, 136, 211–12, 221, 244, 256,
    258, 265, 268, 275–6, 278, 291, 308–9, 338,
    344, 358, 360–1, 371, 373, 387, 389, 438, 452,
    470, 487, 510, 515
seal of God's counsels 90
second Adam 46, 58–9, 280, 405
seed 85
servant 60–1, 187, 276–7
shepherd 214, 275; of Israel 94
shield 275
sibling 456, 458
sinner 215, 231
sinner's friend 265
slave 107
soldier of the Cross 390
Son; Son of God 16, 19–20, 24, 32, 34, 36, 41,
    44, 46, 49, 53–4, 57, 59, 72, 77, 81, 86–91,
    95, 97, 99–100, 113–14, 116, 120, 125, 128,
    131, 134, 136–42, 147, 150, 162, 166, 172,
    194, 209, 211, 215, 219, 230, 232, 250,
    256–9, 270, 282–3, 291–2, 294–6, 304, 314,
    316, 322, 346, 352–5, 365, 368, 372, 380, 399,
    406–7, 424, 436, 441–3, 447–8, 451, 466,
    470, 473, 482–3, 489, 502–4, 506–7, 516,
    520, 526; of Abraham 57, 59, 95; of
    David 57, 59, 95–6, 256, 314, 424, 442; of
    Man 17, 22–3, 33, 59, 81, 100, 142, 231, 236,
    283, 292–3, 346, 466, 481, 491, 519, 527; of
    Mary 163; of uncleanness 147; of
    woman 462
source 74
sovereign 109, 306, 457
sower 72
splendour 74
stag 242
stumbling-block 415
sun 106–7, 136, 177, 188, 268, 303, 398, 403; of
    Righteousness 266
sweetness 397
symbol 467, 501
table 187
teacher 47, 212, 275, 279, 325, 344, 382, 520; of
    morality 386; of truth 385–6
thinker 414
thought 397
treasure 85
true God from true God 91, 295
truth 20, 488

unknown one 489; one unknown 346
verb 497
vicar 72
victim 227, 436
victor 259, 455, 496, 509; see also benefit:
    victory
vine 85, 241, 280
water 85
way 20, 85, 179, 241, 283, 488
well of light 74
well-beloved 399
wisdom 87, 128, 496; of God 68, 85
witness 399
wonderful 365
word 44, 48, 52–5, 57–9, 64, 71–2, 76–8, 82,
    85, 87, 91, 94–8, 100–1, 113, 124–9, 137, 150,
    230, 233, 241, 244, 250, 272, 291, 294, 353,
    355–6, 372, 375, 396–7, 404–5, 414, 441, 443,
    488, 491, 498–9, 504, 527
worm 283
youth 377
zaddik 520
zealot 460
Jesus People 452
Jesus Prayer 10, 103, 105, 111–13, 189, 391, 397,
    441–3, 529
Joan of Arc 401
Job 153, 177–8, 472
John of Damascus 128–9, 130–1, 140, 236
John of Lausanne 196
John of Salisbury 114
John of the Cross 241–3
John the Baptist 14, 15, 19, 25, 51, 76, 93, 119, 256,
    304, 309, 339, 359, 370, 423–6, 428, 440
John XXIII, pope 443
John, Acts of 30–1
John, apostle 19, 21, 30–1, 65, 84, 131, 149, 153,
    170–1, 314, 340, 372, 374, 380, 401
John, Gospel of 18, 20, 33–4, 76–7
Jonson, Ben 255
Joseph the Visionary 142–3
Joseph, father of Jesus 13, 27, 95, 113, 146, 339
Joseph, patriarch 63, 205
Josephus, Flavius 66
Joshua son of Nun 336, 390, 526
Judah, patriarch 65
Judaism 16, 50, 60–8, 78, 146–50, 203–5, 311–13,
    330, 337, 342–4, 362, 420, 423–6, 432, 510,
    515–22, 527; see also Jesus: characteristics:
    Jewish
Judas, disciple 147–8, 249, 481, 512; see also life:
    betrayal

Julia Eustochium 59
Julian of Norwich 189–91
Juliana of Mont-Cornillon 195–7
Justin Martyr 71–2
Justinian, emperor 107, 126

Kagawa, Toyohiko 439
Kähler, Martin 370–1, 417
Kant, Immanuel 319, 321–4, 355–66
Käsemann, Ernst 419–21
Kassia 118
Kempis, Thomas à 185, 192–3
Kendrick, Graham 495–6
Kennedy, John F. 518
kenosis 46, 96–7, 99, 107, 117, 134, 145, 298, 322–3,
    347, 352–5, 357, 364, 440, 444, 499, 502–4
kerygma 417, 420–2, 451, 529
Kierkegaard, Søren Aaby 391–4, 414–15
Kim Chi Ha 444–6
kingdom of God, of heaven, of Christ 14–15, 19,
    25–6, 29–30, 47, 108, 214, 244, 277, 289, 293,
    305, 309, 314, 324, 338, 344, 361–2, 370, 374,
    377–8, 383, 421, 425–31, 435, 445–6, 449–50,
    469–70, 498, 512, 516
Klausner, Joseph 516
Koyama, Kosuke 440–1

language, original
  Anglo-Norman 121–2
  Anglo-Saxon 120
  Arabic 151–4, 171–2
  Chinese 119–20
  Danish 391–4
  Dutch 185–6, 228–9
  English 158–61, 180–2, 189–91, 220–1, 223–7,
    248–51, 255–9, 262–9, 271, 284–93, 296–300,
    304–5, 307–8, 327–9, 333–5, 341–2, 347–53,
    356–60, 364–6, 372–7, 381–90, 394–5, 397–
    400, 402–9, 421–39, 440–3, 446–9, 451–6,
    458–62, 465–81, 486–8, 492–501, 505–6,
    510–15, 517–22
  French 269–70, 281–3, 294–5, 303–7,
    313–15, 317, 340–1, 377–8, 400–1, 456–7,
    493–4, 523–4
  German 172, 175, 184–5, 210–14, 218–19, 230–2,
    235–6, 240–1, 272–80, 309–11, 315–17, 321–7,
    330–3, 335–9, 342–6, 353–6, 360–3, 366–71,
    379–81, 395–8, 413–21, 463–5, 481–5, 488–92,
    503–5, 516
  Greek 13–34, 37, 39–43, 46–7, 48, 50–4, 57–9,
    61–3, 66–8, 70–9, 82–98, 105–13, 118–19,
    123–31, 187–9, 243–4

Hebrew 60–1, 66–7, 146–8, 203–5, 311–13
  Italian 177–8, 186–7, 238–9, 246–8
  Japanese 439
  Korean 444–6
  Latin 26, 36, 38–9, 43–5, 48, 55–6, 59, 64–6,
    68–70, 72–3, 80–2, 88–9, 98–100, 113–17,
    131–44, 149–50, 157–8, 161–2, 165–71,
    172–80, 182–4, 191–202, 209–11, 215–17,
    221–3, 226–8, 232–4, 236–8, 300–2, 443–4
  Pahlavi 150–1
  Persian 153, 162–5
  Portuguese 449–50
  Russian 144–5, 350, 382–3, 391, 397, 502–3,
    508–9, 524–5
  Sanskrit 405
  Spanish 241–3, 245–6, 259–61, 506–8
  Syriac 34–6, 49, 142–3
Lao-tse, Taoist author 362
Lateran, Fourth Council 140, 155, 195
law 26, 61–7, 97, 100, 113, 118, 146–7, 203–4,
    209–10, 215, 227, 279, 289, 292–3, 296, 301,
    307, 311–13, 338, 343, 369–70, 382–3, 392, 414,
    426, 430, 435, 516–17
Lawrence, D. H. 474–6
Lazarus 94, 125, 132
Lee, Mother Ann 394
Lent, season of 130
Lentulus, Letter of 161–2, 174
Leo III, Emperor 129
Leo the Great 98–100, 124
Leontius of Jerusalem 126–7, 128, 527
Lessing, Gotthold Ephraim 309, 315–17
Levellers movement 290, 292; see also Diggers
Lewis, Clive Staples 476–8
liberal Protestantism 319, 330, 344, 366, 370, 377,
    379, 411, 420–2, 434, 486
liberation theology 411–12, 443–6, 449–52,
    454–6, 506–8
light 30, 33–4, 39, 50–1, 56, 59, 61, 65–6, 73, 76, 84,
    103, 105–8, 111, 120, 136, 167, 172, 179, 189,
    247, 280, 335–6, 362, 475, 524
Lincoln, Abraham 518
Linton, Eliza Lynn 341–2
liturgy 104, 195–7, 248, 263, 289, 447, 487, 509,
    528
Lives of Jesus see Quest of the Historical
    Jesus
Lloyd Jones, Martin 437–9
Locke, John 298
Loisy, Alfred 377–8
Lombard, Peter 104, 128, 132, 140–2
Lossky, Vladimir 508–9

Loyola, Ignatius 208, **245–6**
Luke, Gospel of 15–19, **22–4**, **26**
Lutgard of Aywières 182
Luther, Martin 207, **215–16**, **216–17**, 218, 221,
   230, **230–2**, 236–7, 417, 436, 439
Lutheranism 209–10, 214, 220, 232–3, 235–6, 240,
   243, 253, 274, 319, 347, 352–3, 355, 364, 370,
   391, 486, 528–9

Macarius of Egypt 105–6, 108
Macrina the Younger 37
Madeleine de Saint-Joseph 282–3
Mailer, Norman 472–4
Maimonides, Moses 146
Manichaeism 130, 150, 394, 527
Marcian, Emperor 12
Marcion; Marcionites 5–6, 80, 394
Mardān Farukh 150–1
Margaret of Oingt 191–2
Margaret of Ypres 184
Mark, Gospel of 14, 16–17, 19–20, 22
Martha, sister of Mary 193, 283
Martin of Tours 43–4, 149
Martyrdom of Saints Carpus, Papylus and
   Agathonicé 41
Marx, Karl; Marxism 411, 529
Mary Magdalen 23, 193, 214, 328
Mary, Mother of Jesus 13–14, 23, 95, 113, 115,
   118–19, 128, 131, 134–5, 146, 151–3, 158, 168,
   170–1, 190, 203, 245, 268, 291, 347–8, 364,
   372, 385, 497, 503; as Theotokos 95, 118,
   130–1; *see also* Jesus: life: virgin birth
Mary, sister of Martha 283
Matthew, disciple 29
Matthew, Gospel of 13–15, 19, 21–2, 24
Mauriac, François 523–4
Maximus the Confessor 128
Mecthild of Magdeburg 169, 172, 175
Meditations on the Life of Christ 175–7
Meier, John P. 427–9
Melanchthon, Philip 207, 209–10, 210–11,
   230, 272
Melchisedek, priest-king 226
Melito of Sardis 62–3
Merezhovsky, Dmitri 524–5
merit 138–9, 194, 197–8, 202, 211, 214, 218, 225,
   269, 301, 307–8, 408, 527–8
messianic consciousness 381; *see also* God-
   consciousness
messianic secret 19
Methodism 253, 264, 319
Methodius of Olympus 48

Meynell, Alice Christiana 351
Michelangelo Buonarroti 238
Mill, John Stuart 329
Milman, Henry Hart 352–3
Milton, John 256–9
Mirror of Perfection 174–5, 183
Mishnah 67
modernism, Roman Catholic 377, 395
Moltmann, Jürgen 503–5
Monophysitism 96, 123–9, 526–7
Montanism 80
Moravians 394
More, Thomas 220–1
Morgan, Thomas 307–8
Mormon, Book of 333–5
Mormonism 320
Moses 19, 23, 33, 50, 63–5, 153, 160, 166, 204, 215,
   220–1, 292–3, 311–12, 336–9, 447, 479, 487
Mott, Lucretia 383–4
Muhammad 103, 151–2, 378
Müntzer, Thomas 217–18, 339
Muslim, Sahih 152
My Dancing Day, Carol 248
mystery 1, 3, 86, 89, 106, 137, 142–4, 179, 195, 236,
   273, 280, 284, 346, 378, 488, 490–3, 495, 503,
   524
mystery plays 158
myth 330, 332, 335–7, 342, 417, 422, 498

Napoleon Bonaparte 319, 417
nationalism 411
naturalism 337
Nazism 434, 463
Neander, Johann August Wilhelm 335, 337–8
neo-Arianism 90
neo-Platonism 73, 106, 526
Nestor the Chronicler 144–5
Nestorianism 127, 394
Nestorius 95–6, 98, 118, 119, 133
Newman, John Henry 372–3, 395
Nicaea, Council of 87, 88, 89–91, 461
Niceta of Remesiana 36
Nicholas of Cusa 201–2
Niebuhr, H. Richard 462, 465–6, 467, 529
Niebuhr, Reinhold 465
Nietzsche, Friedrich Wilhelm 360–3
Nizzahon Vetus 203–4, 528
Noah, patriarch 65, 311, 399, 442
Noel, Conrad 447–9
nominalism 115
Nonconformism 263, 271, 287
Nouwen, Henri 478–81

Ochino, Bernardino 238
Oetinger, Friedrich Christoph 279–80
Olevian, Gaspar 211–14
Olier, Jean-Jacques 253, 269–70, 281
Origen 26, 48, 85–6
original sin 211
Orthodox Church 243, 397, 411; see also
  language: Greek; language: Russian
orthodoxy 11, 42, 80, 88, 97–8, 100, 115, 134,
  235–6, 304, 368, 372; see also creeds; heresy
ousia 88, 90, 123–4, 526
Oxford Movement 319, 372

paganism 60, 67–75
Panikkar, Raymond 514–15
Papylus, martyr 41
Papyrus Ox 840 26–7
Parker, Theodore 375–7, 402
Pascal, Blaise 305–7
Paschasius Radbertus 142–3
Passover 227, 245, 424, 426, 526
Paul of Tarsus 21, 39, 40, 44–6, 50–1, 57, 67–8,
  81, 215, 305, 308, 330, 367, 374, 385, 413, 440,
  460, 517, 520–1
Paula, mother of Julia Eustochium 59
Paulinus of Nola 49–50
Payson, Edward 397–8
Pelagianism 211, 492
Pentecost 280, 395, 435, 500–1, 509
Pentecostalism 412
Perrin, Norman 421–2, 467
personality of Jesus 332, 366–71, 418
Peter of Celle 114–15
Peter of Damaskos 110–11
Peter, Acts of 84–5
Peter, Gospel of 31–2
Pharisees 26, 312, 343, 359, 445, 447, 519
Philimon, Abba 112–13
Philip, disciple 18, 20, 180
Phineas son of Eleazar 166
pietism 189, 240, 253, 264, 272–80, 337, 347, 366,
  388
Pilate 31, 66, 77, 91, 135, 177, 213, 249, 424, 517–18
Pilgrim, Candid Narrations of a 391
Plato; Platonism 71–2, 417–18, 526; see also neo-
  Platonism
Plechtchéev, Russian author 350, 529
Pliny the Younger 68–70
Plotinus 526
pluralism 511
Porphyry 68, 526
Presbyterianism 256, 286, 289, 373

presence of God 284, 324–5, 520
presence of Jesus 24, 168, 220–1, 222, 243, 327
  489; in the Eucharist 194–5, 221, 223–6,
  230, 232, 235, 289; due to divinity 214, 223
  (see also ubiquity); face-to-face 327, 373–4;
  in church 374; in individual 272–3, 278, 290,
  323, 369, 374, 381; spiritual 367–8
Proba, Falconia 72–3
Protestant orthodoxy 253, 272, 319, 411, 486
Protestantism 253, 269, 285, 502; see also
  Anglicanism, Calvinism, Lutheranism,
  etc.
providence 3, 5, 46–7, 53, 56, 59, 79, 83, 96, 99,
  167, 397, 413, 424, 451, 479, 482, 493–4
Prudentius, Aurelius Clemens 56
psychology of Jesus 418, 421
purgatory 227, 305
Puritanism 223, 253, 255, 272, 284–9, 290, 388,
  447

Quakers 272, 290, 319, 383, 394
Quest of the Historical Jesus 9, 319, 321–46, 371,
  411, 417–33, 449–50, 460, 493, 515; Second
  Quest 319–22, 417; Third Quest 417, 423–31
Qur'ān 151–2, 171, 430

Radhakrishnan, Sarvepalli 511–13
radicalism 272, 290–3, 303, 327, 341, 463–5
Rahner, Karl 449, 490–2
Ramabai, Pandita 407–9
Ramakrishna, Sri 405, 513–14
Ramsey, Michael 505–6
Ranke, Leopold von 529
rationalism 321, 337, 344, 418
Ratramnus of Corbie 143–4
recapitulation 57–9
Reformation 9, 138, 143, 184, 207, 215, 217, 226,
  230, 238, 240, 245, 255, 263, 321, 347, 423, 434
Reformed Church 253, 319, 364, 366, 388, 503; see
  also Calvinism
Reimarus, Hermann Samuel 309–11, 315, 333
reincarnation 405, 408
relationship to Jesus
  being a lesser Christ 439
  being conformed to Christ 218, 269
  being contemporaneous with Christ 392–4;
    see also history as problem
  being crucified with Christ 37, 49, 77, 131, 180,
    186–7, 202, 213, 269–70, 276, 239, 401, 439–1,
    450
  being in Christ 3, 39, 214, 224–6, 240, 244, 248,
    281, 285, 289, 394, 435, 465

being in the image of Christ 269, 277–9, 398, 506
being like Christ 106, 259, 383–4, 392
being married to Christ 8, 214, 273, 400
being raised with Christ 202
being united to Christ 107, 116, 202, 224, 272, 281–3, 285, 295, 297, 374, 387, 395–6, 400
Christ born in us 117, 290–1
Christ coming again in us 293
Christ in our suffering 495
Christ in the poor 43, 444, 461, 512
Christ in us 30, 39, 110, 226, 240–1, 279, 285, 289–91, 389
communing with Christ 286–7
communing with God through Christ 354, 369–80
completing Christ 241, 282, 445, 499
eating Christ 241, 395–7
kissing Christ 272, 286–7, 348
meeting God in Christ 486
ministering to Christ 35–6
relating to Christ 331
sharing Christ's story 468
sharing the image of God with Christ 48, 52–3, 179, 188, 233, 392, 407, 497
relics 38, 41, 130, 132
Rembrandt van Rijn 524
Renaissance, the 9, 156–7, 172–4, 207, 209, 220, 240, 253
Rénan, Ernest 340–1, 361
responses to Christ
acceptance 389, 438, 469
admiration 323
affection 373
asceticism 37, 42, 49, 51, 59, 64, 92, 110, 115, 180, 183–7, 189, 238, 269, 382, 515; see also responses: self-denial
awe 227, 247, 284, 350
baptism 3, 24, 51, 91, 188–9, 202, 211, 214, 217, 228, 269, 291, 335, 526
bearing one's cross 407
belief 33, 47, 68, 76, 211, 236, 304–5
blessing 36, 388–9, 438, 442
chastity 48, 244, 273, 382, 394
childlikeness 362
compassion 393
confession; proclamation; mission 9, 24–5, 244–5, 370, 388, 399–400, 440–1, 444, 450
contrition or penitence 183, 247, 264, 297
courage 445–6
cupidity 425
dance 248–9

desire 55–6, 108–9, 242–3, 245, 272–3, 275, 279, 324–5, 327, 466
devotion 373
disbelief 22–3
discipleship; following 3, 30, 73, 439, 449–50, 463, 467–8, 470, 507–8
embarrassment 425
emotion 38, 175, 183, 358
endurance 16, 19, 21, 108, 193, 264–6, 275, 277, 297, 440
faith 18, 77, 81, 120, 142–3, 212, 214, 218, 227, 273–4, 297, 325, 370, 375, 390, 415–16, 421, 435, 443, 460, 465, 488
faithfulness 277
fasting 383
fear 373, 393, 425, 444–5, 465, 477
forgiveness 15
good deeds 34, 43, 69, 110, 211, 214, 217, 244, 273, 279, 283, 286, 367, 384, 438, 443, 467
goodness 376
grief 15, 110, 245–6, 251, 264
hatred of sin 247
honesty 393
humility 48, 109–10, 113, 115–16, 132, 145, 176, 186–7, 191, 226, 244, 263–4, 273, 286, 393, 400, 440, 444, 465
imitation 3, 48, 110, 139, 183–9, 207, 215, 240, 243–4, 270, 276, 283, 322–3, 329, 395, 450
joy; gladness; delight 34, 41, 43, 55, 110, 116, 120, 139, 175, 189, 239, 245, 247, 251, 266, 271, 273–4, 287, 297, 376, 386, 389–91, 398, 407, 409, 441, 477–9, 515
justice 384
learning 48
love (of God, Christ, neighbours, enemies, etc.) 37, 44, 50, 77, 116, 120, 174, 186–7, 189, 191, 201, 238, 247, 262–8, 272–4, 279, 281–2, 287, 307, 323–4, 328, 342, 348–50, 358, 379, 384, 391, 401, 407, 440, 443, 465–9, 507–8
loyalty 467
martyrdom 8, 11–12, 41, 49, 64, 71, 77, 176, 228, 394, 400–1
meditation 8, 9, 86, 103, 105, 107–8, 110–13, 132, 175–7, 178, 183, 186, 194, 240, 245–8, 272–3, 279, 283, 341, 439
meekness 15
mercy 15, 277, 384, 469
monastic life 103–4, 110, 115, 187–8, 214
morality; virtue 244, 273, 279, 329, 420
mysticism 420
obedience 19, 24, 37, 58, 120, 176, 186–7, 236, 277, 286, 305, 367, 382–3, 395, 398

patience 244
peacemaking 15
penance 182, 207, 215
pilgrimage 271, 444
pity 247
poverty 15, 244, 276, 382, 426, 445
praise; worship 36, 73, 137, 187, 239, 245, 267, 335, 373, 375, 406, 487, 495
prayer 15, 42, 38, 176, 273, 281, 286, 288, 376
recognition 368, 427, 479–81
repentance 29, 188, 200, 411, 424, 524
sacrifice 212–13
self-denial 64, 108, 214, 238, 240, 264, 279–80, 287–8, 404, 415, 440, 444, 472
service 245, 469
silence 373
sincerity 227
suffering 115, 444
surprise 515
surrender 389
thankfulness 43, 211–13, 264, 275, 323, 398
trust 36, 47, 369, 469, 479
waiting 288–9
weakness 266
wisdom 376
work 279, 281, 369
wrestling 264
Reuther, Rosemary Radford 497–9
Rolle, Richard 180–2
romanticism 347
Rumi, Jelaluddin 163–5
Rupert of Deutz 113–14
Russian Orthodox Church 10, 144–5, 320, 441, 502, 508

Sa'adi, Persian author 162–3
Sabbath 26–7, 311–12, 424
Sabellianism 505
sacred heart of Jesus 155, 200, 281
Sales, Francis de 294–5
Salvation Army 398
Samson 300
Sanders, E. P. 423–5
Sandmel, Samuel 517–18
Sanon, Anselme T. 456–7
Satprakashananda, Swami 513–14
Sayers, Dorothy L 461–2
Schleiermacher, Friedrich 276, 319, 335, 337, 366–8, 369, 413
Schmidt, Hans 350
Schoeps, Hans Joachim 520

scholasticism 104, 133, 137–142, 155–6, 197–200, 207, 209–10, 230, 321
Schweitzer, Albert 344–6, 417
Scofield Reference Bible 388
Scott, Job 291–2
Scribes 17, 22; see also Pharisees
Scupoli, Lorenzo 246–8
Sen, Keshub Chunder 402–4
sentimentality 319, 337, 347, 351
Sergieff, John Ilyitch 397
Sergius the Grammarian 123–4, 526
Severus of Antioch 123, 124–6
Shakers 394
Shakespeare, William 255
Sharrar, archaic Marronite liturgy 35–6
Shem Tob, Joseph ibn 204–5
Sibbes, Richard 286–7
Sibylline Oracles 70–1
Simeon 118, 511
Simeon the New Theologian 108–9
Simon of Cyrene 79
Simon Peter, apostle 18–19, 21, 23, 29–31, 65, 77, 84–5, 94, 143, 149, 181, 215, 283, 286, 314, 338, 340, 374, 434, 481
Sirmium, Council of 88–9
Smith, Amanda Berry 389–90
Smith, Joseph 333–5
Sobrino, Jon 506–8
Socinus, Fausto Paulo; Socinianism 300–1
Socrates 360, 378, 489
Solomon 34, 38
Solomon, Odes of 34–5
Spener, Philipp Jakob 272, 276
Spirit 4, 16, 25, 51, 55, 57, 75, 81, 88, 90–2, 96, 111–12, 114–15, 130, 152, 172, 179, 188, 212, 250, 272, 275, 279–80, 285, 287, 292–3, 324–6, 345–6, 364–6, 369, 371, 374, 392, 398, 400, 441, 505; and church 40, 217, 269–70, 443; and Jesus 50, 98, 232, 366, 378, 384, 404–5, 500, 502–3; and Jesus' baptism 14, 72, 248, 424, 509; and Jesus' conception 13, 95, 128, 212, 222, 296, 365, 435; and Jesus' presence 214, 221, 289, 458; and salvation 49, 63, 105–6, 109, 143, 189, 194, 211, 240, 287, 297, 396, 435, 507; and sanctification 225, 228, 270, 366
Spufford, Margaret 10, 494–5
Stephen, martyr 367
stigmata 176, 269, 527 see also wounds of Christ
Stoics 72
Stott, John R. W. 436–7

Strauss, David Friedrich 335–7, 338, 340
Sufism 153–4, 163–5
Sulpicius Severus 43–4
Suso, Henry 184–5
Synesius of Cyrene 73–5

T'ai-tsung, emperor of China 119
Talmud 66–7, 146
Tauler, Johann 165–6, 184
Tchaikovsky 350
Te Deum 36
Teilhard de Chardin, Pierre 493–4
temple 22, 26, 94, 106, 119, 147, 245, 257, 261, 273, 279, 359–60, 375–6, 381, 400, 407, 424, 430, 432, 511; see also life: presentation; and life: cleansing of the Temple
Temple, William 510–11
Tersteegen, Gerhard 278–9
Tertullian 26, 80–2
Theatine Order 208, 246
Theodora, Empress 129
Theodoret 98
Theodoric 133
Theodosius, Emperor 56, 91
Theoleptos of Philadelphia 155, 187–8
theologia crucis 439, 504
Theophilus, emperor 118
Therapeutics 394
Thérèse of Lisieux 400–1
Thomas de Cantimpré 182, 184
Thomas of Celano 157–8
Thomas, apostle 20, 29
Thomas, Gospel of 26, 28–30
Thomas, Infancy Story of 27–8
Thomasius, Gottfried 353–5
Thompson, Francis 351–2
Tillich, Paul 434–6, 529
Tol'doth Yeshu 146–8
Tolstoy, Leo 382–3
Torrey, Reuben Archer 388–9
Traherne, Thomas 1, 3, 284
Trajan, Emperor 68, 70
transubstantiation 42–3, 195, 208, 220, 224–5, 305
Trent, Council of 226–8
Trinity 6, 9, 14, 19, 24, 28, 86, 89, 93, 120, 127, 134, 136, 140, 160, 172–3, 194, 209–10, 243–4, 254, 335, 356–8, 364–6, 411, 487, 501–3, 505–9, 516
Troeltsch, Ernst 331–3, 465
Turner, Steve 446
two natures 81, 83–6, 91–101, 133, 207–8, 210–11,
214–16, 222–3, 230–9, 250, 259, 283, 285, 296, 325, 352–5, 357, 378, 405, 443, 487, 491, 495, 527; see also humanity; divinity
typology 11, 33, 336–7, 426, 442

ubiquity 30, 45, 58–9, 83, 96, 129, 150–1, 214, 221–3, 230, 232–5, 306, 353, 357
uniqueness 329, 356, 370, 380, 496, 510; see also exclusivism
Unitarianism 300, 319–20, 352, 356–8, 375, 385
Upadhyay, Brahmabandhab 404–5
Ursinus, Zacharias 211–14
Ursula of Münsterburg 214, 228
Utilitarianism 329

Valentinus 79
Vatican, First Council 395
Vatican, Second Council 411, 443–4, 449, 490
Vedanta 404
Vere, Aubrey Thomas de 347–8
Vermes, Geza 519–20
Vermigli, Pietro Martire 233–4, 428
Virgil 72
Vivekananda, Swami 405–7
Vives, Juan Luis 172–4
Vulgate 64

Waldensians 155, 394
Watts, Isaac 263–4
Wecelin, cleric of Franconia 149
Wernle, Paul 330, 528
Wesley, Charles 264–6
Wesley, John 253, 264, 389
Westminster Assembly: Catechism 296–8; Directory 289
Wilde, Oscar 348–50
Wiles, Maurice 486–8
William of St-Thierry 113
Wilson-Kastner, Patricia 499–501
Winstanley, Gerrard 292–3
Wolfson, Elliot R. 520–2
Wollebius, Johannes 300–2
womanism 460–1
Wordsworth, William 385
wounds of Christ 21, 121, 171, 176, 182, 184, 186–7, 190, 246–7, 250–1, 264, 268, 278, 350, 527; wound in side 182, 192, 249, 262–3, 334, 474; see also instruments of the passion

Wright, N. T. 429

Zachariah 153
Zealots 337, 460, 519

Zinzendorf, Nikolaus Ludwig Graf von 272, 276–8
Zoroastrianism 142, 146, 150–1
Zwingli, Huldreich 221–3